Fabric à la Romantic Regency

A Glossary of Fabrics from Original Sources
1795 – 1836

Including their Uses, Contemporary Opinions, Technical Information, and the Occasional Definition.

A Record of Who Wore What, and When, From Royalty to the Charity Poor

Compiled by Deb Salisbury

Editor of
Elephant's Breath & London Smoke:
Historic Colour Names, Definitions & Uses
and
Victorian Bathing and Bathing Suits:
The Culture of the Two-Piece Bathing Dress from 1837 – 1901

Published by
The Mantua-Maker Historical Sewing Patterns
Abbott, Texas

Published by
The Mantua-Maker Historical Sewing Patterns
100 PR 232
Abbott, TX 76621
deb@mantua-maker.com
http://www.Mantua-Maker.com

Cover arranged by Deb Salisbury
Cover photo from *La Belle Assemblée*, 1826

Salisbury, Deb.
Fabric à la Romantic Regency: A Glossary of Fabrics from Original Sources 1795 – 1836 /
Deb Salisbury
p. cm.
Includes biographical references

Dedication: A special thanks to my mom, Dona Salisbury.

Table of Contents

Introduction

Alamode, marabout pluche de soie, zybeline.

When I decided to do research a new Regency dress pattern, I discovered I had a fantastic new set of resources available. And an appalling sensation of inadequacy. What did these hundreds of fabric terms mean? What was gas net, rock silk, or pelian satin?

I started a list. The list became rather long.

Before I was halfway satisfied, I had a dictionary on my hands.

I can't pretend to fully define all the entries in this dictionary – I'm working from sources where almost everyone knew exactly what most of the terms meant. I won't say I've covered all materials. I have focused on the times when a magazine felt the need to define a term, or when I notice something new or different. I've tried to hunt down the poorly (or un-) defined entries.

You will find modern sources that define many of these terms. Those definitions are correct – for certain decades, years, or sometimes only for certain months. This book provides a series of snapshots of the terms used in fashion.

This glossary covers English fashion from 1795 to 1836, technically the Directoire, Empire, Regency and Romantic eras. It also covers many French fabric terms as recorded by the English. Other fabrics were imported, and were often named for their area of origin, such as Madras, Calico, or Nankeen; Indian silk, Italian net, or French lace.

At the beginning of this period, fashion very rapidly changed from the stiff Georgian styles into the soft and flowing Directoire dresses, somewhat imitating ancient Greek clothing. Stays were discarded by the *haut ton* – for a short while. By the beginning of the Romantic age, tastes gradually shifted into harder and more angular lines. Wide skirts and wider sleeves, plus constricting corsets became the rage. The fabrics they used changed accordingly.

Who wore what types of fabric also changed. What was fashionable with the *haute ton* one year might be considered far too common the next, when the middle class was able to buy it. Machine-made lace became popular during these decades, fashionable at first, but becoming less and less expensive. Many lace makers were put out of work before handmade lace became fashionable – and extremely costly – again.

Some materials were considered appropriate only for the working poor. And the cheapest, roughest, worst-woven fabrics were deemed suitable for work house inhabitants and slaves.

Reading between the lines can tell you much about the society of this period. For example, consider this entry on the word "cloth" –

~~~ Cloth, in commerce, a manufacture made of wool, wove on the loom. Cloths are of divers qualities, fine or coarse, according to some, consists of the following particulars: 1. That the wool be of a good quality, and well dressed. 2. It must be equally spun, carefully observing that the thread of the warp be finer and better twisted than that of the woof. 3. The cloth must be well wrought, and beaten on the loom, so as to be every where equally compact. 4. The wool must not be finer at one end of the piece than in the rest. 5. The lifts must be sufficiently strong, of the same length with the stuff, and must consist of good wool, hair, or ostrich-feathers; or, what is still better, of Danish dog's hair. 6. The cloth must be free from knots and other imperfections. 7. It must be well scoured with fuller's earth, well fulled with the best white soap, and afterwards washed in clear water. 8. The hair or nap must be drawn out with the teazel, without being too much opened. 9. It must be shorn close without making it threadbare. 10. It must be well dried. 11. It must not be tenter-stretched, to force it to its just dimensions. 12. It must be pressed cold, not hot pressed, the latter being very injurious to woollen cloth. Encyclopædia Britannica, 1797

This definition tells you not only the basic structure of cloth and some now-exotic components, but the possible problems in its production and many of the underhanded tricks manufacturers used to cheat their customers.

Sometimes opinions were gently inserted. The commentator here probably *was* offended:
~~~ Damasked silks, figured with flowers of various colours, on a ground shot with two colours, are great favourites. They are exceedingly rich, and if chosen tastefully, do not offend the eye by their gaudiness. *Lady's Magazine*, March 1830

Unless otherwise noted, all entries in this book are from writers of this period, usually found in fashion magazines, but I also used newspapers, encyclopedias, and dictionaries. My comments are enclosed in square brackets [ ] and I have attempted to insert myself as rarely as possible, and only for clarity.

When looking for a particular term, use a little imagination. Spelling was just becoming standardized in the seventeenth century, and drift was still occurring in the nineteenth, as in *checkered, checquered* and *chequered*. British and American words also had different spellings, such as *grey* and *gray*, and *colour* and *color*, a condition that began in the early nineteenth century. French spellings – and misspellings – were common in period publications.

French is the language of fashion, and has been for many centuries. I've searched for English descriptions of French terms, and when I thought it might help, I've included a simple translation from eighteenth or nineteenth century sources.

At the end of each entry is the title of the publication I have quoted and the year it was issued. *Italics* indicate a periodical, while underline indicates a book.

If I have removed words, … will show in their place.

When a new source begins within an entry, ~~~ will appear.

Fabrics à la Romantic Regency is intended for the use of costume historians, literary scholars, Regency enthusiasts, Regency re-enactors and dance enthusiasts, historical writers and history buffs. Anyone who has questions about fabric from 1795 to 1836 will find many answers in these pages.

Period Comments on Fabric in Dress

Ladies' Dresses *on her* Majesty's Birth-Day. *Her Majesty.* White crape petticoat, embroidered with white satin, in waves across, intersected with spotted blue shaded satin, and black velvet stars, ornamented with an elegant double border of painted satin in shaded spots, festooned and trimmed with black lace; under and upper drapery of white satin and spotted crape, trimmed with black lace, and blue shaded satin border; the pocket-holes trimmed with black lace, with a flounce of black lace round the bottom; the body and train of tea green striped shag, trimmed with fine black lace and blue shaded ribbon in spots.
Lady's Magazine, January 1797

The clothing given yearly to the children is as follows: … Girls. A grey linen shift, with white linen sleeves, a linsey-woolsey petticoat, an olive coloured twilled cotton gown, a check apron.
First Number of the Reports of the Society in Dublin, for Promoting the Comforts of the Poor, 1800

[in 1800 & 1801] the value of the dress of the poorest labourer, at the lowest prices might be, … *Dress of a Woman.* … Gown for 2 years, stuff or camblet, at 10*s*.
County of Kilkenny, 1802

[Gentlemen's] Morning Dress – A bronze-coloured single lappelled coat, with covered buttons – fancy toilinet waistcoat, light kerseymere pantaloons, and Swedish hussar boots.
For Full Dress – A dark blue double-breasted coat, with gold basket buttons; no silk lining. A white waistcoat, single breast. Black silk stocking-breeches and stockings, all in one piece; no buttons at the knees, or strings. This longitudinal pantaloon terminates with round-toed Spanish leather shoes and silk strings. Great coats of dark bottle green cloth, with velvet collar and facings: no silk linings, they being exploded as completely *outré*. An opera hat.
The National Register, May 1, 1808

Morning and walking gowns … We have observed several in the corded cambric, in imitation of the corded sarsnet, confined in at the waist with a correspondent ribband. The straw striped muslin is likewise a favourite article, in this style of dress. In the afternoon, or intermediate rank of dress, the bosoms of gowns are either cut low and square, in the Egyptian manner, or made high, after the costume of the Romans, with a plain falling collar of antique lace; the sleeves are worn long and not transparent. Imperial and coloured bombazeens, with broad satin striped sarsnets, are well adapted to this class of attire;
La Belle Assemblée, November 1809

… the proper materials for the Shooting Jacket – in the early and warm season, *jean, satteen,* or *nankeen*; for late Autumn and Winter, *fustian* or *velveteen* are to be chosen, the shooting waistcoat being made of the same stuff.
British Field Sports, 1818

The materials used in grand costume continue to be of the richest and most varied description: nothing could be more magnificent than the dresses of the ladies who attended the drawing-room which his Majesty held to celebrate his birthday on Thursday, the 15th of June. Gold and silver tissue, coloured and white satin, both figured and plain, white and coloured *gros de Naples, reps* silk, levantine, *velours épingle,* white and coloured net, blond net, gauze, tulle, blond, and thread lace, were the materials of the dresses. The trimmings were silver fringe, gold and silver lamas, point lace, blond lace, pearls, rouleaus of various materials, Brussels lace, embroidery in coloured silks, artificial flowers intermixed with satin and net, and Roman pearls intermixed with blond and satin.
Repository of Arts, September 1820

[in Bedfordshire] Lace making, a more sedentary employment, and the women and children generally appear sickly. There are school mistresses for teaching both straw plaiting and lace making. Begin to learn lace at six or seven years of age; do little good for two years, at ten years earn two shillings a week, at sixteen as much as can be made by the business, or nearly six shillings a week; work in summer from six o'clock in the morning till sunset, and in winter from nine till eleven at night; maid servants scarce in consequence, but poor rates kept down.

Encyclopædia of Agriculture, 1825

London Gentlemen's Fashions for February.

Walking Dress. – This coat is of a light green milled superfine cloth, and is to be worn without a great coat, as it is of a stout texture, for that purpose. It is made double-breasted, with broad lappels at top to button up across the neck if required; the length of the coat should be between that of an ordinary frock coat and a great coat; the collar and lappels are of black Genoa velvet; the skirts are lined with silk, the same color, or black velvet, the same as the collar and lappels; the sleeve is rather full to the elbow, and from thence to the wrist it fits the arm rather tight, the pockets are in the folds behind, and a breast pocket horizontally across the left breast. The trousers are of a milled kersey, tight about the hips and waist, and of moderate width at bottom, not to cover the boot; they are not so long at the bottom, nor so wide as last month.

An Evening Dress. – The coat is of a dark green; the length of the waist is the same as list month, but the lappels are longer in front, and more pointed; the buttons are a habit size, and six on each lappel; they are near to the edge at bottom, but at top are wide, running towards the shoulder; it is intended that only one button of this coat should be buttoned, which is the second from the bottom. The waistcoat has still a rolling collar, with dead gold buttons, or silk the same color; it is left very open on the chest, and consequently only three button! are fastened; an under waistcoat of fine white marcella is cut to correspond, so as to just make its appearance round the collar and bosom. Dark blue or black single kerseymere trousers; they are made tight about the hips, and with a falldown, and are straight at the bottom, not lower than the ankle bone, they are made rather tight about the thigh to the small of the knee, marking out the leg to the ankle, and worn without straps.

An Evening Dress Mantelet. – This mantelet, which is a half circle, is of a fine olive or brown cloth; the collar flats like a great coat; the outside is of velvet, and the front is faced with the same; the cape, has the same quantity of fulness as the cloak, and by being put in the same as the neck, it falls in folds like the cloak, and looks very handsome. The mantelet, or cloak, is of superfine claret cloth, made extremely full, and lined with blue velvet, the collar descends low on the person, and is very capacious. The coat is made to button over in front. The collar is large, and falls gracefully over. The coat is dark blue, double-breasted, with a blue velvet collar. The waistcoat is of a delicate yellow kerseymere, made single-breasted. The pantaloons are of a dark fawn superfine cloth, made full, projecting well over the boot, and are fastened underneath by a strap.

A Morning Dress. – This is a dark fawn frock coat, lined in the skirts with a silk serge the same colour as the coat, made single breasted. It has a small cape, which just covers the shoulders; the collar is full, and rather longer than a frock without a cape: the sleeve has wadding in the top, which carries the cape well off, and gives the shoulders a square appearance. The waistcoat has a short, stand-up collar, without a step, and buttons up to the top. Superfine claret cloth pantaloons. For morning trousers the newest colours area saffron coloured kersey, a reddish dove colour, and a fawn drab, with a nut brown. They are not worn so long on the instep as last month, but, instead of covering the boot, the trousers are cut hollow a little to show the foot; the straps are, therefore, longer at the bottom, and button with two buttons under the foot.

The Casket, April 1830

LIVERIES.
Best Qualities.

Footman's Suit   £3 3 0

Namely, plain Coat, cloth or striped Waistcoat, and Velveteen Breeches.

Groom's Suit   3 10 0

Namely, short Frock Coat, cloth or striped Waistcoat, and Velveteen Breeches.

Coachman's Suit 3 13 6

Namely, long Frock Coat, cloth or striped Waistcoat, and Velveteen Breeches.

The above are subject to the following extras: –

Plush Breeches, 17s., Cassimere Breeches, 5s. 6d., cloth Trousers, 7s. 6d., Scarlet or fancy Cassimere Waistcoats, 3s. 6d., coloured edging, 3s. 6d., notched holes, 6d. each.

Doudney Brothers, 1830

Cheapness of Female Clothing in Modern Times. – The wife of a labouring man may buy at a retail shop a neat and good print as low as 6d. per yard, so that, allowing six yards for the dress, the whole material shall only cost three shillings. Common plain calico may be bought for 2½d. per yard. Elegant cotton prints, for ladies' dresses, sell at from 10d. to 1s. 4d. per yard, and printed muslins at from 1s. to 4s., – the higher priced having beautiful patterns, in brilliant and permanent colours. Thus the humblest classes have now the means of as great neatness, and even gaiety of dress, as the middle and upper classes of the last age. A country-wake in the nineteenth century may display as much finery as a drawing-room of the eighteenth; and the peasant's cottage may, at this day, with good management, have as handsome furniture for beds, windows, and tables, as the house of a substantial tradesman sixty years since.

Baines's History of Lancashire. Imperial Magazine, September 1833

The quantity of material employed in making a dress seems to augment every year. Fifteen years ago, the short waist, the *Amadis* sleeves, and the narrow skirts, did not require more than seven or eight yards of silk. Subsequently the increased dimensions of the sleeves, and the ungored skirts rendered a greater quantity requisite. Now the dress-maker requires nearly a whole piece. If the dress be of satin, *gros de Naples,* or velvet, no less than fourteen or fifteen yards will suffice, including long sleeves and a pelerine mantelet.

A slight change is, however, observable in the dimensions of sleeves. They are now less wide at top than they have been for some time past. But this diminution occasions little difference in the quantity of stuff. Sleeves appear likely to undergo a change of form this winter. The fullness which is diminished at the shoulder is slightly enlarged towards the wrist; but this fashion is as yet rarely adopted. Eight breadths are frequently employed for the skirt of a dress.

Court Journal, November 2, 1833.

Period Comments on Fabric in Mourning

Morning Mourning Dress *for the* Month *of* March. The front hair dressed upon the forehead in large loose curls, the hind hair turned up plain. – Small white chip hat, trimmed with black ribband, and a wreath of black satin flowers. Round gown of muslin, with a solid embroidered border in black silk; short sleeves, embroidered the same. Black ribband tied round the neck. Large muslin shawl, embroidered the same as the gown. Gray gloves, with black. Elastic glove-strings. Black and white sandal slippers.

The toupee dressed *en chenille,* the hind hair in a-double *chignon,* a white satin ribband intermixed with the hair. Black and white *bouquet* placed on the right side. Petticoat of plain muslin, trimmed with a black net border; *corset* and *epaulettes* of black peeling satin; white satin sleeves covered with black net. Black silk cord and tassels round the waist. – Black ribband, with a black enameled *croeix a la Jeannette,* round the neck. Long black ear rings. White gloves and shoes.

Lady's Magazine, March 1797

Orders for the Court's going into mourning on Sunday the 29th ult. for his late Royal Highness, Prince Henry of Prussia, viz. – The Ladies to wear black silk, fringed or plain linen, white gloves, necklaces and ear-rings, black or white shoes, fans and tippets. – Undress, white or grey lutestrings, tabbies, or damasks. – The Gentlemen to wear black full-trimmed, fringed or plain linen, black swords and buckles. – Undress, grey frocks.

The Court to change the mourning on Sunday, the 5th of September inst. viz. – The ladies to wear black silk or velvet, coloured ribbons, fans, and tippets; or plain white, or white and gold, or white and silver stuffs, with black ribbons. – The Gentlemen to wear black coats, and black or plain white, or white and gold, or while and silver stuff waistcoats, lull-trimmed coloured swords and buckles.

Corbett's Weekly, September 4, 1802

A Mourning Dress. As many of our discerning and tasteful correspondents have hinted to us the utility of occasionally presenting them with a mourning, we take advantage of the present period to comply with their wishes. … In slight mourning habits, the dress is composed of black gossamer net, or imperial gauze, worn over a white satin slip. A demi-train. A round frock front, and short French sleeves, each edged with a rich Vandyke lace. A cestus of white satin, edged with gold bullion, finished in front with a rich cord and cone tassels, suspended from topaz studs. Pearl necklace and bracelets, with topaz snaps. Hair in the eastern style, with a Spartan diadem, and comb of topaz or gold. A Circassian scarf of grey Spanish silk, with a Tuscan border in black embroidery, and tassels to correspond; confined on one shoulder with a topaz broach. Shoes of grey satin, with clasps of jet, or rosettes of black bugles. White gloves of French kid; and fan of black crape, with gold spangled devices.

In deep mourning, this robe should be formed of black crape, and worn over black sarsnet. The ornaments and trimmings of every description must be of bugles or jet. The shoes of queen's silk. The scarf, black crape pr imperial silk, spotted and bordered with bugles. Jet tassels and broach.

Weekly Entertainer, September 11, 1809

People are allowed to go to court in private mourning, except on the birth-days. Their uniforms, with a piece of black crape tied round the arm, are reckoned sufficient for officers in the deepest mourning.

Gentlemen not in uniform, wear what are called weepers in deep mourning, which are merely cambric cuffs, with broad hems turned back upon the sleeves.

A Book Explaining the Ranks and Dignities of British Society, 1809

The mourning ordered for the Court on the melancholy occasion of her Majesty's death, consists of bombazeen, black crape, long lawn, and plain muslin for dress. Norwich crape for undress. It is probable, that these materials will not be worn according to the strict letter of the Lord Chamberlain's orders, by any ladies but those connected with the Court, for though the mourning is general and deep, we observe satin, sarsnet, and velvet, adopted by several very elegant women; though we must observe, that, with these materials, there is always a mixture of crape.

Ladies' Monthly Museum, December 1818

The melancholy event of her Royal Highness the Duchess of York's death, which took place early in August, has caused a delay in the autumnal fashions. The court mourning ordered for her Royal Highness was, in consideration, we presume, for the interests of trade, of a shorter continuance than the public expected: it commenced on the 13th of August, and will terminate on the 3d of September. The materials ordered by the Lord Chamberlain were, for dress, black silk, with plain muslin, long lawn, crape, or love hoods; black silk shoes, black glazed gloves, and black paper fans. For head-dress, black or grey unwatered tabbies. The mourning changed to black silk, with white gloves and ornaments, on the 29th; and on the 31st, to black silk with coloured ribbons, and white and silver or gold stuffs with black ribbons.

The mourning was ordered only for the court, but it was nevertheless general with all persons who had any pretensions to fashion.

Repository of Arts, September 1820

There are two kinds of mourning, the full and the half mourning. The full mourning is worn for a father, mother, grandfather, grandmother, husband, wife, brother and sister. It is divided into three periods.* For the first six weeks, we wear only woollen garments; in the six weeks following, we wear silk, and the three last months, we mingle white with the black.

Half mourning is worn for uncles, aunts, cousins, and second cousins. The first fortnight we wear black silk, and the last week, white mixed with black.

Custom requires that a woman should wear mourning for her husband a year and six weeks, while that of a widower is only six months. This difference, which may appear singular, is founded upon reasons of convenience and social relations.

In the three first months of mourning for her husband, a woman wears only woollen garments; the six first weeks, her head dress and neck-kerchief are black crape or gauze; in the six following weeks, they are white crape or linen. The next six months, she dresses in black silk; in winter, gros de Naples; in summer, taffetas. Head dress, white crape. The three last months, she wears black and white, and the six last weeks, white only.

The mourning on the death of a wife, is a black cloth coat without buttons,** dark shoes, woollen-hose, black buckles, and a sword-knot of crape, if the person carries one. At the end of six weeks, we may wear a black coat with buttons, black silk hose, silver buckles, and a black ribband upon the sword. The half mourning of the three last months is a black coat, a sword and silver buckles, white silk stockings, and a sword-knot of black and white.

It is altogether contrary to propriety to select for yourself at the shops the articles of mourning, to have them made in your presence, or to make them yourself; and, for a fortnight at least, and sometimes even for the six first weeks, ladies ought not to sew, even while receiving their relations and intimate friends, so much are they supposed to be depressed by their affliction. ...

* Several of the particulars which follow, are not observed in this country [USA]. – *T.* ...

** It is not the custom among us to dispense with buttons. – *T.* ["translator"]

<u>Gentleman and Lady's Book of Politeness</u>, 1833

Fabrics

Abaca - Atlas

abaca – a kind of hemp or flax, made from the fibrous part of an Indian plantane, the white makes very fine cloth, but the grey is used for cordage and cables. General Dictionary of Commerce, 1810

Abbas Mirza – A new dress made of an article called *Abbas Mirza*, has been much admired; it had a corsage *à la Grecque,* the plaited drapery of which discovered an embroidered chemisette. The skirt was very full all round the waist; the ground was plain with an oriental border formed of broad stripes of twelve different shades; it was too rich to require any trimming. ... A turban of Abbas-Mirza-cachemire, is always adopted, *Ladies' Monthly Museum,* December 1828

Aboukir – Ball dresses of the *Mouseline* [sic] *d'Aboukir* have a splendid effect. This new article of manufacture presents a mosaic pattern, in which every variety of tint is intermingled with gold foliage. It is beautifully soft and pliant, being composed of the finest wool. For turbans, nothing is more appropriate and elegant than the *Mouseline d'Aboukir,* ornamented by a bird of paradise, or a diamond aigrette. *Court Journal,* December 19, 1835 ~~~ A beautiful new material called *mousseline d'Aboukir,* has just appeared for ball-dresses; it is composed of Cashmere wool, and is exquisitely soft and fine; the pattern is a kind of mosaic, in which various colours are intermingled with gold foliage. This material is also employed for turbans; *Court Magazine,* January 1836 ~~~ Some new materials have appeared both for dinner and evening dress. One of these, *satin d'Aboukir,* a mixture of silk and wool, flowered in various hues, in a running pattern, is extremely beautiful; *Ladies' Pocket,* January 1836 ~~~ Evening costume is still of a light kind; several new materials have, however, appeared for it. We may cite among them the *satins d'Aboukir,* ... These rich and beautiful materials will be in great request as soon as the winter has fairly set in. *Ladies' Pocket,* November 1836

Adatais – Adatais, Adatsi, or Adatys, in commerce, a muslin or cotton-cloth, very fine and clear, of which the piece is ten French ells long, and three quarters broad. It comes from the East-Indies; and the finest is made at Bengal. Encyclopædia Britannica, 1797 ~~~ *Aditis,* a fine Bengal muslin, 13 yards to the piece. New Universal Gazetteer, 1832 [see also *Bengal muslin*]

aeraphine – [see *aerophane*]

aerienne – Dinner Dress. Dress of figured *gaze Aerienne.* ... [Paris] A dress of *crêpe Aeriènne,* of a delicate lilac colour, over an under dress of rich lilac satin. *Repository of Fashions,* May 1829 ~~~ As to gauzes, we hardly know to which to give the preference; but the *gaze aérienne* embroidered on a plain ground is, perhaps, the most beautiful: it is much used for grand costume. *La Belle Assemblée,* December 1830 ~~~ Aérien, ne, *a. ethereal, airy.* Boyer's Royal Dictionary, 1794

aerophane – Ball Dress. A dress of white *crêpe-Aerophane, La Belle Assemblée,* March 1828 ~~~ the ornaments on the crown, which are often of crape aerophane or gauze. *Ladies' Monthly Museum,* May 1828 ~~~ The most approved ball dresses were of the new light material, called *crêpe-Aerophane ... La Belle Assemblée,* [review of the first six months] 1828 ~~~ Black velvet turbans and those of white crêpe-aerophane are much in request with matronly ladies; they are finished with exquisite taste, and it is a kind of head-dress which seems to set off every female countenance. *Lady's Magazine,* March 1829 ~~~ [court dress] A white aerophane dress over satin, splendidly embroidered in green and gold, *Royal Lady's,* May 1831 ~~~ A bridal dress of white *aéraphine* gauze, embroidered in white silks, *Atkinson's Casket,* March 1835 ~~~ Aérophane – Se dit d'un corps transparent à l'air. [French: Said of a transparent body in the air.] Des Termes Appropriés Aux Arts et Aux Sciences, 1824

African – [court dress] A dress of white satin a Brandenbourg, ... train rich mais velours d'Afrique, broché a colonnes, lined with white satin, *Court Journal,* June 1, 1833 ~~~ A new material for hats and bonnets has been imported from Paris. It is called *velours d'Afrique.* The bonnets made of it are usually lined with satin, and trimmed with satin ribbon. *Court Journal,* November 7, 1835 ~~~ Some new silks, of a very rich kind, will appear very shortly. They are the ... *velours d'Afrique,* ... It is expected that, both in form and materials, the style of the seventeenth century will be revived in winter evening dress. *Court Magazine,* October 1836 ~~~ [court dress] Costume, siecle de Louis XV., superb blonde, over white satin petticoat; rich lilac gros d'Afrique manteau, *Lady's Magazine and Museum*, June 1836 ~~~ Some *élégantes* ore trying to bring the Maintenon into vogue, it is a kind of lingree pelerine with a large square collar descending low upon the shoulders, composed of an extremely rich black silk, *gros d'Afrique*, and trimmed with old fashioned black lace; it is wadded, and of course will he sufficiently comfortable till the weather becomes very cold; it will certainly be very fashionable, as it is elegant without being shewy. *New Monthly Belle Assemblée*, October 1836 ~~~ [Paris] The *Maintenon mantelet*, composed of a sort of long scarf, with rather a long cape … is much admired. I saw one of African *gros*, black, with a deep trimming of lace, *Blackwood's Lady's Magazine*, December 1836 [see also *reps Africain*]

aigrette – "The Aigrette is of the Heron family, and distinguished by long silky feathers on it's [sic] back, used to form ornaments for the head-dresses of Ladies, Knights, Sultans, and are snow white," &c. – Fitzgerald's Ornithology. Sporting Magazine, November 1798 ~~~ The finest aigrettes are formed by the tails of the bird of paradise; three or four of these beautiful birds are thus sacrificed to procure a lady several aigrettes, and give an immense value to the trimming of a hat. This is in the highest degree of luxury. *Ladies' Monthly Museum*, June 1827

alamode – in commerce, a thin glossy black silk, chiefly used for womens hoods and mens mourning scarfs. Encyclopædia Britannica, 1797 ~~~ In modes, principally used for cloaks, we already emulate the best productions of that kind in England; and, however high the character of English modes may be in Ireland, it is certain that the consumption of Ireland, is, in a great degree, supplied by the Irish manufacturers. A majority, indeed, of what is sold, is called by the mercer, English; but this arises from his wish to profit by the vulgar prejudice in favour of English modes. Instances daily occur of a piece of Irish mode being cut into two parts, one of which is shewed to a customer as Irish, the other, as English; the latter is always preferred, and by this artifice, the mercer secures custom, a high price, and the character of having assortments. The manufacture of modes is worth attention for another reason; it is not variable, as the other branches of the silk manufacture, from the caprices of fashion. They are a species of goods, which are always likely to be in demand, and, therefore, always likely to occupy a considerable number of people. Manufactures of Ireland, 1798 ~~~ [1776] A remarkable cause was tried before Lord Chief Justice Parker, and a special jury, in the court of Exchsquer, wherein Mr. Reboul, merchant, was plaintiff, and a customhouse-officer defendant, for the illegal seizure of a parcel of alamode silks; which were siezed under pretence that they were French. But it appeared, to the great satisfaction of the court, they were manufactured in Spitalfield, by Messrs. Freemount and Son. The jury, after withdrawing a quarter of an hour, gave a verdict for the plaintiff, with 225*l.* damages. Annual Register, 1803 ~~~ Black mode, four shillings and four pence to five shillings and eightpence per yard. [in 1801] A Voyage Round the World, 1805 ~~~ (*a la mode*, French.) According to the fashion: a low word. It is used likewise by shopkeepers for a kind of thin silken material. New Encyclopædia, 1807 ~~~ The *taffetas noir lustre*, or black and glossed taffety, is what the English call alamode or mode: General Dictionary of Commerce, 1810 ~~~ *Modes* are something like sarcenets, but have the warp and woof of different thicknesses. *Persian* is still thinner, and more flimsy. Book of Commerce by Sea and Land, 1834~~~ "To be sure, fine black cloth or cassimere is the most fashionable for mourning coats. But many very genteel people wear black levantine or black mode trimmed with crape. Handsome silk coats would scarcely cost above twenty or twenty-five dollars a piece." [story: Constance Allerton] *Casket*, January 1836 ~~~ Here is a cloak, rather out of condition, made of *mode,* which is somewhat like sarcenet, but with the warp and woof of different thicknesses. It is an article not now much in use. Scenes of Commerce, 1836

Albanian – [court dress] Draperies of purple Albany net with silver acorns; *La Belle Assemblée*, June 1807 ~~~ *Albaniennes, odalisques,* and other fancy materials are worn in dinner dress, *Ladies' Pocket,* June 1830

Albion – Full Dress. … Albion net-gloves; … A pink full dress gown, made of pink Albion net, *La Belle Assemblée*, March 1806 ~~~ [ad] Fitch and Co., encouraged by the extraordinary demand for their ALBION WASHING POPLINS, for Ladies' Morning or Home Dinner Dresses, at 24s and 26s each, *Repository of Arts*, May 1815 ~~~ Britain was first called by the antients Albion, from its *white* cliffs; and afterwards in the language of the natives, Britain. Description of Britain, 1809 [see also *British* and *English*]

Alençon point – Brussels-points and *points d'Alençon* were in greater request, and fetched higher prices than ever. Desportes, a French merchant, who is settled in Weimar, sold a lace-veil of extraordinary beauty to a Russian princess for one hundred pounds. *Monthly Magazine*, April 1802 ~~~ The manufacture of fine laces, known by the name of *Alençon point*, affords the most agreeable prospect. The old established factories are not capable of supplying the incessant orders for this article, both for the foreign and home consumption. *Monthly Mirror*, August 1802 ~~~ The newest kind of trimming sported by the wealthy is the Alençon point lace; it is a beautiful and novel manufacture, exceeding every article in lace that has yet appeared in Europe. *La Belle Assemblée*, May 1820 ~~~ It has a manufactory of very beautiful lace, known by the name of point d'Alençon, where a single pair of ruffles may be made to cost between 5 and 6000 francs. <u>Itinerary of France and Belgium</u>, 1822 ~~~ Grand Festival Dress. … Robe of point d'Alençon, exquisitely embroidered à colonnes, with a deep flounce; … This magnificent dress is worn over another of blue moire *Lady's Magazine and Museum*, July 1834 [see *point lace*]

alepine – Alepínes, *s. f. pl.* Bombazeens. <u>English and Spanish Languages</u>, 1809 ~~~ I shall now proceed to the display of some minutiæ regarding the out-fit of a gentleman about to embark in a chartered ship; … For wear on board-ship, nothing can equal pantaloons, of which two pairs of thick, and two of thin, should be provided; together with as many pairs of wove cotton long-drawers, to wear under them. The thick kinds may be milled broad cloth, or wove worsted; the thin ones of light corderoy, aleppine, &c. *East India Vade-Mecum*, 1810 ~~~ [Spain] Wool and hair manufactured, including goats hair, bristles, horse hair, feathers, and human hair. … Colored alepin, to one yard and half wide <u>Digest of the Commercial Regulations</u>, 1824 ~~~ The painted dresses of Alepine or Chaly, are all made with a stomacher in front: *Ladies' Pocket*, December 1829 ~~~ Woollen goods, viz. alepine, <u>Tariff</u>, 1829 ~~~ Bombazine, *alépine*, a material of the same description, but somewhat lighter, and *gros des Indes*, are the materials employed for undress; … Carriage Dress. A gown of *alépine*; the colour the darkest shade of *gris lavande*; *La Belle Assemblée*, August 1830

Algerian – *Satin d'Algar* has taken the place of velvet in evening dress; *Royal Lady's*, April 1831 ~~~ [Paris] *drap d'Alger*, … a mixture of silk and worsted, of a slighter kind than poplin, but very much resembling it, are the materials of promenade dress. *Ladies' Museum*, May 1831 ~~~ Gros d'Alger – a mixture of silk and worsted, of a slighter kind than poplin, but very much resembling it, are the materials of promenade dress. *Ladies' Museum*, May 1831 ~~~ Evening Dress. A dress of *Satin d'Alger*, striped canary colour and white. *Casket*, July 1831 ~~~ Materials of Half Dress… *drap d'Alger* are new and very fashionable materials; … composed of silk and wool, is extremely light and brilliant, and likely to continue in favour during the spring. *Casket*, July 1831 ~~~ Some new materials, as *gaze d'Alger*, … have recently been introduced in evening dress; the gauzes are figured, and of a very rich description; *Ladies' Museum*, November 1831 ~~~ [Paris morning dress] The scarf is of gold-coloured gaze Algerienne, with very rich ends. *La Belle Assemblée*, December 1831 ~~~ Make and Materials of Evening Dress. … It is expected that turbans will be very much worn. The most elegant are of *gaze satinée d'Alger*. *Atheneum*, February 1832 ~~~ Tartan silks, tigrine, Siam taffitas, and Algiers satin, form the majority of the dresses worn at evening parties in Paris. *Court Journal*, February 7, 1835 ~~~ Breakfast Dress. Peignoir of *mousseline d'Alger*. *Court Magazine*, September 1835 ~~~ Public Promenade Dress. … *Gros d'Alger* hat; the colour is a milk white, *Ladies' Pocket*, December 1835 ~~~ The *modistes* and *conturiers* of Paris are at present busily occupied in preparing *costumes de soirées*. For this purpose they employ the richest and most splendid silks and satins, which almost stand upright of themselves. Among the articles most in request are *reps Algerien*, figured in satin flowers; *Court Journal*, December 19, 1835 ~~~ Half transparent materials, of the very finest Cashmere wool, are in great request. The most fashionable are the … *mousseline d'Algar*, … of small Turkish patterns patterns, presents a dazzling assemblage of hues; *Ladies' Pocket*, June 1836 ~~~ Morning Dresses. … Hat of pale pink gros d'Alger, *New Monthly Belle Assemblée*, November 1836

Algileck – [Paris] The evening dress silks that have appeared, are all in the superb but heavy style of Louis XIV's reign. The satins *Salomon, Esmeralda,* and *Pharamond,* are expected to be in great request; as are also the *Velours Algileck,* and *Leocadie,* and the *Velontées de la Mosquée,* and *Carlina. New Monthly Belle*

Assemblée, November 1836 ~~~Evening costume is still of a light kind; several new materials have, however, appeared for it. We may cite among them the … *Velours, Algibeck*, and *Omasis* … These rich and beautiful materials will be in great request as soon as the winter has fairly set in. *Ladies' Pocket*, November 1836 ~~~ [Paris] Some superb materials have appeared for evening dress; the most *distingué* are the *velours Algibeck* and *Ornasis, Court Magazine*, November 1836

Alhambra – The muslins *à Alhambra* are so called because they are printed with arabesques taken from that celebrated place. *Lady's Magazine*, March 31, 1830

alibala – Sarsnets of various colour, with the Alibala and thicker sort of India muslins than those worn on evenings, are most prevalent at friendly meetings or social home parties: these … muslins [are ornamented] with lace. *La Belle Assemblée*, March 1812

allegeas – Allegeas or Allegias, a stuff manufactured in the East Indies. There are two sorts, one of cotton, and the other of several kinds of herbs, which are spun like flax or hemp. <u>Dictionary of Commerce</u>, 1810 ~~~ Their length and breath are 8 ells by 5, 6, or 7 eighths, and of 12 ells, by 3 fourths or 5 eighths. <u>Encyclopædia Perthensis</u>, 1816

alpaca – The so perfectly fine Spanish cloth, which has the softness of velvet and satin, and which we generally see come in presents to other countries, is not worked from the wool of Spanish sheep, but from the wool taken from the Peruvian Vigogna, Lama, or Alpaca *(camellus glama et pacos Linnæi),* which is of the camel species, and which will scarcely (it is probable) be introduced into Europe, though it should seem that, they ought to thrive equally well on the Spanish, as on the Peruvian mountains, which are still higher, and covered with snow. <u>Communications to the Board of Agriculture</u>, 1797 ~~~ *The paco, or the alpaco, and the vicugna are two animals of the same genus, but of very different species.* <u>History of Chili</u>, 1808 ~~~ The Pacos is smaller than the Lama, but resembles it in shape and in all its qualities; the wool is, however, finer, being as good and as precious as silk, making excellent gloves, stockings, and cloth, and constitutes a valuable branch of commerce to the Spaniards. These animals are natives of South America. *Atheneum*, December 1808 ~~~ The picked wool of the Alpaca, whether dyed, or in its natural colour, produces stuffs of exquisite gloss and fineness; it is much more valuable than any of the other species of wool, except the Vicuna. *American Farmer*, June 8, 1821 [see also *vigonia*]

aman – Aman, a sort of blue cotton cloth, which comes from the Levant by the way of Aleppo. <u>Dictionary of Commerce</u>, 1810 ~~~ The Bengal cotton goods which go under the names of *casses, amáns,* and *garats*, have been exported in considerable quantity by the English; <u>Universal Geography</u>, 1825

amen – [see *lasting*]

American nankeen – A sample of American Nankeen has been shown us, (says the Baltimore Patriot,) made of the nankeen colored cotton raised in Georgia on the estate of Senator Forsyth. It is sold at two dollar, the piece, and is finer than the India nankeen ordinarily worn; still finer samples are intended to be manufactured. It differs advantageously from the India, in the important particular of not fading from wear; on the contrary, a sample was shown us which had been in wear two years, and grown of a darker and richer color. *American Railroad Journal*, August 18, 1832 ~~~We have before us a beautiful specimen of American nankeen, made from nankeen colored cotton, raised by Mr. Forsyth, of Georgia. The nankeen cotton was first raised in the south, eight or ten years ago, but was not then thought much of – as is the case with all new articles, it was with difficulty that persons could be found to try it. … Mr. Nathaniel F. Williams, merchant of this city, agent for the sale of the nankeen, to whom we are indebted for an opportunity of examining it, informs us that a friend of his had accidentally got a large spot of ink on a new pair of pantaloons, which he considered had spoiled them. Mr. W. advised him to apply a little lemon juice and salt to the spot, and expose it to the sun, which was done, the ink extracted, and the color of the cloth remained unchanged. … We have accidentally learned that, when certain contracts have expired, the American nankeens will be made of the cassimere width; and, we hope, sold by the *yard*, like other goods, instead of by the piece – *Niles' Register*, June 19, 1833 [see *nankeen*]

American silk – *American Silk.* – It is with pleasure we notice the high reputation in which American Silk is held. As yet but little has been brought into market, but specimens have been exhibited to those who are capable of judging, and they have pronounced it excellent. ... American Silk is fine, nervous, good, regular, clean, of a fine colour; in a word, it unites all the qualities that can be wished for. Its market price in the state of raw Silk, well reeled, according to its different qualities, well prepared, would be 26 francs a pound, and the sale of it at Lyons, would be very easy, particularly if there was a constant supply of bales weighing from 100 to 150 pounds. *Southern Agriculturist*, May 1830 ~~~ Carriage Dress. ... The pelisse is of reps Americain, of a light shade of aventurine; *La Belle Assemblée*, February 1832 ~~~ [Paris] Bottines for the promenade are generally composed of *reps Americain*, and should correspond in colour with the dress. *La Belle Assemblée*, May 1832 ~~~ Pelisses are also expected to be very fashionable in carriage dress. We have just been favoured with a sight of one of a very rich material, *reps Americain,* which we consider very novel and elegant. *Maids, Wives, and Widows*, November 10, 1832 ~~~ Archery Dress. ... *Bottines* of *gros Americain* to correspond with the dress. *Court Magazine*, August 1833

American squirrel – it is bordered all round ... with a fur of the American squirrel, or leopard spot. *La Belle Assemblée*, November 1806 ~~~ the American Squirrel is of an uniform ash colour, <u>New Encyclopædia</u>, 1807 ~~~ A Russian mantle of bright velvet crimson, lined throughout with the spotted American squirrel skin, with broad facings and high collar of the same. *Edinburgh Annual Register*, February 3, 1810 ~~~ Promenade Dress. ... A Cossack mantle of pale ruby, or blossom-coloured velvet, lined with white sarsnet, and trimmed entirely round with a broad skin of light sable, ermine, seal, or the *American squirrel*; a short tippet of the-same: *Repository of Arts*, April 1814 ~~~ A pelerine tippet, with long ends, of the light grey American squirrel, *La Belle Assemblée*, January 1829 ~~~ fur pelerines of the American-squirrel are much in vogue; these are beautifully variegated with the fore and back part of that valuable animal. *Ladies' Pocket*, December 1829

amethyst gauze – [see *metallic gauze*]

amianthus – [see *asbestos*]

amiantines bouclees – [see *epinettes*]

Amy Robsart – A new and splendid material for full dress, that is expected to be very fashionable, is called *satin Amy Robsart*, – it is a soft rich satin, printed in gold and colours. *Court Magazine*, December 1835 [see also *Walter Scott*]

Ancre – Another beautiful material [for full dress], but of a less expensive kind [than Amy Robsart], is the *satin d'Ancre*; it is a mixture of cachemire and silk, is twilled, a white ground quadrilled in wood colour, with a running pattern of green foliage, and small Bengal roses mingled with other flowers. *Court Magazine*, December 1835

Andrinople – After the Scotch stuffs, the *Andrinoples* are now the principle attraction: the ground of these is always of a deep red (red Rouen cotton); but the designs in black begin to vary in their pattern: sometimes they are in the form of twisted columns, and again in detached crossing; however, the greater part still have large black stripes. The white canezout is indispensable with this costume, in order to soften the harshness of the colour on approaching too near the figure. These Andrinoples having made their appearance among the second class of fashionables, we believe the stuff will not continue long in vogue. *Ladies' Monthly Museum*, October 1825 ~~~ October Fashions, in Rhyme. ... *Andrinople*, or *Barège*, For walking gowns is quite the rage; Whether zig-zag, striped, or plaided, *Spirit of the Times*, October 8, 1825

Anglaise – *English*. La langue Anglaise *or* l'Anglais, *the English tongue.* Un Anglais, une Anglaise, *an English man or woman.* <u>Dufief's French Dictionary</u>, 1810 [see *British* and *English*]

Anglo-Merino cloth – [see *Merino*]

Angola – The round French robe, ... are formed of undrest crape, Angola silk, or muslin. *Emerald*, September 26, 1807 ~~~ In the campaign of Angora, according to M. Tournefort, they breed the finest goats in the world. They are of a dazzling white; and their hair, which is as fine as silk, naturally curled in locks of eight or nine inches long, is worked up into the finest stuffs, especially camlet; but little of this hair is exported unspun, because the people of the country get their livelihood by spinning it. <u>Travels through Turkey</u>, 1810 ~~~ Angola stockings, (a new article manufactured in Leicestershire), are said to consist of a mixture of cotton and Angola wool. <u>Dictionary of Commerce</u>, 1810 ~~~

Evening or Ball Dress. – A Grecian round robe, of lilac or apple-blossom crape, … Angola silk, round the bottom of the robe. *Edinburgh Annual Register*, July 1, 1813 ~~~ Pelisses … in the Angola cloth, … Merinos, half twills, kerseymeres, and Angolas, are universal. *La Belle Assemblée*, December 1814 ~~~ Angola, for *Angora*. The best-educated people frequently say, an Angola shawl; an Angola cat: – it should be *Angora*. Angola is a kingdom of Africa; whereas, Angora, or Angoura, is a town of Turkey in Asia, where the inhabitants breed the finest goats in the world; the hair of which is of a beautiful white, and almost like silk, which they work into the finest stuffs. Errors of Pronunciation, 1817 ~~~ Shawls rivalling those of Cashmere are fabricated from the hair of the Angora goat. It is long and of a silken texture. Universal Gazetteer, 1823 ~~~ Angola shawls are now greatly in favor; they are generally of a very large size, and are not worn over pelisses, but with silk, poplin, or Merino gowns. It is only the beautiful silky kind of Angola shawl that is in so much estimation. *Ladies' Monthly Museum*, January 1823 ~~~ [ad] Angola do. [ditto: flannels] a superior article, and warranted not to shrink in washing. *New England Farmer*, December 10, 1834 ~~~ [ad] Dry Goods at Reduced Prices. … 2 bales of Angola Flannel, an excellent article for summer wear. *New England Farmer*, July 1, 1835 [see also *camlet* and *mohair*]

angora – [see *angola*]

apron check – cottons, … those bed and apron checks, … Indeed the demand for these commodities is so unlimited, and the wages of labour are so often lower here [Norfolk] than at Manchester, *Monthly Magazine*, January 1804 ~~~ [ad] apron and furniture checks; which, together with his formerly advertised Stock, will be found worthy attention. *Colonial Times*, May 5, 1826 ~~~ [October 20, 1832] To whom paid. John H. Kinzie … 20 pieces 4-4 apron checks 692 ½ yds at 24 cents, Emigration of Indians, 1835 [see also *checked*]

arabesque – A painting or ornament consisting entirely of foliage. Sheridan's English Dictionary, 1797 ~~~ Evening Full Dress. – This dress which for elegance and interest has never yet been exceeded, … the border may be enriched with Moresque and Arabesque ornaments according to fancy; *National Register*, September 4, 1808 ~~~ An almost unlimited number of objects are introduced in the Arabesque; but the scroll in all its varied and undulating forms is the chief and most characteristic ornament. Thus we may see it in its simple leafy elegance of curvature; or, more complex, with the outline of some vegetable production, entwining itself with numerous evolutions, until it loses its character, and shoots forth into the varied forms of animated existence. These scrolls are frequently made to terminate in the body of some fabulous figure, or even in exquisite representations of the human form. The whole kingdom of animate and inanimate being is called up by the artist to grace his design, and to these existing creatures, fancy adds a new creation, by blending the forms which are presented to her view. House Decorator and Painter's Guide, 1811 ~~~ [court dress] A blue "Arabesque" gauze and gold robe, elegantly trimmed with feathers and gold vine-leaves; *Royal Lady's Magazine*, April 1831 ~~~ *Out-Door Costume, New Materials for Mantle Dresses*. … We close our list with a material of a very economical kind: it is a washing silk, in a very striking pattern of *Arabesques*. *Maids, Wives, and Widows*, November 10, 1832 ~~~ Arabesques of ruby velvet ornamented the front of the skirt. *Court Magazine*, March 1836

arabia – [see *model linen* and *ticking*]

Arachne – [Patent] To Messrs. Pouillot, Fayolle, and Hullin, of Paris, for five years, for a machine for making the lace, called *tricot de Berlin, toile d'araignée, oeil de perdrix*. *Monthly Magazine*, November 1809 ~~~ Araignée, spider … Toile d'araignée, cobweb. Tardy's French Dictionary, 1808 ~~~ A deep border of fine Arachne net *La Belle Assemblée*, March 1819 ~~~ We have seen a very elegant dress just completed for a ball given by a lady of rank and fashion: it is a frock of gossamer, or Arachne net, over white satin, trimmed with clusters of early spring flowers of various colors. *La Belle Assemblée*, May 1823 ~~~ Evening dress is this winter likely to be extremely magnificent. Among the new kinds of light materials expected to be most in favour, are the *esmeralda*, and *tulle araché*. These, which have but just appeared in France, are now made here, and are confessed to be fully equal to the French articles of the same names. The *tulle* is of an extremely clear kind, and embroidered in light patterns with a mixture of gold, or silver, and silk. The silk is of rich full colours, as crimson, *aventurine*, green violet,

&c. *La Belle Assemblée*, December 1831 ~~~ Make and Material of Ball Dress. – *Gaze Esmeralda, tulle-Arachné*, and crape, are the materials of the new ball dresses. ... The second, a new kind of embroidered *tulle* crape, is, however, most in favor. The favorite for is *à la Jardinière*. *Atheneum*, April 1832 [see also *cobweb, gossamer net* and *spider*]

araignee – [see *arachne, cobweb* and *spider*]

areophane – Another very rich dress is of silver gauze *aréophane*: *La Belle Assemblée*, January 1831 [probably *aerophane*]

Argus – There are a few feathers in the wing of the Argus pheasant, of great beauty. They do not possess a great variety of colors, for the marks are only different shades of a lightish brown, or stone color; but they appear in regular rings and spots, from end to end, in a manner which gives the idea of their being artificially produced. They form a very elegant ornament. Book of Commerce, 1834 ~~~ white crape petticoat, worn over white satin, ornamented all over with tufts of the Argus feather. ... Argus feathers were blended with the ostrich, which composted the head-dress. *La Belle Assemblée*, January 1807

Armenia – [Paris] Cloak of velours d'Arménie, lined with satin and wadded. *Lady's Magazine and Museum*, December 1834

Armion Dunoise – [Paris] There were also several materials of a very light kind of silk and wool. One is the *Armion Dunoise*; *Court Magazine*, May 1836

armoisin – a silk stuff, or kind of taffety, manufactured in the East Indies, at Lyons in France, and a Lucca in Italy. That of the Indies is slighter than those made in Europe. Encyclopædia Britannica, 1797 ~~~ [in 1789, in the estate of a bankrupt] one hundred and fifty yards of armozeen, Complete System of Pleading, 1798 ~~~ taffetas d'armoisin, *Persian*. Dufief's French Dictionary, 1810 ~~~ The merchandises of Europe, China, and India, fit for the trade of Japan, are ... black and coloured armoisins, Dictionary of Commerce, 1810 ~~~ The bridal spencer of white Armozeen silk, ... has just issued from the tasteful repository of Mrs. Bell, for the hymeneal ceremony of a lady of distinction. *La Belle Assemblée*, February 1819 ~~~ Armosin, *s.* (sarcenet; a silk-stuff, a kind of taffety) Wilson's French Dictionary, 1833 [see also *persian* and *sarsnet*]

armure – If you entrust me with any commission for the present season, I shall send you a dress of *velours epingle armure* of dalia, as this is still a choice colour for dress. *Casket*, February 1833 ~~~ [ad] Highly Important to the Fashionable World. RICH FIGURED and PLAIN SILKS Satineés, Sylphidé, Quadrillé, Ecossais, Quadraute, Satinnette, Brillantine, Armure, *Court Journal*, March 28, 1835 ~~~ For those who prefer a more humble style of *robe-de-chambre*, the material may be silk, marceline, armure, or *satin-de-laine. Court Journal*, October 24, 1835

army cloth – the produce of the Merino sheep, is manufactured into superfine cloth, at from 20s. to 30s. per yard; English wool, on the contrary, is manufactured into army cloth, blanketing, kersies, &c. the price of which is under 12s. per yard. *Monthly Magazine*, December 1818 ~~~ The coarse cloths and kerseys, called army cloths, are about six-quarter yards wide when finished. American Tariffs, 1828 [see *kersey*]

artificial – [see *imitation*]

artificial flowers – *The Princess Royal* – Appeared at court in a dress of her own work; a green and gold embroidery, with artificial flowers worked in the front; *Lady's Magazine*, January 1797 ~~~ Artificial flowers are made, sometimes of very fine coloured paper, sometimes of the inside linings upon which the silk-worm spins its silk, but principally of cambric, which is a kind of linen made of flax, first manufactured at Cambray, in France; of which great quantities were imported into this country: but now, persons convicted of wearing, or selling, or making up for hire, any cambric or French lawns are liable to a penalty of 5*l*. Book of Trades, 1806 ~~~ Artificial flowers belong to a second order of dress, from whence too they are likely soon to be banished, not bearing the contrast of nature; flowers of stamped or cramped satin and lace are now a more approved ornament for hats or caps. *La Belle Assemblée*, May 1811 ~~~ Artificial flowers, which we have no longer occasion to import from France, since our own are hardly to be distinguished from the productions of nature, are universally adopted in full dress by juvenile *belles*; they are also used to ornament the *toques* and turbans of matronly ladies. *Repository of Arts*, July 1817 ~~~ Flowers, made of feathers, from a beautiful head-dress for young ladies; *La Belle Assemblée*, January 1818 ~~~ These flowers are of velvet, feathers, or transparent whalebone. *La Belle Assemblée*, December 1827 ~~~ Our younger females are fond of sticking a single flower here and there, among their tresses. This has a very pretty effect at rural parties: the flowers are not only correct copies from nature, but are exquisitely scented. *La Belle Assemblée*, August 1828 ~~~ Among the newest artificial flowers, tulips, of various colors, have been introduced. *Atheneum*, April 1832

Asbestos – The asbestos is a sort of fossil stone, which may be split into threads and filaments, and wrought into cloth. ... Cloth made of the extraordinary fossil production now under consideration, is endued with the wonderful property of remaining unconsumed in the fire. <u>Arithmetical Questions</u>, 1795 ~~~ The amianthus, called also *incombustible flax,* and *asbestos,* is a mineral substance found in several parts of the earth. It consists of fibres of a white colour, more or less greyish, which adhere strongly to each other. Means however are found to separate them, and when well washed, they have the appearance of the whitest flax. The amianthus is found in the Pyrenees, the Alps, &c. <u>Recreations in Mathematics and Natural Philosophy</u>, 1803 ~~~ ITALY. *Fires.* – M. Aldini, of Milan, has invented a dress which enables the wearer to traverse with impunity the flames of a large fire, for the purpose of rescuing those who have been exposed to their fury, or of saving property from destruction. This dress is composed of a tissue of asbestos, which it is well known is not combustible, covered with metallic gauze, through which it is also well known flame will not penetrate. *Atheneum*, April 8, 1829 ~~~ Another Longchamps novelty is the *chapeau amiaté*, said to be composed of amianthus, but the peculiar merit of this non-combustible certainly down not lie on the surface. *Godey's Ladies Book*, June 1831

Asia – *gaze d'Asie jaconie* ... are the new materials for evening dress. *La Belle Assemblée*, May 1831 ~~~ Evening Dress. (World of Fashion.) A dress of white *gaze d'Asie, corsage uni* cut low, and trimmed round the bust with blond lace mancherons, set on very broad and full. *Atheneum*, September 15, 1831 ~~~ Asiatic *adj.* (of Asia) *Asiatique. d'Asie; né en Asie.* <u>Wilson's French Dictionary</u>, 1833 ~~~ [Paris] Satin d'Asie, that *à la Keine*, and one still more rich, called *satin Isabelle*, have appeared for half-dress. *Ladies' Pocket*, November 1836

Astracan fur – At Astrachan they have great quantities of lamb-skins, grey and black; some waved, others curled, all naturally, and very pretty, having a fine gloss, particularly the waved, which, at a small distance, appear like the richest watered tabby; they are much esteemed, and are much used for the lining of coats, and the turning up of caps, in Persia, Russia, and other parts. <u>Annual Register ... for the Year 1767</u>, 1800 ~~~lamb-skins ... The fleeces of Astracan are smooth, glossy, and black. They are used in the Levant for trimming caps, turbans, and other articles of dress. <u>General Dictionary of Commerce</u>, 1810 ~~~ [Paris] a kind of green pelisse made of fine Merino cloth, its colour is between the deep Spanish fly-green and the *Pomona*; pelisses and mantles of this beautiful colour are generally trimmed with sable or Astracan fur. *La Belle Assemblée*, March 1811 ~~~ The Polonese half-boot ... are lined with silk plush, trimmed with Astracan fur, and laced with silk cords and tassels. *La Belle Assemblée*, January 1820 ~~~ There are, however, some satin pelisses which have not so wintry an appearance: these are generally black, and their trimming consists of a mixture of Astracan fur and the small feathers of the toukan, orange-colour and red. *Ladies' Monthly Museum*, April 1828 [see also *lamb skin* and *Moscow ribbon*]

Athenian – The dress stuffs are ... the Athenian: ... a sort of smooth bark, knit in silk: the prettiest are of a very pale sea-blue ground, knit in shaded vine-lees. *Ladies' Monthly Museum*, June 1826 ~~~ [in January] The Parisian ladies were very fond of dresses made of what they called *Athenian* cloth. *La Belle Assemblée*, [review of the first six months] 1828 ~~~ [ad] Fall Goods. ... 2 case Athenian Camlet, an excellent article for ladies' Habits, Cloaks, &c. 1 case Athenian Cassimeres, suitable for ladies' Habits, Cloaks, &c. *New England Farmer*, December 17, 1834

atlas – a rich kind of silk. <u>Sheridan's English Dictionary</u>, 1797 ~~~ in commerce, a silk-satin, manufactured in the East Indies. There are some plain, some striped, some flowered, the flowers of which are either gold or only silk. There are atlasses of all colours; but most of them false [not colour-fast], especially the red and the crimson. The manufacture of them is admirable; the gold and silk being worked together after such a manner as no workmen in Europe and imitate; yet they are far from having that fine gloss and lustre which the French know how to give to their silk stuffs. <u>Encyclopædia Britannica</u>, 1797 ~~~ Atlas, once generally used for winter-dresses, is now employed only for covers and state-cloaths. *Monthly Magazine*, April 1802 ~~~ in commerce, a sort of silk or sattin manufactured in the East Indies, in which gold and silk are so wrought together, as no workman in Europe can imitate. In China they weave long strips of gilt paper into their silks. The same slips of paper are twisted about silk threads, so artificially, as to look finer than gold thread, though of no great value. <u>General Dictionary of Commerce</u>, 1810 ~~~ Princess Charlotte of Wales' Wedding Dress and Jewellery. 1. The wedding dress is a slip of white and-silver atlas, worn under a dress of transparent silk net elegantly embroidered in silver lama, with a border to correspond, tastefully worked in bunches of flowers, to form festoons round the bottom; the sleeves and neck trimmed with a rich suit of Brussels point lace. The mantua is two yards and an half long, made of rich silver and white atlas, trimmed the same as the dress, to correspond. *Niles' Weekly Register*, June 22, 1816

Bagnos - Buzin des Indes

bagnos – Shawls *en bagnos* (which is an imitation of China crape), *Repository of Arts*, August 1829

bailloque – or Bayoque. Thus the French call those ostrich-feathers, which are of a dark brown colour, mixed with white. This kind of feather is seldom dyed; but the feathers are well washed with soap, which gives them a bright glossy appearance. These *bailoque* feathers are the least valued. General Dictionary of Commerce, 1810 [see also *boiteuse*]

baize – There are two kinds of dresses worn by the Indian women, made in the same plain manner with those worn by the men in general, the whole consisting of a short petticoat and a veil of American baize. View of the United States of America, 1795 ~~~ Bays, in commerce, a sort of open woollen stuff, having a long nap, sometimes frized, and sometimes not. This stuff is without wale; and it is wrought in a loom with two treddles, like flannel. It is chiefly manufactured at Colchester and Bockin, in Essex, … Their chief use is for dressing the monks and nuns, and for linings, especially in the army. … The breadth of bays is commonly a yard and a half, a yard and three quarters, or two yards, by 42 to 48 in length. Encyclopædia Britannica, 1797 ~~~ [extracts from a will, 1800] thirty yards of baize of the same colour [drab] at about 14d a yard for petticoats for ten poor elderly women of Mansfield, to be given some time in the month of October annually, for ever, History of Mansfield, 1801 ~~~ this baize is used in America for the slaves? – It is; and in Holland a great deal is used; … I think for petticoats, or something of that kind. Reports from the Committees, 1821 ~~~ A General Collection of Words of variable spelling, in which those of the best usage are printed in Roman character, … baize, *bayze, bayes, baise, bays, bayz*. Practical Orthography, 1828 ~~~ *Bockings and Baizes* – 42 inches wide, cost 6d. to 1s. 3d. – For lining the pea-jackets of sailors and boatmen, and the great-coats and round-jackets of farmers, mechanics, and laborers, and for table and floor cloths, &c. *Niles' Weekly Register*, March 8, 1828 ~~~ Baize (for which some would write Bays, from the name of a City in France,) is a coarse, open, plain cloth, of worsted warp and woollen weft, which is sometimes sold white, but more usually dyed. When Baize is perched on both sides, it has the appearance of coloured Flannel; but it is often perched on one side and napped on the other, and is then commonly called Frieze, although the word Frieze is more properly a general than a particular denomination. Analytical Dictionary, 1830 ~~~ 2 pieces green baize 106 yards – 90 [cents, totaling $] 84.80 [letter dated October 26, 1832] Emigration of Indians, 1835 [see also *bocking* and *frieze*]

baleine – [see *whalebone*]

balloon net – There is also a species of nets called BALLOON NETS. These are also mounted like the patent net. The cording is so disposed, that the crossing of the gauze may be continued regularly, while every crossing of the whip part is twice repeated. In this net, the gauze part is slackened, and the whip part kept always tight. By these means the gauze, being drawn alternately to the right and left, forms a waving, or serpentine appearance, instead of being perfectly straight. There are many varieties of these nets. Art of Weaving, 1808 ~~~ It is observable in the allover dropped whip net, that the two threads *i* and *a* form a twist resembling a splitful of gauze warp, thrown into a zig-zag or serpentine direction, which gives this pattern the appearance of one which was frequently woven on the silk, and known by the name of the balloon net; on which account it sometimes passes under that name. Art of Weaving, 1831

baltic moss – In *November* [1822], there are, however, some new invented materials this month, for hat and turbans, likely to meet with much encouragement, namely, Irish velvet, crystallized velvet, and Baltic moss. Museum of Foreign Literature, 1823 [see also *moss*]

Baltimore crape – For half-dress, a new material called Baltimore crape, and which is sprigged, has lately made it appearance; the colour is that of the dried date leaf: *La Belle Assemblée*, August 1820

bamboo – *Morning Dress*. Chinese hats of Bamboo cane, *Lady's Magazine*, July 1798 ~~~ That *bamboo hats* fairly come under the general classification of "all hats, or bonnets of straw, chip, or grass," *Public Documents*, December 1830 ~~~ It appears from them that the proprietors, … distribute to their slaves one suit per annum, or else the materials for making; in general only the latter; and that it consists of the following articles: – To the men, a short jacket of coarse and flimsy woollen, called *baize* or *bamboo*,

… The customary allowance of negro clothing has generally been *two yards and a quarter, or two yards and a half of a coarse woollen stuff*, known in many of the islands by the name of *bamboo*, to grown negroes; and less in proportion to smaller ones. <u>Slavery of the British West India Colonies Delineated</u>, 1830 [see also *baize* or *cane*]

ban – in commerce, a sort of smooth fine muslin, which the English import from the East Indies. The piece is almost a yard broad, and runs about 20 yards and a half. <u>Encyclopædia Britannica</u>, 1797

bandanna – From an important recent investigation it appears, that 1200 pieces of Bandana Handkerchiefs and six cases of Playing Cards, were, by the connivance of the Captain, and Revenue Officers, landed, from a Vessel bound to Embden, in April 1795. <u>Commerce and Police of the River Thames</u>, 1800 ~~~ the silk-manufacturers and weavers of this place [Macclesfield], have just received the pleasing intelligence, that the East-India Company will wave their privilege of selling Bandanna silk-handkerchiefs for home consumption. This communication was made to them, by authority, on the 26th of January, 1815. <u>Encyclopædia Londinensis</u>, 1816 ~~~ It is stated in the weavers petition, that in the year 1813, 8*s.* 6*d.* per dozen was paid for weaving double-warped yard-wide bandanna handkerchiefs, or 4*s.* 11½ *d.* per cut of seven yards, and 9*s*, 6*d.* per dozen for single warp, or 5*s.* 6½ *d.* per cut; … So that upon bandannas the general earnings are not more than 11*s.* or 12*s.* a week? – 12*s.* 6*d.* if they work hard; but those bandannas are not made by what we call our prime weavers; they will not touch one; it is a common thing for a weaver to have from three to five looms in his house; out of those I can say it is common to give one bandanna, the rest all coloured works; that bandanna is generally made by a boy or a girl; and I am of opinion, that although the bandanna is the worst paid of any work a man has, I consider either the master or the man could not do well without it; there are several months in the year with all silk manufacturers, that he does not know what to turn his attention to. <u>Reports from the Committees</u>, 1818 ~~~ Bandanna handkerchiefs, and bandanna cloths for garments, were begun to be made at Glasgow about the year 1802, by Mr. Henry Monteith, and are now manufactured there to a considerable amount. The cloth is dyed a bright Turkey red, and the colour is discharged from those parts in it which form the pattern or figure, by passing a chemical mixture through them. This article is made no where but at Glasgow. <u>Encyclopædia Britannica</u>, 1824 ~~~ Bandana; the name applied to a peculiar species of handkerchief, the fabric of which may be either silk or cotton, having a dark ground of Turkey red, blue, or purple, varegated with patterns of white, or bright yellow. These Handkerchiefs were formerly manufactured in the East Indies, and thence imported into Europe; but the beauty and durability of their colours caused such a demand for this commodity in England and the nations of the continent, as to stimulate our British manufacturers, not only to imitate, but even surpass the Eastern Bandana. At first, the imitations were made by the common process of printing with blocks, which never produced such durability of colour or clean outline of pattern. … It is to be observed, in the outset, that the process for the formation of bandanas is the converse of calico printing, the cloth being first dyed of a uniform dark colour, and the pattern being afterwards formed by the application of a chemical agent to those parts where the spots or figures are meant to appear, which discharges or extracts the colour from these parts only. The cloth employed is usually cotton, sometimes woven plain, but more frequently tweeled; and the dye for the ground is most commonly Turkey red <u>Popular Encyclopædia</u>, 1836

baragan – in commerce, a sort of stuff, not diapered, something like a camblet, but of a coarser grain. It is used to make cloaks, surtouts, and other such garments, to keep off the rain. … Those of Valenciennes are the most valued; they are all of wool, both the warp and the woof. <u>Encyclopædia Britannica</u>, 1797 ~~~ Barracan or Barragan, … a French woollen stuff, resembling the English *banagon*, but inferior in quality. <u>General Dictionary of Commerce</u>, 1810 ~~~ Barracan (*Com.*) a French woollen stuff resembling the English *barrage*. <u>Universal Technological Dictionary</u>, 1823 ~~~ Barragon, for flowered woollen stuffs, to one yard and one third wide – watered or plain, to one yard <u>Digest of the Commercial Regulations</u>, 1824 ~~~ [men's] Shooting Dress. … The trowsers are of Russia Baragan, with broad stripes; *Casket*, January 1831 ~~~ That called "*baragan*"-fustian is by far the *best and most durable.* <u>Instructions to Young Sportsmen</u>, 1833 [see also *barrage*]

barege – [Paris] For the promenade, white gowns are most prevalent, either at Tivoli or at the Thuilleries;

over these is often worn a dark red scarf shawl of *Barege* crape, with the ends ornamented by a rich knotted fringe, *La Belle Assemblée*, June 1819 ~~~ [Paris] a small scarf composed of *crépon de Barèges*: it is trimmed with knotted fringe, is very narrow, and is tied carelessly at the throat: *ponceau* is the favourite colour for these scarfs. *Repository of Arts*, June 1819 ~~~ [Paris] Dresses of *Barèges* silk, trimmed with flounces, exquisitely embroidered with coloured silks, are much in favour with those of rank and opulence, who only can afford to wear them. *La Belle Assemblée*, December 1819 ~~~ [Paris] Gowns are, silk, muslin, *bourre de soie*, *baréges*, *crêpe des baréges*, and *crêpe des Merinos*: these two last materials are transparent, and are worn in white and colours; the latter is most prevalent in out-door costume, the former in full dress. *Repository of Arts*, May 1823 ~~~ Coloured *barège* still continues the favourite material for half-dress gowns; striped *barège* is more fashionable than that of a diamond pattern. *Repository of Arts*, June 1823 ~~~ Barêge silks, which are now quite the rage, are generally either striped or chequered; sometimes the ground of these patterns is figured in that way, as to give to the silk the appearance of having been watered. *La Belle Assemblée*, December 1823 ~~~ Many evening dresses are of *Barége-gauze*, either figured or plain. *La Belle Assemblée*, February 1827 ~~~ it must be recollected that the entire warp is composed of silk, ... an article called *barege*, being composed of similar materials and wove in a similar manner with *Italian nett*, *Public Documents*, January 1829 ~~~ Carriage and Promenade Dress. – Gown of lilac barege. *Lady's Book*, November 1830 ~~~ We have seen also a few light shawls of the *baréges* kind, worn by genteel women, but their price is so moderate, that they are not likely to become fashionable. *Ladies' Museum*, August 1831 ~~~ A dress of the same colour as the above, but of a different material, almost rivalled in beauty the rich production of the Indian loom. It was composed of puce Barege-muslin, lined throughout with gros-de-Naples of the same colour. The softness of the long folds, thus supported, had a most elegant effect. *Court Journal*, February 2, 1833 ~~~ In all the lighter fabrics of silk and worsted, such as bombasins, Norwich crapes, barege, &c. *Public Documents*, October 1833

barege cachemire – [Paris] For the promenade, square shawls of *Barége* cachemire, with the ground of a lilac, or of a red-currant color, or a cinnamon brown, are much in favor; they are striped with green and orange color. These shawls are extremely beautiful. *Ladies' Monthly Museum*, September 1821 ~~~ a scarf shawl of Amaranthine colored *Barége* cachemire is tied round the throat; *La Belle Assemblée*, January 1823 ~~~ [Paris] Scarf-shawls of Barège-Cachemire are red, chequered with lines of black. *Lady's Magazine*, October 1825

bariga – a species of raw silk, brought from the East Indies. General Dictionary of Commerce, 1810 ~~~ Cabeca (*Com*) or cabesse, the finest kind of India silks, in distinction from the *bariga*, which is the inferior sort. Universal Technological Dictionary, 1823

barns – The womens apparel is chiefly a variety of stuffs of their own manufacture; as ... *barns*, and other course linens of various kinds, Statistical Account of Scotland, 1795 ~~~ The principal manufacture in this county [Kinross-shire] is that of coarse linens, commonly called Silesias, woven from twenty-seven to thirty inches in breadth, some coarse fabrics, provincially called *tweels*, *barns*, and *straikens*. Beauties of Scotland, 1806

barracan – [see *baragan*]

barrage – a linen interwoven with worsted flowers, manufactured in Normandy. General Dictionary of Commerce, 1810 ~~~ Barrage, *m. Normandy table linen*. Dufief's French Dictionary, 1810 ~~~ [ad] Veils, Fancy Silk and Gause Hdkfs. Barrage and Thibet, do. Silk and Cotton, Plain and Fancy Hose, Kid Gloves, Horse Skin, do. Blond Gause and Barrage Veils. *New England Farmer*, April 27, 1831

barrege – Barrege, a silk from France. ... of silk and worsted, *Public Documents*, March 1832 [see *barege*]

Bath coating – The winters of 1797 and 1798 he [writer James White] passed in the neighbourhood of Bath, and many persons noticed in the pump-room, the streets, or vicinity of the city, a thin, pale, emaciated man (between 30 and 40), with a wild, yet penetrating look, dressed in a light coat, of Bath coating. *European Magazine*, April 1799 ~~~ Fashions for Gentlemen. Great coats are generally worn of olive, olive brown, dark bottle green, superfine cloth, or superfine Bath coating; *Jersey Magazine*, February 1810 ~~~ For promenade dress, ... [mantles] are usually made of Bath coating, lined and trimmed with black. *Ladies' Monthly Museum*, December 1818 ~~~ Dresses for Wildfowl Shooting. ...

the waistcoat, both before and behind, should be made of either *shag*, or Bath-coating, which certainly, taking all weather, answers best, and is the most comfortable. Instructions to Young Sportsmen, 1825 ~~~ There was several years ago a manufactory of coarse woollen cloth, called Bath-coating, and kerseymere, carried on here and in the neighbourhood, but it has ceased to exist. Gazetteer of England and Wales, 1836 [see also *coating*]

batiste – in commerce, a fine white kind of linen cloth manufactured in Flanders and Picardy. There are three kinds of batiste; the first very thin; the second less thin; and the third much thicker called *Holland batiste*, as coming very near the goodness of Hollands. The chief use of Batiste is for neck-cloths, head-cloths, surplices, &c. Encyclopædia Britannica, 1797 ~~~ Batiste, *sf. cambric, lawn.* Nugent's French Dictionary, 1817 ~~~ Morning dress. A round dress, composed of *batiste*; the bottom is embroidered in a running pattern of *pensées* in yellow silk, *Manchester Iris*, May 11, 1822 ~~~ Dresses of striped batiste are much worn in home costume; the texture of these cheap dresses is light and cool, but the elegance of their patterns, and brilliancy of their summer tints, are greatly improved; and when these dresses are well-made and tastefully trimmed, they form a very pretty home attire for young persons. *Ladies' Monthly Museum*, August 1828 ~~~ Dresses of coloured batiste are also much in fashion for home attire: they are most admired when the ground is of some light and unobtrusive colour, and the figures in large chequers. The tints of these chequers are so various and vivid, and so beautifully shaded off, one colour into the other, in the stripes that form the diamonds, that they have an effect equal to the finest painted velvet. *Ladies' Monthly Museum*, October 1828 ~~~ Batiste; cambric; a very fine, thick, white, linen cloth. It is made of the best white flax, called *ramé*, … Different kinds of batiste are called *linons, claires, cambrics,* &c, and manufactured not only in France and the Netherlands, but also in Switzerland, in Bohemia and Silesia. The best come from India. Encyclopædia Americana, 1829 ~~~ [mourning for George IV.] Black *batiste* or plain black gingham are, we presume on account of their being a cooler dress than silk, adopted by many genteel women. *Ladies' Museum*, August 1830 ~~~ [Paris] Aprons have a very delightful effect when worn under the dressing-gowns, which I admired above all things. The latter are made of India muslin or in *batiste linon*, worked all over, or *a colonnes gothiques*; *Casket*, February 1833 [see also *cambric* and *lawn*]

batiste de laine – [Paris] The materials of promenade dress are silks of different descriptions, muslins, *batiste de laine*, *La Belle Assemblée*, June 1830 ~~~ One of the prettiest mourning dresses that we have seen is a *peignoir* of *batiste-laine*, of that shade of iron grey that approaches nearly to black; *La Belle Assemblée*, August 1830 ~~~ Morning Dress. – A redingote of *batiste laine*, striped in broad grey and white stripes. *Lady's Book*, October 1830 ~~~ A simple style of morning dress, but one that is at this moment very fashionable, is a pelisse robe, of plain *batiste de laine*, *Court Magazine*, October 1836

batiste de soie – Evening Dress. It is composed of printed *batiste de Soie*, a low corsage very open on the bosom, and with a lappel of the pelerine kind. *Ladies' Museum*, June 1832 ~~~ [Paris] Grand Festival Dresses. … A dress of mousseline de soie, or batiste de soie, écrue, pearl grey, apricot, pale rose, or hanneton brown, richly embroidered in floss silks, *Lady's Magazine and Museum*, July 1834

bats' wings – Evening Dress. … Short full sleeve, composed of Urling's net, finished at the bottom by a narrow satin band, and ornamented with satin in the form of bat's wings. *Manchester Iris*, April 6, 1822 ~~~ A new pattern in Cachemire shawls has lately appeared, and these shawls are favourite out-door envelopes; they are figured all over in half *rosaces*, vulgarly called bats' wings: the first that were in this pattern, just shewed themselves last winter; they were then on a black ground; now the ground is white, and the bats'-wings are of the most glaring colours. *La Belle Assemblée*, September 1823

Bauces – We may cite also the satins *Bauces* and *Hosalba* as equally remarkable for their richness and elegance. *Ladies' Pocket*, November 1836

bay-yarn – A term sometimes used promiscuously with woollen yarn. Sheridan's English Dictionary, 1797

bayadere – The Morning Occupations of a Pretty Woman. … We soon stopped at Noustiers, to select some kerchiefs of shot-silk a-la-Bayadère; they are pretty, but will soon become common; in eight days they will be no longer wearable. *Paris Spectator*, May 1813 ~~~ [Paris] In order to shew that they are not in mourning, our *élégantes* usually throw a Bayadere scarf, either of orange, light blue, or *ponceau*, loosely over their shoulders: these colours contrast very well with the black, and contribute to enliven it.… As the bosom is now very much exposed in full dress, a fashionable *belle,* in order to guard against the cold, throws a Bayadere scarf round her shoulders as soon as she takes off her pelisse: this scarf is always of two or three colours, and terminated by large tassels surmounted by sliders, which the wearer raises or lowers at pleasure, according as she wishes to have her scarf wide or narrow. *Repository of Arts,* December 1821 ~~~ Make and Materials of Out-Door Costume. … Dresses are composed of a variety of new spring silks, as *Gros de Naples, Bayadères, Thessaliennes Chines Perses,* and *Foulard du Bengale,* a mixture of silk and thread, and a perfect imitation of Indian materials. *Atheneum,* July 15, 1831 ~~~ Be it known to you my fair countrywomen, that every Indian shawl for which you pay so high a price, is second-hand, and that, too often, it has been worn by some *Bayadere,* (Indian dancing girl) *Niles' Weekly Register,* August 16, 1834 ~~~ An English lady of rank wore a dress of lilac *poult de soie,* figured with flowers. … The *ceinture* composed of a green and lilac Bayadere riband, the ends descending to the bottom of the dress. *Court Journal,* May 30, 1835 ~~~ There is a great variety of new and beautiful ribands both for hats and scarfs. The *ruban fleur des champs* is flowered in a beautiful and delicate pattern, those with fringed *dents* are extremely rich; the *Bayadere* and the *gaze oiseau* are of a lighter but a very pretty kind. *Court Magazine,* June 1835 [see also *buyadire*]

bays – [see *baize*]

bayoque – [see *bailloque*]

bead fringe – [Paris] I was also much attracted by a dress formed entirely of silver-grey velvet, ornamented round the train, petticoat, and drapery, with a white beaded fringe, *La Belle Assemblée,* January 1807 ~~~ Ball Dress. … the sleeve is made of chequered satin riband and white crape, tucked to sit very full, and finished with a rich bead fringe, … Turban, of black crape, twisted over a very broad, and richly embroidered jet bead bandeau, carelessly tied on the left side, the end trimmed with a rich jet fringe, terminating with a jet tassel; *Ladies' Monthly Museum,* January 1818 ~~~ in 1822, … *Miss Whitehead* – A figured lace dress over white satin, festooned with flounces of lace and beads, the body ornamented with Brussels lace, a rich bead fringe and stomacher; <u>Authentic Records of the Guild Merchant of Preston</u>, 1822

bear fur – Morning Dresses. … Party-coloured bear muff. *Lady's Magazine,* January 1797 ~~~ Mourning Dresses. … Grey gloves, black shoes, black bear muff, with tow white roses in the front. *Lady's Magazine,* February 1797 ~~~ Curricle caps, made of bear-skin, are among the new articles worn by our dashing belles. *Lady's Magazine,* November 1800 ~~~ Black bear muffs and tippets, long before, and in the form of handkerchiefs, are general for morning, and walking dresses; *Port Folio,* February 27, 1802 ~~~ Bear skins make a Fur in great esteem, used in housings, on coach boxes, &c. Of the skins of Bears' cubs, are made gloves, muffs, and in some countries, cloths. <u>Dictionary of Merchandise</u>, 1805 ~~~ Bear-skins, a sort of fur very much esteemed, and which gives rise to a large trade. The old bear skins are use for housings or horse-cloths, &c. The skins of the young bears server to make muffs, tippets, &c. for ladies' wear. Of Bear skins the principal colours are black, brown and silver grey. The skins are brought from the northern parts of Europe and Asia. <u>General Dictionary of Commerce</u>, 1810 ~~~ The following prices for articles which are required to be worn by all officers in the British army, … Round hat, with cockade and feather, and bear skin – 2*l.* 12*s.* 6*d.* <u>Regimental Companion</u>, 1811 ~~~ Morning, or Carriage Costume. … With this dress, it is sometimes fashionable to adopt the muff of silver bear, or blue fox. This very comfortable and useful article is making great advances towards a fashionable celebrity. *Repository of Arts,* December 1812 ~~~ I humbly think the uniform of our cavalry was the handsomest in all the armies of Europe, and in point of beauty could not be improved by alteration even by a committee of tailors. The helmet of the horse brigade of artillery with bear-skin cannot be surpassed. *Royal Military Chronicle,* January 1813 ~~~ The American furs which are at present brought to London are: Bears of several species and colours. The black are used for hammer-cloths, for grenadiers' caps, and other military equipments. (In the United States for coverings of sleighs.) The russet, or Isabella bear, for muffs. The silver or gray. The white, or Polar bear, for rugs. <u>Transactions of the Society</u>, 1833 [see also *Isabella bear*]

bearskin cloth – Witney, a populous town in Oxfordshire, noted for its manufacture of the finest blankets, and other thick woollens, called bearskins and kerseys. <u>Universal Gazetteer</u>, 1795 ~~~ woollen cloths

... The coarse cloths however for men, such as bear skin duffles, and even coarse stockings, were chiefly brought from England. <u>Review of the Events and Treaties</u>, 1796 ~~~ A top-coat for a boy twelve years old, of the cloth called bear-skin, eight dollars; <u>Tour of America</u>, 1805 ~~~ [in Leeds] more recently very large quantities of fancy articles have been made, such as swan-downs, toilonets, and kerseymeres; to which may be added a thick coarse cloth, much in use among travellers, called bear-skins. <u>Pocket Gazetteer of England and Wales</u>, 1807 ~~~ [deposition to the magistrates] He cautiously went down stairs, and looking through the glass window of the tap-room, saw a powerful well-made man, six feet high, and dressed in a drab shaggy bearskin coat, stooping over the body of Mrs. Williamson, apparently rifling her pockets. *New Annual Register*, December 1811 ~~~ [14th November, 1808] Arklow Charter School, for Girls. ... for Sundays they had a cloak of a stuff called bear-skin, and a straw bonnet. <u>Reports from the Commissioners of the Board of Education in Ireland</u>, 1813 ~~~ these wools [from middle-woolled sheep] are now employed in flannels, army and navy cloths, friezed coatings, Petershams, bear-skin and other coatings, <u>Useful and Ornamental Planting</u>, 1832

beaver cloth – [re: Patent Waterproof Cloth] the firmer the texture of the cloth, the more durable is the waterproof. Though nankeens, thin casimer, and other light wearing apparel, &c. will resist a middling rain, they will not do it in the degree of a superfine broad, or second cloth, or stout beaver, such as is generally used for box and driving coats, which are thus rendered impenetrable to any rains that ever fall in any of the four quarters of the globe; <u>Analytical Hints</u>, 1802 ~~~ The following Address of the Cotton Weavers of Ireland, lately appeared in the Irish papers. "After thirty years unwearied attention to bring the Manufacture of Cotton to its present), state of perfection, in this Country, the Cotton Weavers, finding themselves on the one side, fully competent to execute any fabric of Cotton Goods equal to any other nation in Europe, and on the other side, distressed in a material manner, for want of employment, in consequence of a preference being given to a certain description of goods, not one yard of which is manufactured in this Kingdom, and are sold under the denomination of Cassimeres, Beavers, Satin and Peruvian Cloths. "It is therefore become indispensably necessary for us, thus to appeal to the feelings of a generous Nation for redress, being fully convinced, that when out burden is made known, we cannot be disappointedly and as we can boldly assert that we can vie with any other people for quality, or texture, in the manufacturing of Velveteens, Cords, Thicksets, and every other article of Cotton Goods. *Monthly Magazine*, July 1, 1806 ~~~ A Morning Walking, or Carriage Habiliment. ... A mountain hat of white imperial beaver, or fur, tied under the chin with a ribband the colour of the coat. *La Belle Assemblée*, December 1807 ~~~ A manufactory of coatings, &c. is established at Ennis by Mr. Carney; I have seen some of his beaver coating at 11s. 4½ *d.* per yard, and think it superior to any sold in Dublin for a much higher price. <u>Statistical Survey of the County of Clare</u>, 1808 ~~~ this is a piece of beaver, for ladies cloaks, the only piece we have attempted, it is made completely from the wool, and dyed in the gaol; <u>Reports from the Committee</u>, 1819 ~~~ Then you had not, the February before, bought twenty-two yards of mixed beaver? – Oh, yes, I beg to correct my statement; I did purchase twenty-two yards of beaver, which I paid for, 6*l.* 7*s.* 6*d.* February 16th, 1820. ... I am not at all aware of the value of the wool; I don't manufacture goods, nor have I ever seen them manufactured. Seventy-seven yards of beaver at 5*s.* was the raw material not worth more than what you gave for the cloth? <u>Investigation at Ilchester Gaol</u>, 1821 ~~~ [ad] Gentlemen's Dress. ... Also, a great variety of Pea Jackets, in Pilot Cloth, Turkey Beaver, &c. *Court Journal*, December 12, 1835

beaver fur and leather – The Princess of Wales travelled in a mantle of green satin, trimmed with gold, with loops and tassels á la Brandenburgh; and wore a beaver hat. *European Magazine*, April 1795 ~~~ Beaver, an animal, otherwise named the castor, amphibious, and remarkable for his art in building his habitation; a hat of the best kind; <u>Sheridan's English Dictionary</u>, 1798 ~~~ Beaver-Skins, in commerce. Of these, merchants distinguish three sorts; the new, the dry, and the fat. The new beaver, which is also called the *white beaver*, or *Muscovy beaver*, because it is commonly kept to be sent into Muscovy, is that which the savage catch in their winter hunting. It is the best, and the most proper for making fine furs, because it has lost none of its hair by shedding. The dry beaver, which is sometimes called the *Iran beaver*, comes from the summer hunting, which is the time when these animals lose part of their hair. Tho' this sort of beaver be much inferior to the former, yet it may also be employed in furs; but it is chiefly used in the manufacture of hats. The French call it *summer castor* or *beaver*. The fat beaver is that has contracted a certain gross and oily humour, from the sweat which exhales from the bodies of the savages, who wear it for some time. Though this sort be better than the dry beaver, yet it is used only in the making of hats. Encyclopædia Britannica, 1797 ~~~ Beaver hats and bonnets superseded those of velvet. *Gentleman's Monthly*, March 1, 1803 ~~~ PLATING is likewise applied to the mode of covering felt hats with a coat or surface of beaver, which gives the article nearly the appearance of a fine castor hat, but not its durability. Dictionary of Commerce, 1810 ~~~ Winter Walking Dress. ... Beaver gloves, *La Belle Assemblée*, January 1812 ~~~ They vary in their colour; the finest are black, but the general colour is a chesnut brown, more or less dark; some have been found, but very rarely white. Encyclopædia Perthensis, 1816 ~~~ Large bonnets are universally adopted for walking; the are composed of beaver, velvet, and Leghorn; *Ladies' Monthly Museum*, March 1818 ~~~ The *hair* is of two kinds, of which the upper is long and thick; and the lower, or that immediately next to the skin, is of dark brown colour, short, close-set, and as soft as down. In commerce a distinction is made betwixt fresh, dry, and fat beaver' skins. Of these the first are obtained from animals that are killed in the winter; the second sort from those during the summer; and the third or fat sort are such as have been carried, for some time, on the bodies of the American Indians, who, as it were, tan the skins with their perspirable matter. It is the fur of the first sort which is chiefly manufactured into hats; but the fat skins are esteemed the most valuable in consequence of the long hairs having been worn off, and the fine downy fur being left perfectly free from them. Each full-grown beaver yields about twenty-four ounces of fur. This, besides hats, is wrought into gloves, caps, stockings, and other articles of dress. The *skin* of the beaver, as leather, serves for saddles, the upper leathers of shoes, gloves, the covering of trunks, &c. Useful Knowledge, 1821 ~~~ Riding habits ... Hat of light drab-coloured beaver, or Brazil straw. ... Hat of very pale grey beaver, with three short feathers. *Court Journal*, September 19, 1835

beaverteen – Men's Lappel Coatees, or Short Coats. This garment is generally made of ¾ Fustian or Beaverteen. Sectum, 1825 ~~~ and a very strong sort of cotton goods called *beaverteens*. All these are cheap – much cheaper than such necessary articles were ever before supplied for our consumption; *Niles' Weekly Register*, October 22, 1831 ~~~ [ad] Have received by the ships Hark-away and Jefferson, direct from Liverpool, ... 1 case 7-8 olive jeans and heavy beaverteens. *Farmer's Register*, May 1835 ~~~ Smooth fustians, ... when shorn after being dyed, are called beaverteen: they are both tweeled fabrics. ... Trowser velveteens are woven 19 inches wide, if they are to be cut up; if not, they are woven 30 inches, and called beaverteen. ... Shorn, dyed, and finished as drab beaverteen. 9½ *d.* to 2*s.* Cotton Manufacture of Great Britain, 1836 [see also *fustian* and *York beaver*]

Bedfordshire lace – [July 1794] A number of ingenious French emigrants have found employment in Buckinghamshire, Bedfordshire, and other adjacent counties in the manufactory of lace; and it is expected that, through the means of these artificers, considerable improvements will be introduced into the methods of making English lace. Annual Register, 1799 ~~~ Bedfordshire partakes less than most parts of the kingdom in the benefits of trade and manufactures. The poor have scarcely any other employment than a little lace-making, chiefly on the Buckinghamshire side, which goes to the shopkeepers in exchange for goods; England Delineated, 1800 ~~~ Children are taught to make lace at about six or seven years old, and they occupy so much of the attention of their school-mistress, that the expense of teaching them amounts to 3*s.* per week, for a month or six weeks, according to their capacity. After they have learned the rudiments of the art, their ordinary schooling is 6*d.* per week. ... At about ten years of age, those of an ordinary capacity will earn about 2*s.* per week; and at thirteen, if well attended to, they are supposed to cause little further expense to their parents. A young girl of sixteen, if not neglected by her friends, will be capable of earning as much money at the lace-pillow, as at any time in future life; and the average earnings of full-grown females is supposed to be very nearly 6*s.* per week. There are some, I am informed, who scarcely clear 5*s.* per week, and a few extreme cases have been mentioned, of earnings as high as 8*s.* or 9*s.* per week. The expense of thread is stated at about one-eighth of the gross value of the lace, and a portion of time is consumed in washing and mending of clothes, selling of the lace, &c. \ The lace-makers begin their work in summer at six or seven in the morning, and finish at sun-set, or the dusk of the evening. In the winter, little is done till eight or nine o'clock in the morning, or after breakfast, when they continue their work till ten or eleven at night, and sometimes later. Agriculture of the County of Bedford, 1813 ~~~ The principal manufacture, of this county is thread-lace, formerly known by the name of bone-lace; a term now grown obsolete, but still retained as synonymous in the statute-books. Lace is made in every part of the county, excepting in a few villages, where it has been superseded by the straw manufacture. The texture is not so fine as that of the lace made in some parts of Buckinghamshire, nor are the earnings of the persons employed in it so large; the average day's work of an adult producing about a shilling only; and children earning from two-pence to five-pence. The trade is nevertheless flourishing, and the demand for the manufacture increasing. Lace-making has been generally esteemed particularly prejudicial to health, and persons travelling through the counties where this manufacture prevails, have been struck with the sickly appearance of the women and children employed in it; which, exclusively of the pernicious effects attributed by some to the posture of the manufacturers, might be sufficiently accounted for by the sedentary nature of their employment, and their habit of working together in small crouded [sic] rooms. Magna Britannia, 1813 ~~~ The lace manufactured in England is generally called Buckinghamshire or Bedfordshire lace, after those districts wherein it is made; it is also called pillow lace, or bobbin lace, because it is woven upon a pillow or cushion by means of bobbins. Edinburgh Encyclopædia, 1830 ~~~ Full Dress. Robe of pale blue *aerophane,* over a dress of white sarsenet. It is made *à la schall,* and folds on the right side; a half *chemisette,* trimmed with the finest Bedford lace, is seen at the front and back of the *corsage; Lady's Magazine,* August 1830 ~~~ Bedfordshire and Honiton lace is so highly prized in Paris that it is to be hoped our fair countrywomen will not despise it because it is produced by the fingers of their own industrious poor. *Lady's Magazine,* September 1830 ~~~ The staple manufacture of Bedford is thread or pillow lace, which is still carried on to a considerable extent, and occupies nearly all the female population of the working classes, notwithstanding the cheapness and perfection to which machinery has brought the cotton lace (which in wear and durability is far surpassed by that manufactured by manual operation). It is however to be regretted that, by this means, the industrious poor who were formerly able to earn a comfortable livelihood, have been reduced to such a state as to render the most toilsome application insufficient to obtain a bare subsistence: Bedford and its Environs, 1831 ~~~ The manufacture of thread or pillow-lace, in the counties of Buckingham, Bedford, and Northampton, is in the same depressed and deplorable state [as bobbin-net]. The miserable workers, after labouring sixteen hours a day, cannot earn more than from 1*s.* 6*d.* to 2*s.* per week! In the very best of times these poor creatures could not earn more than from 8*s.* to 10*s.* a week; but their present distressed and pauperised situation is truly piteous. *New Monthly Magazine,* October 1832 [see also *Buckinghamshire, bone lace* and *pillow lace*]

beggar's lace – *Merchandize employed in the Guinea trade, from Goree to the Gambia, with the common price, in the year* 1789. … Beads, beggar's lace, paper, tobacco, small bells, Statistics of France, 1815 ~~~ [ad] Have received by the ships Hark-away and Jefferson, direct from Liverpool, … English thread laces and edgings and beggar's lace. *Farmer's Register,* May 1835 ~~~ [a simple, white thread lace common in France before 1723, called gueue (= beggar)]

beige – Beige-Serge, called so by the people of Poitou; it is black, grey, or tawny coloured. It is also called sheep-coloured serge, or natural serge; because the wool of which it is manufactured is never dried [dyed?], being employed for both warp and woof, such as it comes from the sheep. *Beiges* ought to be composed of thirty-eight or thirty-nine reeds at least, each reed being of twenty threads. General Dictionary of Commerce, 1810 ~~~ Beige, s.f. sort of serge. Boyer's French Dictionary, 1816

Belzoni – A favorite dress for the evening is a white satin slip, under a dress of Urling's black Chantilly lace; with a sash tied behind of the Belzoni or *Egyptian* plaid. *Ladies' Monthly Museum,* January 1822 ~~~ Belzoni tartan silks are worn in half-dress; *La Belle Assemblée,* November 1825

Bengal – The womens apparel is chiefly a variety of stuffs of their own manufacture; as *Bengals,* a kind of cloth of linen warp, and cotton weft; Statistical Account of Scotland, 1795 ~~~ Bengal, Indian cotton-stuff <u>Perry's English Dictionary</u>, 1795 ~~~ Bengal, *n.s.* a sort of thin slight stuff, made of silk and hair, for women's apparel. <u>American Encyclopædia</u>, 1806

Bengal foulard – The new materials are *foulards du Bengale*, composed of silk and thread, *La Belle Assemblée*, May 1831 ~~~ Make and Materials of Out-Door Costume. … Dresses are composed of a variety of new spring silks, as *Gros de Naples, Bayadères, Thessaliennes Chines Perses*, and *Foulard du Bengale*, a mixture of silk and thread, and a perfect imitation of Indian materials. *Atheneum*, July 15, 1831 ~~~ Plain *gros de Naples* of fancy colours, is now the favourite material in half dress, although printed muslins, *foulards du Bengale, palmyriennes*, and several other fancy materials, are fashionable. *Ladies' Museum*, August 1831

Bengal muslin – Cotton is brought to much greater perfection; it is fit for every thing, and is usefully employed in a variety of different manufactures, which are consumed over the whole globe. That for which there is the most universal demand, and which more particularly comes from Bengal, is plain, striped, or worked muslin. It is easily manufactured in the rainy season, because then the materials are more flexible, and do not break so readily. The weavers, during the rest of the year, supply, as much as possible, this moisture in the air, by vessels full of water, which they take care to put under their looms. <u>History of the Settlements and Trade of the Europeans in the East and West Indies</u>, 1798 ~~~ India Muslins, we understand, are again coming much into wear; and for the information of our Fashionable Readers, we have observed, at the house of Millard, in the City, some of the choicest productions of the East Indies from the Company's recent Sale of Bengal Muslins, &c. Their beauty is exquisite, and from the extreme low prices that house (which for many years has been the principal mart of the Company's goods) is selling them at, it is evident the Honourable Company can have but little export trade. *La Belle Assemblée*, February 1812 ~~~ The Elizabeth *negligée* for breakfast *costume*. It is made of the finest Bengal muslin, and profusely trimmed with vine Mechlin lace; *La Belle Assemblée*, February 1818 ~~~ Some cotton fabrics made by the Hindoos, are of the finest and most beautiful kind. At Shantee-pooru, and Dhaka, muslins are made which sell at a hundred roopees a piece. At two places in Bengal, muslins are made by a few families so exceedingly fine, that four months are required to weave one piece, which sells for four or five hundred roopees. When this muslin is laid on the grass, and the dew has fallen upon it, it is no longer discernible. <u>A View … of the Hindoos</u>, 1824 ~~~ [ad] *Domestic Goods, manufactured of Cotton cultivated by free labor, and for sale at the store of Lydia White,* … India, Book, Mull, and Nansook Muslins – Seersuckers, Bengals, &c. &c. *Genius of Universal Emancipation*, December 1832 ~~~ Bengal, which for some thousands of years stood unequalled in the fabric of muslins, figured calicoes, and other fine cotton goods, is rivalled in several parts of Great Britain. <u>History of the Cotton Manufacture of Great Britain</u>, 1836 [see also *Decca muslin*]

Bengal silk – *Considerations on the Attempt of the East-India Company to become Manufacturers in Great-Britain.* … The reason assigned for this by the company is, that they, deeming it necessary to enlarge their imports of Bengal raw-silk, have devised a plan, the object of which is to occasion an increased consumption of the commodity, by throwing some portion of it into *organzine,* to serve as a substitute for part of the organzine at present imported from Italy. And as the merchants and others interested in the silk trade have objected to the measure, the company have published some Reports to correct any mistaken ideas that may prevail. … But his more immediate arguments regard the respective qualities of the Bengal and Italian silks. He asserts that it is not pretended by the most sanguine abettors of the company's experiment, that their commodity can ever be expected completely to rival that of Italy. 'How then,' he asks, 'would the silk manufacturer, already smarting under the neglect of the public, be able once more to fix the caprice of fashion in his favour, if he should imprudently substitute the dingy and woolly produce of Bengal, for the brilliant and firm staple of Italian organzine?' <u>Critical Review</u>, 1796 ~~~ The greatest part, however, of the silk produced in Bengal and other parts of India is exported *raw*, and in its original yellow colour. <u>Indian Antiquities</u>, 1800 ~~~ The East India Company have for some years past persuaded themselves that by throwing Bengal silk into organzine they should gradually do away the necessity of importing organzine from Italy; the deficient supply of the latter has lately induced the manufacturers to endeavour to substitute Bengal organzine in almost every article in which Italian silk was before used; but the result has been a conviction, that for some principal articles Bengal silk never can be used with equal advantage to that of Italy, from an inherent deficiency in its quality. In some articles, however, it is found to answer very well, *Monthly Magazine*, September 1808 ~~~ For half-dress, the Indian turban claims a pre-eminent rank: it is reckoned most elegant when formed of the white Bengal silk, in a beautiful pattern of squares of white satin on a delicate Indian ground; *Repository of Arts*, November 1819 ~~~ The commoner sorts of ribands are composed altogether, both warp and shoot, of Bengal silk. Those of better quality are manufactured with a mixture of Italian and Bengal silk; and the finest descriptions are made of Italian silk without any mixture. Silk Manufacture, 1832

Bengal stripes – [see *gingham*]

Berlin – [Patent] To Messrs. Pouillot, Fayolle, and Hullin, of Paris, for five years, for a machine for making the lace, called *tricot de Berlin, Monthly Magazine*, November 1809 ~~~ Are you not aware that the single worsted that Berlin is made of, is very different from that that is made into stockings? – With this difference, that being twisted a little harder, of course it will shew the imperfections the more. In fact it is a worse article, because it is spun from one roving, whereas the yarn generally used for stockings is spun from two. Reports from the Committees, 1812 ~~~ The principal manufactures of Berlin are in silk, serge, fustian, muslin, camlets, and other woollen, linen, and cotton stuffs; also stockings, carpets, embroidery, New Universal Gazetteer, 1821 ~~~ Tulle de Berline, Tulle de Flandre, (Thread Lace Gowns) Commercial Directory, 1823 ~~~ To Mr. W. Seymour, Odiham, for 5 pieces of printed Cotton, … 5 ditto of Worsted Berlin, *Evangelical Magazine*, February 1823 ~~~ Though there are many different kinds [of gloves] worn, those mostly in repute among the higher orders are the Doe-skin, Kid and Berlin, which latter was first introduced into fashion two seasons ago. … We now come to the Berlin. These, looking equally as well as Doe-skin or Woodstock, I would particularly recommend to notice, for the great economy attending their wear. Gray and white are the most desirable colours. These gloves are made of a kind of strong cotton, which, while it should possess great strength, should be very thin and neat. The great advantage derived from their use (an advantage no other kind possesses), is their bearing washing the same as linen, which, when their texture is good, they will at least sustain twenty times, without showing any symptoms of wear. Great care, however, ought to be taken in their cleansing; and when boiled with a little pearlash, it will be found an excellent thing for producing a snowy whiteness that nothing can surpass. Whole Art of Dress, 1830

Berlin silk – the gros de Naples and gros de Berlin, of the house of Arquillière and Mourron, deserve particular notice from their strength and fineness, and their quality of preserving their lustre to the last; *Foreign Quarterly Review*, January 1829 ~~~ [Paris] Dinner Dress. The dress is a rich *gros de Berlin*, trimmed at the knees with satin of the same shade made into a border of elephant's ears; *Lady's Magazine*, February 1830 ~~~ Morning Dress. – Coat dress, gros de Berlin of celestial blue, with plaited bosom and falling collar – handkerchief sleeves. *Godey's Ladies Book*, April 1832

bettilla muslin – There are several sorts of muslins brought from the East Indies, and more particularly from Bengal; such as doreas, betelles, mulmuls, tanjeebs, &c. New Encyclopædia, 1807 ~~~ Bétille, *sf. a sort of muslin* Nugent's French Dictionary, 1808 ~~~ the new Japanese bettilla muslins brought out and sold by the house of Millard in the city. They are an excellent specimen of the ingenuity of the British manufacturer, and since the interchange with Parisian fashions and the rage for colours have taken place, they are become the leading article of the day. *Repository of Arts*, May 1815 ~~~ On the coast of Coromandel, a striped muslin is made, called *dorea*, and in the Tamul language *betille*, quantities of which are exported by the caravans to Persian, Arabia, and the Levant. Very little of it goes to Europe, where the fabric is skilfully imitated. Universal Geography, 1822 [see also *Bengal muslin*]

bird of paradise – [court dress] her head richly dressed, gold, and a beautiful bird of paradise in the front. *Lady's Magazine*, June 1798 ~~~ This bird is valuable, in a commercial point of view, on account of its plumage, with which of late years, ladies of the first rank, in this country, have ornamented their head-dresses. There are five species of the genus to which the bird of Paradise belongs. 1. The largest bird of Paradise. The description of its plumage is as follows: the head and back part of the neck are lemon-coloured, a little black about the eyes; about the neck is of the brightest glossy emerald-green, soft like velvet, as is also the breast which is black; the wings are chesnut coloured; the back part of the body is covered with long, straight, narrow feathers of a pale brown colour, similar to the plumes of the ostrich. On both sides of the belly are two tufts of stiff and short feathers, of a golden yellow, and shining. From the rump proceed two long stiff shafts, which are feathered on their extremities. This species is found in the Aroo islands, and in New Guinea. 2. The smaller bird of Paradise. The head and neck are of a dirty yellow, the back of a greyish-yellow, the breast and belly of a dusky colour, and the wings chesnut. The colours of this bird are less bright than the former, to which in other respects it is pretty similar. 3 and 4. The larger and smaller black birds of Paradise. On both these the plumage of the head, neck, and belly, is black and velvety, with a hue of purple and gold which appears very strong. The plumes of this bird are only to be procured from New Guinea, and from one particular part of that country. 5. The king bird of Paradise. This creature is about seven inches long, and somewhat larger than a titmouse. The crown of the head is flame-coloured, the neck and breast are of a chesnut colour, with a ring of the brightest emerald-green. Its wings are red and shining, with spots and stripes. Two naked black shafts project from the rump, having at their extremities semi-lunar twisted plumage, of the glaring green colour above, and dusky below. The belly is white and green sprinkled, and on each side is a tuft of long plumage feathered with a broad margin, being on one side green and on the other dusky. The rack is blood-red and brown, shining on silk. This bird is also an inhabitant of New Guinea. General Dictionary of Commerce, 1810 ~~~ The court head-dresses consist chiefly of white satin *toques*, ornamented with marabouts or the bird of paradise plume. *La Belle Assemblée*, January 1820 ~~~ The finest *aigrettes* are formed by the tails of the bird of paradise; three or four of these beautiful birds are thus sacrificed to procure a lady several *aigrettes*, and give an immense value to the trimming of a hat. This is in the highest degree of luxury. *Ladies' Monthly Museum*, June 1827 ~~~ [Paris] Birds of Paradise are often seen in the public walks as ornaments on white chip hats, on an evening, *Lady's Magazine*, June 1829

birds down – [ad] Birds-Down – This Hosiery is made of the fine down of Swans, Eider Ducks, and other Birds, mixed with fine wool; it exceeds in warmth and delicacy every other except Patent Fleecy Hosiery, and as it does not shrink in washing it is consequently very durable. *La Belle Assemblée*, December 1807

birds eye – *Napt a couple of birds eye wipes*. He had stolen a couple of handkerchiefs of a particular pattern, called the Bird's-eye. Life's Painter of Variegated Characters, 1790-1800? ~~~ *Premiums on Scottish Manufactures* … For the best twenty pieces of bleached diaper, in imitation of the Russian, of a light texture, and to be taken up very soft; the length of each piece to be twenty-one yards, and to stand full twenty-two inches and a half in breadth, when white (though a high colour is not necessary), the pattern known by the name of *Treble bird's eye*; the length and the price to be marked on the ticket of each piece, 15*l*. *Tradesman*, May 1, 1811 ~~~ Fogle. A handkerchief. *Cant*. A blue handkerchief with white diamond spots, commonly called a *blue bird's eye*. *Ex. gv.* "My handkerchiefs, of *bird's eye blue*, / Bear them to Belcher when I'm gone." Classical Dictionary of the Vulgar Tongue, 1823 ~~~ [Tariffs] Diapers for napkins, brown and white, plain, spotted, bird's eye, diamonds, large and small, and other similar patterns, Message from the President of the United States, 1824 ~~~ [boxing match] a referee having been chosen, (after a considerable time spent in electing the latter,) and the *colours* of the belligerents tied to the stakes – blue bird's eye for Ward, and green with yellow spots for Byrne – they prepared for action. *Sporting Magazine*, August 1831 ~~~ [ad] Damask Table Cloths of every description, both colored and white – Birdeye and Damask Diaper Boston Annual Advertiser, 1832 ~~~ Stuff goods, worsted, viz; bird's eye, bombazetts, calimancos, camblets, Trade between Great Britain and the United States of America, 1833 ~~~ [ad] Have received by the ships Hark-away and Jefferson, direct from Liverpool, … 1 case fine bird's eye, Russia and 3-4 Scotch diapers. *Farmer's Register*, May 1835 [see also *diaper*, *stuff*, and *worsted*]

bishop lawn – Baptism therefore (the true Uses and Intent whereof will be seen presently) contributeth no more towards Salvation, without it's Uses and Fruits, than the triple Cap on the Pope's Head, and the Sign of the Cross on his Shoes, contribute towards his pontifical Supereminence; or than a Cardinal's purple Robe contributeth to his Dignity; or than a Bishop's Lawn Sleeves to the true Discharge of his Ministry; True Christian Religion, 1795 ~~~ [ad] Have received by the ships Hark-away and Jefferson, direct from Liverpool, …1 case 9-8 and 6-4 plain Swiss muslins and bishop lawns. *Farmer's Register*,

May 1835 ~~~ [ad] Dry Goods at Reduced Prices. ... Bishop lawns, from 20 cents to 5s 3d per yd *New England Farmer*, July 1, 1835

black Spanish – [obituary] John Brown, a native of Abbey Holm, in Cumberland. This ingenious man, who was a shoe-maker, in concert with two Italians, first introduced that preparation of leather called Black Spanish or Morocco; but his associates contrived to exclude him from all the benefits of an invention, *Gentleman's Magazine*, December 1798 ~~~ Black Spanish, an article now brought to such perfection, and in general use for womens' shoes and other purposes, was scarcely known in this country fifteen or twenty years ago; *Monthly Magazine*, April 1802 ~~~ [ad in 1823] morocco skins of all colours, black Spanish leather, shammy ditto, calf skin boot legs, and yellow tops for gentlemen's boots, British Settlements in Australasia, 1824

blond – *The Queen*. A Royal purple coat, covered with beautiful fine blond, drawn up in festoons, *Lady's Magazine*, June 1796 ~~~ *Blond-Lace*, a lace made of fine linen thread or silk, much in the same manner as that of gold and silver. The pattern of the lace is fixed upon a large round pillow, and pins being stuck into the holes or openings in the patterns, the threads are interwoven by means of a number of bobbins made of bone or ivory, each of which contains a small quantity of fine thread, ins such a manner as to make the lace exactly resemble the pattern. Encyclopædia Britannica, 1797 ~~~ The *blond* lace, as to its fabric, resembles the thread laces, but it differs as to its material, which are white silk; but this silk being of a very inferior kind, and not equal to the beautiful thread used in manufacturing other laces, will not permit the bland to be bleached, a process on which depends its chief beauty. Hence the blond lace is not only infinitely less durable, but is also of less value than the ordinary laces. Literary Panorama, 1808 ~~~ Blond-lace. ... Is manufactured of silk, in imitation of thread lace, and large quantities of it are made in different parts of France and Flanders. Of late years the manufacture of blond-lace in England has been so much improved, as to equal, if not surpass that produced on the continent. London Commercial Dictionary, 1819 ~~~ Black and white *blonds* are worn at the edges of morning bonnets, as best pleases the fancy of the wearer: with a pink bonnet, the curtain-veil is generally black. The patterns of these broad *blonds* are exquisite; they are very expensive, and are more than four times the value of the bonnet which they trim. *La Belle Assemblée*, May 1827 ~~~ Blonde Lace is of silk, both black and white, and has a more shining appearance than the Chantilly; arising from the texture of the silk, which is not so hardly twisted. It is usually employed for the trimmings of dresses. The flowers and leaves are in general distinguished by one of their sides being worked very thickly, and the other formed by open work. Young Lady's Book, 1829 ~~~ Blond lace, or an imitation of it, now forms a part of almost every dress. *Ladies' Museum*, May 1831 ~~~ [court dress] A blonde dress over a petticoat of lavender satin; body tastefully ornamented with blonde, forming a stomacher; train of lavender satin, prettily trimmed with blonde to correspond. *Court Journal*, June 22, 1833 ~~~ Blond (blon'd) *s*. (bone-lace, coarse lace] *Blonde*, f. Blond-lace made in the shape of a parsley-leaf. Wilson's French Dictionary, 1833 ~~~ For ball-dresses, blonde is occasionally worn, though it is by no means so general as during former seasons. The old blondes, with massive flower patterns, are intirely [sic] laid aside. Those now used for open robes or flounced dresses, are the *blondes dentelles*. They are double the thickness of the old blonde, and are worked in light patterns. These *blondes dentelles* are among the most beautiful *fantasies* of female dress, combining the richness of lace with the lightness and delicacy of blonde. *Court Journal*, January 10, 1835 [see also *bone lace*]

blond antique – [Paris] We may cite among the most distinguished head-dresses, caps of *blonde antique* ornamented with *velours épingle*, and flowers. *Ladies' Pocket*, December 1836

blond Chantilly – [see *Chantilly blond*]

blond de Cambray – A rich but narrow blond lace, called *blond de Cambray*, ... is an article of English manufacture, quite equal to the French blond, and considerably less expensive. As it has always been our plan to recommend our own manufactures in preference to those of foreigners, especially when equal in quality, we have pleasure in inviting the attention of our readers to this newly invented addition to their ornaments. ... or else a very broad *blond de Cambray* forms an upper sleeve, *La Belle Assemblée*, March 1830 ~~~ We have no hesitation in saying, not even the celebrated *magazin* of Le Roi, ... can furnish any blond lace more beautifully made, or of richer patterns, then the *blond de*

Cambray. We have seen some of the vaunted *blond de Chantilly*, which was far from equalling it. *La Belle Assemblée*, April 1830 ~~~ Those [under dresses] of *blond de Cambray* are in high request, the lightness and openness of the ground, with the uncommon beauty of the patterns, the style of which is fully equal to the most novel French blonds, have procured them very high patronage. This may, perhaps, also, in some degree, be owing to the combining economy with elegance, as the price is not above a third of the French article, though even connoisseurs cannot tell the difference. ... above all, blond lace, are in request, both for *soirées* and balls. Some of the most beautiful dresses of the latter material are those of the *blonde de Cambray*. Some have the grounds lightly sprigged, others are striped, *à colonne*, and trimmed *en biais* with superb flounces; *Court Magazine*, February 1835

blond de fil – [see *thread lace*]

blond dentelle – [see *blond*]

blond gauze – Dinner Party Dress. ... Long sleeve of blond gauze, confined a little above the elbow by a white satin rouleau, and terminated by a cuff a la Marie Stuart of pink crape; *Repository of Arts*, August 1829 ~~~ The sleeve called *à la belle Paule* is a slight variation from that *à la Donna Maria*. They are made of the elegant new blonde gauze. *Lady's Magazine*, February 1830 ~~~ Full Dress. ... The mantilla scarf that falls from the headdress is white and silver blonde gauze. *Lady's Magazine*, July 1830 ~~~ [court dress] Black blonde gauze dress; train of black satin; *Royal Lady's*, April 1831 ~~~ *gaze blonde*, ... are all fashionable for dancing dresses. *Court Magazine*, February 1835 ~~~ [turbans] of rich but light materials, as *gaze blonde*, *Court Magazine*, February 1836

blond illusion – [see *illusion*]

blond net – although various trimming are fashionable, lace, particularly blond, is in the highest estimation; it is, however, more generally appropriated to full than to dinner dresses, except blond net, but is quilled very full on dinner dresses, *La Belle Assemblée*, November 1814 ~~~ *Cornettes* of different forms, but all with low cauls, are generally worn both in morning and half dress: in the former they are composed of English lace; in the latter, of blond net trimmed with blond lace: *Repository of Arts*, April 1823 ~~~ Turbans seem a very general head-dress again with matronly ladies. Those of a certain age wear with them a *mentonnière* of plaited blond-net, which renders them an infinitely becoming and suitable *coiffeure* to ladies in the decline of life. *La Belle Assemblée*, November 1828 ~~~ Dress caps of colored blond net, and trimmed with blond lace to correspond, have just made their appearance; *Ladies' Museum*, February 1830 ~~~ [court dress] A dress of white blonde tulle, trimmed with lilies of the valley, worn over white satin, body and sleeves trimmed with blonde; ... A white blonde tulle dress, lined with satin, *Royal Lady's*, June 1831 ~~~ [court dresses] A dress of tulle blonde, trimmed with gold, over a slip of white satin; ... Embroidered blonde tulle dresses, over white satin: corsages and manteaus of broche green silk, *Court Journal*, June 1, 1833 ~~~ A good many mantelets are of plain blond net, ... Half dress bonnets are ... trimmed with a *ruche* of blond net at the edge of the brim, *Court Magazine*, October 1833 ~~~ *Tulle* blonde, embroidered in white or coloured floss silk, is much employed for ball and evening dress. *Court Journal*, November 14, 1835 ~~~ Nothing is so fashionable at present for grand parties as robes of *tulle blonde* over slips of white *pou de soie glace*. *Ladies' Pocket*, July 1836

blond tulle – [see *blond net*]

blonde – [see *blond*]

blonze – [court dress] A rich gauze petticoat, ... body and train purple velvet, richly trimmed with blonze. *Lady's Magazine*, January 1797 [probably *blonde*]

blue cloth – Manufactures (woollen). ... All *long coloured cloths*, called plunkets, azures, and blues, and long white cloths made in *Suffolk*, *Norfolk* and *Essex*, or elsewhere of like making – 29 to 32 [Yards long.] Whole Law Relative to the Duty and Office of a Justice of the Peace, 1794 ~~~ [In 1809, superfine] Blue cloth rose to 34s. per yard and upwards; but the extravagant cost of Spanish wool, and of the cloth, checked the manufacture. There was more parsimonious use of it, and inferior cloths were worn. Now the blue cloths which sold for 34s. are reduced to their former prices, viz. 24s. Literary Panorama, 1811 ~~~ superfine blue cloth, 2l. 18s. 6d; to 3l. 7s. 6d. per yard; Sketches of America, 1818 ~~~ [in Demerara] Their usual clothing consists of a blue cloth jacket, blue cloth trowsers, a hat,

4 ells of Osnaburgs, 4 ells of checks, each, and a cap *for the men; the women,* a hat, blue-cloth wrapper, blue-cloth petticoat, 6 ells checks, 6 ells Osnaburgs, and a handkerchief, each: <u>Considerations on Negro Slavery</u>, 1824 ~~~ [ad] MR. JOHN P. DEANE respectfully informs his Friends, it being his intentention [sic] to proceed to Sydney, the following GOODS will be disposed of at the under-mentioned Prices, being at least 30 per cent, under the retail Prices: ... broad blue cloth, 20s. ditto [per yard]; *Colonial Times,* March 3, 1826 ~~~ [ad] Proposals will be received at the Office of the Commissary General of Purchases, in Philadelphia, for making Army Clothing for the year 1837, and for sundry articles ready made, as hereafter enumerated, viz – ... Blue cloth, 6-4 wide, dyed in indigo, and in the wool. *Army and Navy Chronicle,* December 8, 1836 [see also *broad cloth* and *superfine*]

blue nap – [see *pennistone*]

blunk – in the Scottish phraseology, the term calico is seldom used; *blunk* is more common, but this properly signifies the application of cotton woof to linen warp. <u>Edinburgh Encyclopædia</u>, 1814 ~~~ Linen Blunks are used for light shirting. <u>Linen Manufacturer</u>, 1817 ~~~ About the year 1780, small spinning jennies were introduced, which led to the introduction of a new fabric called blunks. These goods were a combination of linen warp and cotton weft, and being preferred by the printers, their manufacture took a number of hands from the linen trade. <u>Traditions of Perth</u>, 1836

bobbin lace – [see *Bedfordshire* and *Buckinghamshire lace, bone* and *pillow lace*]

bobbin-net lace – [patent] March 20. [1809] For a machine for the making and manufacturing of bobbin lace, or nearly resembling foreign lace. To John Heathcoat, *Edinburgh Annual Register,* 1811 ~~~ But a more important alteration has taken place in Lace-Making, by substituting the loom: at Nottingham, and some other places, is now manufactured a lace of finer quality, more even in its texture, and considerably more elegant in its appearance than any bone-lace whatever, and at about one-third the price of bone-lace. This lace is made of two kinds: the coarsest is called *Mecklin-net*; the other, *bobbin-net,* because it is woven by bobbins in some such way as the bone-lace is made, and for which, we believe, a patent was obtained. Not only lace, but veils, cloaks, and handkerchiefs, are made in this way, both of silk and cotton: the only inconvenience attending this mode of manufacture is, that the figures in the lace must be fixed by hand after the lace is woven: notwithstanding this defect, the introduction of this method has considerably reduced the demand for bone lace. <u>Book of English Trades</u>, 1818 ~~~ Bobbinet is a late invention. It is the ground-work of lace, formed by machinery; it is therefore done very rapidly, and can be sold cheap. Upon this is worked any pattern by the needle, and this is formed an elegant article, which threatens to ruin all our industrious lace-makers, till its cheapness makes it common. Then the opulent will return to the more expensive article, to distinguish themselves, and real lace may come into fashion again. <u>Scenes of British Wealth</u>, 1825 ~~~ [Paris] Another evening dress that has been much admired, is of *tulle Anglaise,* or, as you call it, net, over a satin under-dress *La Belle Assemblée,* February 1832 ~~~ BEDFORDSHIRE. *Lace-makers* ... The manufacture of an article of lace, made by machinery (principally in Leicestershire and Nottinghamshire), called bobbin-net, has experienced a still greater depreciation in value. The yard-wide bobbin-net, which about ten years ago met with a ready sale at sixty shillings per yard, is now retailed at sixteen-pence! *New Monthly Magazine,* October 1832 ~~~ English tulle, (bobbinet,) <u>Commercial Relations</u>, 1834 ~~~ The beauty of bobbin-net lace depends, not only upon the quality of the threads, but principally upon the perfectly hexagonal shape of the holes, and the equality of their sizes. ... Turbans ... may be made of ... bobbinnet. *Court Journal,* January 17, 1835 ~~~ [ad] Dry Goods at Reduced Prices. ... Bobbinet Laces, fm 9d to 5s 3d per yd *New England Farmer,* July 1, 1835 ~~~ Bobbin-net is usually brought into the market in pieces, of from 20 to 30 yards, or even more, in length, and of very variable breadths. ... Bobbin-net lace is a thin semi-transparent web of fine cotton thread, arranged in hexagonal holes or meshes. ... The fine cotton yarns which are used for making bobbin-net lace-thread, and for the hosiery trade, are generally subjected, first of all, to a singeing process by the flame of the coal-gas, in a peculiar machine, to free them from their loose, divergent fibres, <u>Cotton Manufacture of Great Britain</u>, 1836 [see also *lace* and *net*]

bocking – a large village in Essex in England, ... There is a large manufactory of bays, chiefly for exportation. <u>Encyclopædia Britannica</u>, 1797 ~~~ Bockingstreet, a populous village in Essex, ... a certain kind of baizes have received from this place the name of *bockings*. <u>Union Gazetteer</u>, 1807 ~~~ Undyed Bocking Baizes, 5 to 6 quarters wide, at 2 shillings to 2 shillings 2 pence sterling, per yard. *Weekly Register*, September 21, 1811 ~~~ Bocking – commonly called bocking baize, being in fact a species of baize, *Public Documents*, April 1827 ~~~ *Bocking and Baizes*. 42 inches wide, cost 6d. to 1s. 3d. – For lining the pea-jackets of sailors and boatmen, and the great-coats and round jackets of farmers, mechanics, and laborers, and for table and floor cloths, &c. *Niles' Weekly Register*, March 8, 1828 ~~~ Bocking (woollen) *Public Documents*, March 1832 ~~~ [ad] 1 bale printed Bocking. 1 do. [ditto] plain do. *New England Farmer*, December 10, 1834 [see also *baize*]

boiled silk – *Boiled silk*, is that which has been boiled in water, to facilitate the spinning and winding. This is the finest of all sorts of silk manufactured in France, and is seldom used, but in the richest stuffs; as velvets, taffeties, damasks, brocades, &c. There is also another kind of boiled silk, which is prepared by boiling, to be milled; and which cannot receive that preparation, without being first through hot water. <u>Guy's Pocket Cyclopædia</u>, 1810 [see also *raw silk*]

bois de Spa Cresontine – [French] A new material for hats, but one that has not yet been generally adopted, is of the fancy kind; it is called *bois de Spa Cresontine*, and made in difference colours, some plain, others quadrilled. *Court Magazine*, August 1833

boiteuse – *Plumes boiteuses*, or marabouts, ornament these hats … *La Belle Assemblée*, January 1827 ~~~ On black velvet hats are often seen willow feathers of blue and black, mixed together, with the hat lined with Navarin-blue; the feather is of a prodigious length, and is one side blue, one black, bearing the appellation of *une plume boiteuse*. *Ladies' Pocket*, March 1829 ~~~ Ostrich feathers, half white, half colored, called *plumes boiteuses*, are much worn at dress parties, and at those theatrical representations which require a peculiar style of *parure*, cherry-color and white, and lilac and white, are the most approved in these party-colored plumes: *Ladies' Pocket*, October 1829 [see also *bailoque*]

bolster cloth – [see *bolting*]

bolting – bolting-cloths, or those kinds of cloth through which meal is sifted in mills. As this cloth is universally used, a considerable quantity of it is consumed. For one bolting-cloth, five yards are required; we may allow, therefore, twenty-five to each mill in the course of a year. When this is considered, it will not appear improbable that the electorate of Saxony, according to a calculation made towards the end of the last century, when manufactories of this cloth were established, paid for it yearly to foreigners from twelve to fifteen thousand rix-dollars. That kind of bolting-cloth also which is used for a variety of needlework, for young ladies' samplers, and for filling up the frames of window-screens, &c. is wove after the manner of gauze, of fine-spun woollen yarn. … A bolting-cloth of English manufacture will continue good three months, but one of German will last scarcely three weeks. The wool necessary for making this cloth must be long, well washed, and spun to a fine equal thread, which, before it is scoured, must be scalded in hot water to prevent it from shrinking. The web must be stiffened; and in this the English have an advantage we have not yet been able to attain. Their bolting-cloth is stiffer as well as smoother, and lets the flour much better through it than ours, which is either very little or not at all stiffened. <u>History of Inventions and Discoveries</u>, 1797 ~~~ *Bolting-cloth*, or *Bolster-cloth*, sometimes also called *Boulting-cloth*, denotes a linen or hair cloth for sifting meal or flour. <u>Encyclopædia Britannica</u>, 1810 ~~~ Bolting-Cloth, whether coarse, made of Hair; or made of Flax or Silk. <u>Commercial Directory</u>, 1823 ~~~ [ad] Have received by the ships Hark-away and Jefferson, direct from Liverpool, … 1 case real anchor bolting cloths, allowed to be the best article imported, at prices very much reduced in the last 30 days. *Farmer's Register*, May 1835

bombasin – [see *bombazine*]

bombazeen – [see *bombazine*]

bombazet – [ad] Family Mourning very cheap, consisting of Bombazeens, Bombazets, Italian, Imperial, and other new Nets; *La Belle Assemblée*, November 1807 ~~~ The second indictment traversed, was for stealing one black silk, and one bombazet gown, valued at ten dollars each, *New-York City-Hall Recorder*, February 1816 ~~~ Elizabeth-Town, Oct. 20th, 1817 ~~~ Bombazette for dress, 4d 25d <u>Trial of Eunice Hall vs. Robert Grant, for Slander</u>, 1821 ~~~ [ad] Summer Goods, … Bombazetts, … of all colour and qualities. <u>Boston Annual Advertiser</u>, 1823 ~~~ Ursuline Community, *Mount Benedict*, *in Charlestown.* … The uniform of the young ladies, consists, on week days, of a grey bombazett dress, and white on Sundays. Picture of Boston, 1829 ~~~ Presents furnished the [Chickasaw] Indians, by order of the commissioners, … 5 ½ yds. bombasette, at 3s. 9d. p. yd. [1830] Executive Documents, 1832 ~~~ Worsted Stuff Goods, from Manchester to New York … Bombazetts … actual [width] inches 18 *a* 19 ~~~ Price per yard s.d. [shillings.pence] 0.5 *a* 0.8 Trade between Great Britain and the United States of America, 1833 ~~~ Worsted stuffs, made in imitation of Bombazeens, whether tweeled or plain, are Bombazets. Both these sorts of cloth are dyed, of any required colour, but never glazed. Analytical Dictionary, 1835

bombazine – Bombasin, a slight stuff for mourning Perry's English Dictionary, 1795 ~~~ a name given to two sorts of stuffs, the one of silk, and the other crossed of cotton. Encyclopædia Britannica, 1797 ~~~ For home or dinner dresses, …Imperial and Spanish bombazeens may probably be considered of too close a texture for the season, they are, however, as is also velvet, still worn among the most fashionable circles. *La Belle Assemblée*, March 1811 ~~~ superior coloured Bombazeen, 3s. and 3s. 6d. usually sold at 4s. and 4s. 6d. *Repository of Arts*, March 1815 ~~~ Sept. 18. [1819] … Mr. Justice Best called Maria Stent, the wife of the prisoner, who stood up in the witness-box, and was sworn. She was plainly dressed in a coloured bombasin gown, Annual Register, 1820 ~~~ White bombasine begins to be a good deal used in dinner gowns: *Repository of Arts*, October 1820 ~~~ Bombasine is another stuff much used in mourning, though when white it does not imply death; this is either all silk, woven so as to appear dull, or else it is silk crossed with a fine worsted. Scenes of British Wealth, 1825 ~~~ A General Collection of Words of variable spelling, in which those of the best usage are printed in Roman character, … bombizine?, bombazine, bombasin 1, *bombysine, bombycine, bonbasine, bumbasin,* … 1 This word, in English, ought to be spelt Bombazene, or Bombizene. Its French dress is aukward, in English company, The *I* is from *y* in *Bombyx*, a silk worm. Practical Orthography, 1828 ~~~ We have only to say, that the sudden heat of the weather, and Midsummer season, has prevented our mentioning bombazin in our fashions; black silk and crape are perhaps deeper mourning, as we see them used as badges of woe on the most solemn occasions; and though bombazin is not equally unknown as tammy and camblet, still mentioned in the court circulars, it is equally unwearable at Midsummer. *Lady's Magazine*, July 1830 ~~~ [mourning for George IV.] ladies appear in black silk dresses (for bombazine is rarely worn) … [Paris] The mourning is of the deepest kind, that is to say, black bombazine, trimmed with crape, for walking or home dress; *Ladies' Museum*, August 1830~~~ is a twilled manufacture, having its warp of silk and its shoot of worsted. The use of this article was at one time restricted to the making of mourning garments; but at a later period, no longer condemned, like the gondolas of Venice, to wear alone the sable hue of night, bombasins appeared in colors as gay and as various as the Protean wand of fashion could call forth. Their manufacture, which once employed a vast number of looms in Spitalfields, has for some time been almost wholly confined to the city of Norwich. Bombasins are all woven gray, that is, with silk of the natural color, and they are dyed in the piece after being taken from the loom. Silk Manufacture, 1832 ~~~ Bombasin, or Bombazeen, (Latin *bombyx*, the silkworm,) is properly of silk manufacture, but the name is now given to a fine closely-woven satin-tweeled fabric, of which the warp only is silk and the weft worsted. Analytical Dictionary, 1835 ~~~ In the corner, I perceive a black dress, made for the late general mourning. It is of *bombasine,* a fabric with a silk warp, crossed with fine worsted. This is manufactured most excellently at Norwich. In black, it is appropriated for mourning; but in colours, it constitutes an elegant article of general dress, though now less in use than it was a few years ago. It is worthy of remark, that a difficulty long existed in dyeing bombasine, because the colouring matters which fasten upon wool will not naturally hold permanently upon silk. At one period only one dyer in London possessed the secret by which the dye could be made to strike on both at the same time; he consequently got the whole trade into his hands, and made a rapid fortune; but now almost every dyer knows the process. Scenes of Commerce, 1836 ~~~ The changes of fashion have thrown the coloured bombazine out of use, and the article is now made only in black for mourning and for exportation. It must however always continue in demand while custom prescribes it as the mourning dress appropriate to females. Penny Cyclopædia, 1836 bone lace – Bone-Lace, *s.* a cheap sort of flaxen lace, woven with bobbins made out of bones. <u>Barclay's English Dictionary</u>, 1799 ~~~ Lace is not woven, and of course it requires in the operation neither warp not woof. It is made of silk or of thread, which is wound on little bobbins, made of bone or ivory, about the thickness of a skewer: hence the name bone-lace. <u>Book of Trades</u>, 1806 ~~~ Bone-Lace, … a thread lace manufactured in different parts of France and Flanders, *with bones* on a cushion, instead of bobbins, whence it takes its name. <u>Dictionary of Commerce</u>, 1810 ~~~ The principal manufacture, of this county [Bedfordshire] is thread-lace, formerly known by the name of bone-lace; a term now grown obsolete, but still retained as synonymous in the statute-books. <u>Magna Britannia</u>, 1813 ~~~ *Cotton* has been spun of so neat and fine a texture, that the use of it, even in the making of bone-lace, has completely, in England, superseded the use of flax; and great quantities of cotton finely spun, are exported continually for the making of lace abroad, although we are not prepared to say that, on the Continent, cotton has wholly superseded the use of flax. <u>Book of English Trades</u>, 1818 ~~~ Bone lace is said to have been the invention of a poor woman in Germany, about the time of our Queen Elizabeth. Her husband, a miner, being out of employment, she endeavoured to support the family by her own labour. Her ingenuity succeeded; lace became a very fashionable article of female adornment, and has continued so to the present day. <u>Scenes of Commerce</u>, 1836 [see *lace*, *pillow lace* and *thread lace*]

bonton – [see *model linen*]

book linen – Book linen is called so from its being put up in the form of a book; it is commonly 1 ¼ ell in width, and 24 Leipsic ells in length; three pieces of it are usually tied together with a red linen riband. It is a blue-striped and checked kind of linen, manufactured in Bielfeld, and likewise in Saxony; the chief markets for it are America and the West Indies; where, in particular, the checked sort is used for seamen's shirts, and the striped for curtains, trousers, jackets, &c. <u>European Commerce</u>, 1805

book muslin – Cotton goods are divided into 7 different classes, each proportionally lighter the than other. The heaviest of these are, 1st. *Shirtings*, 2d. *Cambrics*, 3d. *Cossas*, 4th. *Jaconetts*, 5th. *Lawn grounds*, 6th. *Mulls*, 7th. *Books*. <u>New Encyclopædia</u>, 1807 ~~~ The long sleeve, is very generally introduced in evening dress, but is ever composed of the clearest materials. Sometimes of lace, patent, or spider-net, and embroidered book muslin. *La Belle Assemblée*, January 1807 ~~~ dresses made for her Royal Highness the Princess Elizabeth, ~~~ A fine India star book muslin dress … worn over a satin slip. *La Belle Assemblée*, May 1818 ~~~ Indeed, fine book muslins are made up in evening-dresses, with satin bodices, more than any other article, while gauze, crape, and net, are confined now to the ball-room. *Ladies' Monthly Museum*, June 1821 ~~~ Book-muslin is woven very transparent, and by dressing made very clear and rather stiff; it is not so rough and knappy, nor so soft as other muslins. <u>Scenes of British Wealth</u>, 1825 ~~~ BOUK, Buke, or Book Muslins, known also by the name of *Wire Muslin,* from the transparency of the fabric, is the lightest and most flimsy species of all the varieties of Indian manufacture. The British imitation originated in Scotland about the year 1785, since which time it has been prosecuted to great extent. In England it has been attempted without much success, for the excessive lightness of the fabric, and consequently the great care which is required to preserve the warp from breaking, requires great delicacy, both of pressure in opening the warp, and nicety or hand in striking it equally home in the cloth. … After being bleached, bouk muslins are always stiffened with starch, to give them that clear appearance, from which they derive the name of *wire muslins*. … From the circumstance of transparency being the chief recommendation of bouk muslins, every operation which would tend to flatten the threads in finishing them, so far from adding to their appearance, would be excessively injurious. They are, therefore, never put through any operation of calendering, but merely folded with regularity, and thin pressed, with a smooth board between every piece. <u>Edinburgh Encyclopædia</u>, 1830 ~~~ Book-muslin is upon the whole considered most elegant, particularly when finished above the hem with an *entre deux* of embroidered English net. *La Belle Assemblée*, September 1831 ~~~ *Book muslin,* of which Emma can shew you a specimen in her late ball dress, is the clearest and finest of all the muslins. It is woven very transparent, and, by dressing, made very clear, and rather stiff; so that it is neither so nappy nor so flimsy as other sorts of muslin. It is sometimes worn over coloured silk, and looks very beautiful. <u>Scenes of Commerce</u>, 1836 ~~~ thin wiry fabrics, such as book-muslins, … Book and jaconet muslins are now currently woven by power-looms, especially in the Glasgow district. <u>Cotton Manufacture</u>, 1836

Booka – The dresses for evening parties … are of every material: muslin does not prevail much, except it is the clear Booka; *La Belle Assemblée*, March 1828 ~~~ A fichu of fine Booka muslin is worn under the dress, *Ladies' Museum*, October 1829 [see *book muslin*]

Borgiennes – Several new materials for robes have already appeared, … *Borgiennes* and *Lithuaniennes*, either figured or flowered, are also remarkable for the beauty both of their fabric and colours. *Court Magazine*, October 1833

Bottilla grounds – Among the newest articles worthy the notice of the fashionable world, are the *Regency Spots*, or the beautiful Bottilla grounds, for ladies' morning dresses; these have an agreeable effect, having a pleasing fall, and giving a graceful effect to the shape. *La Belle Assemblée*, March 1811

boucle – Bouclé, ée, adj. curled, etc. … Buckle, *s. boucle*, <u>Boyer's Royal Dictionary</u>, 1794

bouclée – Others [hats] are trimmed with … *plumes bouclées* – these are also ostrich feathers, the backs of which are knotted. *La Belle Assemblée*, February 1832

bouk – [see *book muslin*]

boulting – [see *bolting*]

Bourracan – [see *barracan*]

Bourracan nankin – The article called "*Bourracan Nankins,*" which has but a small proportion of wool in it, *Public Documents*, June 1831 [see also *nankeen*]

Bragance – [Paris] The most elegant of the former [mantles] are in velvet, satin, and *tissu Bragance. Court Magazine*, December 1833

braid – Braid (*v. t. from the* Sax brædan) To weave together. Braid (*s. from the verb*) A not or complication of something woven together, a kind of flat cord or lace. <u>Ash's English Dictionary</u>, 1795 ~~~ [court dress] A white crape petticoat, striped with silver braid and rich border, *Lady's Magazine*, June 1798 ~~~ Short gown of French double-sided silk, made very short in the waist, and tight to the shape: … the back is braided at each side with silk twist, in waves, and finished at each hip with a rich silk ornament. *La Belle Assemblée*, December 1814 ~~~ The jacket for the riflemen will be of green cloth, hussar fashion, collar, body, back, seams, cuffs, and welts to be bound round with black silk braid for officers, and black worsted for the enlisted men; two blind buttonholes on each side of the collar, of black braid, terminating in crows-feet; and a button at the upper end of each hole. Three rows of nine buttons on the breast; buttonholes of black braid, a little circular in their form. <u>General Regulations for the Army</u>, 1821 ~~~ Walking Dress. The braided pelisses, which were but partially patronised on their first appearance, are now in high favour with those ladies of rank who may be said to lead the fashions. Over a round dress of milk-white bombasin, or Norwich crape, is a close pelisse of puce-coloured cachemire, ornamented down the front and round the border with a peculiarly rich braiding in silk, the flowers of which represent the Caledonian thistle; two beautiful branches of the same braiding rise from the points that terminate the bottom of the facings, and form a superb ornament in front, on each side of the border. The ornament across the bust consists of a braiding in foliage only; but it has a very rich appearance, being composed of several rows reaching across the front to the forepart of each shoulder. The mancherons are plain, and are almost close to the sleeve; these are finished with one row of leaves in braiding. *Manchester Iris*, January 11, 1823 ~~~ The most novel [scarfs] are those of white muslin, ornamented at the bottom in gold braiding, in exact imitation of the embroidery of a Polish lancer's uniform. We have seen some embroidered in silk braiding of different colors, but those of gold are most *distingué. Atheneum*, September 1831 ~~~ [men's] Walking Dress. … Trowsers of chequered kerseymere, buttoned in the front with two rows of black braid up the side seams. *Day*, February 10, 1832 [see also *gimp* and *twist*]

branched – [see *ramaged*]

Brandenburg – [April] The Princess of Wales travelled in a mantle of green satin, trimmed with gold, with loops and tassels a la Brandenburgh; and wore a beaver hat. <u>Annual Register</u>, 1795 ~~~ For the promenade … as the season advances it is imagined that rich silk Brandenburg trimmings will receive an added portion of fashionable approbation; what appeared heavy and superfluous in summer, will confessedly add much to the comfort and elegance of the winter costume. *La Belle Assemblée*, August 1811 ~~~ the Brandenburgh trimming, though it has long been the mode, is yet very prevalent, in all colours. *La Belle Assemblée*, November 1811 ~~~ Walking *Dress*. – A round robe of jacconot muslin, with a boddice of violet sarsnet, trimmed with rich silk Brandenburgs of Austrian green; *Edinburgh Annual Register*, July 31, 1811 ~~~ Some ladies wear a dress of white Merino crape, ornamented with scarlet *brandenburghs* from the top to the bottom; *La Belle Assemblée*, December 1818 ~~~ [Paris] a new envelope is there often sported, called the Polish wrap, it is of dark blue, trimmed and ornamented with Brandenburgh chain work; *Ladies' Monthly Museum*, February 1821 ~~~ When cambric dresses are flounced with muslin, the flounces are eleven or twelve in number : they are trimmed down the bust with Brandenburghs of cotton. The new Brandenburghs, however, called bead-Brandenburghs, are most in favor; The are made of hair, and are of the most delicate workmanship. *Ladies' Monthly Museum*, June 1821 ~~~ Dresses of *gros de Naples*, for half-costume, are greatly admired. ... in the front of the bust is and ornament resembling a bias fold; ... and, on each side are two Brandenburgh ornaments, spreading out, at each end, next the arms, in *fleurs de lis*. *Ladies' Monthly Museum*, June 1825 ~~~ [Paris] Evening Dress. ... *Corsage* rather high, which is ornamented, as is also the skirt with *Brandenbourgs* in matted silver. *Royal Lady's*, January 1831 ~~~ With *redingotes* open in front, and with deep cut *corsages*, muslin *guimps* are worn, embroidered in chevrons or *Brandebourgs* which correspond with the design, forming a ladder-step in front of the skirt. *Maids, Wives, and Widows*, November 10, 1832 ~~~ [court dress] A dress pf white moire a Brandenburg, garni de blonde, *Court Journal*, June 1, 1833 [see also *frog*]

brillante – [Paris] I do not, however, believe you have yet seen our *crêpe brillanté*. This is a most *unique* and novel article, and whether checquered, striped, or spotted, may boast a richness and variety hitherto unparalleled. *La Belle Assemblée*, April 1819 ~~~ [Spain] Wool and hair manufactured, including goats hair, bristles, horse hair, feathers, and human hair. ... Calamancoes, known as Harlequins, Batavias, Brillantes, &c. all of wool, plain or worked, pressed Digest of the Commercial Regulations, 1824 ~~~ A very pretty article for turbans made its appearance [in December], called gauze *brillanté*, which had a good effect by candle-light. *La Belle Assemblée*, (year in review) 1825 ~~~ For the full-dress winter balls, young ladies wear gaze-brillante, *Lady's Magazine*, January 1829 ~~~ for grand balls, are dresses of tulle, or of *gaze-brillantee,* ornamented with gold or silver: *Ladies' Pocket*, February 1829 ~~~ A *ruche* composed of a new and very light and beautiful material called *gaze* brillantie, *Ladies' Pocket*, July 1830 ~~~ [court dress] The train is composed of bright grey gros de Tours: the trimming consists of a *bouillon* of *gaze brillantée*, to correspond with the dress, wreathed in pearls. ... [Paris] Evening Dress. A gown of *gaze brillantée*: the colour is *bleu de Berry*, over a gros de Naples slip to correspond. *Ladies' Museum*, August 1830

brillantine – Brilliantine (French silk) *Public Documents*, March 1832 ~~~ [ad] Highly Important to the Fashionable World. RICH FIGURED and PLAIN SILKS. – Satineés, Sylphidé, Quadrillé, Ecosaais, Quadrante, Satinnette, Brillantine, Armure, Challis, *Court Journal*, March 28, 1835 ~~~ [ad] Have received by the ships Hark-away and Jefferson, direct from Liverpool, ... 1 bale 4-4 Prussians and brillianteen hdkfs. *Farmer's Register*, May 1835 ~~~ We have to announce several new materials for *négligé*, half dress, and evening dress. Among the first, we think that *brillantine*, a very light material of Cashmere wool quadrilled with silk, may take precedence. *Court Magazine*, May 1836

Britannia – Upwards of fifteen thousand looms are constantly employed in the manufacture of linen and cotton in Perth, and as many more in the country around it. The fabrics thus manufactured consist chiefly of Silesias, Britannias, Journey from Edinburgh through Parts of North Britain, 1802 ~~~ The descriptions of linen goods for which this place [Dundee] is famous, are sail canvas, Osnaburghs, cotton baggings, sheetings, a kind of white linens called *Britannias*, and another called *Shirtings*, &c. Union Gazetteer, 1807 ~~~ Britannia is something heavier than Silesia, and is used for the same purpose; and also for sheets and trowsers in the West India settlements. Linen Manufacturer, 1817 ~~~ The French in Britanny made very substantial useful linens, that the Spaniards and West Indians were very fond of; these were imitated in Germany, and hence came the name Britannias and *Creas a la Morlaix*; they derive their names from the French fabricks. Reports from the Committees, 1820 ~~~ [ad] Britannia and coloured handkerchiefs; *Colonial Times*, January 13, 1826 ~~~ What may be considered as the staple articles are yard wide *Britannias*, which still form a large proportion of the printing trade; Glasgow Delineated, 1826

Britannia pearl fur – The trimming which ornaments the wrap is the newly invented Britannia trimming, far more elegant than fur, and the best substitute for fur hitherto discovered. It has, we understand, cost Mrs. Bell much trouble and expence, to bring it to its present perfection; it is intended not only for triinings, but also for hats, bonnets, &c. a purpose for which it is most admirably adapted. One of the chief recommendations of this trimming, is its novelty, nothing of the kind having ever been introduced before; and, perhaps, no article which has ever been brought before the public, is so well calculated to answer the purposes for which it is intended. As a substitute for fur, its merits are obvious, while from the lightness of its texture it is considerably more elegant than fur; for muffs and tippets, it is far superior to swansdown; and our fair fashionables consider it so elegant in hats and bonnets, that they order scarcely any thing else. … Mrs. Bell, whose correct and elegant taste enables her to new-model the Parisian fashions in the most becoming manner, has, we understand, produced an improved D'Angouleme bonnet, in her beautiful newly-invented Britannia trimming; we have no doubt that it will be found attractive; the material itself is, in fact, the most beautiful and appropriate thing for bonnets, trimmings, &c. that we have ever seen; it is at once light, rich, elegant, and novel; the latter recommendation would, with most of our fair fashionables, be of itself sufficient; but the Britannia trimming has more solid claims to general favour than novelty, its effect as a trimming is far superior to that of any description of fur for which it is intended as a substitute, and it is not only appropriate to pelisses, &c. but it is also admirably calculated for every description of dinner dress, its effect on velvet is particularly striking and beautiful: *La Belle Assemblée*, November 1814 ~~~ Improved French bonnet of black Britannia pearl fur, … The various hats and bonnets worn by *belles* of taste, in the walking costume, have been so completely superseded by Mrs. Bell's newly invented Britannia pearl fur, and silk mole skin bonnets and hats, that it is superfluous to describe them; … A piece of rich worked muslin, or pointed lace, stands up round the bosom, and partly shades an elegant small tippet of the newly invented Britannia pearl fur. – These tippets, which are now much worn, are particularly appropriate to dark silk, or velvet pelisses, as they considerably heighten their effect. Head-dress, the Britannia pearl fur hat; it may be termed the most tasteful and appropriate head-dress of the season; it is lined with white satin, and ornamented in a most tasteful style, with a beautiful plume of white feathers. The Britannia hat is exquisitely adapted to the first style of promenade dress, and is unquestionably an elegant improvement on the French bonnets, and possessing infinitely more taste. The materials of this hat are extremely appropriate for head-dresses; it is so much richer, and considerably lighter than either velvet or seal skin, and more adapted to the season than satin or any sort of silk. Large sized muff, composed also of Britannia pearl fur. *La Belle Assemblée*, December 1814

British blond – [court dress] A rich British blonde dress, handsomely trimmed with riband, blonde, and flowers, over white satin; a beautiful train of blonde, lined with white satin; *Royal Lady's*, April 1831 [see *blond*]

British cashmere – in *November* [1822] the pelisses began to assume a wintery appearance, and as now, to be fabricated of the fine cloth, called British cachemire; of this material the dresses began to be prepared that are now adopted. Museum of Foreign Literature, 1823 ~~~ Pomeranian mantles of the cloth called British cachemire (why, we know not, as it is totally unlike cachemire) *La Belle Assemblée*, January 1826 ~~~ Those [shawls] most in favour are the British cashmeres; they are of the finest texture, and of uncommon softness and lightness. *Ladies' Museum*, November 1831

British lace – a bonnet of the same colour (the latter edged with a deep veil of British lace,) … the rain spotted the lilac silk, and shrunk up the British lace veil. *Monthly Epitome*, January 1797 ~~~ on a machine, in the same manner as our British lace; *La Belle Assemblée*, March 1811 ~~~ But a more important alteration has taken place in Lace-Making, by substituting the loom: at Nottingham, and some other places, is now manufactured a lace of finer quality, more even in its texture, and considerably more elegant in its appearance than any bone-lace whatever, and at about one-third the price of bone-lace. This lace is made of two kinds; the coarsest is called *Mecklin-net;* the other, *bobbin-net* because it is woven by bobbins in some such way as the bone-lace is made, and for which, We believe, a patent was obtained. Not only lace, but veils, cloaks, and handkerchiefs, are made in this way, both of silk and cotton: the only inconvenience attending this mode of manufacture is, that the figures in the lace must be fixed by hand after the lace is woven; but, notwithstanding this defect, the introduction of this method has considerably reduced the demand for bone lace. All these laces made by the loom are, in the trade, contradistinguished by the name of *British* lace, particularly that made of *black* silk, a lace which has lately, most unaccountably, gone a good deal out of fashion. Book of English Trades, 1818 ~~~ Evening Dress – British lace dress: the waist rather long, and the *corsage* plain, *Kaleidoscope*, December 9, 1823 ~~~ Parisian Evening Dress. … It is of English lace in a pattern of stripes representing foliage, and is worn over a satin slip; *Lady's Magazine*, May 1829 ~~~ a cap of *dentelle Anglaise* (Bedford or Honiton lace); *Lady's Magazine*, December 31, 1830 ~~~ The King gave the bride away. The bride wore a dress of British lace, *Royal Lady's*, January 1831 ~~~ Lace made by the loom is generally known as *British* lace. British Cyclopædia of the Arts and Sciences, 1835 [see *lace*; *Bedfordshire, Buckinghamshire,* and *Honiton,* plus *bobbin-net* and *Nottingham*]

British Leghorn – [see *cotton straw* and *imitation Leghorn*]

British net – Dress of British net, embroidered in wreaths of roses in floize silk, ornamented with point, and silk cord and tassels. *La Belle Assemblée*, June 1816 ~~~ [Ball dress] English net is also in favour, particularly for very young ladies. *Repository of Fashions*, August 1829 ~~~ We see with pleasure that English net begins to be very fashionable in evening-dress. Some of the prettiest robes we have seen for a long time are composed of it. We may cite among them one that had the *corsage* draped *à la Tyrolienne,* and the back and shoulders trimmed with a pelerine of the same material embroidered round the border in a wreath of red rose-buds, with a foliage of two shades of green. *Ladies' Pocket*, August 1836 [see also *bobbin-net* and *Nottingham*]

British shirting – Mr. Lowe, of Cheapside, has at length accomplished what has long been a desideratum in the English manufactures, in having produced a fabric that he has denominated "British Shirting," which being made partly of flax and partly of cotton, is equally durable with Irish linen, and will wash as well as that substance. – As a non-conductor of heat, it answers the same purposes as calico, in not producing the sense of coldness to those wearers who are subject to perspiration; and it is said to be only about half as expensive as Irish linen of the same width and fineness. *Universal Magazine*, September 1811 ~~~ LOWE'S PATENT BRITISH SHIRTING CLOTH, The only Manufacture in Great Britain in which the advantages of English Flax and Cotton are united in one Thread. Established in 1808. This Fabric, from its commencement, has been manufactured with a view for sale to private families and home trade, and has, by progressive improvement, been brought to a degree of perfection unequalled. Its peculiar texture frees it from the injurious cold or chill experienced in the wear of Irish or other linen, and the unpleasant sensation peculiar to fabrics made wholly of cotton. For Durability, beautiful Appearance, Comfort in Wear, and great Economy, it stands unrivalled. Sold at about HALF the PRICE of Irish or other fine Linens, *Repository of Arts*, January 1815 [see also *shirting*]

broad cloth – a manufacture made of sheeps wool of our own cloth mixt with that of Segovia in Spain, the staple commodity and honour of this nation, so called from its breadth, which is so great that it is weaved by two persons who sit at each side, and fling the shuttle to one another. Royal English Dictionary, 1775 ~~~ Halifax. … the principal fabrics are … broad and narrow cloths. They are generally woven by poor manufacturers, and sold in an unfinished state to the merchants, who dye and prepare them for foreign and home consumption. State of the Poor, 1797 ~~~ Our broad cloths form the principal article of the dress of men of the superior classes; and a more perfect manufacture, with respect to beauty and utility, cannot easily be conceived. The threads in it are so concealed by a fine nap or down raised on the surface, and curiously smoothed and glossed, that it looks more like a rich texture of nature's forming, than the work of the weaver. Arts of Life, 1802 ~~~ A riding coat of fine broad cloth, the colour a dark lavender blossom; *La Belle Assemblée*, December 1806 ~~~ The Spanish and British wools are worked up together in the manufacture of *fine* cloths. It is a common question, in the cloth-halls of Yorkshire in England, to ask – How much Spanish wool is there in this piece? – and the answer generally is – half and half; – that is, half Spanish and half English wool. Fine broad cloth, up to the price of 15s. or 16s. a yard, is made entirely of English wool; cloth from 15s. to 20s. a yard, is made of Spanish and English wool, mixed; and superfine cloths, from 20s. to 30s. a yard and upwards, is made altogether of Spanish wool. These prices relate to cloth in its *undressed* state: when it comes into the hands of the consumer, of course the cost is considerably enhanced. In the year 1809, the price of woollen cloths in the West of England, and in Yorkshire, was considerably lowered, owing to the manufacturers using *British* wool instead of that imported from Spain; and, except in the superfine cloth, it answers completely, especially that from the *Anglo-Merino* breed of sheep. Resources of the British Empire, 1811 ~~~ Broad cloth, a fine woollen cloth Webster's Dictionary, 1817 ~~~ *Broadcloths* – 45 inches wide, cost 1s. 10d. to 2s. 5d. – The most inferior would come under this provision; … This quality is used by mechanics, sailors, fishermen, boatmen, and laborers. … *Broadcloths*, of common quality, 50 to 54 inches wide, 3s. 3 1-8d. to 6s. Worn, very generally, by farmers, mechanics, sailors, boatmen, fishermen, and laborers. *Niles' Weekly Register*, March 8, 1828 ~~~ Broad cloth is from 60 to 63 inches wide, and there are from 40 to 60 yards in a piece; the lower sorts being the longest. A Million of Facts, 1835 ~~~ A more perfect manufacture than our broad cloths, with respect to beauty and utility, cannot easily be conceived. The threads in it are so *concealed* by a fine nap or down raised on the surface, and curiously smoothed and glossed, that it looks more like a rich *texture* of nature's forming than the work of the weaver. Fourth Book of Lessons, 1835 [see also *superfine*]

brocade – A silken stuff variegated. Sheridan's English Dictionary, 1797 ~~~ Formerly the word signified only a stuff, wove all of gold, both in the warp and the woof, or all of silver, or of both mixed together; thence it passed to those of stuffs in which there was silk mixed, to raise and terminate the gold or silver flowers; but at present all stuffs, even those of silk alone, whether they be grograms of Tours or of Naples, satins, and even taffeties or lustrings, if they be but adorned and worked with some flowers or other figures, are called *brocades*. Encyclopædia Britannica, 1797 ~~~ brocades, by the caprice of fashion, are at present not worn, yet as they may soon become fashionable again, New Encyclopædia, 1807 ~~~ Brocaded ribbands have just appeared, consequently confined for the present to fashionable circles; … In regards to shoes, the brocaded silk is happily just introduced; and works up so elegantly into Grecian sandals, and when composed partly of silver, as well as silk thread, into that fascinating ornament the *Cinderella slipper*, it must afford infinite pleasure to some of our fair friends show more particularly lay the stress of beauty on the foot. It is to no clumsy cobbler that we owe this pleasing trifle; it is the ladies who have taken this art into their own hands, and so much improved upon it. *La Belle Assemblée*, June 1810 ~~~ [dress belonging to Princess Charlotte] the mantua of an extremely rich gold brocade, with blown roses, richly woven in, very thickly all over the dress, *Niles' Weekly Register*, June 22, 1816 ~~~ Brocades. – This term came from the French word *brochées*; which was applied to figured silks, among which was interwoven patterns in gold, silver, &c. *Ladies' Museum*, July 1829 ~~~ Her Majesty has caused patterns of figured silk to be forwarded for inspection, and ordered several for ordinary purposes; and for the Royal visit to Guildhall the Queen has commanded a white silk of splendid fabric, magnificently figured with leaves and flowers; some part of the blossoms of which are to be enriched with silver woven into the silk, displaying at once what can be done by the trade of London, and originating a taste for magnificent brocade silks, which will at once become general among the higher classes, and create a new means of giving bread to thousands. We shall simply add to the following directions, that after the 9th of November, ladies will do well to adopt, in place of other material, wherever they can do so, some of the magnificent silks which will by that time become general among the higher classes. *Lady's Magazine*, October 1830 ~~~ Rich brocaded satins of all descriptions are worn in dresses a l'antique; velvet dresses, made à l'antique, are also tres à la mode. *Lady's Magazine and Museum*, December 1834 ~~~ The materials for evening dress rival in splendour those of several seasons past; brocades richly flowered in antique patterns of lively colours, sometimes intermingled with gold; *Court Magazine*, November 1835 ~~~ Her Majesty. … cerise satin train, richly brocaded in silver (Spitalfields manufacture), with handsome silver border, … H.R.H. the Duchess of Kent. … beautiful cerise tabinet train, richly brocaded in silver, … train of Irish manufacture. *Lady's Magazine and Museum*, June 1836 [see also *silk* and *Spitalfields*] brocaded gauze – [ad] Satin Brocade Gauzes, 8s. 6d. usually sold at 10s. 6d.; *Repository of Arts*, May 1815 ~~~ [court dress] White satin petticoat, trimmed with blond and rolio of white satin, draperies of white brocaded gauze, trimmed with blond, *La Belle Assemblée*, May 1816 ~~~ This new and beautiful manufacture of brocaded gauze is the most fashionable article for evening dresses for the young; *La Belle Assemblée*, January 1819 ~~~ The autumn produced in Paris two new materials for the fabrication of hats: one is a brocaded satin, the other a brocaded gauze. ... The hats of brocaded gauze are of the same shape as those that have been worn all the summer: the brocaded figures are of the same colour as the ground – white on white, pink on pink, &c. *La Belle Assemblée*, November 1819 ~~~ [court dress] A dress of gold-brocaded gauze, trimmed with borderings of Indian barbs; body and sleeves trimmed with blonde; train of crimson brocade; *Royal Lady's*, May 1831 ~~~ A new kind of brocaded gauze of a very light but rich description, is coming much into favour in evening dress; one of the prettiest dresses we have lately seen was composed of it. *Ladies' Museum*, August 1831

brocado – [see *brocade*]

broche – [past tense of] Brocher, *va to * knit, * stitch; * do in a hurry; * work with gold, silk, &c.* New Pocket Dictionary, 1830 ~~~ [court dress] A splendid silver poplin broche dress, *Royal Lady's Magazine*, June 1832 ~~~ at a grand ball ... Another lady wore a dress of satin *perse rayé*, *broché* in very glaring colours – orange and black; *Court Magazine*, March 1833 ~~~ [Paris] Grand Festival Dresses. – Morning Concert Dresses. Ensemble De Grande Toilette, No. 1. A robe Dubarry of gros grains. This is a most splendid material, in imitation of the rich ribbons worn as ceintures, and broché in beautiful patterns of natural flowers. A small delicate branching flower runs all over it in diamonds, and in the centre of each diamond is a single flower or bouquet: in one suppose a tulip, in another a rose, in a third a marguerite, and so on; in every square a different flower, or else a different bouquet. *Lady's Magazine and Museum*, July 1834 ~~~ [Paris] Another beautiful dress was *à l'antique*, of light blue satin, *broché* all over in a running pattern with silver; *Lady's Magazine and Museum*, February 1835 [see also *brocade*]

brochellas – An extra premium is also due to Cunningham & Anderson, of Richmond, Virginia, for specimen No. 415, deposited by Hacker, Brown & Co., being their Brochellas, dyed blue in this city. They are well calculated for a cheap wearing apparel, and being stout and well made, will supply a desideratum which has been anxiously looked for. These are also interesting to us, as being the first specimens of cotton goods received from a manufactory south of the Potomac; these five pieces were found in the warehouses in this city, and not sent expressly by the manufacturers, they may, therefore, be inferred to be a fair specimen of the goods they make. *Journal of the Franklin Institute*, November 1831 ~~~ ARTICLES known by the names of Brochellas, and Summer Cloth, cannot be admitted at 10 percent, duty, as Worsted Stuff Goods, if composed in part of Cotton, but must pay the Wollen's [sic] duty, 50 per cent. Tariff, 1832 ~~~ Worsted stuff goods, such as Bombazines, Bombazetts, Brochellas, *Examiner*, July 8, 1835 [see also *summer cloth*]

brown Holland – The staple manufacture of Perth is linen; and of late, a considerable quantity of cotton-cloth. ... Four-fourths wide brown and white country linen, chiefly used for hat-linings, buckrams, &c. Brown Hollands, Hessians, pack-sheetings, and other coarse fabrics, manufactured in the neighbourhood; Statistical Account of Scotland, 1796 ~~~ [when storing clothes] There should be a brown Holland cloth to cover the coats, to keep the dust from them. Footman's Directory, 1823 ~~~ Brown Holland (flax) *Public Documents*, March 1832 ~~~ [ad] Have received by the ships Hark-away and Jefferson, direct from Liverpool, ... 2 cases brown Holland; *Farmer's Register*, May 1835 ~~~ *List of prices paid by the clothiers of Baltimore for work performed for them by the seamstresses.* ... Brown Holland jackets. 12 ½ cents *Niles' Weekly Register*, October 31, 1835

Brussels lace – [court dress] A rich gold-spangled crape petticoat, trimmed round the bottom with fine Brussels point, over purple satin, *Lady's Magazine*, January 1797 ~~~ Her Royal Highness the Princess Charlotte of Wales. – A pink and silver slip, with a beautiful Brussels lace frock to wear over it, and a pink and silver girdle. *La Belle Assemblée*, June 1807 ~~~ [belonging to Princess Charlotte] Two Brussels lace dresses, with border and trimming of point lace to match; the one cost 350 guineas, the other 300 guineas. *Niles' Weekly Register*, June 22, 1816 ~~~ Brussels Point-Lace has always been deemed the most valuable, and is the only sort used in court-dresses, for gentlemen's frills and ruffles, and the principal one for the trimmings of ladies' dresses. The most beautiful and expensive veils are also of this manufacture. It may be distinguished by the appearance of some parts of its ornamental leaves, which resemble French cambric; and by a thick and bold prominent thread round their margin, which appears worked over in button-hole stitch with another very fine thread; it has also a peculiar yellow hue, which tint is studiously preserved by rinsing the Lace, after having been washed, in a weak solution of coffee. Young Lady's Book, 1829 ~~~ The lace made here is of two sorts, called English or Brussels lace, according to its ground. The best is very expensive; a single veil, of handsome pattern, costs about £40. This will not appear a very large sum, when the time taken in the manufacture is considered; a flower, about two inches in diameter, will occupy one of the workwomen a whole day. *Saturday Magazine*, supplement for July, 1835

Bruxelles – [see *Brussels lace*]

Buckinghamshire lace – The principal manufactures in this district [Buckinghamshire] are those of paper and lace. Lace is made in many parts of the county by women and children; the best hands can earn from one shilling to eighteen-pence per day. Agriculture of the County of Hants, 1794 ~~~ [in Buckingham] Women, on an average, earn 8d. or 9d. a day, by lace-making. State of the Poor, 1797 ~~~ In all the accounts we have read of Buckinghamshire, it is stated that *bone* lace is the chief manufacture; but some of the oldest makers, whom we consulted, were totally ignorant of the term. The principal sort made is fine thread-lace, black and white: the former commonly worked with a french-ground, or perfect diamond squares; the latter generally executed with a roundish hole, called the point-ground. The maker is furnished with a round pillow, on which a slip of parchment is fixed, perforated with a great number of holes, correspondent to the pattern required to be executed. These holes are filled with pins, which are placed and displaced as the bobbins are moved, or stitches finished. The thread is fixed on the top of small bobbins, or gimps; the first are used in making fine lace and ground; and the latter for coarse lace, and to work in the flowers, &c. Beauties of England and Wales, 1801 ~~~ blond or bone-lace, which is produced in England, chiefly in the county of Buckingham. Domestic Encyclopedia, 1802 ~~~ New Patents. ... Charles Lacy, of Nottingham, and John Lindley, of Loughborough, lace manufacturers, for machinery for making bobbin or Buckinghamshire lace net, and the aid of which lace net may be made with greater facility and less manual labour than by any machinery or method now in use. ... John Heathcoat, Loughborough, lace manufacturer, for improvements upon machinery in making bobbin net, or Buckingham lace net. *New Monthly Magazine*, January 1817 ~~~ [in 1816] she announced her firm determination to support the arm of British industry, and accordingly ordered her wedding dress to be of Buckinghamshire lace, in preference to the gaudy frippery of Brussels manufacture. Biographical Memoir of the Much Lamented Princess Charlotte Augusta, 1818 ~~~ Ruff of Buckinghamshire lace; cap of the same, *Repository of Arts*, March 1823 ~~~ The lace manufactured in England is generally called Buckinghamshire or Bedfordshire lace, after those districts wherein it is made; it is also called pillow lace, or bobbin lace, because it is woven upon a pillow or cushion by means of bobbins. Edinburgh Encyclopædia, 1830 ~~~ Her Majesty. Dress of white satin, ... train of white velvet, lined with white satin, elegantly trimmed with Buckinghamshire blonde and geraniums to correspond; *Court Journal*, March 2, 1833 [By the end of this period, Buckinghamshire lace usually meant handmade lace, not machine made (for which see *Nottingham*); see also *Bedfordshire lace*, *bone lace* and *pillow lace*]

buckram – a coarse cloath made of hemp, gummed, calendered, and dyed; used by taylors to stiffen their garments; ... they are sometimes made of old sheets or pieces of sails gummed. Royal English Dictionary, 1775 ~~~ The linen is whitened at the bleachfields in the neighbourhood [of Coupar], is used for buckram and hat linings, and is worth about 9d. per yard. Statistical Account of Scotland, 1796 ~~~ A sort of strong linen cloth, stiffened with gum, used by taylors and staymakers. ... Buckram is more generally, if not always, stiffened with glue, and used in the making of garments to keep them in the form intended. It is also used in the bodies of women's gowns; ... Buckrams are sold wholesale by the dozen small pieces or remnants, each about 4 ells long, and broad according to the piece from which they are cut. New Encyclopædia, 1807 ~~~ When I say this, I mean to eulogize the taste which yet prevails with persons of real judgment, to maintain the *ease and gracefulness* of our assumed Grecian mode, against a new race of stay-makers, corset-inventors, &c. who have just armed themselves with whalebone, steel, and buckram, to the utter destruction of all the naturally-elegant shapes which fall into their hands. Mirror of the Graces, 1811 ~~~ *For an Improvement in the manufacturing of Gentlemen's Stocks.* – G. R. Lillibridge, *New York.* The foundation, or stiffening part of this stock, is formed of two pieces, joined together lengthwise, say of doubled buckram. They are to be so joined that they move on each other, as on a hinge, and are hence called "Hinge-Stocks." When thus formed, they are to be covered and lined in the usual way. The buckram may be rendered waterproof by shellac varnish. London Journal of Arts and Sciences, 1830 ~~~ A somewhat similar article [to catgut], but more closely woven and stiffened with glue, is termed Buckram: Italian *Bucherame* (from *bucheráto*, full of holes) alluding to its sieve-like texture. Analytical Dictionary, 1835 [see also *canvas*]

buck skin – The following written notice was stuck up at the gate of an inn in a village on the western road, previous to the commencement of the late Whitsun Holidays. ... a good pair pf buck-skin, breeches to be wrestled for, the best man to have the breeches; no dispute about falls, but three go-down's. *Sporting Magazine*, July 1795 ~~~ "Do you not remember," resumed Edward, "our calling one morning at your chambers, when we found you struggling, with all your might, to squeeze yourself into a new pair of buckskin breeches? I am sure I shall never forget the strenuous efforts you made on that occasion." Edward: Various Views of Human Nature, 1796 ~~~ The gloves that gentlemen wear are in general of doe or buck skin, such as will wash and clean: if they are white or yellow, they often want washing, and if attention is not paid in doing it, they are soon spoiled. Footman's Directory, 1823 ~~~ The buck-skin, as dressed for the use of our glovers, is remarkable for its thickness, softness and pliability, and with these advantages it has the great superiority of not being liable to injury from moisture, as tannin is made use of in its preparation. In relation to its warmth, durability and agreeableness to the wearer, it appears to be much preferred to similar leather made from any other skins, whether of European or American deer. Within a few years past the use of buckskin shirts has very much increased among invalids, and often with great advantage. But it is generally believed that these shirts render the body extremely susceptible to changes of temperature, and, all things considered, do more injury than shirts made of flannel or other commonly used materials. American Natural History, 1826 ~~~ The common dress of the labouring mechanic, not a century ago, consisted of this leathern doublet; and the buckskin breeches of the sportsman are still worn. Useful and Ornamental Planting, 1832

buckskin cloth – coloured Buckskin Trousers, of the finest quality, 30s. *Geo. D. Doudney's Monthly Fashion Sheet*, March, 1835 ~~~ [ad] Have received by the ships Hark-away and Jefferson, direct from Liverpool, ... 2 cases low priced cotton fustians. 1 case stout moleskins and champion buckskins. *Farmer's Register*, May 1835 ~~~ Monthly Report of the Woollen Trade. ... The trade in middle priced and fine single milled goods has also been checked by the increasing consumption of buckskins, which have been so much in demand during November and October, that they have been bought, or ordered, whilst in the loom; as these are chiefly manufactured in the neighbourhood of Huddersfield, and in Saddleworth, the trade of those places has been marked by considerable animation. *Farmer's Magazine*, January 1836 ~~~ Excellent Winter Buckskin Trousers, for 20s. per pair; the best Buckskins that are made, for 28s. *Eminent Foreign Statesmen*, March 1836 ~~~ Wolcottville Manufacturing Company, Conn., for an excellent specimen of buckskin and other sattinets, made of Mogadore wool, Wolcott & Goodwin, agents, 29 Pinestreet. *Gold Medal. Mechanics' Magazine*, December 1836

buff – Buff, leather for military accoutrements, prepared from the buffalo, and dressed with oil, after the manner of shamony. Leather of other preparation is however sometimes substituted for this buff skin. British Military Library, 1804 ~~~ Buff-leather is used for sword belts, and for other purposes where its exceeding thickness and firmness is required. Dictionary of Merchandise, 1805 ~~~ What is the price of raw material for buff leather? – The raw material for buff leather, to buy it in Leadenhall market, is the same to the tanner. What is that price? – They are about 4½ *d.* or 5½ *d.* What is the material worth when manufactured per lb.? – From 2*s.* 6*d.* to 4*s.* per lb. What should you suppose is the difference in value between the Bristol hides made into buff and London hides made into buff? –

Full 1*s.* out of 4*s.* Twenty-five per cent? – Yes. Then that twenty-five per cent in value entirely arises from the difference between well and ill flaying? – Entirely so. <u>Reports from the Committees</u>, 1824 ~~~ [General Rogniat] The General gives to the legionary cavalry exactly the same defensive armour as he does to the infantry of the line, with the addition merely of large buff-skin gloves reaching to the elbow. ... "To recapitulate: the legionary of the line will be armed with a simple firelock and bayonet, a brass helmet with chin-straps, a buff-skin cuirass, and shoulder-straps of brass scales: his officer will carry a half pike instead of a firelock. ... SUBSTANCE OF COL. MARBOT'S REMARKS. ... The additional weight of a buff-leather cuirass will be more sensibly felt after rain, when it will soon weigh from eighteen to twenty pounds. Besides, buff-leather is very difficult to dry, and contracts; and if this defect were to be remedied by a covering of varnished leather, the cuirass would become too stiff, and would be a hindrance to the soldier both in stooping and in the handling of his firelock. However, the advantages of this kind of armour are such as to render it very desirable that some material could be found which would prove to be at the same time *light, pliant, water-proof,* and *bullet-proof. United Service Journal,* March 1829 ~~~ Ordnance Office, *January* 5, 1819. ... Agreements have been made between the Ordnance Department and Robert Dingee, of Yonkers, near New York, for two thousand sets of accoutrements for infantry, with buff belts, and breastplate of brass, at the rate of three dollars a set: and for two thousand five hundred sword belts for infantry, to be made of buff leather, at one dollar and twenty-five cents each, including buckle, hook, and clasp. <u>American State Papers</u>, 1833 ~~~ Formerly, when metallic armour was going out of use, but while it was still considered advisable to cover the body in battle with a better protection than ordinary clothing, a species of very thick but pliant leather was made from the hide of the urus, or wild bull, at that time plentiful in the forests of Poland, Hungary, and the middle and southern provinces of Russia. The name by which this animal was commonly known was that of Buffe, whence is derived the term buff-leather as designating the hide of this animal prepared in a particular way. The Russia Company, which was chartered by Henry VIII., was obliged to import a certain number of "buffe-hides," which were manufactured into leather for military use. Real buff-leather would turn the edge of a sword and was pistol-proof. The time of its principal use in this country was during the great civil war in the reign of Charles I., after which it gradually declined and at length became obsolete. Besides the hides of the urus, I believe those of the real buffalo of Italy were employed for the same purpose. The buff-leather of modern times is prepared from cowhide, and is used for little else than soldiers' belts. <u>Transactions of the Society</u>, 1836

bugles – Bugle, *s.* a shining bead, of a cylindrical from, and made of glass. <u>Barclay's English Dictionary</u>, 1799 ~~~ In the evening, Her Royal Highness's was extremely elegant, train and drapery of white crape, spangled bugles embroidered at bottom *Boston Weekly,* August 20, 1803 ~~~ Lady Frances Pratt. Was dressed in one of the most beautiful dresses at Court, made of pale green velvet, ornamented with green bugles, in wreaths and fringes. *National Register,* January 24, 1808 ~~~ Bugles, are small glass beads, of different colours, of which large quantities are exported to Africa, and there bartered on the Coast, for slaves, ivory, gums, &c. &c. <u>Dictionary of Commerce</u>, 1810 ~~~ Bugle, small glass tubes of different colours, stitched to the tassels and flounces of women's gowns, to make them appear more brilliant. <u>Newman's Spanish Dictionary</u>, 1823 ~~~ Bugles constitute an elegant ornament in mourning, but of late years they have declined in favour. *La Belle Assemblée,* February 1827 ~~~ [Court dress] A black aerophane dress, over black satin, embroidered in white bugles and opals; *Court Journal,* June 22, 1833 ~~~ A shining bead of black glass. <u>Critical Pronouncing Dictionary</u>, 1837

buke muslin – [see *book muslin*]

bumbazeen – [see *bombazine*]

bunting – Bunting, a thin slight stuff used for ship's colours; <u>Perry's English Dictionary</u>, 1795 ~~~ Bunting, thin linen cloth <u>Webster's Dictionary</u>, 1817 ~~~ Buntine is a thin sort of woollen stuff, very pliable, though strong; it is wove in strips, blue, white, red, &c. which strips are afterwards strongly sewed together, into the form needed for the specific flag, <u>Scenes of British Wealth</u>, 1825 ~~~ Buntin, or Bunting, which is used for ships' colours, is also a stout sort of Tamy. It is usually either ten or twenty inches in breadth and sold undressed. <u>Analytical Dictionary</u>, 1835

buridan – *Buridan.* – A wide striped silk material, light and deep garnet, light and deep green, &c., with satin cloaks of the same colour. … *Out-Door Costume, New Materials for Mantle Dresses.* … *Buridan,* a silk of a new and uncommonly rich kind; it is striped horizontally in very broad stripes, in two shades of the same colour, as emerald upon dark green, &c. &c.; the stripes are figured in satin, which also corresponds. *Maids, Wives, and Widows,* November 10, 1832

buyadire – Colour muslins are also worn in home dress, though not so much as white: there have been some just introduced, the ground of which is either blue, rust colour, or lilac; they have broad borders round the bottom of the skirt, which are called *buyadires*; these borders are of a different colour: these dresses are sometimes finished by flounces, but in general they are ornamented only with the borders. *Repository of Arts,* June 1819 [see also *bayadere*]

buzin des Indes – Home Dress of a Paris Lady. – The robe is composed of a new silk, buzin des Indes; *New Monthly Belle Assemblée,* August 1836

Cabbage - Cypress feather

cabbage – A Taylor who cabbag'd, as taylors will do, Not an inch from an ell, but a yard out of two; <u>Mirth and Metre</u>, 1807 ~~~ pieces purloined from their employers by Taylors and Sempstresses; the act is 'cabbaging.' <u>Slang</u>, 1823

cachemérienne – [see *cashemirienne*]

cachemire – [see *cashmere*]

cachemire bombasin – Among the new materials for winter dresses is the *Cachemire-bombasin*; an article of a soft and supple texture, and highly glazed. *La Belle Assemblée*, January, 1830

cachemire de laine – [see *cashmere wool*]

cachemire gauze – [see *cashmere gauze*]

cachemire muslin – [see *cashmere muslin*]

cacique gauze – And now *December*, dreary *December*, closes the year of 1822, wherein we find … for the warm atmosphere of the ball room or crowded evening party, has been invented the cacique gauze, of the most rich and varied hue; which by adapting as turbans on their graceful heads, they may vie with the beauties who composed the court of Mexican monarchs, while the Montezuma plume waves magnificently over their brow, and the Mexican diadem encircles their glossy tresses. <u>Museum of Foreign Literature</u>, 1823

caddas – [1793] Caddas, or crewel riband, the dozen pieces, every piece containing thirty six yards <u>Statutes at Large</u>, 1796 ~~~ Caddas, are ribbons manufactured of silk and worsted; called also cruel ribbons. <u>Dictionary of Commerce</u>, 1810

caddis – Caddis, a kind of stuff; <u>Perry's English Dictionary</u>, 1795 ~~~ When a wound penetrates deep, it is not safe to keep its lips quite close: this keeps in the matter, and is apt to make the wound fester. In this cafe the best way is to fill the wound with soft lint, commonly called *caddis*. It however must not be stuffed in too hard, otherwise it will do hurt. <u>Domestic Medicine</u>, 1800

caffa – Silk wrought, viz. … Grograms broad, Caffa, or Damask, <u>Ship-Master's Assistant</u>, 1795 ~~~ (Sound Duties.) Stuffs, Barattas, Caffa, damasks, rattins, satins, taffeties, and all sorts of silk stuffs, <u>Ship Owner's Manual</u>, 1795 ~~~ Caffa, painted cotton cloths, manufactured in the East Indes, and sold at Bengal. <u>Encyclopædia Britannica</u>, 1797

caffart damask – There is also a stuff in France called the *caffart damask*, made in imitation of the true damask, having woof of hair, coarse silk, thread, wool, or cotton. Some have the warp of silk and the woof of thread; others are all thread or all wool. <u>Encyclopædia Britannica</u>, 1797 ~~~ The French had long since a manufacture in imitation of the old fashioned silk damask, which they called *Cafard* (counterfeit) damask: <u>Silk Manufacture</u>, 1832

calabar skin – [see *Siberian squirrel*]

calamanco – Calamanco, a sort of woollen stuff, with a glossy surface. <u>Barclay's English Dictionary</u>, 1799 ~~~ Halifax. … the principal fabrics are … callimancoes, … They are generally woven by poor manufacturers, and sold in an unfinished state to the merchants, who dye and prepare them for foreign and home consumption. <u>State of the Poor</u>, 1797 ~~~ a sort of woollen stuff manufactured in England and in Brabant; it has a fine gloss, and is chequered in the warp, whence the checks only appear on the right side. Some calamancos are quite plain, others have broad stripes adorned with flowers, some with plain broad stripes, some with narrow stripes, and others watered. <u>Encyclopædia Britannica</u>, 1797 ~~~ The greater part of the combing wool is consumed in worsted for making what is called new drapery in the Book of Rates, viz. … callimanco, 9d. to 2s. 2d. … per yard. <u>Origin of Commerce</u>, 1801 ~~~ Flannel, it is true, in spite of Dr. Darwin, has regained among men even more, perhaps, than it has lost among the women, but calamanco with its stiff ungraceful fraternity of stuffs seems irrecoverably banished, except among a few old fashioned people, and the lowest classes of the community, and œconomy has joined with fashion to prevent a recal. *Universal Magazine*, November 1810 ~~~ Estimate of the Expense for clothing a … Nurse, … belonging to the Royal Military Asylum, Chelsea; for 1816. ~~~ 1 Calimanco Petticoat per annum – 6s. 5¼d. <u>Reports from the Committees</u>, 1816 ~~~ Calamanco and lamparillas, with flowers or spots of silk wrought in the loom. [exported from Spain to

America] Digest of Commercial Regulations, 1824 ~~~ [Paris] Walking dresses of Merino Caroline, with Calimanco stripes, are increasing in favour: *Ladies' Monthly Museum*, December 1826 ~~~ A General Collection of Words of variable spelling, in which those of the best usage are printed in Roman character, ... calamanco, *callimanco*, *calimanco*, Practical Orthography, 1828 ~~~ Calamanco (Spanish *calamaco*) is made wholly of worsted, and is glazed, or not glazed, and dyed of such colours as fashion may dictate. Calamancoes are woven with a satin tweel and are often striped, lengthwise, by alternately reversing the tweeled side. Analytical Dictionary, 1830 ~~~ Calamanco; a woollen stuff, principally manufactured in the Netherlands. The English manufactures of it have declined of late years. The warp is sometimes mixed with silk or goats' hair. British Cyclopedia, 1835

Caledonian silk – The new manufacture of Caledonian silk is likely to be universally adopted among the higher circles as a *demi-saison* dinner dress; indeed its firm texture seems likely to ensure its patronage next winter: it appears equally strong with the poplin, but has a more silky surface. These silks are in beautiful chequers of various colours on a white ground; but for the present season lilac, or pale green, is most prevalent. *La Belle Assemblée*, September 1819 [see also *plaid* and *tartan*]

calender – a machine used in manufactories to press certain woollen and silken stuffs and linens, to make them smooth, even, and glossy, or to give them waves, or water them, as may be seen in Mohairs and tabbies. This instrument is composed of two thick cylinders or rollers, of very hard and well polished wood, round which the stuffs to be calendered are wound: Encyclopædia Britannica, 1797

calf skin – *Calf-Skins,* in the leather manufacture, are prepared and dressed by the tanners, skinners, and curriers, who fell them for the use of the shoe-makers, saddlers, book-binders, and other artificers, who employ them in their several manufactures. ... The English calf-skin is much valued abroad, and the commerce thereof very considerable in France and other countries; where divers attempts have been made to imitate it, but hitherto in vain. What is like to baffle all endeavours for imitating the English calf in France is, the smallness and weakness of the calves about Paris; which at 15 days old are not so big as the English ones when they come into the world. Encyclopædia Britannica, 1797 ~~~ KIP SKINS are the skins of the Calf, at a certain age bordering on maturity, which are always passed in London as Calf Skins. Practice of the Customs, 1812 ~~~ [ad] Boot and Shoes, Among which are Ladies' Prunell, Sattin, Morocco, Seal and Calf skin BOOTS, Prunell of all colours, Kid, Sattin, Morocco, Seal and Calf skin Shoes; Directory for the Village of Rochester, 1827 ~~~ THE WELLINGTON, ... are commonly made of calfskin, though among the *ton,* for the sake of expense, doubtless, Spanish leather is used. This, I think, except in dress shoes, for which it only is qualified, should never be used; as it never possesses a quarter the jet brilliancy well-polished calf-skin can boast; while, in point of wear, it is far inferior. Whole Art of Dress, 1830 ~~~ A green chariot, with a drab lining (No. 300), the Jarvey with a calf-skin waistcoat, and a cat-skin collar to his coat. Fur collars will certainly go out of fashion after this. The *tout ensemble* is, however, destroyed by a hay-band round his hat. *Sporting Magazine*, December 1830 ~~~ 150 pair calf skin boots sell for 4 dollars 50 cts. per pair; Manufactures in the United States, 1833 [see also *neat's leather*]

calico – Calico, an Indian stuff Perry's English Dictionary, 1795 ~~~ *Dresses for April. ... Morning. ...* Round gown of French grey-checquered calico; *Lady's Magazine*, April 1797 ~~~ in commerce, a sort of cloth resembling linens made of cotton. The name is taken from that of Callicut, a city on the coast of Malabar, ... Callicoes are of different kinds, plain, printed, painted, stained, dyed, chints, muslins, and the like, all included under the general denomination of *callicoes*. Some of them are painted with various flowers of different colours; others are not stained, but have a stripe of gold and silver quite through the piece, and at each end is fixed a tissue of gold, silver, and silk, intermixed with flowers. Encyclopædia Britannica, 1797 ~~~ Servants in reputable places cannot reasonably be expected to keep to the very plain and homely dress of former days, ... And even those, who, till they go to service, have had no better garment than the uniform of the Charity School, should, on their going into respectable families, be permitted to dress a little above their former condition. The *callico gown* and its suitable appendages may now take place of the *serge* or the *camblet* for the Sunday dress; Oeconomy of Charity, 1801 ~~~ The callico-printer is employed in printing this cloth. The first hint towards this branch of business was had from the Indian chintzes. The callico-printing was introduced into London in the year 1676, and it has since been encouraged by divers acts of parliament. In the East Indies, they paint all their callicoes with the pencil, which they must do with great expedition, as the price there is very low; but here the following method is adopted: The pattern is first drawn on paper, the whole breadth of the cloth intended to be printed; the workman then divides the pattern into several parts according to its size, each part being about eight inches broad, by twelve inches long; each distinct part of the pattern thus divided, is cut out upon wooden blocks; the cloth to be printed is extended upon a table; and the types, being covered with the proper colours, are laid on after the manner represented in the plate, and the impression is left upon the cloth. The workman begins to lay on the types at one end of the piece, and so continues till the whole is finished: great care must be taken that the patterns join with accuracy, and that there is no interstice or vacancy left. Cutting the pattern in wood being the most curious part of the process, we shall describe that particularly. The cutters in wood begin with preparing a plank or block of the proper size: beech, pear-tree, and box, are used for this purpose; but the boxtree is the most fit for the business, as being the closest, and least liable to be worm-eaten. As soon as the wood is cut into the proper size and made very smooth, it is fit to receive the drawing of the design. Sometimes ink is used, and to prevent its running, it is rubbed over with a mixture of white lead and water, and after it is dry it is rubbed off and polished. On this the design is drawn; and those who cannot draw themselves, make use of designs furnished by others whose profession is to draw patterns. The drawing marks out so much of the block as is to be spared, or left standing. The rest they cut off, and take away very curiously with the point of exceedingly sharp knives, or little chisels, or gravers, according to the bigness or delicacy of the work; for they stand in need of no other instruments. … The manner of printing with wooden prints is easy and expeditious, if there be only two colours; as green and blue; or black, and a white ground, then the block requires only to be clipped in the printing-ink, and impressed on the cloth. If more colours are used, than they are to be laid on with a brush or brushes, and the impressions to be made as before with the hand. When the whole piece is printed, the cloth is washed and bleached to take away any accidental stains it may have acquired in the operation: it is then dried, calendered, and laid up in folds fit for the shop. Book of Trades, 1806 ~~~ *Territory of Michigan, district of Detroit.* Personally appeared before me, the subscriber, Aaron Thomas and Agnes Thomas, his wife, who both made oath on the Holy Evangelist of Almighty God, that the Indians have taken from them, from the house of Mr. Atwater, on the 16th of August, 1812, one chintz gown, valued seven and a half dollars, one calico gown, valued three dollars seventy five cents, Authentic History of the Second War for Independence, 1815 ~~~ Printed calico gowns are universally worn in undress, with flounced of the same material, *La Belle Assemblée,* July 1818 ~~~ A Letter from a Young Married Lady to her Sister in the Country. *Brighton.* … But I know you are eager to learn how we were attired on the wedding-day: we were dreadfully troubled to make the bride-elect attend to reason; it was so horrid vulgar to be dressed in white at a wedding; for her part, she would like to be married in a printed calico, and her hair in papers: *La Belle Assemblée,* August 1818 ~~~ *Calico Printing.* The method of transferring engraved designs from steel plates to copper, as proposed by Messrs. Perkins, Fairman, and Heath, (see our first volume) is now practising with very great success in aid of Calico Printing. By this process very beautiful designs of any character, particularly intricate scroll work, are transferred to the surfaces of copper cylinders, and a description of coloured goods, such as the finest sorts of calico and muslin, are now by these means preparing for the Spring fashions, which, from their extreme delicacy, are expected to take among the upper circles. London Journal of Arts and Sciences, 1823 ~~~ Calicoes, for instance, which in London may be purchased at eightpence per yard, *European Magazine,* September 1823 ~~~ In your opinion what is the proper distinction between calicoes and muslins? – It would be very difficult to distinguish; but the opinion I have formed is, that calicoes commence with a very coarse article of 22 to 24 inches wide, those are made of yarns about thirties and forties, the finer reeds are increased in breadth from 25 to 27 inches: the breadth seems to be the principal criterion to judge by. Sessional Papers, 1823 ~~~ Stuff forwarded every year to make a suit of clothes for each teacher would cost but little in England, but here [Madagascar] it would cost a good deal of money. … Fine English calico at 1*s.* per yard for trowsers; and common calico at 6*d.* per yard for shirts, *Evangelical Magazine,* March 1825 ~~~ [ad] MR.

JOHN P. DEANE respectfully informs his Friends, it being his intentention [sic] to proceed to Sydney, the following GOODS will be disposed of at the under-mentioned Prices, being at least 30 per cent, under the retail Prices: – Calico, for linings, 6d. per yard; calico for sheeting, 1½ yards 1s. 3d. ditto; calico shirting, 1s. 6d. ditto; *Colonial Times*, March 3, 1826 ~~~ [ad] Calico, from Manchester, 5d. to 7d. per yard. *Political Guardian*, April 22, 1831 ~~~ The pattern to be impressed on the calico was formerly cut out in relief on a wooden block of the requisite size, exactly like a wooden cut for figures or diagrams. The wood used was generally holly, and the cutting of the pattern formed a separate trade called block-cutting. The perishable nature of wood, however, involved the printer often in much expense, and hence a great improvement has taken place by using slender pieces of brass or copper, which are fixed on the wood so as to produce the pattern, and which give greater sharpness and precision to the impressions. ... Another kind of calico printing, called *resist work,* is now in common use. A resist paste is composed of sulphate, nitrate, muriate, or acetate of copper, of which the sulphate is the best, mixed with flour paste, or any of the other gums, or with pipe clay and gum. With this paste the pattern is printed on the calico, which when sufficiently dry is repeatedly dipped in the blue vat, till they have received the requisite depth of tint. The goods are then washed and passed through diluted sulphuric acid, and all the parts printed by the preparation of copper are found to be of a good white, in consequence of having resisted the action of the indigo, though all the rest of the calico has been permanently dyed. The deep blue calicoes, with white figures or white spots, are generally executed by the resist process with indigo; and by a peculiar method, with subsequent dying or madder, weld or bark, red or yellow spots or figures may be produced upon a blue ground. ... The introduction of cylinder printing into the calico manufacture, is a most important step in its progress. Cylinders from 18 to 42 inches long, and from 3 ½ to 5 inches wide, are now formed by hammering plates of copper into a circular form, though sometimes they are bored out of a solid mass of copper. The pattern is enchased on the surface. The cylinders furnish themselves with colouring matter, placed in a trough, and are kept clear by a steel knife, called the *doctor,* which passes over the surface, when they are charged with the thickened colour. The cylinder, thus coloured, rolls over the piece of calico, from one end to the other, and communicates the pattern with the greatest certainty and accuracy. Sometimes two cylinders are used to give two different colours at the same time. Mr. A. Parkinson of Manchester, has invented a machine, on which one cylinder and two surface rollers give three distinct colours. Other machines have been employed, called *surface machines.* They consist of cylinders of wood, with the pattern formed upon them, exactly like the pattern blocks already described. By means of those cylinder machines, a piece of calico, which employs a man and a boy *three hours,* may be done in *three* or *three and a half minutes.* Hence the British calico printer has been able to finish calico goods, in which the printing consists of precipitating the colouring matter of logwood and other vegetable dyes, without using any mordaunt or previous preparation whatever, at the rate of *one penny per yard,* including every expense of colour, paste, and printing. In such goods, the pattern will be washed out by the first shower of rain. Edinburgh Encyclopædia, 1832 [see also *chintz* and *pullicat*]

calimanco, callimanco – [see *calamanco*]

callico – [see *calico*]

camblet – [see *camlet*]

cambleteen – [see *camletine*]

cambray – Cambray, of silk only 20 [percent tariff] Tariff, 1832 ~~~ [court dress] Tulle de Cambray, elegantly trimmed with roses, over white satin petticoat; *Lady's Magazine and Museum*, May 1836 [see also *blond de Cambray, Cambray, cambric,* and *chambray gauze*]

cambric – Cambrick is a species of linen, made of flax, very fine and white; the name of which was originally derived from the city of Cambray *, where cambricks were first manufactured. The cambricks allowed to be worn in this country are fabricated in Scotland and Ireland. Cambrick is much used for ruffles and handkerchiefs. ... *Cambray is one of the most opulent and commercial cities in the Netherlands. Arithmetical Questions, 1795 ~~~ Any persons convicted of wearing, selling, (except for exportation,) or making up for hire any French cambrics or lawns, are liable to a penalty of 5*l*. Encyclopædia Britannica, 1797 ~~~ I was charged by a friend to buy some lace and cambric [in

Paris]; but, independent of the illegality of such merchandise, it is so dear, that I believe it might be bought almost as cheap in London. A friend of mine at Paris shewed me the cambric of his cravat, which he declared cost him eighteen livres (fifteen shillings) a yard. *Scots Magazine*, January 1801 ~~~ Morning Dresses. ... The dress is a fawn-coloured cambric muslin, inlaid with white worked muslin in front. ... The gown a blue cambric muslin, with black checks. *Ladies' Monthly Museum*, June 1802 ~~~ [reported in October 1803, Madame Napoleone] All her *chemises* are of the finest cambric, with borders of lace that cost ten Louis-d'ors each. Six dozen of chemises with lace, are made up for her every month. *AntiJacobin Review*, March 1804 ~~~ A kind of fine linen, used for ruffles, women's sleeves, and caps. Book of Trades, 1806 ~~~ Walking dress pantaloons of corded cambric, trimmed round the bottom with lace or fine muslin. ... Equal striped cambric muslins are coming into fashion for morning dresses, *La Belle Assemblée*, May 1806 ~~~ [ad] Superfine Yard-and-half-wide Corded Cambric, at 2s. the general price 3s. 6d. ... 100 Pieces of full Two Yards-wide Cambric Muslin, at 2s.; *La Belle Assemblée*, March 1807 ~~~ Cotton goods are divided into 7 different classes, each proportionally lighter the than other. The heaviest of these are, 1st. *Shirtings*, 2d. *Cambrics*, New Encyclopædia, 1807 ~~~ Morning Dress. A round robe of fine Cambric jaconot muslin, fastened down the front with cotton ball tassels; *Repository of Arts*, February 1815 ~~~ French fashions are now very prevalent in town. The Morning Dress is of striped, or plain muslin, or cambric, tastefully finished by a body of embroidered cambric, formed of detached pieces, and making a beautiful temporary *corsage*, of the ingenuity and elegance of which, no idea can be given from a description alone. *Ladies' Monthly Museum*, July 1816 ~~~ Can you state what the price of the Irish cambric is, that which is thrown out of consumption by the smuggling in of the French cambric? – I cannot accurately state that; I am aware, that the consumption or demand for fine lawns has very much decreased within the last two years. Which decrease you attribute to the smuggling in of French cambrics? – Undoubtedly, to the quantity of French cambrics that are now sold in our markets, and also to their being got in without paying the duty. ... What price did the finest cambric, made before two years ago, in the north of Ireland, bear? – Perhaps ten or twelve shillings. Sessional Papers, 1824 ~~~ The fine season has lasted with the French the same as it has with us, and white dresses still prevail: they are generally of cambric, and are trimmed at the border with three very broad bias folds; *Lady's Magazine*, September 1825 ~~~ [Paris] Some dresses for *demi-parure* have very light-coloured grounds, which are figured over in patterns of very lively colours. They are of fine cambric-muslin, very highly glazed, and have much the appearance of chintzes. *Ladies' Museum*, September 1829 ~~~ Cottons, ... Cambric, 12 yds. by 40 to 45 in. *Asiatic Journal*, February 1830 ~~~ [ad] Ladies' Outfits. ... For the Overland Journey to India. ... 12 Cambric Drawers [at] 4/ ... 2£ 8s. ... 12 Cambric Drawers [at] 1/9 ~~~ 12s. *Overland to India*, c1830 ~~~ The robe is cambric of the clearest kind, the *corsage* partially high; amadis sleeves. The skirt is embroidered *en tablier*; on each side of the front is a wreath of feather stitch. Cambric *canezou*, rounded and deep behind, falling very low over the shoulders, and cleft in the centre. *Court Magazine*, October 1833 ~~~ The most novel morning dresses are *peignoirs* of French cambric trimmed with Valenciennes lace; *Court Magazine*, July 1835 ~~~ *Cambric muslins*, being closer woven than jaconots, are of stronger fabric, and frequently printed. They are also used for cravats. Scenes of Commerce, 1836 [see also *batiste*, *lawn*, *French cambric* and *Scotch cambric*]

cameleon – [on an improved loom, patented December 18, 1824 by Pierre Gosset] I must not omit to mention an article of great value, which can also be manufactured with my shuttle in the most beautiful manner, which article I call *Camelion*, from it continual change of colour as it is moved about, and which is superior in brilliancy to any other article hitherto made of silk, possessing great richness and softness, and from its novelty and beauty likely to become very much in demand. *Repertory of Patent Inventions*, October 1825 ~~~ Gowns in full dress ... A new material, called *Cameleon des Irlandaises à colonnes perses* is coming much into favour; it is light and rich. *Repository of Fashions*, February 1829 ~~~ *Gros de Naples caméleon*, a new and very pretty changeable silk, is much worn in half dress. *La Belle Assemblée*, April 1831 ~~~ A series of new materials for cloaks have appeared; the following are a few of those which we think particularly well adapted for cloaks: – *Cameleon*. – Figured large *bouquets* on the outside in elegant designs, and with stripes inside. This material requires no lining, and the cloak is made so as to be worn on both sides. ... *Out-Door Costume, New Materials for Mantle Dresses.* – The first is the *Cameleon,* which well deserves its name: one side flowered in large bouquets, and striking colours; the other is striped. These mantles are not lined, and are so made that either side can be worn. *Maids, Wives, and Widows,* November 10, 1832

Camelia – A quantity of what is denominated Camelia wool, was imported into England by the East India company, seven years ago, but it only sold for 3s. 6d. per lb. and from having both scurf and hair in it, was not suited for the manufacture of hats. It was perhaps shorn at an unseasonable moment, for had it been divested of these two objections, it would have been worth 10s. to the hat trade, or of an equal value with Vigonia. *Agricultural Magazine,* October 1811 ~~~ A favourite article for morning dresses is the newly-invented manufacture entitled Camelias; *La Belle Assemblée,* November 1823 ~~~ A new material, called *Camelia,* is in favour in morning dress, but it is not so generally adopted as poplin, *reps* silk, or *gros de Naples. Repository of Arts,* January 1824

camica – Camica, stuff made of camel's hair <u>Perry's English Dictionary</u>, 1795 ~~~ in old records, camelot. <u>New Encyclopædia</u>, 1807 [see *camlet*]

camlet – Camblet is a stuff sometimes made of wool, sometimes of silk, and sometimes of hair, especially that of goats, with wool or silk. The true or oriental camblet is fabricated from the pure hair of a sort of goat, described by travellers as an extraordinary species, the most beautiful in the world; their hair being of a silvery whiteness, as fine as silk, and naturally curled in locks eight or nine inches in length. ... We have no camblets made in Europe of the goats hair alone; it being found necessary to add a mixture of woollen thread. England, France, Holland, and Flanders, are the chief places of this manufacture. But Brussels exceeds them all in the beauty and quantity of its camblets; and those of England are reputed the second. Some give the name of mohair to the camblets or stuffs made of the hair now under consideration. <u>Arithmetical Questions</u>, 1795 ~~~ Camelot, or Chamblet, ... The manufacturer, &c. of camblets are to take care they do not acquire any false and needless plaits; it being almost impossible to get them out again. This is notorious, even to a proverb: we say, a person is like camblet, he has taken his plait. <u>Encyclopædia Britannica</u>, 1797 ~~~ The greater part of the combing wool is consumed in worsted for making what is called new drapery in the Book of Rates, viz. ... camblet, 10d. to 1s. 8d. [per yard] <u>Origin of Commerce</u>, 1801 ~~~ This word is spelled *camblet* in the tariffs of the custom-house, and the correspondence of the East-India Company. ... The first camlets were made of mohair, which is the hair of a goat, but which, as it comes from the Levant, might well pass for camel's hair. *Monthly Magazine,* August 1805 ~~~ I shall now proceed to the display of some minutiæ regarding the out-fit of a gentleman about to embark in a chartered ship; ... It will be proper to have two or three coats to wear on board-ship: two should be of broad cloth, and one of camlet, or some other light stuff: *East India Vade-Mecum,* 1810 ~~~ Camblets are manufactured in Holland and Flanders, and in Ireland and England. Dublin exceeds them all in the beauty and quality of its camblets; those of England are next in repute. ... *Figured Camblets* are those of one colour, whereon are stamped various figures, flowers, foliage, &c. by means of hot irons, which are a kind of moulds passed together with the stuff under the press ; these were chiefly brought from Amiens and Flanders. The commerce of these was formerly much more considerable than at present. *Water camblets,* after weaving, receive a certain preparation with water, and afterwards pass under a hot press, which gives them a smoothness and lustre. *Waved camblets* are those whereon waves are impressed, as on tabbies, by means of a cylinder, under which they are passed several times. <u>Guy's Pocket Cyclopædia</u>, 1810 ~~~ [ad] Ready Made Clothing, Viz. ... Camlet Great COATS. CLOAKS, Plaid and Camlet. <u>Boston Annual Advertiser</u>, 1823 ~~~ These directions apply to such Gowns as are frequently wanted for the purpose of being presented to Charitable Institutions, and which are usually made of brown serge, or camlet. If serge, 30 inches wide, then 2 ½ breadths must be allowed for the skirt. If camblet, from 18 to 20 inches wide, the skirt will require 4 breadths. The length of the skirts will be 40, 42 ½, and 45 inches. The quantity of serge will be 4 ½ yards; or of camblet 6 ¾ yards – the body-lining will take a yard of 4-qr, brown irish. <u>Sectum</u>, 1825 ~~~ Watered camblets are often called moreens, moraine being the French term for that kind of wool which the tanner or currier removes from the hide by the application of quick lime. <u>History of Inventions and Discoveries</u>, 1827 ~~~ A General

Collection of Words of variable spelling, in which those of the best usage are printed in Roman character, ... camlet, *chamblot, chamelot,* camlot, *camelot, chamlet, camelet, camblet,* Practical Orthography, 1828 ~~~ *Mr. Ward.* Is a tailor: made about fifty cloaks last winter: two thirds imitation camblet, one third silk or German camblet, Trial of John Francis Knapp, 1830 ~~~ Worsted Stuff Goods, from Manchester to New York ... Camblets ... actual [width] inches 27 *a* [to] 32 ~~~ Price per yard s.d. [shillings.pence] 1.4 *a* 2.6 Trade between Great Britain and the United States of America, 1833 ~~~ The *Angora* Goats ... are famous for the milk-white colour and silky softness of their wool. From this, usually intermixed or interwoven with silk, or with sheep's wool, is fabricated the cloth called Camlet, or Camblet, of which there are many spurious imitations. Analytical Dictionary, 1835 ~~~ 1 do [piece] indigo blue camlet 49 do [yards] 45 [cents per yard, from a letter dated October 26, 1832] Emigration of Indians, 1835 [see also *angora, mohair* and *moreen*]

camletine – a slight stuff, made of hair and coarse silk, in the manner of camblet. It is now out of fashion. Encyclopædia Britannica, 1797 ~~~ Extract General Letter to Canton, dated 19th February 1802. Para. 59. By the ships David Scott and Cussnels, we have consigned you six hundred pieces of Cambleteens, being an article which we understand has occasionally been carried out in American ships, ... for our proceedings relative to the sale of the Cambleteens; with much persuasion, and after considerable difficulty, we prevailed on the Merchants to allow the Invoice Cost, or 8 Dollars per piece; ... We have not, after the most strict enquiries, been able to ascertain that goods of this description were ever imported by the Americans, nor were they at all known to the Chinese, Report from the Select Committee, 1812 ~~~ [visited in the Autumn of 1808] Trim School, for Girls. ... They are all well clad in blue *Camleteen,* which is bought in Dublin and made up at home; ... [14th November, 1808] Arklow Charter School, for Girls. ... They were all very well dressed in a dark green coloured *camleteen,* Board of Education in Ireland, 1813

Canadian drake – At the beginning of May, when the weather still continued damp and chill, we saw a beautiful pelisse of cinnamon-brown *gros de Naples,* trimmed on each side of the front (where it was fastened down the skirt) with the neck of the Canadian drake. Nothing can equal the brilliant green of this glossy plumage, the soft texture of which is superior in delicacy to the finest Chinchilla fur. *Lady's Magazine,* May 1829

cancanias – [see *concan*]

cane – Cane hats; see hats. Canes; viz. reed canes, the thousand – 11s. [duty] ... Canes; viz. rattans, the thousand – 16s. 6d. [duty] ... Chip, cane, or horse-hair hats or bonnets, each hat or bonnet not exceeding 22 inches in diameter, the dozen – 3s. 6d. [duty] Ship Owner's Manual, 1795 ~~~ Hats are also made for women's wear, not only of the above stuff, but of chips, straw, or cane, by plaiting, and sewing the plaits together; beginning with the centre of the crown, and working round till the whole is finished. New Encyclopædia, 1807 ~~~ [Paris] A few cane hats have also appeared worked in diamonds. *La Belle Assemblée,* July 1816 ~~~ Promenade and Carriage Costumes. ... Shade bonnet of fine black cane, embroidered with chenille and velvet flowers round the front; the crown, of black satin, very full, and high in the back, is made of cane and chenille like the front; *Ladies' Monthly Museum,* January 1818 ~~~ A new carriage hat of white cane is in great repute; it is lined with light blue sarsenet, and has long folded sarsenet lappets instead of strings falling loose, and each terminated by a small bow of the same; *Ladies' Monthly Museum,* November 1822 ~~~ [Paris] We give to the English the most graceful fashions, and they in return introduce to us those that are both useful and agreeable; such, for example, is the invention of the *calèshe,* which all our ladies are prepared to adopt this winter for the prevention of coughs and colds. These *calèshes* are a species of large hoods made of taffeta, stiffened by canes of sufficient strength to sustain a shawl. This contrivance has been for many years used in London, where the ladies even make it add to their attractions: their blooming complexions, and their lovely light curls, never appear more seducing than from under one of these hoods lined with rose colour or blue. *Lady's Magazine,* January 1830 ~~~ Asylum for Poor Lunatics in Maine. ... We have seen the very best results from labor. Patients who without it were noisy and troublesome, have become quiet with it. One patient, who was brought to the institution in irons, and who, until employed, was constantly raving and excited, when furnished with occupation, became quiet; he braids and sews four or five cane hats a week, besides spending his evenings at games, and, except when interrupted by the entrance of strangers, is peaceable and quiet. *Prison Discipline Society,* May 1836 [see also *bamboo* and *straw*]

Canterbury – The silk trade here, from the general use of cottons, has been declining for some years past. To supply this loss in part, Mr. John Callaway, an industrious and ingenious silk-manufacturer, introduced in 1789, looms in the cotton branch, and erected mills for the purpose of carding and spinning the wool into yarn; which by a mixture of silk in the fabric, he converted into the light and elegant piece-goods, known by the names of Canterbury muslins, Canterbury damasks, &c. These articles were so well received by the public, as to induce many manufacturers in other parts of the kingdom to imitate them, and, as is too often the case, to the injury of the original inventor. <u>A Walk in and about the City of Canterbury</u>, 1796

canton cord – [ad] Grace, Prime &Co., offer for sale, … 3 cases Cantoon Cords. *American Railroad Journal,* May 18, 1833 ~~~ *On Cotton Goods.* … Cantoon crape and Cantoon Cord. These are exceedingly good imitations of the foreign article, and very durable and desirable goods. *Journal of the Franklin Institute,* December 1833 ~~~ [ad] Have received by the ships Hark-away and Jefferson, direct from Liverpool, … 1 case 3-4 drab cantoons and Pittsburg cords.. *Farmer's Register,* May 1835 ~~~ Old Humphrey on Consistency. … What affinity, what possible connexion could there be between "Watt's Psalms and Hymns," and "Imperial Saxony Cloth, Canton Drill Trowsers, and Petersham Great Coats?" *Weekly Visitor,* June 9, 1835 ~~~ Cantoon is a fustian with a fine cord visible upon the one side, and a satiny surface of the yarns running at right angles to the cords upon the other side. The satiny side is sometimes smoothed by singing. The stuff is strong, and has a very fine aspect. Its price is one shilling and sixpence a-yard. <u>Cotton Manufacture of Great Britain</u>, 1836 ~~~ [ad for men's] Cantoon and Drill Trousers, 10*s.* 6*d.* per pair, *Eminent Foreign Statesmen,* March 1836 [see also *drill* and *fustian*]

canton crape – *Letters from Boston.* … "brother L." and "sister S." in a very learned and ingenious discussion of the question, *whether a gown of pink canton crape became her complexion more than one of buff lustre.* At length I was appealed to for my judgement; and as the lady contended for the crape, and my politeness would not suffer me to give judgement against the lady, the crape won the cause. *Polyanthos,* April 1812 ~~~ There are large quantities of clothing imported from England, and many individuals have their regular London taylors. Black and coloured Canton crape, black stuff, white jean, white drill, and Nankin are worn for trowsers; … [prices of] Canton crapes for ladies' dresses very moderate – in England they are prohibited: perhaps there are few articles to equal these for gentility combined with economy and elegance. <u>Sketches of America</u>, 1818 ~~~ [ad] Ladies having real India Shawls, or Canton Crape Shawls, or dresses to dispose of, or exchange, will be treated liberally. *Evangelical Magazine,* April 1821 ~~~ [ad] Canton Crape Shawls and Scarfs – from 2 guineas to 3 guineas each; *Evangelical Magazine,* April 1822 ~~~ [ad] Canton, or China Crape Shawls and Dresses; *Examiner,* July 16, 1826 ~~~ Canton Crapes. These fabrics are an imitation of a species of silk shawls imported from Canton, … These shawls are sometimes woven plain, and sometimes flowered in the draw loom. The plain ones are, for the most part, ornamented with needle work. The grounds are plain texture; but the flowered parts of those woven in the draw loom are tweeled with an eight-leafed satin tweel, the same as the finer kind of damask. <u>Art of Weaving</u>, 1831 ~~~ [ad] Silks at Reduced Prices. … Black Canton Crape at 1s. per yard. *New England Farmer,* March 25, 1835 ~~~ [ad for men's trousers] Broad linen cords, diagonal craped cantoons, gambrooms, &c., of various colours, of which there is an infinite variety, will also be much worn. *Geo. D. Doudney's Monthly Fashion Sheet,* April 1835 [see also *China crape* and *crape*]

canton flannel – [in 1810] substitutes for woollens made of cotton, will be found peculiarly convenient, saleable and profitable.* … * Blankets, counterpanes, coverlets, Canton flannels, cotton velvets, corduroys, and other warm, stout and heavy goods. <u>Arts and Manufactures</u>, 1814 ~~~ 48. For the best sample of green and red canton flannel, not less than twenty-six inches wide, and two hundred yards to be exhibited, *A Silver Medal.* 49. For the best sample of white Canton flannel, twenty-six inches wide, *Journal of the Franklin Institute,* May 1831 ~~~ That premium No. 94 be awarded to the York Manufacturing Company, for Nos. 53 and 54, canton flannels; a superior fabric of uncommon regularity of nap, and presenting a beautifully smooth surface. To Mr. William Almond much credit is also due for his specimen of Canton flannels, a substantial article, well calculated for general use. The consumption of this article is very extensive. *Journal of the Franklin Institute*, January 1834 ~~~ [ad] Have received by the ships Hark-away and Jefferson, direct from Liverpool, … 3 cases bleached jeans, and brown and bleached Canton flannels. *Farmer's Register*, May 1835 ~~~ [ad] Proposals will be received at the Office of the Commissary General of Purchases, in Philadelphia, for making Army Clothing for the year 1836, as hereafter enumerated, viz – … Drawers of Canton Flannel, &c. *Army and Navy Chronicle*, January 14, 1836 [see *flannel*]

Canton silk – It appears that the Canton silks are cheaper than the French, but there is not so much service in them. The Americans prefer cheapness to durability, *Asiatic Journal*, December 1821 ~~~ The most elegant of the new materials for dinner and evening dress are the *carreaux écossais, gros de Canton* and *Pekins Chines*. These are silks of the richest kind: *Court Magazine*, May 1834 [see also *China silk*]

cantoon – [see *canton*]

canvas – Cavalry. – … 1 pair of canvas, or woolen over-hose. 1 canvas, or woolen frock or jacket. Treatise of Military Finance, 1796 ~~~ in commerce, a very clear unbleached cloth of hemp, or flax, wove regularly in little squares. It is used in working tapestry with the needle, by passing the threads of gold, silver, silk, or wool, through the intervals or squares. Canvas is also a coarse cloth of hemp, unbleached, somewhat clear, which serves to cover womens stays; to stiffen mens clothes, and to make some other of their wearing apparel, &c. Encyclopædia Britannica, 1797 ~~~ Canvas for family, 7 yards to each per ann. with other purposes included, 100 yards, at 9*d.* per yard Communications to the Board of Agriculture, 1806 ~~~ [September] A gang of 14 or 15 pickpockets, the eldest of whom assumed the title of "captain," being under the age of 15 years, was brought for examination before the sitting alderman at Guildhall. … Ned Stedwick, captain, about 15 years of age, dressed in a thickset jacket, and coarse canvas trowsers. Annual Register, 1807 ~~~ Canvass is used for sail cloth, except that of fine numbers, which is applied to the same purpose as Dowlas. The warp is made double, and the weft single, and is made either of hemp, flax, or tow. The various kinds are distinguished by numbers, from number 1 to number 9, &c. … The manufacture of Canvass or (Duck,) Dowlas, Osnaburgh, Hushing, and Sheeting, are chiefly confined to Aberdeen, Brechin, Montrose, Arbroath, Forfar, Kirriemuir, Dundee, and Kirkaldy, and small villages adjacent. Linen Manufacturer, 1817 ~~~ [in New South Wales] The summer clothing to the convicts in the barracks, consists of a canvas smock frock, one linen or cotton shirt, two pair of trowsers, (one of which ought to be reserved for use on Sundays) one pair of shoes, and one cap. Until the end of the year 1820, these supplies were furnished from the old canvas and sheeting that were found in the commissariat stores, and that had remained there for several years. Sessional Papers, 1822 ~~~ [Paris] quantities of tapestry-work, as slippers, ceintures, portefeuilles (pocket books), visiting card cases, comb-trays, baskets, pincushions, &c. worked on silk canvas, to save the trouble of filling in the ground: the patterns, bouquets, guirlandes, birds, landscapes, or Greek patterns. … The robe de chambre … Slippers embroidered on black silk canvas, which is more becoming to the foot than any other, *Lady's Magazine and Museum*, April 1835 [see also *buckram* and *duck*]

caoutchouc – [see *Indian rubber*]

carding wool – [see *long wool* and *wool*]

Carlina – [Paris] The evening dress silks that have appeared, are all in the superb but heavy style of Louis XIV's reign. The satins *Salomon, Esmeralda,* and *Pharamond,* are expected to be in great request; as are also … the *Velontées de la Mosquée,* and *Carlina. New Monthly Belle Assemblée*, November 1836 ~~~ [Paris] *Velonti Carlina* and *Velonti de la Mosquée* are new and very beautiful silks for evening dress. *Ladies' Pocket*, November 1836 ~~~ [Paris] Some superb materials have appeared for evening dress; the most *distingué* are the … *veloutée Carlina, Court Magazine*, November 1836

carmantine – Hats from the promenade are of *paille d'Italie, paille de riz,* a new fancy material called *carmantine écossaise,* and *moire. The carmantine* is of dust colour, either light or dark, or silver white; it is an imitation of *moire,* and in some degree surpasses it by the variety and richness of the patterns. *La Belle*

Assemblée, June 1832

Caroline plaids – Walking dresses of Merino Caroline, with Calimanco stripes, are increasing in favour; *Ladies' Monthly Museum,* December 1826 ~~~ *Caroline plaids,* composed of *cotton* and *worsted, or combed wool, Public Documents,* October 1828 ~~~ *Caroline plaids* – 27 inches wide, cost 6d. to 9d. ... This is an article composed of cotton and worsted, and would pay the higher or woollen duty. – The consumption is very great among the farming, mechanic, and laboring interests; and it is not, at present, manufactured in any port of the United States. The quality principally consumed costs 7d. sterling. *Niles' Weekly Register,* March 8, 1828 ~~~ 2 pieces Carolina plaid 72 yards – 60 [cents; total $] 43.20 [letter dated October 26, 1832] <u>Emigration of Indians</u>, 1835 ~~~ Caroline Plaids, all stuff, [duty] free. Caroline Plaids, cotton and wool, . . . 50 per cent. —— cotton. *See Cotton.* 25 do. —— stripes, cotton. <u>Jones's Digest</u>, 1836

carreaux – English Ball. Dress. – Round dress of Urling's Patent Lace over white net and satin, *en carreaux,* between each diamond, a blue satin quatrefoil with a pearl in the centre: this bordering is surmounted by sprigs formed of blue satin, in bias; with a *corsage en carreaux,* to correspond with the border of the dress. *Kaleidoscope,* April 9, 1822 ~~~ The most elegant of the new materials for dinner and evening dress are the *carreaux écossais, gros de Canton* and *Pekins Chines.* These are silks of the richest kind: *Court Magazine,* May 1834 ~~~ Carreau, kà-ro, s. m. square, any thing that has four sides; goose or pressing-iron; cushion; (at cards) diamond; <u>Boyer's French Dictionary</u>, 1835

Casanova – Evening costume is still of a light kind; several new materials have, however, appeared for it. We may cite among them the *satins ...Casanova,* ... These rich and beautiful materials will be in great request as soon as the winter has fairly set in. *Ladies' Pocket,* November 1836

cashmere – SHAWLS, are woollen handkerchiefs, an ell wide, and near two long. The wool is so fine and silky, that the whole handkerchief may be contained in the two hands closed. It is the produce of a Tibet sheep; but some say that no wool is employed but that of lambs torn from the belly of their mother before the time of birth. The most beautiful shawls come from Cashmire: their price is from 150 livres (about six guineas) to 1200 livres (or 50l. sterling.) ... The shawls of Mr. Knights' manufacture [in Norwich], it is said, can scarcely be distinguished from Indian shawls, though they can be afforded at one twentieth part of the price . When the shawl is 16 quarters square, Mr. Knights says it may be retailed at 20l.; if it consisted of 12 quarters, and embroidered as the former, it will cost 15l. if plain, with a fringe only, a shawl of 16 quarters square may be sold at 8l. 8s.; if 12 quarters and fringed, at 6l. 6s. Mr. Knights maintains, that his counterpane of four yards square is equal in beauty, and superior in strength, to the Indian counterpanes which are sold at 200 guineas. The principal consumption of this cloth is in train-dresses for ladies; as likewise for long scarfs, in imitation of the real Indian scarfs, which are fold from 60l. to 80l. whereas scarfs of this fabric are sold for as many shillings, and the ladies square shawls in proportion. <u>Encyclopædia Britannica</u>, 1797 ~~~ [Evening Dress] a long occasional scarf of crimson Cashmire, richly bordered at the ends. *Repository of Arts,* December 1812 ~~~ Our promenade costume has at present an uniformity which fatigues the eye, not on account of white dresses only, but because *belles* of all ages now appear in square shawls; go where you will you see nothing else. Ladies of the highest rank wear those of Cashmere, but as their price is immense, those of French manufacture are of course much more general: they are worn in scarlet, royal purple, orange, lavender, and dark green; the middle plain, and the border very rich. French ladies laugh at our formal taste, but in this instance, I think, we have the laugh against them. *Repository of Arts,* November 1816 ~~~ the most costly and elegant gowns are of Cachemire, with a border of large palm leaves. *La Belle Assemblée,* November 1818 ~~~ Parisian Evening Dress. Cashmire dress with a broad shawl border, beautifully variegated in different colors. *Ladies' Monthly Museum,* January 1822 ~~~ The newest cachemires are in small diamond-checquers, with a few light flowers. *La Belle Assemblée,* June 1827 ~~~ Dresses of cachemire, (we do not mean the cloth so misnamed) but a light kind of material, something like the *barége*: these dresses in shawl patterns, from a charming costume for half dress: *Ladies' Monthly Museum,* June 1828 ~~~ The coat is a mixture of long coarse hair, and of short fine wool: this latter begins to be loose early in April; and is collected easily and expeditiously by combing the animals two or three times, with such a comb as is used for horses' manes. A good deal of the long hair comes off at the same time, but the manufacturer has found no difficulty in separating it. The produce of a male is about four ounces, and of a female about two ounces. Two pounds of wool as it comes off the goat's back may be estimated to make one shawl, fully four inches square. It will therefore require ten goats, male and female, to furnish materials for one shawl. <u>Encyclopædia of Agriculture</u>, 1831 ~~~ One of the most expensive dresses that has been seen this season, is an Indian cachemire; a red ground, thickly strewed with small bouquets. The cachemire has cost, at Constantinople, three thousand francs. *Atheneum*, April 1831 ~~~ Boots should be made of the same colour and as far as possible of the same material as the dress. We lately noticed a dress of flowered Indian cashmere worn with boots to correspond. *Court Journal*, May 11, 1833 ~~~ We assure them, from good authority, that plain Cashmere will be in very great request both for mantles and dresses. It is a material that may be worn with propriety in promenade-dress, while at the same time its intrinsic value renders it appropriate for carriage-costumes. *Ladies' Pocket*, November 1836 [see also *British cashmere, casimir, Lyons cashmere, shawl cloth* and *Thibet wool*]

cashmere de Lyon – [see *Lyons cashmere*]

cashmere gauze – A new kind of gauze called cachemire gauze is now much worn to trim the brims of both *chapeaux* and *capotes*, *Ladies' Monthly Museum*, May 1818 ~~~ [in December] Toques, turbans, and *berréts* were made of *barége* or of cachemere gauze; the pattern being a Scotch tartan, we can find no reason for its bearing the appellation, since, though gauze is fabricated in China, Japan, Cyprus, and in most of the states of Barbary, we never heard of its being manufactured in the valley of Cachemere. *La Belle Assemblée*, (year in review) 1825 ~~~ The city dress, as reported in the Ladies' Courier for October last, was much richer, and consisted chiefly in Cashmere gauzes, or rose, straw-colour, or white crapes, with cannerous or under dresses of satin; *New-York Mirror*, January 27, 1827 ~~~ Scarfs, of Cashmere gauze, are the sole out-door addition to a high dress, and they are merely throat-scarfs; though they are more ornamental than useful, yet they give a beautiful finish to a dress. ... Another ball-dress was of rose-colour gauze-cachemire, with large satin stripes, *Ladies' Monthly Museum*, January 1828 ~~~ Beautiful articles for summer dresses are now brought forward, consisting of Cachmire gauze, Chinese Crape, and white crape, *Lady's Magazine*, June 1829 ~~~ [Paris] Dresses of Cashmere gauze, of oriental green, embroidered in silk of the same colour, though in different shades, are trimmed with flounces cut in sharp points. *Ladies' Museum*, July 1829 ~~~ a variety of light and beautiful materials, as *tissu Cachemire, mousseline de laine,* &c. &c. are all in request. ... Shawls and scarfs of painted China crape are much in favour; but those of *tissu Cachemire* are more in request. They are singularly light and elegant. *La Belle Assemblée*, July 1830 ~~~ in evening dress, ... *Gaze cashmere*, and *gaze satinnée*, are most in favour for young ladies. *Ladies' Museum*, January 1832 ~~~ Boas begin to give place to scarfs, they are of China crapes with *tissu de Cachemire*, and *tissu Tyrolienne*; these last resemble grenadine gauze in richness, softness, and brilliancy, but they are thicker. *La Belle Assemblée*, May 1832 ~~~ A much prettier material [than Satin-Montespan] is called cachemire gauze; it is half transparent, a white ground striped in a narrow Turkish pattern: there are generally three colours, not too full, and well-contrasted in the stripes. *Maids, Wives, and Widows*, March 16, 1833 ~~~ Shawls are also in favour; some of those most generally adopted in carriage-dress are of *gaze Cachemire*, a material, as its name implies, of Cashmere wool, but almost transparent. The shawls are square, of a large size, and of Egyptian patterns, in beautiful, but rather full colours. *Ladies' Pocket*, June 1836

cashmere muslin – Printed muslins, called cachemire muslins, obtain the greatest favour at the present. The variety of colours in the design of the borders of shawls is perfectly imitated: the greater part of the designs represent small twisted columns. *Ladies' Monthly Museum*, September 1825 ~~~ The Cachemire muslins fully merit their name by the exquisite softness of their texture. *Lady's Magazine*, April 1830 ~~~ The materials we spoke of last month, with the addition of *mousseline Cachemire* and *tissu Cachemire*, are in favour in full dress. *La Belle Assemblée*, July 1830 ~~~ For dinner parties or *petites soirees* nothing is more elegant than a robe of *mousseline de soie*, cashmere muslin, or any other transparent material, *Court Journal*, May 11, 1833 ~~~ Half transparent materials as ... *mousseline cachemire*, ... are yet fashionable; they are made in the pelisse style, and are worn over richly embroidered muslin dresses. ... Shawls are adopted for the evening promenade. ... Others, more appropriate to the season, are of *mousseline Cachemire* of beautiful delicate patterns. *Court Magazine*, July 1835

cashmere satin – *Satin Cashmere.* – A tissue which has the brilliant appearance of the richest satin, superior by its elegance to *chaly. Maids, Wives, and Widows*, November 10, 1832 ~~~ Satins Ecossais, satins Quentin Durward, satins Marie Stuart, and plaids des Montagnards. All the above are imitations of the Scotch plaids, made in Cachemere wool and silk. Satin Damas; also Cachemere wool and silk: *Lady's Magazine and Museum*, November 1834 ~~~ Thus out-door dress offers little variety; pelisses of satin cachemire are the last novelty, they are of different colours, but emerald green predominates: *Court Magazine*, April 1835 ~~~[for evening dress] Besides those rich materials we may cite *satin cachemire*, light, soft, and yet rich; *Court Magazine*, November 1835 ~~~ [walking dress] A robe of cream-colour satin Cashmere spotted with red flowers; *Godey's Ladies Book*, March 1836 ~~~ A dress of lilac cashmere satin, *Godey's Ladies Book*, September 1836

cashmere wool – or with light shawls: the most novel among the latter are of *Cachemire de laine*, with very rich borders. *La Belle Assemblée*, October 1830 ~~~ Small shawls composed of *laine-cachemire*, a material which is nearly as light as muslin, are in great request for the morning promenades. *La Belle Assemblée*, September 1831 ~~~ Mantles … are of cachemere wool, light as silk, but much warmer. … Several new materials for winter dresses, composed of cachemere wool, have appeared at Delisle's and Gagelin's, but none have yet been made up; they are figured and printed in various patterns, and very vivid colours: it is supposed that they will be very fashionable in another month. *La Belle Assemblée*, November 1831 ~~~ Tartan shawls of *laine Cachemire* are already adopted by some *élégantes*, for the promenade. *Court Magazine*, November 1834

cashmirienne – Fancy black begins to be very much in favour both in full and half dress, but particularly in the latter. We have seen several *douillettes* in black satin, figured poplin, and *cachemirienne. Repository of Arts*, January 1829 ~~~ English *cashemirienne*, a material quite as good, if not better than the French one, is now much worn in morning dress. *Ladies' Museum*, March 1831 ~~~ One of the most elegant of the half dress novelties of the month, is a morning visiting dress, of *cashmirienne*, a material originally French, but now made here in equal perfection. The ground is chamois, printed in a running pattern of chocolate and *aventurine. Ladies' Museum*, February 1832 ~~~ Evening Dress. A white *gaze cashmirienne* dress, embroidered *à l'Esmeralda*, in a highly raised pattern, in floize silk; the colour are citron, green, blue, and pink. *Ladies' Museum*, April 1832 ~~~ Shawls are either of *cashmirienne* or *crepe de Lyon, Ladies' Museum*, June 1832 ~~~ The most elegant among the half dress materials are … Cashmerienne stripes. *Court Magazine*, April 1836 ~~~ *Robes de chambre* … are composed of fine merinoes or of plain or printed Cashemérienne. *Court Magazine*, December 1836

casimir – Cassimer or Casimer, the name of a thin tweeled woolen cloth, much in fashion for summer use. Encyclopædia Britannica, 1797 ~~~ Those pieces of Cashmire cloth which we call *Casimir*, are in length more than 60 ells, and are about five eights of an ell in width; their price in the manufactories is not more than four or five shillings. These cloths are greatly superior to those which are made in France, or in England, though not one quarter of the price of those made in the country last named. There is also a prodigious superiority in their duration, those of Cashmire being extremely lasting. This superiority they derive intirely [sic] from the softness and length of their staple, and the manner in which they are cleaned and prepared. Literary Panorama, 1807 [see *cashmere* and *cassimire*]

casinette – [see *cassinet*]

cassimire – Cassimer, or Cassimere, *s.* the name of a thin tweeled woollen cloth, much in fashion for summer use. Barclay's English Dictionary, 1799 ~~~ Amongst the ladies who, in spite of the shivering breeze chose rather to accommodate their attire to the *season* than its *temperature*, the most prevalent novelties which caught observation were the Spanish cloak, with embroidered Egyptian border, and fashioned of various materials and colours, as velvet, taffeta, lace, and cassimere; *La Belle Assemblée*, April 1806 ~~~ Cassimere, called at first *kerseymere*, was a mere handsome *improvement on the kersey* in England, about 40 or 45 years ago. *Weekly Register*, March 21, 1812 ~~~ [walking costume] It is simply a pilgrim's cloak, made of a very dark fine cloth or cassimere, *Edinburgh Annual Register*, January 31, 1813 ~~~ [ad] London CASSIMERES, of white buff, blue, black, light and dark drab, leather and olive drab, Oxford mixt, grey do. hareback do. – with a variety of embossed CASSIMERES a new and superior article for Pantaloons. <u>Boston Annual Advertiser</u>, 1823 ~~~ *Cassimeres* – 27 inches wide, cost 1s. 9d. to 5s. These prices include almost all imported. The quantity above 5s. is very limited, and is annually decreasing. This is an article of general consumption, *Niles' Weekly Register*, March 8, 1828 ~~~ Having thus furnished a Table applicable to most of the various kinds of "*cloth*" imported into this country, it is necessary to make a similar statement with regard to "*cassimer*," which is known to all consumers as a twilled woollen stuff most generally used for making pantaloons, and about 27 or 28 inches in width. Before the passage of the Tariff of 1828, large quantities of cassimer were imported, but the minimum system increased the cost so much as to cause the entire prohibition of most of those of the lower prices. Very few cassimers are now imported except such as are used by the wealthier classes. <u>An Exposition…of the Tariff System</u>, 1832 ~~~ Cassemere, or cassimere or kerseymere, *Public Documents*, March 1832 ~~~ Cassimere, woolen, [duty] 50 per cent. —— cotton, wool being a component part, 50 do. <u>Jones's Digest</u>, 1836 [see also *kerseymere*]

cassinet – [ad] Summer Goods, … Cassinetts, … of all colour and qualities. <u>Boston Annual Advertiser</u>, 1823 ~~~ A new article called Circassian, or Cassinette, is now manufacturing in the neighbourhood of Huddersfield, Yorkshire, in very considerable quantities, principally for exportation to the continent; the warp is of cotton, and the weft of wool, and all colours, quantities, and widths, may be had. It wears well, and in some colours looks very genteel. The chief recommendations of this fabric are its cheapness, durability, and incombustibility; not that it will not burn, but it takes fire with difficulty, and is on that account well adapted for children's wear. The Cassinette makes a pleasant dress, particularly in winter; and though it is little more than the same price as calico, it will wear three times as long, and save a fourth dress in washing. *Economist*, July 17, 1824 ~~~ [men's] A Walking or Riding Dress. … The waistcoat is of buff casinette; *Casket*, January 1831 ~~~ [men's] Still we have observed some new casinets for trousers: they are mostly fawn colour, with broad check formed with a small black stripe. *Day*, February 10, 1832 ~~~ [ad] super mix'd, drab, and olive Merino Cassinetts for children's summer dresses. *New England Farmer*, July 10, 1833 ~~~ *List of prices paid by the clothiers of Baltimore for work performed for them by the seamstresses.* … Casinet pantaloons. 25 cents. … Casinet roundabouts. 18 ½ cents *Niles' Weekly Register*, October 31, 1835 ~~~ Cassinet, I believe, is an article very little used? – There are a great many cassinets wove; I believe they are made up as low as from 20*d.* to 2*s.* … What is it? – A low article of pantaloons, exported at a low price. <u>Reports from Committees</u>, 1835 [see also *Circassian*]

Caston de Bristol – [Paris] Watered silk bonnets are, upon the whole, most fashionable, but those of fine split straw, of a fancy material called *payne*, and of *Caston de Bristol*, are also worn by many elegant women. *Ladies' Museum*, September 1831 [see also *imitation Leghorn*]

castor – [see *beaver*]

Castorine – [at Louviers] Mons. D. has now made some of the finest and most beautiful cloth that has ever yet been seen, of the pure undyed Peruvian, or Vigonia wool, if it may be so called, for it is not produced by a sheep; … *Castorine rayé en soie*, [striped with silk] <u>Voyages and Travels</u>, 1809 ~~~ [Paris] Next to the Scotch cloaks, which are only worn on returning from the theatres, or in brilliant equipage, cloaks of *Vigontine* (a sort of superfine Castorine) and those of cloth of the first quality, are adopted by ladies of high fashion. *Ladies' Monthly Museum*, December 1825 ~~~ Castorine lize (woollen cloth) <u>Jones's Digest</u>, 1835 ~~~ These varieties of wool serve for the manufacture of various stuffs and fabrics used for raiment and other purposes, under the name of broad cloths, kerseymeres, baizes, flannels, worsted stuffs, merinos, castorine, vigontines, cachemires, &c. <u>Philosophy of Manufactures</u>, 1835

catgut – a kind of open-worked stuff, composed of cotton, flaxen, or silken threads, and stiffened with starch or glue. It is generally used in the formation of females' caps and bonnets. <u>General Dictionary of Commerce</u>, 1810 ~~~ In this species of cloth, which is called catgut, … the threads are alternately raised and sunk in the twining and untwining. The stuff commonly employed in the texture of catgut is linen thread, and it is used for stiffening those parts of female dress where transparency is required, as buckram is used for the same purpose in men's clothes. <u>Edinburgh Encyclopædia</u>, 1830 ~~~ A sort of

Cotton, or Linen, Cloth, in which the threads of the Warp and the Weft are twisted and stiffened so as to produce a fabric something like wire-cloth, used for stretching out bonnets and other articles of female dress, is also called Catgut. Analytical Dictionary, 1835

catiste de laine – a pelisse of grey *Catiste de laine*; *Ladies' Pocket*, March 1830 [probably a typo for *batiste*, see *batiste de laine*]

cerecloth – Cloth smeared over with glutinous matter. Sheridan's English Dictionary, 1797 ~~~ Cerecloth, a cloth dipped in wax Webster's Dictionary, 1817 ~~~ Sear-cloth (*Surg.*) or *cere-cloth*, a particular kind of cloth like wax-cloth, which is applied to wounds. Universal Technological Dictionary, 1823

Ceres gauze – the Ceres gauze … forms a light and beautiful *toque* turban, or hat, for the evening party at this mild season of the year. *La Belle Assemblée*, April 1819 ~~~ I myself saw the beautiful ball-dress of Ceres gauze, made for a lady of rank, who visited Paris, *La Belle Assemblée*, May 1819

chagreen – [see *shagreen*]

chagrin – [see *shagreen*]

chain gauze – the more matronly adopt … the chain *reps* silk, or the gossamer satin. *La Belle Assemblée*, January 1819 ~~~ The chain gauze, of a fine silky and shining texture in rich stripes of chain-work very close together, is a light and beautiful article for ball dresses: its trimming should be fine blond, interspersed with *rouleaux* of satin, light wreaths of artificial flowers, or embossments of white *chenille* on satin of some light spring colour. *La Belle Assemblée*, February 1819 ~~~ Evening Dress. Frock of chain gauze, over white satin, *La Belle Assemblée*, March 1819 ~~~ A beautiful dinner dress has been finished by Mrs. Bell for a lady of fashion, of that beautiful article the chain *reps* silk: *La Belle Assemblée*, December 1820

chain gimp – For receiving friends at home, or for social dinner parties, … the Merino crape which is much worn also on these occasions, has little other trimming than a neat chain gimp, the same colour as the gown. *La Belle Assemblée*, October 1811 ~~~ the trimming most in requisition is a kind of chain gimp composed of dark chenille, intermixed with small white beads. *La Belle Assemblée*, February 1812 ~~~ The trimmings of gowns are chiefly composed of light gossamer fringe, or chain gymp of various colours intermingled, something in the style of the old French trimming; for very full dress they are of silver. *La Belle Assemblée*, June 1812 ~~~ Walking Dress. A jaconact muslin round dress: the skirt is gored, and sufficiently wide to hang in easy folds round the figure; it is ornamented at the bottom of the skirt with a rich flounce of work, headed by a chain trimming *en bouillonné,* composed of soft muslin; this is surmounted by another flounce headed in the same manner, and that by a third. *Ladies' Monthly Museum*, September 1820 ~~~ Some [dinner gowns] have the corsage quite tight to the shape, bat the front is ornamented with a gimp, or chain trimming of wrought silk, disposed in the *gerbe* or fan style. *Ladies' Pocket*, June 1830 [see also *gimp*]

chain pearl straw – [see *pearl straw*]

chain work net – the most elegant novelty for the carriage is the Russian imperial spencer of plain black satin, trimmed in a beautiful and novel manner with an entire new kind of chain-work net silk trimming. *La Belle Assemblée*, March 1820 [see *net* and *Nottingham lace*]

chainette – a trimming, silk and cotton, *Public Documents*, March 1832

chaly – The CHALONS. (*Net-Work.*) The *châli* of England, vulgarly called the châlon, is a species of crossed serge, which has for some time past been gaining favour in the Levant. This stuff is of a texture superior to the finest French serges, and has revenged the English for the discredit into which their woollen cloths had fallen, by giving a mortal blow to our woollen-cloth trade. The châlon of England contends even with advantage against the *châli* of Angora, whose texture is incomparably the finest, but which has neither its lustre or celebrity. What has extended the consumption of the châlons, is their good look. Our wools of Berry and of the Bourbonnais are, for their lightness, equally as proper as those of England for the texture of these stuffs, and we might contend advantageously with the English by the brilliancy of our colours and the excellence of the workmanship. The manufacture of châlons merits greater encouragement, as these stuffs might become one of the richest branches of our commerce in Turkey. View of the Commerce of Greece, 1800 ~~~ Various new materials, with a great diversity of names, signifying their importation from distant lands, though manufactured in the work-shops of Paris, have been introduced for gowns this spring: amongst these is … the *chaly de Constantinople*: … remarkable … for the softness of its texture. *Ladies' Museum*, May 1829 ~~~ [Paris] A *tissu* from camels' hair from the Morea, and named *Chaly*, is very much in favor for dresses among the *merveilleuses*; *Lady's Magazine*, December 1829 ~~~ *Chaly*, though not so much in favour as muslin, is still adopted by many elegant women. This material is now brought to such perfection that is lightness equals its beauty; that of light grey, the patterns of which are rose, or blue, is most in favour. *La Belle Assemblée*, September 1830 ~~~ *Chali* is in equal favour in half dress, and full dress. It is composed of wool, and is as light and fine as cachemire. Many are printed in India patterns; others are flowered: the prettiest of the latter are those in flowered wreaths. *La Belle Assemblée*, November 1830 ~~~ Ball dress of white *chalis*, over pink satin. This beautiful dress has the skirt trimmed with leaves of pink satin. *Royal Lady's*, March 1832 ~~~ [Paris] *Chalys* seem likely to be still worn during this season; but if you purchase any, pray take notice, that the patterns now in fashion are very large and excessively *bariolés*. Chaly dresses with shawl patterns at the bottom are in very good taste; but to tell you the truth, I prefer it in a beautiful plain coloured pink, *vert, perruche, maïs*, and so forth. This is really more elegant than the patterns; but every one, you know, is not of my taste. *Court Magazine*, April 1833 ~~~ I saw Mademoiselle de D – yesterday. She was better dressed than ever. You know her passion for *chalis*. We always see her with the newest patterns, but I never saw any thing so pretty as she wore yesterday. It was striped, blue, orange, and white, in *bouquets de cashemire*. As she is rather stout, the stripes suit her admirably. *Casket*, February 1833 ~~~ [court dress] A white embroidered chali dress; body and sleeves trimmed with blonde; *Court Journal*, May 11, 1833 ~~~ [ad] Grecian Shalys of superior fabric and figures 3s.9 [per yard] *New England Farmer*, March 25, 1835 ~~~ [men's] A very neat variety of striped and checked Challis Waistcoats are introducing, which, with a few new silks, will be the fashion for this month. *Geo. D. Doudney's Monthly Fashion Sheet*, April 1835 [see also *serge*]

chaly-cashmere – Chaly, though far from being out of favour, is less generally worn that it was last year. A new article, called chaly-cashmere, which approximates more nearly to muslin, is preferred, on account of its thinness and lightness. *Court Journal*, June 15, 1833

chambery – [see *chambray*]

chamblee – Chamblee (China, silk) <u>Commercial Directory</u>, 1823 ~~~ [letter:] Treasury Department, *February* 8, 1819. ~~~ Chamblee … 30 yards long and 45-100 wide. <u>American State Papers</u>, 1835 [see also *chambley*]

chamblet – [see *camlet*]

chambley – To Chambley, to be variegated; to appear like cloth or silk watered by the calenderer. <u>Barclay's English Dictionary</u>, 1799 [see also *camlet*]

chambray muslin – [court dress] The prevailing colours were lilac, yellow, green, and some slate colours: Chamberry muslins were much worn; *Lady's Magazine*, June 1800 ~~~ Round dress of blue chambray muslin. *Boston Weekly*, October 22, 1803 ~~~ [ad] Yard-wide Chambrays, at 1s. per yard; … Ell-wide Grey and Brown Chambrays, at 1s. 6d. *La Belle Assemblée*, March 1807 ~~~ [April 20, 1820] The cotton goods manufactured in this country are to the greatest extent are plaids, stripes, chambrays, and cotton shirting of the coarser qualities, which now cost in England less than 25 cents the square yard, … 100 yards of plaid stripe, or chambray, 24 inches wide, at 6d, cost £2 10s. sterling. <u>American State Papers</u>, 1834 ~~~ Chambray, silk and cotton [or] silk and wool, *Public Documents*, March 1832

chambray gauze – Silver chambery is extremely fashionable and elegant, both for turbans and dresses. *La Belle Assemblée*, April 1806 ~~~ Next in favour to crape for ball-dresses is *gaze de Chambery*. … Ball Dress. The colour of the dress is Turquoise blue, or *vert de lumière* – the material *gaze de Chambery* over satin of the same colour: *Lady's Magazine*, February 1830 ~~~ Rich silks and silver gauzes are still in favor in grand costume. At a late *soirée*, remarkable for its brilliancy, a newly married lady appeared in a dress of white Chambery gauze, *Ladies' Pocket*, June 1830 ~~~ Chambray gauze, cotton, 25 [percent tariff], cotton and silk, 25 [%], if wool is a component part, (*See Woollens*). <u>Tariff</u>, 1832

chameleon – [see *cameleon*]

chamois – SHAMOIS, Chamois, or Shammy, a kind of leather, either dressed in oil or tanned, much esteemed for its softness, pliancy, &c. It is prepared from the skin of the chamois, or shamois, a kind of rupicapra, or wild goat, called also ifaid [isaid?], inhabiting the mountains of Dauphiny, Savoy, Piedmont, and the Pyrenees. Besides the softness and warmth of the leather, it has the faculty of bearing soap without damage; which renders it very useful on many accounts. Encyclopædia Britannica, 1797 ~~~ Shammy, or Chamois leather. ... The real shammy is prepared from the skin of the chamois-goat. The true chamois leather is counterfeited with common goat, kid, and even sheep-skin; Dictionary of Commerce, 1810 ~~~ [mourning for Princess Amelia; ladies and gentlemen to wear] shamoy shoes and gloves, *Edinburgh Annual Register*, November 5, 1810 ~~~ *Gloves, Breeches, &c.* – Buff, shamoy, and buckskin leathers, dressed in oil for soldiers' belts and other accoutrements, gloves, breeches, aprons, &c. are prepared in considerable quantities at Silvermills near Edinburgh, Pollockshaws near Glasgow, and some other places. The skins, which are chiefly those of the cow, calf, sheep, and deer, after having been charged with oil, are subjected to a process of milling, similar to that of wauking or fulling. General Report of the Agricultural State ... of Scotland, 1814 ~~~ [for rheumatism] After trying innumerable other remedies without success, he was advised, by a most respectable member of the medical profession, to put on both drawers and an under waistcoat of chamois leather, which, in a very few days, gave him so much relief, that he could walk, and even ride, without pain; and in the course of three weeks at the most, he was entirely cured. This was in the year 1807-8; and he has had no return of the complaint since. ... The leather washes like linen ; only it must not be washed in hot water. The chamois leather feels cold and uncomfortable for the first day or two; but it soon becomes more comfortable than flannel. The price is about sixteen shillings a set. It is proper to have several sets, and to change them frequently. Code of Health and Longevity, 1816 ~~~ Evening Dress. ... Gloves of black shamoy leather; *Ladies' Monthly Museum*, December 1817 ~~~ [mourning for Princess Charlotte] chamoy shoes and gloves, Biographical Memoir of the Much Lamented Princess Charlotte Augusta, 1818 ~~~ Black chamois shoes and gloves. *Kaleidoscope*, September 4, 1821 ~~~ [mourning for King George the Fourth] The ladies to wear black bombazines, plain muslin, or long lawn linen, crape hoods, shamoy shoes and gloves, and crape fans. *Lady's Magazine*, June 1830 [note: chamois is also a colour; see also *washing leather*]

changeable silk – like a changeable silk, we can easily see there are two different colours, but we cannot easily discover where the one ends, or where the other begins. Manual of Liberty, 1795 ~~~ Some were of primrose, peach blossom, purple, and changeable coloured sarsnets, *La Belle Assemblée*, June 1806 ~~~ Changeable silks increase in favor; the fringes that ornament these dresses are formed of the two colors with which the silks are shot. *Lady's Magazine*, November 1829 ~~~ [Paris] Walking Dress. – A pelisse of gros de Naples, of a changeable color, mazarine-blue, shot with orange color, forming either a reddish purple, or a rich and lively brown, with a gold tinge, according to the manner in which the two colors are interwoven. *Ladies' Pocket Magazine*, January 1830 ~~~ Changeable silks are coming much into favour in dinner dress: they are of a richer kind than those so much in fashion two years ago. Ruby, green, *aventurine*, and crimson, all shot with white, are the favourite colours. *Ladies' Museum*, February 1832 [see also *shot silk*]

Chantilly blond – For the full-dress winter balls, ... Velvet dresses for the same occasion, and those of watered *gros de Naples,* or of satin, are all bordered with two flounces of white Chantilly blond; one of which is set on straight, while the other is festooned, and has a very full and broad head. *Lady's Magazine*, January 1829 ~~~ French Fashions. Wedding Dress. A dress of *blonde de Chantilly*, over white satin; ... The wedding veil, also of *blonde de Chantilly*, *La Belle Assemblée*, March 1831 ~~~ [court dresses] Dress of blonde Chantilly over white satin; ... White blonde dress, a colonnes; train of white satin, trimmed with deep Chantilly blonde. *Court Journal*, May 11, 1833 ~~~ There is a great difference between a real Chantilly veil and an imitation, if you know where to look for it; the blond, instead of forming intrinsically a part of the whole, is only laid on the lace foundation: they will say it is all blond, true blond, and swear to you nothing can be more perfect; they are right, blond it certainly is; but examine the edges, and you will find that they have been sown on, and the foundation cut away at the back; therefore, it is not the real Chantilly veil manufactured in one piece. The imitation is called "application," and apparently the same, but of course the difference would be perceptible by its inferior durability. <u>Letters from Brussels</u>, 1835 ~~~ [court dress] Train of Chantilly blond: à la colonné, *Lady's Magazine and Museum*, June 1835

Chantilly lace – [Paris] Over this dress is thrown a rich large black lace half-handkerchief: those of Chantilly are most in request, from the peculiar elegance of the border. *Repository of Arts*, September 1816 ~~~ [Paris] The Duchess de Berri, ... now wears, for the promenade, ... Chantilly half-handkerchiefs are thrown over this dress: it consists of large black lace of the finest texture, elegantly bordered. *Ladies' Monthly Museum*, October 1816 ~~~ *Though the court mourning may now be said to have finally ended, yet many ladies seem determined to wear black silk till after November; and this without any spirit of party, but as a convenient dress for short and wintry days, now fast approaching: black, therefore, is yet very prevalent, but it is merely the gown, which often consists of Urling's black Chantilly lace over white or grey sarsnet;* *Ladies' Monthly Museum*, October 1821 ~~~ *a veil of Chantilly lace is thrown carelessly across the brim of the bonnet, but this is not always adopted;* *La Belle Assemblée*, January 1823 ~~~ *The dress of the parties next undergoes a strict investigation, in order, if the rank be doubtful, to ascertain the extent of the property; and here the ladies are the keenest critics. An experienced dowager, herself arrayed in all the glories of Chantilly lace, Indian cachemires, and diamonds of the first water, will detect at a glance mock* blond, *Norwich shawls, or any other contrivance which a slender purse may suggest, and treat the wearer accordingly.* *Atheneum*, August 1, 1827 ~~~ White Chantilly lace, also over white satin, is much worn by young ladies in full dress: *La Belle Assemblée*, July 1829 ~~~ *By Chantilly, is generally understood a Lace formed of the finest black twisted silk. The veils of this kind are very much admired. The thicker parts of the flowers seem composed of several thicknesses of silk, having the appearance of being darned in afterwards. The lighter parts are formed in the making of the Lace.* <u>Young Lady's Book</u>, 1829 ~~~ Black lace veils, of our own manufacture, but offering an excellent imitation of Chantilly lace, are very much in favour in carriage dress. *Ladies' Museum*, January 1832 ~~~ [court dress] Most magnificent black crape elegantly embroidered in silk, the body trimmed with Chantilly lace. *Godey's Ladies Book*, August 1836 [see also *English Chantilly* and *tissu Chantilly*]

checked – Check (*s. in commerce, from* checker) Checkered linen, checkered stuff. <u>Ash's English Dictionary</u>, 1795 ~~~ Check for aprons [per ell, in 1794] ... 1s. 4d. <u>Case of Labourers in Husbandry</u>, 1795 ~~~ The prices of checks run from 6d. to 1s. 6d. per yard; <u>Statistical Account of Scotland</u>, 1796 ~~~ Checquered or Burdett handkerchief is very generally worn by the loungers of both sexes, in their Bond-street perambulations. *Lady's Magazine*, November 1800 ~~~ Hats of the Yeoman form, with triangular fronts, formed of velvet, quilted satin, or scarlet kerseymere, checked with white satin or velvet, are new and elegant articles. *La Belle Assemblée*, October 1807 ~~~ *Checks. The patterns of checks may be either similar, or dissimilar, in the warp and weft. The former is the most prevalent. Checks being merely combinations of the two methods of striping, require no further description; and as they contain most frequently a mixture of colours, their beauty depends more upon the taste and fancy of the manufacturer, and the skill of the dyer, than upon that of the weaver, whose business is merely to make the cloth of a good quality, and insert his weft according to his pattern. Stripes and checks are manufactured in great quantities from all the different materials, especially from woollen, silk, and cotton. When the patterns of checks differ at the borders, from the middle, or bosom of the web, they are called shawls, or handkerchiefs. It is very common to weave these with borders only, the bosom being left plain. In this case, the check work is only at the corners, the rest of the four borders appearing as stripes, two by the warp, and two by the weft.* <u>Art of Weaving</u>, 1807 ~~~ Bonnets of coloured figured sarcenet, lined with a different colour, and of a different pattern; for instance, the bonnet is, perhaps, of pink, chequered with black, in diamonds, and lined with yellow *spotted* with black. *La Belle Assemblée*, November 1826 ~~~ Many ladies, when the weather is chill, wear cloaks of fine cloth, chequered with black on scarlet; *Ladies' Pocket*, May 1829 ~~~ The drawn bonnets, which are tolerably numerous in London, are at present almost universal in Paris. ... are made chiefly of checquered silks: pink and white, lilac and white, blue and white, &c. ... A pelisse of checquered Gros de Naples, the colours green, white, and lilac. *Court Journal*, May 16, 1835 [see also *plaid* and *tartan*]

chef – *the fag end (of a piece of cloth)*; <u>Dufief's French Dictionary</u>, 1810 chenille – [court dress] An elegant dress in yellow crape, and white chinelle, with a drapery of rich blond, ... a flounce of blond and chinelle; *Lady's Magazine*, June 1797 ~~~ [Paris] The open-worked hats are either of yellow straw or silk chenille; *Lady's Magazine*, December 1800 ~~~ For full dress, gowns ... are bordered alternately with borders of chenille in embroidery; *Port Folio*, June 1809 ~~~ Hungarian mantle, with double capes, trimmed with chenille fur, composed of the same material as the robe, *Edinburgh Annual Register*, December 2, 1811 ~~~ The crowns of bonnets are made round, and they vary as to the style of their trimming: chenille is a material much made use of at the edge; and this, when of the very best quality, has a rich and splendid effect. *La Belle Assemblée*, January 1820 ~~~ Chenille is a fine silk poil, or nap, twisted spirally around a thread, ... has derived its name from its slightly caterpillar-like appearance. Young Lady's Book, 1829 ~~~ Chenille, *s.* (among trimming-makers; a sort of silk cord much like a caterpillar) A French and English Dictionary, 1833 ~~~ List of New Patents. ... Andrew Baldrence, Chenille Cutter, residing in Paisley, for a machine for cutting chenille, chenille cloth into chenille thread, and for making weft or part of weft, for shawls now called and know by the names of Chenille, Kamtschatka Moss, and Velours de Soi, or one other of these names. – Sealed September 19, 1835 *Repertory of Patent Inventions*, November 1835

chenille granite – A new kind of granite material has also been invented for hats, which is formed of little pieces of *chenille,* worked into a kind of tissue; this is called the *chenille* granite: the ribbons used in ornamenting those winter hats, are striped, or edged with, down. The most favourite trimmings are grey *chenille* granite on rose-colour, and violet on olive green. *La Belle Assemblée*, December 1819 ~~~ [for winter chapeaux] new and very beautiful stuffs. ... The other is called *granite*, or chenille stuff: the reason of this double appellation is, that it is composed of plaited chenille. *Repository of Arts*, December 1819 ~~~ and chenille stuff, are the materials most used for bonnets; ... is composed wholly of chenille. ... Bands of chenille stuff, edged with satin, are now very much used to trim dresses. *Ladies' Monthly Museum*, February 1820

chevaux de frise – Chevaux-de-Fri'se, *s.* a military fence composed of a piece of timber, traversed with, wooden spikes, pointed with iron, five or six feet long, used in defending a passage or tourniquet; a kind of trimming. Johnson's English Dictionary, 1804 ~~~ [evening dress] If composed of crape, or any light article, it is trimmed, at its several terminations, with a *chevaux-de-frise* border, composed of double folds of alternate satin and crape; but if composed of a more substantial material (such as satin, sarsnet, or lustre), the trimming is either silver, or silk fringe, or a border of feathers, or matted crape. I must not forget to observe that the *chevaux-de-frise* trimming is the most fashionable decoration at this moment for every sort of evening or dress robe; it has a most pleasing effect, when formed (as I have often seen it) of two colours, happily and tastefully contrasted. *Repository of Arts*, September 1812 ~~~ Evening Dress. A black crape frock over a black sarsnet slip. The skirt of the frock is finished by full flounces of the fashionable *chevaux de frise* trimming. *Repository of Arts*, December 1817 ~~~ Some ball-dresses are trimmed at the border with two rows of full *chevaux-de-fris*, very distinct from each other, and of a very bright or dark colour on white gauze. *Ladies' Monthly Museum*, February 1821 ~~~ the newly entwined *cheveux de frize* trimming, formed of notched, or pinked silk. *Ladies' Monthly Museum*, February 1824 ~~~ Carriage Dress. High round dress of *gros de Naples*, the color of the Parma violet, elegantly ornamented at the border with a full shell-puckering of the same material; over which is a row of united chevrons, in chevaux-de-frize. *Lady's Magazine*, December 1825

chicken skin – [see *Limerick*]

chicoree – *Chicorée* trimmings in distinct rows are often seen on evening dresses, and have a very pretty effect: flounces on gowns for half-dress prevail much; there are generally five, one above the other, which ascend within three hands' distance of the waist; so that the petticoat appears one mass of trimming, for above every flounce are five very small tucks; *La Belle Assemblée*, July 1825 ~~~ For the promenade, silk dresses are trimmed with one deep flounce, scolloped and pinked at the edge, over which is a row of *chicorée,* and at about a hand's breadth distance above is another row of the same trimming: *Ladies' Monthly Museum*, June 1826 ~~~ The new flounces are headed with a *ruche*, or *chicorée*, when of crape or silk. *La Belle Assemblée*, May 1827

China crape – The principal silk stuffs manufactured by the Chinese are ... crapes, brocades, plush, different kinds of velvet, and a multitude of other stuffs, the names of which are unknown in Europe. <u>View of the Chinese Empire</u>, 1795 ~~~ a new and beautiful manufacture for ladies' winter dresses, from the above house, where it may be obtained in any quantity, and of various colours. It does not exceed mediocrity in price, although it possesses the useful property of never creasing in the wear; added to which, it resembles the genuine China crape, by its falling naturally into the most graceful folds. *Repository of Arts*, November 1812 ~~~ A figured China crape silk, admirably adapted for the approaching summer months, forms a cool and elegant domestic evening dress, is worn with loose white muslin sleeves, and trimmed round the bottom with a silk ball fringe of corresponding colour. It is equally calculated for a morning or promenade costume; and is sold, at 30s. the dress, *Repository of Arts*, June 1814 ~~~ Our imitations of China crape and French silk, both for dresses and scarfs, are now universally adopted; the former in particular are uncommonly good. ... China crape scarfs, richly embroidered in colours at the ends, are much worn in the carriage costume, *Repository of Arts*, July 1816 ~~~ [Paris] Ball dresses are made of Chinese crape, decorated with three rows of white satin, in bias, interspersed with one large fold of crape round the border. *Ladies' Monthly Museum*, July 1817 ~~~ China crape for ladies' dresses is also cheap; sufficient for a dress, from 9 to 12 dollars. <u>An Account of the United States of America</u>, 1823 ~~~ Next in favor to these pelisses are those truly elegant shawls the Chinese crapes, that set so well to the form, discovering its contour, while they impart warmth sufficient for the temperature of spring: the most genteel are those of the true Indian white, approaching to cream-color; but as the expense attending these valuable articles generally confines them to the higher orders of society, we see them of pink, blue, orange-color, and lilac; the new ones are distinguished by the extreme breadth of their fringe. *Lady's Magazine*, May 1825 ~~~ [ad] Real China crape shawls, at 21s. such as other houses are selling for 63s.; *Examiner*, April 23, 1826 ~~~ Beautiful articles for summer dresses are now brought forward, consisting of Cachemire gauze, Chinese crape, and white crape, painted in patterns of various hues; and these materials are also seen in shawls, and scarfs, adorned at the ends with light but rich broad silk fringe. *Lady's Magazine*, June 1829 ~~~ Make and Materials of Dinner Dress. – White China crape, striped or figured in satin, is coming much into favour; *Day*, February 6, 1832 ~~~ Shawls, *fichus* and scarfs of black China crape, embroidered in coloured silk, are much in favour, and appear almost to have superseded boas. The richness of their patterns, and the pliancy of their texture, render them extremely elegant. *Court Journal*, March 23, 1833 [see also *canton crape* and *crape*]

China croisé – Among the number of rich materials introduced for half [dress] ... *China croisé*, a material of the same kind [as China satiné], but more elegant; *Court Magazine*, November 1835

China gauze – The principal silk stuffs manufactured by the Chinese are plain and flowered gauzes, of which they make dresses for summer; <u>View of the Chinese Empire</u>, 1795 ~~~ The sylph-like form of early youth, adorned with the roseate blush of uninterrupted health, will receive additional attraction by adopting the newly invented evening dress of Chinese gauze, which, in its varied tints, represents a *fac simile* of the Chinese grass, so well known for its verdant and versatile beauty. *La Belle Assemblée*, March 1816 ~~~ Many matronly ladies, however, in the country, wear at evening parties small equestrian hats of Chinese gauze or satin, *La Belle Assemblée*, August 1818 ~~~ In the ball-room, ... white Chinese gauze is often worn at dances by young persons, over white satin, *Lady's Magazine*, February 1825 ~~~ [Paris] The sister of the Duchesse de Berri, the princess of Bavaria, had a most elegant fitting out on her marriage; among the most elegant of her dresses was one of real Chinese gauze, – the colored flowers and those of silver were really admirable on this material; *Ladies' Pocket*, September 1829 ~~~ Different kinds of gauze are worn in evening dress, particularly gaze de Chine, and gaze de Turin; the first is of uncommon richness; the other of a lighter description, and much in favour for ball dresses. Both kinds of gauze are striped, spotted, and figured in a great variety of patterns. *Ladies' Museum*, December 1830

China satin – Sir G. Staunton's *Account of the Embassy to China*. [published 1797] ~~~ The flowered and embroidered satins, and other branches in the manufacture of silk, every part of which is done by women, occupy vast numbers of them in Han-choo-foo. *Analytical Review*, November 1797 ~~~ The Chinese satins are most valued, because of their cleaning and bleaching easily, without losing any thing of their lustre ; in other respects they are inferior to those of Europe. British Encyclopedia, 1809 ~~~ [Paris] Chinese satin, and *embroidered linon,* make beautiful, ball dresses. *Ladies' Monthly Museum*, December 1828 ~~~ Chinese satins, richly embroidered, were once in high estimation, but our own manufactures are at present equal in most respects to the foreign. The colours and flowers are various, and the price is regulated accordingly. Dictionary of Mechanical Science, 1829 ~~~ Several new materials for robes have already appeared, ... *Satin de Chine* is equally rich [as satin trianon], but of different patterns. *Court Magazine*, October 1833 ~~~ *Satin de Chine* is a new material, that may be worn in half-dress or for evening parties; it has the richness but not the brilliancy of satin, and is generally of light colours, rose, blue, pea-green, &c. *Court Magazine*, January 1834 [see also *India satin* and *peeling satin*]

China satiné – Among the number of rich materials introduced for half [dress] ... *China satiné*, a mixture of silk and wool; *Court Magazine*, November 1835

China silk – Chinese silk is deemed the best in the known world, *Monthly Review*, May 1799 ~~~ [ad] Collyer's Silk Stockings. ... Ladies' and Gentlemen's stout and fine black, white, and coloured China silk, from 7s. 6d. or three pair for a Guinea, *La Belle Assemblée*, May 1807 ~~~ A shawl of Chinese silk, thrown negligently over the shoulders. ... the Pedlar's cloak, and Rugen mantle, of Chinese silk, trimmed with Vandyke brocade ribband; *La Belle Assemblée*, September 1807 ~~~ Even when the best soap is used, it is generally suspected that it injures the whiteness of the silk. The splendour of the Chinese silk is brighter than that of the European, and the Chinese employ no soap in their operations. Dictionary of Commerce, 1810 ~~~ Evening Dress. ... The head-dress is a toque, composed of Chinese silk and white net: *Repository of Arts*, March 1819 ~~~ When silk is intended for the manufacture of blonds, laces, and gauzes, it should have its natural stiffness and elasticity. The greater part of the silk produced in our climates has a yellow colour. The white silk of China is therefore principally employed for these objects, and a few others. It is not yet positively ascertained whether the Chinese silk is naturally white, or rendered so by some unknown process. According to Poivre, this silk is bleached by exposing it to the sun. But some other circumstance is necessary; for this method has been tried without success. Elements of the Art of Dyeing, 1824 ~~~ [ad] Dresses of various designs for Morning, Dinner, Evening, and Ball Costume, in China Silk, *Declaration of the Catholic Bishops*, September 1826 ~~~ [ad] Rich figured, checked, and plain China Silks. At Messrs. Jones & Cooke's Sale, on Saturday next, will be sold, *Colonist*, March 6, 1828 ~~~ A few days ago eleven hundred cases of China silks were sold at auction in New York by John Hone and Sons. The sales amounted to more than half a million dollars!! *New England Farmer*, April 27, 1831 ~~~ [Paris] I have another dress for rainy weather. It is of China silk, with a bronze ground; it has small *ramages* of bright colours, a flat *corsage* and pelerine to match, *Court Magazine*, July 1833

China velvet – The principal silk stuffs manufactured by the Chinese are ... different kinds of velvet, and a multitude of other stuffs, the names of which are unknown in Europe. View of the Chinese Empire, 1795 ~~~ Here the various caprices of taste and fancy are most eminently displayed; here the Parisian beauty attracts the eye, as she sometimes spurts a hat of cloth, of the same colour as her pelisse; another challenges admiration, and sometimes envy, by a scarce and costly article, a hat of Chinese velvet, stamped in clouds, or of a snow-like whiteness: *La Belle Assemblée*, December 1814 ~~~ The Chinese likewise manufacture velvets; but, if we are to judge from the specimens which have been imported into Europe, their success in this branch has been but very moderate, the quality of Chinese velvet being far inferior to even the most indifferent of European production. Silk Manufacture, 1832 ~~~ [court dress] A dress of white moire a Brandenburg, train of celeste velours Chinois, lined with white. *Court Journal*, June 1, 1833

chinchilla – the chinchilla, a kind of squirrel, in shape like a lap-dog. Its fur is of a bright grey colour, and finer than the most delicate silk. Literary Panorama, 1807 ~~~ Muffs of all kinds stem to be universal; but the most elegant are those of fine swansdown, chinchilla, and the pale fox. Pellerines are now getting, by their generality, almost too common for the refined taste of our *elegantes* of high ton, and the round tippet of swansdown or chinchilla is much more in favour. *La Belle Assemblée*, December 1811 ~~~ The practice, in London, is to enter red squirrel skins, *ad valoreum*, under the name of *Chinchilla* skins. <u>Practice of the Customs</u>, 1812 ~~~ *Chinchilla, (Mus Paca.)* – A species of rat or field mole, greatly esteemed for the fine fur with which the body is covered instead of a skin, which is as soft as the silk deposited by the garden spiders. The fur is of an ash colour, and of sufficient length to be spun. This little animal is about six inches long from the nose to the tail, the ears small and pointed, the snout short, the teeth like those of the domestic mole, the tail of a moderate length, and thickly set with very soft hair. ... The skin is now generally used for the purpose of carrying tobacco by those who smoke. [translated from 1786 original] <u>Dictionary of America and the West Indies</u>, 1815 ~~~ elegantly trimmed with that light and valuable fur, the chinchilla; *La Belle Assemblée*, March 1819 ~~~ [Paris] For the out-door costume some variety is observed, and mantelet pelerines of Chinchilla fur or black marten, *Lady's Magazine*, February 1825 ~~~ [velvet pelisses] lined and faced with costly fur, as ermine, chinchilla, or sable; *Ladies' Museum*, February 1830 ~~~ The Chinchilla, or Chinche, ... is a native of South America. Notwithstanding the great variety of skins, taken from the animal, brought into our markets, until very recently very little of the Chinchilla was known. The animal, in general, is about nine inches in length, with a tail of nearly five. ... The fur is long, thick, close, woolly, somewhat crisp and entangled, grayish, or ash-coloured above, and paler beneath. ... The fur of the Chinchilla is highly valuable, being extensively used in the manufacture of hats, caps, &c. *Atkinson's Casket*, February 1832 ~~~ Fine dark chinchilla, and squirrel back, will rank next to ermine and sable. *Court Magazine*, November 1833 ~~~ No fur has fallen in price this winter, but chinchilla is less in demand than some others. *Schoolmaster*, March 9, 1833

chinelle – [see *chenille*]

chintz – a fine cloth manufactured of cotton, in the East-Indies, generally printed with lively and durable colours. <u>Royal English Dictionary</u>, 1775 ~~~ Morning Dress. ... Round gown of salmon-colour flowered chintz; *Lady's Magazine*, February 1796 ~~~ Great improvements have of late years been made in this art, and chintz printed in England, has, for art and beauty, surpassed any that has been brought from the East-Indies. These chintz patterns are generally drawn and painted with three reds, two purples, blues, greens and yellows, from which, being blended one with another, a variety of other colours are produced, so as to appear upon the cloth like a curious painting; for by that means are introduced the crimson, orange, olive, buff, chocolate, and several other changes and shades. <u>Laboratory</u>, 1799 ~~~ It was a new fact to me, that the most beautiful of the chintses are stamped by means of copper cylinders, on which the figures are engraved; these cylinders are covered with the proper substance, and then impressed on the stuffs by rolling. <u>Journal of Travels</u>, 1806 ~~~ With respect to drawing of patterns for the calico printers, they are, for the generality, in imitation of the flowered silk manufactory, with such variations as may best answer the nature of the different sorts of works, of which there is great variety. The principal are the whole chintzs, in which they imitate the richest silk brocades, with a great variety of beautiful colours: these make the best appearance on an open white ground. The fashion, as with the brocaded silks, has run upon natural flowers, stalks, and leaves; sometimes intermixed with ornaments, after the French taste, sometimes in groupes or festoons of flowers, or fruit, or in sprigs and branches carelessly flung, in a natural and agreeable manner. Of late, the ground has, by some printers, been dyed of a cloth colour, and the white has only appeared in the heightening of the flowers, and in the ground colour, where it is preserved by a paste, in imitation of a silk tobine: this makes, especially when first new and glazed, a very rich and handsome show. In like manner blue grounds are done, which are more lasting. Black, or dark ground chintz patterns are done with the same variety of colours, but differ from the former in the ground being more closely covered with flowers and leaves, and the white being preserved in the heightening of them. This has a great effect, if well managed by the pattern-drawer, and by the hands it must pass through in the printing. Great improvements have of late years been made in this art, and chintz printed in England, has, for art and beauty, surpassed any that has been brought from the East Indies. These chintz patterns are generally drawn and painted with three reds, two purples, blues, greens, and yellows, from which, being blended one with another, a variety of other colours are produced, so as to appear upon the cloth like a curious painting; for by that means are introduced the crimson, orange, olive, buff, chocolate, and several other changes and shades. Next to the whole chintz are the half chintz: these differ from the former, as they are printed with only two reds, and no purple. The patterns that serve for one, will, in the management of the printing, serve for the other, both with respect to the white, as for the coloured or black grounds. We now come to patterns for five colours: these are drawn with one, or a full single red; and a black out-line for all the rest of the colours, as blue, green, and yellow: sometimes the yellow is shadowed off with the red. Both white and black grounds are printed in these colours, in stripes, sprigs, or other whimsical fancies. Next to these in order are the three coloured patterns; these are intended for the common or coarse cottons, on account of the small variety of colours, which consist only of black, red, and blue; and the pattern-drawer is obliged to make as much show as he can in his design. However, some work of this kind has been done on fine cottons, in imitation of needle-work, to great perfection, and worn by ladies of the first rank and fashion, for a dishabille or undress. To these three-coloured patterns we may add those for two purples, and blue. The last of all are the single purples: these are commonly done with small flowers, some with an open ground, and some much covered. Some patterns are with running trails, others are set, and in sprigs; some are for white, and some for black, or shagreen grounds. In short, there is no end of fashions and changes, which of course must cause great study, and labour to a pattern-drawer. Laboratory, 1810 ~~~ We are happy to see that the very beautiful dark English chintzes are now much patronized by the higher classes, for morning and home deshabille; they are of various patterns, but the wave stripe of a light colour, over which is entwined flowers of a bright red, and the spaces between the stripes elegantly figured with variously coloured flowers, seem to be the most admired. *La Belle Assemblée*, November 1823 ~~~ Chintzes of most elegant patterns, colours, and fine texture, are preferred by ladies of taste; universally worn, on mornings in the retired promenades, and sometimes retained through the day; only, however, by the young, when the chintz is peculiarly beautiful; then, with elegant ornaments and the hair tastefully arranged, these exquisite specimens of British manufacture form a very charming home attire. *La Belle Assemblée*, July 1827 ~~~ Chintzes are much worn; they are in various patterns; and it is impossible to speak decidedly on which is most preferred, either plaided, striped, or flowered, though we may individually prefer the latter, because the colors and designs are so extremely rich and beautiful; yet we find, from our observations, that the plaids seem to be regarded as most genteel: to speak the real truth, costly as these dresses may be as to texture and price, they are but colored washing-gowns, at best; and the slightest silk, at half the expense, is far more elegant: the Spitalfields manufacturers would be glad if every one was of our opinion. *Ladies' Pocket*, June 1829 ~~~ [ad] dark Persian chintzes, for morning wear; *Court Journal*, February 9, 1833 ~~~ Chintz is a fine cotton fabric; the patterns, as of all Indian goods, are peculiar and showy, though not elegant. The English have succeeded in imitating the chintz patterns; and the Swiss are very expert at these imitations. Book of Commerce by Sea and Land, 1834 [see also *calico*, *muslin* and *white chintz*]

chip – Walking Dress. Coloured chip hat, tied under the chin, and ornamented with flowers in front. … The large sewed gipsey chips, pressed chips, chips of all kind, and superfine Leghorn, in the poke, in all shapes, are in general wear. *Lady's Magazine*, July 1800 ~~~ Walking Dress. A black chip hat, with black ostrich feathers and ribands; *Ladies' Monthly Museum*, April 1802 ~~~ For the latter [the promenade] we have to recommend the *al Fresco* hat in white, unbleached chip; it is of a rural elegance and simplicity well suited to the season and the occasion; … We have noticed, on some very gay people, flat chip hats, prettily enough ornamented with artificial flowers, but we consider them to belong to that pert, flippant style of dress, ill suited to the *quiet* elegance of genteel or fashionable life, or only adapted to "the gay fantastic hour." *La Belle Assemblée*, June 1810 ~~~ Chip Hats are manufactured on the same principles as those of straw, the chips being generally plaited in the same manner, although sometimes they are interwoven in the manner of basket work, particularly the common kind used by the country people. The only particularities are the methods adopted to obtain the chips, and the manner of whitening them. As to the first, the wood usually chosen for this manufacture is that of the lime tree, poplar tree, willow tree, and some others, which have a white wood without knots. The wood is taken green, and divided into very fine chips by means of a plane with two irons. The first plane iron is furnished with several cutting teeth, and the second has as usual a plain chisel edge; of course the shavings are divided lengthways into as many slips, and one more, as there are teeth in the first plane iron. The plane is pushed forward between guides placed for that purpose, in order that the teeth may always repass in the same place. Several machines have been invented for the cutting of these chips; but this double iron plane is the simplest, and perfectly answers the purpose for which it is intended. The chips are whitened, or the hats, after they are made, by soaking them in cold soap water, with a little stone blue among it; after which they are exposed for some days on the grass, taking care to sprinkle them with clear water as often as they grow dry. These chips, or the hats made from them, may be dyed in the same manner as straw plait or straw hats. *American Mechanics' Magazine*, August 13, 1825 ~~~ Chip hats being composed of the shavings of wood, *Godey's Ladies Book*, December 1832

chitterlings – the frill at the bosom of a shirt. <u>Sheridan's English Dictionary</u>, 1797

chryseon – [ad] Court dress, exhibiting the application of the newly invented Chryseon, or gold fringe; *London Literary Gazette*, January 8, 1831 ~~~ Gold and silver fringes, of a description very far above any that have hitherto appeared, are now manufactured upon a new principle, from a beautiful material called *Chrysson*. Mr. Burgis, the inventor, has obtained a patent for this superb addition to court and ball dresses, so superior in every respect to any thing of the kind that has ever yet been introduced: it never tarnishes, not will it soil any, the most delicate, material; it is perfectly unequalled for brilliancy and lightness, and will retain its lustre many years; whereas fringes made upon the common principle are sure to tarnish in a short time. *Ladies' Museum*, March 1831 ~~~ Chrysson. – Court and ball dresses are now beginning to be ornamented with gold and silver fringes, made upon a new principle, and from a very beautiful material, for which a patent has been obtained. It is called *Chrysson*, as its name imports, and possesses a great number of advantages over everything we have hitherto seen, particularly in respect to its brilliancy, lightness, and, above all, its permanency, as it will never tarnish, or soil the most delicate satin, as is the case with other gold and silver fringes upon exposure to a humid atmosphere, besides being very heavy; whereas fringes made upon the new principle, by Mr. Burgis, the inventor and patentee, retain their elegance and beautiful lustre for many years, and are not heavier than silk of the same size. *Atheneum*, April 1831 ~~~ Court Dress. … shoes made of the chryseon gold, and also silver, new present as an elegant addition to the decorative department of costume. *Godey's Ladies Book*, May 1831

chrysson – [see *chryseon*]

Circassian – [Paris] Pale olive-coloured promenade coats, of a fine Circassian cloth, are much worn: *Lady's Magazine*, March 1807 ~~~ [Paris] Riding coats of Circassian silk. *La Belle Assemblée*, July 1807 ~~~ [court dress] Petticoat and train of white satin; superb Circassian cloth drapery embroidered in gold, *La Belle Assemblée*, January 1809 ~~~ Patterns of British manufacture. No. 1 is an animated and lively sample of the true Circassian cloth, beautifully coloured, and similar in effect to that worn by those formerly celebrated and graceful people, … This article of seasonable introduction is admirably adapted, both for dresses of various descriptions, and also for the coat *à la surtout*. It is nearly two yards wide, extremely light and adhesive, and, like the Chinese crape, falls in graceful folds with the movements of the figure. *Repository of Arts*, November 1813 ~~~ Circassian gauze for Turkish and Persian *toques*, is much in requisition; it is of fine net, and appears to be powdered with pearls, or is adorned with pearls in various devices; … The Circassian wave silk forms a beautiful material for carriage bonnets; *La Belle Assemblée*, April 1819 ~~~ The newest ball dresses are of Circassian gauze: *Ladies' Pocket*, April 1830 ~~~ Some [riding] habits have been seen of light blue satin *Circassienne*, which is a manufacture of cachemire wool and cotton. *Lady's Magazine*, May 31, 1830 ~~~ *Circassiennes*, … are among the new materials in half dress; they are changeable, being a mixture of silk and English wool of different colours. *Ladies' Museum*, February 1831 ~~~ Circassian (worsted stuff) *Public Documents*, March 1832 ~~~ [ad] 4 cases Circassians, very superior qualities and various colors *New England Farmer*, September 25, 1833 ~~~ Worsted Stuff Goods, from Manchester to New York … Circassians … actual [width] inches 24 *a* [to] 27 ~~~ Price per yard s.d. [shillings.pence] 1.0 *a* 3.0 <u>Trade between Great Britain and the United States of America</u>, 1833 ~~~ 1 piece Circassian plaid calico 38 ½ [yards] 75 [cents; total $] 28.87 ½ [letter dated October 26, 1832] <u>Emigration of Indians,</u>

1835 [see *cassinet*]

cisele – Velours … ciselé, *cut velvet*. Dufief's French Dictionary, 1810 ~~~ Ciselé, ée, *.p engraved, carved*. Velours ciselé, *flowered velvet*, or *cut flowers*. Boyer's Royal Dictionary, 1814 [see *cut velvet*]

clear lawn – [Paris] *Chemise à l'Indienne*. – This is a beautiful undress, the waist is formed by plaits artfully arranged, and by bows of ribband; the train falls to the ground in an elegant drapery; it is made of delicate clear lawn. *Lady's Magazine*, June 1796 ~~~ Clear lawn should be made of clean evenly yarn, or else it will not answer the end for which it is intended, as it is used for women's head dresses, (tho' not so much as formerly,) and dresses, where any colour such as red, blue, green, yellow, &c. is wanted to show through; it is also made into strips, by interspersing at certain intervals, double or heavy yarn, and sometimes ornamented by hand sewing, &c. Linen Manufacturer, 1817 ~~~ [Paris] this morning promenade dress is worn a bonnet of fine clear lawn, with full-blown red roses, or a *bouquet* of tulips, finely grouped together. *La Belle Assemblée*, August 1819 ~~~ Morning dresses of … India muslins, richly embroidered, are highly esteemed by ladies of rank. The *corsages* of these splendid dresses are made half-high; and a fine *chemisette* tucker, of clear lawn, laid in small plaits, and edged with narrow lace, appears above the dress, across the bust. *Ladies' Monthly Museum*, June 1827 [see *lawn*]

clear muslin – Dress of clear white muslin, with a train of lilac, fastened between the shoulders, and tied loosely on the left side with a silk cord: *Lady's Magazine*, July 1798 ~~~ Caps of clear muslin, with three rows of edging, add many charms to the possessors of unaffected ease and simple beauty. *Lady's Magazine*, December 1800 ~~~ An Evening Dress. A round train gown of clear muslin, or leno, over white satin, tamboured in a snail pattern, and ornamented at the feet and round the bosom with rosets of gold, or coloured velvet; *La Belle Assemblée*, October 1807 ~~~ Muslins are usually worn very clear, and the petticoat so short, as to exhibit the ankle through, which is laced in the sandal style, ornamented with the open-wove stocking. *La Belle Assemblée*, November 1807 ~~~ Muslin is the only thing worn in dinner-dress. … A round dress of clear muslin, trimmed at the bottom with a full flounce of broad lace, *Repository of Arts*, November 1816 ~~~ Clear muslin, lightly embroidered in coloured silks, is in great favour for ball dress with unmarried ladies, to whom fashion imperiously prescribes a simple and unexpensive dress. [Paris] *Repository of Fashions*, July 1829 ~~~ Clear muslin embroidered round the border, either in white or colors is much worn in evening dress: *Ladies' Pocket*, October 1830 ~~~ Clear muslin pelisses, lined with coloured sarsnet, or *gros de Naples*, … Clear muslin, printed in delicate patterns, and in colours partly full, and partly light, is fashionable for dresses, *Court Magazine*, August 1833 ~~~ Clear India muslin, a white ground figured in squares, with a *filet* of purple Cashmere, is also a half-dress material, the high price of which renders it likely to be fashionable. *Court Magazine*, May 1835

Clementine – Evening dress. – A dress of Canary-colored *gaze Clementine* satin to correspond; *Godey's Ladies Book*, June 1831

clodia crape – Ball dresses are trimmed with three rows of satin in bias *rouleaux*; … this is always the way in which striped crape, flock gauze, clodia crape, rainbow gauze, plain *barége* silk, or *tulle* dresses are trimmed. *La Belle Assemblée*, April 1823

cloth – Any thing woven for dress or covering; Sheridan's English Dictionary, 1797 ~~~ Cloth, in commerce, a manufacture made of wool, wove on the loom. Cloths are of divers qualities, fine or coarse, according to some, consists of the following particulars: 1. That the wool be of a good quality, and well dressed. 2. It must be equally spun, carefully observing that the thread of the warp be finer and better twisted than that of the woof. 3. The cloth must be well wrought, and beaten on the loom, so as to be every where equally compact. 4. The wool must not be finer at one end of the piece than in the rest. 5. The lifts must be sufficiently strong, of the same length with the stuff, and must consist of good wool, hair, or ostrich-feathers; or, what is still better, of Danish dog's hair. 6. The cloth must be free from knots and other imperfections. 7. It must be well scoured with fuller's earth, well fulled with the best white soap, and afterwards washed in clear water. 8. The hair or nap must be drawn out with the teazel, without being too much opened. 9. It must be shorn close without making it threadbare. 10. It must be well dried. 11. It must not be tenter-stretched, to force it to its just dimensions. 12. It must be pressed cold, not hot pressed, the latter being very injurious to woollen cloth. Encyclopædia

Britannica, 1797 ~~~ CLOTH. *s.* Term given to cloth that was never coloured or dyed, ray-cloth; sort of cloth made of hair and silk, grogram, grogeram or grogran; name of a coarse sort of woollen cloth, penistone; canvas cloth used for making sails, mildernix; sort of linen cloth used for table-cloths, coverlets, &c. huckaback; cant phrases used by taylors for stealing fragments of cloth, to cabbage, to prig. Dictionary of the Synonymous Words, 1806 ~~~ *The Woollen Manufacture* includes the several commodities into which wool is wrought; as broad cloths, kerseymeres, baize, serges, flannel, says, stuffs, frize, stockings, caps, rugs, &c. 6. *Cloths.* The word cloth is more particularly applied to a web, or tissue of woollen threads, interwoven; of which some, called the *warp*, are extended longitudinally, from one end of the piece to the other; the rest, called *woof*, are disposed across the first, or the breadthway of the piece. Cloths are woven on the loom, as well as linens, druggets, serges, camblets, &c. The goodness of cloth depends on many peculiar circumstances. The cloth should be well wrought and beaten on the loom, so as to be every where equally close and compact. The wool must not be finer and better at one end of the piece than the rest. The lists should be sufficiently strong, and of the same length with the stuff. For *coarse* cloth they should consist of course wool and cow hairs from Scotland; for *fine* cloth, of Vigonia, or Alpaca wool (taken from the lama,) from South America. The cloth must be well cleared of the knots and other imperfections; be well scoured with good fuller's earth, then fulled with the best white soap, and washed in clear water. The hair, or nap, must be well *rowed,* or drawn out with the teazle *dipsacus fullonum,* L. [Latin name of the teazle plant]) without being too much opened; it must be shorn close, yet without laying the ground or thread bare; be well dyed; not stretched or pulled, further than is necessary to bring it to the just length and breadth; and lastly, it must be properly pressed. New Pocket Cyclopædia, 1813 ~~~ CLOTH, in commerce, in its general sense, includes all kinds of clothing woven or manufactured in the loom, except silk; whether the threads be of wool, cotton, hemp, or flax. Cloth is, however, more peculiarly applied to woollen threads interwoven, some of which are called *warp,* and extend lengthwise, from one end of the piece to the other; the others are called the *woof,* and disposed across the first, or breadthwise of the piece. Cloths are of various qualities, fine, coarse, strong, &c.; some are of different colors; others are wrought white, and afterwards dyed in the piece. Their breadths and lengths are various. ... Cloth is distinguished by being either *plain* or *kersey* woven. The first method consists simply in the threads crossing each other at right angles; in the last they are crossed so as to give an additional strength to the cloth; hence it appears in diagonal lines or rows running obliquely across the piece; and, in general, this style of weaving adds thickness as well as strength to the fabric. In the cotton manufacture, cloth, so woven, is called *twilled.* New Family Encyclopedia, 1835 [see also *wool*]

clothing wool – [see *wool*]

cloud – the veins or stains in stones, or other bodies; ... to variegate with dark veins. Sheridan's English Dictionary, 1797 ~~~ [threads] are formed into hanks, some of which are tightly bound round at certain intervals, previous to their being dyed, in order to prevent the parts so tied from taking the colour. This is done, that the threads may be disposed in the warp, so as to produce the clouds which are seen in various species of the cotton goods, particularly *gingams.* [sic] *Monthly Magazine,* October 1797 ~~~ The principal silks manufactured by the Chinese are ... napped, flowered, clouded, and pinked taffeties; New Universal Gazetteer, 1798 ~~~ Statement Of British Cotton Manufactures Suitable For Sicily. ... Clouds invoiced at *1s. 2d.* per yard. Voyages and Travels, 1812 ~~~ Clouded, ... variegated with colored spots or veins. American Dictionary, 1830

cloud net – [belonging to Princess Charlotte] Two dresses of British cloud net, elegantly trimmed with cloud, and another to wear over satin slips. *Niles' Weekly Register,* June 22, 1816

coarse – 2. Not soft or fine: used of cloth, of which the threads are large. Encyclopædia Perthensis, 1816

coarse silk – [see *floret*]

coating – The woollen clokes are made of grey coating, one yard and three quarters wide, at 5*s.* 6*d.* per yard, but the discount allowed for ready money, and one yard which it is customary to give when twenty yards are purchased at one time, reduce the cost of this article to 5*s.* per yard. The clokes are made up in different sizes, from one yard and a quarter to two yards in each; the two yards size, with binding, strings, and thread, cost 10*s.* 10*d.* In this estimate no charge for making is included, as they are made by the children in the school. Promoting the Comforts of the Poor, 1800 ~~~ Coatings are cloths, or rather broad cloths, which are in fact made as nearly as possible in a similar way to those which are intended for the press, though not so stoutly milled, and the main difference in the manufacturing is in the finishing; they are raised considerably upon the gig, the long wool is raised upon them; in most instances it is so left as to appear like a shag. Reports from the Committees, 1821 ~~~ a cloak … made of a find kind of cloth, which we [in France] call coating, *Repository of Arts*, February 1823 ~~~ even very elegant ladies are seen in the modest cloke of humble coating. *Lady's Magazine*, December 1825 ~~~ *Coatings* – 50 inches wide, cost 1s. 8d. to 5s. … Consumed by the farming, mechanic, and laboring interests, and for women's cloaks and coats. The principal consumption is by the farmers, mechanics, and laborers, of a quality which costs about 2s. 6d. *Niles' Weekly Register*, March 8, 1828 ~~~ The fabrics formed of wool … *Coatings,* which are of a coarse open texture, are used for great coats and other inferior purposes. Scenes of Commerce, 1836

cobweb muslin – a description of the wedding-dr ess of Lady H. Villiers; for a bridal costume possesses considerable interest for us young girls who one day hope to be ranked amidst the votaries of Hymen. This dress, my dear Julia, was composed of the finest India cobweb muslin, made round with a train, and worn over a soft and highly polished satin slip; *La Belle Assemblée*, January 1807 ~~~ I'll send her a piece of the true cobweb muslin. You may see through as many folds of it as Ajax had in his shield, *European Magazine*, April 1808

cobweb net – Her two daughters … will each wear a Carthage cymar of cobweb net, bordered and spotted with silver. *La Belle Assemblée*, March 1809 ~~~ a long sleeve of fine cobweb net placed over [the short sleeve], and confined at the wrist with a diamond clasp; *Port Folio*, June 1809 [see also *Arachne, gossamer net,* and *spider*]

cock feathers – Many velvet hats are ornamented with cock's feathers, grouped together, and floating over one side, like the tails of the birds-of-paradise. *Ladies' Pocket*, January 1830 ~~~ Tufts of cock's feathers have also been adopted by some very elegant women. *Ladies' Museum*, February 1830

cockade – A bow of ribband worn in the hat. Sheridan's English Dictionary, 1797 ~~~ on less particular occasions [than public parties, bonnets] are worn plain, or with a simple rose or cockade in front. *La Belle Assemblée*, July 1808 ~~~ [French morning dress cornette] a large cockade of ribbon and net mixed ornaments it in front; *Repository of Arts*, July 1816 ~~~ [Paris hats] at one side a cockade of Marabout feathers, *Ladies' Monthly Museum*, November 1818 ~~~ A great many [bonnets] in walking dress, and even for morning visits, are trimmed with a large cockade of ribbon, which is placed only on one side. *Atheneum*, July 15, 1831 ~~~ Bonnets are generally trimmed with an enormous cockade, composed of six rows; three of tulle and three of ribbon. *Casket*, September 1831

colbertine – A kind of lace worn by women. Sheridan's English Dictionary, 1797 ~~~ *Princess Augusta*. A white satin petticoat, richly embroidered wit gold spangles and foil, … and gold Colberteen and laurel at the pocket-holes; *Lady's Magazine*, January 1800 ~~~ *Princess Amelia* was elegantly attired, in a petticoat composed of two silver embroidered white crape draperies over lilac satin, … with bows of real silver colberteen at pocket-holes, *Lady's Magazine*, June 1800 ~~~ It is termed "a lace resembling network, of the fabrick of Mons. Colbert, superintendant of the French King's manufactures," in the Fop's Dictionary of 1690. Johnson's English Dictionary, 1827

Colerain – In the Linen Laws and resolutions of the Board, the different kinds of plain Linen were denominated from the places in which they were generally manufactured; they are now, except Colerain's and Drogheda's, distinguished by their breadth, and number in the reed. … Colerain's, when brown, [should measure] thirty-two, when white thirty. [inches wide] Select Papers of the Belfast Literary Society, 1808 ~~~ The coarser [flax] yarn is carried to L. Derry, the finer to Coleraine, Newtown, &c. The fabric of Coleraine is the finest. All of this fabric, though made and sold in other places, goes under the name of *Coleraines*. Memoir … of the County of London-Derry, 1814 ~~~ Where are Coleraine linens chiefly made ? – In the neighbourhood of Coleraine they are manufactured, and in the county of Derry; the average prices of the cloth, that is sold in the market of Coleraine, is 18*d.* to 2*s.* 8*d.* a yard in the brown state; in former times, they used to go up as high as 5*s.* or 6*s.* a yard, perhaps higher; the linens, coming into the London market, purporting to be Coleraines, stamped with the spurious seals, are sold in the London market at 10 ½ *d.* and 11*d.* average, in the white state. [June 19, 1822] Report [on] … the Linen Trade of Ireland, 1824 ~~~ Colerain (Irish linen) *Public Documents*, March 23, 1832

Combing wool – [1794] What Sort of Articles in the Woollen Manufactory must necessarily be made of Combing Wool? he said, Sagathies, Duroy plain, Duroy figured, Draughts, Estamanes, Shalloons, Serge plain, Tamies, Poplins, Lastings, Bombazines, Bombazette, Callimanco, Harratines, Stuff Damask, Barragon, Camblets, Sattinette, Crapes, *English* Shawls, Moncriefs, Russells, Buntings, Grograms, Carpeting, Worsted Plush, Worsted Hose, Worsted Fringe, Lace and Bindings, Worsted Crewels, Drugetts, Rackers, Long Ells, *German* Serge, Sanfords, Frays, Coarse Ells, and Baize. Journals of the House of Commons, 1803 ~~~ Sheep's wool may, therefore, be divided into two kinds, short wool or clothing wool, and long or combing wool; each of these kinds may be subdivided into a variety of sorts, according to their degrees of fineness. This process is the proper labour of the wool sorter. … Long or combing wool may vary in length from three to eight or ten inches; it is prepared on a comb or instrument, with rows of long steel teeth, which open the fibres, and arrange them longitudinally; in the thread spun from combed wool, the fibres or filaments of the wool are arranged in the same manner, or similar to these of flax, and the pieces when woven are not subjected to the process of felting. The shorter combing wools are principally used for hose, and are spun softer than the longer combing wools; the former being made into what is called hard worsted yarn, and the latter into soft worsted yarn. *New England Farmer*, September 25, 1824 [see also *wool* and *worsted*]

concan – [ad] Summer Goods, … Concans, … of all colour and qualities. Boston Annual Advertiser, 1823 ~~~ [letter dated February 8, 1819] Concan, (30 yards,) [Original cost] 9 00 per piece, … 30 yards long and 45-100 wide. American State Papers, 1834 ~~~ Many substantial and beautiful fabrics are formed of a combination of silk and cotton. Varieties of vestings, varieties of heavy damask, Concan, Seersuckers, &c. &c. American Silk Grower's Guide, 1835

coney – [see *rabbit*]

contil de soie – Aprons are universally worn in the latter [home costume]: they are still *à la bonne*, but those of *foulard* have given place to plain *gros de Naples*, or *contil de Soie*. *La Belle Assemblée*, December 1830 ~~~ [Paris] Two kinds of silk have lately appeared; the one called *contil de soie à mille raies* … is a rich silk, striped like a small corded dimity; *La Belle Assemblée*, June 1831 ~~~ Wadded pelisses, composed of rich twilled sarsnet, called *contil de Soie*, are also in favour for the promenade; *Ladies' Museum*, December 1831 [see also *coutil de soie*]

corded gingham – Morning dresses are of a very pretty novelty, called corded gingham; and this material, at present, is preferred for *déjeûné* costume to either white cambric or chintz. They are most admired when of pink; and the corded stripes are placed so close together, that the dress appears as though it were all of one colour, while the very small portion of white gives to it a most soft and delicate shade. *La Belle Assemblée*, November 1828 [see *gingham*]

corded long cloth – Sarsnet dresses make like plain frocks, and cambrics, or corded long cloth, a new Oriental article, are much worn in half dress. *Ladies' Monthly Museum*, August 1821

corded muslin – Rather a novel article has appeared for morning dresses; a corded muslin, the cord about the size of fine twine; *La Belle Assemblée*, April 1810 ~~~ [Paris] The undress of a modish *belle* is now composed entirely of English manufacture: plain jaconot, or striped or corded muslin, has superseded, in a great measure, Scots or English cambric. *Repository of Arts*, July 1816 ~~~ [ad] corded muslins, 4s. per yard; *Colonial Times*, March 31, 1826 [see *muslin*]

cordeline – Cordeline, *sf. list of a silk stuff* Stone's French Dictionary, 1823 ~~~ [Paris] Redingotte of a new silk, called *cordeline*. *Lady's Magazine and Museum*, June 1835 ~~~ Although silk bonnets are fashionable, that is to say those of *pou de soie, cordeline*, and *gros de Naples*, *Court Magazine*, July 1835

cordonnet – [see *twist*]

cordovan – But the unpromising appearance of the weather did not dismay either the real or *would be* sportsmen; … an incredible number of horsemen, among whom were many cockney nimrods, in smart frocks, cordovan boots, and long-necked spurs, each capering his hack Bucephalus, to attract the attention of those they passed. *Sporting Magazine*, April 1795 ~~~ Half boots, up to the knee, made of cordovan leather, which draw on by means of hooks, are worn by many females of dashing ton. *Lady's Magazine*, December 1800 ~~~ About six and thirty years ago, boots were then beginning to be fashionable, … After trying a number of experiments on various kinds of leather, they at last hit upon a prohibited article which was of very little value at that time, but it fully answered their most sanguine wishes, viz. horse-hides. There was at that time a law against making boots and shoes of horse-leather; but a. few years ago it was repealed. Perhaps that law was proper at the time it was made, but the great improvement in the art of tanning has made it proper also to be repealed. Now, to evade this law, that stood in their way, was their next consideration. They at last resolved to give it the name of *Cordovan*, from Cordova in Spain, a town famous for making leather of goat-skins, which we in this country call Spanish leather. This said Cordovan leather was manufactured by Mr. Fell, in such an ingenious way, that the small of the boot-leg was elastic, and fitted close to the leg like the stocking, that in a very little tune they were so highly esteemed, and became so fashionable, that every jemmy gentleman was unhappy until be got up to his knees in Cordovan boots. That capricious dame, Fashion, has long since discarded her then-favourite Cordovan, and has now taken the clumsy hessian into her good graces. *Monthly Magazine*, March 1813 ~~~ There is also a leather called Cordovan leather, or vulgarly Spanish leather, which differs only from the Morocco in its being dressed with bark; the other being prepared with sumac and gall, and they are both made of buck and goat skins. County and City of Cork, 1815 ~~~ The usual legal appellation of *Cordwainer* is derived from *Cordovan*, a peculiar kind of leather, originally made of goat skins at *Cordova* in Spain; but all leather made of horse-hides and curried is at present so called. *Gentleman's Magazine*, supplement 1818 ~~~ CORDOVAN. A sort of leather made of goat skin at Cordova in Spain. Dictionary of General Knowledge, 1833

cords – Patents for New Inventions. … To George Tennant, of Great Ormond-street, in the county of Middlesex, gent., and Alexander Galloway, of Holborn, in the same county, machinist, for a machine or machines for cutting all sorts of fustians usually denominated constitution cord, tabby cord, shaft cord, thickset, tabby velveteen, Genoa velveteen, velveret, and every other species of fustian, velveret, and velveteen, also velvet, plush, and other cloths or goods made of cotton, silk, woollen, or any mixture thereof, usually cut in the manufacture of such articles. June 14. *Philosophical Magazine*, August 1808 ~~~ Patent cords, toilinets, and other woollen goods mixed with thread and other yarn, New Annual Register, 1825

corduroy – He has corduroy breeches; *Scots Magazine*, June 1796 ~~~ I shall now proceed to the display of some minutiæ regarding the out-fit of a gentleman about to embark in a chartered ship; … For wear on board-ship, nothing can equal pantaloons, of which two pairs of thick, and two of thin, should be provided; together with as many pairs of wove cotton long-drawers, to wear under them. The thick kinds may be milled broad cloth, or wove worsted; the thin ones of light corderoy, aleppine, &c. *East India Vade-Mecum*, 1810 ~~~ Corduroy, or *cord du Roi*, (in English king's cord), was originally a manufacture of silk, but is now imitated in cotton; from its name it will easily be recognised to be of French invention. The manufacture is now extended over many parts of Europe; and in England, it is carried on to a great extent in the north western counties of Lancashire, Cheshire, and some parts of Yorkshire. There are several varieties of this article, all in imitation of French or Italian patterns. Encyclopædia Perthensis, 1816 ~~~ corduroy, or king's cord, is merely striped velvet. Dictionary of Mechanical Science, 1829 ~~~ *List of prices paid by the clothiers of Baltimore for work performed for them by the seamstresses.* … Corduroy do. [ditto: pantaloons] 10 cents *Niles' Weekly Register*, October 31, 1835 ~~~ *Apparatus for cutting the Pile or Cords of Fustians, Velveteens, Corduroys, etc.* … Eight-shaft cord, vulgarly called corduroy. … Eight-shaft can be made at prices from 6*d* a-yard to 20*d*. The stuff is 18 inches wide when finished. If they be 27 inches wide, their price is from 13*d*. to 2*s*. 6*d*. Cotton Manufacture of Great Britain, 1836 [see also *fustian*]

Corinthian – For half dress we cannot forbear calling the attention of our fashionable readers to the new trimming lately invented, and which we first saw at the Repository, in St. James's-street, of the *Marchande de Modes* to her Royal Highness the Duchess of Kent: it is called the Corinthian trimming, and is chiefly used for ornamenting the borders of dresses, as flounces, &c. It is of fine clear lawn or Bengal muslin, and is finished by scallops of a light, novel, and elegant kind of work; not so heavy as embroidery, but which affords equal diversity of effect. *La Belle Assemblée*, February 1819

cork – Cork is the exterior bark of a tree belonging to the genus of the oak, which grows wild in the southern parts of Europe, particularly France, Spain, Portugal, and Tuscany. ... A third use of cork, among the Romans, was its being made into soles, which were put into their shoes, in order to secure the feet from water, especially in winter; *Weekly Magazine*, May 26, 1798 ~~~ Head-dress, a hat composed of cork, cut in a new manner; it is intermixed with green satin, and lined with the same material: ... a beautiful plume of feathers, to correspond in colour with the cork: *Repository of Arts*, May 1819 ~~~ [Paris] a new sort of clogs, which reflect much credit on the inventor. The soles are of cork, and arc at once light, and impenetrable to the wet; *La Belle Assemblée*, February 1826

Cosmo gauze – The most favourite evening dress is the Austrian bridal robe of Cosmo gauze; this to be properly appreciated must be seen, description cannot do it justice; the front of it is peculiarly beautiful, for while it modestly conceals it heightens female attractions; and the superb richness of the flounces, and their exquisite lightness combined, render it one of the most unique habiliments ever produced for a youthful and royal bride. ... Cosmo gauze and satin are reckoned most elegant for evening. *La Belle Assemblée*, October 1816 ~~~ for evening dress velvets, French silks, particularly the rich levantine, are most in requisition for the matron ladies, while the younger sport the Cosmo gauze, *La Belle Assemblée*, November 1816

cossae – The Bengal ships, with two from Columbo, brought the following cargoes: ... Cossaes. *Monthly Magazine*, October 1798 ~~~ Indian words imported with the goods, just as we now use *jaconet, cossae, mul-mul* for denominations of Indian fabrics. Annals of Commerce, 1805 ~~~ Cotton goods are divided into 7 different classes, each proportionally lighter the than other. The heaviest of these are, 1st. *Shirtings*, 2d. *Cambrics*, 3d. *Cossas*, New Encyclopædia, 1807 ~~~ Cossae is a term applied to a species of cotton cloth, like most others originally imported from India, and differs to very little from calico in almost any particular, ... The cossae is generally finer than the calico, and like it, is chiefly used for the purpose of printing. It is rather lighter in the fabric, forming a kind of intermediate texture between that and the jacconott. Edinburgh Encyclopædia, 1830

cote pali – Dresses of *côte-pali*, with shaded lines, are still in vogue; the prettiest are of vine-lees and rose-colour, yellow and brown. *Ladies' Monthly Museum*, July 1826 ~~~ That cool material, *cot-pali*, was in high favour for almost every style of dress. Some dresses made of this article have very broad stripes, *La Belle Assemblée*, [review of the last six months] 1828 ~~~ "You'll dirty my cote-pali merino," Almack's Revisited, 1828 ~~~ Other evening dresses are of spotted cot-pali, and some of white gauze, *Ladies' Monthly Museum*, August 1828 ~~~ Morning Dress. Dress of *cottà pali, oiseau de Paradis* colour. *Repository of Fashions*, May 1829 ~~~ [Paris] a high dress, or a spring pelisse; the first is compose of silk, or of some of the numerous light materials manufactured of silk and cotton, which have been, during some years, in favour with the Parisian belles, such as *Cotpalis, palmyriennes*, &c. *Ladies' Museum*, May 1830

cottage straw – Dr Hodgson also informed Townsend of the robberies that were continually committed in the church; in consequence of which Townsend went to the church yesterday morning, and as soon as he entered it, he observed in the aisle Mary Blakeman, *alias* Hills, a well known female pickpocket, genteelly dressed in a black velvet pelisse and a cottage straw bonnet. She is celebrated for robbing females. *Edinburgh Annual Register*, April 6, 1810 ~~~ Riding dress. ... Bee-hive hat of fine moss or cottage straw; *Edinburgh Annual Register*, December 2, 1811 ~~~ Leghorn, fine Dunstable, and the coarse, rustic cottage straw, are the materials for sea-side morning bonnets, and rural retired walks. *La Belle Assemblée*, August 1828

cotton – Cotton is separated from the seeds of the plant by a mill, and then spun and prepared for all sorts of fine works, as stockings, waistcoats, quilts, tapestry, curtains, &c. With it they likewise make muslin; and sometimes it is mixed with wool, sometimes with silk, and even with gold itself. ... Of cotton-thread, that of Damas, called *cotton d'ounce*, and the of Jerusalem, called *bazas*, are the most esteemed; as also that of the West India islands. Encyclopædia Britannica, 1797 ~~~ *The clothing given yearly to the children* [in the charity school] *is as follows*: ... Girls. A grey linen shift, with white linen sleeves, a linsey-woolsey petticoat, an olive coloured twilled cotton gown, a check apron. ... The twilled cotton was chosen for gowns after the following experiment was made: In the year 1794, four gowns were made up for four children of the same size, and at the same time. One of green camblet, one of plain blue linsey-woolsey, one of brown-and-white crape stuff, and one of olive coloured twilled cotton. Those gowns were very nearly the same price. At the expiration of three months from the time they were given, the three first were broken, and the cotton was not; but since that time this article has risen in price about one-third; and perhaps on that account another may be adopted. Reports ... for Promoting the Comforts of the Poor, 1800 ~~~ The fabrics made from cotton are probably more various and numerous than from any other material. They comprehend stuffs of all degrees of fineness, from the transparent muslin of a robe or a turban, to the thick, plush and warm bed-quilt. The commerce of Great Britain has of late years been peculiarly indebted to the cotton manufactory, which produces cloathing for people of all ranks, from Russia to Guinea, and unites elegance with cheapness in an unrivalled degree. Arts of Life, 1802 ~~~ Neither was a handsome cotton gown attainable by women in humble circumstances; and thence the cottons were mixed with linen yarn to reduce their price. But now cotton yarn is cheaper than linen yarn; and cotton goods are very much used in place of cambrics, lawns, and other expensive fabrics of flax; and they have almost totally superseded the silks. Women of all ranks, from the highest to the lowest, are clothed in British manufactures of cotton, from the muslin cap on the crown of the head to the cotton stocking under the sole of the foot. The ingenuity of the calico-printers has kept pace with the ingenuity of the weavers and others concerned in the preceding stages of the manufacture, and produced patterns of printed goods, which for elegance of drawing exceed every thing that ever was imported, and for durability of colour generally stand the washing so well, as to appear fresh and new every time they are washed, and give an air of neatness and cleanliness to the wearer beyond the elegance of silk in the first freshness of its transitory lustre. But even the most elegant prints are excelled by the superior beauty and virgin purity of the muslins, the growth and the manufacture of the British dominions. With the gentlemen cotton stuffs for waistcoats have almost superseded woollen cloths, and silk stuffs, I believe entirely and they have the advantage, like the ladies' gowns, of having a new and fresh appearance every time they are washed. Cotton stockings have also become very general for summer wear, and have gained ground very-much upon silk stockings, which are too thin for our climate, and too expensive for common wear for people of middling circumstances. Annals of Commerce, 1805 ~~~ Cotton goods are divided into seven different classes, each proportionally lighter than the other. The heaviest of these are, 1st, *Shirtings*; 2d, *Cambrics*; 3d, Cossaes; 4th, *Jaconets*; 5th, *Lawn grounds*; 6th, *Mulls*; 7th, *Books*. New Encyclopædia, 1807 ~~~ About the year 1769, cotton was introduced into Scotland as a material for the fabrication of cloth. It was used at first as woof only, the warp being linen yarn. The fabrics thus produced were stout chequered and striped goods, and also plain cloth, which was either printed or dyed. General Report of the Agricultural State ... of Scotland, 1814 ~~~ *Cotton* has been spun of so neat and fine a texture, that the use of it, even in the making of bone-lace, has completely, in England, superseded the use of flax; and great quantities of cotton finely spun, are exported continually for the making of lace abroad, although we are not prepared to say that, on the Continent, cotton has wholly superseded the use of flax, Book of English Trades, 1818 ~~~ The spinning of cotton was once a very tedious process; one thread at a time, by a pair of hands, could make but little progress. This spinning is also now performed by machinery, in a manner most ingenious, and, to those unaccustomed to it, very surprising. That the pliant fingers should be superseded, and excelled by a pair of rollers whirled round by a steam-engine, a body of water, or any other inanimate power, seems to be an astonishing effort of art. Yet such is the case, and a thread much more thin, even, and strong, is the result. The credit of inventing this wonderful mode of operation is due to Mr., afterwards Sir Richard, Arkwright. Book of Commerce by Sea and Land, 1834 ~~~ Cotton may be considered as an intermediate substance between animal wool and linen; it increases warmth and perspiration, imbibes and retains the perspired humors, to the injury of the wearer, and, like wool, readily attracts infectious matter. The Toilette of Health, Beauty, and Fashion, 1834

cotton flannel – [see *domet*]

cotton lace – [see *bone lace* and *bobbin-net*]

cotton of Siam – [see *Siam*]

cotton straw – [Paris] straw hats, for the promenade, with the newly fabricated cotton straw and Leghorn, and fancy straw, are very prevalent. *La Belle Assemblée*, June 1818 ~~~ With respect to bonnets, nothing appears likely to be so fashionable during the remainder of the mourning as the British Leghorn; which, by the bye, was a French invention, and is still worn in Paris under the name of *la paille-coton*: it is cotton plaited to imitate straw, and as the plaits are extremely fine, it really has a great resemblance to Leghorn: it is, however, much more calculated for summer than winter wear, and will very probably be generally adopted towards the end of the spring. *Repository of Arts*, January 1819 ~~~ [Paris] The cotton hats, in imitation of straw, are no longer white, but of various colours. *La Belle Assemblée*, August 1819 ~~~ The materials for *chapeaux* are, white straw, *gros de Naples*, Leghorn, gauze, *paille de soie*, and *paille de coton*: this last is now always worn in straw-colour, in which it looks so like Leghorn, that it can scarcely be distinguished from it. *Repository of Arts*, August 1819 ~~~ [Paris] the most prevailing hat was of cotton straw, ornamented with foliage of black crape; *Ladies' Monthly Museum*, October 1821 ~~~ [Paris] Leghorn, rice straw, and cotton straw, are all worn for walking bonnets and hats. *Ladies' Museum*, August 1830

cotton thread – [Newark, in Nottinghamshire] The cotton manufacture is the principal business of consequence carried on in this parish: a mill, for making cotton-thread for stockings, employs about 300 hands; chiefly women and children: they earn, at present, from 1s. to 5s. a week. State of the Poor, 1797 ~~~ [in South Carolina] We have obtained and possess the common hand spinning jenny, which makes by one person, male or female, from 40 to 120 cotton threads at one time; also the carding machine to go by hand, horse, ox, or water; also the roving machine, to reduce cotton wool into ropes or yards of the size of a goose quill ; also the mule, spinning by hand 120 fine threads; also the water-spinning machinery of Arkwright, to spin perpetually at any mill seat. We also possess the machinery for doubling and twisting thread, for hosiery, and the British and German stocking-weaver's looms, for making every article of hosiery, from feel-socks to pantaloons. Cobbett's Annual Register, 1803 ~~~ *British cotton manufactures* – We lately gave an account, from authentic documents, of the woollen manufactures carried on in Great Britain. From the same source, we have ascertained that about 240,000 hands, or persons, chiefly children, are employed in the spinning of cotton thread. These manufacture as much thread, by the power of water and steam, and the application of the new improved machinery, as could have been done by 28 millions eight hundred thousand persons, by the finger only. *Niles' Weekly Register*, November 8, 1823 ~~~ Cotton thread for sewing has been brought to great perfection, so as almost to supersede that made of flax. It was formerly sold in skeins, but great quantities are now disposed of already wound, upon small wooden spools. These being wound by machinery are afforded about as cheap as the skeins, and save much trouble. Book of Commerce by Sea and Land, 1834

cotton velvet – [in Whithorn] The modes of clothing and living were in proportion, and consisted of the poorest fare and coarsest apparel: Now they live as well as any in Great Britain of their rank. The men are clothed, sometimes with homespun, but more commonly with Yorkshire narrows, cotton velvets, and corderoys. The women appear in printed linens, cottons and muslins. Here I speak of men and women of the lowest ranks in life; servants, cottagers, and mechanics. Statistical Account of Scotland, 1795 ~~~ The French papers state, that the English goods already seized in Paris only, are in value upwards of three millions. The following articles are subject to arbitrary decree: 1. All kinds of cotton velvet; *European Magazine*, January 1798 ~~~ Cotton velvets were first made [in England] by Jeremiah Clarke in 1756; Beauties of England and Wales, 1807 ~~~ It is an instructive fact, that the woollen manufactures of Great-Britain have been steadily computed at a little more than sixteen millions sterling per annum, for the whole period between the peace of 1783, and the beginning of the present war in the year 1803. – The weight of the wool annually consumed there, varies little from the weight of our whole *surplus* cotton, as exported in the greatest year. If our cotton shall be impeded by the belligerents in its way to foreign markets, we must and shall manufacture many cotton goods, so as to rival foreign woollens. The American will not be uncomfortable in his own cotton velvets, velverets, corduroys, swanskins, and cotton blankets. <u>Archives of Useful Knowledge</u>, 1811 ~~~ [novel] "Another breadth or two would make it full enough, and cotton velvet will do, and come cheap," said Mrs. Falconer. "Cotton velvet!" cried Miss Georgiana, " I would not wear cotton velvet like the odious, shabby Miss Chattertons, who are infamous for it." <u>Patronage</u>, 1814 ~~~ Some ladies have taken it into their heads to patronize cotton velvet, because not of home manufacture; *La Belle Assemblée*, January 1816 [see also *Manchester*, *velveret* and *velveteen*]

cottons – [see *Kendal cottons*]

coutil – Coutil, or Coutis, (cou-ti) m. *tick, canvass-ticking, tent-cloth*. … Coutil, *ticking, ticken*. <u>Dufief's French Dictionary</u>, 1810 ~~~ Men of fashion not longer hunt in leather gaiters; they now have *pantalons ecru* in double twilled *coutil*; *Casket*, January 1831 ~~~ Coutils (German flax) *Public Documents*, March 1832 [see *ticking*]

coutil de soie – *Redingotes* composed of *coutil de soie*, of a rich winter colour, as bottle green, chesnut, or beet red, are also in favour in promenade dress. *La Belle Assemblée*, January 1831 ~~~ Make and Materials of Out-Door Costume. … Others [mantles] are of *coutil de soie*, lined and trimmed with *peluche* of a strongly contrasted colour, as ponceau for dark green, azure for *avanturine*, &c. &c. *Day*, February 6, 1832 [see also *contil de soie*]

crape – [court dress] Petticoat in blue crape, with squares of silver lamé; train of blue crape and silver; *Lady's Magazine*, June 1797 ~~~ Crapes are either craped, *i.e.* crisped, or smooth; the first double, expressing a closer mourning; the latter single, used for that less deep. Note, White is reserved for young people, or those devoted to virginity. The silk destined for the first is more twisted than the second; it being the greater or less degree of twisting, especially of the warp, which produces the crisping given it when taken out of the loom, steeped in clear water, and rubbed with a piece of wax for the purpose. Crapes are all dyed raw. <u>Encyclopædia Britannica</u>, 1797 ~~~ The greater part of the combing wool is consumed in worsted for making what is called new drapery in the Book of Rates, viz. … worsted crapes, from 7d. to 9d. per yard. <u>Origin of Commerce</u>, 1801 ~~~ *Crape* is a very light transparent stuff, in some respects like gauze; but it is made of raw silk, gummed and twisted on the mill, and woven without crossing. It is used for mourning, and is a very fashionable article in court dresses. Crapes used for mourning are either *crisped* or *smooth*: the first is *double,* and denotes the deeper mourning; the *single* or smooth crape is for the slighter. Crapes are of different colours, but the silk is always dyed in its raw state. The chief manufacture for this article of dress is at Lyons, but a great deal is made in various parts of this kingdom. Crapes when made into court dresses are ornamented in a thousand different ways: sometimes as caps, or turbans, they are ornamented with *spangles, artificial flowers,* and with *diamonds.* <u>Book of Trades</u>, 1806 ~~~ At a meeting of the gentleman of the bar of the state of Delaware, attending the high court of errors and appeals, it was unanimously recommended that, in testimony of their great respect for the memory of their late friend, to wear crape on their left arm for the space of thirty days. *Niles' Weekly Register*, August 19, 1815 ~~~ [Paris] Crape is a good deal used for grand costume, as is also silver gauze; both are worn over white satin. *Repository of Arts,* July 1820 ~~~ *Recent Patents. To* John Francis, *of the City of Norwich, Shawl and Bombazine Manufacturer, for Improvements in the Process of making or manufacturing a certain Article or Fabric, composed of Silk and Worsted, for useful Purposes.* [Sealed 12th April, 1823.] The article or fabric alluded to in the above ambiguous title is crape, and the proposed improvements seem to be rather in the introduction of some novel feature in that article, than in an improved process of manufacture. The patentee proposes to make crape with satin stripes, or satin figures raised above the surface, and this is said to be done by "forming in the ground a *Tammit work,* with or without a figure," or it may be done by a *twill*. <u>London Journal of Arts and Sciences</u>, 1824 ~~~ [ad, June 1823] 16-inch black crape, 5s. per yard; yard wide ditto ditto, 10s. 6d. per yard; <u>British Settlements in Australasia</u>, 1824 ~~~ A fashion, altogether new, has been adopted in the last days of March; it is to line crape dresses with another under crape of a different colour; as rose-coloured crape under white, white under rose, blue over white, likewise a delicate purple pink over white crape. No one that has not seen the effect can imagine how delicately soft these dresses appear, they are made exceedingly full, and worn over stiffened petticoats, and trimmed simply. *Lady's Magazine*, March 1830 ~~~ [mourning for George IV.] Evening Dress. A black crape dress over a black gros de Naples slip; *Ladies' Museum,* July 1830 ~~~ When three, four, or more sets of gauze mounting are thus employed to form figures of plain on a gauze ground, such patterns have assumed the name of crapes, although the crapes which are manufactured for mournings are of the plain texture, and the crisped appearance is given them in the process of dressing, after they are out of the loom. Art of Weaving, 1831 ~~~ Crape is a light and transparent article of plain weaving; it is nude with hard silk of the natural color, and the peculiar appearance which it is made to put on is given to it in the operations of dying and dressing after it quits the loom; a further quantity of *gum* being then added to the silk, the threads are impelled, by the stiffness thus acquired, to unwreathe the twist which had been given to them in the mill, and hence the apparent irregularity of texture assumed by crape. This may be easily proved by washing it in water hot enough to discharge the gum; the fabric will then assume an appearance very similar to that of gauze. The warp of crape is usually composed of singles; the shoot is frequently formed of the same material; and sometimes, when it is wished to make it of closer texture, of two-thread tram, the two threads, by partially untwisting, then give a more crinkled and intricate appearance to the cloth. Silk Manufacture, 1832 ~~~ *Crape* is also made of raw silk; it is woven without crossing, and is highly stiffened with wax and gum. Having a peculiarly dull appearance, it is appropriated to mourning. Book of Commerce by Sea and Land, 1834 ~~~ That elegant light summer dress is of *crape,* an article made of raw silk, in the chain manner, and highly stiffened with wax and gum. It is either figured or plain, and much in use for various purposes, as for shawls, scarfs, neckerchiefs, &c. When dyed black, it has a peculiarly dull appearance, and is used for bonnets, hatbands, and other appendages to mourning. A fabric of this sort, called *China crape,* because introduced to us from China, constitutes a beautiful article for summer wear, either in shawls or dresses. Norwich is the chief place of this manufacture. Scenes of Commerce, 1836 ~~~ Crape de Lyons, silk and worsted, Jones's Digest, 1836 [see also *crepe*]

crape aerophane – [see *aerophane*]

crape blond – The most approved ball dresses are robes of … *crape blonde,* worked like *tulle.* All these transparent dresses should be worn over slips of the richest white satin. *Court Journal,* January 17, 1835

crape lamé – [court dress] A superb petticoat of yellow crape lamé, *Lady's Magazine,* June 1797 [see also *lamé*]

crash – A coarse sort of narrow Russia Linen, not exceeding 22 ½ inches in breadth, commonly called Crash, and generally used as Towelling only, Practice of the Customs, 1812 ~~~ [ad] Dry Goods at Reduced Prices. … 5 bales Russia Crash, *New England Farmer,* July 1, 1835

creas – Creas, are made in Saxony and Bohemia, and likewise attempted in Silesia; they are 1 5/8, 1 1/2, 1 1/4, and 1 1/8 Leipsic ells wide, and each piece contains 108 ells in length. The yarn of this linen is made, is bleached before it is woven. The assortments are chiefly the following: 1. Those which are 1 1/8 ell wide, are called in Italy, tele corame 7/4; and in England dowlas of 32 inches; and these two countries are the chief markets for it; but considerable exportations of this sort are made from Hamburg, Lubec, and Bremen, direct to America, and to the West Indies, where this sort of linen meets with quick and advantageous sales. 2. Those of 1 1/2 ell wide, are called in Spain, creas anehas; and in France, créas larges; they are distinguished according to their quality in density and fineness, as well as to the countries to which the different sorts of them are mostly exported. The common kind, called sleeked dowlas, is but ill adapted for the Spanish trade, and the lowest in quality; yet, on account of their fine weft, are finer than the rest. The middling quality is only adapted for the Italian trade. English sleeked dowlas, are of a dense quality; and loom dowlas is an uncommon fine and dense kind of linen. These two sorts are only woven of the best Meissen, Brunswick, and Halberstadt yarn, and solely destined for the English market. 3. Those that are 1 1/8 ell and 1 1/2 ell in width, are of the same quality. The chief markets for this sort of linen, are the upper parts of Italy and Spain; yet it is likewise sent in considerable quantities to Barbary, and in particular to Algiers and Tunis, by the way of Leghorn, where it is principally used as winding sheets for the dead. 4. Dowlas 3/4, as they are called in England,, is the fourth sort of creas 1 1/4 ell wide; they bear the same distinction with those of 1 1/2 ell wide, and both sorts are in pieces of an equal length, except that this sort is commonly made up in half pieces. The creas derive the name of morlaix from the city of Morlaix, in Bretagne. To these creas belong likewise the rough dowlas, from 1 1/4 to 1 1/2 ell wide, and 108 Leipsic ells in length, which only differ from the common sort of creas, by being woven of raw yarn. They are mostly exported to Portugal, where they are called Pano Ferro. European Commerce, 1805 ~~~ *Selection of a Cargo suited, on a general scale, for the Spanish Settlements in America,* ... Linens, folded and marked as Creas a la Morlaix. Present State of the Spanish Colonies, 1810

crebe – [see *grebe*]

crepe – [French = crêpe, English = crape, but often used interchangeably. See also *crape*]

crepe aerienne – [see *aerienne*]

crepe Aerophane – [see *aerophane*]

crepe brillante – [see *brillante*]

crepe Dauphine – [see *Dauphine*]

crepe de bareges – [see *barege*]

crepe de Borege – The material at present most in favour for dinner dress is *crepe de Borege*: it is a plaid gauze of a very coarse worsted kind, and the most glaring vulgar-looking thing I ever saw: however, it is at present very much the fashion. Some dresses of it have appeared within the last few days, which are striped instead of plaided; these do not look so bad, because the colours are not so *outré*: the ground is white, and the stripes are rose colour, lilac, and blue; they are ways trimmed with flounces of the same material, the stripes of which are placed in an opposite direction to those of the robe. *Repository of Arts*, July 1821 [probably *barege*]

crepe de Lyon – [Paris] They [shawls] are mostly of a light description, such as *barges*, China crape, or *crepe de Lyon*; *Ladies' Pocket*, August 1830 ~~~ *crepe de Lyon*, (this last is an imitation, and a very good one, of China crape); *Ladies' Museum*, June 1832

crepe de Merino – [see *Merino crape*]

crepe lisse – Crêpe lisse, *tiffany*. Dufief's French Dictionary, 1810 ~~~ Ball Dress. White *crêpe lisse* dress, worn over a bright pink satin slip; *Repository of Arts*, January 1823 ~~~ [Paris] Evening dresses are now generally of gauze *crêpe lisse*, or *tulle*, over white satin; *Ladies' Monthly Museum*, March 1825 ~~~ Crepe-lisse must be washed in the same way [as blond lace], after which it must be dipped into a starch prepared thus – to two table spoonfuls of starch boiled in the common way, add a very small bit of lump sugar, and stir it till it is dissolved, then take one table spoonful of unmade starch, well worked, so as to have a perfectly smooth surface, and beat it in that state when ready to be thinned for boiling, then beat it very well with the made starch before the crepe-lisse is put through it: when taken out it must be well clapped, and pinned straight upon a frame or a bed. *New England Farmer*, August 11, 1826 ~~~ At evening parties, ladies wear dresses of beautifully striped *crêpe-lisse*, *Lady's Magazine*, May 1829 ~~~ long white sleeves of white *crêpe lisse* (we give the French name, because it is known by no other), *Maids, Wives, and Widows*, December 1, 1832 ~~~ Long sleeves of *crêpe lisse*, *Royal Lady's Magazine*, February 1833 [see *tiffany*]

crepe velours – and some [ball dresses] of a very superb description, are of a new material, *crêpe velours*, worked round the border in light wreaths of flowers, intermixed with ears of corn. *Court Magazine*, December 1835

crepon – Crépon (kre-pon) m. *a very thick woollen stuff that looks like crape*. Dufief's French Dictionary, 1810 ~~~ [court dress] A robe of crepon d'Indostan, in an oriental pattern of gold and green, trimmed with blonde; *Court Journal*, June 1, 1833

crescent gauze – In the month of *August* [1822], ... Turbans of crescent gauze, or of gold moss gauze, confined their tresses, and white lace dresses, with a drapery of crescent gauze, formed a chaste and elegant evening costume. Museum of Foreign Literature, 1823

cretonne – *a sort of linen cloth* Dufief's French Dictionary, 1810 ~~~ *Cretonne*, a kind of mixed cloth of hemp and linen, made in Normandy – the chain of hemp and the woof of linen. System of Universal Geography, 1834

crewel – A kind of worsted yarn, yarn twisted and wound on a ball. Ash's English Dictionary, 1795 ~~~ [1794] What Sort of Articles in the Woollen Manufactory must necessarily be made of Combing Wool? ... Worsted Crewels, Journals of the House of Commons, 1803 ~~~ Waistcoats; *viz*. ... wrought with crewel, <u>Dictionary of Commerce</u>, 1810 ~~~ [Paris] Blouses are still in fashion; … these dresses are of clear muslin, embroidered between broad tucks, with coloured crewel: the patterns represent various summer flowers. *Ladies' Monthly Museum*, July 1824 ~~~ Organdy dresses promise to be ad much in favour as they were last summer: some have appeared beautifully embroidered in different colours, in crewel. *La Belle Assemblée*, June 1826

crewel ribbon – [see *caddas*]

crimped satin – A new satin has lately been introduced which has the appearance of being crimped small, or ribbed, this has a very pleasing effect when made up into bonnets, and is of the newest invention. *La Belle Assemblée*, April 1811 ~~~ headed with a row of crimped satin, formed into Spanish puffs. *Ladies' Monthly Museum*, February 1818 ~~~ Besides watered *gros de Naples*, and crimped satin, which are very much in favour for carriage bonnets, <u>Ladies' Museum</u>, August 1831

crin – Crin, *horse-hair* <u>Dufief's French Dictionary</u>, 1810 ~~~ Ribands are expected to be profusely employed in every department of the toilette in which they can be used, and some very beautiful new ones have just appeared. … One that is likely to be extremely fashionable is the *gase crin*. It is half horse-hair and half silk, and is beautifully shaded. *Court Magazine*, October 1835

crinoline – [Paris] *Crinoline*, a material fabricated from horse-hair, is much used in the country for bonnets; these bonnets are grey, or a shade of yellow. *Ladies' Museum*, September 1829 ~~~ A new material has just been introduced for *capotes*, which promises to be a favourite: it is called *crinoline*, from *crin*, horse-hair; it is a fine clear stuff, not unlike in appearance to leno, but of a very string and durable description: it is made in different colours; grey, and the colour of unbleached cambric, are most in favour. *Repository of Fashions*, September 1829 ~~~ *Bottines* [shoes] of *crinoline*, the upper part grey, the lower black. *La Belle Assemblée*, August 1830 ~~~ [men's] Pantaloons composed of *crinoline*, whether green, granite, or *ecru*, are also in request. This material is much admired for its freshness and firmness. *Casket*, January 1831 [see also *horse hair*]

cruel ribbon – [see *caddas*]

crystal – [Spain] Cristal, a shining woollen stuff, also called gauze, plain, striped or printed, up to 1 1/8 yard wide <u>Digest of the Commercial Regulations</u>, 1824 ~~~ A very fine wide Durant, termed Crystal, (Spanish *crystalla*, transparent,) is exported, always white, for Nuns' Veils. <u>Analytical Dictionary</u>, 1830 ~~~ [court dress] Rich white satin dress, double flounce of queen's blonde, headed with a plat of silver crystal; *Royal Lady's*, May 1831 ~~~ Ball Dress. – It is composed of christal gauze, a very clear but rich material, over rose-coloured sarsnet. *Maids, Wives, and Widows*, January 12, 1833 ~~~ On the paille de riz, the ribbons are what are called crystal ribbons, a smooth shining gauze ribbon. *Lady's Magazine and Museum*, July 1834 ~~~ [Paris] The ribbons are satin, sarcenet, and rich crystal ribbons broché in flowers. *Lady's Magazine*, May 1835 ~~~ [Paris] These hats are ornamented with flowers, and trimmed with Foulard or crystal ribbons, pink, light green, paille, or lilac. *Lady's Magazine*, June 1835

crystallized velvet – In *November* [1822], there are, however, some new invented materials this month, for hat and turbans, likely to meet with much encouragement, namely, Irish velvet, crystallized velvet, and Baltic moss. <u>Museum of Foreign Literature</u>, 1823 ~~~ For evening full-dress, nothing is thought more elegant than the Ottoman turban; the front is of basketwork, formed of white satin, and white crystallized velvet, or else of silver lace: *La Belle Assemblée*, January 1823

cubica – [see *shalloon*]

Cupid's net – [ad] coloured Silk Figured Netts: among which is the Cupid's Nett, which are very elegant for Dresses; *La Belle Assemblée*, January 1808

Cupid's wings – The trimmings consist of satin cut in leaves, curled plush, in the form of Cupid's wings, ribbons and flowers. *La Belle Assemblée*, December 1820 ~~~ A black velvet bonnet, lined with that sort of silk plush which the French call Cupid's wings; the ground is rose colour; the long curled silk which forms the pile is of lavender. *Gazette of Fashion*, February 2, 1822 ~~~ A carriage bonnet of white satin is the favorite; it is trimmed at the edge with that beautiful gossamer plumage, called Cupid's wings. *Ladies' Monthly Museum*, March 1822

curled silk – CRESPINO, s.f. a sort of coif or head-dress made of curled silk; <u>Baretti's Spanish Dictionary</u>,

1800 ~~~ another fabrication from the same inventress, of real British manufacture, the curled silk for bonnets; … Bonnets are worn very large, of various materials, but the most elegant are those made of curled silk, with a bunch of flowers over the left ear. *La Belle Assemblée*, September 1816 ~~~ Evening Dress, for the Opera, Theatre, &c. This dress has been considered by the fashionable world as singularly elegant, and highly attractive. It consists of the Roxburgh mantle, made of a rich and beautiful curled white silk, producing an effect almost, enchanting. Nothing has certainly ever been introduced for mantles equal to it, and if worn by a fascinating lady, a grandeur and importance is given to her figure quite surprising. *Ladies' Monthly Museum*, December 1816 ~~~ [Paris] The materials used for *chapeaux*, are … *pluche bouclée*; this last is a very beautiful material; it is a curled silk *pluche* which has at once a very light and rich effect. *Ladies' Monthly Museum*, January 1821 ~~~ [Paris] White watered *gros de Naples*, figured satin, and *diamantine*, are also in favour in full dress. … The bottom of the skirt is trimmed with a very broad *biais* of curled silk plush; a *rouleau* of the same material edges the *corsage* and the jockeys: *La Belle Assemblée*, December 1830

cut velvet – [court dress] A white satin crape petticoat, elegantly trimmed with crimson *cut velvet*; body and train of crimson velvet to correspond, interwoven with showers of silver spangles. *Lady's Magazine*, January 1807 ~~~ Cut velvet is that whereon the ground is a kind of taffety, or *gros de tours*, and the figures velvet. General Dictionary of Commerce, 1810 ~~~ [Paris] Some hats are made of white silk checquered with green, and these are finished by several bands of green cut velvet round the crown, with a trimming of ribband or blond set round the edge in very large plaits. *La Belle Assemblée*, December 1816 ~~~ spencers of figured or cut velvet are much more general; *La Belle Assemblée*, November 1820 ~~~ [Paris] Hats and bonnets are often made of cut velvet. *La Belle Assemblée*, December 1823 ~~~ ornamented with braiding embroidery, or cut velvet, according to the texture of the dress: *Atkinson's Casket*, March 1835 [see *velours epinglé*]

cuttanees – a species of callico. General Dictionary of Commerce, 1810

cygnet – [Paris] *Cygnet* swan's-down is coming into favour with our belles. *Lady's Magazine and Museum*, December 1834 [see also *swan*]

Cypress cord – Carriage Dress. A dress composed of brown Cypress cord, *Ladies' Monthly Museum*, May 1824

Cypress gauze – [see *cyprus*]

cyprus – Cyprus, a thin stuff or silky gauze Perry's English Dictionary, 1795 ~~~ [sales of] Plain Gauze (or Cyprus) has improven [since last month], and the manufacturers are increasing their hands. Prices of weaving remains steady. *Weavers' Magazine*, May 1819 ~~~ [mourning for the King] Amongst the head-dresses, we remarked a *cornette* for the breakfast table of white cypress gauze, *La Belle Assemblée*, March 1820 ~~~ Cyprus crape is a favourite article for full dress, and hangs on the female form most gracefully; *La Belle Assemblée*, April 1823 ~~~ Morning Dress. High dress of Cyprus crape, of a pale lavender colour, *Repository of Arts*, April 1823 ~~~ Evening dresses are of Cyprus gauze, richly striped with satin. Dresses of this article in pink or amber, are very elegant; *La Belle Assemblée*, November 1823 ~~~ [Paris] Square shawls of Cyprus crape appearing like old-fashioned damask, by their large flowers, are in high estimation for young persons. Some of these are of a deep red, others of very pale colors: *Lady's Magazine*, October 1825 ~~~ [mourning for the Duke of York] Evening dresses of black crape, or Cyprus gauze, are sometimes trimmed with black bugles. *La Belle Assemblée*, February 1827 [In this instance, Cypress might refer to a black color, rather than a type of gauze.] ~~~ Dresses of Cyprus crape, elegantly figured, are a charming article for evening and dress dinner parties; *La Belle Assemblée*, February 1828 ~~~ Dresses of Cyprus crape, of a bright crimson, figured in oriental patterns, are often worn in fire-side costume, *Ladies' Museum*, January 1830 [see also *crape*]

cypress feather – Black velvet *toque* ornamented with jet, and black cypress feathers. … The bonnets are still worn very large; cypress feathers are more worn that we expected. *La Belle Assemblée*, November 1818 ~~~ When they are worn in evening parties the addition of a drooping plume of crimped cypress feathers, renders them a head-dress of the most striking and superb appearance. We first beheld this beautiful plume at the *Magazin de Modes*, in St James's-street (patronized by her Royal Highness the Duchess of Kent), on a newly invented turban cap, formed of fine net, striped gauze, and summer rose-coloured satin: the stem of this feather seems covered with pink, which beautiful colour shoots its roseate hue through the crimped white plumage that trembles over it. *La Belle Assemblée*, August 1819 ~~~ [mourning] The feathers that have appeared in hats are of the weeping-willow kind, which are truly appropriate; to these, according to the manner in which the plumage is drest, the fashion-mongers give the name of Cypress feathers. ... We have seen one carriage hat of white crape, trimmed with black, and ornamented with a long black Cypress feather. *La Belle Assemblée*, February 1827

Dacca - Durant

dacca – [see *Decca*]

Dalmatia – and the new Dalmatia cloth, are the most favoured articles which compose the dinner dresses. *La Belle Assemblée*, October 1816

damaras – Damaras, an Indian taffeta <u>Perry's English Dictionary</u>, 1795

damas – [see *damask*]

damask – a manufacture of linen and silk woven with raised flowers; <u>Royal English Dictionary</u>, 1775 ~~~ Damask, silk or woollen woven into flowers; a red colour <u>Perry's English Dictionary</u>, 1795 ~~~ *Damask patterns* require the boldest stroke of any; the flowers and leaves should always be large, and the small work omitted as much as possible, except it be in the middle of a leaf or a flower. An attempt was made to introduce small flowers for the fashion, and a great number of looms were set to work accordingly; but this fashion was soon over, and the large designs continued in vogue; nor will a damask figure of whimsical fancies be of long continuance. Several attemps [sic] have been made that way, but without success. A bold stroke with the line of beauty, and well shaped stalks, leaves and flowers, natural or imaginary, are the only things a designer has to observe in compleating [sic] a well-designed damask pattern. <u>Laboratory</u>, 1799 ~~~ Damas, *m. damask*. <u>Dufief's French Dictionary</u>, 1810 ~~~ a silk stuff, with a raised pattern, so that the right side of damask is that which has the flowers raised or saturated. Damasks should be of dressed silk, both in warp and woof; and in France, half an ell in breadth: they are made at Chalons, in Champagne, and some places in Flanders, as at Tournay, &c. entirely of wool, 3-8ths. of an ell wide, and 20 ells long. <u>General Dictionary of Commerce</u>, 1810 ~~~ *Damask.* – The first piece seen of this silk was brought from *Damascus,* in Syria, from whence it derived its name. *Ladies' Museum*, July 1829 ~~~ Damasked silks, figured with flowers of various colours, on a ground shot with two colours, are great favourites. They are exceedingly rich, and if chosen tastefully, do not offend the eye by their gaudiness. *Lady's Magazine*, March 1830 ~~~ Figured silks are so much worn that I cannot refrain from again mentioning it to you, although I have done so several times before. Damasks *à grands ramages* are now all the rage. We pay so high as fifty francs an ell for them, for our ancient costumes; and so much has been used that they are now very scarce at Paris. The morning dresses are not subjected to the old fashions of our forefathers; these fashions are confined only to ball and dinner dresses. *Court Magazine*, April 1833 ~~~ Elite of Parisian Fashions. For Morning Costume, the rich damask silks are at present preferred. Every variety of pattern courts attention, but the most *distinguès* are of two colours in relief, or rather, two shades of the same colour, in imitation of the old-fashioned damasks, on a rich stripe, with coloured flowers between; *Casket*, March 1835 ~~~ [Court dress] Orange damask dress, *Lady's Magazine and Museum*, June 1835 ~~~ [court dress] An elegant white crape dress, richly embroidered on soi a bouquets, over a rich while satin slip; corsage of rich pink and while Damas, profusely trimmed with blond: manteau of rich Damas roses and blanc, *Niles' Weekly Register*, July 18, 1835

damask caffart – [see *caffart damask*]

damask satin – [ad] 30 Pieces Plain and Ribbed Damask Satins, (black and drab) being an elegant, durable and fashionable article for Gentlemen's Pantaloons. <u>Boston Annual Advertiser</u>, 1823 ~~~ Some satin damask hats, of lively colours, are lined with velvet, of the same shade as the hat. *La Belle Assemblée*, December 1827 ~~~ Hats of damask satin, a very splendid article, are of jaune-vapeur; *Lady's Magazine*, November 1829 ~~~ Damask satin is a very brilliant and approved article for hats: *La Belle Assemblée*, December 1829 ~~~ The most fashionable materials for cloaks are – ... Satin Damas; also [made of] Cachemere wool and silk: the pattern an exact imitation of the ancient damask. *Lady's Magazine and Museum*, November 1834 ~~~ Tariff. *Of the Duties payable at the time of the passage of the Compromise Act of March 2, 1833.* ~~~ Worsted stuff goods, such as ... Damask Satins, *Examiner*, July 8, 1835 ~~~ [Court dress] Train of jonquil and white damask satin, *Lady's Magazine and Museum*, June 1835

damasse – or *petite venise*, a kind of wrought linen manufactured in Flanders, so called from its being adorned with large flowers or figures, like silken damasks. It is used chiefly for table-cloths, napkins,

&c. There is also a silk stuff so called, which looks like a damask on one side, and on the other is plain. <u>General Dictionary of Commerce</u>, 1810 ~~~ Carriage Dress. Robe of green *satin damassé*, a rich dead ground with satin sprigs highly raised. *Court Magazine*, February 1835 ~~~ [Court dress] White silk damasse, elegantly trimmed with blonde on each side, *Lady's Magazine and Museum*, June 1836

dammiers – [Paris] At the same ball I observed several dresses of gaze *à dammiers* (in squares, like those of a chess-board) in two colour, or two shades of one colour: *Lady's Magazine and Museum*, January 1835

Danae – [Paris] There were also several materials of a very light kind of silk and wool. ... another, called *Danae*, is printed. The patterns of both are new and pretty. ... Turbans are expected to continue in favour in evening dress: two new materials, *tul-Sylphide*, and *tul-Danae* have just appeared for them. *Court Magazine*, May 1836 ~~~ French Opera Dress. Robe of blue *satin Danae*, *New Monthly Belle Assemblée*, November 1836 ~~~ There are also some beautiful materials of silk and Cashmere wool, both for half-dress and *robes habiltées*; the *satin Danaé* and the *tissu d'Issachar* are the most remarkable of the latter. *Court Magazine*, December 1836

Dauphine – [Paris] The gauze of which ball dresses are made is quite a new article, and is styled *crêpe Dauphine*: its texture is like that of the finest crape, and it is crossed by rich broad stripes about an inch distant from each other. Between the stripes are very narrow lines in chequers. *Lady's Magazine*, December 1825

Decca – India muslins, of every description, particularly the fine Decca, are in peculiar favour, *La Belle Assemblée*, April 1812 ~~~ dinner dress ... of fine Decca muslin, striped, *La Belle Assemblée*, September 1818 ~~~ The pelisses are of the thin *decca*, *La Belle Assemblée*, June 1819 ~~~ Dacca, in the eastern quarter of the province of Bengal, has long been celebrated for the manufacture of the finest muslins. <u>Edinburgh Encyclopædia</u>, 1830 ~~~ fine India muslin manufactured at Decca – transparent and soft as the web of the gossamer spider; *Atheneum*, January 21, 1832 [see also *Bengal muslin*]

denim – [Rhode Island] Jeans, fustians, denims, thicksets, velvets, &c. are here manufactured and sent to the southern States. <u>View of the American United States</u>, 1795 ~~~ Many kinds of stuff are called from the towns in which they were first made. Thus, ... at Halifax, Denims (originally De Nismes); *Monthly Magazine*, September 1805 ~~~ [Cincinnati] The products of the loom have not been great; but several handsome pieces of carpeting, diaper, plaid, denim and other cotton fabrics, deserve to be mentioned. *Niles' Weekly Register*, September 15, 1815 ~~~ A *premium of twenty five dollars* for the best piece of denims, manufactured from cotton, to contain not less than 25 yards, to be 1 1-3 yards wide, twilled, stout and thick, and to be deemed sufficiently warm for clothing slaves in the winter. ... The warmth, durability, and cheapness of cotton point it out as an article altogether suitable for the manufacture of blankets, and coarse denims, for clothing not only the slaves of the South, but also that portion of the white population, who, either from economy or patriotism, are disposed to encourage domestic manufactures. *American Farmer*, October 5, 1827

Denmark satin – Half boots ... are most in favour; but the material most in requisition for the promenade is the Denmark satin, which is at once durable and adapted to set off a well shaped foot and ancle. *La Belle Assemblée*, January 1816 ~~~ Lasting is woven either with a double tweel, or a satin tweel, in which latter case it is called Denmark Satin. <u>Analytical Dictionary</u>, 1830 ~~~ Satin, Denmark (worsted stuffs) *Public Documents*, March 1832 ~~~ Denmark satin, or sateen, if cotton and wool is component material, 40 per cent. Denmark satin, or sateens, entirely stuff, 25 do. <u>Tariff</u>, 1832 [see also *lasting* and *satteen*]

dent de loup – [see *wolves teeth*]

dentelle – *lace*. <u>Dufief's French Dictionary</u>, 1810

dentelle Anglaise – [see *British lace*]

dentelle au fuseau – *bone-lace*. <u>Dufief's French Dictionary</u>, 1810

dentelle de fil – *thread-lace*. <u>Dufief's French Dictionary</u>, 1810

dentelle de point – *point-lace*. <u>Dufief's French Dictionary</u>, 1810

dentille de lin – *tape-lace*. <u>Dufief's French Dictionary</u>, 1810

dentille de soie – *or* blonde, *silk-lace, blond-lace*. <u>Dufief's French Dictionary</u>, 1810 ~~~ [Court dress] Magnificent dentelle de soie, beautifully embroidered in bouquets, flounces of blonde, *Godey's Ladies*

Book, August 1836

diamantine – [Paris] White watered *gros de Naples*, figured satin, and *diamantine*, are also in favour in full dress. *La Belle Assemblée*, December 1830

Diana de Poietiers – [Paris] New Materials. – For grandes toilettes d'hirer, the newest materials are the … Satin *Diana de Poietiers* – a satin striped *à Colonnes*, with cut velvet. *Lady's Magazine and Museum*, November 1834

diaper – Diaper is a sort of linen cloth woven in flowers, and other figures; by some reckoned the finest species of figured linen after damask. The word diaper is used by Shakespeare to denote a napkin or towel. Dunfermline in Fifeshire, Scotland, had a good trade in diapers. Arithmetical Questions, 1795 ~~~ Diaper is the name given to a linen-cloth with a rhomboidal figure or pattern, which is used to make napkins and night-caps. *Monthly Magazine*, September 1805 ~~~ diapers, or damask, as they are more frequently called, A View of Society and Manners in the North of Ireland, 1813… Linen cloth woven in flowers, and other figures; the finest species of figured linen after damask. Encyclopædia Perthensis, 1816 ~~~ Diapers, cotton [or] linen (Russia diapers are always linen) *Public Documents*, March 1832 [see *damask*]

diaphane – Diaphane, *diaphanous*; transparent, Dufief's French Dictionary, 1810 ~~~ One of the prettiest of these last [turbans], is composed of a new material, *gaze diaphane*, of peculiar richness and beauty. *La Belle Assemblée*, March 1832 ~~~ gaze Diaphane … worn in ball dress. *La Belle Assemblée*, May 1832 ~~~ [London] *coiffure à la Sultainne*, *diaphane* satin, [Paris] Morning Costume … the satin *diaphane* is almost as transparent as a gauze, and belong exclusively to the toilette *parée*. *Casket*, March 1835

Dieppe lace – The grounds of the Dieppe lace, instead of being close are more like a net, and consequently lighter than the others. Many are prejudiced against these laces, asserting that they spread in washing, but this is only when they are badly made. The designs are usually well executed, and with some taste. Their prices vary from 7 ½d. or 8d. to 8s. 6d. per yard, some is as high as 1s. per yard. Literary Panorama, 1808

dimity – A fine kind of fustian, or cloth of cotton. Sheridan's English Dictionary, 1797 ~~~ Mary amused herself for a full hour at the unpacking of my portmanteau, … Mercy on me! a double dimity petticoat! *La Belle Assemblée*, November 1806 ~~~ a species of cross-barred stuff entirely composed of cotton, similar in fabric to fustian. Dimity has usually several longitudinal stripes or cords which in the weaving are raised just above the surface of the piece. These cords are generally about the thickness of small twine, though they are occasionally thinner and sometimes thicker. *Single-corded dimities,* are those whose stripes are narrow and round; in the *broad striped dimities* they are flatter and broader. The manufacture of dimities was first established at Lyons, about 1580, and for several years the French supplied us with the article; but since the introduction of the manufacture into Manchester, we have scarcely had occasion to seek abroad for what we have in such abundance and perfection at home. Dimities of every description are imported, from the East Indies, and immense quantities are frequently put up at the company's sales. General Dictionary of Commerce, 1810 ~~~ Gowns of India dimity, with flounces embroidered in different colours, and rows of coloured embroidery between each flounce, is a novelty much admired; *La Belle Assemblée*, August 1818 ~~~ A General Collection of Words of variable spelling, in which those of the best usage are printed in Roman character, … dimity, *dimitty*, Practical Orthography, 1828 [see *fustian*]

doe skin – The equestrian heroes who so very gallantly assisted a *certain* lady in her fall from her horse, felt a very severe mortification in the discovery of her doe-skin breeches, *Sporting Magazine*, April 1800 ~~~ [Woodstock] About fifty years ago, the manufacture of leather into breeches and gloves began to be established here; and has gradually risen to a degree of reputation unrivalled, and to an extent which furnishes employment to the poor for many miles round. The making of breeches, indeed, from the disuse of leather in that article of dress, except among military men, has dwindled away to little; but in the same proportion the manufacture of gloves has been rising. Between 60 to 70 men are now employed as grounders of leather and cutters of gloves, who can earn from a guinea to 30s. weekly; and no fewer than 1400 or 1500 women and girls are engaged in making of gloves, whose wages, according to their diligence, will run from *8s.* to 12s. per week. The leather grounders have a peculiar art, in dressing the skin in such a manner as to give it at once fineness of grain and tenacity of substance. The sewers too produce very durable work, and the neatness of the fabric is universally admired. Woodstock gloves likewise possess this advantage: they may be washed several times, and look well and feel comfortable to the hands till they are quite worn out. A pair of doe-skin gloves, which will cost about 5*s.* will last a gentleman who rides daily, nearly twelve months; hence they are not only more elegant, but cheaper than the gloves generally made in other places. Agriculture of Oxfordshire, 1809 ~~~ The Roe-Buck. … The flesh of the roe is always reckoned the best venison, and their skins, when dressed, are sold at a high price, under the name of doe-skin. *La Belle Assemblée,* January 1818 ~~~ The *horns* of the fallow deer are used for all the same purposes as those of the stag; and their hides, under the name of *buck-skin* and *doe-skin,* have long been celebrated for their softness and pliability: and the manufacturing of them into breeches and gloves affords subsistence to a very numerous and industrious class of people. Domestic Encyclopedia, 1821 ~~~ light doe-skin gloves, finish this promenade dress, in which is combined richness, elegance, and simplicity. *La Belle Assemblée,* January 1823 ~~~ [ad] gloves … Doe skin, 2s., or 22s. 6d. per dozen; *Examiner,* January 15, 1826 ~~~ Doe-skin [gloves] are chiefly adopted by the ton for riding and driving; for either of which, from their extreme softness, warmth, and thickness, they are very admirably contrived. Whole Art of Dress, 1830 ~~~ [men's] A Walking or Riding Dress. … The trowsers are of doe-skin, of a fawn or buff colour; *Casket,* January 1831 ~~~ *Uniforms.* … Of the Light Artillery. … *Pantaloons –* White cassimere or doe-skin for parade, dark blue cloth for service. American State Papers, 1834 [see also *buck skin*]

doeskin cloth – the Third Class, though not as fine, is of an excellent stout Saxon cloth, admirably adapted for Gentleman's travelling or hack wear. … [Third Class] Doeskin, and a large variety of excellent Riding and Travelling Trousers . . 0 13 0 [13*s.*] Doudney Brothers, 1830 ~~~ A new colour will be introduced for this month, the Persian-green doe-skin – also, some light drabs and mixtures of the same material, which, with the doe-skin cords and buck-skins, will form a good variety for Gentlemen's Morning Trousers. *Geo. D. Doudney's Monthly Fashion Sheet,* March 1835 ~~~ The newest materials for Morning Trousers are … striped merino doe-skins, which, in contrast with their almost-numberless rivals, will obtain the decided preference with all who study neatness and gentlemanly taste. *Geo. D. Doudney's Monthly Fashion Sheet,* April 1835

dog skin – *Letter of a Fribble to a Friend.* … I was forced to scrub my hands with filthy wash-ball, which has so ruined their complexion, that laying in dog-skin gloves, will not recover them this fortnight. *Sporting Magazine,* April 1799 ~~~ Dog-skin gloves keep the skin soft; they also allay itching, and correct the contraction of the hands. There are women who beneficially apply the same skin to the bosom; which they cover with pieces at night to keep the skin soft and elastic. Medicine has also availed itself of the assistance of this skin; it has prescribed stockings made of it to relieve the gout, to strengthen the legs, and to prevent swelling. Toilette of Health, Beauty, and Fashion, 1834 ~~~ The skin of the dog is thin but tough, and makes leather of excellent quality. The supply is entirely of home growth, and has fallen off so much of late years that at present it is in a manner extinct, and has been superseded, in part at least, as a material for thin dress-shoes, by horse-leather and by tanned rat-skins. Transactions of the Society, 1836

doily – A species of woollen stuff; a small coarse napkin. Sheridan's English Dictionary, 1797

domet – A kind of plain cloth, of which the warp is cotton and the weft woollen, is called Domett, or Cotton-flannel. It is made, principally, for exportation, except what is dyed black and sold to the Undertakers for the purpose of covering coffins. Analytical Dictionary, 1835 ~~~ [ad] Dry Goods at Reduced Prices. … 1 bale Domet Flannet, … 4 do [ditto: bales] col'd [colored] Dometts, *New England Farmer,* July 1, 1835

Donna Maria gauze – [Paris] Dress gowns are either of white satin, *gaze Donna Maria,* or crape; *La Belle Assemblée,* April 1831 ~~~ The Venetian sleeves made of blond or Dona Maria gauze, (brocaded gauze,) are very fashionable; *The Day,* January 24, 1832 ~~~ Evening Dress. It is composed of rose-coloured Donna Maria gauze, over satin to correspond. *La Belle Assemblée,* February 1832 ~~~ An open dress of white crape, lined with Donna Maria gauze. *Court Journal,* June 8, 1833

Dorcas – Among the new materials that are expected to be fashionable in evening-dress, we may cite the

... *tissu Dorcas*, a new silk, printed in large patterns; *Court Magazine*, May 1833

dorea – The Bengal ships, with two from Columbo, brought the following cargoes: ... Doreas. *Monthly Magazine*, October 1798 ~~~a sort of fine India muslin. Ceneral Dictionary of Commerce, 1810 ~~~ On the coast of Coromandel, a striped muslin is made, called *dorea*, and in the Tamul language *betille*, quantities of which are exported by the caravans to Persian, Arabia, and the Levant. Very little of it goes to Europe, where the fabric is skilfully imitated. Universal Geography, 1822 [see also *Bengal muslin*]

dorine – [court dress] An elegant and rich gause dorine dress, trimmed with a deep flounce of superb blond, and a tasteful torsade of satin and gold above; *Royal Lady's Magazine*, March 1831 ~~~ An embroidered white crape dress à colonne, over white satin, and a beautiful pink and silver dorine fringe below the embroidered border, *Royal Lady's Magazine*, April 1831

dornick – Dornick is weaved 2, 3, and sometimes 4 threads in the split, but most commonly 3 threads; and is used for kitchen towels, brats, bibs, &c. In the weaving of Dornick respect must be paid to the figure, as some figures require to be heavier set than others, and must be set accordingly; a figure that has a great portion of plain, will not require to be so heavy set as that which has little plain, &c. Linen Manufacturer, 1817

double cloth – Double cloth is, for the most part, composed of two similar fabrics, generally plain, which are interwoven at various intervals, and formed into a diversity of figures, agreeably to the design of the pattern to be produced. This is the method usually pursued in carpet weaving. Sometimes one of the fabrics is superior in quality to the other, as in quiltings; in which the superior fabric is called the face, and the inferior, the back. It will therefore be necessary, in explaining the principles of this branch of weaving, to take these two methods separately into consideration: and, in discussing the former, the reader would do well to keep in view the plans and descriptions of diaper weaving, given in the last chapter, to which the mountings and processes of weaving double cloth bear a strong analogy. Art of Weaving, 1831

double merino – [see *Merino*]

double press lace – [see *single press lace*]

double sided silk – The ladies who have recently returned from Paris have brought with them French silks, which might vie with the brocades of our grand-mammas for substance and durability; nothing can indeed be more beautiful than those double-sided silks, as they are called; but as their importation is strictly prohibited, many of our fair fashionables are obliged to content themselves with our imitation of them, some of which are excellent. *La Belle Assemblée*, November 1814 ~~~ For dinner dress, ... French double-sided silks, are, we think, highest in request; ... Short gown of French double-sided silk, *La Belle Assemblée*, December 1814

douillette en gros de Naples glacé – Watered *gros de Naples* are new and elegant, called in French *douillette en gros de Naples glacé*. *Lady's Magazine*, March 1830 [see *gros de Naples*]

dowlas – A coarse kind of linen. Sheridan's English Dictionary, 1797 ~~~ The Philadelphia fashion ... The heat of our climate compels both sexes to consult comfort, rather than splendor. ... Vulgar nankeen and filthy dowlas are in great request. *Port Folio*, June 18, 1802 ~~~ [for soldiers in the West Indies] the pantaloons, or rather trowsers, of strong brown linen, or dowlas, Systematic View, 1804 ~~~ Dowlas is often made of bleached yarn, and is used for pocketing, linings soldiers' gaiters, trowsers, &c. Linen Manufacturer, 1817 ~~~ a sort of course linen cloth, manufactured principally in the north of Ireland, in Lancashire, &c. General Dictionary of Commerce, 1810 ~~~ Dowlas, (German) flax *Public Documents*, March 1832 [see *creas*]

down – Down, are the shortest, smoothest, softest, and most delicate feathers of birds, particularly geese, ducks and swans; growing on their neck and part of their stomach. Down is a commodity of most countries: but that in most repute, for fineness, lightness, and warmth, comes from Denmark, Sweden, and other northern countries. Dictionary of Merchandize, 1803 ~~~ For the carriage costume, and for morning visits, hats of white moss silk with a plume of down feathers, are most in favor, and never was this article more in requisition than at present: *La Belle Assemblée*, March 1816 ~~~ The brims of hats are worn much extended; and down feathers are reckoned more elegant than flowers. *La Belle*

Assemblée, October 1818 ~~~ Down feathers are the most fashionable: they are worn in plumes; and a down-feather edging is now the only trimming that adorns the brims of hats. ... I must not forget to say, that down feathers are rose-colour, white, fawn, and grey. *Repository of Arts*, March 1819 ~~~ A new kind of ornament, of the chaperon form, composed of down feathers and sprigs of silver foliage, placed alternately, has a very elegant appearance, particularly in dark hair. *Ladies' Museum*, June 1830 [see also *marabout*]

dozens – Manufactures (woollen). ... All *Devonshire* kerseys, called dozens, 12 & 13 [Yards long.] Whole Law Relative to the Duty and Office of a Justice of the Peace, 1794 ~~~ Woollen bays ... Devonshire dozens Digest of the Commercial Regulations, 1824

drab – Drab, thick double-milled woollen cloth; Perry's English Dictionary, 1795 ~~~ Drab is a sort of thick woollen cloth, woven purposely for great-coats, and it is sometimes double-milled. This kind of cloth is manufactured in Yorkshire, and also in many parts of the west of England in the greatest perfection. General Dictionary of Commerce, 1810 ~~~ Dresses for Wildfowl Shooting. ... Under the waistcoat, should be worn a Flushing frock, and over it, a short jacket, of either drab cloth, or swanskin. Instructions to Young Sportsmen, 1825 ~~~ The cloths noted in the Table, as costing 2s. 6d. are drabs, such as are used by stage-drivers, watermen, and other labourers, for great-coats, pea-jackets, &c. – No article of this kind, so far as our information extends, is manufactured in the United States. A large part of those imported into Philadelphia and New York are designed for the Western states; and, after affording the importer, as has been the case for a year past, a higher profit than the one specified in our Table, together with the country merchant's profit, are retailed to consumers in the Western states at $1.75 to $1.87 per yard – being about three times the price which the English labourer has to pay for the same kind of clothing. An Exposition...of the Tariff System, 1832 ~~~ 1 piece super drab cloth – 24 yards – [price $] 5.50 [amount $] 132.00 ~~~1 piece double mill'd drab cloth, 12 ½ yds [price $] 3.00 [amount $] 37.50 [letter dated October 26, 1832] Emigration of Indians, 1835 [see also *drill*]

draft – [see *lasting*]

drap – *cloth; woollen cloth.* Dufief's French Dictionary, 1810

drap d'Alger – [see *Algerian*]

drap d'été – [see *ete* and *summer cloth*]

drap de soie – the superb Drap de Soie, [on sale for] 6s.; rivalling the most costly production of French genius in brilliancy of the colours and delicacy of execution; much worn on visits of etiquette or bridal congratulations. Ladies of high rank and splendid fortune will be delighted with this new and facinating [sic] British production. *Examiner*, February 5, 1826 ~~~ Walking Dress. ... shoes of drap de soie. *Lady's Magazine and Museum*, April 1836

drap de St. Maur – [see *St. Maur*]

drap fin – *superfine or broad cloth.* Dufief's French Dictionary, 1810

drill – cotton drilling for vests, pantaloons, guetres, bedsacks, working frocks and trowsers, rifle frocks and overalls, *Weekly Register*, September 21, 1811 ~~~ Drilling, in the retail shops, is known by the name of Russia Drab, and is in general about 28 inches broad, and the pieces from 30 to 36 Archines in length. It is distinguished from all other Cloth by its being twilled. Practice of the Customs, 1812 ~~~ [ad] Summer Goods, Such as Drab and White Drills, Striped and Ribbed do. [ditto] Boston Annual Advertiser, 1823 ~~~ Drills, from Manchester to New York. Cotton only, Nominal width, 3/4, actual do. 21 a [to] 25 inches, Length 40 a 45 yards. Cotton & Linen, (Union) ... actual [width] 24 a 26 ~~~ Linen only, ... actual [width] 25 a 27 [inches] Trade between Great Britain and the United States of America, 1833 ~~~ [ad] Have received by the ships Hark-away and Jefferson, direct from Liverpool, ...1 case 3-4 brown French and English white linen drillings. *Farmer's Register*, May 1835... [Washington] Cadets of the Military Academy ... Fatigue dress – of unbleached Russia drilling. ... For summer, all officers to wear plain white drilling. *Army and Navy Chronicle*, December 2, 1835 ~~~ Drilling. *s.* A kind of strong, twilled linen, worn by soldiers at the drill. Gentlemen's Lexicon, 1835

drogget – [see *drugget*]

Druck linen – Druck linen, a Silesian manufacture, which by some is bleached quite white, and by others only half bleached. It is 1 ½ ell in breadth. By some manufacturers it is left in its full length, as the pieces are made; by others it is divided into pieces containing 58 ells each. It is taken off from the bleaching ground, without being dressed up. Many merchants or manufacturers leave the one end of the piece out, to which a piece of paper is fixed, marked with the number of ells it contains. Merchants, who give orders for this linen uncut, ought to notice precisely the length of the piece. The chief market for this sort of linen is England, but much is also exported to America and to the West Indies. European Commerce, 1805

drugget – Drugget, a slight kind of woollen cloth Perry's English Dictionary, 1795 ~~~ The womens apparel is chiefly a variety of stuffs of their own manufacture; as … *drugget*, composed of linen warp and woollen weft; Statistical Account of Scotland, 1795 ~~~ Drugget, in commerce, a stuff sometimes all wool, and sometimes half wool half thread, sometimes corded, but usually plain. Those that have the woof of wool, and the warp of thread, are called *threaded druggets*; and those wrought with the shuttle on a loom of four marches, … are called *corded druggets*. As to the plain, they are wrought on a loom of two marches, with the shuttle, in the same manner as cloth, camblets, and other like stuffs not corded. Encyclopædia Britannica, 1797 ~~~ [Berwick] The women's gowns are made of a coarse cotton, called French Drogget, purchased at 1s. 6d. per yard. History of Berwick upon Tweed, 1799 ~~~ An emigrant possessing, say 500*l.* capital, might, with advantage, take with him the following articles for his own use in the settlements. … Twenty blue drugget jackets. Twenty blue drugget trousers. British Settlements in Australasia, 1824 ~~~ Drugget, cloth pressed so as to be water-marked like camelot; Etymons of English Words, 1826 ~~~ The grey Drugget, so much used, at present, for Soldiers' great coats, carpet covers, &c. is a double-milled Baize; but other fabrics, if sufficiently coarse and having the warp differing in kind from the weft, have also the same name. Druggets may be either plain or tweeled, the latter being termed Corded Druggets; and, when the warp is of Linen yarn and the weft woollen, they are Threaded Druggets. Analytical Dictionary, 1830

Dubarry – [French] Grand Festival Dresses – Morning Concert Dresses. Ensemble de Grande Toilette, No. 1. A robe of Dubarry gros grains. This is a most splendid material, in imitation of the rich ribbons worn as ceintures, and broché in beautiful patterns of natural flowers. *Lady's Magazine*, July 1834 ~~~ [Paris bonnet] the ribands were of *gaze Dubarry*, flowered in sprigs of roses. *Court Magazine*, October 1834

ducape – Ducapé, a kind of silk Perry's English Dictionary, 1795 ~~~ What are Ducapes? Coloured silks, made with a small Figure upon it. Are they called so from some Manufacturer? No, they are of French Extraction; some call them Figured Gros de Naples. House of Lords Sessional Papers, July 3, 1823 ~~~ splendid Ducapes, [on sale for] 4s. 6d., usual price 6s. 6d.; *Examiner*, February 5, 1826 ~~~ [ad] Du Cape, 4s. per yard. *Political Guardian*, April 22, 1831 ~~~ Ducapes are likewise plain-wove stout silks, but of softer texture than the last. [gros de Naples] Silk Manufacture, 1832 ~~~ [Court dresses] manteau apricot figured ducape, … train of blue ducape, watered in leaves; … A rich vapeur ducape dress, *Royal Lady's Magazine*, June 1831 ~~~ [ad] Real Spitalfields Ducapes, 1s. 11d. to 2s. ½d. *Court Journal*, November 30, 1833 [see also *gros de Naples*]

duck – The trowsers are to be made of dark brown Russia duck, and made full large enough to button all the way up, over breeches and leggins. Rules and Regulations for the Cavalry, 1795 ~~~ To those engaged in mercantile concerns, we conceive the follow price current of goods, wares, &c. as they actually were at Philadelphia in January, 1794, … Duck, Russia, per piece of 42 yards . . 14 0 [$14.00] View of the American United States, 1795 ~~~ Duck, one shilling and ninepence farthing per yard. [in 1801] A Voyage Round the World, 1805 ~~~Ducks, a sort of strong brown cloth, used chiefly by sail-makers; the best is manufactured in Prussia. General Dictionary of Commerce, 1810 ~~~ I spun some tow and flax, and wove a bolt of duck; … Mr. Colt will exhibit at your Fair, a bolt of his cotton duck, *American Farmer*, March 11, 1825 ~~~ Dresses for Wildfowl Shooting. … I shall now add one recipe for a surtout, by way of a dread-nought, which, as wet weather has of late years been "so much in fashion," will, I trust be doing service, not only to gunners, but to every class of the community, except the tailors, who might lose business by it, and the satellites the dandies, who would faint at the sight of it. … Larry Rogers, who calls it his *"Sou'wester,"* and gets it all for nine shillings. … Make, with an article called *Russia duck* (which, *as well as swanskin*, should be previously wetted and dried, to prevent shrinking), a loose over-all frock coat, and a hood; <u>Instructions to Young Sportsmen</u>, 1825 ~~~ Flax and its Manufactures ... the bolt of *best* Russia duck, which costs about $16 per bolt, *Niles' Weekly Register*, March 22, 1828 ~~~ Yearly Allowance of Clothing [for slaves] ... 1 pair of duck trousers <u>Bulletins of State Intelligence</u>, 1834

duffle – Duffle and silk cloaks, printed and muslin gowns, by all ranks of women. <u>Statistical Account of Scotland</u>, 1799 ~~~ [for soldiers] A cloak with a hood, in the form of a Portugal cloak – the material a close, strong, duffle, light and warm, manufactured expressly for the purpose, rendered less penetrable to wet, by incorporating grease or oil with the manufacture of the cloth, <u>Systematic View</u>, 1804 ~~~ Duffield, or *Duffel*, a village in Derbyshire, ... famous for being the place where the species of woollen cloth called *Duffle* or *Duffel*, was first manufactured. <u>Union Gazetteer</u>, 1807 ~~~ Duffle is a stout milled Flannel, but of greater breadth and differently dressed. It may be either perched or Friezed (napped) and is sold of all colours. The Grey Duffle, being a mixture of black and white, must necessarily be dyed in the wool. – Duffle should have a different orthography, if it has had its name from Duffel, a town in France. <u>Analytical Dictionary</u>, 1835 ~~~ [ad] Have received by the ships Harkaway and Jefferson, direct from Liverpool, ... 3 do [bales] point and duffle ditto [blankets]. *Farmer's Register*, May 1835

Dunstable – [in Dunstable] In the straw work, which is the staple manufacture of the place, a woman can earn from 6s. to 12s. a week; children, from 2s. to 4s. a week. This business has given employment, for the last 20 years, to every woman, who wished to work: and, for 10 years back, straw work has sold well, particularly in the spring. Earnings in this line, have, for the last four years, been exceedingly great, which, in some measure, perhaps, accounts for the Poor's Rates not having risen during that period. The straw is chiefly manufactured into hats, baskets, &c. <u>State of the Poor</u>, 1797 ~~~ *Morning Dress*. ... Dunstable hat, trimmed round with a narrow ribband, and across the crown with a fancy wreath of artificial flowers. *Lady's Magazine*, July 1798 ~~~ Though the fine Dunstable straw hat is in high favour, it cannot destroy the predilection for the Leghorn, which yet prevails. *La Belle Assemblée*, July 1825 ~~~ these bonnets have now succeeded to the heavy, coarse dunstable, which affectation only could ever have adopted. *Ladies' Monthly Museum*, August 1828 ~~~ The precise period when the Dunstable bonnets made of straw-plat, that is of entire wheat-straws platted in long narrow strips, and afterwards sewn together, were invented, is unknown. The *Dunstable* bonnet is probably a century and a half old. ... Of the different *plats,* which are numerous, the principal are the following. First: the Dunstable, or whole straw; a considerable improvement has taken place in the imitation; *Saturday Magazine*, January 26, 1833 ~~~ Fine Dunstable straw bonnets begin to be a good deal in favour in walking-dress, as do also those of sewed Leghorn straw. *Ladies' Pocket*, June 1836

durant – [awarded in 1795] Second Rate Premium [loosely: second place prize] ... Gown and durant petticoat. <u>State of the Poor</u>, 1797 ~~~ durants, or stuffs made of single worsted, three-quarters of a yard wide, <u>Manufactures of Ireland</u>, 1798 ~~~ *Durance*, the stuff used in female dress now termed Durant. [in glossary of:] <u>Queenhoo-Hall</u>, 1808 ~~~ A glazed woollen stuff, called by some everlasting. <u>Knowles English Dictionary</u>, 1835 ~~~ Durant, which is merely a better sort of Tamy, is little used in this country, but is exported, in considerable quantities, to Spain and Portugal. Both Tamies and Durants are hotpressed and glazed, but the former are kept at the full width of the cloth, while the latter are Creased, that is, they are folded, selvage to selvage, which leaves a marked line, called a Crease, running lengthwise, along the middle of the piece. <u>Analytical Dictionary</u>, 1835 [see also *tammy*]

Ecossais - Everlasting

ecossais – *Scot, Scotch*; Dufief's French Dictionary, 1810 ~~~ écossais (plaid) … *Lady's Magazine and Museum*, July 1834 ~~~ The most fashionable materials for cloaks are – … Satin Ecossais … are imitations of the Scotch plaids, made in Cachemere wool and silk. *Lady's Magazine and Museum*, November 1834 ~~~ [Paris] in requisition for carriage or public promenade dress, which for us is the same thing, so will also be some new materials of wool and silk intermingled: they are called *ecossais satins*, *New Monthly Belle Assemblée*, November 1836

edging – Edging, a narrow lace; a border Perry's English Dictionary, 1795

effile – Effilé, *fringe, a kind of trimming.* Porter de l'effilé, *to wear fringed ruffles.* … *slender, thin, unwoven;* Dufief's French Dictionary, 1810 ~~~ They are bordered with a silver fringe of that very light kind called *effilé*; *La Belle Assemblée*, March 1831 ~~~ A light silk fringe of that kind called *effilé*, borders the lapel. *Ladies' Museum*, September 1831 ~~~ A party-coloured *effilé*, in which the three colours of the dress are interwoven, border the lappel. *Ladies' Museum*, February 1832

egret – The Egret, a small sort of heron, bears on his head a very beautiful tuft of feathers. In the days of chivalry, warriors wore them on their helmets. They are now in request as ornaments for ladies' head-dresses; and the Turks and Persians wear them, in their turbans. The bird was once very plentiful in England, but is now scarce; though it may be found in most places, in all the temperate climates of the globe. Book of Commerce, 1834 [see also *heron*]

Egyptian – Egyptian ribbons, about six inches in breadth, with a border forming a row of pyramids, is a novelty much used in the trimming of hats: *La Belle Assemblée*, May 1819 ~~~ [Paris] Before I quit the promenade costume, I must mention to you two articles, which appear at present indispensable to it: the first is a sash, composed of either Egyptian or plaid ribbon; the Egyptian ribbon is always of two colours, the middle of one sort, and a little stripe at each edge of another; the favourite contrasts are, dark puce and apple-green, gold colour and white, *pouceau* and pale blue. These ribbons are worn excessively broad, some are six inches in width; they are tied on one side, near the front, in a bow and long ends. *Repository of Arts*, June 1819 ~~~ A favorite dress for the evening is a white satin slip, under a dress of Urling's black Chantilly lace; with a sash tied behind of the Belzoni or *Egyptian* plaid. – We cannot forbear remarking the absurdity of the term Egyptian to the Scotch word *plaid*, when given to the chequers on a mummy's tomb of two thousand years old. – It is a pity the venders of silks and ribands should be so very *unclassical*; *Ladies' Monthly Museum*, January 1822

Egyptian cloth – Walking Dress. High round dress of Egyptian cloth of the fallen leaf colour, … Few cloth pelisses have as yet made their appearance, except those which are made of that satin-like texture which is so conspicuous in the Nile, or Egyptian cloth, a faithful imitation from that woven from the finest camel's hair, and worn only by the higher order of the inhabitants on the banks of the Nile. This desirable material for ladies' dresses, so superior to the Merino, the kerseymere, or any light cloth for female wear, has been fabricated at an immense expence in this country, and it is impossible to form an idea of any thing more beautiful, more light, or appropriate than this charming material for winter dresses, habits, and pelisses. *La Belle Assemblée*, October 1820 ~~~ On the fine Egyptian cloth [pelisses] we find the rich plush silk, the grey squirrel, or the glossy satin. *La Belle Assemblée*, November 1820

Egyptian muslin – Various new materials, with a great diversity of names, signifying their importation from distant lands, though manufactured in the work-shops of Paris, have been introduced for gowns this spring: amongst these is the Egyptian muslin, … remarkable for the brilliancy of its colours and the originality of its designs; *Ladies' Museum*, May 1829 ~~~ [Paris] Among the lighter materials for the promenade, … we may add to them … the *mousselines Egyptiennes*: these last are very much in favour. *Repository of Fashions*, June 1829

Egyptian satin – White satin scarfs with borders of the Egyptian satins, in crimson cloth, velvet, or chenille, are very elegant and tasteful ornaments for full dress; *La Belle Assemblée*, December 1808 ~~~ High dresses, of the pelisse kind, composed of *moire*, or of *satin d'Egypte*, are much in favour in half dress, particularly for morning visits; *Ladies' Museum*, November 1831 eider down – Eider down is imported from Denmark; the ducks that supply it being inhabitants of Hudson's Bay, Greenland, Iceland, and Norway. Our own islands west of Scotland breed numbers of these birds, which turn out a profitable branch of trade to the poor inhabitants. ... Encyclopædia Britannica, 1797 ~~~ These birds pluck it from their breasts and line their nests with it. ... [Down] of the eider duck is the most valuable. That found in the nest is most valued, and is termed *live down*; it is infinitely more elastic than that plucked from the dead bird, which is little esteemed in Iceland. General Dictionary of Commerce, 1810

ell – A measure containing 45 inches, or a yard and a quarter. ... The ell is a measure, which obtains, under different denominations, in most countries, whereby cloths, stuffs, linens, silks, &c. are usually measured; answering nearly to the yard of England, the canna of Italy, the vara of Spain, the palm of Sicily, &c. ... The ells most frequently used with us are the English and Flemish; the former containing 3 feet 9 inches, or one yard and a quarter; the latter only 27 inches, or 3 quarters of a yard; so that the ell English is to the Flemish ell as 5 to 3. In Scotland, the ell contains 37 2-10ths English inches. Encyclopædia Perthensis, 1816

elysienne – [Paris] Redingotte of a new silk called *Elysienne*. *Lady's Magazine and Museum*, May 1835 ~~~ A bonnet of pink *Elysienne*, trimmed with pink fringed riband *Court Journal*, September 12, 1835

embossed – [patent granted to] Paul Newman, of Melksham, in the county of Wilts, Clothier; for a method of figuring and ornamenting, by means of pressure, embossment, or otherwise, cloths or stuffs of woollen, linen, cotton, velvet, silk, or satin, or any mixture of those materials. Dated July 16, 1799. Repertory of Arts, 1799 ~~~ [court dress] A dress of jonquil crape embossed with silver, and looped up with wreaths and bunches of yellow roses; *La Belle Assemblée*, June 1807 ~~~ the *Emigré* mantle or Brazilian cloak. It is formed of purple velvet embossed on a topaz satin ground, *La Belle Assemblée*, December 1807 ~~~ Of the ball-dresses ... a border of a most novel material of embossed silk stripes, on a net of exquisite workmanship: *La Belle Assemblée*, December 1820 ~~~ The surfaces of plain silk goods, and particularly of ribands, are sometimes embossed, so that very elegant patterns are produced upon them. This operation is likewise performed by passing the silk between rollers, the surfaces of which contain the pattern which it is intended to produce. In one of the cylinders the pattern is sunk, and in the other raised, so that the eminences of one coincide exactly with the cavities of the other cylinder. This process has of late been very extensively employed for ornamenting waistcoat patterns, producing a very rich and tasteful appearance; but it can be more appropriately applied to ribands or other fabrics which are not much exposed to friction; the inequalities of surface are otherwise found to be unfavourable to the durability of the material. Silk Manufacture, 1832

emerald gauze – [see *metallic gauze*]

eminet – [ad] on Sale, every Article Connected with the Silk Trade, as well as Fine Prunello, Eminets, and Moreens; *Yorkshire Observer*, December 7, 1822 [see *erminet*]

English blond – [see *blond* and *British blond*]

English Chantilly – as a convenient dress for short and wintry days, now fast approaching: black, therefore, it is yet very prevalent, but it is merely the gown, which often consists of Urling's black Chantilly lace over white or grey sarsnet; *Ladies' Monthly Museum*, October 1821 ~~~ We have, a few days ago, seen a dress which was completed for a young bride of high distinction; it was entirely of fine lace; and was worn over a slip of white satin: a scarf of the same hung in graceful negligence over her shoulders. ... So fine was the texture of the wedding-dress, and so exquisite its pattern, that is was taken by many for Brussels', and the wearer constantly blamed, when our own manufactures are so excellent, and so many of their workmen in want; it was, however, we well know, only a most wonderful specimen of the lace called *English* Chantilly. *Ladies' Pocket*, May 1829 ~~~ Black lace veils, of our own manufacture, but offering an excellent imitation of Chantilly lace, are very much in favour in carriage dress. *Ladies' Museum*, January 1832 [see *Chantilly*]

English lace – [see *British lace*]

English muslin – *Imports of L. Derry, for the Year ending January the 5th*, 1802. *From England.* ... English muslin, coloured and worked, 74 yards. Statistical Survey of the County of Londonderry, 1802 ~~~ White muslin dresses of large checquers are much in favour, all of English muslin. *La Belle Assemblée*,

September 1827 ~~~ [Paris] Among the new materials for gowns are *mousselines Anglaises*; they are jaconot with a thick stripe, the stripes are beautifully shaded, and at considerable distances from each other; in the space between the stripes are *bouquets* of five or six flowers, coloured after nature. *Repository of Fashions*, September 1829 ~~~ There is at this moment little or no difference between evening dress and half-dress; in fact, the materials of both are frequently the same; as for example, chaly printed gros de Naples and English muslins; some of the prettiest of the last are in diamond patterns, thick and thin alternately; *Casket*, September 1831 [see also *muslin*]

English net – [see *bobbin-net*, *British net* and *Nottingham*]

English organdy – The charming material of improved leno, called English organdy, is justly appreciated, and much worn by females of rank and fashion; it is striped with narrow satin stripes, with of peach-colour *tourterelle* or blue, and constitutes one of the prettiest summer costumes yet worn. *La Belle Assemblée*, September 1825 [see *leno* and *organdy*]

English point – The lace *improperly* called *English point*, is made with bobbins, and (as far as regards the patterns) is an imitation of Brussels lace, but the edging of the flowers is not lasting, and the flowers themselves quickly separate from the ground. <u>Literary Panorama</u>, 1808 ~~~ The favourite head-dress at the Opera is a cap made of English point lace: the richness of the pattern, and the elegant manner in which this lace is made up, render them much more admired than caps of the more costly blond. *La Belle Assemblée*, November 1829 ~~~ The edge of the brim may be trimmed according to the fancy of the wearer, with a black or white blond lace veil, but one of English point lace is considered much more *distingué*. *Court Magazine*, December 1833 ~~~ [Paris] Grand Festival Dresses … Hat of poux de soie, … and a short veil of point d'Angleterre completes the costume. *Lady's Magazine and Museum*, July 1834 ~~~ [Paris] The Duchess de V – wore a robe of *point d'Angleterre*, looped up on one side by a bow of blue riband. *Court Journal*, August 1, 1835

English tulle – [see *bobbin-net*]

English-figured stuff – many [cloaks] are to be seen of what they call English-figured stuff; the only disadvantage of this material is, that it is hard, et cela ne drappe pas, comme nos étoffes. [and it does not drape like our stuffs.] *Lady's Magazine and Museum*, January 1836

entredeux – there were two rows, separated by an *entre-deux* of embroidered muslin; *Ladies' Monthly Museum*, June 1827 ~~~ it is trimmed with a row of *entre deux* (insertion), *Court Magazine*, May 1833 ~~~ Costume de Bal or de Soiree. – Dress of organdi (book muslin), … The corsage is *à l'Enfant*, gathered top and bottom. It is finished at the neck by an *entredeux* (in which coloured ribbons are inserted), and a narrow lace. *Lady's Magazine and Museum*, October 1834 ~~~ [Paris] In white muslin dresses these bands may be in *entre deux* (insertion), *Lady's Magazine and Museum*, May 1836 [see *insertion* and *letting-in lace*]

epinettes – a new description of *pluche de soie*, which is sometimes called *èpinettes*, and sometimes *amiantines bouclées*: this last name arises, I suppose, from the pile of the *pluche* being very long and rather curled. *Repository of Arts*, November 1821 [see *pluche de soie* and *plush*]

ermine – Royal Marriage. … In the procession to the chapel, and during the ceremony, her Royal Highness wore a crimson velvet mantling, trimmed with ermine, and over the shoulders hung a rich silver cord and tassels. *Scots Magazine*, April 1795 ~~~ The erminea, or ermine, has the tail tipt with black, and has been distinguished by authors into two varieties, the *stoat* and the *white ermine*, though the difference seems chiefly to depend on climate and the season of the year; the stoat of a pale tawny brown or reddish yellow colour in summer, becoming the white ermine of winter in cold countries. … scarcely ten inches long nose to rump, and the tail about five and a half; the hair is likewise shorter and less shining than in that animal. [the martin] In the northern regions, the fur of the ermine becomes entirely white, except the outer half of the tail, which remains black. The skin is reckoned valuable, and sells in Siberia from two to three pounds Sterling a-hundred; but in ancient times it was in much greater request than now. <u>Encyclopædia Britannica</u>, 1797 ~~~ Walking dress. … The gown of white India muslin, made high in the neck, with an erect lace collar; ermine fur tippet. *Lady's Magazine*, October 1810 ~~~ The ermine is remarkable for the softness, the closeness, and the warmth of its fur. In the north of Europe and Siberia, their skins make a valuable article of commerce: than are found in some parts of the United States, particularly in Vermont. <u>Youth's Companion</u>, 1813 ~~~ In Russia ermines' skins of good quality are sold at the rate of about a shilling each. They are usually sewed in lengths of three Russian ells, and these parcels are estimated, according to their quality, at from two to five guineas each. Many deceptions, however, have been practised respecting ermines' skins, which have tended to depreciate their value; the principal of these is to conceal and sew small bits of lead in the feet, to increase their weight. <u>Useful Knowledge</u>, 1821 ~~~ the silk pelisses are truly elegant; we saw one lately, on a lady of high distinction, of *gros de Naples,* of a beautiful lavender colour: it was trimmed all round with a broad border of real ermine, of which valuable fur was an entire mantelet-cape: higher up, near the collar, was a row of the black tails of this superb little creature, which were so placed on the snow-white fur, as to give the appearance of a smaller cape, falling over that which hung over the shoulders. *La Belle Assemblée,* April 1828 ~~~ Ermine, so long the most expensive, and considered as the most elegant of furs, is now less fashionable, are far less expensive than sable, or even than Isabella bear, which is next to sable in estimation *La Belle Assemblée,* December 1831 ~~~ Ermines, which are delicately white, are found in all the colder parts of the North, and their skins become an important article of commerce with Norway, Lapland, Russia, &c., where they are found in prodigious numbers. They are taken in traps, baited with flesh, and made of two flat stones, the uppermost of which, in falling, crushes them; or they are shot with blunt arrows. This animal, in warmer climates is called a *stoat,* but its fur is coarse there, and of no value. <u>Book of Commerce by Sea and Land</u>, 1834 ~~~ ermine, which for a long time had been out of favour, has now nearly regained its former vogue; it is expected to be particularly in request for trimmings of mantles and mantelets. *Court Magazine,* December 1835 ~~~ [Paris] Ermine is very fashionable, both for the promenade and evening wraps. It is now the most fashionable fur for both muffs and boas; *Court Magazine,* February 1836

erminet – [ad] Fur Trimmings, Norwich, Paisley, Seal, Erminetta, Vicuna, *Kaleidoscope,* November 11, 1823 ~~~ Custom House, London, 31st October 1823. To the Commissioners of Customs, Ireland. Gentlemen, Having had under consideration your letters of the 9th ultimo, stating that a question has arisen as to the definition of the article termed "Ornamental Old Drapery," in the Act 4 Geo. IV. c. 26. that it appears to you, that the term comprises all kinds of fancy waistcoating, under the following names; Swansdown, Manillas, Toillenets, Erminets, and Shalloons, <u>Accounts and Papers</u>, 1824 ~~~ 1 piece erminette, 38 yards – [Price $] 1.50 [Amount $] 57.00 [letter dated October 26, 1832] <u>Emigration of Indians</u>, 1835

esmeralda – Evening dress is this winter likely to be extremely magnificent. Among the new kinds of light materials expected to be most in favour, are the *esmeralda,* and *tulle arachné.* These, which have but just appeared in France, are now made here, and are confessed to be fully equal to the French articles of the same names. … The *esmeraldas* are of crape, or gauze, the latter are most beautiful; both are white, and embroidered in a pretty, but somewhat fantastic pattern, in black and gold. Their name is derived from the heroine of a fashionable romance. *La Belle Assemblée,* December 1831 ~~~ Make and Material of Ball Dress. – *Gaze Esmeralda, tulle-Arachné,* and crape, are the materials of the new ball dresses. The first is a rich white gauze, embroidered in fantastic patterns, in dark colored silks, mixed either with gold or silver. *Atheneum,* April 1832 ~~~ [Paris] The evening dress silks that have appeared, are all in the superb but heavy style of Louis XIV's reign. The satins *Salomon, Esmeralda,* and *Pharamond,* are expected to be in great request; *New Monthly Belle Assemblée,* November 1836

espirit – Afternoon Dresses. … Armenian turban, … A white ostrich and a blue esprit feather on the left side. *Lady's Magazine,* February 1796 ~~~ Instead of the stiff plumes called *Espirits,* sometimes a long and waving feather is substituted in their place. *Port Folio,* February 27, 1802 ~~~ The *espirit* feathers now worn in turbans are very long. *La Belle Assemblée,* January 1827

Essen linen – Essen linen is a very strong kind of linen, made near a little place called Essen. It is almost of the same quality as the Osnabruck linen, <u>European Commerce</u>, 1805 [see *osnaburg*]

estaing – Among the new materials for [men's] pantaloons are *satin de laine,* and *estaing,* either black, brown, *grenat noisette,* or *ecru. Casket,* January 1831

estoffe de laine croisée – [see *kersey*]

estrich – or Estridge, … is the fine soft down which lies immediately under the feathers of the bird called the ostrich. The finest is used as a substitute for beaver in the manufacture of hats, and the coarser or stronger sort is employed in the fabrication of a stuff, which resembles a fine woollen cloth. We usually import our estridge from the Levant, from Italy, and from other parts of the Mediterranean. General Dictionary of Commerce, 1810

etamine – Etamine, *buntine, the woollen stuff of which a ship's colours are made. … tammy, bolting cloth.* Dufief's French Dictionary, 1810 ~~~ Taminy, (a woollen stuff) *Estamine,* Chambaud's French Dictionary, 1815 [see *tammy*]

ete – Eté, *summer. Un jour d'été, a summer day.* Tardy's French Dictionary, 1799 ~~~ the new silk, called *gros-d'Eté, La Belle Assemblée,* November 1819 ~~~ For dinner parties of ceremony, and as an evening dress, is a beautifully striped material of the *gros d'Eté* texture, of Queen's eye colour; *La Belle Assemblée,* August 1820 ~~~ *gros d'été,* which, in fact, is but another name for lutestring, are the silks at present most in favour. *Repository of Arts,* June 1823 ~~~ *List of French Patents.* [in 1823] … for a stuff which they call *drap d'été* (summer-cloth). *Repertory of Arts,* November 1824 ~~~ Evening Dress. A gown of rose colour *gaze de Smyrne* over a slip of *gros d'été* to correspond. *Repository of Fashions,* July 1829 ~~~ Two beautiful sisters war dresses of *brocard d'eté,* the one pink, and the other lilac. *Court Journal,* August 1, 1835 ~~~ The new *gros d'étés* are next in requisition; they are watered, quadrilled, or striped, with small patterns in the stripes. *Court Magazine,* June 1836 ~~~ Paris Public Promenade Dress. – Robe of green striped *gros d'été, New Monthly Belle Assemblée,* August 1836 [see also *summer satin*]

etoilee – [evening dress turban] in *gaze etoilée,* a rich gauze spotted with silver, *Court Magazine,* November 1835 ~~~ Etoilée, starry, full of stars. Boyer's French Dictionary, 1835

ettamine – [see *etamine*]

European cachemire – Cloaks with sleeves, called *Turkish mantles,* were also much in request for out-door envelopes: they were generally of that fine, soft cloth, called European-Cachemire; *La Belle Assemblée,* [review of the first six months] 1828 ~~~ Many riding-habits are made of figured merino, but the fine cloth, called European cachemire, is preferred, as it has the singular advantage of never being creased; nor does the rain affect it. *Ladies' Monthly Museum,* August 1828 [see *cashmere*]

everlasting – [willed in 1789] one hundred yards of everlasting, Complete System of Pleading, 1798 ~~~ The greater part of the combing wool is consumed in worsted for making what is called new drapery in the Book of Rates, viz. … everlasting, 1s. 3d. to 4s. … per yard. Origin of Commerce, 1801 ~~~ a coarse cloth used by tailors for stuffing the pudding collars of our modern dandies. It is employed in small scraps or slips. Slang, 1823 ~~~ Worsted Stuff Goods, from Manchester to New York … Lastings … actual [width] inches 25 *a* [to] 26… Price per yard s.d. [shillings.pence] 1.4 *a* 3.0 Trade between Great Britain and the United States of America, 1833 [see also *lasting* and *durant*]

Fabric - Fustian

fabric – a texture of silk or stuff. <u>Royal English Dictionary</u>, 1775 ~~~ FABRIC (in Commerce). The same as manufacture; lace of the fabric of Brussels, &c. <u>Dictionary of General Knowledge</u>, 1833

fag end – The end of a web of cloth. <u>Johnson's English Dictionary</u>, 1812

Faliero – printed cambrics, called *Falieros*; these last are of read and black grounds, with patterns of different colours. *Repository of Fashions*, September 1829

fancy net – *List of Patents granted in Scotland* [in 1825] … a description of cloth made of cotton, and commonly called Fancy Net, in imitation of French Net, or to be made of silk, woollen, and linen, or a combination of these, or part of these; <u>Edinburgh Philosophical Journal</u>, 1826

fausse Valenciennes lace – [see *mock Valenciennes*]

favorite – French Fashions. Opera Dress. A dress composed of a new material called *gaze favorite*; figured in perpendicular wreaths of small blue and yellow flowers alternately, on a white ground. *La Belle Assemblée*, August 1831

feathers – [on his Majesty's birth-day] Feathers were universally worn; four or five in an head-dress, of different colours, mostly half white, half lilac. *Lady's Magazine*, June 1794 ~~~ Feathers make a considerable article of commerce, particularly those of the ostrich, heron, swan, peacock, goose, &c. for plumes, ornaments of the head, filling of beds, writing-pens, &c. … The best method of curing them is to lay them in a room exposed to the air and sun; and when dried, to put them in coarse bags, and beat them well with poles to get out the dirt, &c. <u>Encyclopædia Britannica</u>, 1797 ~~~ The feathers generally worn are the Argus pheasant, the Indian macaw, the argilla, the flat and porcupine ostrich, and the Scringapatam plume. *Lady's Magazine*, April 1800 ~~~ THE FEATHER-WORKER This is another business in which women are chiefly employed. … Before the feathers come into the hands of the person who makes them up for sale, they undergo several operations. They are curled, either by being baked, or by means of hot irons; when necessary, they are also dyed. The feathers principally in use are those of the ostrich, heron, the common cock, swan, peacock, and goose: of these, some are adapted to plumes with which hearses and horses are decorated at the funerals of the great; others are fitted for ornaments to the human head: to some we are indebted for the beds on which we lie, and to others for the pens with which we write. … Military feathers are chiefly made of the *hackle* feathers, as they are called; these are plucked from the neck of the cock. The feathers of this bird are in great demand: his neck and back are clothed with long streaming feathers, intermixed with orange, black, and yellow; his tail is made up of stiff feathers, with two large ones waving over the rest in form of a sickle. The plumage of the *wonderful Indian cock* is very beautiful, and consists of five different colours, viz. the black, white, green, red, and blue; and the tail is made up of twelve very beautiful feathers. But ostrich feathers are the most valuable: they are such as are represented in the plate. In their natural state they are mostly black and white: the largest feathers are at the extremeties of their wings and tails. The feathers of the … Round feathers, such as the woman in the plate is at work upon, are composed of a number of smaller ones: if they are taken from the cock's neck, they are neatly tied on wire with thread; but if they are small ostrich feathers, they are twisted round an upright wire. The single ostrich feathers have usually a small piece of wire at the end, for the purpose of fixing into the cap, turban, or hair. Women that work at this business can earn two shillings a clay. <u>Book of Trades</u>, 1806 ~~~ We cannot say we admire the very long drooping feathers now adopted in full-dress, which descend as low as the elbow: they by no means add grace to a good figure, and on the little short-necked woman, who will wear them because they are fashionable, they are most ridiculously unfitting. *Lady's Magazine*, February 1825 ~~~ Peacocks' feathers, those of the paroquet, and the plumage of birds of paradise dyed, are the ornaments employed for hats and turbans. White ostrich feathers are also in favour, particularly for crimson velvet hats. *Court Magazine*, December 1835

feather fringe – [Paris ball dress] A dress of gros de Naples, the colour oriental-green, is much admired at evening parties: it is trimmed with feather-fringe, as high as the knee. *Ladies' Museum*, October 1829 ~~~ On dresses of crape, feather-fringe forms a beautiful trimming. *Ladies' Pocket*, December 1829 ~~~ Feather-fringe is much used in the ornamenting of velvet hats, and forms a light and very elegant trimming; scarlet and orange-colour, mixed, in this material, have a very pleasing effect on black velvet carriage hats. *La Belle Assemblée*, January, 1830 ~~~ feather fringe is a delicate and beautiful article, made from the barbs of the ostrich, and having all the quality of the finest silk; this trimming is reserved fro the full-dress evening party. ... On velvet dresses, for the evening, feather-fringe constitutes the favourite trimming. ... all the black bonnets, however, that we have yet remarked, in carriages, whether of satin or velvet, are trimmed with ribands of some gay and striking colour, and often with coloured feather fringe; scarlet and yellow are the most favourite associations. *Ladies' Museum*, January 1830

feathered silk – But a new trimming has just been invented at Lyons for dresses, in imitation of Chinchilla fur; it is called feathered silk, and sells at thirty-five francs per yard. *La Belle Assemblée*, October 1819 [see also *plume silk*]

felt – a kind of stuff or cloth, either of wool alone, or of castors, camels, conies hair, and lambs wool, neither spun, crossed, nor woven, but wrought and fulled with lees and size, and afterwards shaped into the form of a hat upon a block; a hide or skin of animals; Barclay's English Dictionary, 1799 ~~~ Felt, in commerce, a sort of stuff deriving all its consistence merely from being fulled, or wrought with lees and size, without either spinning or weaving. Felt is made wither of wool alone, or of wool and hair. Those of French make, 3 ½ yards long, and 1 ½ broad, for cloaks, Encyclopædia Britannica, 1797 ~~~ Fur is used either growing to the skin, or separated from it. In its detached state, it is usually employed in making a stuff called felt. ... It is in the manufacture of hats that felting is chiefly practised; and the fur used for this purpose is that of the beaver, the rabbit, and the hare. Fourth Book of Lessons, 1835

ferret – Ferret or floret silk, Filozel, sleeve-silk, coarse Dictionary of Commerce, 1810 ~~~ A kind of narrow woollen tape. Encyclopædia Perthensis, 1816 ~~~Ferret, a small animal, a silk tape Webster's Dictionary, 1817 ~~~ Ferret, A kind of silk tape used for trimming or ornament; F. *fleurette*; B. *floret*; Etymons of English Words, 1826 ... We call ferret, or flock silk, those coarse fibres which the worm in spinning casts about, as it were by chance, before it begins its cocoon. ... It is from this species of silk, called by the Piedmontese floretta, that the narrow ribband, so well known by the name of ferret, is manufactured. I have also seen several kinds of passable cloth, and likewise stockings, made of this carded flock silk. But the price of every thing that I have seen produced from it was much inferior to the worst productions of the milled silk. Methodical Treatise…on Silk, 1828 [see also *filoselle*, *floret* and *floss*]

feuille des Indes – the most admired materials for dresses which have just appeared in Paris. ... *Feuille des Indes*: – Somewhat resembling the *Velours Medicis*. The pattern consists of an elegant leaf, in bright relief on a dark ground. It may be had in every variety of colour, and is peculiarly appropriate to full dress. *Court Journal*, October 17, 1835

figured – Figured camblets, are those of one colour, whereon are stamped various figures, flowers, foliage, &c. by means of hot irons, which are a kind of moulds, passed together with the stuff, under a press. These are chiefly brought from Amiens and Flanders; the commerce of these was anciently much more considerable than at present. Encyclopædia Britannica, 1797 ~~~ Figured velvet, that is, adorned and worked with divers figures, though the ground is the same with the figures, that is the whole surface velveted. Dictionary of Commerce, 1810 ~~~ marked with figures. The term is chiefly applied to stuffs, whereon the figures of flowers, and the like, are either wrought or stamped. Encyclopædia Perthensis, 1816 ~~~ Dress hats are of figured velvet, granite or scabious colour, *Lady's Magazine*, December 1830

fil – [see *thread*]

filet – Silk-twist, *filet*, Chambaud's French Dictionary, 1815 ~~~ Scarfs are still as fashionable as ever; The most novel are of black silk *filet*, excessively fine, and with patterns in application which have a very rich effect. *Court Magazine*, September 1836

filet de Lille – Gloves of silk and *filet de Lille* have again made their appearance this summer. *Court Journal*, June 6, 1835 [see *Lisle*]

filet de Vulcain – A dress has been prepared at Paris for the queen of Prussia: the pattern is called *Filets de*

Vulcain. The ground is pink, and this net, which seems spread over it, is like that on a balloon; the threads are composed of yellow and black silk: … It is impossible to imagine the beautiful effect of the black and yellow net on the rose-colour ground. *La Belle Assemblée*, February 1827 ~~~ [court dress] dress of tulle filet de Vulcain, over superb satin slip, *Lady's Magazine and Museum*, June 1836

fille d'honneur – If the gown is not adorned with *ruches*, it is trimmed *à la fille d'honneur*, that is with narrow flounces scollopped, or rather notched like the teeth of a saw, and put very close to each other: *Repository of Arts*, December 1821

filling – [see *weft*]

fillozel – [see *filoselle*]

filoselle – Note I. Raw, long, short, China, Morea silk, &c. are weighed by a great pound of 24 oz. But Ferret, Filosella, sleeve silk, &c. by the common pound of 16 oz. Schoolmaster's Assistant, 1800 ~~~ *ferret-silk* Tardy's French Dictionary, 1799 ~~~ Ferret or floret silk, Fillozel, sleeve-silk, coarse Ship-Master's Assistant, 1801 ~~~ Fillozel or Paris Silk Sessional Papers, 1825 ~~~ Filoselle, … *Grogram-yarn, a kind of ferret or coarse silk, floss-silk*. Boniface's French Dictionary, 1828 ~~~ The thread called, in France, filoselle, is made in part from pointed cocoons, formed by feeble worms, or in cold seasons; the ends are slightly covered with silk, and, not being entirely close, the water enters and precipitates them to the bottom. More or less are met with in every parcel. They are first deprived of their gum, by being immersed in plain water, or in soap and water, when the filoselle is wished to be white, as before directed. When dried, this filoselle is spun upon the distaff in France, and practice enables the women to form an even and fine thread. The filoselle thread made from the tow of the seed cocoons, is esteemed of the first quality, giving no waste. It is spun upon the distaff, in France, but may be spun on the wheel. It is prepared as above directed, and is used to make stockings. The bourre, or waste, is the produce of the remains of the various manipulations which silk undergoes when manufacturing, as reeling, doubling, and milling. It is carded and spun upon the distaff, and sometimes on a wheel. Growth and Manufacture of Silk, 1828 ~~~ The *filoselle* or floss silk which will issue from the filatures, and needs not be thrown, but only carded and spun in the usual way, will be immediately employed by our industrious workmen in making stockings, caps, vestings, and other kinds of hosiery. Growth and Manufacture of Silk, 1830 [see *floret* and *floss*]

fisher – By some information of due authority which has been recently made public, we learn, that the *fur-trade* of the British Canadian Provinces, is now in a flourishing state. Its produce in the year 1798, consisted of … 1650 fisher skins, *Monthly Magazine*, January 1802 ~~~ The fur of the marten is valuable. There are two kinds in America; the Pine marten, and Pennants marten, called Fisher. Dictionary of General Knowledge, 1830 ~~~ The Fisher, sometimes called the black Fox, greatly resembles the Martin; his colour is black, and his fur valuable. New Brunswick, 1832 ~~~ Peckan, or fisher. In quality inferior to the mink and pine martin, but twice the size of this latter, and exported to the continent. Transactions of the Society, 1833 [see also *fox* and *marten*]

fitch – GOODS PROHIBITED TO BE IMPORTED FOR SALE, BY ANY PERSONS, EXCEPT MADE AND WROUGHT IN IRELAND, OR TAKEN UPON THE SEAS, OR WRECKED. … Furs tawed, viz. Badger, Bear, Beaver, Calabar, Cat, Ermine, Fitch, Fox, Ship-Master's Assistant, 1795 ~~~ the Polecat, Fitchet, or Foumart. – The length of this animal is about 17 inches, exclusive of the tail; that of the tail six. … The sides are covered with hairs of two colours, the ends of which are of a blackish hue, like the other parts; the middle of a full tawny colour. … Though the smell of the polecat, when alive, is rank and disagreeable, even to a proverb, yet the skin is dressed with the hair on, and used as other furs for tippets, &c. and is also sent abroad to line clothes. Encyclopædia Britannica, 1810 ~~~ The furs most fashionable, after ermine and sable, are Chinchella, Fitch, and dark squirrel. *Ladies' Monthly Museum*, December 1819 ~~~ [ad] Sable, Fitch, Ermine, *Kaleidoscope*, November 11, 1823 ~~~ [story] a green hunting boddice, or spencer, tastefully trimmed with fine fitch fur, covered without concealing the perfect contour of her bust; *European Magazine*, November 1824 ~~~ the foumart of the north of England most decidedly is not the weasel, or the *Mustéla vulgaris*, but the polecat, or *Mustéla Putòrius* of Linnæus; which, from the strong smell it emits, when frightened, is called the foumart, quasi foul marten, … The foumart of Yorkshire is the same animal which yields the fur, which, when imported from abroad, is called fitch. *Magazine of Natural History*, April 1832 ~~~ [novel: Finesse] a boa of that evil-smelling fur, termed *fitch*, *Monthly Review*, June 1835 ~~~ The Polecat, Fitchew, or Fitchet, *(mustela putorius,)* the Foomart of Scotland, is about a foot and a half long, and extremely active. It lurks in crevices, or burrows in the earth. Like many other species of the Weasel, it secretes a fluid, the smell of which is highly offensive. Its fur is of a dark brown colour, and very beautiful. Analytical Dictionary, 1835

flannel – a kind of slight, loose woolen stuff, very warm, composed of a woof and warp, woven on a loom, with two treddles, after the manner of bays, &c. Royal English Dictionary, 1775 ~~~ A soft nappy stuff of wool. Sheridan's English Dictionary, 1797 ~~~ Welsh flannel, two shillings and a halfpenny to two shillings and fivepence farthing per yard. [in 1801] A Voyage Round the World, 1805 ~~~ Grouse-shooting is very laborious, and requires both judgment and experience, particularly in such mountains as the sportsman is a stranger to. As the season is generally the hottest in the year, it becomes necessary to be clothed accordingly. The lighter the dress the better, taking care at the same time to let the garments next your skin chiefly consist of flannel. A flannel shirt and drawers are the best things that can be used for this purpose, and ought, in fact, to be considered as indispensable. Shooter's Guide, 1816 ~~~ The uneasy sensation occasioned by flannel is of very short duration; use will very speedily not only accustom it to the body, but render its wearing pleasant and agreeable: that it may make the skin red and inflamed, if it be too much rubbed and scratched, cannot be denied; but it is a palpable error that it produces cutaneous eruptions; it having quite a *contrary* effect, as it preserves the pores open, increases perspiration, and thus *removes the cause* of cutaneous diseases, which arise chiefly from a checked and irregular state of excretion by the pores. In answer to another objection against flannel, upon the score of *cleanliness,* we observe, that it is certain that a flannel shirt or waistcoat will preserve the body, not only as clean, but *much cleaner* than linen, if as frequently changed. *Wool,* on account of its rough surface, may be more calculated to absorb infectious morbid matter, than a more smooth substance; but we have nothing to apprehend from *flannel next the skin.* We are rather of opinion that it is a better preventive against contagion, than any other; because, while it encourages perspiration, it at the same time *removes* the inhaled poisonous particles; particularly if, in cases of danger, perspiration be increased by other suitable means. Hence, those who wear flannel next their skin never suffer from cold. Female's Encyclopædia, 1830 ~~~ Flannel - some flannels have a little cotton mingled. Book of Commerce by Sea and Land, 1834 ~~~ Flannels are made of Woollenyarn, slightly twisted in the spinning, and of open texture, – the object in view being to have the cloth soft and spungy, without regard to strength. Such as have the pile raised on one side (which is done by teasels, or by cards, and called Perching,) are termed *Raised* Flannels – when both sides are so covered, they are *Double-raised* Flannels. There are also Milled and Double-milled Flannels; and all the sorts are, occasionally, dyed, though more usually sold white. Analytical Dictionary, 1835 ~~~ The dress consists of a robe de chambre of flannel, so excessively fine in its texture that it might almost be taken for Cachemere: they sell this flannel here at an amazing high price, as English. *Lady's Magazine and Museum*, April 1835 ~~~ *List of prices paid by the clothiers of Baltimore for work performed for them by the seamstresses. … Flannel shirts. 8 cents. … Flannel under shirts. 6 ½ cents Niles' Weekly Register*, October 31, 1835 ~~~ [ad] Proposals will be received at the Office of the Commissary General of Purchases, in Philadelphia, for making Army Clothing for the year 1837, and for sundry articles ready made, as hereafter enumerated, viz – … Flannel, of cotton and wool, 7-8 wide. *Army and Navy Chronicle*, December 15, 1836 [see also *canton flannel* and *cotton flannel*]

flannelle – *flannel.* Dufief's French Dictionary, 1810 ~~~ [Paris] Mantles have already become very general in the promenades. Several of those for *negligé* are of *flannelle a mouchee* – it is a woollen material, quadrilled in large squares of red, green, or blue with black; the spots are red on the black, or black on the red. *Court Magazine*, December 1835

fleecy hosiery – *Practical Observations concerning Sea-Bathing,* … "flannel and fleecy hosiery are to be found under the shirts among half of the young men of the age. Debility, irritation, the premature approaches old age, and a pale and sickly countenance, are the effect of this pernicious fashion." *European Magazine*, 1805 ~~~ to shelter themselves from the piercing attacks of the cold, by a judicious adoption of her bosom friend. – This article does not now (as formerly) consist in an insignificant piece of fur, just fitted to the chest; but in conformity to the enlarged sense, which its comprehensive name implies, affords a more extensive protection in the sensible under-wrap of fleecy-hosiery, or lamb's-wool   *La Belle Assemblée*, December 1808 ~~~ Fleecy-hosiery, a very useful kind of manufacture, in which fine fleeces of wool are interwoven into a cotton piece of the common stocking texture. The following is the specification of the patent granted to Mr. Holland, of Broad-street, Bloomsbury, in the county of Middlesex, for a method of making stockings, socks, waistcoats, and other clothing, for persons afflicted with complaints requiring warmth, and for common use in cold climates, and for making false or downy calves in stockings. It is dated September 22, 1788. <u>Pantologia</u>, 1819

fleur des Anges – A gauze called *fleur des Anges*, destined for ball dresses and turbans, is still more elegant than the Donna Maria gauze that has been such a favourite. *Court Magazine*, October 1833 ~~~ Evening Dress. The robe is composed of a new kind of gauze, called *gaze fleur des anges*, a rose-coloured ground, flowered in separate sprigs in a blond lace pattern, and worn over a satin slip to correspond. *Court Magazine*, November 1833 ~~~ An evening dress of white *fleur d'Ange* gauze tissue, *Casket*, January 1834

fleuret – In sorting the cocoons, you will always find some perforated cocoons among them, whose worm is already born; these you must set apart for fleuret. <u>Dictionary of Merchandize</u>, 1803 ~~~ Fleuret, *m ferret silk, ferret ribbon.* – le blancard, *a kind of linen.* <u>Dufief's French Dictionary</u>, 1810 [see *floret* and *floss*]

flock gauze – fine muslin, silk net, and flock gauze are most in favour for evening costume. *La Belle Assemblée*, September 1818 ~~~ Ball dresses are of flock gauze, some white, some rose-colour, with *corsages* of velvet, *La Belle Assemblée*, December 1820 ~~~ At select evening parties, dresses of striped flock gauze are worn, the stripes very broad: *Ladies' Monthly Museum*, June 1828 ~~~ Dresses for evening parties still continue to be ornamented with beautiful embroidery; the most elegant are those of light texture, such as palmyrene, flock gauze, and silk *batiste*; *Ladies' Pocket*, February 1829

flock silk – [see *ferret*]

floize – A beautiful ball dress ... is worn the Spanish *corsage* of bright crimson sarsnet, beautifully finished with a white trimming of floize silk: nothing can be more appropriate than this dress for the winter season, yet it boasts all the lightness so requisite to be adopted by the votaries of the ball-room. *La Belle Assemblée*, December 1816 ~~~ The Madrid robe is also another novelty for fancy mourning; it is of black spotted gauze, with broad flounces of white figured *tulle* of a rich pattern, each flounce caught up in festoons, and edged with a light and elegant floize silk trimming. *La Belle Assemblée*, December 1818 ~~~ For dinner-dress parties, ... The tulle dress is also richly embroidered in floize silk, *Ladies' Monthly Museum*, May 1821 ~~~ Ball Dress. ... Round the border of the petticoat are two rows of trimming, en tirebouchons of blue crape lisse, entwined with a rich guimp of floize silk; *Kaleidoscope*, August 10, 1824 ~~~ [evening dress flounce] A light but rich trimming, composed of floize silk, finishes the points and dents, each of which has, in the centre, a lozenge embroidered in gold. *Casket*, April 1830 ~~~ [story] employed in reeling off a tangled skein of floize silk. ... But floize silk is (as all fair ladies are aware) one of the most adhesive things in the world *Lady's Magazine and Museum*, March 1835 [see also *floss*]

Florence – [see *florentine*]

Florence net – an elegant dress for evening parties, or for concerts, of black Florence net over a rose colour slip: ... For dinner parties, or for the home reception of company, nothing is deemed more elegant than a dress of French violet, trimmed with blue satin and violet, in alternate folds or puckerings: this beautiful, though fragile colour, is either of satin, poplin, Italian crape, or the more admired article of Florence net, according to the taste or youth of the wearer. *La Belle Assemblée*, March 1816

florentine – [Paris] In dresses of *éclat*, white satin is preferred to figured muslins. The taste for silk perseveres. Besides brown Florence and plain white satins, we see coloured, figured, and striped satins. *Lady's Magazine*, May 1800 ~~~ For Gentlemen. Full dress. ... those also [breeches] of black florentine silk are very fashionable *Edinburgh Annual Register*, May 1, 1810 ~~~Statement Of British Cotton

Manufactures Suitable For Sicily. ... Florentines at 1s. 8d. are the kinds that suit. <u>Voyages and Travels</u>, 1812 ~~~ Muslin walking scarfs, lined with florentine silk are in high estimation, *La Belle Assemblée*, July 1814 ~~~ [Thomas Smith convicted of stealing] half a piece of Florence silk, and two shawls, *New-York City-Hall Recorder*, March 1816 ~~~ Florentine, a species of silk cloth <u>Webster's Dictionary</u>, 1817 ~~~ English Evening Dress. Of Florence gauze, over a white slip of *gros de Naples*, or satin trimmed with a rich border of puckered net, or gauze, *Ladies' Monthly Museum*, February 1821 ~~~ [ad] Florentine stripes for trowsers, *Colonial Times*, January 13, 1826 ~~~ A few ladies of distinguished taste in dress were seen in crape *redingotes*, some lined with satin, others with *Florence*. *La Belle Assemblée*, July 1830 ~~~ The cloaks are wadded and lined with Florence (sarsnet), or any other light silk. *Lady's Magazine and Museum*, November 1834 ~~~ I have found nothing better for a light summer jacket than what is made at Manchester by the name of *satteen, jeanet,* or *florentine*, which is printed on each side, in imitation of cloth. This stuff far surpasses the others for lightness, comfort, durability, and every thing that can be required for warm weather; <u>Instructions to Young Sportsmen</u>, 1833 ~~~ The cloaks are wadded and lined with Florence (sarsnet), or any other light silk. *Lady's Magazine and Museum*, November 1834 ~~~ plain silks such as Sarcenets, Satins, Gros de Naples, Florentines, Plushes, and Velvets; *New England Farmer*, July 1, 1835 ~~~ For morning visits nothing is more elegant than a dress of chesnut-coloured florentine, sprigged with small detached bouquets in bright colours. *Court Journal*, October 24, 1835 ~~~ Florence or florentine silk, coming from beyond the Cape of Good Hope, 10 per cent. [Tariff.] <u>Jones's Digest</u>, 1835 ~~~ only think of having to give two dollars a yard for slight Florence silk; such silk as before the war *we* would not have worn at all *Godey's Ladies Book*, November 1836 [see also *sarsnet*]

floret [figured fabric] – Florets, (linnen) *Sound-Tariff*, August 1821 ~~~ it was a new Article; it was for what we term Floret, Royal Floret, a richer Article, on a similar Principle to that before made under the Head and Figure of Florets; but it was a richer Article by Three and Four Threads in the room of Two. ... Floret ... is a regulated Article greatly in Demand; but from the Restrictions and Regulations of the Magistrates entirely lost to London. Where is it carried on? In Macclesfield and Manchester, and other Parts of the Kingdom. ... sold to the Consumer in London for One Shilling and Four-pence, ... Floret, Fifty-four Inches wide. <u>House of Lords Sessional Papers</u>, 1823 ~~~ [1821] forty-five [weavers] are employed upon figured work, and their earnings amount to 33s. per week. ... the fact is, that the journeymen weavers who are most actively engaged in obtaining the price fixed upon labour by the magistrate, are those who are constantly employed upon the figured work, and their attention is directed solely to their own immediate interest; this inequality of wages in favour of particular work has lately taken from Spitalfields the whole of the manufacture of Handkerchiefs; it is now removing more rapidly the manufacture of Florets, which are made in Cheshire and Lancashire, from one-third to one-half less than the charge for weaving which the Middlesex magistrates have settled, and will, at no distant period, remove from Spitalfields the whole Silk manufacture, and leave a population of 50,000 persons to be a charge upon the public. <u>Reports and Papers of the House of Commons</u>, 1824 ~~~ figured silks, such as Florets, Tobines, Tissues, and Damasks; *New England Farmer*, July 1, 1835

floret [raw silk] – The nymphæ which come from the cocoons that are reeled off, are not thought fit for preserving the eggs of them; but those: which they keep for that purpose, are suffered, when they become moths, to eat their way through the balls; and of these perforated cocoons they make an inferior kind of silk, called floret. <u>Voyages to the East-Indies</u>, 1798 ~~~ Ferret or floret silk, filozel, sleeve-silk, coarse, <u>Practical Book of Customs</u>, 1801 ~~~ It deserves to be remarked, that, during the first day of its labours, the silk-worm spins only the exterior, irregular texture, which is known, in commerce, under the name of *floret*, or coarse silk, serving for inferior stockings, gloves, &c. <u>Domestic Encyclopædia</u>, 1802 [see *floss*]

florine – The dress stuffs are the *florine*, ... which may be compared to the double *grenadine*, has beautiful designs of pillars formed of small knit ornaments, placed very near each other; these pillars are distant about an inch and a half between each. *Ladies' Monthly Museum*, June 1826

floss – The next business is to wind off the silk. After separating a downy matter from the outside of the cocoons, called *floss*, <u>Arts of Life</u>, 1802 ~~~ White sarsnet parasol, with Vandyke floss fringe. *La Belle*

Assemblée, April 1807 ~~~ a very pretty trimming of silk net, the edge of this trimming, which is composed of floss silk is extremely beautiful; *La Belle Assemblée*, November 1814 ~~~ Floss silk (coarse waste silk). *Soie de bourres, filoselle,* Chambaud's French Dictionary, 1815 … [court dress] White satin petticoat, with floss silk net draperies; train to correspond. *La Belle Assemblée*, May 1816 ~~~ [ad] Ready Made Clothing. For the accommodation of Gentlemen travelling, he keeps constantly on hand, … Lambs' wool, Floss and Flannel drawers, Directory for the Village of Rochester, 1827 ~~~ In winding off the silk from the cocoons, whether perfect or imperfect, the finest and best threads are not those which are first spun out; on the contrary, the first threads which come off the cocoon are coarse, uneven, and unfit for use in the silk manufactories, either for the stuffs, twist or sewing silk. This loose, furzy substance, which is about one-tenth part of the whole silk on the cocoon, is called in French *fleuret,* and in English *floss,* from the Latin *flos,* flower; a name which reminds us of *lucus à non lucendo.* As soon as the threads of silk in the process of reeling come out fine and regular, this floss is separated from them and put aside for use, as will be presently mentioned. To it are added all the threads which, either from some defect in the cocoons, or from the awkwardness of the women employed in the different operations of reeling, winding and doubling, either break off so as not to be easily united to the other threads, or come out uneven or otherwise unfit for use; these are called the *waste silk,* and added to the *floss,* assume with it the same name. This mass, boiled in soap and water, afterwards carded and spun in the spinning wheel, takes the name in French of *bourre de soie* or *filoselle.* Boyer, in his dictionary, translates the word *filoselle* into English by *ferret-silk* or *flurt silk.* This last name is evidently a corruption, or an English pronunciation of the French word *fleuret, floss silk.* This floss, ferret or flurt-silk, by whatever name it may be called, is employed in making silk stockings, mittens, gloves, suspenders, night caps, and, in general, all kinds of silk hosiery. I have heard that the women of Connecticut knit silk stockings and mittens out of the silk which they extract from the cocoons. Essays on American Silk, 1830 ~~~ [court dress] A white gros de Naples dress, embroidered with gold, and white floss silk corsage à la Sevigné; *Royal Lady's Magazine*, June 1831 ~~~ Even one kind of silk which occurs in entangled tufts, called floss, is spun like cotton, by the simultaneous action of stretching and twisting. … There are three kinds of raw silk, organzine, tram, and floss. Philosophy of Manufactures, 1835 ~~~ [court dress] Body and sleeves of a magnificient blue and silver brocaded Irish tabbinet, … rich figured white satin petticoat, with elegant flounce, richly embroidered with blue floss silk to correspond. *Lady's Magazine and Museum*, June 1836 [see also *ferret, floret* and *spun silk*]

flurt silk – [see *floss*]

flushing – Before proceeding further, it may be proper to explain what is known, among weavers, by the appellation of *flushing.* When any thread, or portion, whether of warp or woof, is not regularly interwoven with the fabric, as in plain weaving, that thread, or portion of threads, is said to be flushed. Art of Weaving, 1807 ~~~ Dresses for Wildfowl Shooting. … Under the waistcoat, should be worn a Flushing frock, … Having put on the boots, there must be drawn over all a pair of short loose sailcloth * (or, if cold frosty weather, Flushing-coating) trowsers. Instructions to Young Sportsmen, 1825 ~~~ *Flushings and Lionskins* – 48 inches wide, cost 1s. 5d. to 3s. …These articles are used for great coats, jackets, &c. and are worn by farmers, mechanics, laborers, sailors, fishermen, and boatmen. *Niles' Weekly Register*, March 8, 1828 ~~~ The term flushing is of frequent use in the art of weaving. Any quantity of weft which passes over or under more threads of warp than one, or extends beyond the range of the plain texture, is said to be floated or flushed. Tweels, lined work, and all the varieties of corduroys, &c. are, therefore, merely the effect of flushing, but the term is commonly restricted to a few of the inferior branches of fancy weaving, Art of Weaving, 1831

fly – Evening Dress. … it is finished at the bottom by a single row of fly trimming, which is a new invention, of a light and pretty description, composed of floss silk. *Repository of Arts*, April 1819 [see also *floss*]

flying squirrel – The American flying Squirrel, is much less than the European, being not above five inches long, and of a russet, grey, or ash colour on the back, and white on the under parts. Dictionary of Merchandise, 1805 ~~~ A new kind of Witzchoura has lately appeared, without any pelerine; the trimming of which commences at the knees, which is of chinchilla fur, or that of the flying squirrel. *La*

Belle Assemblée, January 1820 ~~~ The flying squirrels are of a beautiful slate colour, with a fur so fine, that, although a small animal, the hatters here give a quarter dollar for every skin. *London Literary Gazette*, August 25, 1827

foil – [worn at the Prince of Wales's marriage] A crape petticoat, embroidered with silver spangles, and stripes of silver foil, *Gentleman's Magazine*, May 1795 ~~~ [Court dress] A white and silver petticoat, richly spangled and divided in waves by stripes of silver foil, ... on the left side a rich drapery of foil stripes, forming a star drapery, *Edinburgh Magazine*, June 1802 ~~~ richly embroidered in dean and bright gold foil, *La Belle Assemblée*, January 1807 ~~~ *Foil*, among jewellers, a thin leaf of metal placed under a precious stone, in order to increase its brilliancy, or give it an agreeable and different colour. These foils are made of either copper, gold, or gold and silver together; the copper foils are commonly known by the name of Nurenberg, or German foils. <u>Dictionary of Commerce</u>, 1810 ~~~ I here allude to the preparation of foils, or coloured laminae, used with so much success in the manufacturing of buttons, in embroidery, and for ornamenting a variety of toys, of which there is a very extensive and daily consumption. These very thin laminae of silver, copper, brass, or tin, perform the same office, under the name of foil, and may be distinguished by the name of *false enamel,* as enamel covered with coloured or uncoloured copal varnish. ... When the nature of the colouring parts which ornament different kinds of foil is examined, it does not always appear to be owing to coloured varnishes. In the course of my researches I think I have observed, that some of these colouring parts belong to that kind of compositions called *sauce,* covered afterwards with a transparent varnish, which preserves them from the influence of moisture, and which produces with the metallic splendour that beautiful effect with which they are generally attended. The processes may be varied, with regard to the tone and shades of the colours, which may be easily rendered stronger or weaker. ... * Sauce is a technical term used to describe the compositions employed in making foil. <u>Painter and Varnisher's Guide</u>, 1816 ~~~ [court dress] A white crape dress, embroidered in bouquets of gold lama and amethyst foil; *Court Journal*, June 1833 ~~~ Court Dress. ... A blue satin petticoat, finished at the bottom by a silver foil trimming, *Court Magazine*, May 1835

fontange – Another silk, something of the same kind as foulard, and likely to be equally fashionable, is called *fontange*; it is figured in very small patterns in vivid colours. The prettiest are blue, on wood colour, white on granite, green on black, and fire colour on black. ... will be very generally adopted in elegant morning dress. *Court Magazine*, April 1834

forest cloth – a peculiar kind of broad cloth. <u>Royal English Dictionary</u>, 1775 ~~~ *Premium 3. – Thirty Dollars.* For the best piece of forest cloth, twenty-five yards long, and one yard wide – made of [wool shorn from the living sheep.] *Universal Magazine*, February 1809 ~~~ I saw the new clothing for the year, ... it consisted of a jacket and waistcoat of excellent forest cloth, <u>Board of Education in Ireland</u>, 1813 ~~~ [debate on the Wool Bill] forest cloths, for sailors, watermen, fishermen, farmers, mechanics, &c.; *Niles' Weekly Register*, April 27, 1827

foulard – conversational French ... "*foulard*" is a silk handkerchief; *New Monthly Magazine*, 1821 ~~~ Shawls *en foulard* are exceedingly fashionable in undress. ... The other novelty is a gown composed of white *foulard uni*. [*uni*: plain] *Repository of Arts*, August 1829 ~~~ Printed and painted silks are also likely to be in favour. The prettiest of the former are the *foulards*, originally a French material, but now made in a very superior manner in England. *La Belle Assemblée*, November 1830 ~~~ Ball Dress. A turban composed of blue crape and *foulard* intermixed, the crape forms the foundation of the turban, the *foulard* is arranged *en papillon*, by folds of crape, placed in the centre; *Casket*, January 1831 ~~~ Dresses of *foulard*, or washing silk, are every day becoming more and more numerous. Their extreme lightness and softness render them peculiarly appropriate to the present season. They are worn in every variety of colour and pattern. A mantelet of the same material as the dress, and trimmed with black lace, has a very pretty effect. *Foulard* promises to supersede chaly, at least until the cool autumnal weather shall restore the latter to its wonted favour. *Court Journal*, June 22, 1833 ~~~ Silks are expected to be very fashionable this summer, both for morning and evening dress. A great variety of foulards have appeared, some of very large and grotesque patterns; others flowered in running patterns, which resemble the chintzes of our grandmamma's early days; and some of a singular but rich description, called *foulard-moyen-age*. ... The new materials most likely to be in favour in evening dress are, *Foulard Pompadour*: the pattern dates from Louis XV.'s time; it is rich, but heavy; *Court Magazine*, April 1834 ~~~ [ad] Foulards at 5s. [per yard] *New England Farmer*, March 25, 1835 ~~~ Plaid silk *foulards*, ... for half-dress. *Court Magazine*, May 1835

foulard baziné – *Foulards bazinés* are printed silks of new and striking patterns. *Court Magazine*, May 1836

foulard Coraline – among the most elegant for the morning promenade, ... the *foulard Coraline*. This last is a new kind of *foulard*, not printed but figured. *Court Magazine*, April 1836

foulard d'Orient – [see *oriental*]

foulard de Bruxelles – A new material, just come into favour for promenade dress, is a washing silk, *foulard de Bruxelles*: it is a small chequered pattern of white, green, or lilac, but the ground is always dust colour. *Court Magazine*, July 1834

foulard de laine – [Paris] Promenade dresses are composed of ... *foulard du laine*, (a material which at a distance resembles printed muslin, but is composed of wool); *Ladies' Museum*, June 1831 ~~~ [Paris] New materials for dresses are this year very numerous. Several of these for morning *negligé* are of the finest Cashmere wool, and of a slighter kind than Chali. These are ... the *foulards de laine*, both plain and printed, *Court Magazine*, May 1835

foulard du Bengale – [see *Bengal*]

foulard satin – Another full dress equally becoming, though less brilliant, consists of a robe of satin foulard, the pattern bouquets of roses on a blue ground. *Court Journal*, February 14, 1835 ~~~ Tea Parties (*des Thés*) are becoming very fashionable at Paris. ... The toilette of our hostess was at once simple and elegant; a dress of foulard satin, the colour of unbleached cambric (called *cindre*), with a delicate running pattern all over of the little blue flower called "forget-me not;" *Lady's Magazine and Museum*, April 1835 ~~~ Pelisse of *satin foulard*; a cashmere design on a brown ground, lined with blue silk, *Court Journal*, May 9, 1835 ~~~ We have observed ... foulard satins in new and elegant patterns, consisting of sprigs and richly shaded checks and stripes. *Court Journal*, October 17, 1835

foulard Ulemas – The new materials most likely to be in favour in evening dress are, ... *Foulard Ulemas*, a grenadine silk, of Egyptian patterns; *Court Magazine*, April 1834

foumart – [see *fitch*]

fox – Mourning Dress. ... Fox tippet. ... Half Mourning Dress. ... Silver fox muff. *Lady's Magazine*, December 1796 ~~~ The scarf is ... invariably trimmed with skin, either blue fox, squirrel, or leopard. *La Belle Assemblée*, November 1806 ~~~ Walking Dress. A Polish Robe of purple velvet, ... the whole trimmed entirely round with the red fox, mole, leopard spot, or gray squirrel. *La Belle Assemblée*, February 1807 ~~~ Large shawls and scarlet mantles are, however, still much worn on these occasions [the Opera]; with which the white fox, or swansdown tippet, also blends. *Port Folio*, June 1809 ~~~ Fox-skins. There is, perhaps, no animal whose fur is subject to greater variety than the fox. The skin of this quadruped in the south of Europe is generally red; but in some parts of America, Asia, and the north of Europe there are black, white, grey, variegated, and fawn-coloured foxes. ... Fox-skins are employed in the making of muffs, tippets, trimmings for garments, &c. General Dictionary of Commerce, 1810 ~~~ The black fox, or, as it is termed in the neighbourhood of Detroit, the fisher, is found in the woody country bordering on the coast. How it should have acquired this appellation it is difficult to imagine, as it certainly does not prey upon fish. ... The silver fox is an animal very rare, even in the country he inhabits. ... It has a long deep lead-coloured fur, for foil, intermixed with long hairs, either of a white or black colour at the lower part, and invariably white at the top, forming a most beautiful silver gray. Annual Register, 1817 ~~~ a muff of the white Siberian fox, with half-boots of puce-colored kid, and light doe-skin gloves, finish this promenade dress, in which is combined richness, elegance, and simplicity. *La Belle Assemblée*, January 1823 ~~~ We have seen a carriage pelisse of satin, of a bright crimson hue; it was trimmed with the fur of the black Moscovy fox, *Lady's Magazine*, January 1829 ~~~ Russian fox, French martin, and grey squirrel are genteel, though not expensive furs. *Maids, Wives, and Widows*, November 10, 1832 ~~~ The American furs which are at present brought to London are: ... Fox. Of this, also, there are many kinds. The white, or Arctic fox, is now coming a little into use here for muffs and tippets; it is a fine fur, and has nothing of the rank smell of other species of fox. The silver, or black, and the cross-fox,* are chiefly sent to Russia. The decided taste in Russia is for dark-coloured furs: hence those which are at the same time black and fine are the most costly. The black fox of America, though a far more valuable fur than that of any other American fox, is not comparable to the Russian, the skins of which are popularly said to be worth their weight in gold, and have actually been sold for 300 or 400 roubles a-piece. The red fox, a much larger and fuller fur than the European fox, and of a bright rust-colour. It is used here for muffs and trimmings, and a considerable demand exists for them in Greece. ... * The cross- fox has a thick long fur, mottled black and white dashed with rust-colour, with certain cruciform markings on the shoulders. Transactions of the Society, 1833 ~~~ The *isatis,* called also the blue fox, is of a deep ashen color; but it is often white in winter. It roams over the north of Siberia. The fur of this species is very valuable, *Lady's Magazine,* February 1825 ~~~ Black foxes are highly esteemed; a single skin will fetch a hundred guineas. Book of Commerce by Sea and Land, 1834... [mantles] the trimming a new kind of fox fur; it is close and very light, of a tawny orange, but black at the extremity. *Court Magazine,* March 1835 [for *black fox,* see also *fisher*]

fox brush feather – [army staff undress, 1800] plain round hat with a fox tail feather over the center of the crown, Bombay Army, 1801 ~~~ [full dress] The cap is Austrian, composed of satin and blond, ornamented with fox-tail feathers, either white, or tipped with blue, and when worn by an attractive lady, has a most beautiful effect. *Ladies' Monthly Museum,* November 1816 ~~~ But the most elegant head-dress *for grande costume,* is the *plume aigrette*; in the front of which is a full bunch of garden lilies formed of white feathers; in the midst of each is a moss rosebud on the point of opening into bloom. White feathers, of the heron kind, are seen spiring [sic] above, and two drooping fox brush white feathers fall over the left side, and complete this unique and truly splendid head-dress. *La Belle Assemblée,* August 1819 ~~~ trimmed with round ostrich, or what, I believe, you call fox-brush feathers. *La Belle Assemblée,* February 1820 ~~~ Bonnets worn by the sea-side ... ornamented with fox-brush feathers. *Ladies' Monthly Museum,* October 1821 ~~~ *List of prices paid for Indian goods in England,* ... Foxtail feathers – pr. doz. $2 50 *Public Documents*, March 5, 1832 [see also *ostrich*]

fragaletta – [Paris] The French ladies are so fond of the clear printed muslins, to which they have given the name of *fragaletta,* that the wear them at concerts, and other assemblies: they have white, or very light coloured grounds, figured over in a pattern of green-leaves and wood-strawberries. *Ladies' Pocket,* October 1829

Française de Foix – [Paris] New Materials. – For grandes toilettes d'hirer, the newest materials are ... Satin *Française de Foix* – the same material [as Scarron], without being striped. *Lady's Magazine and Museum,* November 1834

freeze – [see *frieze*]

French cambric – While French cambrics were subjected to a duty amounting to a legal prohibition, almost every linen draper in London, perhaps every one, sold them; and all of them pleaded custom on the one hand and necessity on the other. The necessity was the necessity of pleasing their customers, who scarcely knew that the cambrics were French and illegal. Each shopkeeper was afraid that, if he could not furnish his customer with a frill to his shirt, both frill and shirt would be bought at a neighbouring shop, where no scruples would be found. The law was very objectionable, and is now repealed. But while it existed, the introduction of cambrics to sale was the most palpable smuggling. Enquiry into the Duties of Men, 1797 ~~~ [Paris] Walking Dress. A plain frock of French cambric, simply open, hemmed at the bottom; ... [London] A few of our *haut ton,* distinguished for youth and beauty, have adopted the short frock of French cambric, *La Belle Assemblée,* October 1806 ~~~ Walking Dress. A gown of white French cambrick, or pale pink muslin, with long sleeves, ... made rather short, and worn over trowsers of white French cambric, *Jersey Magazine,* September 1810 ~~~ Dress for the Fashionable Promenades. A purple velvet pelisse, with a full standing-up collar, worn carelessly open over a round white dress of fine French cambric; *La Belle Assemblée,* February 1812 ~~~ A series of experiments have been lately instituted by the patentee of the British shirting cloth, which promise considerable advantages to the manufacturers of this country. After repeated trials and variations of process, a method has at length been discovered of bringing flax of English growth to a degree of perfection never before attained, and likely to produce a fabric equal in fineness and beautiful appearance to the most costly French cambric. This discovery at the present crisis is of some moment as it is calculated to supersede the importation of an important branch of French manufacture. *Monthly Magazine*, February 1812 ~~~ *Morning Costume*. – The Cobourg *accouchement robe* appears to be making a general appearance in the higher circles; it is made of the finest French cambric, rather in the chemise style, barely to meet in front, &c. &c. *Literary Gazette*, October 11, 1817 ~~~ Peignoirs of jaconot muslin, or French cambric embroidered down the front on each side, and worn with mantelets of the same material, also embroidered, are considered most elegant in morning dress; *Court Magazine*, September 1833 ~~~ French cambric (*batiste*) <u>Hand-Book for Travellers on the Continent</u>, 1836 [see also *batiste*, *cambric*, and *Scotch cambric*]

French cambric – While French cambrics were subjected to a duty amounting to a legal prohibition, almost every linen draper in London, perhaps every one, sold them; and all of them pleaded custom on the one hand and necessity on the other. The necessity was the necessity of pleasing their customers, who scarcely knew that the cambrics were French and illegal. Each shopkeeper was afraid that, if he could not furnish his customer with a frill to his shirt, both frill and shirt would be bought at a neighbouring shop, where no scruples would be found. The law was very objectionable, and is now repealed. But while it existed, the introduction of cambrics to sale was the most palpable smuggling. <u>Enquiry into the Duties of Men</u>, 1797 ~~~ [Paris] Walking Dress. A plain frock of French cambric, simply open, hemmed at the bottom; … [London] A few of our *haut ton*, distinguished for youth and beauty, have adopted the short frock of French cambric, *La Belle Assemblée*, October 1806 ~~~ Dress for the Fashionable Promenades. A purple velvet pelisse, with a full standing-up collar, worn carelessly open over a round white dress of fine French cambric; *La Belle Assemblée*, February 1812 ~~~ A series of experiments have been lately instituted by the patentee of the British shirting cloth, which promise considerable advantages to the manufacturers of this country. After repeated trials and variations of process, a method has at length been discovered of bringing flax of English growth to a degree of perfection never before attained, and likely to produce a fabric equal in fineness and beautiful appearance to the most costly French cambric. This discovery at the present crisis is of some moment as it is calculated to supersede the importation of an important branch of French manufacture. *Monthly Magazine*, February 1812 ~~~ *Morning Costume*. – The Cobourg *accouchement robe* appears to be making a general appearance in the higher circles; it is made of the finest French cambric, rather in the chemise style, barely to meet in front, &c. &c. *Literary Gazette*, October 11, 1817 ~~~ Peignoirs of jaconot muslin, or French cambric embroidered down the front on each side, and worn with mantelets of the same material, also embroidered, are considered most elegant in morning dress; *Court Magazine*, September 1833 ~~~ French cambric (*batiste*) <u>Hand-Book for Travellers on the Continent</u>, 1836 [see also *batiste*, *cambric*, and *Scotch cambric*]

French ground – [see *pillow lace*]

French lace – It appears that French lace, being so little bulky, has been last year smuggled into this counter in prodigious quantities. *Monthly Magazine*, July 1803 ~~~ Over the cap, or suspended from the edge, is seen a short veil of French lace. Indeed we remark, that no female of fashionable pretensions appears in a cap or small hat, without this chaste and becoming appendage. The veil is so graceful and interesting an ornament, that which ever way disposed it must ever produce a distinguishing effect. We take upon us however to recommend some attention to the size and disposition of this generally becoming ornament; in which particular it should at all times be adapted to the style of feature and stature of the several wearers; a short woman obscures the possible symmetry of her figure by a long or wide veil, while a female of commanding height, graceful carriage, and imposing air, receives from the long veil considerable advantage. *La Belle Assemblée*, August 1807 ~~~ [Patent] John Brown, of New Radford, near Nottingham, Lace-net Manufacturer; for a machine or machines for the manufacture of bobbin-lace or twist-net, similar to and resembling the Buckinghamshire lace net and French lace-net, as made by the hand with bobbins on pillows. Dated April 24, 1811. *Repertory of Arts*, June 1811 ~~~ *belles* of high *ton* sport French lace veils, but the extravagant price of foreign lace makes our bobbin net more generally worn, and it looks as well. *La*

Belle Assemblée, October 1814 [see also *bobbin net* and *lace*]

French sable – [see *marten*]

French net – [may sometimes be the same as French lace] The Parisian chemise is trimmed round with plain French net; … [Paris] Ball-dresses, dear Julia, were never more attractive than this spring. Frocks of French net, over white satin, painted in natural flowers. *La Belle Assemblée*, April 1807 ~~~ *Evening or Full Dress.* … [patent granted to] John Brown, of New Radford, near Nottingham, Lace-net Manufacturer; for a machine or machines for the manufacture of bobbin-lace or twist-net, similar to and resembling the Buckinghamshire lace-net and French lace-net, as made by the hand with bobbins on. pillows. Dated April 24, 1811. *Repertory of Arts*, June 1811 ~~~ The Maria Louisa *pelerine* of the most delicate French net, trimmed round with a broad lace, *Edinburgh Annual Register*, June 30, 1810 ~~~ Ball-Dress. A skirt of deep rose-coloured French net, of moderate length, ornamented with a full, but novel trimming of the same material and satin, *Ladies' Monthly Museum*, December 1826 [see *net* and *Paris net*]

frieze – Frieze, a coarse kind of woollen cloth; <u>Perry's English Dictionary</u>, 1795 ~~~ Frize, or Freeze, in commerce, a kind of woollen cloth or stuff for winter wear, being frized or knapt on one side; whence, in all probability, it derives its name. Of frizes, some are crossed, others not crossed: the former are chiefly of English manufacture, the latter of Irish. <u>Encyclopædia Britannica</u>, 1797 ~~~ Freeze, or Frieze, … a coarse kind of woollen stuff, or cloth, for winter wear; so called as being friezed or napped on one side. The manufacture of friezes is chiefly confined to Yorkshire. <u>General Dictionary of Commerce</u>, 1810 ~~~ I saw in a store-room two complete sets of clothing for each child, very little the worse for the wear; one was a jacket and waistcoat of brown frieze faced with yellow, <u>Board of Education in Ireland</u>, 1813 ~~~ The *frize* is a sort of coarse ratten, <u>Encyclopædia Perthensis</u>, 1816 ~~~ friezes (Swanskins) <u>Sessional Papers</u>, 1827 ~~~ A General Collection of Words of variable spelling, in which those of the best usage are printed in Roman character, … freeze, *frieze*, <u>Practical Orthography</u>, 1828 ~~~ Jacket and trousers of blue frieze *Schoolmaster*, February 9, 1833 [see *baize*]

friezed – (napped) <u>Analytical Dictionary</u>, 1835

friezing – Frizing of cloth, a term in the woollen manufactory, applied to the forming of the nap of stuff into a number of little hard burrs or prominences, covering almost the whole ground thereof. Some cloths are only frized on the back side, as black cloths; others on the right side, as coloured and mixed cloths, ratteens, bays, friezes, &c. Frizing may be performed two ways. One with the hand, by means of two workmen, who conduct a kind of plank that serves for a frizing instrument. The other, by a mill, worked either by water or a horse; and sometimes by men. This latter is esteemed the better way of frizing, by reason the motion being uniform and regular, the little knobs are formed more equably and regularly. <u>Encyclopædia Britannica</u>, 1797… The Friezing, or Frizing of woollencloth depends on a similar principle. The hairs of the pile are twisted into each other so as to form little raised naps, or burls, which are thickly and regularly spread over the surface of the cloth. This effect is produced either by working with the hand, or by a Friezing Machine. In either case the cloth is stretched on the Friezing Table and, having its surface moistened with a thin solution of honey or other glutinous substance, the pile is twisted into little knobs by the semicircular motion of the Friezer or Crisper which is a board incrustated with a kind of cement made of glue, sand, &c. The cloth is gradually taken from the Friezing table by means of a wooden roller, beset with short wire points in the manner of Cards. Every sort of woollencloth, or of woollen and worsted, may be Friezed; but worsted cloths, having no pile, cannot admit of that operation. <u>Analytical Dictionary</u>, 1835

frimatée – Others [hats] are trimmed with *plumes frimatées* – ostrich feathers which appear as if covered with hoar frost; *La Belle Assemblée*, February 1832 … the feathers appear frosted, they are called *plumes frimatées*. *La Belle Assemblée*, June 1832 [see also *frosted*]

fringe – an ornament consisting of threads, which are fastened at one end by weaving, but hang loose at the other. <u>Royal English Dictionary</u>, 1775 ~~~ [court dress] White crape petticoat, with silver fringe at the bottom, *Lady's Magazine*, June 1796 ~~~ [Paris] Fringe is in almost general use. The bags called *ridicules* are always trimmed with it. *Lady's Magazine*, August 1800 ~~~ Fringe, … a well-known ornament for dress or furniture, usually composed of silk, thread, gold, silver, or flaxen threads. The making of gold and silver *fringe,* frogs, and tassels, is performed by the lacemen; but is chiefly done by women upon the hand. The making of silk fringe is performed in the loom by the livery-lace weavers. Silk fringe is prohibited from being imported. Dictionary of Commerce, 1810 ~~~ We have noticed also a broad pointed silk fringe, which has a heading, richly wrought of floss silk leaves, with open spaces between. *Repository of Arts,* March 1819 ~~~ the fringes on these shawls exceed in beauty and richness all we have ever yet seen of the kind; they are, however, by no means heavy, but *au contraire,* and fine as gossamer. *La Belle Assemblée,* July 1827 ~~~ Fringe, long as it has been worn, is still more in favour than any of the trimmings we have mentioned. Our *merveilleuses* carry this fashion to a ridiculous extreme, not only the skirt of the gown and the pelerine are trimmed with a deep rich fringe, but a similar fringe must encircle the bottom of the waist, and the ends of the *ceinture* and the tops of the gloves must be finished with a light narrow fringe; nay, we have even seen some instances in which the shoes were fringed. *Repository of Fashions,* August 1829 ~~~ Evening dress. ... The skirt ... [is] trimmed rather below the knee with a fringe of uncommon breadth and beauty. It has an open-worked head, very richly wrought in lozenges. *La Belle Assemblée,* February, 1830 ~~~ When the dress is of changeable silk, the fringe is always party-colored. *Ladies' Pocket,* February 1830 ~~~ The skirt is finished with a fringe, that everlasting trimming, which, as a lady observed to us the other day, is worn on every thing and by every body; but be it remembered that there are fringes of all prices, and that that which ornaments the dress of a woman of fashion, must not only be elegant but of a very expensive kind. ... Many dresses were trimmed with fringe, which was of the most varied description: gold, silver, feathers, and beads. *La Belle Assemblée,* March 1830 ~~~ [ad] Have received by the ships Hark-away and Jefferson, direct from Liverpool, ... 2 cases white cotton fringes, well assorted. *Farmer's Register,* May 1835

frivolity – HER majesty, as usual on her own birth-day, was plain, though tastefully attired, in a salmon-coloured satin petticoat, ornamented with a patent lace trimming, in perpendicular folds, and two draperies of the same drawn up on each in festoons, with goats' beard, headed with wreaths of puce-coloured frivolity, and a deep flounce of the same round the bottom of the coat. Body and train of puce-coloured velvet, trimmed with goats' beard and frivolity. *Lady's Magazine,* January 1798 ~~~ We have remarked at the promenades, a lady of rank attired in a dress of smooth grenadine, trimmed with more than fifty rows of small ribands (formerly called *frivolités*) of satin, laid flat, and very close to each other. *Ladies' Monthly Museum,* August 1826

frize – [see *frieze*]

frizette – Frizettes, hair or silk, Tariff, 1832

frog – Dress of buff Chambray muslin, ... The back made plain, with white silk frogs. *Boston Weekly Magazine,* August 27, 1803 ~~~ A Cossack spenser and cap of lilac twill sarsnet, ornamented with silk frogs, cords, and tassels of the same colour; *La Belle Assemblée,* May 1807 ~~~ [Paris] a new pelisse of sarsnet, ... ornamented with embroidery, frogs, tassels, and fancy trimming, in tasteful windings of black and jonquil; *Ladies' Monthly Museum,* May 1816 ~~~ [Paris] The front of the pelisse is ornamented all the way down with steel frogs. *Ladies' Monthly Museum,* March 1818 ~~~ The prettiest [dresses] are those trimmed in the shawl style with velvet; it forms a straight-falling collar behind, slopes down almost to a point on each side of the breast, and, if cut, as is sometimes the case, to resemble frogs, or, as they are fashionably styled *Brandelburgs,* has a very dressy look. *Schoolmaster,* January 12, 1833 ~~~ for the carriage and promenade, however, silk pelisses are preferred. They are richly ornamented with frogs and braiding, or with various kinds of fancy trimming, composed of silk or velvet. *Court Journal,* November 9, 1833 [see also *Brandenburg*]

frosted – Frostwork, work in which the substance is laid on with inequalities, like the dew congealed upon shrubs. Sheridan's English Dictionary, 1797 ~~~ A Patriotic hat of ... frosted velvet, *La Belle Assemblée,* January 1809 ~~~ a white feather frosted with silver; *La Belle Assemblée,* May 1809 ~~~ A mirza turban of frosted sattin, *Lady's Weekly Miscellany,* June 30, 1810 ~~~ a rich white silk trimming, which is called frost work; it is the lightest and most elegant thing we have seen for some time, and is universally worn; *Edinburgh Annual Register,* March 1, 1813... materials which are called frosted, or rock-work, are much in use; the silky part of the figured velvet is most beautiful, and shines exactly like satin, while the ground resembles fine spangled velvet. It is very seldom that the same velvet or the same granite material, or rock-work, consists of two colours, though they are of every one that the rainbow can boast; but still it is rose on rose colour, and given on green, &c. *La Belle Assemblée*, November 1819 ~~~ Most of the new hats are trimmed with feathers; frosted ones are likely to be very much in favour. *Court Magazine*, November 1834

full – To cleanse cloth from its oil or grease. Encyclopædia Perthensis, 1816

fur – Animals prized for their furs – The Sable, Mar-mot, Stout or Ermine, Glutton, Marten, Chalon, Beaver. Geographical Extracts, 1796 ~~~ Fur, or Furr, in commerce, signifies the skins of wild beasts, dressed in alum with the hair on; and used as a part of dress, by princes, magistrates and others. The kinds most in use are those of the ermine, sable, castor, hair, coney, &c. It was not till the latter ages that the furs of beasts became an article of luxury. The refined nations of antiquity never made use of them; those alone who were stigmatized as barbarians were clothed in the skins of animals, Cæsar might be as much amazed with the skin-dressed heroes of Britain, as our celebrated Cook was at those of his new discovered regions. ... During Captain Cook's last voyage to the Pacific Ocean, besides the various scientific advantages derived from it, a new source of wealth was laid open to future navigators, by trading for furs of the most valuable kind on the NW. coast of America. New and Complete American Encyclopædia, 1807 ~~~ Furs were formerly imported from Italy until the conquest of Canada, and the more northern parts of America, since which they have been obtained from the Indians. The furs used at present are brought from the remotest parts of North America by the Hudson's Bay Company, and from Russia, and are of great value, particularly the skins of ermines, black foxes and sables. The skins of hares and rabbits are mostly brought from the northern parts of England, and Ireland. The wool which these skins yield, as well as that of the beaver, is principally employed by hatters. The other species of fur are used as a part of the dress, of princes, magistrates, and females. Dictionary of Commerce, 1810 ~~~ Muffs are much worn, swansdown, martin and grey squirrel, with Russian fox, sable and the breast of the grebe: this last is in feathers, and shines like silver; ermine is also much in favour. *La Belle Assemblée*, December 1820 ~~~ The fashionable furs are the fox, the white wolf of Siberia, and chinchilla: *La Belle Assemblée*, February 1823 ~~~ In despite of the unusual mildness of the humid winter, never were furs so much in request; every one adopting them, according to circumstances, and their intrinsic value indicating the rank of the wearer. Martens, foxes, chinchillas, zibelines, and ermines, all are tributary to beauty; and the skins of the rabbits and Persian cats are made to imitate those of higher price. *La Belle Assemblée*, March 1828 ~~~ In the article of fur, which promises to be much worn this winter, the most in favor is the lynx, the beautiful light-grey American squirrel, and the light sable and marten, intermingled, forming stripes, and fancy patterns, which appear like feathers; this latter seems such an ephemeral fashion, that it is not likely to be durable: the two furs, thus diversified, had a very beautiful appearance; but it seems a pity to mingle any inferior fur, such as the marten, though now much the rage, with such a valuable skin as that of the little light zibeliac, which sells at an immense price, even in America, of which it is a native; and, after all, it has very much the semblance, when thus variegated, of the Norway rat. *Ladies' Pocket*, January 1829 ~~~ Ermine, so long the most expensive, and considered as the most elegant of furs, is now less fashionable, and far less expensive than sable, or even than Isabella bear, which is next to sable in estimation. *La Belle Assemblée*, December 1831 ~~~ Sable and ermine are considered the most elegant furs, particularly the former; but as they are very costly, ladies who do not choose to go to that expense adopt grey squirrel, or French marten: the last is in great favour, and is a remarkably light and elegant fur. *Ladies' Museum*, February 1832 ~~~ [ad] New and Fashionable Furs. ... Sable, Squirrel, Lynx, Ermine, Russian Fox, French Sable, Swan, Isabella Bear, Chinchilla, and Fitch. *Court Journal*, January 5, 1833 ~~~ These furs may be classed according to the purposes for which they are used, into *Hatting-furs*, employed in making hats, consist of those of the Beaver, the Musquash (*Fiber Zibeticus*), Otter, Neutria (*Myopotamos bonariensis*), Hare, and Rabbit. Furs used as parts of dress, are those of the Fox, Sable, Ermine, Marten, Weazle, Racoon, and many others, in China, and other countries. Furs used for furniture, &c., – Bear, Wolf, Panther, Lynx, &c. *Saturday Magazine*, February 27, 1836 [see each fur type] furbelow – Fur or fringe sewed on the lower part of the garment; an ornament of dress. <u>Sheridan's English Dictionary</u>, 1797 ~~~ Furbelow, an ornament of ruffled or plaited silk, linen, stuffs, etc. sewed on women's garments. <u>Barclay's English Dictionary</u>, 1799

fustian – Fustian, cloth made of cotton; <u>Perry's English Dictionary</u>, 1795... A kind of cloth made of linen and cotton; <u>Sheridan's English Dictionary</u>, 1797 ~~~ Fustian, in commerce, a kind of cotton stuff, which seems as it were whaled on one side. Right fustians should be altogether made of cotton yarn, both woof and warp; but many pieces are made, the warp of which is flax, or even hemp. There are fustians are made of various kinds, wide, narrow, fine, coarse; with shag or nap, and without it. <u>Encyclopædia Britannica</u>, 1797 ~~~ the cloth of the coat ought also to be of a light texture, – a coarse cassimere, a camlet, or red fustian; <u>Systematic View ... of Armies</u>, 1804 ~~~ *Patents for new Inventions, &c. granted in the Year* 1803. ... William Boond, of Manchester. Lancashire, cotton manufacturer; for a new invented manufacture of mixed and coloured cotton velvets, velveteens, velverets, thicksets, cords, and other cotton piece goods, commonly called fustians. Dated April 5. <u>Annual Register</u>, 1805 ~~~ the term *fustians* includes, cords, velveteens, velverets, pillows, barragons, cotton velvets, and most other heavy fabricks; <u>Sessional Papers</u>, 1823 ~~~ for a man, who, at all times, uses but one kind of jacket, fustian would be about the medium. ... a pair of trousers, which may be made of fustian or leather, <u>Instructions to Young Sportsmen</u>, 1833 ~~~ *Apparatus for cutting the Pile or Cords of Fustians, Velveteens, Corduroys, etc.* ... The fustian, by passing through this machine, has its cut-up surface made uniformly shaggy. Smooth fustians, when cropped or shorn before dyeing, are called moleskins; but when shorn after being dyed, are called beaverteen: they are both tweeled fabrics. Cantoon is a fustian with a fine cord visible upon the one side, and a satiny surface of yarns running at right angles to the cords upon the other side. The satiny side is sometimes smoothed by singeing. The stuff is strong, and has a very fine aspect. Its price is one shilling and sixpence a-yard. Common plain fustian, of a brown or drab colour, with satin top, is sold as low as 7*d.* a yard. A fustian, with a small cord running in an oblique direction, has a very agreeable appearance. It is called diagonal. Moleskin shorn, of a very strong texture, and a drab dyed tint, is sold at 20*d.* per yard. <u>Cotton Manufacture of Great Britain</u>, 1836

Galloon - Gymp net

galloon – A kind of close lace, made of gold or silver, or of silk alone. Sheridan's English Dictionary, 1797 ~~~ Galloon, a narrow thick kind of ferret or lace, used to edge or border cloths, sometimes made of wool or thread, and at others of gold or silver, but commonly mohair or silk. It is mostly used for binding hats, and other parts of wearing apparel; there are two kinds for binding hats, the coarsest is principally made at Spitalfields, the finer at Coventry. General Dictionary of Commerce, 1810 ~~~ Binding, Galloon, of silk and cotton 25 [percent]. entirely of Silk 20 [percent]. Tariff, 1828 ~~~ Galloons, cotton or cotton and silk, … silk, … Galloons, if wool be a major component part, Tariff, 1832 ~~~ Evening Dress. … Dark shoes tied with galloon of the same colour. Godey's Ladies Book, April 1832

gambroon – The mixed stuffs, gambroons, and flannels of Rheims are in much esteem, and from their cheapness and durability, are an excellent article of clothing for the poor. Foreign Quarterly Review, September 1828 ~~~ Horse-Guards … Green Gambroon Trowsers for Summer. Army List, July 1829 ~~~ [ad] Excellent Travelling, or In-door Coats, of Gambroon, and a variety of other Materials, very light and gentlemanly – 10s. 6p. The same, Waterproof – 13s. Summer trousers, of White Drill, Gambroon, and other Fashionable Fabrics – 10s. 6d. Doudney Brothers, 1830 ~~~ There are some circumstances in which colour is of great consequence; for instance, stalking a deer, &c. In such a case, the dress should be of the same colour as the surrounding objects; mohair gambroom, of a bottle green, is an unremarkable colour. Hints to Grown Sportsmen, 1832 ~~~ Grouse Shooting. – The 12th of August is at hand, and the Sportsman who contemplates a trip to the moors, must already have commenced preparations. After having exercised his skill and judgment upon the more essential points, his dog and gun, the next matter which invites his attention is personal comfort. To promote this there is nothing more important than dress of proper materials. Formerly the fatigue of mounting hill and crossing moor, was in no small degree increased by the weight of a thick heavy velvet jacket, but here too the "march of intellect" has stepped in, and a Gambroon Jacket is now substituted for the antique velvet one. Were it in our power to indulge in an excursion to the North, there is no sporting dress we have ever met with, which, whether as regards lightness and imperviousness to rain, without confining perspiration, at all equals that which we have seen at Messrs. Doudney and Sons, Lombard-street. Equipped in one of Doudney's Gambroon Jackets, his shooting, waistcoat, and long tanned-leather gaiters, the Sportsman may defy the effect of sun, fog, or rain and that, too, at a most moderate charge. Farmer's Magazine, August 1835

Ganges – [see merino]

gas lace – The object of my invention is to remove from every kind of lace or net, or other goods of the description above-mentioned, all superfluous and loose fibres or ends of fibres, which are not so bound and twisted into the thread or yarn of which the lace or net, or such other goods, is composed, as to form a part of the solid body thereof; these superfluous fibres do not contribute to the strength of the thread or of the lace or net, or such other goods as aforesaid, but form a kind of fur or wool around the threads which make them appear thicker than they really are, and also fills up the meshes, holes, or interstices of the lace or net, or such other goods as aforesaid, and makes them appear indistinct and woolly. My method of improving lace or net, or such other goods as aforesaid is, by passing them through or at a very small distance over a body of flame or fire produced by the combustion of inflammable gas, while the said flame or the intense heat thereof is urged upwards, so as to pass through the holes or meshes of the lace or net, or such other goods as aforesaid, by means of a current of air, which is produced by a chimney fixed over the flame immediately above the lace or net, or such other goods as aforesaid. The action of the flame is to burn, singe, and destroy as much of the said superfluous fibres or fur, as may be removed without injury to the lace or net, or such other goods as aforesaid. … The apparatus for the production of the inflammable gas may be the same which is well known and in use for the purpose of illumination. Repertory of Arts, September 1818 ~~~ turban of gas net; La Belle Assemblée, May 1819 ~~~ a very becoming and beautiful carriage hat for Hyde Park; it is of the white Circassian wave silk, trimmed at the edge with gas lace, La Belle Assemblée,

September 1819

gas net – [see *gas lace*]

gauffree – [Paris] Girdles of gauffre satin, or ponceau twisted crape, formed at the ends into light flowers, have just been invented. *Lady's Magazine*, December 1800 ~~~ Gaufre, *honey-comb*; ... Gaufrer, *to figure (stuffs, &c.) with an iron divided into several little squares.* ... Gauffré, *figured.* Dufief's French Dictionary, 1810 ~~~ [Paris] Now let me speak to you of *chapeaux,* the favourite materials for which are, *gros de Naples, gaze gauffrée, perkale,* and crape: *Repository of Arts*, October 1819 ~~~ *Gauffré* gauze is the only material now in use of transparent hats; *La Belle Assemblée*, October 1819 ~~~ [Paris] At the last sitting of the *Institut,* the hats were chiefly white: they were of rice straw, cotton *tissu,* and silk, *gauffrée;* the hats of *gauffrée* silk are figured in narrow stripes, very close together; *La Belle Assemblée*, August 1823 ~~~ A pelerine of clear muslin, *gauffré* at the edge, *La Belle Assemblée*, June 1829 ~~~ *Gauffrée.* – Crape or gauze *gauffrée* is imprinted with hot irons. The term *gauffrée* is taken from a French pastrycook, who invented a kind of paste, extremely thin, baked between two irons, and bearing the marks of the irons on each side. *Ladies' Museum*, July 1829 ~~~ *Tulle* cap, ... the front, *en papillon,* is composed of gaufred *tulle, Ladies' Pocket,* September 1836

gauze – [see also *gaze,* and check the word preceding or following *gauze* or *gaze*]

gauze – Gauze, a very thin silk or linen Perry's English Dictionary, 1795 ~~~ The principal silk stuffs brought from China are, ... Plain and painted gauzes, singles or double. *New-York Magazine*, February 1795 ~~~ [Court dress] petticoat of rich striped gauze, ... turban of striped gauze, *Lady's Magazine*, June 1797 ~~~ There are figured gauses; some with flowers of gold and silver, on a silk ground: these last are chiefly brought from China. Encyclopædia Britannica, 1797 ~~~ *Gauze* is a very thin, slight, transparent kind of stuff, woven sometimes of silk, and sometimes only of thread. The gauze-loom does not differ very much from the common weaver's loom, but it has some appendages which are peculiar to it. There are a great variety of gauzes; some with flowers on a silk ground, some wrought with gold and silver. Gauze is chiefly made in this country, but part of what is used here is brought from China. Book of Trades, 1806 ~~~ [ad] Satin Brocade Gauzes, 8s. 6d usually sold at 10s. 6d. [per yard]; ... Italian Gauzes, 2s. 9d.; *Repository of Arts*, May 1815 ~~~ New Patents ... process for manufacturing a new kind of lawn and gauze in cotton, silk, gold, or silver. *Monthly Magazine*, October 1818 ~~~ Evening dresses of spotted gauze *La Belle Assemblée*, August 1819 ~~~ A new kind of brocaded gauze of a very light but rich description, is coming much into favour in evening dress; *Ladies' Museum*, August 1831 ~~~ *Gauze* is a silken fabric, quite transparent, held together by artificial stiffening. Paisley, in Scotland, is famous for this delicate material, which is used chiefly as a trimming to ornament stouter fabrics. Book of Commerce by Sea and Land, 1834

gauze satinée – [see *satin gauze*]

gaze – *gauze*; Dufief's French Dictionary, 1810 [see *gauze*]

gaze à plumes – Ball dress is extremely magnificent, except for unmarried ladies, who are still young. Gauzes of various kinds, particularly... the *gaze à plumes,* are the favorite materials. The latter is a novelty of the most elegant kind: it is embroidered in differently coloured silks, in imitation of very small feathers. *La Belle Assemblée*, February 1832

gaze crin – One [riband] that is likely to be extremely fashionable is the *gaze crin.* It is half horse-hair and half silk, and is beautifully shaded. *Court Magazine*, October 1835

gaze d'orient – [see *oriental*]

gaze de laine – [see *wool gauze*]

gaze dentille – A new gaze, called *gaze dentille,* which offers an excellent imitation of Brussels lace, has just appeared for ball dresses and turbans. *Ladies' Pocket,* January 1836

gaze Elisabeth – *gaze Elisabeth,* are all fashionable for dancing dresses. *Court Magazine*, February 1835

gaze salamandre – [see *salamandre*]

gaze satinée – [see *satin gauze*]

Genoa velvet – Prince of Wales wore a blue Genoa velvet coat and breeches, *Scots Magazine*, April 1795 ... From the Female Tatler of 1709, ... any right Geneva (Genoa) velvet, *European Magazine*, June 1818 ~~~ A pelerine, made quite plain, of beautiful black Genoa velvet, is much admired by many fashionable ladies, and is worn over a high dress, for the morning promenade. *Ladies' Monthly Museum*, December 1825 ~~~ the velvet now most approved [for hats] is the best Genoa velvet, in preference to the usual silk bonnet-velvet. *La Belle Assemblée*, February 1826 ~~~ for February … the new hats were all of the most costly Genoa velvet; a valuable and durable, but heavy material, and having very much, at the first glance, an appearance resembling that of cotton velvet. It has, however, on great advantage; the nap does not wear off, nor does it imbibe every particle of dust, like other velvets. *La Belle Assemblée*, [summary of the last six months] 1826 ~~~ The figure represents a piece of velvet cut in section, and of that kind which, being woven on a tweeled ground, is known by the name of Genoa velvet; a pretty strong presumption, that the origin of this manufacture at least, in Europe, is Italian. Dictionary of Mechanical Science, 1829 ~~~ [court dress] rich sapphire blue Genoa velvet manteau, lined with white silk, and richly trimmed with blonde; *Lady's Magazine and Museum*, March 1836 [see *velvet*]

Gentlemen's cloth – [see *men's cloth*]

Georgian cloth – A Zealand wrap, of crimson Georgian cloth, … [Paris] Your pelisse, I have chosen of fine Georgian cloth; because it is quite as genteel, and more appropriate for your purpose than velvet. *La Belle Assemblée*, November 1807 ~~~ the manufacturers of Georgian broad-cloth Spirit of the Public Journals, 1808 ~~~ The Roman mantle, in orange, scarlet, or blue Georgian cloth, edged with a narrow gold tape, is a very graceful and convenient defence against the night air. *Port Folio*, March 1810 ~~~ A round robe of fine Georgian cloth, *Repository of Arts*, December 1812

Georgiana cloth – Incognito hat of French grey, or pigeon's wing, formed of sarsnet, velvet or the Georgiana cloth. *La Belle Assemblée*, January 1807 ~~~ a most whimsical robe of dark brown Georgina cloth, *National Register*, December 4, 1808

ghenting – [see *kenting*]

Gilmerton Livery – Gilmerton livery, a sort of woolen cloth, Statistical Account of Scotland, 1799 ~~~ Athelstaneford, … where a species of striped woollen cloth is manufactured, called *Gilmerton Livery*. Union Gazetteer, 1807

gimp – Gimp, a kind of silk twist; edging Perry's English Dictionary, 1795 ~~~ Guipure, *f guimp lace, vellum lace*. Dufief's French Dictionary, 1810 ~~~ but the trimming most in requisition is a kind of chain gimp composed of chenille, intermixed with small white beads. … these sarsnets are generally ornamented with feather gymp, *La Belle Assemblée*, March 1812… chiefly ornamented with rich fringes, elegantly wrought buttons, and twisted moss gimp. *Ladies' Monthly Museum*, December 1822 ~~~ The few spencers that were seen, were either of blue silk with hard silk gimp trimming, disposed in the military style, *Repository of Arts*, May 1823 ~~~ in some instances a very deep flounce cut *en biais*, is substituted for the fringe, and when that is the case, it is headed by a broad rich gimp; *Repository of Arts*, July 1829 ~~~ the front of the dress, and the cuffs, are frequently ornamented with silk braiding, guimp, and other kinds of wrought silk trimming variously arranged. *La Belle Assemblée*, June 1830 ~~~ LACE is a delicate kind of net work, which is much for the ornament of female dresses. The meshes of this kind of net are of a hexagonal figure, and are formed by twisting or plaiting together very fine threads of silk, flax, or cotton. Thick threads are also woven into the net to form the figures or pattern, according to some design; and these thick threads, which are called gimp, form the ornament of the lace. Edinburgh Encyclopædia, 1830 ~~~ The *Hiermoloff* [cloak] is long, with hanging sleeves, and a double pelerine with long ends, trimmed with guimp and tassels. *Court Journal*, October 26, 1833 ~~~ Much *gimp* is here [Dedham, Mass.] manufactured and used in the structure of the bonnets. A stout cotton thread having been prepared by being wound around and completely covered with silk, a large cotton cord twenty yards in length is next attached to a swivel, and the other end to a spindle – this cord is made to revolve with astonishing speed, and the fine prepared cord, which a workman carries at a good walk is speedily wound round it as a covering, the whole having the appearance of silk. This thread or finer cord is first wound round with the silk in the same manner. The simplicity of this machinery, the rapidity of its execution, the singular sound it produces, are calculated to strike the beholder with sudden surprise and admiration. American Silk Grower's Guide, 1835 ~~~ Gimp and fringe are daily increasing in favour, especially as trimmings for the *soieries ecossaises* [plaid silks]. *Court*

Journal, May 16, 1835 [see also *braid, passementerie, twist* and *vellum lace*]

gingham – [threads] are formed into hanks, some of which are tightly bound round at certain intervals, previous to their being dyed, in order to prevent the parts so tied from taking the colour. This is done, that the threads may be disposed in the warp, so as to produce the clouds which are seen in various species of the cotton goods, particularly *gingams*. *Monthly Magazine*, October 1797 ~~~ The Bengal ships, with two from Columbo, brought the following cargoes: … Ginghams. *Monthly Magazine*, October 1798 ~~~ [Paris] The Gingham robes, silk handkerchiefs, and shawls, are almost all striped in large diamonds. *Lady's Magazine*, August 1800 ~~~ Mr. B. shows clearly that *machinery*, which has opened the way to the harvest of British muslins, calicoes, dimities, ginghams, &c. has had a contrary effect in the woollen manufacture, thrown thousands out of employment, without improving the manufacture, either in texture or variety, or reducing the price. *Gentleman's Magazine*, July 1801 ~~~ *Ginghams*, are a striped fabrick and the colours are given to the yarn before it is woven, on which pretence, it was contended that they were not included in the description of callicoes *printed*, or *stained*, Transactions of the Royal Irish Academy, 1803 ~~~ A variegated check gingam, for the intermediate order of costume, or for the sea-side trowser or bathing wrap. Plaitings of net-lace or scallopped flounces of plain muslin, are best appropriated to dresses of this order. *Repository of Arts*, August 1813 ~~~ in the state of Rhode Island, … Ginghams, [sold at] 40 to 50 [cents per yd.] Sketch of the United States of North America, 1814 ~~~ Gingham, a cloth of cotton and linen striped and glazed Webster's Dictionary, 1817 ~~~ A gingham robe, with very small squares, rose, blue, or lilac, composes the rural toilet. *Ladies' Monthly Museum*, September 1825 ~~~ *Gingham* – a striped kind of cotton, took its name from *Guingamp*, a town in Bretagne, where it was first woven. *Ladies' Museum*, July 1829 ~~~ Black *batiste* or plain black gingham are, we presume on account of their being a cooler dress than silk, adopted by many genteel women. *Ladies' Museum*, August 1830 ~~~ BENGAL Stripes, known also by the appellation *of Ginghams,* is one of the numerous varieties of the cotton manufacture which have been derived from Indian sources, and recently cultivated to very great extent in Britain. A very near relative of the writer of this article, was the first person who manufactured them to any extent, for the purpose of sale in Scotland; and their introduction in Lancashire, where they have been carried to a prodigious height, is still more recent. The Bengal or gingham, is a stout but generally rather fine fabric, of coloured striped cotton; and these stripes are sometimes crossed, with either similar or dissimilar stripes, by the woof, so as to form a check. The fabric of the Bengal stripes is generally designed to assimilate it to the heavier kinds of printed cottons used for women's apparel. A kind of a much denser fabric, and generally of much larger patterns, is also manufactured for hangings of beds, window curtains, sofa and chair covers, and other kinds of domestic furniture. A great part of their excellence, when well manufactured, consists in strength of fabric and brilliancy of colour. Edinburgh Encyclopædia, 1830 ~~~ Some of the new ginghams are flowered in large white bouquets in rose, blue or lilac grounds; others are brown and white striped, *a mille raies*; and several are string in very broad stripes *chinees. Casket*, September 1831 ~~~ For the early morning walk, dresses of plain or striped gingham are very generally adopted; *Atheneum*, August 1832 ~~~ Ginghams, from Manchester to New York. Width called 4/4, is actually from 24 to 26 inches. Trade between Great Britain and the United States of America, 1833 ~~~ [ad] Have received by the ships Hark-away and Jefferson, direct from Liverpool, … 2 cases 3-4 plaid and striped cambric ginghams. 1 case 3-4 plain black, blue, buff, pink and orange ginghams. *Farmer's Register*, May 1835 ~~~ For the best samples of 4 4 fancy striped or checked gingham, in imitation of the Scotch, … Colours of all cotton goods to be permanent. *Hazard's Register of Pennsylvania*, May 1835 ~~~ Morning Dress. Of plaid Swiss gingham, *Court Magazine*, January 1836

gingham-sarcenet – Bonnets of striped sarcenet, the stripes so narrow, that the material is named gingham-sarcenet, are very fashionable: *La Belle Assemblée*, June 1829 [see *sarsnet*]

glacé – Taffetas glacé, *glazed silk*. Dufief's French Dictionary, 1810 ~~~ Frosted (said of a brocade). *Glacé*. Chambaud's French Dictionary, 1815 ~~~ [Paris] a dress of coloured poux de soie, rose or blue, glacé de blanc (shot with white) *Lady's Magazine and Museum*, July 1834 [see *glazed* and word preceding *glacé*; see also *changeable* and *shot silk*]

Glasgow leno – Another half-dress is of the new Glasgow leno, which is much patronized by our nobility; the ground is white, with narrow stripes of Nakara, or wild poppy colour; *La Belle Assemblée*, September 1819 [see also *leno*]

Glasgow silk – We have noticed some pelisses made of the new Glasgow silk, but we do not much admire them; the material is of too hard a nature for out-door costume in the present season: yet, for dresses for matronly ladies during the months of December and January, they will, no doubt, be very prevalent. *Repository of Arts*, November 1819

glazed – Gowns, of highly glazed cambric, are made with sleeves tight to the arm, *Ladies' Monthly Museum*, September 1817 ~~~ [Manchester] The first factory we entered, was a glazing house; that is, a place where calicoes are glazed. All the machinery in these factories, (or nearly so,) is propelled by steam. The process of glazing is a very curious one, varying in its nature according to the quality of the stuff, and the degree of polish to be given to it. The first thing is to cover the stuff with a very thin coat of bees-wax. This is done by causing the calico, chintz, or whatever it may be, to pass between two cylinders or rollers, which are longer than the breadth of the stuff, in one of which are grooves filled with long cakes of bees-wax, that project a little above the surface of the cylinders. These cakes are perhaps an inch thick, and placed five or six inches apart. The upper cylinder contains the wax, the lower one is kept warm by steam, which circulates through it by pipes. The cloth passes between the cylinders, and becomes in that manner slightly covered by the wax. Another process is to pass the stuff between two cylinders, one of which is of polished steel, and the other of paper; the former being kept hot either by iron heaters, placed inside of it, or by the introduction of steam. The glazing material is applied to it by a sponge. The cloth enters very smoothly into the aperture of the two cylinders, and is pressed with prodigious force as it passes through. This gives a fine and beautiful polish to the stuff, as well as the stiffness observed in well glazed calicoes. Year in Europe … in 1818 and 1819, 1824 ~~~ The hats and bonnets are made of glazed plush; and this gloss has a beautiful effect, giving to the plush the same appearance as the changeable silks, now the reigning mode. *Lady's Magazine*, December 1829 ~~~ Full Dress. … A short tunic, composed of blue glazed satin, is worn over the dress; *La Belle Assemblée*, October 1830… In the thick fabrics of cloth, including both those kinds which are used for many parts of household furniture, and those for female dress, the operation of glazing is used both to add to the original beauty of the cloth, and to render it more impervious to dust or smoke. The glazing operation is performed entirely by the friction of any smooth substance upon the cloth; and to render the gloss brighter, a small quantity of bleached wax is previously rubbed over the surface. The operation of glazing by the common plan is very laborious, the apparatus being of the most simple kind. Edinburgh Encyclopædia, 1830 ~~~ There is more variety in the materials than in the make of these dresses [*demi toilette*]: they are composed of very rich silks, as … *gros de Naples, Glacée*. *Ladies' Museum*, February 1832

gold lace – Court Dress. … Body and train of purple satin, richly ornamented with gold lace: epaulettes of the same, looped with diamonds: *Lady's Magazine*, February 1797 ~~~ The fact is, that what is called *Gold Lace* should rather be called *Gilt Lace*, being only silver lace gilded. There is no such thing as real gold lace. Encyclopædia Perthensis, 1816 ~~~ Velvet dresses … for full dress have a broad gold lace near the hem, and over it a slight embroidery. *Lady's Magazine*, December 1825 ~~~ [Court dress] A white watered silk embossed in gold, à colonnes; train of rich figured mais satin, trimmed with a deep flounce of gold lace. *Court Journal*, June 1, 1833

gold thread – *Gold-Thread* or *spun-gold*, is a flatted gold, wrapped or laid over a thread of silk, by twisting with a wheel and iron bobbins. To dispose the wire to be spun on silk, they pass it between two rollers of a little mill; these rollers are of nicely polished steel, and about three inches in diameter. They are set very close to each other, and turned by means of a handle fastened to one of them, which gives motion to the other. The gold-wire in passing between the two is rendered quite flat, but without losing any of its gilding; and is rendered so exceedingly thin and flexible, that it is easily spun on silk thread, by means of a hand-wheel, and so wound on a spool or bobbin. Encyclopædia Britannica, 1797

golden pheasant – A new and distinguished head-dress at such an occasion [full winter dress ball] has been seen in the form of a coronet, made of the feathers of the golden-pheasant, *Ladies' Pocket*, February

1829

gossamer net – Dresses of coloured gossamer net, worn over white sarsnet or satin, gave a sort of silvery rainbow lustre, and are remarkable for delicacy and beauty. *National Register*, October 2, 1808 ~~~ Short Polanese robes of coloured gossamer net, over white satin under dresses, have a very light and elegant effect in the ball-room. *La Belle Assemblée*, February 1809 ~~~ In slight mourning habits, the dress is composed of black gossamer net, or imperial gauze, worn over a white satin slip. *Weekly Entertainer*, September 11, 1809 ~~~ In full or evening dress, ... coloured crapes, gossamer nets (worn over white satin) with black or coloured velvets, are in the most fashionable request. *Jersey Magazine*, January 1810 ~~~ In full dress, there is more ample scope for taste and invention; here we see white and coloured crape, gossamer net, muslin and leno, worn over white and coloured satin, *Repository of Arts*, July 1813 ~~~ The most fashionable materials for evening dress, are gossamer nets and gauze of the thinnest fabric over white satin; *Ladies' Monthly Museum*, February 1818 ~~~ Caps of *blond*, or of gossamer net-work, ornamented with autumnal flowers, were much in favour for home costume, and for half dress. *La Belle Assemblée*, [review of last six months (November)] 1827 [see *net*]

gossamer satin – Evening Dress. A white gossamer satin petticoat and vest, with a Turkish hanging sleeve. *La Belle Assemblée*, November 1808 ~~~ A square mantle of white net, ... sometimes this graceful appendage is formed entirely of lace, at others of gossamer satin, edged with swansdown. *Port Folio*, June 1809 ~~~ *Evening Costume. –* A white or pearl colour gossamer satin gown, with a demi-train; *Edinburgh Annual Register*, February 1, 1812 ~~~ coloured muslins, crapes, Opera nets, gossamer satins, and French sarsnets, for evening parties; *La Belle Assemblée*, July 1812... full-dress, which still consists of gossamer satins, sarsnet, and figured gauzes. *Ladies' Monthly Museum*, May 1821 ~~~ the mantle is lined throughout with figured sarcenet or gossamer satin of a lighter shade, *European Magazine*, April 1823 ~~~ Ball Dress. Over a gossamer satin slip is warn a dress of Urling's patent lace, *La Belle Assemblée*, May 1823 ~~~ Berêts and turbans are still worn at evening dress parties, ... formed of very rich though light materials; such as ... gossamer satin, sprinkled with stars of silver. *Ladies' Monthly Museum*, July 1828 ~~~ Evening costume. A dress of white gossamer satin, with a very broad hem at the border of the skirt, *Atheneum*, December 1, 1828

gothic – Gothic ... having ornaments wild or chimerical, built after the manner of a cathedral. <u>Ash's English Dictionary</u>, 1795 ~~~ *Evening or Opera Dress* ... A white sattin slip *a la antique*, trimmed with gothic lace; *Lady's Miscellany*, June 30, 1810 ~~~ Walking Dress. ... The [pelisse] trimming goes all round; it is a plain band of black crape, cut at one edge, in the Gothic style, in a scroll pattern; this edge is finished by lutestring cords. *Ladies' Monthly Museum*, March 1820 ~~~ [Paris] A new material has been seen for dresses, which is Indian long-cloth in Gothic patterns. *Ladies' Museum*, June 1829 ~~~ Black lace veils of Gothic patterns are expected to be much in favour, with bonnets of dark hues. We understand that several rich and elegant patterns of a similar description have recently appeared in *blonde de Cambray*. *Court Magazine*, November 1834 ~~~ Muslins of Gothic and Oriental designs, stamped or painted in gold and enamel, are in great demand by the court, and the numerous parties now formed in high society. *Lady's Magazine*, May 31, 1830 ~~~ [Paris] A variety of new materials are in favour in home dress; among these are Chinese, Turkish, Moorish, and Gothic muslins, all of which are of singular, and we had almost said very ugly, patterns. Some have excessively large and glaring stripes; others, and these last are prettiest, are flowered. *Ladies' Museum*, June 1830 ~~~ Black lace veils of Gothic patterns are expected to be much in favour, with bonnets of dark hues. We understand that several rich and elegant patterns of a similar description have recently appeared in *blonde de Cambray*. *Court Magazine*, October 1834 ~~~ *Gaze gothique* ... are in request, both for *soirées* and balls. *Court Magazine*, February 1835

gourgouran – The principal silk stuffs brought from China are, ... Plain gourgourans, of 13 ells by ½, and of 14 ells by 5/8. *New-York Magazine*, February 1795

granite – [cornettes] of a new material called granite; ... A beautiful watered silk, imitating granite, is among the novelties for winter: *La Belle Assemblée*, November 1819 ~~~ [for winter chapeaux] new and very beautiful stuffs. ... The other is called *granite,* or chenille stuff: the reason of this double appellation is, that it is composed of plaited chenille. *Repository of Arts*, December 1819 ~~~ a new

French material, called *granite*; it is a stuff made of *chenille*. *The Ladies' Monthly Museum*, January 1820 ...... [Paris] Shag silk, granite plush, and quadrille gauze, form favorite materials, also, for those hats that are worn at the public promenades; *La Belle Assemblée*, December 1820 [see also *rock-work*]

grass cloth – brown India grass cloth ... 50 pieces 4-4 India grass cloth, a good substitute for corded skirts ... 1 do white grass cloth round jackets, a very excellent article. *Farmer's Register*, May 1835

grebe – The urinator, or tippet-grebe, ... are killed for the sake of their beautiful skins. The under side of them being dressed with the feathers on, are made in to muffs and tippets; each bird sells for about 14 shillings. Encyclopædia Britannica, 1797 ~~~ Crested Grebe. ... Of the skin of the belly of this species, in some countries, are made ladies muffs, and other ornamental articles of their dress, which are of a dazzling whiteness. It takes five skins to make a muff, which sells so high as four or five pounds. Elements of Natural History, 1801 ~~~ the article which is to compose the trimming is of the most rare, expensive, and novel kind; it is entirely composed of feathers from the neck of a beautiful bird of Otaheite, wherein variegated shades of amber form a striking predominance. *La Belle Assemblée*, December 1818 ~~~ superb trimming of the Otaheitan grebe bird round the bottom: *La Belle Assemblée*, November 1819 ~~~ [Paris] Muffs are much worn, ... the breast of the grêbe: this last is in feathers, and shines like silver; *La Belle Assemblée*, December 1820 ~~~ Grebes ... The semi-metallic lustre of their plumage has caused it to be occasionally employed as fur. Animal Kingdom, 1831 ~~~ [court dress] A dress of white satin, trimmed with grebe skins; *Court Journal*, March 2, 1833 ~~~ An attempt is making to bring a new kind of fur, which has something of the appearance of feathers, and is in reality manufactured from the feathers of a kind of wild duck; it is called *crébe*, the colour is somewhat of mother-o'-pearl. It has been introduced by two or three foreign ladies of distinguished rank, but is not likely to become a favourite fur. *Court Magazine*, January 1836 ~~~ [court dress] Emerald green Genoa velvet manteau, lined with white silk, trimmed with blonde lace and grebe; rich white satin petticoat, trimmed with two rows of grebe; *Lady's Magazine and Museum*, March 1836 ~~~ An attempt was made a year or two ago, and is now again making, to introduce a new kind of fur which we have imported from Germany, as you may see from its harsh name, *Grébe*; it is manufactured from the plumage of a sea fowl, and it is intended to rival swansdown, but assuredly will never in any respect be able to compete with that delicate fur. Some of our *merveilleuses* however affect to patronize it, as they do every thing else that is new, scarce, and dear; but it is not likely ever to become fashionable. *New Monthly Belle Assemblée*, December 1836

Grecian net – a kind of lace called the Grecian net, being at this time rather fashionable, History ... of the County of Derby, 1829 ~~~ Ball-Dress. Dress of white Grecian thread-net, *Lady's Magazine*, August 1830 ~~~ Small caps are very generally worn in evening dress. ... *Tulle grec* is also a favourite material. *Court Journal*, March 28, 1835 ~~~ Toilette d'Interieur. ... Cap of Grecian net, with a plain round caul and a double border of the same, ... [Paris] a simple cap of tulle blonde, or tulle Grecque, completes this charming attire. *Lady's Magazine and Museum*, April 1835 ~~~ [ad] Dry Goods at Reduced Prices. ... Grecian do [ditto: lace] superior quality, at 2s per yard, *New England Farmer*, July 1, 1835 ... [court dress] Very handsome Grecian net dress, over white satin, trimmed with puffing of net and pink flowers; *Lady's Magazine and Museum*, May 1836 ~~~ The pusher machines are very limited in number, but they are kept up on account of a kind of lace, called a Grecian net, a showy fabric, for which they are peculiarly adapted. Cotton Manufacture of Great Britain, 1836

Grecian satin – The Grecian satin, a material precious for its softness, and beautiful shades, is recommended to those ladies who are preparing furred dresses, pelisses, &c, for the approaching winter. *Ladies' Monthly Museum*, November 1826

Greek chaly – [Paris] The riding habits are very elegant; ... of a new material, named Greek *chaly*: *Ladies' Museum*, October 1829 ~~~ Morning dresses are of ... Greek Chaly, with colored branches on a white ground. *Ladies' Pocket*, December 1829 [see also *chaly*]

Greek velvet – Evening Dress. A dress of white Greek velvet, or satin, painted *en colonnes* of flowers, in various colours: *La Belle Assemblée*, April 1829 ~~~ [court dress] A white crape dress, ornamented with gauze riband; body trimmed with blonde lace; train of lavender-coloured velours Grec; *Royal Lady's*, June 1831 ~~~ Hat of *velours Grec*, *Lady's Magazine and Museum*, March 1836

Gregorian cloth – York Mantle and Hat, seal-skin, or Gregorian cloth, *La Belle Assemblée*, February 1806 [Georgian cloth?]

grenadine – The silk used in the making of black laces is dyed and prepared at Lyons, where it is called *Grenadine*; <u>Literary Panorama</u>, 1808 ~~~ We have noticed a great many blue scarfs, of *barège*, or *grenadine*, set *en ceinture*; that is fixed behind, … At a late brilliant concert, we observed a young lady, attired in a beautiful dress of white barége tissue, trimmed with bias of Scottish plaid *grenadine*. *Ladies' Monthly Museum*, June 1826 ~~~ Among the quadrilled grenadines which are considered the prettiest, we have remarked one, in particular, of a white ground, quadrilled with red and brown; the lines imitate satin perfectly, and produce a rich and elegant effect: they form delightful dresses. *Ladies' Monthly Museum*, November 1826 ~~~ elegant shaded Grenadines for evening wear, 15s. 17s. 6d. and 20s. the full Dress; *Examiner*, November 19, 1826 ~~~ [court dress] Dress of rich white figured Grenadine gauze, *Royal Lady's*, March 1831 ~~~ Crape, gauze, and tulle, are the materials for grand costume. The only novelty is a grenadine gauze, of a rich but slight kind, figured with silver; it is worn both for dresses and berets. *La Belle Assemblée*, September 1831 ~~~ [Paris] Half-transparent materials of Cachmere wool, of silk and wool, and *foulard grenadin* are also made *en peignoir*. *Court Magazine*, August 1833

grenoble – gloves of Grenoble so light and fine: <u>Lex Mercatoria</u>, 1813 ~~~ [Isere, France] its leather gloves, known by the name of Grenoble gloves, are held in great estimation; <u>London Encyclopædia</u>, 1829

grey squirrel – This most graceful habit is styled the Hibernian vest, and is formed of velvet, the colour pigeon's breast; it is formed as a flowing robe in front, so as occasionally to wrap round the figure; the back is cut round in form of a high gown, without cape or collar, and is trimmed entirely round with a full waving skin of grey squirrel. The vest is formed by a width of velvet fastened down on the inside of the waist, brought across the bosom, and gathered into a brooch on the left shoulder; it is hemmed on the edge next the throat, with the same skin. *La Belle Assemblée*, February 1807 ~~~ [Paris] our promenade dresses are always composed of Merino cloth, and invariably trimmed with fur: the most fashionable at present is the skin of the grey squirrel. Some pelisses have a very broad band of this round the bottom; a narrower band goes up each side of the fronts; the collar and the epaulettes are also fur, and the bottoms of the long sleeves are trimmed to correspond. … I had forgotten to say to you, that we are so fond of furs, that we even have our walking shoes ornamented with the skin of the grey squirrel, which is at present the only fur the *tonish belle* will be seen in. *Repository of Arts*, April 1819 ~~~ High cachemire dresses are also worn in the morning walks, with only a fur tippet or a satin pelerine trimmed with fur; the favourite fur is that of the artic grey squirrel. *La Belle Assemblée*, November 1820 ~~~ Tippets, and Russian mantles, of the American grey squirrel, are much worn over high cloth dresses. *Ladies' Monthly Museum*, March 1826 ~~~ [Paris] Several Cashmere mantles are lined with grey squirrel fur, and a few are bordered with swans' down. Fur trimmings are not, however, as yet generally adopted, but muffs and tippets form an indispensable part of promenade dress. Sable is the only fashionable fur for married ladies; but most unmarried ones wear grey squirrel back. *Court Magazine*, December 1833 ~~~ Grey squirrel, always a favourite out-door fur with ladies of moderate fortune, will not be considered good enough for trimming evening dresses, but will probably be employed for *negligé*. *New Monthly Belle Assemblée*, December 1836 [see also *squirrel*]

gro – [see *gros*]

grogram – Grogram, a kind of stuff made of silk and mohair. <u>Encyclopædia Britannica</u>, 1797 ~~~ Grogeram, Grogram, or Grogran, *s.* a sort of stuff, all silk, woven with a large woof, and a rough pile. <u>Barclay's English Dictionary</u>, 1799 ~~~ "Grogram" is nothing more than "Gros grain;" <u>Communications to the Board of Agriculture</u>, 1806 ~~~ We might as well dress up fashion in a puritanical grogram at once, *AntiJacobin Review*, August 1809 ~~~ Du gros de Naples *or* de Tours, *grogram*. <u>Dufief's French Dictionary</u>, 1810 ~~~ Grogram Yarn is a mixture of silk and mohair, which makes a stuff somewhat coarser and thicker than taffety. <u>Practice of the Customs</u>, 1812 ~~~ he did not recollect me until I mentioned my name. 'Tis no wonder; for instead of this mean grogram stuff, I used to wear rich taffeta silk [story: The Bridal Robe] *La Belle Assemblée*, November 1826 ~~~

Comparing the modes of dress of the present day, with those which prevailed in the age of our great-grandmothers, ... The magnificent grogram, and the silk stiffs which stood alone, displayed a finery quite a fanciful and certainly more magnificent than the light, airy gossamer garments, which now deck all classes, *Royal Lady's Magazine*, September 1833 ~~~ [Paris] Grand Festival Dresses – Morning Concert Dresses. Ensemble de Grande Toilette, No. 1. A robe of Dubarry gros grains. This is a most splendid material, in imitation of the rich ribbons worn as ceintures, and broché in beautiful patterns of natural flowers. *Lady's Magazine and Museum*, July 1834 [see also *gros de Naples*]

gros – *big, great in bulk; coarse; thick; rich, wealthy*; ... Gros drap, *coarse cloth*. Grosse soie, *course or sewing silk*. <u>Dufief's French Dictionary</u>, 1810 ~~~ Gros (*French*); thick, strong; a word used in many compositions for silks, as *gros de Naples, gros de Tours, gros de Berlin*, &c., all strong fabrics. <u>Encyclopædia Americana</u>, 1831 ~~~ She knew very well what gros de Naples was, (or gro de nap, as it is commonly called,) but she was at a loss to distinguish gros de Berlin, gros de Suisse, gros de Zane, and all the other gros. [story: Laura Lovel] *Casket*, May 1834

gros Americain – [see *American silk*]

gros d'Afrique – [see *African*]

gros d'Alger – [see *Algerian*]

gros d'Antwerp – [Paris] *Mantelets, Shawls*, and *Scarfs*, of taffetas or *gros d'Antwerp*, as it is now called, *Lady's Magazine and Museum*, May 1836

gros d'Automne – Opera Dress. A dress of changeable *gros d'Automne*, peach-blossom, shot with lavender of a very dark shade. *La Belle Assemblée*, October 1830 ~~~ A new and very rich kind of *gros d'automne* has just appeared for hats and bonnets. *Ladies' Pocket*, September 1836

gros d'Eté – [see *ete*]

gros d'hiver – stout silks of different kinds: the most fashionable is a silk of a very substantial fabric, called *gros d'hiver*. *Repository of Arts*, December 1821 ~~~ the new and justly admired Gros d'Hiver, [on sale for] 5s. 6d. manufacturers price, 7s; *Examiner*, February 5, 1826 ~~~ Pelisses are of a material called *gros d'hiver*, *Lady's Magazine*, December 1830 ~~~ [Paris] Walking Dress. A redingote of bright brown *gros d'hiver*, opening upon the chest in the form of a heart, *Casket*, January 1831 ~~~ Wintery, *adj.* d'hiver, <u>Boyer's French Dictionary</u>, 1835

gros d'orient – [see *oriental*]

gros de Berlin – [see *Berlin silk*]

gros de Chine – [Paris] A new material, however, has been seen lately of a mixture of silk and stuff, called *gros de Chine*; *Ladies' Museum*, November 1829... [Paris] A new material, called *Gros de Chine*, is much admired for pelisses and walking dresses; it is a mixture of silk and stuff, and warm and appropriate to the winter; pelisses of this kind are trimmed with twisted fringe, shaded in various colors, to correspond with the Cachemire patterns, with which the ground of the dress is figured. *Ladies' Pocket*, November 1829 ~~~ Many of the pelisses worn this winter are of merino, and some of gros de la Chine; *Ladies' Pocket*, January 1830 ~~~ Dinner Dress. A dress of figure *gros de la Chine* of a bright crimson, *La Belle Assemblée*, January 1830 ~~~ Rich plain silks, as *gros de Chine* ... are also in request. *La Belle Assemblée*, July 1831

gros de Indes – [Paris] Hat of *gros des Indes*, ornamented with Hortensia flowers. Another robe of *gros des Indes*, is much admired. *Ladies' Monthly Museum*, February 1826 ~~~ Dresses of *gros des Indes* are much in favour for young persons. This silk hangs well on the figure, and though the small pattern which runs over it, of the same colour, is ingeniously wrought, there is a flimsiness and unfinished appearance in the material, which we do not admire. A gown never looks new, even on the first time of wearing it. We saw one of pearl-grey, which looked much better than those of lively colours; *La Belle Assemblée*, January 1828 ~~~ Evening Dress. ... The gown rich blue *Gros des Inde*, *Lady's Magazine*, March 1830 ~~~ gros-des-indes is formed by using different shuttles with threads of various substances for the shoot, whereby a stripe is formed transversely to the length of the goods, <u>Silk Manufacture</u>, 1832 ~~~ We see also some [bonnets] of a very rich plain silk; it is known here by the name of Reps; in France it is called *gros de Indes*. *Maids, Wives, and Widows*, December 1, 1832 ~~~ [Paris] *New Materials*. ... *Gros des Indes*. – A thick ribbed silk for walking dresses. *Lady's Magazine and*

Museum, May 1836 ~~~ [court dresses] trains of gros des Indes in white, trimmed with puffings of net and pink flowers, handsomely lined; *Lady's Magazine and Museum*, May 1836 ~~~ Gros des Indes is formed by using different shuttles, with threads of various substances as the shoot. Encyclopædia Americana, 1836 [see also *reps*]

gros de la Mecque – Some new silks, of a very rich kind, will appear very shortly. They are the *gros de la Mecque*, … It is expected that, both in form and materials, the style of the seventeenth century will be revived in winter evening dress. *Court Magazine*, October 1836

gros de Mascara – [Paris, new materials] *Gros de Mascara, broché* or *quadrille*. – A rich silk in the style of gros de Naples broché, all over in flowers. *Lady's Magazine and Museum*, May 1836

gros de Naples – *grogram*. Boyer's Royal Dictionary: French and English, 1794 ~~~ grograms of Tours or of Naples, Encyclopædia Britannica, 1797 ~~~ Tariff of 1797. … at present all stuffs, even those of silk alone, whether they be grograms of Tours or of Naples, satins, and even taffeties or lustrings, if they be but adorned and worked with some flowers or other figures, are called *brocades*. Encyclopædia Britannica, 1797 ~~~ silk, … gros-de-tours and gros-de-Naples serge and sattins, plain and single coloured, View of the Russian Empire, 1800 ~~~ The stuffs for hats are *gros de Naples*, satin, and Paduasoie. *La Belle Assemblée*, March 1810 … [Paris] The bonnets that are made of green *Gros de Naples*, are ornamented with a bunch of daisies of a mazarine blue; *La Belle Assemblée*, November 1818 ~~~ Gray hats, of *Gros-de-Naples*, are invariably worn, at present, by ladies belonging to the court; *La Belle Assemblée*, January 1819 ~~~ Walking-Dress. A round dress, composed of lavender-coloured *gros de Naples*. *Repository of Arts*, April 1819 ~~~ [Paris] Dress gowns are composed either of levantine, satin, or the rich silk called gros de Naples, which, in France, is of a much thicker fabric than the silk which we call by that name. *Ladies' Monthly Museum*, January 1820 ~~~ the most beautiful Gros de Naples [on sale] at 3s. 6d., worth at least 5s. 6d.; *Examiner*, February 5, 1826 ~~~ [Paris] a very stout kind of *gros de Naples* is also worn, which gives notice of its approach by its loud *rustling*. *Ladies' Magazine*, December 1829 ~~~ Among the novelties in carriage bonnets, the most elegant are … of figured gros de Naples; the last are peculiarly beautiful; the ground is either white, canary yellow, or a delicate shade of grey, covered with a light running pattern, in the most varied and brilliant colours. *Ladies' Museum*, February 1830 ~~~ Watered *gros de Naples* are new and elegant, called in French *douillette en gros de Naples glacé*. *Lady's Magazine*, March 1830 ~~~ [ad] Gros de Naples, 3s. per yard. *Political Guardian*, April 22, 1831 ~~~ There are several descriptions of silk goods, or, to speak more correctly, several modifications of the same class, which are each known popularly by distinctive names, but which yet require no particular description. Thus the plainest mode of silk-weaving takes the name of Persian, sarsnet, gros-de-naples, ducapes, &c., varying only in the thickness of the fabric, or the quality of the material of which it is composed, and not at all differing in the arrangements of its interfacings. … [gros-de-naples] is made of stouter and harder thrown organzine silk, and is put together with more care and labor, containing a greater number of threads, both warp and shoot, in a given surface. Silk Manufacture, 1832 ~~~ *gaze gros de Naples* … are in request, both for *soirées* and balls. *Court Magazine*, February 1835 ~~~ *Gros de Naples* hats and bonnets continue in fashion; they will be much worn at the sea-side, lined with rose-coloured crape, *Court Journal*, August 8, 1835 ~~~ Morning Dress. – Pelisse robe of green chequered *gros de Naples*, … Carriage Dress. – Robe of figured rose-coloured *gros de Naples*, *New Monthly Belle Assemblée*, August 1836 [see *grogram*, *gros de Tours* and *lustring*]

gros de Perse-diaphone – [Paris] *Gros de Perse-diaphone*, a transparent, figured material, is an admired novelty for evening costume; *Ladies' Pocket*, February 1829

gros de Tours – grograms of Tours or of Naples, Encyclopædia Britannica, 1797 ~~~ There is this difference between satin and the gros de tours, namely, that satin must be plain and smooth, and wholly of one colour, whereas the gros de tours, having the wool of one colour, and the chain or warp of another, present a thousand different shades or gradations of colours. The liveliness and motion of these shades or gradations constitute the principal beauty of the gros de tours, the finest of which come from Naples, and are thence denominated *gros de Naples*. The assortments are composed of tender and delicate colours; A View of the Commerce of Greece, 1800 ~~~ Du gros de Naples *or* de Tours, *grogram*. Dufief's French Dictionary, 1810 ~~~ [Paris] It [redingote] is composed of the new silk called *gros de Tours*, *Repository of Fashions*, June 1829 ~~~ Evening Dress. A gown of gros de Tours, *Casket*, April 1830 ~~~ *Gros de Tours* satin, and *gros des Indes*, are equally fashionable in half-dress. *La Belle Assemblée*, February 1831 ~~~ Velvet is coming into favour in full dress, but it is not yet so generally adopted as various rich kinds of silk. That called *gros de Tours*, is the richest, and the most decidedly fashionable. *Ladies' Museum*, January 1832 ~~~ Make and Materials of Evening Dress. – Among the new materials which belong to winter rather than autumn, but for which many orders have already been given, ... A new article, called *gros de Tours à rubans de satin*, will, it is expected, be much in favor; it fully equals the finest velvets. *Atheneum*, February 1832 ~~~ The most elegant of these dresses are composed of that very rich silk called *Gros de Tours*: in appearance and substance it strongly resembles Terry velvet. *Maids, Wives, and Widows*, February 16, 1833 [see also *grogram* and *gros de Naples*]

gros de Varna – Evening Dress. A gown of rose-coloured *gros de Varna*, *Royal Lady's*, April 1831 ~~~ The gown was of figured gros de Varna, colour bleu celeste; *London Literary Gazette*, June 18, 1831 ~~~ Materials of Half Dress. *Gros de Varne* ... new and very fashionable materials; ... as its name implies, a silk; *Casket*, July 1831

gros de Varsovie – Two new silks have appeared, ... The other material is called *gros de Varsovie*, it is a very rich silk, a dead ground with a running pattern of a very light description, in satin of the same colour. *Ladies' Museum*, May 1832 ~~~ Public Promenade Dress. It is composed of a new fancy silk, called *gros de Varsovie*; the ground is a light shade of emerald green, figured in the most delicate manner with black, and with a small black flower. *Ladies' Museum*, June 1832

gros drap – *coarse cloth*. Dufief's French Dictionary, 1810

gros grain – Gros-grain, *grogram*. Dufief's French Dictionary, 1810 [see *grogram*]

gros orient – [see *oriental*]

gros Polonais – the new material, *gros Polonais*; this last is an extremely rich silk. *Lady's Book*, December 1831

gros princesse – [Paris] Some half season capotes of plain but very rich silk, called *gros-princesse*, it resembles *gros des Indes*, have already appeared. They are of full colours, as puce, *violet deveque*, or dark green. *Court Magazine*, October 1833 ~~~ Carriage Dress. A Pelisse of lemon-coloured *gros princesse*, plain, high corsage. ... Winter materials will this year surpass, both in richness and variety, those of many preceding seasons. *Gros princesse*, plain satin, *reps*, and Cashmere, are expected to be most fashionable in out-door dress, for which the only novelties that have yet appeared, are pelisses of the three first of these materials. *Court Magazine*, November 1833

guimp – [see *gimp*]

guinea hen – Guinea hen's feathers and peacocks' feathers, cut short, are favorite ornaments; they are prettily grouped together, forming a king of palm leaf, at the edge of a gauze ribbon. *La Belle Assemblée*, May 1820

guingan – Guigan, *sm.* gingham, a kind of striped cotton-cloth. Cobbett's French Dictionary, 1833 [see *gingham*]

guingan de soie – Two new kinds of silk have lately appeared; ... *guingan de soie* ... is of small square patterns, like a gingham. *La Belle Assemblée*, June 1831 ~~~ *Guingans de soie*, ... are the materials most in favour for half-dress gowns, *La Belle Assemblée*, October 1831

guipure – [see *gimp* and *vellum lace*]

gymp net – Court of Fashion for November 1809 ~~~ For the out-door costume, pelisses ... [are] confined to the waist with a band of gymp net and a small square buckle. *Port Folio*, March 1810

Haberjects - Hunter

haberjects – (*Com.*) a sort of cloth of a mixed colour. Universal Technological Dictionary, 1823

habit cloth – The width of pongee is half a yard, habit cloth yard and half. Trial of Twenty-Four Journeymen Tailors, 1827 ~~~ To the list we have just given of the various foreign cloths imported into the United States, we must add the thin fabrics, known under the name of pelisse and habit cloths – the former used almost exclusively for women's wear – the latter for women's wear and for men's summer clothing. An Exposition…of the Tariff System, 1832 ~~~ [ad] 1 case very nice Habit cloth, Brown, Blue, Claret, &c. *New England Farmer*, September 25, 1833 ~~~ [ad] ladies Habit Cloth, of superior quality. *New England Farmer*, December 10, 1834 [see also *ladies' cloth*]

hackle – raw silk, or any filmy or fibrous substance unspun; Royal English Dictionary, 1775

hackle feather – Military feathers are chiefly made of the *hackle* feathers, as they are called; these are plucked from the neck of the cock. Book of Trades, 1806

hair – [French] our girdles now are made of hair, or of hard silk to resemble hair, plaited in the same manner as the neck-chains which have been so long in use: *Repository of Arts*, August 1821

hair silk – [see *singles*]

haircloth – stuff woven of horse-hair. Royal English Dictionary, 1775 ~~~ Stuff made of hair, very rough and prickly, worn sometimes in mortification. Sheridan's English Dictionary, 1797 ~~~ Hair-cloths, indeed, are made from long hair of any kind; but those, in general, are too hard and rough for cloathing, and are employed in other services. I suppose it will not much recommend this manufacture to you, to be told that some superstitious people, who fancied that tormenting themselves in this world would entitle them to the favour of their maker in another, have thought it a good expedient to wear hair-cloth shirts. Arts of Life, 1802 ~~~ The Parisian ladies congratulate themselves on the invention of a sort of haircloth for shoes, which they say are light, elastic, and durable. *Lady's Magazine*, May 31, 1830

Haitiénne – [Paris] Silks are the only materials for promenade robes and *redingotes*; a beautiful kind of *gros de Naples*, called *Haitiénne*. *Court Magazine*, May 1835

half chintz – Next to the whole chintz are the half chintz: these differ from the former, in that they are printed with only two reds, and no purple. The patterns that serve for one, will, in the management of the printing, serve for the other, both with respect to the white, as for the coloured or black grounds. Laboratory, 1799 [see *chintz*]

handkerchiefs – [see *checked*]

harlequin – [Spain] Wool and hair manufactured, including goats hair, bristles, horse hair, feathers, and human hair. … Calamancoes, known as Harlequins, Batavias, Brillantes, &c. all of wool, plain or worked, pressed Digest of the Commercial Regulations, 1824

heath-cock – [Paris] On several hats are seen feathers of the heath-cock, disposed as those of the bird-of-paradise. *Ladies' Museum*, January 1829

hegemane – The new materials are … a half transparent material called *hegemane*. *La Belle Assemblée*, May 1831

hemp – a plant of which cordage and cloth is made, Royal English Dictionary, 1775 ~~~ Only the coarser kinds of hemp are employed in making cordage, the better sorts being used for linen, which, though it can never be made so fine as that from flax, is yet incomparably stronger, and equally susceptible of bleaching both in the old and new way. Cloths made of hemp also have this property, that their colour improves by wearing, while that of linen decays. The English hemp is much superior in strength to that which grows in any other country. Encyclopædia Perthensis, 1816

hernani – [ad] The new Hernani's just introduced, a tasteful and handsome Dinner Dress, at only 17s. 6d.; and although so reasonable, are the most fashionable material worn. *Court Journal*, June 15, 1833 ~~~ Have received by the ships Hark-away and Jefferson, direct from Liverpool, … 20 cartoons rich foulard, silk, Hernani, blonde, gauze, and other fancy shoulder hdkfs. *Farmer's Register*, May 1835

heron – The peasant bonnet of figured silk, with an heron plume, and shaded mistake ribbands. *La Belle Assemblée*, May 1806 ~~~ a full plume of heron's feathers bent down like the bird of paradise plume.

La Belle Assemblée, March 1818

Hindostan – a new kind of gauze, called Hindostan, or Mogul gauze, is much used in the arrangement of these truly elegant and tasteful head-dresses [theatre and evening turbans]. *Ladies' Monthly Museum*, February 1823 ~~~ *Hindostan* and *Memphis* are composed of a mixture of silk and wool; the first is figured and quadrilled with flowers in the squares, *Court Magazine*, May 1836 [see also *Indostan*]

Holland – Holland, in linen-drapery, is a fine, white, even, close kind of linen cloth, chiefly used for shirts, sheets, &c. Arithmetical Questions, 1795 ~~~ Holland, a fine close kind of linen cloth, so called from its being first manufactured in Holland; but this kind of linen is now made also in Ireland in greater perfection than in any other part of the world. Dictionary of Commerce, 1810 ~~~ Holland is a species of stout shirting, the manufacture of which came from Holland, from which it takes its name; Linen Manufacturer, 1817 ~~~ [ad] Have received by the ships Hark-away and Jefferson, direct from Liverpool, ... 2 cases brown Holland; *Farmer's Register*, May 1835

Holland batiste – There are three kinds of batiste; the first very thin; the second less thin; and the third much thicker called *Holland Batiste*, as coming very near the goodness of Hollands. Encyclopædia Britannica, 1797

honley – Negro Men's Jackets. ... These jackets will require 2 ½ yards of 27 inch Honley or Pennystone, Sectum, 1825

Honiton lace – [court dress] Duchess of Rutland. – This lady was particularly noticed for her great beauty and elegance; her dress well adapted and becoming, entirely of lace, the petticoat of Honiton lace over pink sarsnet, the two draperies of point lace, *La Belle Assemblée*, June 1810 ~~~ All lace worn on this magnificent occasion [the prince's fete] was of the manufacture of this country; a noble example, which we hope will be universally followed in all ranks of life. Honiton lace, as most resembling Brussels point, held the preference. *Edinburgh Annual Register*, July 31, 1811 ~~~ A very costly manufacture of lace once flourished at Honiton, in Devonshire; but laces of that expensive sort are not so much worn as formerly; but it is to be regretted, as ladies who have plenty of money, are supporting industrious manufacturers, when they spend some of it in this way. Scenes of British Wealth, 1825 ~~~ There is also a kind called Honiton Lace, in which the flowers, or sprigs, are made separately, and sewn on afterwards. The Honiton sprigs and trimmings may be purchased alone, for ladies to embroider on Net, and to their own taste. Young Lady's Book, 1829 ~~~ Another kind of lace is made at Honiton in Devonshire, and is called Honiton lace. It is of the same kind as that made at Brussels, and it is also called Brussels lace; two sides of each mesh of this lace are plaited of four threads twisted together. The plaiting renders it much more durable than the twist lace, and it therefore bears a much greater price. Edinburgh Encyclopædia, 1830 ~~~ Bedfordshire and Honiton lace is so highly prized in Paris that it is to be hoped our fair countrywomen will not despise it because it is produced by the fingers of their own industrious poor. *Lady's Magazine*, September 1830 ~~~ Her Majesty. A superb point lace dress, of the Honiton manufacture, over rich white satin; train of beautiful rose-coloured velvet, lined with rich white satin, trimmed with point lace to correspond. *Ladies' Museum*, March 1831 ~~~ [court dress] A Honiton lace dress, trimmed with Brussles point, over white satin; *Royal Lady's*, April 1831 [see *point lace*]

hook and eye – Hooks *and* Eyes. It is directed in all well-disciplined corps, that every officer, non-commissioned officer, and soldier, when regimentally dressed, should have the uniform coat hooked across the chest. This regulation has, in some degree, been dispensed with during the winter months, as far as it regards the officers, who have been permitted to button their coats. In some corps the indulgence is rendered nugatory, as the facings are sewed to the coat. The dressing of a line is certainly rendered more perfect by the use of the hooks and eyes, as they prevent any intermediate obstacle along the line of fight. This nicety is indispensable in parade business; but we shall not pretend to say how far it may be necessary to enforce it strictly on service. The propriety of some general rule being established is manifest, since every soldier knows, that the slightest deviation from the laudable system of uniformity almost always leads to gross neglects. New and Enlarged Military Dictionary, 1802 ~~~ The [pelisse] front is fastened down with hooks and eyes inside, *La Belle Assemblée*, December 1814 ~~~ [Paris] On many gowns, as well as sponsors, that fasten behind, the buttons are merely ornamental; the dress itself is fastened with hooks and eyes underneath; some ladies have even false button-holes worked, to render the illusion more complete. *Ladies' Monthly Museum*, March 1821 ~~~ [Paris] Robes which were formerly made to fasten with clasps, are now attached by hooks and eyelet-holes, which are found to loosen much more conveniently. *Ladies' Monthly Museum*, July 1822 ~~~ [ad] Pelisse and Belt Hooks and Eyes, Gilt, Silvered, and Black; Sheffield Directory and Guide, 1828 ~~~ Pins were first brought from France into England in the year 1543. Previous to that invention, they used ribbons, loopholes, laces, hooks and eyes of brass, silver and gold. *Casket*, June 1831 ~~~ Only a junta of jewellers, dressmakers, and ladies' maids, could give a complete catalogue of the numerous ornaments of gold and silver which have of late been added to the dress of our females in the higher circles of society. ... clasps and buttons of gold the fasten the bodies of gowns, ... gold hooks-and-eyes for the drapery of the gowns, Edinburgh New Philosophical Journal, 1832 ~~~ Gentlemen's Fashions for January. RIDING DRESS. A Snuff-Coloured rolling collar frock coat, single-breasted, fastened with two hooks and eyes at the waist; the front turning down to the very bottom of the waist; *Day*, January 6, 1832

horse hair – chip, cane, or horse hair hats, or bonnets, Statutes at Large, 1797 ~~~ Hats are also made for womens wear, not only of the above stuffs, but of chips, straw, or cane, by plaiting, and sewing the plaits together; beginning with the centre of the crown, and working round till the whole is finished. Hats for the same purpose are also wove and made of horse-hair, silk, &c. Encyclopædia Britannica, 1797 ~~~ Horse-hair is in general use and estimation for belts, bracelets, and other ornaments. *La Belle Assemblée*, August 1823 ~~~ General Statement of Prohibited Goods, ... Tissues of horsehair (excepting Sieve Cloths, Lace, and Hats) Commercial Relations, 1834 ~~~ The long hair from *horses' tails and manes*, is woven into a kind of satin, for covering chair bottoms. A large manufacture of this article is at Worcester. Horse-hair is also woven into a coarse sort of cloth, useful for many purposes in the stable, scullery, and kitchen. The bottoms of sieves are also generally made of horse-hair, woven for the purpose. It is spun into lines for the laundry; and, sometimes, it is twisted or plaited into bracelets for ladies, or into watch-guards for gentlemen. Scenes of Commerce, 1836 [see also *crinoline*]

Hosalba – We may cite also the satins *Bauces* and *Hosalba* as equally remarkable for their richness and elegance. *Ladies' Pocket*, November 1836

huckaback – Huckaback is a kind of linen on which the figures are raised. It is much used for table-cloths and napkins. Arithmetical Questions, 1795 ~~~ The neat and flourishing town of Darlington possesses a good trade in huckabacks and other coarse linens, which has been greatly extended by the introduction of machinery. *Monthly Magazine*, September 1797 ~~~ fine huckaback, for towelling, 5½d. per yard; superiour ditto, 8½d.; *Examiner*, September 24, 1826 ~~~ From one advertisement of the year 1745, ... huckabacks, (a figured worsted for women's gowns) Annals of Philadelphia, by John F. Watson, 1830

humming-bird – Humming-birds, and other small birds of brilliant plumage, are now more in favour as ornaments on the hair than butterflies; *Ladies' Museum*, February 1829

hunter – a double milled forest cloth. Webster's Dictionary, 1817 ~~~ Do you make a particular kind of strong goods at one time of the year? – Yes, they are hunters and double-milled kerseys; hunters of different colour, drabs and brown. Explain what you mean by hunters? – They are double-milled fine kerseys for top-coats. A description of strong thick cloth for great coats? – Yes. Reports from the Committees, 1821 [see also *kersey*]

Iceland moss - Italian straw

Iceland moss – Imitation iceland moss, made of silk, and from Europe *Public Documents*, March 23, 1832 [see also *Lapland moss*]

illusion – Evening Dress. ... gauze, particularly a new kind, called *gaze-illusion*, are all fashionable. *Casket*, July 1831 ~~~ We may cite as a model of lightness and elegant simplicity, the *capote Taglioni*; it is composed of *tulle illusion*. ... [Paris] Rice straw, crape, and *tulle illusion* are the materials in favour for evening dress hats; *Court Magazine*, June 1834 ~~~ Dinner and Evening Dresses. ... The *ruche* which trims the bosom is of *blonde illusion*. ... a small bonnet-cap of *blonde illusion*, *Court Magazine*, March 1835 ~~~ Dinner Dress. ... *Chemisette* of *tulle illusion*. *Court Magazine*, April 1835 ~~~ Paris Morning Dress. – The robe is purple satin, the *corsage* plain, ... nearly covered by a pelerine of *tulle illusion*, the embroidery of which consists in *applications* of muslin; ... *tulle illusion*, are also in request for dress caps, *Ladies' Pocket*, January 1836 ~~~ [Paris] a veil put on at the edge of the front of *tulle illusion*. *Lady's Magazine*, May 1836 ~~~ [Court dress] Tulle illusion dress, elegantly trimmed with orange blossom and white roses, over a satin slip; *Lady's Magazine*, June 1836

imitation Chantilly – [see *English Chantilly* and *Chantilly blond*]

imitation fur – Specification of the Patent granted to Thomas Fryer, ... Woollen-manufacturere; for a Method of manufacturing and finishing Goods from Cotton, Cotton and Silk, Cotton and Linen, or Cotton and Mohair, in such Manner as to make the same appear as if covered with Ermine or Fur, and in Imitation thereof. Dated October 13, 1801. Repertory of Arts, 1802

imitation Leghorn – In the summer of 1805, I had the honour to present to his Majesty, by the hands of Sir Harry Burrard Neale, the first British Leghorn hat made in this country, ... British System of Education, 1810 ~~~ *Patent granted in France. Mademoiselle Julie Manceau, of Paris, for a Process for making with Raw silk Hats imitating the Italian (or Leghorn) Straw hats.* April 16, 1818 ~~~ If instead of raw silk it is preferred to use hair, the hats are to be formed of it in the same manner. These new hats are lighter than those of Italian straw, and they may be washed and redyed of different colours. *New Monthly Magazine*, October 1826 ~~~ Imitation Leghorn Hats. At the late meeting of the Hartford Agricultural Society, several articles of domestic manufacture were exhibited, of superior workmanship; and among the articles of wearing apparel were two elegant imitations of ladies' Leghorn hats, made by two young ladies, from a grass common in the vicinity of Hartford. They were closely compared (says the Editor of the Connecticut Mirror) with the finest Leghorns worn by the ladies in the city of Hartford, and so curiously were they wrought, that one of them, at least, was pronounced equal, if not superior, to those with which it was examined. The material of which they are made so nearly resembles that of the genuine Leghorns, that it would be difficult, if not impossible, to distinguish the one from the other. This grass is commonly known by the name of *ticklematch grass*. *Ladies' Literary Cabinet*, January 15, 1820 ~~~ a communication from Miss Sophia Woodhouse, the daughter of a farmer residing at Weathersfield, in the State of Connecticut, stating that she had manufactured some bonnets in imitation of Leghorn, from the stems of a species of grass growing spontaneously in that part of the United States, and popularly known by the name of *Ticklemoth*. The communication was accompanied by a bonnet of her manufacture, and a few dried specimens of the entire grass. The bonnet being submitted to the inspection of the principal dealers in such articles, was declared by all of them to be superior even to Leghorn in the fineness of the material and the beauty of its colour; and that the introduction of the straw to this country either by importation or by growing it here, would probably be of public advantage, by supplying a raw material superior to any other, and which probably may be manufactured to great advantage in those parts of Great Britain and Ireland where labour is cheap. Transactions of the Society, 1821 ~~~ Miss Woodhouse had told the Society of Arts, that the grass she used was the *Poa Pratensis*. This is the *smooth-stalked meadow-grass*. ... But Miss Woodhouse could only tell the name that was given to her; and it appears pretty evident to me, that the person who gave her the name to send to the Society, mistook the *Agrostis Vulgaris* for the *Poa Pratensis*. ... The *Agrostis Vulgaris* is our *common Couch Grass*, ... In some parts of England, particularly in Suffolk and Norfolk, this wicked grass is called *Spear Grass*, and that is the very name which Miss

Woodhouse's grass goes by in Connecticut. ... The *Couch Grass* has a finer stalk than the smooth-stalked meadow-grass. It is also very tough; and this was probably the reason for selecting it in Connecticut. Cottage Economy, 1824 ~~~ Remarkable French Patents in 1823. ... Silk Bonnets and Hats. ... for a woven fabric of silk, imitating the Leghorn straw, for making men and women's hats, &c. Register of Arts, 1825 ~~~ Imitation Leghorn hats are now extensively manufactured in Ireland, and of a very superior quality. The consumption of this costly article of female dress is increasing. (Large quantities of these hats are made at Ithaca, N. Y. The grass used is said to be preferable to the Tuscan wheat. *Niles' Weekly Register*, March 18, 1826 ~~~ The bonnets, of a material worn last summer, in imitation of Leghorn, have again appeared this spring; *Ladies' Pocket*, June 1829 ~~~ [Paris bonnets] They are either of straw closely platted and sewn together, or of open straw, and sometimes of the Bristol manufacture, in imitation of Leghorn. ... [Paris] It is in vain that so many packing-cases continually arrive from your city of Bristol, containing hats, fabricated with so much ingenuity, to imitate our beautiful Leghorn; nothing can supplant or replace them; ... The price of the Bristol hats, in imitation of straw, has considerably fallen. ... * Such is the opinion of our continental correspondent: the sentiments are not our own. We are happy to see the *real* Leghorn, not so *very fashionable* with us. Our own manufactures are almost unrivalled, and every encouragement ought to be given to native talent and industry. *Ladies' Museum*, August 1829 ~~~ [in 1831] A great number of Females and Boys are employed in Straw Plaiting and imitation Leghorn in the parishes of St. Alban's and St. Peter. Reports and Papers of the House of Commons, 1836 [see also *cotton straw*]

imitation morocco – This is a specimen in imitation of Morocco leather, and is now brought to such perfection, as to be applicable to every purpose to which Morocco leather is converted, even to the manufacture of ladies' slippers. A great advantage in this material is the capability of its being made to any size without the appearance of a seam. This article is appropriated also to covers of piano-fortes, card-tables, carriage linings, &c. Its beauty and cheapness will make it a desirable requisite for these purposes, as instead of diminishing, it will rather augment the ornament of a drawing-room, &c. *Repository of Arts*, August 1812

imitation willow straw – The marine bonnet, made of the new cotton manufacture in imitation of willow straw, must not be forgotten: it is elegantly striped with green, representing Chinese grass; *La Belle Assemblée*, July 1818

imperial beaver – A Morning Walking, or Carriage Habiliment. ... A mountain hat of white imperial beaver, or fur, tied under the chin with a ribband the colour of the coat. *La Belle Assemblée*, December 1807

imperial cloth – The construction of these robes are various, some in velvet and fine imperial cloth, ... a round robe of fine white imperial cloth, trimmed round the bottom with a gold fringe; *La Belle Assemblée*, January 1809 ~~~ The following interesting particulars are extracted from the Lord's Committee's Report on Wool, in 1828. ... "Such has been the improvement in the course of the last twenty years in the quality of our best broadcloths, that if a piece of Sheppard's celebrated imperial cloth were now brought into the market it would not sell. Philosophy of Manufactures, 1835

imperial gauze – [Court dress] Slate-coloured petticoat, over white silk, silver embroidered drapery, ... train, slate-coloured, and silver imperial gauze. *Edinburgh Magazine*, June 1802 ~~~ In full dress, ... we have not been able to decide which has the preference; white and lilac satins, Imperial gauze nets, figured gauze, *La Belle Assemblée*, August 1810 ~~~ Evening Dress. ... A French frock, with demi train of black imperial gauze, worn over a slip of white sarsnet or satin; *Lady's Miscellany*, March 16, 1811

imperial net – [court dress] We have seldom witnessed any thing more splendid than her Ladyship's dress: she wore a petticoat of white Imperial net, bordered with silver, *La Belle Assemblée*, June 1807 ~~~ For evening, or full dress, nothing has appeared to rival the Imperial nets, figured gauzes, sarsnets, ... all of which are held in equal estimation. *La Belle Assemblée*, May 1810 ~~~ Evening dresses of Imperial or Opera grey nets over white satin, *La Belle Assemblée*, December 1810 [may be the same as *imperial gauze*]

imperial satin – Walking, or Carriage Costume. A French coat of imperial satin, ... the yielding and adhesive folds of imperial satin, of gossamer softness. *La Belle Assemblée*, April 1807 ~~~ [Paris] We find among the most elegant silks for half-dress, *satin imperial*, *Court Magazine*, November 1836 ~~~

Satins Imperial à la Reines and *Perline*, may be classed among the richest materials for half-dress; *New Monthly Belle Assemblée*, November 1836

imperial silk – London Half Dress. ... Shoes of fancy kid, or Imperial silk; *La Belle Assemblée*, August 1808

imperial velvet – Evening Half Dress. .. hat of imperial silk velvet *à la Maria Louisa*, *Jersey Magazine*, November 1810

incombustible flax – [see *asbestos*]

India mull muslin – Our gowns ... consisted of India mull muslin, worked in the most delicate and minute sprigs. ... [ad] fine India Mulls, 31s. 6d. for 21 yards; *La Belle Assemblée*, July 1807 ~~~ It is imagined that soft India mull muslins, wrought in small sprigs, with coloured cruels, will be found in great request for the end of autumn and winter; they may not be probably considered to belong to full dress. *La Belle Assemblée*, September 1811 ~~~ Robes of Indian mull muslin, trimmed with a single deep flounce round the border, are beginning to come into favour. *Court Magazine*, August 1835 ~~~ for evening dress. ... Plain organdy and India mull muslin trimmed with lace are also very much in request. *New Monthly Belle Assemblée*, July 1836 [see also *mull*]

India muslin – Indien, ... *Indian; printed callico.* <u>Tardy's French Dictionary</u>, 1799 ~~~ Formerly, all muslins were imported from India; ... It should, however, be remarked, that the British muslins acquire a yellowish cast, after they have been repeatedly washed, while the genuine India-muslins retain their original whiteness. <u>Domestic Encyclopædia</u>, 1802 ~~~ when we speak of "India muslins," we consider them as *imported from* India; but when we call them "Indian muslins," we speak of them as *manufactured there*. *Gentleman's Magazine*, September 1804 ~~~ A long dress of plain fine India muslin, the sleeves made of lace and muslin rolleau, intermixed in cross stripes, over a white satin linen: *Lady's Magazine*, March 1807 ~~~ The three quarter pelisse ... is the most favorite dress for walking; ... India muslins, of every description, particularly the fine Decca, are in peculiar favor, notwithstanding the inclemency of the weather in the commencement of the month of March; ... [evening dress] fine India muslins of almost a cobweb texture, are often seen on a great number of ladies, where there are large parties; they are worn with white satin bodies or cymars, *La Belle Assemblée*, March 1812 ~~~ [Paris] Coloured muslin gowns are of two descriptions: one is soft India muslin; the ground white, but so much covered by a running pattern of flowers, that you see very little of it; these flowers are of various sorts, but extremely small, and the colours of the most vivid and beautiful description. *Repository of Arts*, July 1821 ~~~ Make And Materials Of Evening Dress. – Although gauze and *tulle*, as well as fancy materials of silk and wool, are fashionable, they are not so *distingué* as India muslin. *Atheneum*, September 1, 1831 ~~~ The new *Indiennes* are equal in price to the *Chalys*, and are extremely rich both in pattern and colour. *Court Journal*, September 28, 1833 ~~~ Some rich materials have already appeared for the approaching autumn. Those most worthy of notice are ... the *mousselines des Indes*, which have a mixture of silk; the ground is white, striped, and flowered in single flowers. Both are intended for evening dress; they are rich and beautiful, but we cannot yet say more than that they are likely to be fashionable. *Court Magazine*, September 1834 ~~~ Indian muslin, either clear or thin jacconot, is now so generally employed for robes, for dinner or social evening parties, that nine dresses out of ten ore composed of one or the other. *Court Magazine*, October 1834 ~~~ [Paris] At a *fete champétre*, lately given by the Countess R –, ... A robe of fine Indian muslin, and clear and light as gauze, *Court Journal*, July 18, 1835 ~~~ But the most decidedly elegant dresses are those of India muslin superbly embroidered either *à la Tunique*, or round the border. We observed at some of the late public breakfasts that this robes were in a majority. *New Monthly Belle Assemblée*, July 1836 ~~~ Evening Dress. – Petticoat of India muslin, *New Monthly Belle Assemblée*, September 1836 [see also *muslin*]

India reps – Dinner party dresses are of Indian reps, or Ispahan velvet; the colour celestial blue. *La Belle Assemblée*, March 1829 ~~~ Public Promenade Dress. A high dress, composed of *reps Indien*; *Ladies' Pocket*, February 1830 ~~~ Moire, reps Indienne, and various imitations of cachemire, are all worn in elegant morning dress. *La Belle Assemblée*, January 1831 ~~~ Morning Visiting Dress. .. The *canezou* is of white *reps Indienne*; *Casket*, February 1831 ~~~ [Paris] *Moire, reps Indienne*, and various imitations of cachemire, are all worn in elegant morning dress. *La Belle Assemblée*, December 1831 ~~~ [court dress]

A colonnade gauze dress over black satin, trimmed with blonde lace; train, reps Indian, trimmed with feathers. *Court Journal*, April 20, 1833 [see also *reps*]

India rubber – This elastic resin, more known by the name of *India Rubber*, is the produce of South America, and among the various uses to which it is applied by the Indians, may be reckoned boots, which are impenetrable to water; Memoirs of Planetes, 1795 ~~~ the proper name of this substance, which is vulgarly called Indian rubber from its common application to *rub* out pencil marks on paper, is *caoutchouc*. It is sometimes, though erroneously, termed elastic gum, and is obtained from the milky juice of different plants in hot countries; ... The juice is applied in successive coatings on a mould of clay, and dried by the fire or the sun; and when of a sufficient thickness, the mould is crushed, and the pieces taken out; its colour, when fresh, is yellowish white, but it grows darker by exposure to the air. Dictionary of Commerce, 1810 ~~~ [Recent Patents, August 1820] The material used is *Caoutchouc* (Indian Rubber) cut into strips of a convenient length and thickness, according to the circumstance under which it is intended to be applied, and the degree of elasticity which may be found necessary. If the Indian rubber be not of the best quality, or the spring be not required very strong, then the strips are prepared by steeping them in hot water to prevent them from cracking on the edges. But when the Indian rubber is of the best quality and the spring is required to be strong, it is to be used without such preparation. Springs of this material are applicable to gloves, by forming a case or pipe in the wrist of the glove and passing a strip of the Indian rubber through the pipe; the wrist of the glove must then be gathered up, and the ends of the elastic strip fastened together so as to form a ring considerably smaller than the opening of the glove, but which expands by the introduction of the hand, and contracts again tightly round the wrist when the hand has passed into the glove. These springs may be applied in a similar manner to any other article of dress where tightness and elasticity are required: as, to waiscoats, wristbands, cuffs of sleeves, kneebands, garters, the openings of pockets, braces, and also to* wigs, false curls, and fronts, to keep them tight on the head; and to pocket-books and purses instead of wire springs; to stays and various other parts of female apparel; to the binding of shoes, to riding-belts, stiffeners of neck-cloths, and a great variety of other uses. ... * A Patent for elastic wigs upon this principle was granted about forty years ago. London Journal of Arts and Sciences, 1821 ~~~ *Mode of rendering Cloth Water-proof.* A chemist, of Glasgow, has discovered a simple and efficacious method of rendering woollen, silk, or other cloth completely water-proof. The mode is said to be by dissolving *caoutchouc* (Indian rubber,) in mineral oil, which is procured in abundance at the gas works. – Put five or six coatings of the mixture, with a brush, on one side of the cloth, on which another piece of cloth is laid, and pass the whole through between two rollers. The adhesion is so complete, that-it is easier to tear the cloth than separate the pieces, which appear to consist of only one fly, and are completely impervious to water. This kind of cloth must be a valuable commodity in a rainy climate. London Journal of Arts and Sciences, 1823 [see *Mackintosh*]... Among the recent inventions at Paris – an elastic stiffening of a vegetable substance has been invented, instead of that spiral brass wire now used for shoulder-straps, glove-tops, corsets, &c.: it is valuable, because it neither cuts the cloth that covers it, nor corrodes with verdigris: it is said to be made of Indian rubber, and promises to be exceedingly useful in belts, &c. The French queen was pleased to express her approbation of some useful articles of dress made in the national colours of this material, *Lady's Magazine*, September 1830 ~~~ Shoes and boots are talked of, as light and durable for winter, made of horse hair or Indian rubber. *Lady's Magazine*, October 1830 ~~~ *India Rubber Hats.* – A manufacturer at Portland has succeeded in making very good hats from India rubber. They are very light, weighing on an average about four ounces; and are so elastic, that they may be folded like a handkerchief; may be crushed into any shape, and will immediately return to their original form without being injured in the smallest degree. *Mechanics' Magazine*, March 5, 1831 ~~~ [ad] CAOUTCHOUC; or Indian Rubber Goloshes. – Patronized by her Majesty and her Royal Highness the Duchess of Kent. – The excellence of these Goloshes, in the perfect exclusion of wet, and affording warmth to the feet, being now very generally known, J. LYON, the original introducer, is induced to offer them with confidence to all persons wanting such protection. They may be had, with or without soles, at 41 St. James's street, *Court Journal*, February 2, 1833 ~~~ Mr. Brockedon gave a conversation "On the Application of Caoutchouc to different Manufactures, particularly to elastic Web." The lecturer stated, that although his object was to explain the application of caoutchouc to elastic fabrics, yet, perhaps, it would be interesting to give a short account of the early knowledge of the material in this country; for although it has been known here about 100 years, yet very little of its useful properties were discovered till within the last ten to fifteen years, when Mr. Hancock took out his patent for applying it in its elastic character, and used it as springs for gloves and a variety of other articles, by sewing threads of the elastic gum between two surfaces, as described in his specification. *Repertory of Patent Inventions*, July 1833 ~~~ New Discovery. Mr. Mariner, of N. York, has made an important discovery for the use of persons exposed to fire or water. It is a process by which he is enabled to coat over leather, cotton, linen, silk, etc. or any like material, into durable India rubber garments, wholly impervious to water, without being rendered heavy or clumsy. The editor of the New York Advocate says he has examined a coat and pantaloons made of cotton cloth, covered in every part with the India rubber, without a stich [sic] except in the button holes. These must be excellent articles for firemen, stage drivers, and travellers in open waggons. Ladies' and gentlemen's boots and shoes may be made of any of the above named materials from the coarsest leather or the finest silk. *Niles' Weekly Register*, August 24, 1833

India satin – From the East Indies are imported those light stuffs called Indian or Chinese satins. They are either plain, damasked, striped, open-worked, or embroidered. Both in lustre and execution they are far inferior to the Lyonese satins; they, however, possess this peculiar property, that even after scouring, they retain their original gloss. General Dictionary of Commerce, 1810 ~~~ Evening Dress. A dress of painted India satin, in stripes of etherial blue, or of bright grass-green, on a white ground, figured between the stripes with variegated spots of Indian-red, and other lively colours. *La Belle Assemblée*, March 1828 ~~~ *Taffetas de Siam*, and *satin des Indes*, full dress materials of a very beautiful kind. ... [*satin des Indes*] has a slight mixture of cashmere, which adds much to its softness and beauty; the lightness and delicacy of the patterns, and the beauty of the colours, have very much the effect of embroidery. An evening dress, composed of *satin des Indes*, which forms part of the *trousseau* of a newly married lady, deserves to be cited fro the novelty as well as elegance of its form. *Court Magazine*, October 1834 ~~~ [ad] Have received by the ships Hark-away and Jefferson, direct from Liverpool, ... 1 case heavy black India satins and levantines. *Farmer's Register*, May 1835

India taffeta – Evening Dress. This consists of a dress of amber-colored India taffeta, *Lady's Magazine*, May 1829 ~~~ [Paris] The new mantles are of Indian taffety; very few, however, of these envelopes have yet appeared. *Ladies' Museum*, September 1829 ~~~ Dresses of Indian taffeta, of some light color, trimmed with crape and satin of the same tint, are much admired for evening costume and for dinner-parties: *Lady's Magazine*, December 1829 ~~~ In silks, ... Indian taffeta and sarcenet, as lighter wear for summer, are now preferred; *Lady's Magazine*, July 1829 ~~~ A robe of beautiful Indian taffety, white with pale blue stripes. *Court Journal*, July 4, 1835 [see *taffeta*]

India velvet – [court dress] A white crape dress over white satin, ... a manteau of light blue velours des Indes, embroidered with silver; *Royal Lady's*, June 1831 ~~~ *Velours epinglé* and *Velours des Indes* are two of the most elegant and fashionable materials for dresses. In pale colours they produce brilliant effects of light and shade. In pink and light blue they make beautiful evening dresses, without any other ornament than blonde *sabots* to the short sleeves, and a few bows of gauze riband on the pointed corsage. *Court Journal*, March 9, 1833 ~~~ [court dress] A silver lama dress, over white satin, with manteau of green velours des Indes, trimmed with silver rouleaux; *Court Journal*, May 11, 1833 ~~~ [Hats and bonnets] fashionable for promenade or carriage. Figured satins and *velours Indien* also promise to be much worn. *Court Journal*, October 31, 1835 ~~~ A great variety of materials have appeared for evening dress. We may cite, as likely to be fashionable, *velours Indien*, ... which are in the rich but heavy style *Court Magazine*, November 1835

Indian cock – [see *peacock*]

Indian wool – [see *thibet wool*]

Indienne – [see *India muslin*]

Indonstan – High Dresses composed of Cashmere wool, under the names of *Indonstans* and *Thibitians*, begin to be worn in the promenades. They are painted and figured in various patterns; *Atkinson's*

Casket, January 1832 [see also *Hindostan* and *merino*]

inkle – Incle (*s. not so common a spelling*) Inkle, a kind of tape. <u>Ash's English Dictionary</u>, 1795 ~~~ Inkle, a kind of narrow fillet, a tape. <u>Sheridan's English Dictionary</u>, 1797... [A. D. 1763] And that all white diaper or twilled tapes made of single flaxen yarn, commonly called diaper inkles, shall contain thirty-three threads or more in breadth, and shall be made up in pieces, each piece containing thirty-fix yards, or more; <u>Statutes Passed in the Parliaments held in Ireland</u>, 1795 ~~~ a sort of broad linen tape, principally manufactured at Manchester and some other towns in Lancashire. <u>General Dictionary of Commerce</u>, 1810 ~~~ The Manufactures of all kinds of Tapes, Inkles, Laces, Fringe, and numberless other small wares, employing a considerable number of hands, are very extensive; <u>A Treatise on the Wealth, Power, and Resources of the British Empire</u>, 1814

insertion – Morning Dress, ... The skirt is ornamented with two rows of vandykes, trimmed round with scollop, and surmounted with a broad insertion. *Ladies' Monthly Museum*, March 1823 ~~~ Morning Dress. ... the upper one [flounce] surmounted by a row of delicate insertion-work, *Manchester Iris*, July 5, 1823 ~~~ Strips of work intended for insertion in plain muslin, or lace, should have a row of hem-stitch on each side, <u>Young Lady's Book</u>, 1829 ~~~ The skirt ... is trimmed with a row of entre deux (insertion), *Court Magazine*, May 1833 ~~~ [ad] Have received by the ships Hark-away and Jefferson, direct from Liverpool, ... 1 cartoon rich worked cambric and Swiss muslin edgings and insertings. *Farmer's Register*, May 1835 ~~~ Apron of Scotch cambric, with an insertion let in all round. *Lady's Magazine*, May 1836 [see also *entre deux* and *letting-in lace*]

ipsilentine – Walking Dress. A dress of white *Ipsilentine*, *corsage en petit cœur*, cut very low, and trimmed with a double fall of blond lace. ... Make and Materials of Evening Dress. – Among the new materials which belong to winter rather than autumn, but for which many orders have already been given, are ... *Ipsilentine*, ... These material are of extreme richness. *Casket*, January 1832 ~~~ Make and Materials of Evening Dress. – Among the new materials which belong to winter rather than autumn, but for which many orders have already been given, are the *satin polonis* and *à la reine*, *reps Africain*, *Ipsilentine*, and *moires à colonnes satinées*. The materials are of extreme richness. *Atheneum*, February 1832

Irac – Among the new tissues we have particularly remarked the Scottish plaid, and striped *Irac*. This light and beautiful material unites at once the brilliancy of silk, with all the rich softness of cachemere: the colours are much more delicate than those of the Scottish plaid worn during the past winter, and are composed of a mixture of pale cherry, green willow, and yellow straw-colour. *Ladies' Monthly Museum*, June 1826

iris – [see *rainbow*]

Irish blond – [court dress] Irish blonde dress over white satin; *Lady's Magazine and Museum*, March 1836 [see *blond*]

Irish linen – Irish linen constitutes one of the most useful and necessary parts of an Englishman's dress; *British Critic*, July 1804 ~~~ I shall now proceed to the display of some minutiae regarding the out-fit of a gentleman about to embark in a chartered ship; ... Two good warm waistcoats of woollen must be provided, and about two dozen of white waistcoats, made of fine Irish linen. *East India Vade-Mecum*, 1810 ~~~ Irish linen, which has long been almost generally used in the manufacture of under garments. *Monthly Magazine*, September 1811 ~~~ The 7/8 and yard wide pieces are from about 18 to 25 yards long. The 1 1/8, 1 ¼, and 1 ½ yard wide pieces, are from 60 to 75 yards long. <u>Practice of the Customs</u>, 1812 ~~~ an Irish linen chemise, which the deceased had herself made. [murdered on May 18, 1827] <u>Annual Register</u>, 1828 ~~~ [lost] eleven Irish linen shirts, made of the finest linen, and ruffled, $118.25; <u>Reports of the Committee</u>, 1831 [see *linen*]

Irish poplin – [court dress] a rich silver spangled crape, ... with a body train of blue Irish linen, interwove with silver. *Lady's Magazine*, June 1791 ~~~ Irish poplins have lost nothing of their attraction, but they are generally worn in light colours; bright faun, amber, drab, Clarence blue, and olive-green, are all in general request; *La Belle Assemblée*, November 1814 ~~~ Irish poplin [on sale] at 2s. a yard, what last season was selling at 5s. *Examiner*, February 5, 1826 ~~~ Irish poplins, figured over in large flowers, form another favourite material for evening costume. *Ladies' Monthly Museum*, December 1828 ~~~ Ireland has been celebrated for a manufacture of mixed silk and worsted, known in the country by the name of tabbinet, and in Great Britain by that of Irish poplin. For a long period this fabric was much sought after both at home and in the foreign market; but the fluctuation of female fashion has latterly considerably diminished the demand for it. Universal Geography, 1833 ~~~ [court dress] rich Irish poplin train, lined with satin, tastefully trimmed with blonde and ribbons; *Lady's Magazine and Museum*, May 1836 ~~~ We understand Irish poplins were never more sought after than at present; their richness and durability will always insure them a preference, independent of the vast good done by the employment of so many industrious artisans. *Court Journal*, December 26, 1835 [see *poplin* and *tabbinet*]

Irish tabinet – The real Irish tabinet will never be common, as it is rather an expensive material, for what it is only calculated for, half-dress: it is worn only by a certain set for that sort of costume, who admire its beauty, and are by their independent station in life entitle to wear what they please. The wretchedly-wearing imitations of this beautiful produce of the Irish looms are fast going out of date; and the real tabinet is not likely, at present, to be very general. *La Belle Assemblée*, October 1826 [see *poplin* and *tabbinet*]

Irish velvet – In *November* [1822], there are, however, some new invented materials this month, for hat and turbans, likely to meet with much encouragement, namely, Irish velvet, crystallized velvet, and Baltic moss. Museum of Foreign Literature, 1823

Isabella bear – We have it from good authority, that the beautiful far known among the trade by the name of Isabella bear, will also this winter be exceedingly fashionable. *Ladies' Museum*, December 1830 ~~~ Ermine, so long the most expensive, and considered as the most elegant of furs, is now less fashionable, and far less expensive than sable, or even than Isabella bear, which is next to sable in estimation. *La Belle Assemblée*, December 1831 ~~~ That light and graceful fur, the Isabella bear, is likely to be in request in evening dress: it is a favorite fur of the Queen's; her Majesty wears it very frequently. *Court Magazine*, November 1833 ~~~ The russet, or Isabella bear, for muffs. Transactions of the Society, 1833 ~~~ Sable will be most fashionable: Isabella bear ranks next: grey squirrel is also to a certain degree fashionable. *Court Magazine*, November 1834

Isabelle – [Paris] New Materials. – For grandes toilettes d'hirer, the newest materials are the … satin *Isabelle*, the same material, [as Médicis, a rich satin stamped with velvet flowers] only *broché* in silver. *Lady's Magazine and Museum*, November 1834 ~~~ [Paris] It is very well known that the Parisians always labour under a mania of one kind or other. The present reigning one is *la danse*. Balls succeed each other with such extreme rapidity, that a lady has no time to think of any thing but her dresses for them; for assist at them she must in one way or other, if not as *danseuse,* at least as chaperon: for the latter the robe may be either of a rich or light material, as *tissu de Memphis, satin Isabelle, gaze blonde,* &c. *Court Magazine*, February 1835 ~~~ Satin d'Asie, that *à la Keine*, and one still more rich, called *satin Isabelle*, have appeared for half-dress. *Ladies' Pocket*, November 1836

Ispahan gauze – Evening Dress. …An elegant evening scarf of Isaphan gauze is added. *Ladies' Museum*, April 1829 ~~~ Dinner Dress. … *Canezou* of white *gaze d'Ispahan*; … [Paris ball dress] *Organdy, crêpe, lisse*, and *gaze d'Ispahan*, are the materials most in favour. They are generally embroidered in colours, in a style of uncommon beauty. *Repository of Fashions*, August 1829 ~~~ Evening dresses. … The turban is of white gauze d'Ispahan. The gauze is disposed in light full folds, which are wreathed in gold beads. *Casket*, April 1830

Ispahan satin – [Paris] Several dresses of colored satin have long sleeves of white *crepe Aerophane, a la Mameluke,* or *a la Marie*: those of Ispahan satin cross in drapery over the bust, *Ladies' Pocket,* January 1829 ~~~ [Paris] Velvet, *satin d'Ispahan*, gold and silver muslins, and a great number of fancy silks and stuffs are in favour in full dress. *Repository of Fashions*, January 1829

Ispahan velvet – A new velvet, called *Ispahan velvet* is much admired for evening dresses this winter; it has one great advantage, it is never known to get rumpled; it is light, and extremely supple. *Ladies' Monthly Museum*, December 1828 ~~~ Dresses of Ispahan velvet, painted in stripes of various colors, are as remarkable for their high price as their beauty. *Lady's Magazine*, March 1829 ~~~ *Canezou* of white *gaze d'Ispahan*; … [Paris] Ball dress is as usual, at this season of the year, of the lightest possible description. *Organdy, crêpe, lisse*, and *gaze d'Ispahan*, are the materials most in favour. *Repository of Fashions*, August 1829 ~~~ [Paris ball dresses] Watered velvet, satin, and velours d'Ispahan, were worn by ladies who did not dance. *La Belle Assemblée*, March 1831 ~~~ [Paris ball dresses] Although robes of gauze and tulle were very numerous; there were also a great many of rich silks and even of velvet. We may class among the most elegant of these dresses one of white *velours d' Ispahan*, *Court Magazine*, February 1836

Issachar – There are also some beautiful materials of silk and Cashmere wool, both for half-dress and *robes habilées*; the *satin Danaé* and the *tissu d'Issachar* are the most remarkable of these latter. *Court Magazine*, November 1836

Italian crape – We have lately been favoured with the sight of a most elegant round robe, formed of a delicate white Italian crape, embroidered all over in small silver stars. This dress was made with a train, and worn over a white satin slip; *La Belle Assemblée*, February 1807

Italian grape – Full Dress. ... Fan of Italian grape, with gold spangles, and devices in transparencies. *La Belle Assemblée*, January 1807 ~~~ [Paris] Mary wore a French coat ... formed of pea green Italian grape, of the most pliant texture, with wove satin spots. *La Belle Assemblée*, May 1807 [possibly a misreading of *crape*]

Italian net – [court dress] A petticoat entirely of Italian silver net, with crape drapery, with stripes of shaded yellow ribbon, the stripes covered with costly blond lace, a double drapery of silver net, tied up with silver fringe and tassels. *Lady's Magazine*, June 1796 ~~~ a demi robe of rose colored crape or Italian net. *Lady's Magazine*, April 1809 ~~~ [Ball dress] The embroidery introduced on Italian net is a novelty that is truly attracting: we have seen a very elegant high dress of this material for *demi-parure*; *Lady's Magazine*, July 1825 ~~~ Dresses for home costume are generally ornamented with flounces, especially when the dress is either of Barège, Italian net or colored muslin. *Lady's Magazine*, October 1825 ~~~ Coloured muslin dresses, and those of Italian net, of very bright and striking summer colours, worn over white satin, prevail much at friendly afternoon parties; they are trimmed with *bias* folds of satin the colour of the dress. *La Belle Assemblée*, February 1826 ~~~ That an article called "*Italian nett*," composed of *silk* and *worsted, or combed wool*, *Public Documents*, January 1829 ~~~ [ad] Italianett, at 12 1-2 cts per yard. *New England Farmer*, December 10, 1834

Italian straw – the preference lately given to Italian straw plait, and which is still becoming more fashionable, has deprived a vast number of our country-women and children of the means of obtaining subsistence. <u>London Journal</u>, 1821 ~~~ the importation of the straw hats and bonnets from *Italy*, greatly superior, in durability and beauty, to those made in England. The plat made in England was made of the straw of *ripened grain*. It was, in general, *split*; ... the Italian plat was made of the straw of grain, or grass, *cut green*. Now, the straw of ripened grass is brittle; or, rather, rotten. ... But, besides the difference in point of toughness, strength, and durability, there was the difference in beauty. The colour of the Italian plat was better; the plat was brighter; and the Italian straws being *small whole* straws, instead of small straws made by the splitting of large ones, there was a roundness in them, that gave *light and shade* to the plat, which could not be given by our flat bits of straw. *Manchester Iris*, July 5, 1823 ~~~ The plant which supplies the straw calculated to make the hats from what is termed Italian straw, is a species of wheat known in Tuscany under the name Marzajolo grano gentile rosso, ... however, any other species of wheat will answer the purpose, *New Monthly Magazine*, March 1832 ~~~ [Paris] Italian straw is this season more in vogue that it was last year, and it is now brought to that degree of fineness that its flexibility is equal to silk. Indeed, to be at all fashionable it must be of the plain kind, and of the most exquisite [sic] fineness. Our readers may judge of the price when we tell them that some of these hats have taken two years and a half to plait. *Ladies' Pocket*, June 1836 [see also *Leghorn, straw*, and *Tuscan straw*]

Jaconet - Juive

jaconet – Indian words imported with the goods, just as we now use *jaconet, cossae, mul-mul* for denominations of Indian fabrics. <u>Annals of Commerce</u>, 1805 ~~~ [ad] Fine Yard-and-half-wide curious Jacconets, at 2s. per yard; *La Belle Assemblée*, March 1807 ~~~ Morning dresses are chiefly composed of cambric, or jaconot muslin; *La Belle Assemblée*, October 1807 ~~~ Cotton goods are divided into 7 different classes, each proportionally lighter the than other. The heaviest of these are, 1st. *Shirtings*, 2d. *Cambrics*, 3d. *Cossas*, 4th. *Jaconetts*, <u>New Encyclopædia</u>, 1807 ~~~ *Carriage Costume.* – A high round robe of jaconet or cambric muslin, with plaited bodice, *Edinburgh Annual Register*, April 30, 1813 ~~~ Jaconet, *n.* a kind of coarse muslin. <u>Webster's Dictionary</u>, 1817 ~~~ [Paris] Merino crape and India jaconot muslin, of a very thin kind, being likewise very fashionable. *Repository of Arts*, August 1819 ~~~ *American jaconet muslin.* We have at this moment before us a piece of *jaconet muslin*, of a fabric so perfect in every particular, that we may safely assert it to be equal, in every respect, to any thing of the kind, produced in any part of the world. Familiar with the finest webs of Asia, we can confidently assert, that the piece before us is equal in beauty, evenness, and much superior in the finishing, to the fine *mulls* of Hindostan. This piece is the first experiment made at the factory of Messrs. Thorp and Slidell, of this neighborhood, yet it will bear inspection and comparison with any foreign production of the same *number of yarn.* This jaconet rivals, in beauty and texture, the lawns of Flanders, and for cravats, ruffles, and fine dresses, has no superior; and we earnestly recommend the products of these ingenious manufacturers to the notice and patronage of every friend of American prosperity. *Niles' Weekly Register*, July 29, 1820 ~~~ White dresses are becoming general; the favourite trimming consists of several narrow flounces of muslin: some dresses of fine jaconaut muslin, are much admired for evening parties at home: *Ladies' Monthly Museum*, June 1827 ~~~ *Jaconots are* a thicker sort of muslin, more commonly worn as a female dress. Neckcloths are also made of it. <u>Book of Commerce by Sea and Land</u>, 1834 ~~~ [ad] Have received by the ships Hark-away and Jefferson, direct from Liverpool, … 2 cases 6-4 jaconett, medium and mull muslins. *Farmer's Register*, May 1835 ~~~ *Jaconot muslin* is a thicker kind, more commonly used for ladies' dresses, and very frequently for gentlemen's cravats. It is sometimes woven with stripes or cords running the whole length of the piece. It is also to be had dyed, or printed in various patterns. In all cases, it forms an elegant light article for summer wear. <u>Scenes of Commerce</u>, 1836 ~~~ Several printed jaconot muslins have appeared of new and very pretty patterns; they are expected to be a good deal in request in undress, but it is yet too early to be at any certainty on the subject; *Court Magazine*, May 1836 ~~~ Book and jaconet muslins are now currently woven by power-looms, especially in the Glasgow district. <u>Cotton Manufacture of Great Britain</u>, 1836 [see also *muslin*]

jacquard – [in France] A prize of 3000 francs for a loom for weaving all kinds of gold and silver stuffs, was adjudged to M. Jacquard, an artist of Lyons; to whom the Emperor has also granted a premium of 50 francs for each of these looms, with which he shall supply manufacturers. *Monthly Magazine*, November 1, 1808 ~~~ In the year 1808, Mr. Jacquart, of Lyons, in France, invented a loom intended to do the work commonly effected by draw-boys, in the manufacture of figured stuff † for which he received a premium of 5,000 francs from the Society for the Encouragement of National Industry. This admirable invention remained unknown to the English until the year 1816, when it was seen by Mr. William Hale, and mentioned by him to several silk manufacturers; one of whom, Mr. Stephen Wilson, went over to France, and introduced it into England with improvements. The loom is applicable alike to silk, cotton, woollen, and linen stuffs. …The great advantages of Jacquart's loom, consist in, 1. Enabling every plain weaver to become a figured weaver, to make goods which they have the greatest difficulty in making in Spitalfields. 2. In their being but one treadle; instead of a number of treadles, or cords, which a boy stands to pull up and down, as in the common loom, the weaver has only to tread on that one treadle, and to throw the shuttle. 3. In enabling the weaver to change a pattern in a few minutes, while the common loom requires many days or weeks. The great superiority of this loom over the common kind, is further proved by the following facts: One man can make 100 yards of figured stuff in twenty-five days. † That is, pulling down the cords, to work a number of treadles at a time.

Growth and Manufacture of Silk, 1828 ~~~ In the course of the very few years which have elapsed since its first introduction into this country, the Jacquard loom has entirely taken the place of every other method of figured silk weaving, and has been, in no small degree, instrumental in bringing that curious and beautiful art to its present state of advancement. The elaborate specimens of brocade which used to be brought forward as evidence of skilfulness on the part of the Spitalfields weavers of former days were produced by only the most skilful among the craft, who bestowed upon their performances the most painful amount of labor. The most beautiful products of the loom in the present day are, however, accomplished by men possessing only the ordinary rate of skill, while the labor attendant upon the actual weaving is but little more than that demanded for making the plainest goods. ... the Jacquard machine, by means of which figured satins of the most beautiful textures and patterns may be manufactured. Treatise on ... Silk Manufacture, 1832 ~~~ When was the Jacquard loom introduced [in England]? – The Jacquard loom came into operation about 1821; the patent came out about then; it was Mr. Wilson, of London, that introduced it into the country, and he got the patent for it. Reports from the Committees. 1835

jane – [made in Leigh] janes in imitation of those of India, figured and flowered by *drawboys*, &c. Union Gazetteer, 1807 ~~~ Kensington Garden Dresses. ... Gloves of straw colour, and half boots of green jane. *National Register*, June 12, 1808 ~~~Slippers of leather or jane to correspond with the dress, have superseded half-boots for the promenade costume. *La Belle Assemblée*, July 1814 ~~~ We beheld a man, the other day, fluttering along Prince's Street, with light jane trowsers, and a white straw hat. *Atheneum*, April 15, 1830 ~~~ Jane. *s.* A kind of fustian. Ladies' Lexicon, 1835 [see *fustian*]

Jane grey – Among the new material that are expected to be fashionable in evening-dress, we may cite ... taffetas Jane Grey, in broad stripes, *Court Magazine*, May 1835 [see *taffeta*]

japan – Under-dresses were universally of white japan, and other muslins, with very long trains. *La Belle Assemblée*, May 1806 ~~~ Some [mantles] were of white japanned muslin or transparent figured leno, lined with purple or rose coloured sarsnet, which had an effect extremely rich and elegant; *La Belle Assemblée*, June 1806 ~~~ Walking Dress. A round cottage gown of jaconet, or japan muslin, made high in the neck, *La Belle Assemblée*, October 1807 ~~~ [Paris] the most tonish [coloured muslin] is of a sort which, I think, you used to call Japan muslin; it is striped to resemble lace. Pink, blue, and lilac are the favourite colours of these dresses. *Repository of Arts*, September 1820 ~~~ Hindoos' manufactures are generally imitated in Europe, and even retain their names. Calicoes, cossacs, jaconets, boucks, chintzs, mulls, japans, ballusores, bandannas, pullcates, ginghams, &c. &c. are all Indian names, and mere imitations. A Million of Facts, 1835

Japanese gauze – very young ladies wear white for evening costume, either of Japan gauze, net, or white satin. *Ladies' Monthly Museum*, December 1821 ~~~ Ball Dress. – Over a what satin slip, a dress of Japanese plain gauze, or tulle, with a full rouleaux of gauze next the shoe, *Kaleidoscope*, April 5, 1825 ~~~ a small fichu of Japanese gauze, *Ladies' Monthly Museum*, November 1825 ~~~ A levantine dress is much in favour for dinner parties; ... and has long sleeves of white Japanese gauze. *Lady's Magazine*, November 1825 ~~~ There were also some new materials of a very splendid description, particularly Japanese gauze, which had a beautiful effect. *La Belle Assemblée*, March 1830

jay – Flowers for adorning the hair of young persons are made of jays' feathers and some of the eyes in the peacock's tail; both are extremely beautiful and quite novel. *La Belle Assemblée*, December 1825

jean – In the House of Representatives, March 8, 1787. ... cotton and linen jeans, Memoir of Samuel Slater, 1836 ~~~ [in 1789] the said WD and JG made a certain cotton cloth jean waistcoat, Complete System of Pleading, 1798 ~~~ Fancy-coloured silk, nankin, and jean shoes and buskins were much worn; *La Belle Assemblée*, June 1806 ~~~ white jean [shoes] are more generally worn than kid, but satin in full dress are seen without an exception. *La Belle Assemblée*, January 1807 ~~~ [in Lancashire] about the year 1709. ... India-jeans, ribs, some thicksets, and some strong jeans, were, however, then made solely of cotton. Beauties of England, 1807 ~~~ *Leigh* ... has considerable manufactures, particularly of fine jeans, in imitation of those of India; General Gazetteer, 1812 ~~~ Slippers of silk-coloured jean, and kid of various colours, are worn of an evening, *La Belle Assemblée*, March 1812 ~~~ The Shoe-Maker. Makes covering for the feet, usually of leather; but frequently also of other materials, as silk, jean, nankeen, &c. <u>Book of English Trades</u>, 1818 ~~~ Swiss spencers of fine white jean, promise also to be very general for walking; *La Belle Assemblée*, May 1819 ~~~ Extract of a Letter dated 17th April 1822 ~~~ under the terms, calicoes and muslins, it has been the practice, in Ireland, to class jeans, jeannets, nankinets, ginghams, &c. and indeed most all light fabrics of plain and twilled goods, that were not particularly expressed in the Act of Union. <u>House Of Lords The Sessional Papers</u>, 1823 ~~~ all who can afford it appear in very gay apparel – the men in broad-cloth coats, fancy waistcoats, and nankeen or jean trowsers, <u>Colonial Slavery</u>, 1823 ~~~ [ad for] Striped Jean Dresses; *Kaleidoscope*, November 23, 1824 ~~~ [ad] MR. JOHN P. DEANE respectfully informs his Friends, it being his intentention [sic] to proceed to Sydney, the following GOODS will be disposed of at the under-mentioned Prices, being at least 30 per cent, under the retail Prices: … ladies' superior white jean stays, 10s. each; *Colonial Times*, March 3, 1826 ~~~ [ad] Have received by the ships Hark-away and Jefferson, direct from Liverpool, … 3 cases bleached jeans, and brown and bleached Canton flannels. … superior satteen and jeans corsetts; … 11 bales 3-4 and 7-8 brown jeans or drillings. *Farmer's Register*, May 1835 ~~~ We all know that a jean, nankeen, or any kind of thin jacket, is the pleasantest wear for September, <u>Instructions to Young Sportsmen</u>, 1833

jeanet – [dyeing] Colours to be Raised … For a velveret take 1-2 bundles of welds, for a jeanet somewhat less: <u>Domestic Encyclopædia</u>, 1803 ~~~ Light fustians, such as jeans, jeanetts, *Tradesman*, October 1814 ~~~ I have found nothing better for a light summer jacket than what is made at Manchester by the name of *satteen,* or *jeanett,* which is printed on each side, in imitation of cloth. This stuff far surpasses the others for lightness, comfort, durability, and every thing that can be required for warm weather; <u>Instructions to Young Sportsmen</u>, 1816 [spelled *jeanet* in the 1833 edition] … [ad] White and Coulered [sic] Jeans and Jeanettes. *Honduras Gazette*, July 1, 1826 ~~~ Jeanette. – *See Cotton Manufactures*. [for tarrif] *Public Documents*, March 1832

jersey – Jersey, among woolcombers, denotes the finest wool, taken from the rest by dressing it with a Jersey comb. <u>Encyclopædia Britannica</u>, 1797 ~~~ The general employ of the industrious Poor throughout the county, is knitting stockings, and spinning linen and jersey: in the latter way, most of the wives and children of labourers at Empingham are employed, and earn from 3d. to 8d. a day, according to their ages and abilities. The jersey so spun is woven into tammies, by poor weavers in the south of Rutland, and in Leicestershire, and Northamptonshire. <u>State of the Poor</u>, 1797 ~~~ (from the island of *Jersey*, which is famous for spinning of yard, and its stocking manufacture.) a fine woollen yarn. <u>Complete and Universal English Dictionary</u>, 1799 ~~~ Anno 1603, it was also ordered by a by-law of this fraternity, that "their apprentices should be forbidden … to wear .. worsted or jersey stockings, <u>An Impartial History … of Newcastle Upon Tyne</u>, 1801 ~~~ patent … for a Method of making Stockings, Gloves, Mitts, Socks, Caps, Coats, Waistcoats, Breeches, Cloaks, and other Clothing and Linings for the same, for Persons afflicted with the Gout, Rheumatism, or other complaints requiring Warmth, and for common Use in cold Climates, and for making false or downy Calves in Stockings. Dated September 22, 1788. … begin the work in the common manner of manufacturing hosiery, and having worked one or more course or courses in the common way, begin to add a coating, thus: draw the frame over the arch, and then hang wool or Jersey, raw or unspun, upon the beards of the needles, <u>Repertory of Arts</u>, 1801 [see also *tammy*]

Jerusalem cotton – Bazat, or Baza, in commerce, a long, fine, spun cotton, which comes from Jerusalem, whence it is also called *Jerusalem-cotton*. <u>Encyclopædia Britannica</u>, 1797

joining lace – This evening dress has been much approved of. A French jacket of white or coloured crape, ornamented with rich narrow joining lace, same round the bottom of the dress; *La Belle Assemblée*, June 1806 ~~~ [a dress made for the Princess Mary, on the occasion of her wedding] A very fine India sprig morning dress, tastefully let in with broad Valenciennes joining lace, flounces of the same; *La Belle Assemblée*, July 1816 ~~~ dinner dress … made of India book-muslin; the body is cut low round the bust; the front is plain, and is elegantly ornamented with joining lace let in in small flowers; the back has a similar embroidery up the middle, and three or four small plaits on each side. *Ladies' Monthly Museum*, June 1818 ~~~ A row of what is called joining-lace is let in in a wave round the upper part of the bust, … The bottom of the skirt is trimmed with three flounces of broad lace, between each of which is a deep wave of joining-lace. *Repository of Arts*, September 1819

Juive – [Paris] New materials for dresses are this year very numerous. Several of these for morning *negligé* are of the finest Cashmere wool, and of a slighter kind than Chali. These are the *Etoffes à la Juive, Court Magazine*, May 1835

Kamtschatka moss - Kolinski

Kamtschatka moss – List of New Patents. ... Andrew Baldrence, Chenille Cutter, residing in Paisley, for a machine for cutting chenille, chenille cloth into chenille thread, and for making weft or part of weft, for shawls now called and know by the names of Chenille, Kamtschatka Moss, and Velours de Soi, or one other of these names. – Sealed September 19, 1835 *Repertory of Patent Inventions*, November 1835 [see also *chenille*]

kangaroo – The Gamgarou, or, as Pennant calls it, Kangaroo, is a native of New South Wales, and first discovered by that able and much-lamented navigator Capt. Cook. ... The body is covered with fine hair of a greyish-brown colour, inclining to dirty white on the belly, very thick and woolly; *Gentleman's Magazine*, June 1796 ~~~ exports at Hobart Town for the years 1817 and 1818: ... Seal and Kangaroo Skins. 10,000. *London Quarterly Review*, May 1820 ~~~ In Van Dieman's Land, £10 per annum will hardly find an entire suit, with hats and shoes. These servants generally make Kangaroo-skin jackets, and shoes of something of the same sort. Many of the settlers who are poor, frequently dress in articles of the same description. Voyage to New South Wales, 1822 ~~~ I observed that a great many of the convicts in Van Dieman's Land wore jackets and trowsers of the kangaroo skin, and sometimes caps of the same material, which they obtain from the stock-keepers who are employed in the interior of the country. Report of ... the Colony of New South Wales, 1822 ~~~ the average prices between April and August, 1826, in sterling money, ... Kangaroo-leather boots, 30*s*. to 35*s*. Do. shoes, 9*s*. to 12*s*. Two Years in New South Wales, 1827 ~~~ Kangaroo-leather is often used for shoes for tender feet. Servants' Guide, 1831 ~~~ Kangaroo-skins are essentially useful in the colony, for hats, and also for shoes, which are remarkably durable; when well packed, and of a good size, these skins fetch nearly sixpence a pound in London. Shoemakers make 100 per cent on the raw material. Journal of a Voyage from Calcutta, 1833

Kendal cottons – The original word, which has been thus transformed, was *coating*, which, when hastily pronounced, has a strong resemblance in respect of sound to *cotton*; and that this is really so, admits of the clearest proof, seeing that at this hour a very coarse kind of *woollen* cloth, that is the staple manufacture of Kendal, in Lancashire, is known by no other name but that of *Kendal cotton,* instead of *Kendal coating.* That these Kendal cottons are made of sheeps wool only, without the smallest admixture of cotton wool, properly so called, you may easily satisfy yourself by going into one of the numerous warehouses in this metropolis, where this kind of cloth is sold, ail which you will frequently see advertised in the newspapers. *British Critic*, November 1796 ~~~ The manufactures of Westmoreland ... consist chiefly of coarse woollen cloth, called *Kendall Cottons,* properly, it is said *coatings,* * ... * Rather, I conceive, from COTTWM, – *Welch*, for a sort of coarse woollen cloth. Reports to the Board of Agriculture, 1808 ~~~ Kendall woollen cloths (usually called Kendall cottons) in pieces of twenty yards, 27 and 28 in wide, for nineteen to twenty-four shillings sterling, undyed, used these 10 or 12 years for vest backs – *Weekly Register*, September 21, 1811 ... *A statement shewing the materials for clothing the army purchased* ... Kendall cotton – 392 yards. *Weekly Register*, January 9, 1813 ~~~ The articles chiefly manufactured, in late years, are thick stuffs, termed *Kendal Cottons,* which are exported for the clothing of Negroes, or used for sailors' jackets; Picture of Britain, 1820 ~~~ Kendall cottons imported into the United States, *Public Documents*, December 10, 1835 ~~~ Nay, at the present day a strange solecism remains in the language of Cumberland, where a peculiar woollen article of the coarsest kind still retains its ancient name of Kendal cottons, which it had five hundred years ago, when no such thing as genuine cotton was known in the kingdom. Cotton Manufacture of Great Britain, 1836 [see also *coatings*]

Kensington lace – Saturday, May 25th, ... A tremendous storm of hail took place at Kensington. The lace manufactory there had almost the whole of the windows broken, and it was with difficulty the work-people escaped from the broken glass and pieces of ice, some of which were three inches in circumference, which were flying about in all directions, to the destruction of a large quantity of valuable lace. In the garden attached some of the trees were stripped as if it had been winter, *New Monthly Magazine*, July 1822 ~~~ Evening Dress, Composed of Kensington figured lace, with a deep scolloped border round the bottom, worn over an azure blue satin; *Ladies' Monthly Museum*, August 1822 ~~~ Spencers are, for the most part, composed of a pale pink satin, covered with Kensington figured lace; *Ladies' Monthly Museum*, September 1822 ~~~ The dresses worn at home ... are set off by a lace frill, and a fine cornette, both of Kensington lace, and a gold convent cross. This attire, though simple, is extremely elegant and becoming. *Ladies' Monthly Museum*, May 1823 ~~~ [ad] KENSINGTON LACE ESTABLISHMENT. – SELLING OFF, the immense STOCK, at about half the usual prices, the Proprietor quitting the Business in July next: consisting of the most beautiful Blonde Court Lappets, Stripes, Spriginss, Pelerines, with Honiton and the Genuine Kensington Lace Sprigs, Shawls, Trimming and Pieces, Laces, and every elegant article so superior to any others, with Black Lace Veils, &c. in fashionable variety. *Court Journal*, February 2, 1833

kenting – Linen, ... Kentings, 50,380 ¼ [yards] ... — mixed with cotton, 36 [yards] <u>Annals of Agriculture</u>, 1796 ~~~ In the year 1779, the Irish acts of Parliament of the 14th and 15th of Charles II. laying a duty of 5s. per dozen, on fine needle-wrought handkerchiefs of Holland, were construed to extend to a coarse article, called Kenting handkerchiefs, sent at that time in considerable quantities from Paisley, and its neighbourhood, to Ireland, at the low average price of 12s. per dozen. <u>Origin of Commerce</u>, 1801 ~~~ Upwards of fifteen thousand looms are constantly employed in the manufacture of linen and cotton in Perth, and as many more in the country around it. The fabrics thus manufactured consist chiefly of Silesias, Britannias, Kentings, <u>Journey from Edinburgh through Parts of North Britain</u>, 1802 ~~~ Paisley, ... The manufacturers afterwards went upon lawns, gauzes, kentings, cambrics, and other light fabrics, which were found more profitable. ... Perth is emulating Paisley in enterprise and industry, being, like it, the center of a manufacturing country. Silesias, brittanias, kentings (or ghentings), hollands for shirting and sheeting, low-priced linens, and pack-sheeting, are fabrics made from flax and hemp, which are chiefly imported from Holland, and spun in the adjacent country. <u>Annals of Commerce</u>, 1805

kersey – Kersey, a kind of coarse woollen cloth, made chiefly in Kent and Devonshire. <u>Encyclopædia Britannica</u>, 1797 ~~~ Kersey, a coarse woollen manufacture between a stuff and a cloth. <u>Barclay's English Dictionary</u>, 1799 ~~~ [in 1803] Kersey was then at 4*s*. 6*d*. a yard, and since continued to fall till it came down to 3*s*. 6*d*. but no reduction was made in the contracts [for army great coats] till the present year; *Parliamentary Register*, June 23, 1808 ~~~ a species of coarse woollen stuff, usually woven in ribs. Kerseys are manufactured in large quantities at Leeds, Halifax, and other parts of Yorkshire, as also at Exeter; <u>General Dictionary of Commerce</u>, 1810 ~~~ Ridge-Washed Kersey, *Kersey* cloth made of fleece wool, washed only on the sheep's back. See *stat. 35 Eliz. c. 10.* <u>Law Dictionary</u>, 1811 ~~~ [Baltimore] Kersey is usually made for the army, the navy, the working people and the frugal. It is equally durable compared with *low priced* broad cloths, ... The weight of good *white* kersey, twenty-seven inches wide, is from eleven ounces and one half to twelve ounces and one half, or thirteen ounces per running yard. It is always tweeled, and certainly owes a great part of its strength to *the tweel.* It is made out of the coarsest wooled breeds of sheep in England, *after the long wool fit for combing and stuffs,* is taken out of the heavy fleeces. Hence the cost of good strong kerseys in England, white and undyed, is as low as forty-five shillings sterling for a piece, which is called thirty, and will measure twenty-nine yards; that is eighteen pence and three fifths sterling, or about thirty-four cents and one half. This article, white kersey, makes excellent military vests and overalls, and is peculiarly acceptable to armies. When dyed drab, blue, brown, &c. it is equally good for working people, seamen, fishermen, &c. *Weekly Register*, March 21, 1812 ~~~ Homespun. A Charleston paper says – We had the pleasure of seeing and feeling a stout piece of cloth, of the quality called *grey kersey,* manufactured in the vicinity of Philadelphia. It is 6-4 wide, and, at the rate of $1 50 per yard, is much cheaper than the common plains. It is warmer, stronger, more elastic, and twice as broad. *Niles' Weekly Register*, March 30, 1822 ~~~ [debate on the Wool Bill] drab kerseys, ... for sailors, watermen, fishermen, farmers, mechanics, &c,; *Niles' Weekly Register*, April 27, 1827 ~~~ Kersey (the Dutch *Karsaai,* and the French *Estoffe de laine croisée*) is double-tweeled Say, the word being compounded of the Swedish, Danish, and Scotch *kors,* cross; because Tweeling is woven so as to have the appearance of lines of plaited threads, running diagonally *across* the web. The Kersey of former times was, comparatively, a coarse cloth, and an article of the same description is still manufactured in some parts of the island, and sold, generally white, by the name of Plaiding; <u>Analytical Dictionary</u>, 1835

kersey woven – [the threads] are crossed so as to give an additional strength to the cloth; hence it appears in diagonal lines or rows running obliquely across the piece; and, in general, this style of weaving adds thickness as well as strength to the fabric. In the cotton manufacture, cloth, so woven, is called *twilled*. <u>New Family Encyclopedia</u>, 1835

kerseymere – Our kerseymeres are still far superior to those of the French manufacture; *Gentleman's Magazine*, January 1798 ~~~ Previous to the Revolution, there was an experiment made at the famous cloth manufactory of Sedan in France, by the order of government, to try to equal the English kerseymeres. French kerseymeres had been manufactured and sold for about 3*s*. 6*d*. per yard; the English kerseymeres were fold from about 12*s*. to 14*s*. or more; but when the French kerseymere of equal quality to the English was produced, the manufacturer declared he must have *considerably more* than the English price. <u>Survey of the Strength and Opulence of Great Britain</u>, 1801 ~~~ Kerseymeres, which of late have become an article of considerable importance, <u>Annals of Commerce</u>, 1805 ~~~ Parisian Fashions. Kerseymere dresses, of a silver grey, are now much worn: *Lady's Magazine*, February 1807 ~~~ Mantle of fawn coloured Kersimere, trimmed with white velvet; *Emerald*, May 9, 1807 ~~~ Gentlemen's … *Morning Dress* … drab colour ribbed kerseymere breeches, *National Register*, May 1, 1808 ~~~ a species of thin woollen stuff, generally woven plain, and made from the finest wools. It is manufactured principally in the west of England, and is almost exclusively employed in the formation of breeches, pantaloons, waistcoats, ladies-habits, pelisses, &c. <u>General Dictionary of Commerce</u>, 1810 ~~~ Kerseymere. A kind of fine cloth woven after the manner of a kersey. <u>Johnson's English Dictionary</u>, 1812 ~~~ A General Collection of Words of variable spelling, in which those of the best usage are printed in Roman character, … cassimer, *cassimere*, *kerseymere*, <u>Practical Orthography</u>, 1828 ~~~ Mantles of kerseymere are among the newest inventions, and promise to be general; *La Belle Assemblée*, November 1818 ~~~ January 16, 1828. … We manufacture, principally, narrow cloth, called kerseymeres, of about 31 inches wide, when finished; <u>American Tariffs</u>, 1828 ~~~ [Paris] Riding Dress. – A habit composed of very fine kerseymere; the color is *flamme d'enfer*, *Ladies' Pocket*, June 1830 ~~~ [men's] Walking Dress. … Trousers of chequered kerseymere, buttoned in the front with two rows of black braid up the side seams. *Day*, February 10, 1832 ~~~ but the improved fabric [of kersey], usually termed Kerseymere, is often made of the choicest wool, and, except in being tweeled and of less width, differs in no respect from superfine cloth. A very fine Kerseymere, slightly milled, and of softer texture, is woven in squares, which are bordered with fringes and termed Whittles, or Whittle Shawls. These are worn only by women, but the Saxon *hwitel* was a cloak for either sex, and, as its name imports, was always *White*, although Whittles are now dyed of any colour required. <u>Analytical Dictionary</u>, 1835 ~~~ *Kerseymeres*, which are generally narrow, are twilled, and of various thicknesses. *Kerseys* are nearly of the same fabric with the last mentioned, but much thicker and stouter. <u>Scenes of Commerce</u>, 1836 [see also *cassimere* and *narrow cloth*]

Kerseynet – *Kerseynets*, 27 inches wide, cost 8d. to 1s. 3d. – It is composed of cotton and wool, … This article is used by all classes for summer dresses, and the quality principally consumed costs about 1s. *Niles' Weekly Register*, March 8, 1828

kid – the daughters, only tore two pair of kid leather gloves, with trying 'em on. [from *The Old Batchelor*] <u>British Theatre</u>, 1795 ~~~ [Dated Feb. 5, 1799] Now, the gloves made from leather, particularly from kid and lamb skins, dressed after my way, will be found of a soft, fine, and thin texture, not having been injured by the astringent and hardening qualities of the lime: they will be stronger, and more tough, than other gloves; the leather not having undergone the corrosive, consequently weakening, qualities of the bran-ferment. The colours will be more bright, and the gloves will not be so rotten as those now made use of, on account of there being no salt in them; which not only lessens the brightness of the colours, and spots the gloves, but is found to be ever corroding them, consequently must weaken the leather very much. <u>Repertory of Arts and Manufactures</u>, 1799 ~~~ Shoes of dove-colour kid, plaited round with narrow ribbon, are very genteel, and among the new articles of dress for mourning. *Lady's Magazine*, December 1800 ~~~ On the abolition of pockets in London, three tenderhearted fair ones went to the representation of Romeo and Juliet; the sorrows of the youthful Capulet, drew such plentiful showers down the cheeks of her fair auditors, who unfortunately had but one cambric among them, that it soon was completely deluged; one of the young ladies, to add to the misfortune, had on a pair of purple kid gloves, the fingers of which she frequently applied to her pale cheeks, which were so curiously striped in all directions, that she pretty nearly resembled a Cherokee Chief, to the great diversion of some laughing bucks of fashion in the next box. *Lady's Weekly Miscellany*, January 14, 1809 ~~~ Kid-skins are the skins of young goats, which are chiefly used in the manufacture of women's fine gloves, such as the French gloves, Limerick gloves, &c. We usually import them from France, Spain, and Italy, undressed, and afterwards prepare them for use. General Dictionary of Commerce, 1810 ~~~ The satin or silk half-boot (though certainly inappropriate) is partially introduced in evening and dress parties: those of jean and kid are invariably worn with the morning and walking dress; *Repository of Arts*, September 1812 ~~~ Morning Dress. ... The slippers worn with this dress are of bronze kid, tied *en sandales*. The gloves are of yellow kid. *Atheneum*, October 8, 1828 ~~~ Gloves. Nothing can give a more perfect finish to a handsome dress than the covering for the hands. Though there are many different kinds worn, those mostly in repute among the higher orders are the Doe-skin, Kid and Berlin, ... Kid of all materials is, without exception, the most beautiful, and sits best on the hand, from its exceeding pliability (when good); compressing the hand with a gentle pressure, like a second natural skin over the first. Buff, or white kid, should alone be assumed for full dress. Whole Art of Dress, 1830 ~~~ Many people cannot, or rather fancy that they cannot shoot in gloves, and consequently their hands become as coarse as those of a gamekeeper, which, utterly as I abhor *dandyism*, I must yet observe is not quite in unison with the appearance of a perfect gentleman. I shall, therefore, recommend to them dark kid gloves, which will stand a month's shooting much better than might be supposed; and if they fit nicely to the fingers, are so thin as not to be the least incumbrance between the triggers. Instructions to Young Sportsmen, 1830 ~~~ At present the manufacturers are employed in making men's and women's fine gloves, which pass in the retail shops under the denomination of kid gloves, but are, in reality, made from lamb-skins, imported from Italy, Spain, and Germany. ... History of the Glove Trade, 1834 ~~~ Kid gloves for the ladies must be all manner of delicate colors, straw, pink, light blue, &c. Gentlemen's gloves are either plain yellow, or various greenish shades. Book of Commerce by Sea and Land, 1834 ~~~ [Paris] We observe that black mittens, so often in and out of favour, are now principally confined lo morning-dress. White ones, of a very open kind, are most in favour in evening costume, but they are not so generally adopted as kid gloves of that shade of white that is slightly tinged with rose. *Ladies' Pocket*, September 1836

kincob – Kumehar. A stuff of a silk or sattin ground, with flowers of gold or silver: generally called by Europeans kincob. Narrative of the Operations of Captain Little's Detachment, 1794

king's cord – [see *corduroy*]

kip skin – [see *calf skin*]

kluteen – A green striped French kluteen, designed for the spring spencer or pelisse; but is equally appropriate for evening dress: it admits of fancy trimming of the same nature, or those of quilled net or thread lace. *Repository of Arts*, May 1815 [note: *Klutene* is Norwegian for *cloth*]

knap – [see *nap*]

Kolinski – Mantles trimmed and lined with fur are now beginning to be very generally adopted. Sable, Isabella bear, and that delicate fur called Kolinski, are all employed for that purpose. *Court Magazine*, January 1834 ~~~ [ad] The attention of the Fashionable World is also directed to a New Fur, recently imported by Snieder and Co., intitled the KOLINSKI, which is introduced by their House, under special patronage, for Dress Muff and Boas, the light and elegant appearance of which surpasses all others. *Court Journal*, February 7, 1835 ~~~ we shall name the second rate furs, which, without being very expensive, are nevertheless considered fashionable – Kolinski, *Ladies' Companion*, January 1836 ~~~ Kolinski, also comparatively cheap, but soft, rich, and becoming, promises to be as great a favourite this year as it was last. *Ladies' Pocket*, November 1836

Lace - Lyons silk

lace – The Princess of Wales was very suburb indeed, and the dress was the most costly that could be made. ... The sleeves, and round the bottom of the robe, were covered with rows of the finest point lace. *Scots Magazine*, April 1795 ~~~ New lace to be put to any coats that want it when they are turned; it can always be got from the Clothier at ten-pence per dozen yards. ... they must get their epaulettes and hat-lace from the Regimental Laceman, <u>Rules and Regulations for the Cavalry</u>, 1795 ~~~ Morning Dress. Night-cap of spotted muslin, trimmed with a double border of lace in whole plaits, *Lady's Magazine*, February 1796 ~~~ a platted string with which women fasten their clothes; ornaments of fine thread curiously woven; textures of thread with gold or silver. <u>Sheridan's English Dictionary</u>, 1797 ~~~ [in Nottingham] Lace-workers earn from 20s. to 40s. a week. ... [in Buckingham] Women, on an average, earn 8d. or 9d. a day, by lace-making. <u>State of the Poor</u>, 1797 ~~~ Lace, in commerce, a work composed of many threads of gold, silver, or silk, interwoven the one with the other, and worked upon a pillow with spindles according to the pattern designed. The open work is formed with pins, which are placed and displaced as the spindles are moved. The importation of gold and silver lace is prohibited. <u>Encyclopædia Britannica</u>, 1797 ~~~ Lace is generally worn, it is introduced into all parts of the dress; the petticoats, pocket-holes, sleeves, scarfs, and even the parasols, are trimmed with it. *Port Folio*, August 21, 1802 ~~~ Lace, which is better calculated for ornament than use, forms one of the most profitable and considerable branches of French industry and commerce. The finest, the dearest, the most beautiful, and most fashionable laces are made from flaxen thread; laces are made of gold and silver for decorations, and household furniture, &c., those made for the latter purpose are coarse, and made with little care, having no other merit than that of the matter of which they are composed. The *blond* lace, as to its fabric, resembles the thread laces, but it differs as to its materials, which are white silk; but this silk being of a very inferior kind, and not equal to the beautiful thread used in manufacturing the other laces, will not permit the blond to be bleached, a process on which depends its chief beauty. Hence the blond lace is not only infinitely less durable, but is also of less value than the ordinary laces. The name *lace* is also given to every work resembling lace, made from black silk, or thread. Lace properly so called, is essentially distinguished from *point*, (to which it bears a resemblance), by being worked upon a cushion, *with bobbins*, whereas, the *point* is invariably made with the needle, such as the French or Alençon point, the Venetian, and the Brussels point. Nevertheless, similarity of appearance has caused the denominations to be confounded; thus, many people speak, and, some authors write, concerning Alençon *lace,* and English. *point*; but, this is an error. ... The silk used in the making of black laces is dyed and prepared at Lyons, where it is called *Grenadine*; that for the fabric of the coarser kinds of lace is dyed at Nismes. The makers of black lace earn from 6 to 10 pence *per diem,* the thread lace makers about 4 or 5 pence. The prices are for thread lace from about 2d. to 2s. 6d. per yard: for blond lace from 3d. to 4s. 2d. per yard. The pieces run about 12 yards in length. <u>Literary Panorama</u>, 1808 ~~~ Black lace cloaks are also much worn, sometimes lined, but more frequently not; these are so convenient, so graceful, and elegantly negligent, and withall so valuable in themselves, for we speak only of the real lace, that we cannot help giving them our warmest approbation and decided recommendation; it is a fashion from which good taste can never long dispense; *La Belle Assemblée*, August 1810 ~~~ Evening dress. Light pink satin gown, trimmed round the bottom with a lace flounce, laid on richly, worked and headed with tufts of the same; short full sleeve, trimmed with lace. A shell lace tippet. *Repository of Arts*, January 1815 ~~~ Evening Dress. Dress of Urling's lace over a pink satin slip: *Repository of Arts*, February 1824 ~~~ Lace-making, though formerly practiced by ladies, having now become so important a branch of European manufacture as to furnish employment for many thousands of females, *Lady's Book*, September 1831 ~~~ The cheaper kinds of lace, have long been made by machinery. And recently the invention of Mr. Heathcoat's lace machine, has effected the fabrication of the more difficult or twisted lace, with precision and despatch. This machine is exceedingly complicated and ingenious, and is now in operation in this country and in France, as well as in England. The best *white* lace has usually been made of flax; but *cotton* can now be spun so neatly and finely, that the use of it, even in *bone-lace,* has completely, in England, superseded the use of flax; and indeed *woven lace* is now got up in that country, so neatly as to have also superseded in a great degree, the use of that made by the hand. *Gold* and *silver* thread is also wrought into lace. This is a stout fabric, commonly close, but wrought so as to exhibit some sort of figure. It is made of different widths, but all narrow like ribbon. There is also a *worsted lace,* of a similar texture, commonly wrought with various patterns in colors. This was formerly much used on liveries, and may still be seen occasionally on the lining of carriages. New Family Encyclopedia, 1831 ~~~ The English, in 1786, had effected a method of making *point net* by improved machinery, and re-looping the conjoined thread, made a fast mesh, so as to require little or no care in stiffening. From this period, lace made by machinery began to be in considerable demand; History, Gazetteer, and Directory of Nottinghamshire, 1832 ~~~ *Why does lace exhibit various patterns?* Because the pattern is drawn on a piece of parchment, and fastened to the cushion of a circular box with pins formed on purpose, which are stuck through it in various places, according to the design intended to be represented; the requisite number of threads are then wound upon a small bobbin, one end being tied to each pin, and these are thrown over and under each other in various ways; so that the threads twine round the pins, and thus form the multiplicity of holes or eyes which produce the desired figure. *Why is some knit-lace called point?* Because it has been worked, or embroidered, with the needle: when formed of silk, it is called *blonde. Why was cotton-lace formerly in such disrepute?* Because the quality of lace depends on its transparency, and at first, the meshes of cotton were encumbered with loose fibres, which destroyed its clearness; and to remove these, for some years appeared to be an insuperable difficulty. *Why is lace "gassed?"* Because the flame of the gas may penetrate the meshes, and free them of these loose fibres, which is done without the smallest injury to the fabric. Knowledge for the People, 1832 ~~~ [court dress] Magnificent point lace dress, over rich blue satin; *Lady's Magazine and Museum,* June 1836 [see also *blond, bobbinet, pillow lace, point, net, tulle* and city of origin, ex: *Brussels*]

lace muslin – Lace muslin, a new and delicate article, peculiarly suitable for *dishabille,* and is either formed as a plain high dress with a tie collar, or as a loose robe open down the front; a tippet cape, falling collar, and trimmed entirely round with a narrow white frill. *Repository of Arts,* June 1814

ladies' cloth – Morning Dress. … Amazon dress of lady's green cloth, *Lady's Magazine,* December 1796 ~~~ Morning Dresses. … Opera *pelisse* of ladies' blue cloth, trimmed with the same. *Lady's Magazine,* January 1797 ~~~ *On the Improvement of British Wool.* … June 14, 1799. … Of the enclosed pattern, I beg again to say, that I have shewn it to some very good judges, who say it is one of the best ladies cloths they have ever seen, and will prove better both in look and wear, worth one guinea and a half per yard, than the greater part of ladies cloths at eighteen shillings: this is a great improvement; because, if such ladies can be made of this quality, we are sure those of stouter texture must succeed. The price of this ladies cloth is £.1 1*s.* per yard. Communications to the Board of Agriculture, 1800 ~~~ [ad] Spanish, and every other description of fine Ladies Cloth, for Pelices and Mantles. *La Belle Assemblée,* March 1807 ~~~ This evidence was received in the year 1803. … 1, The finest and thinnest cloths are made for the Turkey-trade; 2, ladies' cloths are in the next degree thicker; 3, the next in thickness are made for the West India trade; 4, the next are for the Russia trade; 5, superfine cloths are thicker still; 6, the thickest of all are double milled superfine, and a species of narrow-cloths named *ratteens. Monthly Magazine,* March 1807 ~~~ Ladies' cloth of the most prevailing colour for riding-habits, pelisses, &c. furnished by William Barry, 55, New Bond-street, inventor of the winter morning and evening cloth dress, given in our *Repository* of Dec. 1813. The chief object of this pattern is, to point out to the public a most valuable discovery made in the improvement of the edges of cloth, ladies' cloth, merino cloth, and kerseymeres, so as to supersede the use of turning in or hemming, which process has been found, by two years experience, fully to answer the so much wanted purpose. The two sides having a small piece cut out, are left in the original state; the other two have undergone the above process, and will be found, by applying a brush, to remain solid, while the others will be found to fray by the same application. *Repository of Arts,* June 1814 ~~~ *Ladies' Cloths* – width 58 inches: cost 5s. to 13s. *Niles' Weekly Register,* March 8, 1828 ~~~ Are the ladies' cloths of a finer description? – They are of a finer description; what is usually termed light woollens. Reports from the Committees, 1830

laine – *wool*. <u>Tardy's French Dictionary</u>, 1799 ~~~ Woollen, (made of wool) *De laine*. <u>Chambaud's French</u>
   <u>Dictionary</u>, 1815 [see *wool*; also *batiste de laine*, *foulard de laine*, *mousselines de laine*, *satin de laine*, *wool gauze*]
laine cachemire – [see *cashmere wool*]
laine d'aguelins – *lamb's wool*; <u>Dufief's French Dictionary</u>, 1810
laine de Moscovie – *fine beaver's wool*. <u>Dufief's French Dictionary</u>, 1810
laine de virogne – *vicugna wool*, <u>Dufief's French Dictionary</u>, 1810 [see *vigonia*]
lama – The Glama, Llama, or South-American camel-sheep, … in a tame state, with smooth short hair, in
   a wild state, with long coarse hair, white, grey, and russet, disposed in spots; … The wool has a strong
   disagreeable scent. <u>Encyclopædia Britannica</u>, 1797 ~~~ Court dress … A white crape petticoat, with a
   rich Vandyke silver foil border, edged with the real silver Lama; *La Belle Assemblée*, June 1807 ~~~
   Over this [frock] is thrown the new wrapping cloak, manufactured from the wool of the female lama;
   unlike most other inventions of a similar nature, it is both elegant and useful: a fine figure appears in it
   to considerable advantage. With respect to the cloth, we never saw any thing so exquisitely beautiful;
   its delicate softness, its transcendent fineness; and, what is, perhaps, a superior recommendation, the
   warmth which it communicates to the frame, renders it an indispensable appendage to the out-door
   costume of ladies of fashion; … The beautiful cloth, … will, it is probable, be adopted by *belles* of taste,
   in the walking costume, as much as it is now worn for wrapping cloaks. Its novelty and elegance, as
   well as the uncommon beauty of its texture, would render it a most superior article for pelisses; *La Belle*
   Assemblée, November 1814 ~~~ Princess Charlotte of Wales' Wedding Dress and Jewellery. 1. The
   wedding dress is a slip of white and-silver atlas, worn under a dress of transparent silk net elegantly
   embroidered in silver lama, with a border to correspond, tastefully worked in bunches of flowers, to
   form festoons round the bottom; the sleeves and neck trimmed with a rich suit of Brussels point lace.
   … 2. A dress of white net, embroidered in gold lama, an elegant border over white satin; *Niles' Weekly*
   Register, June 22, 1816 ~~~ Ball Dress. Dress of pink lama gauze: *Manchester Iris*, October 5, 1823 ~~~
   At parties of *grande parure*, crape dresses, figured in silver lama, bordered with leaves of the same,
   [March] *La Belle Assemblée*, summary of the last six months, 1827 ~~~ [Court dress] Rich gold lama,
   over pink satin petticoat; train … trimmed with gold lama and blonde; *Lady's Magazine and Museum*,
   April 1836
lamb skin – Fashions for Gentlemen. … The leaders of the haut-ton appear at the opera in great coats
   edged with Russia lamb skin, with cuffs, collar, and lappels of the same, *Jersey Magazine*, February 1810
   ~~~ Lamb-skins, … afford excellent leather for the formation of gloves, breeches, and even shoes,
   being usually pliant, and consequently capable of being worked into particular forms with great facility.
   Lamb-skins are, however, principally employed in their natural state, that is, with the wool on, in
   trimming gloves, covering muffs, and adorning different articles of dress. The skins whose wool is
   short and curly, are used in trimming gloves; those with thin, soft wool, are made into muffs; and such
   as are covered with close coarse wool resembling hair, are employed as furs. The price of lamb-skins
   varies according to the fineness, the brilliancy, and the colour of the wool. Black lamb-skins are more
   generally esteemed than those of any other colour. <u>General Dictionary of Commerce</u>, 1810 ~~~
   Gloves, ladies' lambskin, and chickens' skin, glazed, white, and colored <u>Digest of the Recent</u>
   <u>Commercial Regulations</u>, 1824 ~~~ lambskins,* from Russia; … * Of which there are the four
   following varieties:—black, wavy, from Astracan; black, curly, from the Ukrain; gray, curly, from the
   Crimea; gray, knotty, from Persia. <u>Transactions of the Society</u>, 1832
lamb's wool – The lambs' wool of the Merino-Ryeland breed will make finer cloth than the best of that of
   the pure Merino breed. In order to demonstrate this, I beg leave to exhibit three pieces of lambs' wool
   broad-cloth. <u>Letters and Papers on Agriculture</u>, 1805 ~~~ [ad] Mrs. Robertshaw begs leave to inform
   the Ladies that her patent Elastic Spanish Lamb's Wool Invisible Petticoats, Drawers, Waistcoats, and
   Dresses, all in one, are ready for their inspection; articles much approved of by every lady that has
   made trial of them, for their pleasant elasticity, softness, and warmth; and are found very convenient to
   Ladies that ride on horseback, as many Ladies found the first they had shrink in the wash. Mrs. R. has
   made it her study to improve them in that particular, and assures them the kind she now offers, are
   made of the finest Spanish Lamb's Wool, and manufactured in so peculiar a manner, that she will

warrant them never to shrink: with all those advantages, will add less to size than a cambric muslin. *La Belle Assemblée*, December 1807 ~~~ *Promenade Costume.* – An Andalusian robe of superfine Spanish lamb's-wool cloth, of a bright amber colour; *Edinburgh Annual Register*, September 30, 1810 ~~~ For delicate Ladies whose health requires them to wear Lamb's Wool all the year, Mrs. M. has manufactured an article very soft and thin for that purpose, of real Spanish Lamb's Wool, which Ladies will find an excellent substitute in changing their thick Winter cloathing, as they are very thin, but yet Wool, which will prevent them taking cold. *Repository of Arts*, May 1814 ~~~ [ad] Ready Made Clothing. For the accommodation of Gentlemen travelling, he keeps constantly on hand, … Lambs' wool, Floss and Flannel drawers, Directory for the Village of Rochester, 1827 ~~~ At the horse-races at Paris, … Another wore a dress of jaconnet, embroidered in coloured silks or lambs-wool above and below the knees; … The favourite female occupations are needlework in lambs-wool or silk, as borders for dresses, or belts, *Lady's Magazine*, September 1830 ~~~ *Lamb-wool Hosiery.* – This branch of the stocking manufacture was introduced only about thirty years ago. The yarn is made of the short wool of lambs, carded by machinery, and spun on wheels resembling the common cotton-jennies. It is soft and oozy, which constitutes its principal property; as being elastic and spongy, it forms an agreeable and warm covering. Edinburgh Encyclopædia, 1830 ~~~ [ad] Have received by the ships Hark-away and Jefferson, direct from Liverpool, … Lambs' wool and Merino shirts and drawers. *Farmer's Register*, May 1835 ~~~ The processes of spinning worsted and lamb's wool – worsted yarn being spun from what is called long wool, which is produced exclusively in England; lamb's wool yarn is spun from short wool, and also from the refuse of the long wool after it has passed through the hands of the combers. *Farmer's Magazine*, August 1835 ~~~ Those that are made of Woollenyarn are usually termed Lambs-wool Stockings, although the Wool has seldom been taken from so young an animal. Analytical Dictionary, 1835 ~~~ The wool of the lamb is generally softer than that of the sheep from the same flock; and as it has the felting quality in a high degree, is much used in the hat manufacture. The wool of dead lamb-skins possesses less of the felting property, and is employed for flannels, and lamb's-wool hosiery. Philosophy of Manufactures, 1835

lame – [Court dresses] A superb petticoat of yellow crape lamé, … Petticoat in blue crape, with squares of silver lamé; train of blue crape and silver; *Lady's Magazine*, June 1797 ~~~ [court dress] Rich lammy petticoat in yellow, with a white and silver drapery, *Lady's Magazine*, June 1798 ~~~ ball dresses worked in gold and silver *lamé*, *La Belle Assemblée*, April 1806 ~~~ [Court dress] Rich morone velvet, superbly embroidered round; the petticoat and train of gold lame, with beautiful clusters of beads and different shades of chenille intermixed; *La Belle Assemblée*, January 1810 ~~~ Lame, (la-me) f. *plated metal*; Dufief's French Dictionary, 1810 ~~~ Tinsel. (… Fr. *Lame d'or ou d'argent.* [of gold or of silver] … *See* FOIL, Dictionary of Commerce, 1810 ~~~ [Court dress] toque lame d'or feathers and diamonds; *Lady's Magazine and Museum*, June 1835 [see also *foil, tinsel*]

lammy – [see *lame*]

lampas – The principal silk stuffs brought from China are, … Lampases for dresses, of 12 ells by 5/8. Ditto for furniture, of from 21 ½ ells to 22 ells by 3/8. *New-York Magazine*, February 1795

laneous – Woolly, made of wool. Sheridan's English Dictionary, 1797

Lapland moss – Coloured feathers, and in profusion, are worn on black carriage hats; the favourite material for which, either in white or black, is the Lapland-iced moss. *Ladies' Monthly Museum*, February 1821 ~~~ Lapland-ice moss is used as a trimming to light coloured cachemire pelisses for the carriage; we must say, we find this very incongruous; for the light colours now, whether in cachemire, *gros de Naples*, or satin, may be looked on as the harbingers of spring; and the abovementioned moss has so chill an appearance, that we fancy ourselves almost in Lapland at the sight of it; nor do we admire it at all as a trimming; it is a beautiful material for winter-bonnets, but no further. *Ladies' Monthly Museum*, March 1821 ~~~ Promenade bonnets … are finished at the edges with gauze *ruches*, deep falls of blond, or plain bands of the new trimming called Lapland moss. *Repository of Arts*, July 1821 [see also *Iceland moss*]

lappet muslin – The muslins which best suit the market of Tunis, are those of the lowest prices; such as coarse yard-wide, and yard and half wide jacconets; coarse striped low priced lappet muslins, with white, red, or blue, whip; <u>Account of Tunis</u>, 1811 ~~~ Statement Of British Cotton Manufactures Suitable For Sicily. ... Lappet Muslins. – Of the common kinds, those which are commonly invoiced at *1s. 3d.* per yard, of gay colours, alculated for the use of the lower orders, go off to advantage. <u>Voyages and Travels</u>, 1812 ~~~ Spots, brocades, and lappets, are produced by a combination of the arts of plain, tweeled, and gauze-weaving; and, as in every other branch of the art, are produced in all their varieties by different ways of forming the sheds, by the application of heddles, and their connections with the treddles which move them. Indeed, the whole knowledge of the art consists in this part of the apparatus, of a loom. <u>Circle of the Mechanical Arts</u>, 1813 ~~~ Our manufacturers still complain that no sales can be effected, either in plain or fancy cloth, but at ruinously low prices. During the present week, lappets and net have been sold at 5d. per yard. For this kind of fabric, little more than thirty years since, the weaver received 2s. 6d. per yard for the workmanship. *Niles' Weekly Register*, November 21, 1829 ~~~ It is in so far a species of crossed texture, that the figures are formed by crossing a part of the warp, while the rest remains parallel. Goods woven in this way are called lappets; and as it is now unquestionably the cheapest, and consequently one of the most extensive branches of the fanciful manufacture, some account of its principles may, without impropriety, be inserted as the conclusion of this article. Lappets, from whatever quarter the knowledge of them was derived, formed originally in Britain a part of the fanciful manufacture known by the name of silk gauze, the principal seat of which was the town of Paisley. With other branches of that art, they were totally abandoned for some years, and, with very great improvements in the construction of the looms, were again revived in the cotton manufacture. The original plan of weaving lappets was, in some respects, very similar to the apparatus which has just been described, the pattern being farmed by bead lams passing through the reed exactly similar to those which it is proposed to employ for the Russian texture. The lappet consists of two warps of different degrees of fineness, one of which forms the ground work or body of the fabric, and the other, which receives the usual appellation of *whip*, is reserved for the ornamental part. <u>Edinburgh Encyclopædia</u>, 1830 ~~~ Lappets, 10 yds. by 40 to 44 in. [inches] ...There has been a good demand throughout the week for Book Muslins, and for the finer sorts of Lappets, particularly Jamdannies and other small patterns; Cambrics and Mulls have also been in good request. *Asiatic Journal*, February 1836

Lara – Among several light summer scarfs which have recently appeared, we may cite, as the prettiest, those of *tulle* Lara. *Court Magazine*, May 1836 ~~~ White scarfs are almost universally adopted in evening dress, some are of *tulle Lara, Court Magazine*, June 1836 ~~~ Summer shawls of *tulle Lara* ... are both in request, *Court Magazine*, August 1836

lasting – *Aikin's Description of the Country round Manchester.* [published 1795] ... "For some time past the staple manufactory of the place and neighbourhood has been tammies, shalloons, drawboys, known best under the title of figured lastings and amens, superfine quilled everlastings, double russels, serges de Nisme and du Rome. These are all made from combing wool. *British Critic*, June 1796 ~~~ The principal manufacutres of this parish [Halifax] are ... everlastings, russels, figured and flowered amens, <u>New Universal Gazetteer</u>, 1798 ~~~ Amens, a kind of everlasting, or prunella, having wool only on side, plain, striped or flowered, ordinary, middling, or fine <u>Digest of the Commercial Regulations</u>, 1824 ~~~ Lasting, or Everlasting, is a stout, closely-woven worsted stuff, dyed black and other colours, and much used for ladies' shoes. Lasting is woven either with a double tweel, or a satin tweel, in which latter case it is called Denmark Satin. It is also figured and a very fine sort, of various patterns is exported to the continent; which, being chiefly used for Church furniture, is called Amen, or Draft. <u>Analytical Dictionary</u>, 1830 ~~~ Lastings, a worsted stuff, <u>Tariff</u>, 1832 ~~~ [ad] Have received by the ships Hark-away and Jefferson, direct from Liverpool, ... 1 case fine black lastings, *Farmer's Register*, May 1835 ~~~ DURANT, du-rant', a. A glazed woollen stuff, called by some everlasting. <u>Knowles' English Dictionary</u>, 1835 ~~~ Of the Dress and Instruments for the Collector of Insects. ... Dress is an article of great importance, both as to material and make. The best material with which the author is acquainted is called lasting. It has these advantages: it is light; it keeps out much wet; it does not catch the thorns of brambles and other bushes; it does not feel cold when wet. These are matters not to be despised by him who often wanders for hours without a chance of shelter. <u>Grammar of Entomology</u>,

1835 ~~~ *List of prices paid by the clothiers of Baltimore for work performed for them by the seamstresses. …* Lasting pantaloons, double stitched. 25 cents *Niles' Weekly Register*, October 31, 1835 ~~~ [in 1834] Lastings are scarce; the last quotations were 50*s*. 6*d*. for No. 1; <u>Practical Mercantile Correspondence</u>, 1836 [see also *everlasting* and *durant*]

laventine – [see *levantine*]

lawn – Afternoon Dresses. … Lawn petticoat with a broad embroidered border. *Lady's Magazine*, February 1796 ~~~ [Paris] *Chemise à l'Indienne*. – This is a beautiful undress, the waist is formed by plaits artfully arranged, and by bows of ribband; the train falls to the ground in artful drapery: it is made of clear lawn. *Lady's Magazine*, June 1796 ~~~ Lawn – fine linen, remarkable for being used in the sleeves of bishops. <u>Sheridan's English Dictionary</u>, 1797 ~~~ 99 yards of cotton lawn, value L.9, 18s.; [Tried in May, 1782.] <u>Select Criminal Trials at Justice Hall in the Old Bailey</u>, 1803 ~~~ Other lawns, called cobweb lawns, likewise manufactured in that city, are of the same width and length as the former. <u>European Commerce</u>, 1805 ~~~ Mary has ordered a most superb robe … It has a long Bishop's sleeve of the clearest French lawn, striped, and finely plaited between each stripe. *La Belle Assemblée*, October 1807 ~~~ A robe of fine French lawn or cambric, with a great deal of lace let in on the bosom, *La Belle Assemblée*, August 1810 ~~~ Lawn is only a sort of clear or transparent cambric. In the manufacture of lawns finer thread is used than in that of cambrics, and in the proportion of 19 to 27. In Picardy, the warp of lawn, like that of cambric, it framed at 16 ¼ yards, but the former loses less than the latter in the progress of the manufacture, being full 15 ½ yards in length when finished. This results from the lawn not being of so close a texture as the cambric, and the two halves of the warp being less frequently crossed. The breadth of a piece of lawn is about 2/3ds. *Literary Panorama*, March 1810 ~~~ Lawn, a sort of clear or open worked cambric, which, till of late years, was exclusively manufactured in France and Flanders. At present the lawn-manufacture is established in Scotland, and in the north of Ireland, … In the manufacture of lawns finer flaxen thread is used than in that of cambric. … Striped and spotted lawns are made precisely of the same dimensions as the plain ones, .. in order to form the stripes and spots, thick cotton is interwoven in the warp. <u>Dictionary of Commerce</u>, 1810 ~~~ Lawn, *linon, batiste*. <u>Dufief's French Dictionary</u>, 1810 ~~~ Blouses for deshabille are made of undressed lawn, with a border of coloured embroidery. *La Belle Assemblée*, July 1825 ~~~ The light summer dresses were of coloured lawn, cyprus crape, and *gros d'Eté*: they were often trimmed in a very whimsical manner, though not in bad taste. *La Belle Assemblée*, [review of the last six months] 1828 ~~~ Lawn muslin (cotton) *Public Documents*, March 1832… [Paris] For dinner, I have a lawn dress of lilac, *Court Magazine*, July 1833 ~~~ George Smith was indicted for stealing, on the 18th of November, [1835] … 13 yards of lawn, value 30s., … John Goetze was indicted for stealing, on the 1st of February, [1836] … 1 ½ yards of lawn, value 1s.; <u>Central Criminal Court</u>, 1836 [see also *cambric, cobweb, long lawn* and *silesia*]

lawn grounds – Cotton goods are divided into 7 different classes, each proportionally lighter the than other. The heaviest of these are, 1st. *Shirtings*, 2d. *Cambrics*, 3d. *Cossas*, 4th. *Jaconetts*, 5th. *Lawn grounds*, <u>New Encyclopædia</u>, 1807 ~~~ The technical term by which the fabric is known in the manufacturing places, is called lawn grounds, they are known by that name by the manufacturers and workmen; after they are finished, they are known to the dealers by the name of books; they are also known in the India house by the name of India book muslins. <u>Reports from the Committees</u>, February 26, 1824

leather – Stays made of bend leather are worn by all the women of lower station in many parts of England. <u>Domestic Medicine</u>, 1798 ~~~ jockey bonnets of purple leather, seamed with bright yellow, or red, are severally selected by the fashionable female. *La Belle Assemblée*, November 1807 ~~~ [ad] Ladies' Wash-Leather Drawers for riding. *Repository of Arts*, March 1815 ~~~ Parisian Walking Dress. … Slippers of pale blue kid, and washing leather gloves. *La Belle Assemblée*, September 1818 ~~~ Riding-habits … The gloves are of chamois-leather of a camel's-hair brown, or other light color. *Ladies' Monthly Museum*, August 1821 ~~~ English Walking-Dress. … *Coffre* reticule of red morocco leather. *Ladies' Monthly Museum*, October 1821 ~~~ [Boots and shoes] Some years ago the English leather was very superior to the French, but since the plan of forcing leather by chemical means in England has been adopted, I prefer the French. *European Magazine*, May 1823 ~~~ The lighter kinds of leather are frequently dyed in beautiful colours. Kid gloves for ladies, have pink, yellow, blue, and other delicate hues. Gentlemen's gloves are of that yellow, known by the name of *York tan,* or they are of various shades of olive green or drab. Morocco leather is usually of a bright scarlet; Spanish leather is mostly blue or black, and Turkey leather is generally dark blue. All these are grained, in a machine, to imitate the original foreign articles, the use of which is nearly superseded by British art. <u>Scenes of Commerce</u>, 1836 [see also *washing leather*]

leather cloth – Fabric Boots And Shoes. – To Richard Hall, of Plymouth, tailor and woollen-draper, a patent "for a composition applicable to certain fabrics or substances, from which may be manufactured boots, shoes, and various other articles," was granted on the 10th of March, and the specification was deposited in the Enrolment Office on the 9th of September. The object of Mr. Hall's invention is to give to strong linen cloth or other suitable fibrous substances a glossy appearance, resembling dressed leather, and, at the same time, the property of being impervious to wet or moisture. The preparation of the composition is first described, and then the method of applying it to the fabrics intended to be manufactured into boots or shoes. The composition consists of one pound of bees' wax, eight ounces of Indian rubber or gum, four ounces of resin, eight ounces of ivory-black, and four ounces of lampblack, melted together by the application of a continued slow heat, or by boiling, and brought to a consistence which can be applied to the fabric with a brush, ... An establishment has been opened in the Strand, by Messrs. Hall and Co., for the manufacture of boots and shoes of this patent material, which they denominate *pannus corium, or leather cloth:* and they state that their boots and shoes will last longer than those made of curried substances, and that they are adapted to all climates, and have no tendency to crack. From the trial which we have seen made, it appears that they are more easy for Corny feet than common shoes; but, on showing a pair to our friend, who mends shoes, he said, when they begin to wear out, they cannot be repaired, and that there is nothing like leather. *Register of Arts*, October 1, 1829 ~~~ Among the inventions of the day we may notice leather-cloth boots and shoes, also called *pannus corium.* They consist of a cloth saturated with a composition, so as to be glossy, to resemble dressed leather, and to be waterproof. The composition is of bees' wax, Indian rubber, or gum, resin, ivory black, and lamp black, melted together and brushed over the cloth like varnish, in two separate coats. The inventers state that boots and shoes of this material will last longer than leather, and will not be liable to crack. We do not pretend to add our testimony. <u>Servants' Guide</u>, 1831 ~~~ Hall and Co.'s celebrated patent leather cloth shoes are much in use. *Blackwood's Lady's Magazine*, August 1836 [see also *pannuscorium*]

Leghorn – the Leghorn platt, which is imported from Italy, being made of whole straw, is considerably stronger and more durable than the *split* straw. ... In the latter [Leghorn platt], the whole straw is used; but it is the produce of a species of small wheat, sown on poor ground, for that express purpose, and with very little, if any, reference to the production of grain. The stems are very thin, fine, and short, being hardly more than ten inches high; the whole presenting rather the appearance of a crop of hay, on an arid soil, than bearing any resemblance to a field of English wheat. <u>Reports of the Society for Bettering the Condition and Increasing the Comforts of the Poor</u>, 1805 ~~~ *Chapeaux* are now principally of Leghorn, gauze, and crape. Leghorn is considered as merely genteel; but gauze and crape, particularly the latter, are very fashionable. *Ladies' Monthly Museum*, August 1818 ~~~ Bonnets of Leghorn are again in favor; * ... * We cannot help expressing our regret at this circumstance, and we still indulge the hope, that the good sense and patriotic feelings of our fair readers will plead in behalf of the distressed manufactures of their own country, and soon banish a fashion, which has little to plead in its excuse. *Ladies' Monthly Museum*, June 1821 ~~~ The importation of these Italian articles was chiefly from the port of Leghorn; and therefore, the bonnet imported were called, *Leghorn Bonnets.* The straw-manufacturers in this country seem to have made no effort to resist this invasion from Leghorn. And, which is very curious, the Leghorn *straw* has now begun to be imported, and to be *platted in this country.* <u>Cottage Economy</u>, 1824 ~~~ The Leghorn straw being much slenderer than that of English growth, may be employed entire for the finest articles, on which account the plat is rendered more even, pliable, and durable, than that of equal fineness made from split straw: it is also greatly superior in colour. A farther advantage is, that the spiral coil of Leghorn plat of which a hat or bonnet is formed, admits of being joined by knitting the adjacent edges together instead of overlapping and sewing them, as must necessarily be the case with the English plat: on account of which difference of construction, the Italian bonnets and hats are of the same uniform thickness, whereas, the English are an unpleasant alternation of ridges and depressions, and require, besides, a considerably greater quantity of plat. These real grounds of preference, independently of the caprice of fashion, soon began to operate unfavourably on the English straw plat, and in a short time put an end to it as far as regards the finer fabrics. Transactions of the Society, 1821 ~~~ Hat of paille d'Italie (Leghorn), *Lady's Magazine and Museum*, July 1834 ~~~ In Paris Leghorn hats have been much worn for some time past; but they are not considered elegant unless very fine, and trimmed with feathers. ... A Leghorn hat, with three Leghorn colored feathers. *Atkinson's Casket*, August 1836 ~~~ Leghorn hats are worn as dress hats, and sometimes, if good materials, look like silk at a distance. *Blackwood's Lady's Magazine*, August 1836 [see also *imitation Leghorn*]

leno – Some [mantles] were of white japanned muslin or transparent figured leno, lined with purple or rose coloured sarsnet, which had an effect extremely rich and elegant; *La Belle Assemblée*, June 1806 ... Duchess of Roxborough's Half-Dress. A Tunic jacket, and trained petticoat, of striped leno, worn over a primrose sarsnet slip; *La Belle Assemblée*, August 1806 ~~~ These bonnets, so conspicuous for unobtrusive neatness, are best formed of clear leno, with the raised pea spot. They are lined with coloured sarsnet, *La Belle Assemblée*, July 1807 ~~~ Another half-dress is of the new Glasgow leno, which is much patronized by our nobility; the ground is white, with narrow stripes of Nakara, or wild poppy colour; *La Belle Assemblée*, October 1819 ~~~ [Paris] Bonnets of gauze, or leno spotted with velvet, over white sarsnet, are much worn in carriages; they are lined with pink, and ornamented with flowers, or plumage: *Ladies' Monthly Museum*, May 1821 ~~~ a manufacture called leno, something in the nature of Scotch gauze, was for a time universally worn, and all of a sudden as universally left off. *Nic-Nac*, January 25, 1823 ~~~ The improved white leno, with rich satin stripes, is still much admired for home costume; these stripes are now broader than they were at first, and are beautifully shaded. *Lady's Magazine*, August 1825 ~~~ The ball dresses are simple, generally consisting of fine white *leno*, or *tulle*, with three broad bias folds round the border of the skirt, *La Belle Assemblée*, October 1825 ~~~ Persons liable to the bites of mosquitoes, should sleep under the cover of a lawn, gauze, or leno net, Five Thousand Receipts, 1825 ~~~ [ad] MR. JOHN P. DEANE respectfully informs his Friends, it being his intentention [sic] to proceed to Sydney, the following GOODS will be disposed of at the under-mentioned Prices, being at least 30 per cent, under the retail Prices: ... leno, 6d., 9d., and 1s. ditto [per yard]; lenos figured, 1s. ditto; *Colonial Times*, March 3, 1826 ~~~ They [pelisses] were made of organdy, or of fine muslin, and lined with either white or coloured sarcenet: the organdy, or improved leno, looked best, with a white lining; *La Belle Assemblée*, Summary of the last six months, 1827 ~~~ Leno linen ... Leno, muslin (See Cotton Manufac.) Tariff, 1832 [see also *gauze*, *English organdy* and *organdy*]

lenon – An evening dress, composed of *lenon*, elegantly worked in the Etruscan style, is much approved of; *La Belle Assemblée*, April 1806 ~~~ A spenser *à l'Espagnole*, and shaded silks, sprig lenon, or spider-web, trimmed with shaded mistake ribband. *La Belle Assemblée*, June 1806

Leocadie – [Paris] The evening dress silks that have appeared, are all in the superb but heavy style of Louis XIV's reign. The satins *Salomon, Esmeralda*, and *Pharamond*, are expected to be in great request; as are also the *Velours Algileck*, and *Leocadie*, and the *Velontées de la Mosquée*, and *Carlina. New Monthly Belle Assemblée*, November 1836

leonaise – It is the Segovian, and particularly the genuine Leonese wools, which, however, are usually comprehended under the name of *Pilas, Leonesas, Segovianas*, which give to cloth the distinguished softness, on which the courtier sets so great a value. Communications to the Board of Agriculture, 1797 ~~~ A new material for half dress, which appears likely to succeed the *mousselines de laine*, is called *lèonaise*; it is of woollen, but closer than the *mousselines de laine*, and figured in very small patterns. *Court Magazine*, November 1834 ~~~ Neglige Dresses are chiefly made in merino, poplin, or cashmere. The *Leonaise* silk is likewise used for the same purpose, with velvet collar and cuffs; this material should be lined with white silk. *Casket*, March 1835 leopard pattern – Large silk shawls of a new fabric in imitation of Leopard spot, are much worn for the opera and play. *Boston Weekly*, May 5, 1804 ~~~ [horse race] York Races. – *Mrs. Thornton against Mr. Flint*, ... Mrs. T.'s dress was a leopard coloured body, with blue sleeves, the rest buff, and a blue cap. Mr. Flint rode in white. ... No words can express the disappointment felt at the defeat of Mrs. Thornton. *Monthly Mirror*, September 1804 ~~~ *The countess of Ely* – Wore a petticoat and robe of leopard satin, with sable trimming, and handsome black lace drapery; head-dress, superb sable leopard feathers, lace, and diamonds. ... *Lady Stewart* – A leopard satin petticoat, elegantly trimmed with black lace, cord and tassels; black velvet train, trimmed with lace. *Lady's Magazine*, January 1807 ~~~ *Princess of Wales.*—A superb gold and white leopard tissue satin train and petticoat, richly embroidered and inlaid all round with beautiful stones, to form vine leaves and grapes, interwoven with bunches of coral. The drapery and pocket-holes of royal purple and gold tissue satin, with a most superb border all round to correspond with the petticoat and train. The body and sleeves of gold leopard tissue satin, embroidered and inlaid with rich coloured stones, to correspond with the train and petticoat. Her Royal Highness wore over this dress a brilliant Grecian wreath of diamonds, superbly set with bunches of roses and I stars. The splendour and magnificence of this dress was much admired. *La Belle Assemblée*, January 1809 ~~~ Walking, or Carriage Costume. A fine cambric round gown, ... A waistcoat or wrap front of marble, or leopard satin, *La Belle Assemblée*, April 1809 ~~~ Walking Dress. ... French tippet of leopard silk shag. *Jersey Magazine*, November 1810

leopard skin – The leopard's hair is of a vivacious yellow hue, marked on the back and sides with small black spots, arranged in circles, and placed very near to each other; the face and legs ornamented with single black spots; the breast and belly covered with longer hairs than the rest of the body, and of a whitish hue; the spots on the tail large, and of an oblong form: the dimensions of this species, from nose to tail, are about four feet; the tail nearly two feet and a half in length. ... The skins of the leopard are brought to Europe, and are deservedly, for their singular beauty, held in high estimation. *Lady's Magazine*, July 1800 ~~~ The Grecian wrap, of dark fawn-coloured velvet, ... is bordered all round with ... a fur of the American squirrel, or leopard spot. *La Belle Assemblée*, November 1806 ~~~ the Roman mantle. It is composed of a long width of kerseymere, and is trimmed quite round, with a fur of the Leopard's skin. ... A plain hat, ... lined with Leopard's skin. *La Belle Assemblée*, December 1806 ~~~ Walking Dress. A Polish Robe of purple velvet, ... the whole trimmed entirely round with the red fox, mole, leopard spot, or gray squirrel. *La Belle Assemblée*, February 1807

letting-in lace – A round dress of white muslin, the back full and low on the shoulders; the bosom trimmed with lace, the sleeves plain with lace let in round the bottom. *Boston Weekly*, October 30, 1803 ~~~ Walking Dress. A Gown of white French cambrick ... with three rows of letting in lace; *Jersey Magazine*, September 1810 ~~~ [Paris] We remark upon the edges of all the *Chapeau à-la-Pamela* in white straw, a plaiting of *tulle*, (letting-in lace,) *La Belle Assemblée*, August 1814 ~~~ [A frock] Body of white lace, composed of alternate strips of letting-in and plain lace, the latter double the breadth of the former, and sewed very full to the other, which is plain; *La Belle Assemblée*, September 1814 ~~~ Transparent bonnets are composed either of gauze, net, or letting-in lace, and all these materials appear to be pretty nearly equal in favour: *Repository of Arts*, July 1819 ~~~ Evening Dress. ... The *canezou* is cut round the upper part, so as to come nearly, but not quite, to the throat, and the fulness is gathered into a row of blond letting-in-lace. *Godey's Lady's Book*, October 1830 [see also *entre deux, insertion*, and *tulle*]

Levant – Among the new articles just introduced for autumnal dressed, we may mention one called *satin du Levant*, which justly merits the favour it enjoys both in London and Paris. It is figured with coloured flowers on a brilliant ground, and its texture is singularly rich and soft. A distinguished Parisian *modiste* declares it to be *la vraie parure du serail*. *Court Journal*, September 14, 1833 ~~~ These [black blond] mantles have a very elegant effect when worn over pelisses of the newly manufactured *satin du Levant*, or the printed satin. This last mentioned article, which is distinguished by a degree of richness truly oriental, is very generally worn, and promises to maintain its favour throughout the ensuing winter. New patterns are continually appearing. *Court Journal*, September 28, 1833

levantine – Levant, The east, particularly those coasts of the Mediterranean east of Italy. Sheridan's English

Dictionary, 1797 ~~~ The Portuguese sarsnet, an evident imitation of that beautiful article the French levantine, has lately made its appearance; but it has all the thickness of the levantine without its elegant softness, *La Belle Assemblée*, June 1812 ~~~ In the carriage costume sarsnet pelisses are still much worn; they are what the French call levantine, of the stoutest texture and twilled: some with satin stripes are peculiarly beautiful; they are trimmed, in general, with swansdown, and worn either with a swansdown tippet, or a small India or silk scarf tied round the throat. We saw one the other day composed of pale lavender levantine, lined with white sarsnet, and trimmed with swansdown. ... Sarsnet and spotted silk are very general in dinner dress; we think the levantine predominates. *Repository of Arts*, November 1816 ~~~ The Spring pelisses ... are made of the most rich and expensive silks: the double levantine seems the most favorite article, lined with sarsnet of a peculiar good quality, or gossamer satin. *La Belle Assemblée*, May 1823 ~~~ Liverpool Grand Festival ... Brocaded Levantines, *The Kaleidoscope*, September 23, 1823 ~~~ [Ad] Distress in Spitalfields. – In consequence of the unexampled distress in the silk manufactory department HILDITCH & CO. have consigned to them upwards of 10,000 yards of the richest yard-wide Levantine, all of which will be sold at 3s. 6d. per yard, which positively cost the unfortunate makers 6s. *Examiner*, February 19, 1826 ~~~ coloured Levantines, 3s. 3d. *Examiner*, June 18, 1826 ~~~ a scarf of double levantine seems preferred. These new double levantines are not, however, as formerly, of two different colours, but are, on both sides, of the same hue. *La Belle Assemblée*, November 1827 ~~~ The favourite silks are levantines and soft *gros de Naples*, shot with violet and green, green and *rose-julienne, mauve* and blue, and bronzed black. *Lady's Magazine*, December 1830 ~~~ levantine is a stout, close-made, and twilled silk, Silk Manufacture, 1832 ~~~ [ad] 2 cases Satin Levantines, superior quality – 3 cases Levantines, low priced *New England Farmer*, September 25, 1833 ~~~ Dinner dresses ...Satin and rich silk are the materials most in favour for these dresses. Some have been recently ordered of levantine, which it is said will be very fashionable this winter; but in conformity to the present taste for rich materials, it is to be of a stouter fabric than that which was so much admired several years ago. *Court Magazine*, December 1833 ~~~ Laventine, a close-made and twilled silk. British Cyclopedia, 1835 ~~~ [ad] Superior Satins Levantines, 3s.6 [per yard] *New England Farmer*, March 25, 1835

lichen-sur-mousse – For dishabille, a light material is much admired; the ground is a yellow green, with a running pattern of very bright yellow – this is called *lichen-sur-mousse*. They are made up in bathing dresses, and for walking through the flower market, in short, for all loose wrapping gowns. *La Belle Assemblée*, August 1823

lilesia – [ad] White Lilesia for lining ladies dresses. *New England Farmer*, July 10, 1833

limerick – Limerick gloves and shoes. *Lady's Magazine*, July 1807 ~~~ The leather of gloves is not tanned, properly speaking, but cured with alum, which renders it soft and pliable, and easy for the hands. The Limerick gloves, likewise called chicken gloves, are made of leather, and are remarkably fine. These gloves are manufactured in the city of Ireland from which they derive their name, and whence they have, from time to time, been sent to most parts of Europe, the East Indies and America. The Limerick gloves are mostly worn by ladies. ... Beautiful gloves continue to be manufactured here, which are celebrated in other places with the name of *Limerick Gloves*, in the town they are called *Chicken Gloves*; they are for the use of ladies, and notwithstanding the very high price of them, are worn in general only one night, at fashionable balls; they are prepared to such fineness, that a pair may be drawn through a finger-ring. Similar articles are now made in Dublin, and perhaps in other places in Ireland, as likewise at Worcester, and are sold under the name of Limerick Gloves. Dictionary of Commerce, 1810 ~~~ Carriage or Polish walking Costume. ... Gloves of pale Limerick or York tan. *Edinburgh Annual Register*, January 30, 1812 ~~~ Limerick, Dublin, and Cork were formerly celebrated for the manufacture of gloves, which passed under the names of "Irish" and "Limericks." Those made at Limerick were of the most exquisite texture, and were manufactured principally from "morts" and "slinks," the skin of the abortive or very young calf, lamb, or kid. Some of these gloves were so beautifully fine, that they have been enclosed in a walnut-shell. This trade, which gave extensive employment to many thousands of people in Ireland, is now so utterly decayed, that a pair of real Limerick gloves is almost as rare as a black swan. History of the Glove Trade, 1834 ~~~ Limerick gloves are not made in Limerick – never were made in Limerick – never will be made in Limerick. Limerick gloves come from Cork. *Fraser's Magazine*, March 1834 ~~~ [6th April, 1830] It used to be the custom in the south-west of Ireland to slaughter many cows while in calf. The skins of these unborn calves were of extraordinary fineness and delicacy, and from such was prepared the leather of which the celebrated Limerick gloves were made. This practice, however, is now almost discontinued, and whatever merit the Limerick gloves may still possess, is owing to the skill of the manufacturer and not to the superiority of his raw material. Transactions of the Society of Arts, 1836

linen – cloth made of hemp or flax. Royal English Dictionary, 1775 ~~~ The following are the prices of home-made and other articles in Cumberland: ... Women's dress generally consists of a black stuff hat, of the price of 1s. 8d.: a linen bed-gown, (stamped with blue,) mostly of the home manufacture; this usually costs in the shops about 5s. 6d.: a cotton or linen neckcloth, price about is. 6d.: two petticoats of flannel, the upper one dyed blue; value of the two about 11s. 6d.: coarse woollen stockings, home manufacture, value about is. 8d.: linen shift, home manufacture, 2 ½ yards, at 1s. 5d. the yard. [Sir F. Eden *on the State of the Poor.*] *Monthly Review*, July 1797 ~~~ All these latter dresses are of Florence satin, Pekin satin, muslin, plain and embroidered, painted linen, gauze, crape, &c. *Port Folio*, February 6, 1802 ~~~ The various branches of the [linen] trade consist in cambrics, lawns, linens, diaper, damask, and chequers. Statistical Survey of the County of Armagh, 1804 ~~~ linen dresses of an amaranthine ground are again in vogue, *Lady's Magazine*, October 1807 ~~~ The interior clothing of the present period consists of linen, of cotton, or of flannel. The first, usually worn next the skin, must be frequently changed. The effect of frequent change is to keep up perspiration, and it was even supposed to produce emaciation. The only real inconvenience of linen is, that it absorbs moisture slowly; in other words, its hygrometrical affinity is inconsiderable, and if for a short time removed from the body after copious perspiration, it feels damp and cold. We bear, however, with this inconvenience from the comfort we feel in changing it; nor, when used only as the garment, next the skin, is it ever materially injurious. *London Medical Dictionary*, 1809 ~~~ Linen is a commodity of universal use from the prince to the peasant, and a commodity that cannot be supplanted by any thing else near so commodious and agreeable for those uses to which it is applied. The use of the Indian cotton cloth his often been attempted for shirting, but to no purpose, and muslins have not unfrequently been offered as a substitute for cambric, but without success; the valuable articles, the produce of the linen manufacture, cannot be superseded by any others; they afford the most wholesome wear hitherto known, and their durability and neatness of appearance are unquestionable. The species of goods, which come under the denomination of linen, are table-cloths plain and damasked, cambric, lawn, shirting, sheeting, towels, Silesias, Osnaburghs, &c. The chief countries in which linens are manufactured are Russia, Germany, Switzerland, Flanders, Holland, Scotland, and Ireland. Of these Russia, principally manufactures sheeting and sail-cloth; Germany shirtings, sheeting, and bagging; Switzerland both fine and coarse goods; Flanders the finer articles, especially cambric and lawn; Holland, sheeting of the very best description; Scotland, coarse shirting; and Ireland, shirting, damask table-linen, and towelling, all of which, in point of quality, are greatly superior to the same description of articles manufactured in any other part of the world. ... In several parts of Germany, Switzerland, Flanders, and France, linens are frequently embellished with painting, and at London, and the other parts of England the produce of the Irish linen manufacture is beautifully printed in the manner of calicoes. Dictionary of Commerce, 1810 ~~~ Foreign linens have in many parts of the world a decided preference over British linens. France was the first country that took up the trade, as the very names of them will show you; for the German linens, against which the objection now runs, are nothing but imitations of French; and whilst they transited with us between 1803 and 1810, we got up imitations, and continued the names of them: we had, for instance, our Britannias, our Rouens, our Creas, and our Platillas. As the Germans succeeded in imitating the French linens, they had linens of their own, of a new invention, to which they gave peculiar names, which we, during the transit system, again imitated; they had their Osnaburgs, their Tecklenburgs, their Hessians, Hamels, and many other linens, which we are now imitating in the north of Yorkshire and Scotland. By finding a vent for our imitations of the Foreign linens, we introduce again our own; such as Irlandas, which are nothing but Irish linen, and would never have got there unless we had flattered their prejudices by taking some of the Foreign. Reports from the Committees, 1820 ~~~ The manufactures of Ulster include coarse linens and fine; lawns up to five shillings per yard, in a brown state; cambricks, from thence to a guinea, in the same state; (the principal or only markets for these two latter articles are Lurgan and Lisburn; Banbridge may be supplied with them, but we are not certain) strong sheetings, diaper, damask diaper, and damask. Ireland exhibited to England, 1823 ~~~ *Linen Cloth* diminishes the elasticity of the skin, increases the internal warmth, and at the same time, from its compactness, too readily retains the perspirable humors, and does not part with them so easily as wool. Soiled shirts, therefore, produce a disagreeable cooling sensation, and obstruct perspiration, especially if made of thick strong cloth, and not regularly changed. Toilette of Health, Beauty, and Fashion, 1834 ~~~ The inner clothing of the present day, consists of either linen, or cotton, or of wool. … The advantages, however, in point of health, which have been ascribed to the introduction of linen into common use, are with more propriety to be attributed to the greater attention paid to personal cleanliness among the middle classes of society, after the introduction of linen, than previously. Changing the linen at night, and again in the morning, is a practice which merits our commendation. It not only insures cleanliness, but, by renewing the air in contact with the surface of the body, becomes an air bath, which greatly assists insensible perspiration. The chief objections to linen, when worn next the skin, are, that it allows the heat of the body readily to escape; and having little affinity for water, causes the matter of perspiration to accumulate upon the skin. Hence, they who wear linen, when, from any cause, perspiration is increased, experience an uncomfortable sensation of chilliness; and are extremely liable to attacks of catarrh, rheumatism, or pleurisy, if exposed under such circumstances to a slight degree of cold, or dampness, or to a current of air. Family Encyclopedia of Useful Knowledge, 1834 ~~~ Linen; a cloth of very extensive use, made of flax, and differing from cloths made of hemp only in fineness. In common linen, the warp and woof cross each other at right angles; if figures are woven in, it is called *damask.* The species of goods which come under the denomination of linen are tablecloths, plain and damasked, cambric, lawn, shirting, sheeting, towels, Silesias, Osnaburgs, &c. The chief countries in which linens are manufactured are Great Britain, Russia, Flanders, and Holland. … In several parts of Germany, Switzerland, Flanders, and France, linens are frequently embellished with painting; and the produce of the Irish linen manufacture is occasionally printed in the manner of calicoes. The beauty of linen consists in the evenness of the thread, its fineness and density. The last of these qualities is sometimes produced by subjecting it to rollers; hence linen with a round thread is preferred to that with a flat thread. The warp or woof is not unfrequently made of cotton yarn, which renders the cloth less durable. … Cotton has, of late years, taken the place of linen for many purposes, on account of its greater cheapness. British Cyclopædia of the Arts and Sciences, 1835

lino – LINO, OR LINAU. This species of gauze is woven merely by treading the plain and open treadles, of the common gauze mounting, alternately with the cross one: that is to say, the cross treadle is pressed down for every second shot, and the other two alternately. Art of Weaving, 1831

linon – *lawn*; Boyer's Royal Dictionary, 1802 ~~~ Linon, *French lawn.* Dufief's French Dictionary, 1810 ~~~ Chinese satin, and *embroidered linon*, make beautiful ball dresses. *Ladies' Monthly Museum,* December 1828 ~~~ Aprons have a very delightful effect when worn under the dressing-gowns, which I admired above all things. The latter are made of India muslin or in *batiste linon*, worked all over, *Atkinson's Casket,* February 1833 [see *lawn*]

linsey – [in 1800 & 1801] the value of the dress of the poorest labourer, at the lowest prices might be, … *Dress of a Woman.* … Petticoat of linsey, 3*s.* 9*d.* County of Kilkenny, 1802 ~~~ Of the Smyrna wool, of the South American wool, and of the coarsest kind of country wool, we make coarse cloths, and a cloth called "linsey," for negro clothing. … The satinets and the negro clothing are generally about three-quarter yards wide, but the linsey is much wider. American Tariffs, 1828 … 1 piece linsey – 37 ½ yards – [price in cents] 64 [amount $] 24.00 [letter dated October 26, 1832] Emigration of Indians, 1835

linsey-woolsey – Linseywoolsey, made of linen and wool mixed, vile, mean Sheridan's English Dictionary, 1797 ~~~ *The clothing given yearly to the children is as* follows: … Girls. A grey linen shift, with white linen sleeves, a linsey-woolsey petticoat, an olive coloured twilled cotton gown, a check apron. First Number of the Reports of the Society in Dublin, for Promoting the Comforts of the Poor, 1800 ~~~ a petticoat of that glossy and beautiful cloth known by the homely name of linsey-woolsey, which rivalled in lustre much of our modern silk. [in a review of Paul Jones] Inspector, 1827 ~~~ PRISONERS sentenced by Courts to Hard Labour in the House of Correction are clothed in the Prison Dress, which consists of a Woollen Jacket and Trowsers for the Males, and a Linsey Woolsey Jacket and Petticoat for the Females; the Cost of the former is 8 *s*. 9 *d*. and the latter 5 *s*. 7 ½ *d*. Gaols: Reports and Schedules, 1828 ~~~ *Linseywoolsey*, a coarse cloth made of flax, or hemp, and wool mixed, and much worn by the peasantry of Scotland, Wales, &c. New Universal Gazetteer, 1832 ~~~ When the girls who were old enough were got out to service, they frequently went back to the workhouse complaining that they were badly treated, – meaning that they had not been so well treated as in the workhouse. These girls, when they returned, were in consequence made to wear a linsey-woolsey gown, and a close cap, which prevented their hair being seen. This, it was imagined, would operate to deter them from throwing themselves so readily out of their places. Poor Laws, 1834 ~~~ Cloth fabricated with linen warp and woollen weft, is linseywoolsey. Analytical Dictionary, 1835

Lionese silk – [see *Lyons silk*]

lionskin – Their great shipments to foreign countries are in "*worsted stuffs*" of combed wool and in woollen cloths, plains, coatings, kerseys, bockings, draperies, kendalls, flannels, lion skins, carpets, blankets and other goods of *carded* wool, from the heavy fleeced and long wooled sheep of the Lincolnshire, Teeswater, Leicestershire, South Hams, (Devon:) Cotteswold (Gloucestershire) and Kentish flocks, and from various other flocks or breeds that do not bear fine wool. *Weekly Register*, March 21, 1812 ~~~ I got me a watch-coat of Lion skin cloth, ... The oddity of my outside dress, puzzled people to tell what I was. Some thought me to be a Quaker, and some took me for a drovier, and others for a plain country farmer. Memoirs of the Life and Travels of B. Hibbard, 1825 ~~~ coatings and Lionskins, for sailors, watermen, farmers, and laborers; *Gales & Seaton's Register*, February 10, 1827 ~~~ *Flushings and Lionskins* – 48 inches wide, cost 1s. 5d. to 3s. ...These articles are used for great coats, jackets, &c. and are worn by farmers, mechanics, laborers, sailors, fishermen, and boatmen. *Niles' Weekly Register*, March 8, 1828 ~~~ *the "Facilitator," for the napping of hats* ... [uses] coarse woollen cloth (lion skin) Repertory of Patent Inventions, 1831 ~~~ *List of prices paid for Indian goods in England*, ... Blue lion skin – " [per yard] 3s. 3d. *Public Documents*, March 5, 1832 ~~~ Philadelphia, 15*th May*, 1832. ... Flushings or lion skin, or thick heavy twilled coating, of a quality that sold in 1816 at 4*s*. and 6*d*., could now be had at 2*s*. to 2*s*. and 2*d*. Executive Documents, 1832

Lisle lace – [ad] Thomas's Fashionable Warehouse, ... Mecklin, Lisle, Normandy, and other White Laces; *La Belle Assemblée*, February 1807 ~~~ At Paris are made black and white laces; also at Caen, Lisle, (those made here are in imitation of Valenciennes laces) Dictionary of Commerce, 1810 ~~~ Morning Dress. ... Cap of sprig net, with border of British Lisle lace; *European Magazine*, January 1823 ~~~ Morning Dress. ... Round cap of sprigged bobbinet, and a single border of British Lille lace, set on with equal fulness all round, *Brighton Gleaner*, April 1823 ~~~ The Lace of Lisle is strong and useful, but not very fine, and is held in less estimation than those previously mentioned. [Brussels, Mechlin and Valenciennes] Young Lady's Book, 1829 ~~~ The bobbin lace consists of hexagonal meshes; four of the sides of each hexagon are formed by twisting two threads round each other, and the other two sides are formed by the simple crossing of two threads over each other. This is the same kind of lace which is known in France by the name of Lisle lace, being manufactured in that town. Edinburgh Encyclopædia, 1830 ~~~ Morning Dresses ... The pelerines are bordered by a double hem edged with Lisle lace. *Court Magazine*, October 1836

Lisle thread – Lisle threads also constitute a small branch of this manufacture; this species is an imitation of threads made at Lisle in French Flanders. Some of this thread of Scotch yarn made in Paisley is worth above ten guineas per pound, which when spread out would measure from Glasgow to Edinburgh. *Scots Magazine*, August 1806 ~~~ You may actually get there thread made of flax, ... the delicate commodity of Lisle, used for darning muslin. Our Village, 1828

lisse – *sleek, smooth, soft, glossy*. Etoffe lisse, *glossy stuff*. Dufief's French Dictionary, 1810 ~~~ Short full sleeve, over which is a long and very large one of *gaze lisse*: *Atheneum*, March 1829 ~~~ Sometimes only the top of the sleeve is white *lisse* or *tulle*, and the lower part white satin, *Lady's Magazine*, May 31, 1830 [see also *crepe lisse*]

list – in commerce, the border of cloth or stuff; serving not only to show their quality, but to preserve them from being torn in the operations of fulling, dying, &c. Encyclopædia Britannica, 1797 ~~~ LIST (among Clothiers). The border or edge of cloth. Dictionary of General Knowledge, 1833 [see also *selvage*]

Lithuaniennes – Several new materials for robes have already appeared, … *Borgiennes* and *Lithuaniennes*, either figured or flowered, are also remarkable for the beauty both of their fabric and colours. *Court Magazine*, October 1833

live down – [see *down* and *eider down*]

livery cloth – *The clothing given yearly to the children* [in the charity school] *is as follows*: Boys. A coat and trowsers of livery cloth, and: a grey linen shirt. … The same advantages arise in purchasing the livery cloth for the boys clothes. The average quantity for the dresses of twenty boys is twenty-five yards; the smaller boys jackets have not skirts. This cloth is 6*s.* 9*d.* per yard. Reports … for Promoting the Comforts of the Poor, 1800 ~~~ servants livery cloth, dyed in the wool. 1 lb. of wool makes a yard; wool 1*s.* per lb. spinning 1s. per lb. clothing 1*s.* per yard; Communications to the Board of Agriculture, 1800 ~~~ [ad] Woollen Drapers, Tailors, and Habit Makers, … Having a large Stock of Livery Cloths, they can Furnish them on very moderate Terms. They beg particularly to recommend their Saxon Blue and Black Cloths of Extra-Superfine Quality, also Milled Scarlet, for Hunting Coats, and of which they keep a constant and select Stock. *Yorkshire Observer*, March 15, 1823 ~~~ "Those who affect an elegant equipage, usually give their coachman annually, say two handsome suits of what is termed the best second cloth (what is called livery cloth is a little cheaper, but much coarser, and not half so serviceable). *London Magazine*, October 1827 ~~~ We are obliged to use the finest sorts of Woos for the common Livery Cloth, in consequence of the Wool having become coarser than it used to be. Evidence Taken Before the Select Committee of the House of Lords, 1828 [see also *second cloth*]

livery lace – [Dublin] The Lord Mayor's liveries, as also the Sheriffs, are white lined with scarlet, most richly and fully laced with scarlet and white livery lace, gilt buttons, with a profusion of silk tassels, and gold laced hats; *Anthologia Hibernica*, October 1793 ~~~ a sort of lace for the trimming of the clothes of servants, usually made of worsted, silk, or gold and silver threads, worked in a variety of patterns. The texture of these laces is perfectly close. General Dictionary of Commerce, 1810 ~~~ Mr. Mersey's new process for weaving coach and livery lace is also highly worthy of notice, as producing a fabric from the same materials, which far exceeds in beauty any thing which had preceded it. Journal of Science and the Arts, 1818

llama – [see *lama*]

lockram – a kind of coarse linen Perry's English Dictionary, 1795

London silk – The French also frenchify the names of cities and countries; for instance London, they call *Londres*; Dufief's French Dictionary, 1810 ~~~ Some additions have been made to our stock of silks: … the *soie de Londres*, an extremely beautiful silk; it resembles levantine in substance, and satin in glossiness of texture. *Atheneum*, July 1820 ~~~ The spencer worn with this dress is composed of dove-coloured *soie de Londres*, and trimmed with rose-coloured *zephyrine*: *Repository of Arts*, July 1820 ~~~ Walking Dress. .. Spencer of cerulean blue *soie de Londres*: *Repository of Arts*, August 1821 [see also *silk* and *Spitalfields*]

londres – The *Londres* are light, thick, woollen cloths, so called because they were first manufactured at London. The assortment was at first, invariably, one-third green, one-third blue, and one-third red. The demand at present consists wholly of blue. View of the Commerce of Greece, 1800

londrin – Since that time [1731], also, the sale of the *Londres* has diminished progressively by the competition of our londrins, which are made to imitate them. … The woollen cloths that have the greatest sale in the Levant are all light stuffs, made in imitation of the *Londres* of England, and are, on that account, called *londrins*. Of these there are two kinds, the *first* and the *second* londrins. In France, the *first* londrins are made wholly of Segovian wool, both in the warp and in the woof. In Germany, the

Silesian wool is mixed with it, and, in England, the wool of that country. The warp consists of three thousand threads in pieces of two ells, in order that they may return from the fuller one ell and a quarter in breadth between the lists. The *second* londrins consist of common wool for the warp; and, for the woof, of the second Segovian wool in France, and of the *second sort* in the other countries. The warp consists of two thousand six hundred threads, in parcels of two ells all but one-sixth, in order that they may return from the fuller one ell and one-sixth in breadth. <u>View of the Commerce of Greece</u>, 1800 ~~~ Beg de Rieux. [France] The manufactures here are the famous cloths called *Londrins*, which are exported to the Levant; they are made of the wool of Roussillon and Narbonne; <u>Voyages and Travels</u>, 1809 ~~~ Londrin, *sm.* London cloth. <u>Cobbett's French Dictionary</u>, 1833

long lawn – The raw long lawns, or what are called double Silesias, are frequently sent to Harlem, in order to be bleached for the English market. The patterns of the coloured lawns are very different; sometimes they are mixed with red, sometimes with blue, and sometimes with green flowers. This coloured sort of lawn is 1 ½ Breslaw ell-wide, and from 52 to 54 ells long, the same as the white and the raw sorts. <u>European Commerce</u>, 1805 ~~~ The court mourning consists, as usual, of crape, bombazeen, and long lawn; … A very full mourning ruff, which in undress is made either of clear muslin or thin long lawn, is always worn with this dishabille, ... We observe that weepers, composed either of clear muslin or long lawn, are very general in undress. *Repository of Arts*, December 1817 ~~~ [Paris] Many ladies have appeared at the Thuilleries in dresses of long lawn, with trimming and collar of the same material: *La Belle Assemblée*, August 1819 ~~~ Lawn or long lawn, (linen) *Public Documents*, March 1832 [see also *cambric*, *lawn* and *Silesia*]

long wool – Long wool, called also carding wool, requires length and soundness in its staple, in order to admit of being spun in a way suitable for worsted fabrics. The fineness of the fibres, of the first consequence in the clothing wool, is of subordinate importance in the combing variety. There are two kinds of long wool: the one used in the manufacture of hard yarn for worsted pieces, the other in that of soft yarn for hosiery; the former being eight inches at least in length, the latter about four or five. <u>Philosophy of Manufactures</u>, 1835 [see *wool*]

Longchamp moss – [Paris] Riding habits with flat buttons, of a mixed cloth, called Longchamp moss, *La Belle Assemblée*, May 1820 [see *medley*]

love – a kind of thin silk, of a black colour, used for borders on garments during a person's wearing mourning. <u>Barclay's English Dictionary</u>, 1799 ~~~ Undress caps are very generally made of book-muslin, and trimmed with love-ribbon. *Repository of Arts*, December 1817 ~~~ White crape and white love are equally expressive of mourning as black; *La Belle Assemblée*, February 1820 ~~~ [mourning for the Duchess of York] The materials ordered by the Lord Chamberlain were, for dress, black silk, with plain muslin, long lawn, crape, or love hoods; black silk shoes, black glazed gloves, and black paper fans. *Repository of Arts*, September 1820 ~~~ and broad floating strings of grey gauze ribbon, or white love; *La Belle Assemblée*, January, 1830 ~~~ The bonnet, composed of black crape, is worn over a white crape morning cap; it is trimmed on the inside of the brim with French grey love ribbon, *Ladies' Pocket*, July 1830 ~~~ [ad] Have received by the ships Hark-away and Jefferson, direct from Liverpool, … 2 cases black love and gauze hdkfs., *Farmer's Register*, May 1835

lovent – Lovent linen is a good, strong, and dense sort of hempen linen, the yarn of which is spun entirely of hemp, and the weft of hempen tow carefully spun. … The lengths of the pieces are very, different, and contain from 50 to 60, 120 and sometimes 130 double ells. A double ell is what the manufacturers of this linen call a staple measure, containing four feet in length; and 100 of these ells are equal to 175 Flemish ells. But most of the pieces are between 100 and 120. The sales are made by 100 staple ells. The width of this linen ought to be one Flemish ell, … The colour of this linen is indifferent, so that a premium is fixed for that which is the best bleached. … The lowest quality is exported to America and the West Indies, for the use of negro shirts, jackets, trousers, and likewise for cotton and coffee bags. <u>European Commerce</u>, 1805

low cloth – I ought to have stated, that besides pound baize, we are in the habit of manufacturing or buying a great many other cloths of a nearly similar description, only made of a mixture of grey wool, which are called low cloths. … You state that your cloths are low cloths, state the price per yard of your cloths? – The bulk of our cloths are from three shillings to four shillings a yard, there are some as low as two shillings, and some as high as ten shillings. ... besides the baize which we make there, we also occasionally make low cloths, which are made in the same way, precisely similar to low broad cloths. Reports from the Committees, 1821 [see also *baize*]

lustre – Taffetas lustré, lutestring, lustring, alamode. Boyer's Royal Dictionary, 1794 ~~~ [ad] Ell-wide beautiful Lustres, all colours at 2s. 6d. worth 3s. *La Belle Assemblée*, March 1807 ~~~ [ad] Italian Gauzes, Lustres, Sarsnets, &c. *La Belle Assemblée*, January 1808 ~~~ Plain high dresses, made in lustre and bombazeen, are worn. *Edinburgh Annual Register*, January 31, 1813 ~~~ Walking Dress. A round dress, composed of Pomona-green lustre; *Ladies' Monthly Museum*, April 1819 ~~~ Cambric-muslin is still worn in morning dress; but plain poplins, lustres, and tabbinets, are much more in request. *Ladies' Monthly Museum*, December 1819 ~~~ We have bought One Lot of Figured Lustres from the Country at 1*s*. 6*d*.; and as I have always been of the Opinion that the Country Trade has been gaining decidedly on the London Manufacture, House of Lords Sessional Papers, July 4, 1823 ~~~ Poplins and lustres are likewise composed partly of silk and partly of worsted, with a somewhat larger proportion of the former material than enters into the composition of bombasin: they are plain woven goods. Treatise on ... Silk Manufacture, 1832 ~~~ lustres (also a mixture of silk and cotton; there here none of these making previous to 1833 on the Jacquards) in 1833, 8*d*.; 1835, 5*d*. Reports from the Committees, 1835 [see also *lustring*]

lustring – a shining glossy silk, invented by the French. Royal English Dictionary, 1775 ~~~ The principal silk stuffs brought from China are, ... Lutestrings, of 12 ells by from 5/8 to 2/3, and of 14 ells by the same. *New-York Magazine*, February 1795 ~~~ Lutestring – Lustring, a shining silk. Sheridan's English Dictionary, 1797 ~~~ *Lutestring brocades* are either upon a plain or figured ground; the design must be open and airy, composed of various sorts of flowers, carelessly disposed and garnished; care must be taken to prevent, as much as can be, the expence of workmanship, and yet to make as great a show for the money as possible. There are also lutestring tobines, which commonly are striped with flowers in the warp, and sometimes between the tobine stripes, with brocaded sprigs. Some have likewise a running trail with the colour of the ground, as other lutstrings. Laboratory, 1799 ~~~ Mary amused herself for a full hour at the unpacking of my portmanteau, ... as I live, a thick lutestring pelice, that will stand alone! What sort of figure, my dear soul, do you intend to exhibit? While all here is clad in mist, *à-la-Grecian*, you will step forth amongst us in your ponderous costume, like the ghost of my grandmother, and frighten us all out of our wits!" *La Belle Assemblée*, November 1806 ~~~ a species of light, shining silk, first manufactured in France, but which was introduced into this country several years ago. There is at present very little demand for lustrings. They are chiefly made in Spitalfields, and that neighbourhood, and are either plain or delicately figured. ... The *taffetas noir lustre*, or black and glossed taffety, is what the English call alamode or mode: and the *non lustre* or *unglossed* of the former *lustring*. General Dictionary of Commerce, 1810 ~~~ The most fashionable pelisse is composed of sea-green lutestring, edged with a border of small satin cords. *Ladies' Monthly Museum*, October 1822 ~~~ [ad] Have received by the ships Hark-away and Jefferson, direct from Liverpool, ... 1 case jet black Gros de Rhine and Matteoni's black Italian lustring. *Farmer's Register*, May 1835 ~~~ The fabric of this gown, which is woven over and under, like a piece of calico, the warp and the woof, or tram, appearing equally on its face, is called *lustring,* from its lustre, or brilliancy, the propriety of which appellative is lost by the absurd practice of softening down the sound to *loostring* and *lutestring*. The genuine sort is the stoutest of the broad silks; and it sometimes bears the name of *gros de Naples,* from its stoutness, and the place where the best sort are, or used to be, manufactured. But a great deal of flimsy silk is now sold at a cheap rate, under this title. Scenes of Commerce, 1836 [see also *lustre* and *silk*]

luxmore – Walking Dress. A cloak of Luxmore, of a bright brown, with a rich pattern in black; *Court Magazine*, December 1835

Luxor – Ribands were never so rich and beautiful as they are this winter. Some of the new French ribands are sold in Paris as high as 15 francs per yard. They are extremely wide, and have, for the most part, black grounds, figured in various colours, and both sides alike. The Pompadour riband is a sort of *fleur-*

de-lis pattern. The Luxor riband is a chaos of fanciful designs. The ribands, representing black lace patterns over pink, orange, blue, &c. are also very pretty and fashionable. *Court Journal*, December 14, 1833 ~~~ Some rich materials have already appeared for the approaching autumn. Those most worthy of notice are the *Satins Luxor*, of Egyptian patterns on a black or white ground, ... intended for evening dress; they are rich and beautiful, but we cannot yet say more than that they are likely to be fashionable. *Court Magazine*, September 1834 ~~~ These mantles are generally made in *Mazeppa* and *satin luxor*. *Court Magazine*, December 1835

lynx – Ounce skins, undressed, the piece – 3s. 6d. [import duty] <u>Ship Owner's Manual</u>, 1795 ~~~ The animal which the Ancients called *lynx*, known in Siberia by the name of the ounce, is only called the *Wildcat* in Canada, where it is smaller than in our hemisphere. ... he is hunted chiefly for the sake of his skin; the hair of which is very long, and of a fine light grey, but less esteemed that that of the fox. <u>Dictionary of Merchandise</u>, 1805 ~~~ [Paris] Coloured satin spensers trimmed with mole, lynx, or swansdown, is a useful change, and may be worn with white dresses of almost every construction. *La Belle Assemblée*, November 1807 ~~~ Lynx-skins, ... are of a grey colour, more or less approaching to black, according to the climate which the animal inhabits. The darkest shade is on the back, and the hue become gradually lighter downwards to the belly, which is white, are marked with black spots, as are the other parts of the skin. The hair is longest on the belly, and is, therefore, the most frequently employed by furriers in the manufacture of muffs. ... but such as inhabit the vicinity of Hudson's Bay are almost white, on which account their skins are highly valued. <u>General Dictionary of Commerce</u>, 1810 ~~~ Muffs have already made their appearance: they are, at present, of swansdown; they, therefore, do not affright us by their wintry appearance. The grey squirrel, the sable, and the ounce, as the cold sets in, will, no doubt, succeed to the delicate cygnet. *Repository of Arts*, November 1819 ~~~ There is a trade in the *skins* of lynxes, and other animals, betwixt Russia and China. These skins constitute a thick and soft fur, and, when of pale or whitish colour, with the spots tolerably distinct, they are very valuable. The further north the animals are caught, the whiter and better are the skins; those that are most elegant are taken near lake Balkash in Usbec Tartary. They are sold at a rate of from fifteen shillings to five or six pounds sterling each, exclusive of the fore feet, which are so valuable as to be sold separately, and at high prices. <u>Useful Knowledge</u>, 1821 ~~~ The most admired [Venetian mantle] is of richly figured *gros de Naples*, of a fine ruby colour, lined with white, and trimmed all round with black lynx fur, *La Belle Assemblée*, December 1823 ~~~ Pelisses of violet colour, puce, and other dark but appropriate colours, are made plain, and are well suited to the promenade; these pelisses are, for the most part, trimmed with fur; the grey squirrel on the dark colours, and the jetty lynx on those that are light. *Ladies' Monthly Museum*, December 1825 ~~~ fur mantles over high dresses; and these are dark. The fine, black, glossy lynx is much in favour for this article of dress, and also for muff. *La Belle Assemblée*, December 1826 ~~~ Nothing is reckoned more genteel for the out door costume for young persons, than a Merino dress, made partially high, with a pelirine [sic] tippet of lynx, or black fox; *Ladies' Pocket*, January 1829 ~~~ The American furs which are at present brought to London are: ... Lynx – wild cat of the traders. This is a long hoary fur, of no great beauty in its natural state, but, when dyed, meets with a ready sale under the name of *lustered lynx*. <u>Transactions of the Society</u>, 1833 ~~~ Trimmings of sable, lynx, &c. for pelisses and cloaks, are again revived. *Court Journal*, January 17, 1835

Lyons cashmere – [Paris] Cachemire scarfs, of Lyons manufacture, are very much admired; they are generally of bright scarlet, the border ornamented by narrow stripes of yellow. *Ladies' Monthly Museum*, January 1824 ~~~ He assured me, that his waistcoat was of the real Lyons Cashmere; *Port Folio*, October 16, 1824 ~~~ a shawl of *Lyonese cachemire*. This material is striped, and the texture, which is formed of raw silk, is made to imitate the shawls of cachemire. *La Belle Assemblée*, December 1828 ~~~ [Paris shawls] the *cashmeres de Lyon* are more in request; they are the best imitation that has yet been produced of the real cashmeres. *Ladies' Museum*, November 1831

Lyons silk – Lyons before the Revolution, purchased about 27 millions worth of raw silk, which it afterwards exported manufactured. At present, for want of hands, capital, and machines, that City sends its own silks to the manufacturers of Berlin. *British Mercury*, March 15, 1799 ~~~ LYONS, the chief town of the department of the Rhone, in France, famous for its silk, velvet, velvet satin, and cotton manufactories, manufactories of stained paper, printing, &c. Lyons is a considerable depot for French and foreign wool, with which it supplies the manufactories of France. The cloths of Lyons are in much request in Spain, Italy, and in the French American islands. Although little silk is collected in Lyons, this place is nevertheless distinguished for its traffic in this valuable article. Silk stockings are also a productive article of manufacture in this country, which carries on a lucrative trade with Italy and Spain; and previous to the war it carried on a considerable commerce with London, Exeter, and Plymouth; with London for cloths, Exeter for serges, and with Plymouth for lead. Lyons exported to England principally lustrings, taffetas, silk stuffs, and gold and silver brocade. The exports from Lyons to England amounted to three millions of francs per annum, its imports from England only to seven or eight millions of francs, a very considerable balance in favour of Lyons; but this trade has been entirely destroyed by the late war. Commercial Dictionary, 1803 ~~~ Shawls of flowered silk, of the Lyons manufacture, with very deep borders, are in high favour for out-door costume; they are two yards and a half square, are exquisitely light and fine, at the same time strong and durable: their colours are lively, and the flowers most accurately and elegantly designed; the first shawl of this beautiful fabric was presented to the Duchess de Berri. *La Belle Assemblée*, July 1816 ~~~ A new kind of stuff manufactured at Lyons, silk, with broad stripes of gold, is much used in turbans; *La Belle Assemblée*, March 1820 ~~~ although the use of silk in dress has been pretty generally changed for muslin, and other stuffs of fine linen and cotton, the Lyons manufactures continue to be of the greatest consequence. The chief articles are gold and silver brocade, plain, double, and striped velvet, richly embroidered taffeta, and satin; also gold and silver laces or galoons, gauze, ribbons, and silk stockings. Edinburgh Gazetteer, 1822 ~~~ and Lyonese silks with satin stripes, are much in favour; the ground of these latter beautiful articles are as changeful as the glossy neck of the dove; and, in different degrees of light and shade, take as many different colours; the stripe is of some predominant hue, that is suitable to all the different shades, and yet strikingly different. ... Such is the practice of a lady of rank and fashion in Paris; and whose pelisse is of a beautifully spotted Lyonese silk, trimmed down the front with two rows of trefoil, in satin, the colour of the spots; *La Belle Assemblée*, October 1823 ~~~ Evening dresses are frequently of Lionese silk, figured with purple palm leaves. *Lady's Magazine*, May 1825 ~~~ Parisian Walking Dress. A redingote of emerald-green watered Lyonese silk, *Ladies' Monthly Museum*, June 1825 ~~~ To Mr. Hughes have been awarded the silver Isis medal and fifteen pounds, for his improved cards for weavers of figured silks. It is wholly impossible by words to give an idea of this improvement to those who are unacquainted with the mechanism of the Jacquard or Lyonese silk loom; the effect of it, however, is a saving of considerable amount in the expense of the cards, – an advantage which, in the present state of the manufacture, will, no doubt, be duly appreciated by those whom it concerns. Transactions of the Society, 1829 ~~~ every day new specimens of brocade and painted satin are forwarded from Lyons, at the price of from fifteen to twenty guineas a dress, embroidered in large bunches of flowers on a black or white-figured silk ground; or arabesques, painted on a black satin ground, or Persian patterns of the boldest kind. These dressed are made up with stomachers and full-trimmed pocket-holes, in the ancient style, and worn with rich blonde cloaks or scarves. *Court Journal*, October 26, 1833 ~~~ [court dress] Silver lama dress, ... manteau of splendid velours de Lyons bleu azure, garniture chefs en lama d'argent; *Lady's Magazine and Museum*, June 1835

Macabre - Musquash

macabre – A series of new materials for cloaks have appeared; the following are a few of those which we think particularly well adapted for cloaks: … *Macabre* – A light silk and woollen material, figured in small designs, and edged with rich gothic borders or flowers. … *Out-Door Costume, New Materials for Mantle Dresses.* … The *Macabre,* a light material composed of silk and wool, and of small patterns, with rich Gothic or flowered borders. *Maids, Wives, and Widows,* November 10, 1832

Macintosh – On the Patent Waterproof Double Fabrics, *Invented by Charles Macintosh, Esq. of Crossbasket.* … Mr. Macintosh's process is exceedingly simple. The caoutchouc is put between two plies of cloth, which it cements so completely, that, when the cloth is not thick, and both plies the same, it would readily be taken for a single ply. For this purpose, two appropriate pieces of cloth are selected, one for the outside, and the other for the lining. These are stretched on tables, or frames, by the common means employed in calico-printing processes. A thin coating of a solution of caoutchouc, in naphtha, is put on each of them, and is allowed to dry. A second is then put on each and also allowed to dry, and likewise, if necessary, a third, and a fourth. At last, a coating is put on one of the plies, and the other ply (with varnished side to varnished side) is put above it, and spread upon it evenly. It is then dried in a stove, to remove the smell of the oil. Lastly, it is smoothed by being passed through a calender. This process greatly strengthens the cloth, without materially altering its appearance. The different plies of cloth may be either of the same kind, or different; woollen cloth to woollen cloth; cotton cloth to cotton cloth; silk to silk; woollen cloth to cotton cloth; or, cotton cloth to silk, &c. Woollen cloth, with either a silk or a calico lining, makes an excellent cloak. But of the specimens which we have seen, we admire most those of which both plies are calico. This, we think, makes a light, and an elegant cloak, perfectly waterproof. Indeed, we conceive that the great improvement which this process of waterproofing has introduced, consists in affording complete protection from the inclemencies of the weather, and of situation, by means of a light fabric, what has hitherto been afforded, only imperfectly, by means of heavy fabrics. [patent sealed on June 17, 1823] *Glasgow Mechanics' Magazine,* January 1824 ~~~ at present the greatest consumption [of naptha, or pyroligneous ether] is by Mr. Macintosh in dissolving caoutchouc (Indian Rubber) for the preparation of his water-proof and air-proof cloth, for great coats, cloaks, &c.; and indeed to such perfection has he now brought it, that he makes air-tight pillowcases and beds, which only require to be blown full of air by the mouth, to be ready for use when required, and in the morning the air may be let out and the bed folded up and put away into the traveller's trunk. Chemical Essays, 1830 ~~~ Three windows of strong glass (CCC,) protected by stout cross wires, enable the diver to see the objects around him. Over his legs, arms, and body, he draws a watertight dress of Mackintosh's cloth; but this is merely to prevent the inconvenience of getting wet, and has nothing to do with the Diving-bell machinery, which consists in the helmet and air-pipe alone. Arcana of Science and Art, 1833 ~~~ In the Highlands of Scotland, more than in any mountainous country with which I am acquainted, a Macintosh waterproof cloak is peculiarly useful. There is often no time to unfold, much less to unbutton an umbrella; Recess, 1834 [see *India rubber*]

Madras muslin – The cargoes of these vessels consist of the following articles, … Madras goods, viz. of Bettellec 500 pieces, muslins 150 pieces, muslin handkerchiefs 100 pieces, callicoes 90,890 pieces – *Universal Magazine,* September 1807 ~~~ Madras … is the depôt for all the manufactures carried on in the northern circars, and the counties south of those provinces. The stuffs made there, though imported to Madras, take its name, instead of those of the countries where they are fabricated, and are known in Europe as Madras muslins, long cloths, and chintzes. Letters on India, 1814 ~~~ Madras turbans still continue in vogue; those made of the real Madras handkerchiefs, royal blue and orange colour, are most in estimation. *La Belle Assemblée,* March 1819 ~~~ Gowns of Madras cotton or fine stuff of a new manufacture are much in vogue; the ground is what the French call Adrianople-red, a very deep crimson; they are striped in zig-zag with black; with these dresses is always worn a white muslin spencer. Sometimes they have large chequers like the Scotch plaids, alternately red, green, and orange-color, or violet and white: *Lady's Magazine,* September 1825 ~~~ Dinner-Dress. A dress of clear Madras muslin worn over a white satin slip: *Ladies' Monthly Museum,* August 1827 ~~~ [duties on importations into the United States] Madras handkerchiefs, such as are usually imported from Madras, that is cotton - 25 do [per cent] ... Mock Madras handkerchiefs, such as usually come from France and England, if made of cotton - 25 do [per cent] ... if warp of silk, and filling of cotton - 25 do [per cent] Public Documents, 1832

Madras silk – The silks manufactured at Madras are all of an imperfect white, but last much longer than English or French. The coloured silks are scarcely inferior, and stand as well as the best of European manufacture. *Mechanics Magazine*, August 12, 1826 ~~~ A new washing silk has just appeared for home *negligé*; it is called *Madras Ecossais*; it is plaided in sober colours, and moderate sized squares. *Court Magazine*, September 1834

Mameluke muslin – The general out-door costumes in the few fine days of the last weeks, have been sprigged Mameluke muslins, ornamented with a broad ribbon of the same colour as the sprig, *National Register*, May 1, 1808

Manchester velvet – [letter dated November 10th, 1802] Dr. Franklin ... was dressed in a suit of Manchester velvet; Memoirs of Dr. Joseph Priestley, 1806 ~~~ The cotton shrub is a plant of luxurious growth, and one of the staple commodities of Jamaica for exportation to the mother country. All our fustians, calicoes, Manchester velvets, &c. are made of this article; A History of the West Indies, 1808 ~~~ Velveret, (German. *Manchester.* ...) a species of cotton velvet, chiefly manufactured at Manchester, and in its neighbourhood. Dictionary of Commerce, 1810 ~~~ The manufactory of Mr. Ashton is for cotton velvet: this is what they call *Manchester* in Germany. *Literary Gazette*, February 21, 1818 ~~~ Last year, the article of Manchester velveteen (a particular description of cotton velvet) which in London sold for about 2 *s*. or 2 *s*. 2 *d*. per yard, Reports from the Committees, May 18, 1821 ~~~ Gentlemen's Gig or Box Coats. ... The Collar should be lined with Manchester Velvet. Sectum, 1825 ~~~ Manchester – velvet, velveteen. New English-German Dictionary, 1834 [see also *cotton velvet*, *velveret*, and *velveteen*]

mandarin – For evening dress, several splendid novelties have this season been introduced: among the most distinguished, are ... the *gaze du Mandarin*. *Court Journal*, January 10, 1835 [see also *Chinese gauze*]

Manteau des Sultanes – The new materials for mantles are of fine Cashmere wool; ... Others are printed, figured, or embroidered in various patterns, distinguished for their novelty and singularity, particularly those called *Palameda, Zenobia, Manteau des Sultanes*, &c. *Casket*, January 1832

mantua – Mantua, a woman's gown; kind of silk Perry's English Dictionary, 1795 ~~~ Mantua, the capital city of the duchy of the same name, in Italy, seated on an island in the midst of a lake, ... It was greatly noted for it's silks, and silk manufactures, but they are now much decayed, Universal Gazetteer, 1795 ~~~ the Mantuas had been regulated as long back as 1805 or 1806, before any such Work as this was known. A Mantua is all Silk, and by the Regulations is allowed One hundred and twenty Shutes to an Inch, Sessional Papers, July 2, 1823 ~~~ As early as 1770, Mrs. Susanna Wright, at Columbia, Lancaster county, made a piece of mantua, 60 yards in length from her own cocoons; Annals of Philadelphia, 1830

manufacture – MANUFACTURE. Any commodity made by the hand, or any thing formed from the raw materials or natural productions of a country, as cloths from wool, and cotton or silk goods from the cotton and silk, &c. Dictionary of General Knowledge, 1833

marabout feathers – [Paris] White silk beaver hats, lined with rose-colour, and ornamented with a wreath of white marabout feathers round the crown, are much in request. *Ladies' Monthly Museum*, May 1817 ~~~ Marabouts or down feathers have again become fashionable; within these few days, we have seen several rose-coloured hats trimmed with them. Yellow crape hats with full plumes of marabouts to correspond in colour are also considered very fashionable. *Ladies' Monthly Museum*, October 1817 ~~~ The duchess de Berri appeared about a week ago in a bonnet ornamented with marabouts in the weeping-willow style, of cherry-color. *Lady's Magazine*, May 1829 ~~~ Boas of marabouts are added to the costume: the boas for full-dress are likewise made *Lady's Magazine*, February 1830 ~~~ Among other novelties sent over by Herbault, is a Boa of Marabout feathers, for full dress, as white and light as snow; but the price (20 guineas), will prevent it from coming into general use; particularly as there are mock ones for about a third of the sum. *Court Journal*, April 4, 1835 ~~~ The plumes which are so much valued are the under tail-coverts; their texture is inconceivably delicate and floating; "a good idea may be formed of their lightness from the weight of one which measured eleven inches and three-quarters in length and seven in breadth, and only balanced eight grains." Introduction to the Study of Birds, 1835 ~~~ Most evening caps have lappets rounded at the ends, and hanging low on the neck, or sometimes a blond veil is fixed to the bow behind; very delicate flowers or boquets of the drooping marabout feathers, are the usual ornaments. *Godey's Ladies Book*, September 1836 [see *adjutant* and *down feather*]

marabout gauze – The *marabout* gauzes are also beautifully checkered in different colours, like the tartan plaids; they took the name of *marabout* from one stripe being of a silky nature, and the other having a downy appearance, like a feather. *La Belle Assemblée*, July 1819 ~~~ Peruvian embossed silk and marabout gauze are favorite articles for evening dresses; *La Belle Assemblée*, May 1820 ~~~ Parisian Ball Dress. A gown of *gaze marabout*, over a white satin slip; *Repository of Arts*, January 1829 ~~~ [court dress] white marabout gauze dress, over white satin. *Lady's Magazine and Museum*, June 1836

marabout ribbon – [Paris] Several of these head coverings are ornamented with gauze ribbons, which are of so light a texture that they have obtained the name of *marabout* ribbons; they are particularly made use of in ornamenting the edges, at which there are two rows quilled of this material. *La Belle Assemblée*, July 1818 ~~~ When the hat … is very dark, it is generally trimmed with rose-coloured ribbon, and which is generally the newly invented marabout ribbon. *La Belle Assemblée*, November 1819 ~~~ Fashionable ribbons at present are of a very rich description: they are made very broad, and bordered with stripes in imitation of down; the middle part is formed of floss silk, cut so as to form streamers: they are styled Marabout ribbons. *Repository of Arts*, December 1819

marabout silk – the hat part which turns up, is of pink and white striped marabout silk, *La Belle Assemblée*, November 1820 ~~~ in the case of the peculiar material [silk] necessary for the fabrication of gauzes and gauze ribbon (which material is called *marabout*, and which exceeds the sort in use in England much more than the French raw silk exceeds the raw silk which we have, and without which material these gauzes never can be made as good as theirs), the prohibition is still most rigidly enforced. So, in addition to cheapness of labour, the lead and priority of fashion, and their acknowledged or supposed superior skill and aptitude, the French are to have also an exclusive monopoly of the only material out of which the article can be fabricated. Mirror of Parliament, 1834 ~~~The finest Marabout silk, used for gauze ribands, sells from 68 to 72 fr., say 70 fr. as an average. Commercial Relations, 1835 ~~~ There is a peculiar kind of silk called Marabout, often with three threads, made from white Novi raw silk. Being white as it comes from the worm, it takes the purest and most delicate shades of colour at once, without the discharge of its gum. That silk is first thrown into the tram, and then sent to the dyer. When dyed, the throwster re-winds and re-throws it, and thereby converts it into marabout, a thread twisted hard like whip-cord.… When organzine costs 3*s*. 6*d*. to throw, the marabout costs 7*s*. 6*d*. Philosophy of Manufactures, 1835

marabout velvet – A large Leghorn bonnet is much in favour for walking; it is trimmed at the edge with dove-colour marabout velvet, *La Belle Assemblée*, May 1820

marbled ticking – The manufacture of flowered damask and ticken has been brought to the greatest perfection, in Silesia and in Lausitz; it is manufactured in three different modes, plain, marbled, and white flowered. This sort of linen consists in table-cloths, napkins, and towels. European Commerce, 1807 ~~~ Damasked linen, also called marbled ticking, is made at Rouen, Saint Vallery, and Bolbec; Dictionary of Commerce, 1810 [see *damask* and *ticking*]

Marceline – Marceline (French silk) Commercial Directory, 1823 ~~~ [Paris] Dinner Dress. – A rose-colored clear muslin gown over a marcelline slip to correspond. *Ladies' Pocket*, October 1830 ~~~ The most elegant of these last [shawls] are composed of black satin, and lined with ponceau marcelline; *La Belle Assemblée*, December 1830 ~~~ [Paris] They [dressing-gowns] are all lined with *marceline* of different colours. *Atkinson's Casket*, February 1833 ~~~ The most favourite novelty of the moment is *marceline*. This material is much employed for pelisses, and for dresses in *demi-toilette*. *Court Journal*, March 30, 1833 ~~~ We have just seen an elegant *robe-de-chambre*, … composed of brown marceline, lined with blue. *Court Journal*, October 24, 1835 marcella – a marsella quilted petticoat, stout and white as a counterpane; [in *The Farmer*, 1787] <u>Dramatic Works of John O'Keeffe</u>, 1798 ~~~ every draper in London puts Marcella waistcoats, in his printed shopbills, for waistcoats made of Marseilles quilting. *Anti-Jacobin Review*, October 1805 ~~~ [men's] Morning or Walking Dress. ... marcella double-breasted waistcoat. *Weekly Entertainer*, September 11, 1809 ~~~ *For Gentlemen*. Full dress. – ... white marcella waistcoat, single-breasted; *Edinburgh Annual Register*, May 7, 1810 ~~~ An elegant printed marcella for gentlemen's waistcoats, remarkably appropriate to the season, and peculiarly adapted by the *fleurs de lis* to the present circumstances of the times. It is manufactured by Messrs. Kestevens, of York-street, Covent-Garden. *Repository of Arts*, June 1814 ~~~ [men's] A Half-Mourning Morning Dress. ... The waistcoat is of marseilla [sic]; a white ground, with large black spots, ... The general mourning has, of course, interfered with novelty, in the production of manufactured articles, for gentlemen's dress for August; yet it has been the cause of some very elegant silks and Marcella, in black and purple, and also lavender and black; some of these are very handsome, and can be worn at any time. *Lady's Book*, October 1830 ~~~ we lost ... a Marseilla waistcoat ... worth ... 1*s*. 6*d*. <u>Central Criminal Court</u>, 1836 ~~~ [ad for men's] Marcellas Waistcoats, 7*s*. each, or three for 1 £ *Eminent Foreign Statesmen*, March 1836

marcelline – [see *marceline*]

Marie Stuart – The most remarkable of the new autumnal materials are the *satins Walter Scott*, they are of plaided patterns, ... Others, called Marie Stuart patterns, are of an excessive size and damasked. *Court Magazine*, October 1834 ~~~ Satins and cashmeres of Scotch plaid patterns are expected to be very fashionable, both for robes and mantles. The *manteaux Marie Stuart*, intended as *wraps* for the Opera or evening parties, are of satin, in large squares of vivid and brilliant colours. *Court Magazine*, November 1834 ~~~ [Paris] The most fashionable materials for cloaks are – ... Satins Ecossais, satins Quentin Durward, satins Marie Stuart, and plaids des Montagnards. All the above are imitations of the Scotch plaids, made in Cachemere wool and silk. *Lady's Magazine and Museum*, November 1834

maringo cloth – Mantles are mostly made of scarlet Maringo cloth, cut in the bias, *Jersey Magazine*, January 1810

maroquin – [see *morocco*]

Marseilles leno – Morning dresses for the breakfast table are chiefly white, and bordered with muslin flounces richly embroidered: many ladies prefer the Marseilles leno, the ground white, with bright scarlet stripes; *La Belle Assemblée*, November 1820 [see *leno*]

Marseilles quilting – In the parish of Leigh is the new village of Tildsley. "This estate ... now contains ... cotton manufactories of Marseilles quiltings, *British Critic*, June 1796 ~~~ Of that kind of kind of cotton goods which is frequently used for waistcoating, and known by the name of Marseilles-quilting, none is manufactured in Ireland. In the finishing of these goods, however, we are arrived at a very considerable degree of excellence; a great part of what is consumed in Ireland is imported white, and printed or painted here. <u>Manufactures of Ireland</u>, 1798 ~~~ That elegant species of cotton cloth, called *Marseilles quilting*, is also fabricated here [Kidderminster, Worcestershire] to a considerable extent, and great perfection. <u>Union Gazetteer for Great Britain and Ireland</u>, 1807 ~~~ [men's] Waistcoats of Marsailles quilting will of course resume their stations as soon as the mildness of the weather will permit; *National Register*, April 3, 1808 ~~~ For Evening Dress. ... white Marseilles quilting waistcoats, single-breasted, are almost exclusively worn; *National Register*, July 3, 1808 ~~~ There is not mode of weaving peculiar to cotton ... as every cotton stuff is woven in a way resembling that of some other fabric, unless we may except that called Marseilles; ... The loom for weaving Marseilles is somewhat similar to the diaper loom. A good idea of the manner in which it is prepared, may be had, by conceiving two webs woven one under the other in the same loom, which are made to intermingle at all the depressed lines, which form the reticulations on the surface, in imitation of the quilting performed by hand. When the species of Marseilles, called Marseilles quilting, is made, a third warp, of softer materials than the two others described, lies between them, and merely serves as a sort of stuffing to the hollow squares formed by them. <u>British Encyclopedia</u>, 1809 ~~~ *List of Foreign Goods imported for Home Consumption*, ... Marseilles quilting, and the like. <u>European Commerce</u>, 1818 ~~~ [ad] 1 case Marseilles Quilts, from 8 to 10 quarters. *New England Farmer*, July 10, 1833 ~~~ *List of prices paid by the clothiers of Baltimore for work performed for them by the seamstresses.* ... Flowered Marseilles vests. 15 cents *Niles' Weekly Register*, October 31, 1835 [see also *quilting*]

marte zibeline – [see *sable*]

marten silk – A boa tippet of marten-silk is added to this appropriate winter pelisse. *Literary Port Folio*, February 4, 1830

marten skin – Martre, *s.f. a marten or martern*. Martre (zibeline), *a sable*. Martre (peau de martre) *a marten-skin*. Boyer's Royal Dictionary: French and English, 1794 ~~~ *Marten* is a beast very like the *Sable,* the skin something coarser, produced in *England* and *Ireland,* and all countries not too cold; but the best are in *Ireland.* Law-Dictionary, 1797 ~~~ Cambric Bonnet, satin neck-handkerchief, trimmed with Marten-skin. *La Belle Assemblée*, February 1806 ~~~ The martin is an animal of a very elegant appearance. Its general length, from nose to tail, is about a foot and a half, and the tail is ten inches long. The martin is of a blackish tawny colour, with a white throat; and the belly is of a dusky brown; the tail is bushy, and of a darker colour than the other parts; ... The skin of the marten, especially that of the throat, is principally used in trimming the garments of females, and the official dresses of magistrates, &c. The other parts of the skin are made into muffs, &c. The nearer to the north this animal is found, the finer its skin, and the more varied its colours; thus North America furnishes fur of this description, of every colour, from a perfect white to a deep black. General Dictionary of Commerce, 1810 ~~~ [Paris mourning] For the out-door costume some variety is observed, and mantelet pelerines of Chinchilla fur or black marten ... are very general, and look well over grey or white dresses. *Lady's Magazine*, February 1825 ~~~ Walking Dress. ... A long tippet with pelerine back, of marten-skin, or chinchilla; *Ladies' Museum*, January 1829 ~~~ Evening Dress. A dress of rose-coloured satin, trimmed at the border of the skirt with three separate rows of marten-skin. *La Belle Assemblée*, March 1829 ~~~ ladies who do not choose to go to that expense adopt grey squirrel, or French marten: the last is in great favour, and is a remarkably light and elegant fur. *Ladies' Museum*, February 1832 ~~~ Grey squirrel is genteel, and martin particularly so. *Maids, Wives, and Widows*, November 24, 1832 ~~~ Inferior furs, as grey squirrel, or French sable, which last we should observe is marten dyed brown, are generally used to trim walking mantles. *Maids, Wives, and Widows*, January 5, 1833 ~~~ The American furs which are at present brought to London are: ... Martin, or martern, or pine martin. A fur of very general use, here for muffs and trimmings, abroad for the same purposes, and for almost all the uses to which the better kinds of furs are applied. The darkest coloured, from the rocky and woody district of the Nipigon, are the best, and go popularly by the name of sable; but the true sable is not a native of America. The wholesale price of skins of first quality is about twenty shillings a-piece. Transactions of the Society, 1833 ~~~ we shall name the second rate furs, which, without being very expensive, are nevertheless considered fashionable – ... stone martin; some furriers give to the last the name of French sable. *Ladies' Companion*, January 1836 [see also *pine marten*]

martre zibeline – [see *sable*]

mascarine – We may cite also some evening dresses of a new summer silk, called *mascarine*; it as a brilliant white ground, quadrilled in a very small pattern in dead white, and the ground strewed with very small bouquets of coloured flowers. *Court Magazine*, June 1836 ~~~ Public Promenade Dress. – Mantle of a perfectly new form, it is composed of tissu Mascarn, a green ground figured in green, and lined with lilac quadrilled gros de Naples; *New Monthly Belle Assemblée*, December 1836

massaca – [Paris] a novel article has appeared in the latter [plush], the ground of which is gold colour, and the down *massaca*. *Repository of Arts*, March 1823 ~~~ [Paris] Velvet turbans, of auricula brown, are tied down *à la Marmotte,* and have streamers of Massaca gauze and gold; *La Belle Assemblée*, December 1823

Masulipatam – the Masulipatam printed chintzes, were I believe much cheaper, and were an article of very great consumption both at Bombay, the Persian Gulph, and other countries in that quarter of India. Are you quite sure that they were cheaper than the printed chintzes of England? – I am almost positively certain of the fact; I carried great numbers of both European chintzes and Masulipatam with me in all my different missions to Persia, to give in presents to different people who rendered service to the mission, and also with the view of giving them patterns of the different manufactures of England and India; and I can recollect, that the common reward of any small service was a piece of

Masulipatam chintz, while I am sure that I never gave a piece of English chintz to any man who had not a title, or who was not a person of some consideration: the Masulipatam chintz is an article of very general wear all over Persia, *Parliamentary Debates*, April 14, 1813 ~~~ the waters of Masulipatam are said to communicate superior freshness to the colours of its chintzes, which seem to improve in washing. *Oriental Herald*, September 1826 ~~~ Plaid silks *foulards, laines rubannés*, and *tissus Masulipatames*, are a mixture of silk and wool, some in large and small patterns, for half-dress. *Court Magazine*, May 1835

matasse – *raw silk*. <u>Dufief's French Dictionary</u>, 1810 [see *raw silk*]

matted – Pearl ear-rings and necklaces were worn as usual, mixed with matted gold in various forms; *Lady's Magazine*, January 1796 ~~~ The Cottage and Mountain bonnet of matted straw, is considered most genteel for the fair and modest pedestrian. *La Belle Assemblée*, May 1809 ~~~ if [the train is] composed of a more substantial material (such as satin, sarsnet, or lustre, the trimming is either silver, or silk fringe, or a border of feathers, or matted crape. *Repository of Arts*, September 1812 ~~~ Pelisses of *gros de Naples* are trimmed with matted satin, of the same color. *Ladies' Monthly Museum*, June 1821 ~~~ [Paris] Round dresses of *gros d'été* are much admired for dinner costume; they are trimmed with full plaitings of the same material, at the border, in form of chaplets; and two beautiful rows of matting, wadded, are placed next the hem of the skirt. *Ladies' Monthly Museum*, February 1822 ~~~ [Paris] Pelisses of *gros de Naples* … are simply trimmed with matted silk or satin. *Ladies' Monthly Museum*, November 1822 ~~~ [Paris mantles] these are often trimmed with a rich, matted fringe, that sets off, in an admirable manner, the colour of the mantle, being generally a shade or two darker. *La Belle Assemblée*, December 1823 [see also *velours natte*]

Mazeppa – An elegant material for half-dress is called *Mazeppa*, the ground is of *satin de soie sergé*, and the flower or square, thrown up in Cashmere worsted, imitates velvet. The grounds are of different kinds, some in plain satin and others in small lozenges. … These mantles are generally made in *Mazeppa* and *satin luxor. Court Magazine*, December 1835

Mechlin lace – The trade of the Flemings at present consists chiefly of their own manufactures, viz. … delicate laces, for which Mechlin is the grand mart; <u>Elements of Geography</u>, 1797 ~~~ [at her wedding] Lady Georgiana Gordon, now Duchess of Bedford, was attired in a muslin dress of the finest fabric, trimmed with a broad superb Mechlin lace as a flounce; *Gentleman's Magazine*, June 1803 ~~~ An Evening, or Ball Dress. … Drawn tucker of Mechlin lace. … [Paris] A Fashionable Party … A round dress of plain India mull muslin; with … a deep fall of Mechlin lace quite round the bosom. *Lady's Magazine*, April 1807 ~~~ The Mechlin laces are the most beautiful, after those of Brussels, and are rather more durable than the latter: they are made with bobbins; but here, as at Brussels, various grounds are used according to the taste of the designer. The particular character of these laces arises from the flowers being twisted with a sort of flat thread, whence they have obtained the appellation of *Mechlin brodie* (i.e. streaked). <u>Literary Panorama</u>, 1808 ~~~ In full or evening dress, … the necks are either trimmed with a simple chenille trimming, or beads; but if with lace, it must be Mechlin, and full two nails deep, set on full. *Edinburgh Annual Register*, June 1, 1811 ~~~ But a more important alteration has taken place in Lace-Making, by substituting the loom: at Nottingham, and some other places, is now manufactured a lace of finer quality, more even in its texture, and considerably more elegant in its appearance than any bone-lace whatever, and at about one-third the price of bone-lace. This lace is made of two kinds: the coarsest is called *Mecklin-net*; the other, *bobbin-net*, <u>Book of English Trades</u>, 1818 ~~~ Returning to Antwerp, our travellers proceeded through Mechlin (misprinted Mecklin,) *Literary Panorama*, April 1818 ~~~ Walking Dress. … Cottage cap, with full border of British Mechlin lace. *Repository of Arts*, February 1824 ~~~ Mechlin Lace ranks next in estimation for delicacy, firmness, and accuracy in the Net; and the flowers, which are woven in the working, have generally a thicker thread worked in at the same time, and forming their outline. <u>Young Lady's Book</u>, 1829 ~~~ The Mecklin lace (thread) *Public Documents*, March 1832 ~~~ Valenciennes and Mechlin laces are the only ones fashionable. *Court Magazine*, September 1834 [see also *bobbin-net*]

Medicis – Half-dress, or, as it is termed, evening *negligé*, is the style generally adopted for the opera and the French theatre; the dresses are mostly of *gros de Naples*, chaly, or a new material in imitation of chaly, called *Toile de Medicis*; *Maids, Wives, and Widows*, November 10, 1832 ~~~ [Paris] New Materials. – For grandes toilettes d'hirer [winter], the newest materials are the satin *Médicis*, a rich satin stamped with velvet flowers, and *broché* in gold. *Lady's Magazine and Museum*, November 1834 ~~~ the most admired materials for dresses which have just appeared in Paris. ... *Velours Medicis*: – A more rich material than the above [reps Trianon], the white pattern being on a ground of *Valours espirité*, and producing an effect which calls up recollections of the splendour of the Court of Versailles. *Court Journal*, October 17, 1835

Medine – [Paris] At the same ball I observed several dresses ... of *tissu de Médine*, a very beautiful gauze, *broché en soie et or.* [brocaded in silk and gold.] *Lady's Magazine and Museum*, January 1835

medley – Great-Britain sends [to Brazil] woollen manufactures, such as fine broad medley cloths, Historical, Geographical, Commercial, and Philosophical View of the United States of America, 1795 ~~~ This year 1614 produced the discovery of a new species of woollen manufacture in England, on the following occasion The States General of the United Netherlands, having isssued a placart, prohibiting the importation of any English woollen cloth, that was dyed in the cloth, ... Whereupon the English clothiers ingeniously discovered the art of making mixtures dyed in the wool, rather than lose all the advantages of dyeing and dressing. This has ever since got the appellation of Medley Cloth. All woollen cloth before this time being only of one single colour dyed in the cloth, as black, blue, red, &c. Origin of Commerce, 1801 ~~~ The shape of the men's coats has experienced a very considerable variation. ... The coats are of blue, or black cloth; the riding-coats of mixed cloth. *Union Magazine*, December 1801 ~~~ The cloths made here, for the most part, are medleys of 7 or 8s. a yard. Traveller's Guide, 1805 ~~~ [Frome] has extensive manufactures of a kind of cloth called *medleys*, mostly for the London market, Union Gazetteer, 1807 ~~~ Mr. W. of Dursley, allows it to be his opinion, that the medley cloths dyed in the wool will not bear *the pressure of the gig-mill*, like the white cloths of his county; and he goes on to say, "that they leave their lists longer on the cloths meant to be dressed by the gig-mill than on those dressed by hand, *to provide for the necessary degree of straining in the gig-mill*," he adds, that the great advantage of the gig-dressed cloth is in its *appearance*, and that they sell such cloths for a *higher price* than those done by hand." Literary Panorama, 1807 ~~~ With regard to the manufacture of mixed cloths, or those wherein the wools are first dyed and then mixed, spun and woven of the colours intended, the process, except what relates to the colour is mostly the same with that just represented. [normal wool-cloth manufacture] Dictionary of Commerce, 1810 ~~~ [Wiltshire and Somersetshire are celebrated for] blues and medleys, or mixtures, principally for home consumption. ... These cloths are brought in the *rough* to Huddersfield, Leeds, &c. and are sold to the clothiers, or *merchants*, as they are called, who dye and finish them according to order. New Pocket Cyclopædia, 1813 ~~~ State of Pennsylvania – Manufactures. ... Mixed cloth and hempen – dtto chiefly mixed. *Yards made.* ... *Total amount*, ... 1,801,025 Statement of the Arts and Manufactures of the United States of America for the Year 1810, 1814 ~~~ In the manufacture of mixed cloths, wool of the different colors, being weighed out in their requisite proportions, are first shaken well together; they are then further mixed, by being well turned in the wool-mill, and, by being afterwards twice passed through the scribbling engine instead of once, they are generally found to be sufficiently intermixed. London Encyclopædia, 1829

Memphis – For evening dress, several splendid novelties have this season been introduced: ... The *tissu de Memphis*, with its large flowers, edged with gold, or light hieroglyphic designs on a white cashmere ground, has an effect at once delicate and brilliant. It is equally well adapted to balls and dinner parties. Scarfs of the same have been introduced. They are much employed for turbans, and, when tactfully made up, they have a perfectly oriental effect. *Court Journal*, January 10, 1835 ~~~ Dinner Dress. The robe is composed of *satin Memphis*, a black ground figured in white in an Egyptian pattern. The ground is a plain silk of the richest ground, the pattern satin. *Court Magazine*, January 1835 ~~~ *Full Evening Dress.* – Robe of *tissue Memphis*. The ground white, and the pattern consisting of squares of various colours intermingled with gold. The extreme richness of this material admits of no trimming whatever. *Court Journal*, March 14, 1835 ~~~ Among the new materials that are expected to be fashionable in evening-dress, we may cite the *tissu Memphis d'été* of Silk and Cashmere wool; *Court Magazine*, May 1835

~~~ [court dress] white gaze Memphis dress, over white satin; *Lady's Magazine and Museum*, March 1836 ~~~ *Hindostan* and *Memphis* are composed of a mixture of silk and wool; ... the latter is both plain and twilled. *Court Magazine*, May 1836 ~~~ Dinner Dress. – The robe is composed of a half-transparent material of very fine Cashmere wool, called tissu de Memphis; it is a white ground strewed with roses, which are not very thickly placed. *New Monthly Belle Assemblée*, July 1836

men's cloth – Mr. Cockburnsack cloth manufacturer began in the year 1795 to manufacture several kinds of woollen stuffs, such as ... men's broad cloths of an inferior quality. <u>History of Berwick upon Tweed</u>, 1799 ~~~ The shops at Vienna are richly furnished. The articles best worth purchasing seem to be, eyder-down, black-lace, furs, Bohemian kerseymere, and men's cloth. <u>Letters from Italy</u>, 1800 ~~~ Men's cloth or cord trowsers <u>Sectum</u>, 1825 ~~~ [ad] Ladies' Riding Habits, Lined with Silk, and finished by first-rate workmen. ... Fine Gentlemen's Cloth [Habits] . . £7 7s. <u>Doudney Brothers</u>, 1830

merino – In the summer of 1785, Sir Joseph Banks, Bart. procured from France a ram and an ewe of the true Merino breed, ... In the year 1787 ~~~ made from them cloth sufficient for a suit of cloaths; and this cloth was judged by the trade to be equal in goodness to superfine broad cloth. <u>View of the Agriculture of Middlesex</u>, 1798 ~~~ All foreigners agree, that no sheep produce such fine fleeces as the Merino breed. <u>Annals of Agriculture</u>, 1799 ~~~ *An Account of the Produce of Ten Fleeces of Merino Wool, made into Broad-Cloth, from the Flock of Lord Somerville*, ... the present high price of Spanish wool, ... 20s. per yard at least, <u>Letters and Papers on Agriculture, Planting, &c.</u>, 1805 ~~~ Merino is now the rage. ... we shall now probably be excluded, by our inveterate enemy [Spain], from every foreign market for our fine wool; and unless we can grow a sufficient quantity at home, our staple manufacture of superfine cloth must, in a very short time, be nearly annihilated, to the great prejudice of the public, and to the utter ruin of many thousands of individuals. *Farmer's Magazine*, August 1807 ~~~ Lord Somerville has presented her Majesty with a Merino dress of exquisite delicacy, manufactured from his lordship's prime Merino flock, by Mr. Frederick Smith of Norwich – this article, made from English wool, is likely to be much worn by our nobility, and other ladies of fashion. ... *Spanish Wool Produce and Manufacture*. – Of Lord Somerville's Spanish wool clipped in 1807, 739 fleeces of his Merino, and Merino and Ryeland wool, sold for £651. ... Mr. Frederick Smith of Norwich has manufactured, from Lord Somerville's Spanish wool, shawls and some stockings, one pair of which, of the usual size, were so fine as to have been drawn through a ring. ... Ryeland and Merino ewes (half blood) [not mixed wools] *Literary Panorama*, September 1808 ~~~ a walking, or rather carriage habit, formed in a high round robe of fine Merino cloth, the colour Spanish fly. ... *The Duchess of Northumberland*. – A white satin petticoat, with draperies of purple Anglo-Merino cloth, richly embroidered with lamé and Chinese tassels; *La Belle Assemblée*, January 1809 ~~~ cloths made of the pure Merino wool are only suited to the uses of the rich and luxurious. Their costly nature precludes their introduction to the humbler walks of life; *Agricultural Museum*, January 23, 1811 ~~~ The merino and other fine wool cannot be combed. It must be carded, and is fit only for woollen, not *worsted* goods. *Weekly Register*, September 21, 1811 ~~~ Coloured crapes over white satin are much worn on an evening: Merino crape and plain sarsnet yet hold their pre-eminence at the dinner party, *La Belle Assemblée*, February 1812 ~~~ [ad] The distinguished approbation with which Grimes's Merino Cloths for Ladies' Dresses have been received by Her Majesty, the Royal Family, the Nobility, Gentry, &c. having caused many poor imitations; he begs leave to state, that his Cloths are made of very fine pure Merino Wool, two yards wide, twilled on both sides; and that a good way of knowing the genuine make is to try if they will shrink, which the good ones will not do, nor will they cockle on being wet, or ravel at the edge, and the colours my be tried by any acid or boiling vinegar. *Repository of Arts*, May 1814 ~~~ Black *Merino* Bombazine, a new and elegant article for do. [Gentlemen's Pantaloons.] <u>Boston Annual Advertiser</u>, 1823 ~~~ Merino dresses are more in favour than ever, this winter; ... this material is now brought to the highest perfection possible; the fineness of their texture, and the admirable workmanship bestowed on them in flat embroidery of silk, the color of the dress, render them a *parure* fit for any party, howsoever brilliant. *La Belle Assemblée*, January 1827 ~~~ Merino sheep, before the ruinous reduction of the foreign wool-duty, did well in this county, both for the flock-master and the manufacturer; and the prices previously obtained from the English manufacturer by the *Spanish* farmer, as well suited the *English* farmer. I myself had above three hundred head of Merino sheep, from the flocks of Spain imported into this country by his late Majesty, Lord Somerville, Sir J. Banks and by George Tollett and Benjamin Thompson, esqrs. My flock averaged above 4 *lbs.* a fleece, through; and I sold at various remunerating prices, from 7s. 6d. per *lb.* down to 4s. but the mischievous and visionary principles of free trade, between this high-taxed and high-tithed kingdom against non-taxed and non-tithed countries, which have been so warmly advocated by Mr. Huskisson and other political theorists, just then beginning to be *fashionable* (though not now, thank God, so fashionable as they have been) Spanish wool was allowed to be imported into this country at a mere *nominal* duty. From that moment, no English fanner could afford to grow it on their high-taxed and tithed farms, so as to compete with the foreigner, who sent his wool from a comparatively untaxed and untithed country; and hence the majority of *English* fine-wool-growers, immediately gave up the pursuit, solely for want of that protection and encouragement, which I humbly contend they richly deserved. History ... of the County of Derby, 1829 ~~~ Merinos still continue much in favor for the morning walk or home costume. Though the cheapness and the coarse texture of some stuffs bearing the name of Merinos have rendered them rather common, yet the fine, soft, and genuine material, will ever be highly appreciated for winter wear. *Lady's Magazine*, November 1829 ~~~ Merino dresses for home costume are very much in favor; though the fine double merino is certainly expensive, yet we would advise the purchasing of this beautiful article, which appears like a very fine and light cloth, not discovering the twill, which, in the other merinos, always imparts the idea of a stuff gown; *Ladies' Pocket*, December 1829 ~~~ Morning dresses are made in the pelisse form, and are generally made of gros de Naples; those for the breakfast-table, are of dark chintz, or double merino: that latter article is much admired; and, when elegantly made, and of fine texture, is often retained during the day, among even distinguished females; *Ladies' Museum*, January 1830 ~~~ Turbans are also much worn of merino gauze, *Godey's Ladies Book*, June 1831 ~~~ *Merinos* promise this winter to be very much in favour, but under many new names. We have Thibetians, Indostan, and Ganges dresses, all of which are *merinos* of different patterns, either printed or figured. *La Belle Assemblée*, December 1831 ~~~ Winter Fashions. Plain merinos and washing silks are fashionable in home dress. We observe, however, that merino, even of the very finest kind, is seldom worn but for dishabille. We must except the printed ones, which are sometimes adopted in half-dress. *Schoolmaster*, January 12, 1833 ~~~ [ad] yard-wide British Merinoes, notwithstanding the advance in wool, at – 0s. 6½d. The double width ditto, as low as – 1s. 2½d. *Court Journal*, November 30, 1833 ~~~ Worsted Stuff Goods, from Manchester to New York ... Merinos ... actual [width] inches 24 *a* [to] 27 ~~~ Price per yard s.d. [shillings.pence] 1.6 *a* 3.0 Trade between Great Britain and the United States of America, 1833 ~~~ Among the newest articles for winter costume, ... an improved kind of merino, called *Merino de Segovia*, *Court Journal*, November 28, 1835 ~~~ I know no costume more generally becoming than this simple *deshabille*, the merinos always of the finest kind, drapes beautifully, as it falls in full and graceful fold round the figure. *New Monthly Belle Assemblée*, October 1836 ~~~ Merinos of the finest kind will also be in favour, second indeed to Cashmere, but yet sufficiently good to be perfectly genteel for walking-dress. *Ladies' Pocket*, November 1836 [see also *superfine*]

merino crape – For home or dinner dresses, sarsnets, Merino crapes, Opera nets made high, with long sleeves, and small falling collar of lace, trimmed round the hands with the same, are by far the most approved. ... [Paris] for full-dress, the chief covering for the hair is mostly flowers and velvet, on rich caps of patent lace; the gossamer Merino crape in a light wave over one side of the head; ... The gowns are made of Chinese silk, taffety, Merino crape, and gossamer satins. *La Belle Assemblée*, March 1811 ~~~ A transparent striped Merino crape, for evening wear. It is usually formed in short tunics, round frocks, or Turkish loose robes. It is often seen united with fancy trimmings and folds of white satin; *Repository of Arts*, July 1812 ~~~ [Paris] For evening dresses, white Merino crapes, with a cordage of green satin, made short, with three distinct borders of green satin riband, each four or five inches broad, are preferred. *Ladies' Monthly Museum*, June 1816 ~~~ [Paris] Merino crape and India jaconot muslin, of a very thin kind, being likewise very fashionable. *Repository of Arts*, August 1819 ~~~ Gowns are ... *crêpe des Merinos*: these two last materials are transparent, and are worn both in white and colours;

the latter is most prevalent in out-door costume, *Repository of Arts*, May 1823

merino de Couvent – [ad] A new Material has been introduced by BROWN and CO., SILK MERCERS, 204 Regent street, called Merino de Couvent. Though warm, it is so light in its manufacture that no sudden transition of dress is experienced by the wearer, as is usually complained of in the heavy Merinos. It is so durable and reasonable in price (25s. the Dress, in, all colours), as to be found the most economical and useful Winter Dress for Young Ladies and Families, ever Introduced: it is likewise in equal use for cloaks. *Court Journal*, November 16, 1833

metal lace – *Manufacturing Metal Laces, so as to imitate gold and silver, and also for manufacturing Gold and Silver upon laces,* by Mr. Finch, King Street, Soho. – For manufacturing yellow copper lace, the wire is to be drawn down, to be flatted, and spun in the engine upon fine thread, yarn, incle, or cotton of a yellow colour, of various shades or tints, as the work may require, and to be woven on thread, &c. the size of spun silk, of the same colour, the warp to be weighted as a spun silk warp, and to be woven in a loom. For making yellow copper wire lace, the wire is to be drawn, flatted and spun in the engine upon fine thread, &c.; likewise to be platted with loaded bobbins upon a cushion in the same way as the gold French braid is made, and to be calendered the same. For making yellow copper Prussian braids, the wire is to be drawn down, &c. as before, and the warp for the orris and edges to be made of the preceding articles. By similar instructions, the specification points out the method of making yellow copper satin braid; yellow copper open lace; white plated copper lace; white plated copper, wire lace; white plated copper French braid; white plated Prussian braids; white plated copper satin braid; white plated copper open lace and gold and silver superb open lace. *Tradesman*, October 1809

metallic gauze – In 1784 Mr. Roswag of Strasbourg presented to the board of trade some gauze made of iron wire, for which he received a reward; and the loom he invented for it was lodged in the collection of machines of Vancanson. … with a thin coating of plaster they might be employed to preserve ships from fire, and buildings on shore still more easily; or at least that they would render the ravages of fire less frequent, and less terrible. These gauzes might be very useful too for theatrical decorations, which would not be liable to take fire. Their only inconvenience is their being so little flexible; but Mr. Rochon does not despair of means being found by chemistry to remedy this imperfection, *Journal of Natural Philosophy, Chemistry and the Arts*, August, 1807 ~~~ Metallic gauze, a fanciful and curious article, is also much used in the fabrication of dress hats; *La Belle Assemblée*, May 1820 ~~~ Metallic gauze is a favourite material for carriage hats, the gauze is ornamented with spots of plush silk; this material, like the granite crape, now much in requisition, is of all colours. *La Belle Assemblée*, July 1820 ~~~ The new material called metallic gauze bears the names of those different gems which it is made to resemble; such as amethyst gauze, emerald gauze, and topaz gauze. *La Belle Assemblée*, November 1820 ~~~ [Paris hats] though last not in estimation, is a new kind of metallic gauze, of a singularly beautiful quality; it is called after different precious stones, to which it is similar in colour, as ruby, amethyst, emerald, and topaz gauze. *Repository of Arts*, November 1820 ~~~ Metallic- or wire-cloths. … The beauty of these works attracted the attention of the public. We remarked, also, with surprise, metallic gauzes of an equal tissue and exquisite finish, and even a waistcoat made of metallic tissue. These objects shew that this species of manufacture is greatly improved in France, since the Exhibition in 1819. Technical Repository, 1824 ~~~ [on an improved loom, patented December 18, 1824 by Pierre Gosset] *Metallic Gauzes*. – These gauzes, which have always been woven with much trouble, and very slowly, can be made with shuttles on my principle with the same ease as the preceding articles [silk goods, cotton and hemp, flax goods, woollen cloths], in the most perfect manner, and twice quicker than what is usual. … There will be also a considerable saving in manual labour, namely, for gauzes of five feet in width, in making which two workmen are obliged to be employed at each loom; by my method the same width can be made by one workman. … The metallic gauzes, of which I have just spoken, are sold now at four shillings the square foot: than can, on my principle, be manufactured at ten-pence!! *Repertory of Patent Inventions*, October 1825 ~~~ ITALY. Fires. – M. Aldini, of Milan, has invented a dress which enables the wearer to traverse with impunity the flames of a large fire, for the purpose of rescuing those who have been exposed to their fury, or of saving property from destruction. This dress is composed of a tissue of asbestos, which it is well known is not combustible, covered with metallic gauze, through which it is also well known flame will not penetrate. *Atheneum*, April 8, 1829 ~~~ The new carriage hats … [several at Longchamps] are made of a new material – a kind of metallic gauze, of a most beautiful texture, and of different colours; *Ladies' Museum*, May 1830

Mexicans – an article called "*Mexicans*," … He states the warp is composed entirely of cotton, and that the filling, thread, or *yarn*, is also intrinsically made of *cotton*; but that there are fibrous particles of wool which adhere to this thread, *Public Documents*, June 1831

Meyer linen – Meyer linen is a good strong kind of hempen linen, made in the principality of Lippe, and is sometimes called Lippish white linen. European Commerce, 1805

Milanaise – *Evening Dresses*. … also *Milanaise*, a new striped silk, where the dress is made *en robe corsage à mille plis*, are certainly most in request; *Blackwood's Lady's*, October 1836

mille rayes – Shot silks of prismatic rose-colour, and those minute shot stripes, called *à la mille rayes*, are mostly worn in dinner and walking costume. These are cherry-colour and white, green and white, and green and lilac; … a gown of green and white *gros de Naples à la mille rayes*. … Dinner and Carriage Dress. – Hat of rice straw, trimmed with bunches of the pink azalia. Ribbons of light green, shaded *a mille rayes*, the stripes very minute, and shot with white. *Lady's Magazine*, May 1830 ~~~ The *nœuds* which ornament hats trimmed in this manner are of *gaze à mille raies*. This kind of trimming is neither pretty nor elegant, but it is new and singular. *La Belle Assemblée*, June 1830 ~~~ The most fashionable ribbons are of gauze with satin stripes, wither very broad, or *à mille raies*. *The Day*, February 6. 1832 ~~~ [court dress] White crape dresses, trimmed with blonde: train of white mille-raye satin, *Court Journal*, June 1, 1833 ~~~ There is but little variety in the costume of children. That of little girls still continues to be short full dresses, with trowsers beneath them. The trowsers are frequently made of jaconet *à mille raies* edged with narrow lace. *Court Journal*, September 7, 1833 ~~~ Some pretty dinner-dresses are of *satin à mille raies*, either black or brown, on a light grey ground. *Court Magazine*, January 1836 ~~~ An elegant new material has just appeared for evening dress, it is called *Velours à mille raies*, it is a kind of Terry velvet, but softer, and more brilliant. *Ladies' Pocket*, February 1836

minco – [see *calaminco*]

miniver – Miniver, among furriers, is the skin taken off the belly of the squirrel. Dictionary of Commerce, 1810

mink – The mink is about as large as a martin, and of the same form. The hair on its tail is shorter; its colour is generally black, and its fur coaser; [sic] View of the American United States, 1795 ~~~ The skin of the mink is blacker than that of an otter, or almost any other creature; "as black as a mink," being a proverbial expression in America. It is not however so valuable; though this greatly depends upon the season in which it is taken. Dictionary of Merchandise, 1805 ~~~ The principal part of the furs sold in Britain come from our possessions in Canada, or are brought thither to the merchants by the Indians; and in one year there are usually purchased, … 32,000 Marten do. [skins] 1,800 Mink do. Dictionary of Mechanical Science, 1829 ~~~ The American furs which are at present brought to London are: … Vison, or mink. Very similar to the Russian mink, but the fur of inferior quality. It is used here, but more on the continent, for trimmings and muffs. Transactions of the Society, 1833 ~~~ [ad] New Furs. – A large quantity of the following Fashionable Furs, in Muffs, Tippets, and Boas, are retailing by Brown and Co. remarkably cheap, … Russian Lynx, Bear, Minx, Sable, *Court Journal*, November 30, 1833 ~~~ The *Mustela vison*, a brown-coloured Weasel, similar to the Martin, is known to Furriers by the American name of Mink, or Minx; … The *lutreola*, or *lesser* Otter, an inhabitant of Finland, is a much smaller animal, with a blackish brown fur which is sold at a high price. This fur has also the name of Mink; but we believe it should not be confounded with the *vison* formerly mentioned. Analytical Dictionary, 1835

mirabout – Some of these *capotes* are edged with colour pipings, but then they are trimmed with *mirabouts*, *Court Magazine*, May 1836 [see *marabout*]

mistake ribband – The peasant bonnet of figured silk, with an heron plume, and shaded mistake ribbands. *La Belle Assemblée*, April 1806 ~~~ lace caps, … trimmed with shaded mistake ribband, *La Belle Assemblée*, July 1806 ~~~ the ribband … is generally of the changeable, or mistake ribband. … The mistake ribband is much used in trimmings on the gipsy cloak, or at the bottom of a plain muslin dress it has a particularly striking and pleasing effect. *La Belle Assemblée*, August 1806

mixed cloth – [see *medley*]

mock – The variety of fabrics, to the making of which cotton can be applied, is a very important consideration in favour of attempting the .cotton manufacture, in preference to any other. The stoutest and the coarsest blankets can be made of the refuse cotton, and cambric muslins, of the most exquisite fineness, can also be made of cotton; the most beautiful table-cloths and napkins, and coarse carpets; the stoutest corduroys, and muslins light as air; dimities, Marseilles-quilting, shirting, sheeting, tickings, pillow-cases, jeans, jeanets, fustians, denims, cottonades, fine and coarse hosiery for every age and sex, pantaloon, vests, mock cassimers, mock serges, mock coating, mock cloths, neck and pocket handkerchiefs, lining and pocketings, dress and undress, and chamber gowns, bed and window curtains, furniture covers, cravats, swansdowns, mole-skins, plushes, velvets, and in short various goods applicable, as usual, to every purpose, or as substitutes for other fabrics heretofore made of wool, hemp, flax, silk, and hair. Such is the unlimited capacity of the native North American raw material, whose future manufacture, under the protection of our government, we earnestly and respectfully recommend to the immediate consideration of all our public authorities. Corbett's Annual Register, 1803 ~~~ Gloves, Cotton Kid, Deer, Sheep, Wash-Leather, Mock Deer, Peau de Chien, Beaver, Mock Beaver and other Leather Commercial Directory, 1823

mock cachemire – [Paris] Scotch plaid clokes of a material formed of mock-Cachemire and silk prevail much for walking; … For friendly evening parties and half-dress, gowns of plaid, in very large chequers are all the rage. They are of the texture we mentioned in the article of mantles, mock Cachemire and silk: *Lady's Magazine*, December 1825

mock pearl – The finest and most transparent sorts of isinglass are consumed in making mock-pearls, and in stiffening linens, silks, gauzes, Domestic Encyclopædia, 1804 ~~~ Dowger Countess of Ormond. – A sage-colour crape dress, with full and elegant draperies, trimmed with real pearl fringe, and tied up with large bunches of mock pearl; *La Belle Assemblée*, June 1807 ~~~ some few ladies have sported the girdle *à la repentie*; these are made of very rich cordons of silk, and the tassels are a mixture of silk and mock pearl: they are a very elegant finish to a lady's dress, and we hope to see them more prevalent; *La Belle Assemblée*, November 1811 ~~~ [hat] The crown is oval, and front … is composed of three rows of scollops one above another, which are edged with real or mock pearl; *La Belle Assemblée*, July 1814 ~~~ (Mock Pearls) such as are made in Paris and in Tuscany, white (in imitation of real pearls) and colored, made of scale of fish; with or without wax inside, not made up as ornaments for Head dresses Commercial Directory, 1823 ~~~ Another and a more costly description of glass beads, made in imitation of pearls, has long been produced in France. Although the name of the inventor of these ornaments has been faithfully preserved, the period of their invention is not precisely known. Reaumur, on whose assertions the greatest reliance may generally be placed, states this to have occurred in 1656. An anecdote related by Beckmann* of a cheat successfully played off upon a lady by a French nobleman, leads to the conclusion that thirty years later than the period here mentioned, these mock pearls were far from being generally introduced or even known. The manner of their invention was this: – M. Jaquin having observed that upon washing a small fish, the *Cyprinus albumus,* or bleak, the water contained numerous fine particles, having the colour of silver, and a pearly lustre, he suffered the water to stand for some time, and, collecting the sediment, covered with it some beads made of plaster of Paris, the favourable appearance of which induced him to manufacture more of the same kind for sale. These were at first eagerly adopted; but the ladies soon finding that when they were exposed to heat, the lustrous coating transferred itself from the beads to their skin, they were as quickly discarded. The next attempt of M. Jaquin was more successful. He procured some glass tubes of a quality easily fusible, and, by means of a blowpipe, converted these into numerous hollow globules. He then proceeded to line the interior surface of these with the powdered fish scales, which he called essence of pearl, or *essence d'Orient*. This was rendered adhesive by being mixed with a solution of isinglass, when it was introduced in a heated state inside the globules, and spread over the whole interior surface, by shaking the beads which, for that purpose, were placed in a bowl upon the table. These hollow beads being blown exceedingly thin, in order to produce a better effect, were consequently very tender. To remedy this evil, as soon as the pearly varnish was sufficiently dry, they were filled with white wax, and being then bored through with a needle, were threaded for sale. ... * Hist. of Inventions, vol. ii, art. *Artificial Pearls.* Cabinet Cyclopædia, 1832

mock sable – We are very much concerned that our reporter of the streets, who in general is very correct in his intelligence, made a very unfortunate mistake in his account of *Mrs. Jehu.* One of that lady's grooms, who constantly attends her in her excursions about town, having been at our office, by her express command, to assure us that her wardrobe does not contain a pelice which answers to our misrepresentation, and that she wears no skin but her own, and a large tippet of *mock sable. Pic Nic,* January 22, 1803 ~~~ Sable ranks before it; but the numerous imitations of this last fur have rendered mock sable vulgar. *Maids, Wives, and Widows,* November 24, 1832 ~~~ A good many gowns have the skirt bordered with a band or rouleau of sable, real or mock, for we perceive that the latter is once more in favour. *Maids, Wives, and Widows,* January 5, 1833 ~~~ we shall name the second rate furs, which, without being very expensive, are nevertheless considered fashionable – Kolinski, squirril [sic] back, mock sable, *Ladies' Companion,* January 1836

mock Valenciennes lace – *Fausse Valenciennes* or mock Valenciennes lace, is a species of real, but inferior in quality, being less close, the design less carefully chosen, and the flowers not strongly marked. Literary Panorama, 1808

mock velvet – The Traffick in *Flanders* ...chiefly consists of several Sorts of Manufacture, as ... Mock Velvets, *London Magazine,* July 1747 ~~~ These are mock-velvets or plushes, with the nap cut, as finished velvets, or with the nap not cut, as shorn velvets, and carpets in imitation of those of Savona. ... A carpet of mock-velvet sells for twenty or thirty sols a square foot; *Monthly Magazine,* January 1805 ~~~ Tripe de velours, *s. wool, velvet, mock velvet, velure, tripe.* Dufief's French Dictionary, 1810 ~~~ Spencers of mock velvet, of all colours, and of a form that sets off a fine shape to best advantage, are generally worn with white dresses for the carriage costume. *La Belle Assemblée,* November 1820 ~~~ [Paris] Round dresses of rose-coloured mock velvet or *reps* silk are very prevalent at dinner parties: *La Belle Assemblée,* December 1820 ~~~ [Paris] A dress for visits of ceremony, or for English tea-parties, is of pink satin, or mock velvet, trimmed with Chinchilla fur; ... This is an expensive dress, under the affectation of half-dress. *Ladies' Monthly Museum,* March 1821

mock wool – [see *shoddy*]

mode – [see *alamode*]

model linen – Model linen is manufactured in Silesia, Bohemia, and Saxony. It is of different breadths; the first sort is 1 ¼, the second 1 ½, and the third 1 ¾ Leipsic ells. This linen is made of dyed yarn, interwoven into it, either striped or checked, and is divided into three different qualities – common, middling, and fine; but the price of it is fixed according to the width, colour, and nicety of the pattern; for if there are several different colours in a piece, then the piece is higher than that which has only one. It is put up in pieces of 72 Leipsic ells. The chief markets for it are Italy, Spain, America, and the West Indies, where it is made use of for all domestic purposes. Under the name of this linen are other sorts, with different descriptions. l. *Arabias.* The width and length is equal to that above described, and there is no other difference between these two sorts, than that the stripes in the Arabias are of a red colour, interwoven- with Turkish yarn. The price is fixed according to the fineness of the quality. \ 2. *Bontons* are 1 ½ and 1 ¼ Leipsic ell wide, and 60 ells long, mostly blue striped and checked, but of the lowest quality. They are commonly cut into three equal lengths or pieces, either of which contains 20 ells. The chief markets are America and the West Indies, where they are only used for seamen's shirts, cloths, &c. European Commerce, 1805

Mogul – The Malabar turban, made of real oriental materials, still remains in favor, and a new kind of gauze, called Hindostan, or Mogul gauze, is much used in the arrangement of these truly elegant and tasteful head-dresses [theatre and evening turbans]. *Ladies' Monthly Museum,* February 1823 ~~~ a bonnet for morning visits of ceremony of mogul velvet of a pure colour, *La Belle Assemblée, La Belle Assemblée,* March 1823

mohair – Mohair, in commerce, is thread or stuff made of the hair of the Angora goat. Arithmetical Questions, 1795 ~~~ Thread or stuff made of camels or other hair. Sheridan's English Dictionary,

1797 ~~~ Mohair, in commerce, the hair of a kind of goat frequently about Angria in Turkey; the inhabitants of which city are all employed in the manufacture of camblets made of this hair. Some give the name *mohair* to the camblets or stuffs made of this hair; of these there are two kinds: the one smooth and plain, the other watered like tabbies, the difference between the two only consists in this, that the latter is calendered, and the other not. There are also mohairs both plain and watered, whose woof is of wool, cotton, or thread. ... Common buttons are generally made of mohair; ... In order to make a button, the mohair must be previously wound on a bobbin; and the mould fixed to a board by means of a bodkin thrust through the hole in the middle of it. This being done, the workman wraps the mohair round the mould in three, four, or six columns, according to the button. Encyclopædia Britannica, 1797 ~~~ A sea-green shawl of fine mohair, with a rich border of various shades and colours. *La Belle Assemblée*, August 1806 ~~~ A Walking Dress. ... A pelice of fawn-coloured sarsnet, trimmed all round with a mohair fringe, *La Belle Assemblée*, October 1806 ~~~ The long scarf *a la Parisot*, composed of mohair, or shawl muslin in imitation, is a most distinguishing ornament. Its colours are generally salmon, cream-colour, orange, and fawn. It has a rich border, happily contrasted with the ground; and on the latter are large variegated spot, where the gold-coloured silk is chiefly predominant. These scarfs are nearly four yards long; *La Belle Assemblée*, December 1806 ~~~ In mohairs, the woof is usually flax, and the warp silk. Book of Trades, 1807 ~~~ Mohair: a kind of stuff, ordinarily of silk both woof and warp; having its grain woven very close. There are two kinds of mohairs; the one smooth and plain, the other watered like tabbies. The difference between the two only consists in this, that the latter is calendered, the other not. There are also mohairs, both plain and watered, whose woof is woollen, cotton, or thread. Guy's Pocket Cyclopædia, 1810 ~~~ Mohair. A man in the civil line, a townsman, or tradesman: a military term, from the mohair buttons worn by persons of those descriptions, or any others not in the army, the buttons of military men being always of metal: this is generally used as a term of contempt, meaning a bourgeois, tradesman, or mechanic. Dictionary of Buckish Slang, 1811 ~~~ Mohair is produced by a species of goat called the Mohair Goat, a variety of the common goat, having soft and silver white hairs. This hair is commonly imported ready spun, and is woven into camblets and other articles, which are afterwards exported to all parts of the world. Practice of Customs, 1812 ~~~ Walking Dress. Hat ... A very beautiful feather, of various shades of lilac mixed with white, and made of mohair silk, in the shape of a bird of paradise, *Lady's Magazine*, March 1830 ~~~When speaking of the Angora goat, we have had occasion to mention the cloth called Camblet, which is manufactured from the hair of that animal. This woolly hair is the Mohair of commerce and the stuff into which it is woven is also, sometimes, called Mohair. The French *moire* was, originally, the same article, but the name was subsequently given to various imitations, one of which is the English Moreen, so much used for bed and window curtains. Analytical Dictionary, 1830 ~~~ [men's] A Shooting Dress. This coat is of light green mohair or velveteen. *Casket*, January 1831 [see also *angora, camlet, moire* and *tabby*]

moire – Moire, *mohair, tabby.* – de laine, *moreen.* Dufief's French Dictionary, 1810 ~~~ * The word Moiré signifies *watered*, as La Soie Moirée, watered silk. Journal of Science and the Arts, 1818 ~~~ The French speak of *la moire ondée*, which our manufacturers have chosen to call Watered Moreen. Analytical Dictionary, 1830 ~~~ [Paris] A bridal-dress was lately admired by Aglaie, as being both elegant and seasonable. The robe was of *moire blanche*, trimmed with swan's-down, *Lady's Magazine*, February 1830 ~~~ Evening Dress. ... The *tablier* is composed of mallow-coloured *soie moirée*, quilled round with a double fold of the same. *Royal Lady's*, June 1831 ~~~ Pelisses are still more fashionable than last month in carriage dress. They are composed of *moire* of an exceedingly rich kind, *La Belle Assemblée*, May 1832 ~~~ Two new silks have appeared, one is *moire à raies*, it is in stripes of the same colour, but one is dead and the other bright; the former is watered. *Ladies' Museum*, May 1832 ~~~ Carriage Dress. Is composed of *moire*, the ground a dark dust colour, printed in zig-zag of brown and rose colour. *La Belle Assemblée*, June 1832 ~~~ *Make and Materials of Evening Dress.* ... Plain *Chaly* and Cashmere *moire*, and *moire Satinée*, are all likely to be in request. *Maids, Wives, and Widows*, November 10, 1832 ~~~ [Paris – at the Duches d'O–'s dinner party] Her daughter wore a dress of *moire chrysophrase*, [chrysophrase is a green gem, which she also wore] *Court Magazine*, January 1833 ~~~ [court dress] A rich moire silk, striped with satin; *Court Journal*, March 2, 1833 ~~~ a parasol of white *moire*, trimmed with black lace. *Court Journal*, August 10, 1833 ~~~ [Court dress] train of blue moirée gros de Naples, … train of white moiré gros de Naples; *Royal Lady's*, March 1836 ~~~ [Paris] materials for hats and bonnets. … *moire*, are all in favour. You are surprised no doubt that the last material, which is a summer one, and indeed calculated for summer only, should be adopted for winter; it is a caprice of fashion, and may be a transient one, but after seeing velvet worn in the dog days out we to be surprised at anything. *New Monthly Belle Assemblée*, December 1836 [see also *moreen*, *mohair*, *tabby*, and *watered*]

moleskin – [*note*: there are three materials by this name: fur, silk, and fustian.] … *Specification of the Patent granted to Joseph Everett, of Salisbury, in the County of Wilts, Clothier; for a certain Article manufactured of different Materials, and wove in a peculiar Manner, so as to give it an Appearance of Velvet, which he denominates "Salisbury Angola Moleskin."* Dated June 30, 1803. … I manufacture the Salisbury Angola Moleskin on two chains or warps, the upper chain is invariably woollen yarn, but the under chain is of cotton, linen, silk, mohair, or worsted. *Repertory of Arts*, March 1, 1804 ~~~ *Apropos* of French hats, Mrs. Bell finished one the other day for a lady of distinction, which was composed of the newly invented silk mole skin, a bright purple with white feathers, it was intended for the carriage costume, but might be worn for the promenade, … Silk mole skin muffs and tippets are from their novelty and elegance in the highest estimation, swansdown are next to them. *La Belle Assemblée*, October 1814 ~~~ Mole-Skin. (among Clothiers; a coarse stuff to make great-coats) New Dictionary, English and French, 1815 ~~~ There was exhibited a hat made of mole skin, in imitation of *Chinchilli*, which indicated much ingenuity. *New England Farmer*, October 19, 1822 ~~~ Shag or moleskin, of thread and silk, spotted or colored, to two thirds wide Digest of the Commercial Regulations, 1824 ~~~ For walking, or carriage costume, over this dress is worn a new an elegant wrapping cloak, made of grey mole-skin, or fine Bath coating; *Ladies' Monthly Museum*, January 1818 ~~~ [men's] A Half-Mourning Morning Dress. … The trowsers are of white moleskin, and button up the front with a fly. *Lady's Book*, October 1830 ~~~ Making included, a ploughman may clothe himself decently on Sundays for less than 2*l*. 10s.; his working garb (mole-skin) costs about 16s.; History of the Middle and Working Classes, 1833 ~~~ [ad] Have received by the ships Hark-away and Jefferson, direct from Liverpool, … 1 case stout moleskins *Farmer's Register*, May 1835 ~~~ Smooth fustians, when cropped or shorn before dying, are called moleskins; … they are both tweeled fabrics. … Moleskin shorn, of a very strong texture, and a drab dyed tint, is sold at 20*d*. per yard. … Shorn, dyed, and re-shorn, as moleskin. Price 10½ *d* to 2*s* 9*d*. Cotton Manufacture of Great Britain, 1836 [see also *fustian*, and *imitation fur*]

mole fur – Mole skins, undressed, the dozen – 2d. [import duty] Ship Owner's Manual, 1795 ~~~ Common Mole. … The fur is so soft and beautiful, that it would make the most elegant articles of dress, did not the difficulty of curing and dressing the skin deter from experiments of this nature. General Zoology, 1800 ~~~ Walking Dress. A Polish Robe of purple velvet, … the whole trimmed entirely round with the red fox, mole, leopard spot, or gray squirrel. *La Belle Assemblée*, February 1807 ~~~ Coloured satin spensers trimmed with mole, linx or swansdown, is a useful change; and may be worn with white dresses of almost every construction. We find them a comfortable and becoming shelter from the partial air of the theatres; ours are formed of rose-pink satin, trimmed with gossamer fur. *La Belle Assemblée*, November 1807 ~~~ In former times the *skins* of moles were in great esteem for many purposes both useful and ornamental. They were employed for the linings of winter garments, and for trimmings in several kinds of dress, and were even made into coverlets for beds. At present, although, by a late invention, the down or fur, which is as soft as the finest velvet, has been adopted in the manufacture of hats, they are so little esteemed in this country that the mole-catchers in general can find no sale for them. Useful Knowledge, 1821

Montespan – New Materials. – One of the richest is called *Satin-Montespan*. The ground is of a dead white, a plain but very rich silk; it is striped in large squares by a rose-colour, green, or violet stripe, lightly marbled with some opposite colour: in the centre of each square is a bouquet formed at least of four different flowers coloured after nature. These dresses have a rich effect, and look extremely well upon tall fine women, but the largeness of the pattern renders them very unbecoming to *belles* of the dumpy order. *Maids, Wives, and Widows*, March 16, 1833 ~~~ [Paris] New Materials. — For grandes toilettes d'hirer, the newest materials are the ... Satin *Montespan* – a rich satin, the ground in general white, with a delicate and very beautiful running pattern of natural flowers all over; the stems and leaves in gold. This is one of the most beautiful of our new materials. *Lady's Magazine and Museum*, November 1834

Montpelier gauze – [ad] the most admired Montpelier Gauzes for evening dress, at 3s. 6d. per yard, may be now had in all the prevailing colour, *Examiner*, April 23, 1826

moraine – [see *morling*]

Moravian – Parisian Summer Fashions. ... Full Dress. A round train dress of Moravian worked muslin, with correspondent border, *La Belle Assemblée*, August 1806 ~~~ Ball dresses, dear Julia, were never more attractive ... Round train-dresses of Moravian muslin, *La Belle Assemblée*, April 1807 ~~~ *Morning Costume.* — A morning robe of spotted or flowered Moravian muslin, *Edinburgh Annual Register*, April 6, 1810 ~~~ Opera Dress. A blue satin robe, worn over a slip of white satin, let in at the bosom and sleeves ... with silver Moravian work. *La Belle Assemblée*, June 1811 ~~~ [ad] BEAUTIFUL WORK UPON MUSLIN by the Moravians, at Evan's, 95, New Bond-Street. Ladies often find it difficult to suit their taste in Flouncings, Trimmings, Habit-Shirts, Caps, &c. for want of a sufficient variety, are respectfully informed, they may see the greatest assortment at the above warehouse. Ladies who wish to purchase Bobbin Lace Squares, are invited to inspect the curious and inimitable way in which the Moravians can run the borderings to resemble lace – no eye can distinguish the difference. *Repository of Arts*, June 1814 ~~~ Walking Dress. A morning dress, composed of thin jaconaut muslin; the bottom of the skirt is very richly ornamented with Moravian work. *Ladies' Monthly Museum*, July 1818 ~~~ Muslin, worked with glazed cotton, was formerly called Dresden-work, but is now known by the name of Moravian, from its production having formed the principal employment of a religious sect, called the Moravian Sisters, which originated in Germany, and some of whose establishments exist in this country: the shops, in London, called Moravian-warehouses, were, originally, opened for the sale of their work; though they are now become ordinary depôts for the various kinds of Fancy Embroidery, produced by the immense numbers of young females, who, in this country, derive their maintenance from the ever-varying use of the needle. Young Lady's Book, 1829

moreen – St. Margaret, in Durham, ... The parishioners are chiefly employed in the woollen manufactures; viz in making moreens, stuffs, and carpeting. State of the Poor, 1797 ~~~ Watered camblets are often called moreens, or morains. *Moraine* being the French name for that wool which the tanner, or currier, removes from the hide by the application of quick lime. The coarse thick stuffs made of this refuse-wool were the original *morains. Monthly Magazine*, August 1805 ~~~ Worsted and stuff goods, such as ... moreens, &c. which are composed entirely of wool are subject to an ad valorem duty of 15 per cent. National Calendar, 1820 ~~~ Moreens are plain stout cloths, of worsted, the weft of which, in comparison with the warp, is a very thick thread. They are woven white and then dyed of any requisite colour, but their distinguishing characteristic is acquired in the process of Watering, Analytical Dictionary, 1830 ~~~ [ad] Have received by the ships Hark-away and Jefferson, direct from Liverpool, ...1 case 3-4 scarlet, crimson and yellow moreens. *Farmer's Register*, May 1835 ~~~ MOREEN, n. A kind of stuff used for curtains and bed-hangings. Knowles' English Dictionary, 1835 ~~~ [in 1834] moreen, No. 2, 20*s.* 6*d.*; Practical Mercantile Correspondence, 1836 ~~~ CURTAINS. ... Moreen is a stout sort of worsted fabric, artificially figured to look like damask. But the figures, instead of being woven in, as in that article [damask], are produced by what is erroneously called *watering*, and effect obtained by passing the cloth over a hot brass cylinder, engraved in patterns, and pressing it between two wooden rollers, to cause the indentation. Its appearance is rich, and its durability keeps it in favour. Scenes of Commerce, 1836 [see also *camblet, mohair, moire, tabby,* and *watered*]

morlaix – [see *creas*]

morling – Morling, Mortling. *s.* wool plucked from dead sheep. Royal Standard English Dictionary, 1800 ~~~ MORLING or MORTLING is that wool taken from the skin of a dead sheep, either dying of the rot, or killed, called in some counties mort-wool. Dictionary of Commerce, 1810 ~~~ Moraine, *fell wool, morling or mortling.* Dufief's French Dictionary, 1810 ... SHORLING and MORLING, or

MORTLING, Words to distinguish fells of sheep; Shorling being the fells after the fleeces are shorn off the sheep's back; and Morling the fells flayed off after they die or are killed: In some parts of England they understand by Shorling, a sheep whose face is shorn off; and by a Morling, a sheep that dies. Law-Dictionary, 1811

morocco – Morning Dress. ... blue morocco slippers. *Lady's Magazine*, February 1796 ~~~ The peninsula of the Crimea has a considerable trade in what is called Morocco leather, of various colours, which is to be had very cheap, and like satin. New Geographical, Historical, and Commercial Grammar, 1798 ~~~ Mr. William Alison of Long-lane, has recently obtained his majesty's letters patent, securing to him, for fourteen years, the sole right to his invention for *the manufacture of morocco leather from American horse-hides. Monthly Magazine*, April 1799 ~~~ The chief colours communicated to Morocco-leather, are red and yellow, for the preparation of which, the Turks have long been celebrated. ... But these two are not the only colours dyed by the Turks, who likewise manufacture black, green, and blue leather; which last three, however, are not only destitute of lustre, but are extremely perishable. The Turks, indeed, are as inferior to Europeans in preparing the more common species, as they excel them in manufacturing and dyeing the red and yellow moroccos. Domestic Encyclopædia, 1803 ~~~ Slippers of red Morocco are revived in the fashionable world; white satin are considered most elegant in full dress. *La Belle Assemblée*, November 1807 ~~~ The (so called) Morocco leather, prepared from sheep-skins chiefly, and used so largely for coach-linings, pocket-books, and the best kind of book-binding, is thus made. The skin, cleansed and worked in the way already described, is taken from the lime-water, and the thickening thereby occasioned is brought down, not by bran liquor as in tawing, but by a bath of dogs' or pigeons' dung diffused in water, where it remains till sufficiently suppled, and till the lime is quite got out and it becomes a perfectly white clean pelt. If intended to be dyed red it is then sewed up very tight in the form of a sack with the grain side outwards (the dye only being required on this side) and is immersed in a cochineal bath of a warmth just equal to what the hand can support, and is worked about for a sufficient time till it is uniformly dyed, a process that demands much skill and experience. The sack is then put into a large vat containing sumach infused in warm water, and kept for some hours till it is sufficiently tanned. ... The process for the real Morocco leather, as prepared from goat-skins at Fez and Tetuan, is thus described by M. Broussonet. The skins are first cleansed, the hair taken off, limed and reduced with bran nearly in the way already described for the English Morocco leather. After coming from the bran they are thrown into a second bath made of white figs, mixed with water, which is thereby rendered slimy and fermentable. In this bath the skins remain four or five days, when they are thoroughly salted with sal-gem (or rock salt) alone (and not with salt and alum) after which they are fit to receive the dye, which for the red, is cochineal and alum, and for the yellow, pomegranate bark and alum. The skins are then tanned, dressed, suppled with a little oil, and dried. Dictionary of Chemistry and Mineralogy, 1807 ~~~ This is a specimen in imitation of Morocco leather, and is now brought to such perfection, as to be applicable to every purpose to which Morocco leather is converted, even to the manufacture of ladies' slippers. A great advantage in this material is the capability of its being made to any size without the appearance of a seam. This article is appropriated also to covers of piano-fortes, card-tables, carriage linings, &c. Its beauty and cheapness will make it a desirable requisite for these purposes, *Repository of Arts*, August 1812 ~~~ Until within the last few years, the consumers of this kind of leather in England have depended wholly on a foreign supply: there are now, however, several manufactories of it in the neighbourhood of London, from which the most beautiful moroccos may be had at prices that have superseded the necessity of importing it from abroad. For leather of inferior quality, and particularly for such as is to receive a yellow colour, sheeps' skins are often substituted. The reason why goats' skins have been principally adopted for the manufacture of morocco is, that they take the dye better, and that they are susceptible of richer and more beautiful colours, than those of any other animals. Useful Knowledge, 1821 ~~~ Belts of Morocco leather are become very general upon robes of every description. *Ladies' Monthly Museum*, July 1822 ~~~ a reticule, shaped like the shepherd's purse, is of lemon coloured Morocco, *La Belle Assemblée*, October 1823 ~~~ Carriage Dress. ... The gaiters are white silk and the shoes lavender coloured morocco. *Lady's Magazine*, April 1830 ~~~ A shooting-dress, about to be adopted by a man of distinguished fashion, is composed of … a grey morocco leather cap. *Casket*, January 1831 ~~~ The dyed leathers are of sheep or goat skin. The former, technically called roan, is far inferior in strength and softness to the latter, which bears the name of morocco, because it was a first offered in the market as a substitute for, or imitation of, they dyed goat-skins prepared in Morocco and other parts of the north of Africa. Transactions of the Society, 1836

mosaic – [court dress] A white satin petticoat trimmed with … a rich gold and silver Mosaic fringe: *Lady's Magazine*, January 1796 ~~~ MOSAIC, or Mosaic Work, and assemblage of little pieces of glass, marble, precious stones, &c. of various colours, cut square, Encyclopædia Britannica, 1797 ~~~ [court dress] A superb rich petticoat, embroidered in draperies, Mosaic pattern relieved by rich spangled stripes, *Scots Magazine*, June 1804 ~~~ [court dress] A white satin petticoat, with crape drapery, and a rich Mosaic embroidery of gold beads, *La Belle Assemblée*, January 1807 ~~~ [court dress] robe, scarlet and brown Mosaic satin, trimmed with point; *La Belle Assemblée*, January 1809 ~~~ We have also noticed some mosaic trimmings, composed of bands of satin and velvet of different colours interwoven: these trimmings have a very rich and elegant appearance, and are of different forms; some are plain bands, others in waves, and some like the teeth of a saw. *Repository of Arts*, December 1821 ~~~ A new kind of figured velvet, named *mosaic*, is often made use of in lining hats of plain velvet. *Ladies' Monthly Museum*, December 1828 ~~~ Ribbons. … the mosaic satins make the most beautiful girdles. *Casket*, March 1835

Moscow ribbon – some shag silk hats are trimmed with ribbands edged with Astracan fur – these are called Moscow ribbands; *La Belle Assemblée*, December 1818

Mosquee – [Paris] The evening dress silks that have appeared, are all in the superb but heavy style of Louis XIV's reign. The satins *Salomon*, *Esmeralda*, and *Pharamond*, are expected to be in great request; as are also … the *Velontées de la Mosquée*, and *Carlina*. *New Monthly Belle Assemblée*, November 1836 ~~~ [Paris] *Velonti Carlina* and *Velonti de la Mosquée* are new and very beautiful silks for evening dress. *Ladies' Pocket*, November 1836 ~~~ which the Persians call Meskit, the Spaniards Mesquita, the Germans Moschée, the French Mosquée, and the English *Mosque*. *Classical Journal*, December 1825

moss – [court dress] Body and train of moss-velvet, trimmed with point and gold; *Lady's Magazine*, January 1809 ~~~ the French corded, spotted, and moss muslins are rather on the decline; they have the appearance of too much substance for the present season. *La Belle Assemblée*, August 1810 ~~~ In the month of *August* [1822], … the most novel and striking is a carriage bonnet of that rare material the spotted moss plush; the ground is white with small dots of bright geranium. *La Belle Assemblée*, November 1820 ~~~ Carriage hat of moss plush silk, in the Regina form, the ground white, *Kaleidoscope*, December 5, 1820 ~~~ This ornament is very becoming, as is the floize-silk moss trimming for the edge of straw bonnets, and which is much more in request than either blond, or gauze *cheveux de fris*, &c. *Ladies' Monthly Museum*, August 1821 ~~~ chiefly ornamented with rich fringes, elegantly wrought buttons, and twisted moss gimp. *Ladies' Monthly Museum*, December 1822 ~~~ Turbans of crescent gauze, or of gold moss gauze, Museum of Foreign Literature, 1823 [see also *chenille*]

moss gimp – Cachemire spencers … are chiefly ornamented with rich fringes, elegantly wrought buttons, and twisted moss gimp. *Ladies' Monthly Museum*, December 1822 [see *gimp*]

moss silk – Promenade Dress. … The Waterloo hat, made in moss silk or straw of a peculiar fineness, lined with fluted satin, *Examiner*, July 30, 1815 ~~~ Moss silk muffs have a most elegant effect; the lightness of this charming material renders it a real acquisition for many appendages to the toilette. *La Belle Assemblée*, January 1816 ~~~ a white satin dress: it was composed of festoons of white gauze, which were finished at the edge with a rich trimming of damask rose-coloured moss silk, … the moss silk trimming was scarcely an inch in breadth, but very full, and had an uncommonly rich and beautiful effect. *Repository of Arts*, December 1820 ~~~ Bonnet of French white *gros de Naples*, (cottage shape), … lined with a blue and French white Parisian moss turned over the edge; *Ladies' Monthly Museum*, April 1822 ~~~ [Paris] The Dauphiness wore a hat of white Lyons mossed silk, surmounted by several plumes of white ostrich feathers. *Lady's Magazine*, May 31, 1830 ~~~ Coloured moss-silk, particularly pale pink for linings, are considered to throw a delicate glow on the complexion. *Lady's*

Magazine, September 1830 ~~~ Bonnets of pearl gray, lined with pink moss, are favourites: to these are often added a demi-veil of black blonde. A hat cut very slanting, and put on one side, was much admired, made of pineapple-green moss on the outside, trimmed with cut ribbons, and a very full wreath of lilac Michaelmas-daisies: it was lined with white satin. *Lady's Magazine*, October 1830

moss straw – Provincial bonnet of fine split straw, or moss straw, *La Belle Assemblée*, July 1808 ~~~ A bee-hive bonnet of fine moss or plaited straw, ornamented with white sarsnet ribbon. *Edinburgh Annual Register*, November 1, 1810 ~~~ In carriages, the moss straw hat or the cottage bonnet. *National Register*, November 6, 1808 ~~~ A Lavinia hat of fine moss straw – a small cap of lace beneath, *Repository of Arts*, August 1812

mouchetee – Moucheté, e, … *a. spotted, eye-spotted…* Moucheter, … *to pink (silk or stuff); to work or make small spots on (stuff)*. Dufief's French Dictionary, 1810 .. *Soies mouchetées* and printed jaconot muslins will be in favour for deshabille. The first are dotted all over with little black points on green, granite, rose, or blue grounds. *Court Magazine*, April 1834

mountain snow plume – the mountain snow plume: nothing can be more chaste or tasteful than this elegant little ornament; its plumage hangs down like the fantastic fretwork formed by frozen snow; *La Belle Assemblée*, January 1820

mousseline – *f.* mŏos-lĭn. *muslin.* Tardy's French Dictionary, 1799 ~~~ Among the new materials for gowns are *mousselines Anglaises*; they are jaconot with a thick stripe, the stripes are beautifully shaded, and at considerable distances from each other: in the space between the stripes are *bouquets* of five or six flowers, coloured after nature. *Repository of Fashions*, September 1829 ~~~ Little change has yet taken place in indoor dress. Some few dresses composed of *mousselines turques et gothiques* have been seen on ladies equally distinguished for their rank and taste. These muslins are of extreme fineness, and of showy and singular pattern. They are worn in *négligé*. *La Belle Assemblée*, May 1830 ~~~ Walking Dress. A printed muslin dress, of a new pattern, called *mousseline Amalthée*; *La Belle Assemblée*, June 1832 ~~~ Materials of Evening Dresses. A new half-transparent material, composed of silk and wool, called *mousseline moirée*, *The Day*, June 9, 1832 ~~~ *Poux de soie*, *mousseline Indone*, painted Pekin, and *mousseline de Soie*, are the fashionable materials in evening dress. *Court Magazine*, August 1833 ~~~ [Paris] White and printed muslins ore the only materials adopted for the promenade, or for *toilettes de campagne*. The prettiest among the latter are the *mousselines satinèes* of the *grandmère* pattern. They are striped in alternate clear and thick glazed stripes. Some have the thick stripes coloured, the others white, and the whole covered with a small running pattern of flowers; but the most elegant are those striped in bias, the ground white, but the thick stripes lightly edged with brown. A row of violet rings forms a chain, separated by bouquets of delicate flowers strewed irregularly. *Court Magazine*, September 1834 ~~~ Half transparent materials, of the very finest Cashmere wool, are in great request. The most fashionable are the *mousselines Peruviennes, mousseline d' Algar*, and *tissue de Syrie*. The first are of Indian patterns, rather large, and of full colours; the second, of small Turkish patterns, presents a dazzling assemblage of hues; the third is of delicate colours, and flowered patterns. *Ladies' Pocket*, June 1836 [see *muslin*]

mousseline Anglaise – [see *English muslin*]

mousseline cachemire – [see *cashmere muslin*]

mousseline d'Aboukir – [see *Aboukir*]

mousseline d'Algar – [see *Algerian*]

mousseline de laine – a variety of light and beautiful materials, as *tissu Cachemire, mousseline de laine*, &c. &c. are all in request. *La Belle Assemblée*, July 1830 ~~~ *Mousseline de laine*, … are fashionable both in half dress and evening dress; gowns in the former are always made partially high. *Ladies' Museum*, August 1830 ~~~ A woollen muslin dress, cashmere designs on a white ground. *Maids, Wives, and Widows*, November 10, 1832 ~~~ At evening parties several ladies have recently worn dresses of *Mousseline de laine* with short sleeves, and *corsages en pointe*. When these muslins are of striped patterns, the stripes are made to divide in the middle of the *corsage*, both behind and before, in the form of a fan. This gives the waist a very slender appearance. These dresses have for the most part cashmere patterns, or sprigs, on a white ground. *Court Journal*, March 23, 1833 ~~~ *Mousseline de laine*, of an arabesque pattern, makes a pretty dress, either for evening *negligé* or for morning *demi-toilette*. ...*Mousseline de laine Pompadour*, with large bunches of coloured flowers on a black ground, is also a beautiful and fashionable article for dresses. *Court Journal*, November 2, 1833 ~~~ Some new materials for autumn have already appeared, both for elegant *negligé* and evening dress. We may cite some *mousselines de laines* of perfectly new patterns; some of a simple kind, others complicated, but none of that large and glaring description that were so prevalent last year. The most striking among the new patterns are the *Odalisques* of a great variety of colours on a green or grey ground; the *fleurs Chinées*, similar to those of *pou de soie*, and the *palmes à ramages*, traced in red, black, or white, upon a chocolate or grey ground. *Court Magazine*, October 1834 ~~~ [Paris] New materials for dresses are this year very numerous. Several of these for morning *negligé* are of the finest Cashmere wool, and of a slighter kind than Chali. These are ... the *mousselines de laine*, these latter are printed in very small patterns, *Court Magazine*, May 1835 ~~~ Notwithstanding the excessive heat of the weather, dresses of *Mousseline de laine* are still seen. The grounds are, however, white, or of very pale tints, thickly scattered with light and rich bouquets. The beauty of the *mousseline de laine* renders it a hard sacrifice to lay it aside. *Court Journal*, June 13, 1835 ~~~ Half transparent materials as *mousseline de laine*, ... are yet fashionable; they are made in the pelisse style, and are worn over richly embroidered muslin dresses. *Court Magazine*, July 1835

mousseline de soie – [see *silk muslin*]

mousseline des Indes – [see *India muslin*]

mousseline Egyptienne – [see *Egyptian muslin*]

mousseline sylphide – [see *sylphide*]

Mozambique – High Dresses composed of Cashmere wool, under the names of *Indonstans* and *Thibitians*, begin to be worn in the promenades. They are painted and figured in various patterns; that called *Mozambique* is extremely fashionable, and is remarkable for its elegant singularity. *Casket*, January 1832

mull – Under the denomination of Muslins Plain, ... mulmuls New Merchant's Guide, 1798 ~~~ Indian words imported with the goods, just as we now use *jaconet, cossae, mul-mul* for denominations of Indian fabrics. Annals of Commerce, 1805 ~~~ Cotton goods are divided into 7 different classes, each proportionally lighter the than other. The heaviest of these are, 1st. *Shirtings*, 2d. *Cambrics*, 3d. *Cossas*, 4th. *Jaconetts*, 5th. *Lawn grounds*, 6th. *Mulls*, New Encyclopædia, 1807 ~~~ Morning dresses ... Mull muslin, with the raised coral spot, finished at the feet with a similar beading, terminating at the extreme edge with a narrow Vandyke lace, is an article of considerable attraction. *La Belle Assemblée*, October 1807 ~~~ There is in the article of mulmuls, some which were sold at the last sale of March for 19*s.* 2*d.* per piece, and others sold at 90*s.* per piece; Minutes of Evidence ... in the Lords Committees, 1813 ~~~ While the English manufacturer made for the market the coarser kinds of cloth, ... the Scotch directed their attention to the finer qualities. Mull-mulls, and buke or book-muslins were soon very perfectly executed. *Scots Magazine*, December 1814 ~~~ Dinner Dress, OF thin mull muslin, body made with a frilling, composed of the same material, to form a tucker, *Ladies' Monthly Museum*, May 1817 ~~~ For the promenade, either on foot or in the carriage, ... for the spencer and pelisse. The former is of fine mull-mul muslin, elegantly embroidered and trimmed with lace, *La Belle Assemblée*, June 1819 ~~~ Bouk and mull muslins, which are finished with starch at the bleachfield to give them a clear wiry appearance, receive no other finishing at the calender than folding and pressing. Edinburg Encyclopædia, 1830 ~~~ [Paris] The most elegant as well as the most distinguee toilette, consists of a peignoir of India or mull muslin, richly embroidered down the front, and round the bottom, *Lady's Magazine and Museum*, September 1834 ~~~ The most elegant summer spencer, one of which has been just completed for a lady of very high rank, is of fine mull mull muslin over pink sarsnet; *La Belle Assemblée*, July 1820 ~~~ Mull Muslin. *s.* A kind of soft thin muslin. Ladies' Lexicon, 1835 ~~~ Muslin predominates in half-dress robes, ... We have observed some dresses of Indian clear, and mull muslin, made in the pelisse style *New Monthly Belle Assemblée*, August 1836 [see also *India mull muslin*]

musk beaver – [see *nutria*]

muslin – Afternoon Dresses. ... Armenian robe of embroidered muslin, the train with a broad hem; full short sleeves, trimming of blond round the neck, and at the top of the sleeves. *Lady's Magazine*, January 1796 ~~~ a fine sort of cotton cloth, which bears a downy knot on its surface. There are several sorts of muslins brought from the East Indies, and more particularly from Bengal; such as doreas, betelles, mulmuls, tanjeebs, &c. Muslin is now manufactured in Britain, and brought to very great perfection. Encyclopædia Britannica, 1797 ~~~ *Promenade Dresses.* 1. A round dress of thick white muslin. ... A full dress of blue muslin, trimmed with white beads. *Port folio,* June 19, 1802 ~~~ Formerly, all muslins were imported from India; but, at present, very considerable quantities are manufactured in Manchester, Glasgow, Paisley, &c. which, for the fineness and durability, are little inferior to those of the East. It should, however, be remarked, that the British muslins acquire a yellowish cast, after they have been repeatedly washed, while the genuine India-muslins retain their original whiteness. Domestic Encyclopædia, 1802 ~~~ The under-dress still continues to be of snow white muslin, certainly a species of drapery the most congenial ever invented, to the graceful elegance of the female form. *La Belle Assemblée,* April 1806 ~~~ *Muslin,* which is one of the chief articles in the millinery business, is a very fine substance, made wholly of cotton; and it takes its name from the soft downy nap on its surface resembling moss, or in French *mousse.* There are various kinds of muslins brought from the East-Indies: the best is said to come from Bengal. They are subject to a heavy duty upon importation, which is returned if exported into foreign countries. Book of Trades, 1806 ~~~ British *muslins* were first manufactured at Anderton, in this county, in 1764. At this period Mr. Joseph Shaw [of Bolton] manufactured *plain, striped,* and *spotted muslins,* and supplied his looms with yarns spun on the old single spindle hand wheels. But he could not get a quantity sufficiently cheap to cope with the East India Company's muslins, which he had to meet in the home market, and was under the necessity of abandoning the pursuit, without being rewarded for his meritorious labours. In the year 1782, Mr. Samuel Oldknow commenced the manufacture of British muslins at *Anderton,* on his native soil. At that time Sir Richard Arkwright's fine yarn, and other roller-drawn yarns, were become tolerably plentiful, and had induced Mr. Thomas Ainsworth, of Bolton, Sir Richard Arkwright, and others, to begin to make this thin and delicate fabric: but it is generally admitted, that Mr. Oldknow was the first that produced the *Balasore handkerchiefs, the jacconot* and *japaned muslins,* in the style of India; and was the first person who realized 10,000l. by the manufactures of British muslins. Beauties of England and Wales, 1807 ~~~ a Manchester muslin, composed of cotton and silk, and of tastefully contrasted colours. It is equally adapted to the domestic or evening costume, distinguished only by its construction and its trimmings. It is sold ... at 2s. 6d. per yard, silk width. *Repository of Arts,* November 1813 ~~~ When made in washing silks it is similar, but if in muslin it is indeed a most expensive dishabille, *La Belle Assemblée,* October 1814 ~~~ 1 Oct. 1823. The opinion of this Board was, that calicoes and muslins were easily distinguished, and that persons conversant with the articles knew clearly what were each? – That is the point which I feel myself doubtful upon. Should you have any difficulty, if a thing were shown to you, in saying whether it was muslin or a calico? – Indeed, I think I would. Where I draw the line of distinction is thus: we are not generally in the habit of printing any calicoes finer than what we call thirteen hundreds, which will count fourteen threads on the manufacturer's glass, and therefore I conceive that all goods finer than those, and thirty-four inches broad, might be considered muslins. Have you the least doubt, on a piece of cloth being shown to you, whether it is a muslin or a calico? – We buy sometimes under the head of muslins what really are not muslins. Should you have any doubt as a manufacturer, if a piece of cloth was shown to you, whether it was a muslin or a calico? – I should have a doubt. Upon what would your doubt rest? – Upon the point of fineness; there is no difference that I know of except in the fineness. There is no difference in the manufacture? – No. Why the name of muslin, as I understand, was given, was this: calicoes were made of what they call water-twist, and, formerly, muslins of copp-twist, but the improvement in spinning the latter has made it applicable to the making of calicoes, and there are thousands of pieces now so made; it is only the eye and the glass that would govern me, along with the breadth. I have been in the habit of considering nothing muslin but what was yard wide, or nearly so, and made finer than thirteen hundreds; but latterly importers call every thing muslin, so as to get them in duty free. But the basis of the distinction is, that the one is fine, and the other not? – Yes. Can you point out any description of goods to which you cannot apply a distinguishing name? – These are the two handkerchiefs which the surveyor-general showed me [*producing them*]; the texture of one is as fine as muslin, but not so broad as I think should entitle it to be considered muslin: the texture of the other is as coarse as calico, though broader; it is upon these that his difficulty arose. ... What is the difference of price between those two articles? – This, which I consider a calico, may be worth 1 *s.* 2*d.*; and the other, of muslin texture, 1 *s.* 6*d.* Sessional Papers, 1824 ~~~ Coloured muslin dresses, and those of Italian net, of very bright and striking summer colours, worn over white satin, prevail much at friendly afternoon parties; they are trimmed with *bias* fold of satin the colour of the dress. The muslin of which the first-mentioned dresses is composed is remarkably clear, and may at a first glance be mistaken for Italian net. *La Belle Assemblée,* August 1826 ~~~ TO KEEP MUSLINS OF A GOOD COLOR. Never wash muslins, or any kind of white cotton goods, with linen; for the latter deposits or discharges a gum and coloring matter every time it is washed, which discolors and dyes the cotton. Wash them by themselves. *Ladies' Pocket,* February 1829 ~~~ *Muslin* – comes from *Mosul,* a town of Turkey in Asia, where the finest muslins are found; the Europeans imitated them, and called the texture *muslin. Ladies' Museum,* July 1829 ~~~ The new printed muslins of all sorts greatly vary in their patterns from those of last year. Arabesque designs, garlands of roses of a large size, Gothic figuring, and Etruscan vases filled with flowers, are the favourite patterns. They print many of these designs on rayed and columned muslins. ... The muslins *à l'Alhambra* are so called because they are printed with arabesques taken from that celebrated palace. *Lady's Magazine,* April 1830 ~~~ A variety of new materials are in favour in home dress; among these are Chinese, Turkish, Moorish, and Gothic muslins, all of which are singular, and we had almost said very ugly, patterns. Some have excessively large and glaring stripes; others, and these last are the prettiest, are flowered. *Ladies' Museum,* June 1830 ~~~ Muslins, of chintz patterns, still keep their ground in morning dress, but they are of darker and fuller colours than those worn in summer. *Ladies' Museum,* October 1830 ~~~ The ladies' coloured muslin dresses ... cost ten shillings per dress, and each weighs six ounces; On the Economy of Machinery And Manufactures, 1832 ~~~ Muslins, so denominated from the downy nap upon them, which the French call *mousse,* are the finest sort of cloths made of cotton, and are the lightest, most transparent, and beautiful for female dress; though indeed in India, sometimes the men dress in long muslin draperies, which reach, like gowns and petticoats, down to the feet. There are different names of muslins; as *book muslin,* which is the clearest and most transparent sort; this is used by our ladies for a ball dress, and looks very beautiful when worn over colored silk. ... The turbans of the Indian princes are made of a great length of muslin, so fine, and so long, as to be the labor of twenty years of the weaver's life; and the criterion of the value of a dress among the ladies of the seraglio, is, its capability of being drawn through a ring. Book of Commerce by Sea and Land, 1834 ~~~ [Paris] As for muslin dresses in walking costume, no one dare put them on who is fearful of exasperating the influenza into consumption. No great temptation, truly; for the newest muslin dresses are in ugly, mean little patterns, that would make our housemaids most commendable Sunday gowns. I have heard you bestow the most vivacious orations in French on the beauties of our printed muslins and chintzes; much as you admire English productions of this kind, I do not think you could like these mean *fade*-looking things. ...[court dress] gold muslin petticoat over satin. *Lady's Magazine and Museum,* June 1836 ~~~ the ingenuity of the manufacturer frequently sends out some novelty, which becomes fashionable for a time, then is no more heard of. But the three sorts, known under the names of *book muslin, jaconot muslin,* and *cambric muslin;* are of more permanent character; Scenes of Commerce, 1836 ~~~ Muslin predominates in half-dress robes, and white are upon the whole in a majority; those lined with coloured silk, or worn over it, have declined in estimation, probably because they have become so exceedingly common. We have observed some dresses of Indian clear, and mull muslin, made in the pelisse style *New Monthly Belle Assemblée,* August 1836 [see also *India muslin*]

muslinet – Webster, George, Manchester, dimity and muslinet manufacturer, March 1. *European Magazine,* August 1796 ~~~ May 2d, 1797. ... I desired Welsh to get a Bundle containing four Muslinet waiscoats [sic] & a Reg[tle] Coat in your Possession Life of Major J. G. Semple Lisle, 1799 ~~~ Duties. Muslins and muslinets, whether printed, stained, colored or otherwise 12½ per cent. Abridgement of the Laws of the United States, 1805 ~~~ [Paris] *Perkale,* jaconot muslin, and muslinet, are all adopted in the morning costume. *Repository of Arts,* July 1817 ~~~ a coarse cotton cloth

Nankeen - Nutria

nankeen – The principal silk stuffs brought from China are, … Yellow nankeens; … White nankeen cloth, in pieces of 27 ells. *New-York Magazine*, February 1795 ~~~ [Paris, men's fashions] The pantaloons, generally of nankeen, reach within two inches of the ankle, where it is tied with a ribband forming a small rose. *Lady's Magazine*, September 1798 … [Paris] Nothing is now so fashionable as the straw hat. … The ribbands are clouded or striped. These latter are *nankin. Lady's Magazine*, June 1800 ~~~ The Philadelphia fashion … The heat of our climate compels both sexes to consult comfort, rather than splendor. … Vulgar nankeen and filthy dowlas are in great request. *Port Folio*, June 18, 1802 ~~~ This walking-dress will be very fashionable. A short round frock of nankin, *La Belle Assemblée*, June 1806 ~~~ The Bombay cotton is chiefly used by the Chinese for making what is called the white Nankin, but which is rather of a cream color than of a clear white. Perhaps it may not be improper to consider here the effects that might possibly follow from cultivating the brown cotton in India, and sending it to England. East India white cotton wool now (1794) sells for ten pence the pound in London, but suppose it to sell for one shilling a pound, which is about one-third cheaper than the average price of West India cotton, this circumstance then, with the reduction in the cost of labor, by the use of our machinery (never likely to be introduced in China) and the dye saved besides, might enable the people of Manchester to afford their Nankins at so low a rate as in a short time entirely to exclude that article of our present import from Canton. Public Life … of the Earl of Macartney, 1807 ~~~ [men's] Morning or Walking Dress. … Nankeen trowsers and gaiters, *Weekly Entertainer*, September 11, 1809 ~~~ Many attempts have been made to imitate the shade of yellow which nankeens possess, but none have hitherto succeeded, so as to produce a colour whose difference from the real nankeen could not be in general distinguished at first sight. British Encyclopedia, 1809 ~~~ worn by ladies of rank and fashion … Nankeen half boots. *Jersey Magazine*, August 1810 ~~~ Nankeen, Nankin, or Nanqueen, … a species of cotton cloth closely woven. It takes its name from Nankin, a city of China, where the reddish thread of which the stuff is made, was originally, and still is, spun. This manufacture has been carried to the highest pitch of perfection in the East Indies, where vast quantities of white, pink, and yellow nankeens are made. At Manchester, and in other parts of Great Britain, these articles are imitated with success, though the British nankeens are inferior, it must be allowed, to those of India, but a little time may bring them to perfection. The Indian nankeens are not only more durable, but hold their colour much longer than the British; which can scarcely undergo three washings without being altered. The cotton employed by the Orientals in the manufacture of nankeen, is *naturally* of a reddish colour, whereas we are obliged to impart the proper hue to our material by means of dying; … Nankeens are mostly used in England in the formation of trowsers, and waistcoats for men's wear, during the summer, and for women's pelisses, &c. General Dictionary of Commerce, 1810 ~~~ Statement Of British Cotton Manufactures Suitable For Sicily. Nankeens. – Consumption considerable. Largest sales effected in the months of March and April. Clouds invoiced at 1*s*. 2*d*. per yard. Twills 1s. 6*d*. and Florentines at 1*s*. 8*d*. are the kinds that suit. Voyages and Travels, 1812 ~~~ A favourite morning head-dress is a basque cap, made of nankin, embroidered and ornamented with coloured cordons. *La Belle Assemblée*, July 1823 ~~~ AMERICAN NANKEENS. J. B. Nons of Philadelphia, has obtained a patent for a receipt to make buff or nankeen colours, which, are indelible. This discovery is of great value, as we now can have nankeens of a cheap quality, and of American manufacture. *New England Farmer*, May 27, 1825 ~~~ Nankins, whether white, blue, long yellow or short yellow – *Public Documents*, March 1832 ~~~ We all know that a jean, nankeen, or any kind of thin jacket, is the pleasantest wear for September, Instructions to Young Sportsmen, 1833 ~~~ Those made in China, still maintain their superiority in color and texture over the English manufacture. Chinese Repository, 1833 ~~~ [ad] Have received by the ships Hark-away and Jefferson, direct from Liverpool, … 1 case 3-4 domestic nankeens, yellow. 1 case 3-4 American nankeen, made from nankeen cotton grown by the Hon. John Forsyth, of Georgia, warranted not to fade. 1 case 3-4 plain and twilled English yellow nankeens. 1 case real marmee chop and German yellow and India blue nankeens. *Farmer's Register*, May 1835 ~~~ The British cotton manufacturer cannot forget that even the once far-famed fabrics of Bengal have given place to his superior skill, not only in the general market of the world, but in the very field of its production. Already have the nankins of China itself almost ceased to be numbered amongst its staple exports, unable to compete with the nankins of England. Address to the People of Great Britain, 1836

nap – NAP (s. *from the* Sax. knoppa) A kind of down, a roughness on the surface of cloth. Ash's English Dictionary, 1795 ~~~ FRIZING of cloth, a term in the woollen manufactory, applied to the forming of the nap of a cloth, or stuff, into a number of little hard burrs or prominences, covering almost the whole ground thereof. British Encyclopedia, 1809 ~~~ [Patent November 20, 1824] This invention is the application of combs or cards to the surface of woollen cloths, in the operation of dressing or finishing them, for the purpose of laying the pile or nap in a uniform manner in one direction only, and also of retaining the position of the nap, and glazing the cloth when its pile has been so laid, by the employment of heated boxes, passed against the distended surface of the cloth, to effect the same object as is usually performed by smoothing irons. *Mechanics' Magazine*, September 17, 1825 ~~~ Knap, s, fleeciness of cloth produced by fulling; Etymons of English Words, 1826 ~~~ TO RAISE THE NAP ON CLOTH. When woollens are worn thread-bare, as is generally the case in the elbows, cuffs, sleeves, &c. of men's coats, the coat, &c. must be soaked in cold water for half an hour, then taken out of the water and put on a board, and the thread-bare parts of the cloth rubbed with a half-worn hatters' card, filled with flocks, or with a prickly thistle, until a sufficient nap is raised. When this is done, hang your coat, &c. up to dry, and with a hard brush lay the nap the right way. This is the method which is pursued by the dealers in old clothes. *Godey's Ladies Book*, July 1832

nap – These reticules are frequently made of white haircloth, and embroidered with floss silk; but as these materials may not be conveniently procured, we will recommend thick gros-de-nap, lined with stiff linen, muslin, or buckram. Half a yard of silk will be sufficient. American Girl's Book, 1831 ~~~ She knew very well what gros de Naples was, (or gro de nap, as it is commonly called,) [story: Laura Lovel] *Casket*, May 1834 ~~~ [ad] Have received by the ships Hark-away and Jefferson, direct from Liverpool, … 2 cases rich figured Gro de Nap, Poi de Soi, and other plain and figured silks. *Farmer's Register*, May 1835 [see *gros de Naples*]

narrow cloth – Halifax. … the principal fabrics are … broad and narrow cloths. They are generally woven by poor manufacturers, and sold in an unfinished state to the merchants, who dye and prepare them for foreign and home consumption. State of the Poor, 1797 ~~~ The coarser wool of Yorkshire, and the northern counties, is used in the narrow cloths. *Weekly Magazine*, June 2, 1798 ~~~ The cloths of inferior fineness are mostly called narrow cloths, and are made of all qualities as to strength and thickness. Some of those used for great-coats, by their substance and shagginess, resemble the original fleece, or rather the fur of a bear, and render unnecessary the use of furred garments among us. Arts of Life, 1802 ~~~ We manufacture, principally, narrow cloth, called kerseymeres, of about 31 inches wide, when finished; we also make some broad cloths from the two higher qualities of the wool. American Tariffs, 1828 ~~~ The operation of fulling has the further effect of thickening the cloth, and rendering it more firm and *compact*, by mixing the threads with each other, something in the manner of felt. The cloths of inferior fineness are mostly called narrow cloths. Some of those used for great-coats, by their substance and shagginess, resemble the original fleece, or rather the fur of a bear, and render unnecessary the used of furred garments. Fourth Book of Lessons, 1835 ~~~ *Narrow cloths*, which are half the breadth of the broad, are generally of stronger fabric, and not so fine [as superfine broad cloth]. Of these a great exportation takes place. *Kerseymeres*, which are generally narrow, are twilled, and of various thicknesses. Scenes of Commerce, 1836 [see also *broad cloth*]

natalien – The new materials for mantles are of fine Cashmere wool; that called *Natalien*, is of a very original description: being of a double kind it does not require lining. *Casket*, January 1832

navy cloth – To Wm. Dyke, Esq. for great merit in a piece of navy cloth, manufactured from English wool, as the production of a manufactory recently established by that gentleman in his neighbourhood, Annals of Agriculture, 1802 ~~~ [from London to Madras] Cloth and Casimeres. 2 pieces best blue Navy cloth. Oriental Commerce, 1813 [see *kersey*]

neat's leather – Mr Morrison … manufactures calves skins, cordovan, neats leather, cordovan and calves legs for boots, <u>History of Berwick upon Tweed</u>, 1799 ~~~ about the 1st of December 1801 the planting commenced, … The hands of the planters were guarded by a piece of neat's leather, to save the palm, with a hole in it for the thumb, to keep it in its place, and fixed on the hind by a strap of the same sort passing round it. *Farmer's Magazine*, May 1805 ~~~ leather made of the skin of an ox or cow. <u>Universal Technological Dictionary</u>, 1823 ~~~ in 1831 the whole value of boots and shoes made at Lynn was $942,000: … neats leather $14,224, *Niles' Weekly Register*, November 23, 1833 [see also *calf skin*]

negro cloth – *Manufactures of wool, and mixtures thereof with cotton and flax,* form another branch of peculiar importance, from their being principally the productions of domestic industry, at times and seasons which can be spared from other occupations. These are broad and narrow cloths, chiefly common or coarse, …and negro cloth in very large quantities, <u>View of the United States of America</u>, 1794 ~~~ The Acadians manufacture a little cotton into quilts and cottonades; and in the remote parts of the province the poorer planters spin and weave some negro cloths of cotton and wool mixed. <u>An Account of Louisiana</u>, 1803 ~~~ No owner of any slaves, (except liverymen and boys,) shall suffer such slaves to have, or wear, any sort of apparel whatsoever, finer, or of greater value, than negro cloth, duffils, kerseys, oznaburgs, blue linen, check linen, or course garlix, or calicoes, checked cottons, or Scots plaids, under the pain of forfeiting all and every such apparel and garment; <u>A Digest of the Laws of South-Carolina</u>, 1822 ~~~ a sample of what they call "American Negro cloth." In point of strength and durability, it is supposed to hold a decided preference over the foreign article, and during the past season, we are told that 50,000 yards of it were distributed in the southern parts of our country. It is 27 inches wide, and, by the quantity, may be had for 35 cents per yard, if contracted for early in the season the warp is cotton, and the commodity seems as well fitted to resist the cold as any thing at thirty five cents per yard could be expected to be. Indeed, it is a firm, solid article, that will apparently do twice the service of the coarse British goods called "plains," and we should suppose that it would weigh one half more, square yard against square yard. In all coarse goods, the *scale* is the best test of quality. *Niles' Weekly Register*, May 10, 1823 ~~~ It is, however, to be remarked, that the consumption of British manufactured negro cloths during the last four years, has materially decreased, and the importers have not been able to sell any quantity of them at prices to over cost, and the *retailers* say that they make a far greater profit on the American manufactured coarse cloth than on the British. … Must we be "brayed in a mortar" before we shall comprehend that British "free trade" doctrines are manufactured for *exportation* – as "negro cloths" were in Yorkshire, out of old clothes, and *glued* together to make them seem substantial? *Niles' Weekly Register*, November 17, 1827 ~~~ I have no hesitation in saying, that a suit of stout twilled cotton drilling would last as long as two of the miserable trash of woollen, called negro cloths, which cost more than double per yard square; and feel very certain the cotton drilling only requires a trial, to entirely supersede the use of wool for the clothing of slaves, *American Farmer*, January 4, 1828 ~~~ Before the Tariff of 1824, a large part of the negro cloths imported from England were made out of old clothes, torn into tatters by machinery, and reduced again to something like wool. … Of what kind of wool are the fabrics made, commonly called negro cloths, and where is it produced? – They are usually made of the Smyrna, Buenos Ayres, and Adrianople wool, … Do you know of any manufacturing establishment using exclusively the coarsest foreign wool; and what kind of fabrics do they produce? – I know of one … The cloth which they make is called and known as negro cloths. <u>American Tariffs</u>, 1828 ~~~ Negro cloths, of wool, the actual value of which at the place where imported, shall not exceed 33 1/8 cents per square yard – [duty of] 14 cts. per sq. yd. *Public Documents*, March 23, 1832 [see also *plains*]

Nereid – A refinement in the use of colors has taken place at Paris; and the milliners and dress-makers are equally busy in adapting it to hats and robes. It is a worked silk, the grain of which is extremely fine, and has received the appellation of the sea-nymph, (*Nereid*). *Ladies' Monthly Museum*, October 1822 ~~~ a new and very beautiful material called *Néréide*, was most in request with the youthful *belles*; *La Belle Assemblée*, March 1830 ~~~ Among the new materials for dinner dress are oriental muslins and *Nereides*, both fully equal to those made in France. *Ladies' Museum*, June 1830 [same as *nerida* or *nerine*?]

Nerida silk – Carriage Costume. – Amaranth colored high dress of Nerida silk, or fine cachemire, trimmed round the borders with three rows of broad chinchilla fur, *Yorkshire Observer*, November 9, 1822 ~~~ [Paris] A new kind of silk for gowns has recently made its appearance, and is in high estimation; it is of Lyons manufacture, and is called nerida. It much resembles the shagreen *gros de Naples*. *Ladies' Monthly Museum*, November 1822 [see also *Lyons* and *shagreen silk*]

nerine – At Paris the new silk called *nerine*, first made its appearance this month [October 1822]; it is fabricated at Lyons, and has much the appearance of shagreen silk. <u>Museum of Foreign Literature</u>, 1823 ~~~ Nerine silk is much worn in evening dress, chiefly of pink, as being a good color for candle-light; *La Belle Assemblée*, March 1823 [probably also *nereid*; in Greek mythology, Nerine was a Nereid]

net – The Queen, was dressed in a silver tissue petticoat, with a drapery of white velvet net, *Scots Magazine*, April 1795 ~~~ The Society had long considered the Weaving Fishing-nets as an object of very considerable importance, and during many years offered Premiums for obtaining that end, but without success, till this Session j when a proper Specimen of the Netting having been produced, and found, on examination, to have every requisite wished for, the Premium of Fifty Guineas was adjudged to Mr. J. W. Boswell, of Barnstaple, the Inventor of a Machine of which a Plate is annexed, and a Sample of the Netting reserved in the Society's Repository for the inspection of the Public. SIR, I BEG leave to present, for the inspection of the Society, a sample of Net, more than eight feet wide and thirty yards long, made on a machine of my own invention. On this machine sixty-eight meshes are made at the same time, and by the same motion, with a perfect fast knot, the same as used by fishermen, and the net made thereby has a perfect selvedge; circumstances which, as they include whatever is regarded as necessary to perfection in Netting, will, I humbly hope, entitle me to the approbation of the Society for this invention, and procure me the distinguished honour of their Premium offered for the best specimen of Netting. ... I hope soon to present a sample of exceeding fine Net, in imitation of lace, made on a finer machine,- which I have now nearly ready for working. This invention, as a circumstance equally curious and novel, may be of great utility to this country, in diminishing the large sums that annually leave it for the importation of lace. <u>Transactions of the Society</u>, 1795 ~~~ [court dress] A very marked and elegant drapery of scarlet nett, in Vandykes, bordered with black velvet, and embroidered in gold. *Lady's Magazine*, January 1797 ~~~ The Queen. A blue sarsnet petticoat, entirely covered with Turkish silver net, superb fringe and tassels, and a chain bordering; *Scots Magazine*, June 1804 ~~~ *Specification of the Patent granted to* Robert Brown, *of the Town and County of the Town of Nottingham, Lace Manufacturer; for a Machine to be affixed or attached to Horizontal Warp or Vandyke Knitting Frames, for the Purpose of manufacturing, by a more simple, neat and expeditious Method, Lace or Nett Work of various Figures and Qualifies, with Thread, Silk, Cotton, Worsted, or other Material produced from Animal, Vegetable, or Mineral Substances.* Dated May 14, 1804. ... To make Brussels lace, ... To make tactic lace, ... To make Valenciennes lace, *Repertory of Arts*, April 1805 ~~~ An Evening, or Ball Dress. ... The shawl drapery, formed of a large square of pink patent net, ... [Paris] a dress prepared for the Princess Amelia: – It is composed of black net lace, quite plain; ... This dress (whose ground-work is of most transparent texture) is worn over an under-dress of highly polished white satin; and has the most novel, beautiful, and splendid effect I ever witnessed. *La Belle Assemblée*, April 1807 ~~~ [dresses belonging to Princess Charlotte] A dress of white net, embroidered in gold lama, an elegant border over white satin; ... A dress of transparent net, worked in bright and dead silver; *Niles' Weekly Register*, June 22, 1816 ~~~ Nottinghamshire. The activity of trade at Nottingham at this time surpasses all precedent. The demand for net lace, principally by French purchasers, who come over for the purpose of stocking themselves with it, is beyond all calculation. In France the net is ingeniously worked (filled up) with silk or cotton patterns, and thus its value is greatly enhanced: it is then for the most part sent back to England, as French lace, and fetches a very high price. *New Monthly Magazine*, August 1824 ~~~ [ad] Thread Nets, for dresses, beginning at 7d. per yard, *Examiner*, June 18, 1826 ~~~ Lace is a delicate kind of net work, which is much used for ornament in female dress. The meshes of this kind of net are of a hexagonal figure, and are formed by twisting or plaiting together very fine threads of silk, flax, or cotton. Thick threads are also woven into the net to form the figures or pattern, according to some design; and these thick threads, which are called gimp, form the ornament of the lace. ... Mr. Heathcoat has recently invented machinery, by which his second machine is made to interweave the gimp in figures or flowers at the same time that the lace is made. Hitherto the machines have only made the plain net, and the figures have been worked by hand after the net was finished. Edinburgh Encyclopædia, 1830 ~~~ Her Majesty. A net dress, embroidered in silver, over rich pink satin, *Court Journal*, June 22, 1833 ~~~ NET. *s.* A texture interwoven with large interstices or meshes. Ladies' Lexicon, 1835 ~~~ There is a great deal of variety in evening head-dresses. Nets, which have now lost their primitive form, have taken others so varied, and of such different colours, that they have become quite an ornament of fancy. *Court Magazine*, March 1836 [see also *bobbin-net, lace* and *tulle*; *gossamer net, patent lace, Nottingham, Italian net, Opera net*, etc.]

new drapery – In 1567 the persecutions and wars in the Low Countries drove great numbers hither, who first introduced the manufacture of baizes and other slight woollen goods (then called new Drapery) at Canterbury, Sandwich, Maidstone, Colchester, Norwich, Southampton, &c. Woodfall's Parliamentary Reports, 1800 ~~~ The greater part of the combing wool is consumed in worsted for making what is called new drapery in the Book of Rates, viz. shaloon from 6d. to 2s. 8d.; callimanco, 9d. to 2s. 2d.; everlasting, 1s. 3d. to 4s.; satinet, 2s. to 4s.; camblet, 10d. to 1s. 8d.; stuffs, broad and narrow, single and double, 6d. to 1s. 6d ; plush, 8d. to 3s. 6d. and worsted crapes, from 7d. to 9d. per yard. Origin of Commerce, 1801 ~~~ [1821] What is the peculiarity in the manufacture of cassinet? – It has cotton warp, that is a new drapery: kerseymere, the pattern of which is just below, pays eight pence halfpenny, being old drapery; it has a worsted warp. Can you state the distinction between old and new drapery? – New drapery may be made of worsted alone, as stuffs; or manufactures made of woollen, with cotton or linen warps; and woollens that have not gone through the process of milling in the tuck-mill; if they were wholly woollen they would pay that duty, though they had not been through the tuck-mill. Sessional Papers, 1823

Night Thought – [see *patent net*]

Nile cloth – [see *Egyptian cloth*]

Norwich crape – From the beginning of the present century, 'till within these forty years, this kingdom alone took of a very considerable quantity of stuffs of various kinds: the crapes of Norwich were in very common use, and during the administration of Sir Robert Walpole, and it long as the city had powerful friends at court, the public mournings were always ordered to be in Norwich crapes. This unpleasant fabric, unsupported by ministerial influence, soon fell into disgrace, and gave way to more elegant manufactures; *Monthly Magazine*, December 1798 ~~~ The mourning ordered for the Court on the melancholy occasion of her Majesty's death, consists of bombazeen, black crape, long lawn, and plain muslin for dress. Norwich crape for undress. It is probable, that these materials will not be worn according to the strict letter of the Lord Chamberlain's orders, by any ladies but those connected with the Court, *Ladies' Monthly Museum*, December 1818 ~~~ [ad] The best Norwich Crapes, measure ¾ wide – 3*s.* per yard. *Evangelical Magazine*, April 1822 ~~~ a round dress of milk-white bombasin, or Norwich crape, *Manchester Iris*, January 11, 1823 ~~~ [Paris] A dress has appeared of rose-coloured Norwich crape, *Ladies' Museum*, April 1829 ~~~ Norwich crapes, technically so called, being composed of the same materials as *bombasins*, only not *twilled*, and considered in the light of *plain bombasins*, *Public Documents*, February 15, 1832 ~~~ A tissue of silk and worsted, similar in many respects to Bombazeen, but plain, is termed Norwich Crape. Analytical Dictionary, 1835 [see also *bombazine*]

Nottingham lace – [in Nottingham] Lace-workers earn from 20s. to 40s. a week. State of the Poor, 1797 ~~~ The Nottingham imitations of lace are of two kinds, point-net and warp-net. From the names of the machines in which they are made, they are both a species of chain-work, and the machines are varieties of the stocking frame. The warp frame makes a very close imitation of the Brussels lace, but has very little durability. … The Nottingham lace trade was very considerable some years ago, but is at present in a state of stagnation. The lace, when well made, is exceedingly beautiful and regular; and hence it was much esteemed at first, particularly the large pieces for making veils and dresses; but, when the want of durability was detected, it lost its value: Still, as the manufacturers were able to make it at a very cheap rate, they sold immense quantities for some years. Edinburgh Encyclopædia, 1830 ~~~ we have been informed, by persons who seemed to know, that *British lace* is the term used by the

Nottingham manufacturers, to distinguish the wove net-lace from that made with bobbins in Northamptonshire, Bedfordshire, and the neighbouring counties; *Eclectic Review*, October 1812 ~~~ Her Royal Highness the Duchess of Kent. A beautiful Nottingham blonde dress over white satin, train of blue and silver brocaded silk, trimmed with silver; *Royal Lady's Magazine*, May 1831 [see also *British lace* and *warp lace*]

nuns' veiling – [see *crystal*]

nutria – *Importations at Liverpool* [from Brazil] … 10 bales nutria skins, *Tradesman*, November 1809 ~~~ the Nutria, or Musk Beaver, … Musquash (Musk Beaver) *New Monthly Magazine*, September 1828 ~~~ Nutria, or Neutria, … In France, the skins were, and perhaps still are, sold under the name of *racoonda*; but in England they are imported as *nutria* skins – deriving their appellation, most probably, from some supposed similarity of the animal which produces them, in appearance and habits, to the otter, the Spanish name for which is nutria . Indeed, Molina speaks of the *coypou* as a species of water rat, of the size and colour of the otter. Nutria fur is largely used in hat manufacture; and has become, within the last fifteen or twenty years, an article of very considerable commercial importance. … Like the beaver, the coypou is furnished with two kinds of fur; viz. the long ruddy hair which gives the tone of the colour, and the brownish ash-coloured fur at its base, which, like the down of the beaver, is of such importance in hat-making, and the cause of the animal's commercial value. *The Mirror*, October 27, 1832 ~~~ I have sent the skin of a female Nutria, herewith, for your inspection, (from which the fur has been cut by machinery,) with a small sample of the belly fur, prepared for the covering of a hat; the wholesale price of the latter is now three guineas per lb.: it is used as a substitute for beaver-wool in second-rate hats. Our French correspondents term the skins "Ratgondin." The skin is rather above the usual size: its length is 26 inches, the tail being cut off, as is always done before skins are exported: the width of the skin is 15 inches, Import and Export Guide, 1834

Odalisque - Ozenbrig

odalisque – The voices and dresses of the singers seemed to be alike worn out. The young maidens of Sidon, in odalisques of violet colour, blue, &c. had a very bad effect. Private Journal of Madame Campan, 1829 ~~~ *Albaniennes, odalisques,* and other fancy materials are worn in dinner dress, *Ladies' Pocket,* June 1830 ~~~ Some new materials for autumn have already appeared, both for elegant *negligé* and evening dress. We may cite some *mousselines de laines* of perfectly new patterns; some of a simple kind, others complicated, but none of that large and glaring description that were so prevalent last year. The most striking among the new patterns are the *Odalisques* of a great variety of colours on a green or grey ground; *Court Magazine,* October 1834

oil-skin – The author has known severe head-achs [sic] occasioned … by going into the bath with the head covered with an oil-skin cap, a piece of furniture which should be excluded the bathing-room. *British Critic,* October 1805 ~~~ *Oil-skin and Wax-Cloth.* – The art of impregnating silk or linen, with oil or wax, so as to become impervious to water, has also been rendered subservient to the purposes of clothing. Hats have been covered with these substances, – a practice which may be serviceable to those who are much out of doors in the wet seasons of the year. Oilskin dresses may likewise be of use in certain diseases, as the gout, or the rheumatism, where a violent perspiration is necessary. Oil-skin socks, however, by excluding the air, and retaining the perspiration, may create great weakness in the feet and ancles. Code of Health and Longevity, 1816 ~~~ the plaintiff was an army-clothier and tailor of great respectability, … and sought to recover from the defendant, Captain John Jebb, of the Royal Horse Guards (Blue), the sum of 24*l.* for a remarkably large and handsome cavalry cloak, lined throughout with silk oil-skin, water proof, and made to order. Annual Register, 1818 ~~~ Oil-skin, or Wax-cloth, increases perspiration in an uncommon degree, but does not suffer it to evaporate again, and is, therefore, only admissible in certain diseases. Toilette of Health, Beauty, and Fashion, 1834 ~~~ Oil-skin cloaks, or mantles, might be either made of silk or of varnished waxed cloth. I should prefer the latter as being the strongest. Friend of Australia, 1836

oiseaux de Paradis –Turbans are becoming very fashionable – ornamented with diamonds, feathers or oiseaux de Paradis. *Lady's Magazine and Museum,* December 1834 [see *bird of paradise*]

old drapery – [see *new drapery*]

olgatino – A new material, named *olgatino,* is invented for winter dresses; it is of very fine stuff, with large Persian patterns over it. *La Belle Assemblée,* December 1828

Omasis – Evening costume is still of a light kind; several new materials have, however, appeared for it. We may cite among them the … *Velours, Algibeck,* and *Omasis*… These rich and beautiful materials will be in great request as soon as the winter has fairly set in. *Ladies' Pocket,* November 1836 ~~~ [Paris] Some superb materials have appeared for evening dress; the most *distingué* are the *velours Algibeck* and *Ornasis, Court Magazine,* November 1836

opera cloth – [ad for men's] Opera Cloth walking Cloaks £1 16s. *Eminent Foreign Statesmen,* March 1836

opera net – [ad] Opera Nets for Dresses; *La Belle Assemblée,* January 1807 ~~~ For home and dinner dresses, sarsnets, Opera nets and coloured muslin, among those who reject virgin white, seem most prevailing. *La Belle Assemblée,* June 1810 ~~~ Evening dresses of Imperial or Opera grey nets over white satin, muffs, tippets, and trimmings of sable, are in general wear for the promenade; as are those of swansdown in a higher degree of dress. *La Belle Assemblée,* December 1810 ~~~ coloured muslins, crapes, Opera nets, gossamer satins, and French sarsnets, for evening parties; *La Belle Assemblée,* July 1812 [see *net*]

orangelist – A seven quarters wide Baize, dyed in fancy colours, is exported, chiefly to Spain, under the name of Orangelist. Analytical Dictionary, 1830 [see *baize*]

organdy – No person in Turkey, Persia or Europe has yet imitated the *Betille* *, made at *Masulipatan,* and known under the name of *Organdi.* The manufacturing of this cloth, which was known in the time of Job, the painting of it, and the preparation of the colours, give employment in India to male and female, young and old. … * A certain kind of white East Indian chintz. Voyage to the East Indies, 1800 ~~~We saw lately a very beautiful summer gown for half dress; it was of that improved leno, know in France by the name of organdy; the ground was white, and had satin stripes of that beautiful and becoming red lilac, the marshmallow-blossom colour. *La Belle Assemblée*, August 1825 ~~~ In Paris, the heat of the weather this month [September] was intense, and the thinnest muslin pelisse was hardly light enough for the Gallic *merveilleuse*; and as organdy was thinner than muslin, this material was universally adopted for summer pelisses in the morning walks in the country: they were trimmed with very broad lace, set on full and in scallops, the *corsage* was made tight to the shape, and they formed a very smart and becoming summer costume. *La Belle Assemblée*, Summary of the last six months, 1825 ~~~ [Paris] Some charming dresses of *organdie*, with cachemere designs, have just appeared. The designs are printed in such a manner as to form partitions between the large folds, the space of which is calculated in the arrangement of the borders. *Ladies' Monthly Museum*, June 1826 ~~~ painted *organdys* for evening parties. *La Belle Assemblée*, September 1831 ~~~ Costume de Bal ou de Soiree. – Dress of organdi (book muslin), embroidered in coloured worsteds, *Lady's Magazine and Museum*, October 1834 ~~~ Printed *organdis*, though not yet adopted, are likely to be very fashionable, both patterns and colours are of a delicate kind. *Court Magazine*, May 1835 ~~~ The new evening dresses are principally of gauze, crape, and organdy; this latter material is indeed carried to a perfection that almost rivals gauze in beauty and transparency. We have seen some very pretty robes composed of it, and trimmed with rose or blue satin ribbon. *Court Magazine*, April 1836 ~~~ Morning Dress. Of *organdi*, checked with pink. *Court Magazine*, September 1836 ~~~ Organdi, *s. m.* (mousseline de coton) *Clear muslin*. <u>Boniface's French Dictionary</u>, 1836 ~~~ [Paris] At the Opera, … robes are in application of Brussels or fine thread net, or of organdi embroidered in dead white silk, which provides somewhat of the effect of an embroidery in silver. *Court Magazine*, October 1836 [see also *book muslin*]

organzine – *Considerations on the Attempt of the East-India Company to become Manufacturers in Great Britain*. 4to. 34 pp. 2s. Sewell. 1796. … The East-India Company had formed some resolutions of importing raw silk in large quantities, and throwing some portion of it into organzine (silk prepared) in order to serve as a substitute for the organzine now imported from Italy. *British Critic*, August 1798 ~~~ It has frequently been remarked, among other absurdities, that when the machine is completely in motion, "it works 73,726 yards of organzine silk-thread by every revolution of the water-wheel," which turns once round every nineteen seconds. The mere view of the machine is sufficient to convince any person, that the quantity of yards wound every circuit of the wheel cannot be told; neither, indeed, is it open to calculation; for the threads are so continually breaking, (not to mention other difficulties that render the attempt insuperable,) that the power of numbers must ever be inadequate to ascertain the amount. <u>Beauties of England and Wales</u>, 1802 ~~~ ORGANZINE, in commerce, a description of silk usually imported from Italy into this country. It is of the utmost importance to the manufacturer, as none of the principal articles could be fabricated without it; and the Italians aware of this, long kept the art of throwing it a most profound secret. It was introduced into this country by the enterprize and skin of Messrs. Thomas and John Lombe, the latter having at the risk of his life, and with wonderful ingenuity, taken a plan of one of these complicated machines, in the King of Sardinia's dominions, from which, on his return, they established a similar set of mills in the town of Derby; and in consideration of the great hazard and expense attending the undertaking, a patent was granted to Sir Thomas Lombe, in 1718, … The process which the silk undergoes to bring it into this state, consists of six different operations: 1. The silk is wound from the skein upon bobbins. 2. It is then sorted. 3. It is spun, or twisted, on a mill in the single thread. 4. Two threads thus spun are doubled, or drawn together through the fingers of a woman, who at the same time cleans them by taking out the slubs which may have been left in the silk by the negligence of the foreign reeler. 5. It is then thrown by a mill, that is, the two threads are twisted together either slack or hard, as the manufacture may require; and it is wound at the same time in skeins upon a reel. 6. The skeins are sorted according to their different degrees of fineness, and then the process is complete. Organzine was for many years made only from Italian silk, but when considerable improvements were made in the culture of silk in India, it suggested the possibility of throwing some of the finer silks of Bengal into organzine. The experiments of individuals were not very satisfactory, but in the beginning of 1794, the East India Company took up the subject with the view of increasing the annual consumption of Bengal silk in this country; and having it in their power to select from their total import the silks most proper for this purpose, they have been enabled, at each subsequent sale, to put up from 80 to 100 bales of good Bengal organzine. It has been adopted successively in several branches of the manufacture; and in the year 1808, when the prohibition of exportation from Italy produced a scarcity of the silks of that country, attempts were made to substitute Bengal organzine for all the purposes to which Italian organzine was applied; the result, however, appeared to be that, for some particular articles, Italian organzine possesses peculiar properties not to be found in any other kind of silk. British Encyclopedia, 1809 ~~~ Organzine is silk prepared for forming the warp of the stuff designed to be woven in the loom. General Dictionary of Commerce, 1810 ~~~ Organzine, s. (a sort of double-twisted silk, and twisting) New Dictionary, English and French, 1815 ~~~ *Organzine*, in French *organsin*, is the next in fineness. It is employed, in weaving, to make the warp of those stuffs that are made entirely of silk. ... Of the three qualities of raw silk of which those different threads are made, the second, that which makes *organzine*, is the most in demand in foreign markets. *Report of the Committee on Agriculture on the Growth and Manufacture of Silk*, May 24, 1830 ~~~ There are three kinds of raw silk, organzine, tram, and floss. Organzine is used for the warp of silk goods, requires the best quality of silk, usually contains from six to eight filaments in one thread, and it receives a considerable twist to make it strong and free from flocky points. The tram is made from inferior silk, and consists of ten or twelve filaments slightly twisted together. ... To make organzine, the thread of raw silk is first twisted, and two of these threads are then united by twisting. In the process of making tram, the original single thread is not twisted at all, but two of them in their simple state are softly twisted together. Thus, in organzine, there is a compound torsion for giving firmness to warp threads, and in tram there is a single torsion, of only such a degree as to make the thread bear the tension of throwing it by the shuttle across the web. Philosophy of Manufactures, 1835

oriental – Ball Dress. ... Skirt of gaze d'orient of a pale marrow-colour, *Casket*, March 1831 ~~~ Ball Dress. A gown of blue Adelaide gaze orientale; *La Belle Assemblée*, April 1831 ~~~ [Court dress] A white Oriental gauze dress, ornamented with gold, lined with satin, trimmed with blonde; *Royal Lady's Magazine*, June 1831 ~~~ Evening Dress. This magnificent dress, worn in the Parisian circles of the highest rank, is made of the silk called *gros d'orient*, richly brocaded with flowers. The whole style of this beautiful dress may be imitated with great advantage in a less costly, and indeed, less heavy material, by substituting satin for brocaded silk, *Lady's Magazine*, January 1830 ~~~ Pelisses are of *gros orient*, or rich, shot silks; *Lady's Magazine*, October 1830 ~~~ Rich plain silks, as ... *gros d'Orient*, &c., are also in request. *La Belle Assemblée*, July 1831 ~~~ Many undress bonnets are composed of *gros des Indes*, or *gros d'Orient*; both of which, we must observe, are now made of a richness very little inferior to velvet itself. *La Belle Assemblée*, December 1831 ~~~ [Court dress] a train of rich lilac d'orient, ... a morning carriage-bonnet, of white *gros d'orient*; *Royal Lady's*, April 1836 ~~~ [court dress] A dress of white velour d'orient, embroidered in silver, *Court Journal*, April 20, 1833 ~~~ The new materials most likely to be in favour in evening dress are, ... *Foulard d'Orient*, a mixture of cashmere and silk, figured in another shade of the same colour. *Court Magazine*, April 1834

Orleans – As silk manufactures formed a more considerable portion of the annual exportations of France than all her other manufactures together, it is important to observe, that Nantes, Tours, and Orleans, which, next to Lyons, were the most considerable seats of these manufactures, have equally suffered, and are represented as having been totally annihilated under the reign of terror. Historical ... Losses Sustained by the French Nation, 1799 ~~~ [court dress] A white figured silk dress, trimmed with point lace; a train of blue-coloured gros d'Orleans, lined with white, *Royal Lady's Magazine*, June 1831 ~~~ [court dress] A white *aerophane* dress, embroidered in white floss silk, over white satin; corsage trimmed with blonde; manteau of figured lilac Orleans silk and blonde. *Court Journal*, March 16, 1833 ~~~ [court dress] train à la Suedoise of velour d'Orleans de blanc, ... [sisters' court dresses] trains of vert peruche gros d'Orleans, trimmed with blonde. *Court Journal*, June 1, 1833 ~~~ [court dress] A tulle dress over white satin, ... manteau of lilac soie d'Orleans, lined with white, and trimmed with blonde and silver; *Court Journal*, April 20, 1833 ~~~ [court dress] Blonde over white satin, tastefully trimmed with violets and French blonde; mantille and ruffles of blonde; train of white satin gros d'Orleans, trimmed with satin and lined with white silk. *Lady's Magazine and Museum*, May 1836

Ornasis – [see *Omasis*]

orre net – New Articles. ... the Orre Net, which is just brought out by the Inventor, Mr. George Rawlinson of Taunton, and Wood Street, London, in very beautiful patterns, and great variety of colours. These articles are of the same fabric as the Blonde Lace, and very beautiful as well as durable; and we have no doubt will come into very general use, being British manufacture, and giving employment to a large portion of our industrious poor. *Day*, June 9, 1832

orris – Orris, ... a kind of gold or silver lace; Barclay's English Dictionary, 1799 ~~~ [patent] To George Finch, jun., of King Street, Soho, orris weaver, for certain methods of manufacturing various kinds of metal laces, so as to imitate gold and silver laces; and also of manufacturing gold and silver open laces. Feb. 4. *Philosophical Magazine*, March 1809 ~~~ ORRIS, a peculiar pattern in which gold and silver laces are worked. The edges are usually ornamented with conical figures placed at equal distances, with spots between them. Dictionary of Commerce, 1810 ~~~ [ad] the much admired Orris-nets, at 3s. per yard, calculated either for Morning or Evening Dress, *Repository of Arts*, April 1815 [Orray-nets? The ink is smeared]

osagine gauze – Osagine-gauze is worn at evening dress parties; and gowns of this material are generally trimmed with flounces of broad *blond*, and otherwise ornamented with gauze ribbons striped with satin; ... Long sleeves, which those ladies wear who are peculiarly susceptible of cold, are, notwithstanding, of a texture so fine, that they set off the turn of them arm to the best advantage: there is certainly, much warmth in them, though it is not apparent. I am informed that this *tissu* is used for under-stockings; in the fear that wearing cotton or thread, under silk, might make the leg appear too thick. *La Belle Assemblée*, January 1828

osier baleine – [see *whalebone* and *willow*]

osnaburgh – Osnabergs are a kind of coarse linen, first made at Osnaberg, in Westphalia, Germany, of which there are two kinds; the one white, and the other brown. The manufacture of the white is well understood in our own country: but the method practised in Germany of making the brown sort, and giving it its peculiar colour, is not known. Some have supposed, that it depends on the manner of bleaching the flax, and others on that of bleaching the yarn after it is spun. Arithmetical Questions, 1795 ~~~ 1797 ~~~ *for the better regulation of the linen and hempen manufactures*; it is amongst other things enacted, That all brown or unbleached linen cloths, called or known by the name of dowlass sheetings, or ozenbrigs, manufactured or made in the provinces of Munster or Connaught, may be sold, or exposed to sale in any place in the said provinces, without being sealed: And whereas it is expedient that all such linens should be sealed as other linens are required to be, before they are fold or exposed to sale; Statutes Passed in the Parliaments Held in Ireland, 1799 ~~~ Osnabruck is a very strong and solid kind of hempen linen, manufactured in the bishoprick of Osnabruck. Its width is 1 ½ Bremen ells, and from 100 to 108 staple or double ells in length. ... The chief markets for it are America, the West Indies, and Spain. European Commerce, 1805 ~~~ The common dress of the men is an Osnaburgh or check frock, and Osnaburgh trowsers, with a coarse hat, but no shoes; so little are these *in fashion* among the negroes, that they are seldom worn, even when they dress out the most gaudily in other respects, nor are they usually worn even by gentlemen's servants. The common dress of the women is an Osnaburgh or coarse linen shift, a petticoat made of various stuff, according to their taste and circumstances, and a handkerchief tied round their heads. ...The annual allowance of clothing which they receive from their owners, is as much Osnaburgh as will make two frocks, and as much woollen stuff as will make a great coat; with a hat, handkerchief, knife, and needles and thread to make up their clothes. This specific quantity an owner is obliged by law to give to his slaves, and many humanely allow them more. Account of Jamaica, 1808 ~~~ Osnabrug or Osnaburgh linen, ... a sort of coarse linen-cloth, manufactured at Osnaburgh, in Germany, whence its name. The Germans sell this linen to the English, the Dutch, and the Spaniards, who, for the most part, send it to their respective colonies. ... We have an imitation of this linen in many parts of Great Britain, called Osnaburgh. General Dictionary of Commerce, 1810 ~~~ Osnaburg takes its name from a place on the Continent, and is used for wrappers, linings, &c. Linen Manufacturer, 1817 ~~~ The slaves are usually provided with three suits of clothing a year, which they commonly make up themselves from the various stuffs delivered to them. Their hats and woollen caps are made in England, I believe expressly for the West Indies. The frock coats of the men, and the petticoats of the female negroes are usually of baize, or osnaburg; and they have shirts, shifts, cotton handkerchiefs, and linen checks regularly dealt out to them. Four Years' Residence in the West Indies, 1833 ~~~ Yearly Allowance of Clothing [for slaves] … 1 Oznaburg petticoat (4 yards) Bulletins of State Intelligence, 1834 ~~~ [ad] Have received by the ships Hark-away and Jefferson, direct from Liverpool, … 20 bales Petersburg Merchants' Company No. 1 cotton oznaburgs, at factory prices. *Farmer's Register*, May 1835

ostrich – Feathers generally worn, chiefly ostrich. *Gentleman's Monthly*, March 1, 1803 ~~~ *Ostrich's Down*, called otherwise ostrich's hair, and sometimes wool, is of two sorts; that called the fine of ostrich, is used by hatters, in the manufacture of common hats; and that called coarse of ostrich, serves for the making of list for fine white cloth. Dictionary of Merchandize, 1803 ~~~ Court dress … Rich white satin petticoat, with bunches of fine ostrich feathers fringe round the bottom, *La Belle Assemblée*, June 1807 ~~~ Ostrich feathers are very generally used for hats, but not at all for bonnets. *Repository of Arts*, February 1819 ~~~ Flat ostrich feathers, either in pink or white, will be worn without being curled. *La Belle Assemblée*, December 1820

Otaheitan or Otaheite – [see *grebe*]

otter – Pelisses are made to fit tight to the shape, without a band, with a broad trimming of sable or of the Nootka Sound otter. *Lady's Miscellany*, June 30, 1810 ~~~ the body of this animal [sea-otter] is long, and of the same thickness throughout: from the extremity of the tail to the nose they measure five feet. The colour is a uniform dark brown, and, when in good order and season, perfectly black. This animal is unrivalled for the beauty, richness, and softness of his fur: the inner part of the fur, when opened, is lighter than the surface in its natural position: there are some black and shining hairs intermixed with the fur, which are rather longer, and add much to its beauty: Annual Register, 1817 ~~~ [Paris] The head-dress is a small otter skin, or sable cap: the former has a gold tassel and acorn; the latter an ermine band. *Repository of Arts*, March 1823 ~~~ The American furs which are at present brought to London are: … Sea-otter. An exceedingly close, fine fur, jet black in winter, when it is in perfection, exceedingly soft with a silken gloss, interspersed with shining silvery hairs, used a little in England, but chiefly sent to Russia and China. Fine skins even now fetch, at first hand, from 10*l.* to 15*l.* The fur of the young animal is a beautiful brown, like fine velvet, and covered with coarse white hair. Transactions of the Society, 1833 [see also *mink*]

ounce – [see *lynx*]

ozenbrig – [see *osnaburgh*]

Paco - Purl

paco – [see *alpaca*]

pactolus – The materials for turbans are of the most brilliant kind, and well adapted for the mid-night glare of artificial day. … the most superb material for the full dress turban, is the pactolus, or golden sand gauze, it combines both lightness and richnesss [sic], and makes up beautifully; but much care is required in not making it appear heavy, and none but a skilful *Marchande de Modes* can possibly pin up a turban of this material, so as to give it a proper effect; it is peculiarly becoming to those ladies who have dark hair and eyes. *La Belle Assemblée*, February 1823 ~~~ Evening Dress. … The head-dress consists of a turban of the Pactolus gauze, ornamented with full-blown Amaranths, and a rich plume of white feathers. *Kaleidoscope*, April 6, 1824

padding – *Paddings* – 27 inches wide, cost 5d. to 1s. – A stiff coarse cloth, for collars: sometimes worn by laborers. *Niles' Weekly Register*, March 8, 1828 ~~~ As we have several times been asked what "paddings" are – we shall inform our readers, that they are a certain kind of hard and harsh woollen stuff, thrown together, and sold in England at 5*d.* or 6*d.* per yard; and that about a cent and a half's worth of this *important* article is used by a tailor to stiffen the colour of a dandy's coat. That's all. *Niles' Weekly Register*, January 10, 1829 ~~~ Presents furnished the [Chickasaw] Indians, by order of the commissioners, … 5 yds. red padding, at 6s. per yard. [1830] <u>Executive Documents</u>, 1832 ~~~ [ad] Have received by the ships Hark-away and Jefferson, direct from Liverpool, … sail duck paddings. … 3-4 and 6-4 double milled red paddings. *Farmer's Register*, May 1835

padou – *a sort of ferret or ribband half thread half silk.* <u>Boyer's Royal Dictionary: French and English</u>, 1814

paduasoy – The principal silk stuffs brought from China are, … Plain padesos, of 14 ells by 5/8, and nearly 5/8. *New-York Magazine*, February 1795 ~~~ *Paduasoys and double ground brocades* require a grand look; the flowers and leaves are generally natural, and as much as possible to imitate embroidery. Sometimes the brocades are worked on a paduasoy double tissue, the colour of the figure whereof is commonly that of the ground, and the device of a running trail, or ornaments with mosaic, or any think [sic] that may be pleasant and agreeable to the eye. The flowers and leaves are in some rich brocades blue, red, green, yellow, or straw-colour, heightened with silver; and a deep orange, with gold. <u>Laboratory</u>, 1799 ~~~ Many kinds of stuff are called from the towns in which they were first made. Thus, … in Spital-fields, Mantuas and Paduasoys. *Monthly Magazine*, September 1805 ~~~ The stuffs for hats are *gros de Naples*, satin, and Paduasoie. *La Belle Assemblée*, March 1810 ~~~ Paduasoy, *f.* (*Padua de soye*, Fr.) A kind of stuff made originally it is supposed, at Padua, and composed of nearly equal parts of cotton and silk. <u>Encyclopædia Londinensis</u>, 1821 ~~~ A kind of silk. *Sheridan*. Written also *padesoy*. <u>Johnson's English Dictionary</u>, 1830

pagne – [in Guinea] A girdle tied across their loins, and which we call a *pagne*, is the only clothing of both sexes. … The *pagnes* are made only of a plant which grows naturally, and requires no preparation: the length of it constitutes the breadth of the piece. The weaver works it upon his lap, without either loom or shuttle, by passing the trim with his fingers between each of the threads of the chain, in the same manner as our basket-makers make their hurdles. <u>History of the Settlements and Trade of the Europeans in the East and West Indies</u>, 1804 ~~~ Some Terms in Use in Africa. … Pagnes – Cotton cloth made by the negroes; a pagne is composed of five bands, each five inches in breadth, and three cubits long. <u>Travels in Africa</u>, 1820 ~~~ [in bonnets] A fancy material, called *pagne*, though too common to be elegant, is worn by many stylish women; *La Belle Assemblée*, September 1831 ~~~ Treasury Department, *Comptroller's Office, December* 3, 1831. Sir: The Secretary of the Treasury has referred to me a letter addressed to him by Mr. Meigs D. Benjamin, upon the subject of the duty legally chargeable on the article called *satin straw* or *Pagne de I'Inde*. The article in question being generally (if not altogether) used in the manufacture of women's hats or bonnets, it was conceived that they were embraced in the 4th clause of the 1st section of the act of 22d May, 1824, under the general head of "all flats, braids, or plats, for making of hats or bonnets," more particularly as some of *the satin straw* is composed almost entirely of straw. *Public Documents*, February 15, 1832 ~~~ Moire, crape, rice straw, and pagne are the materials in favour for hats and bonnets. … Hats composed of pagne are always either grey, or the new colour called *ecru*, they are lined with cherry colour, and rose of different shades, *The Day*, May 5, 1832 [see also *payne*]

paille – *straw, chaff, flaw* Tardy's French Dictionary, 1799 [see *straw*]

paille coton – [see *cotton straw*]

paille d'Italie – [see *Leghorn*]

paille de riz – [see *rice straw*]

paille de soie – The materials for *Chapeaux* are various, and some new ones have been introduced, but we cannot yet say how far they will become fashionable; one of them called *paille de soie*, is already in some estimation, and seems likely to be in great favour; it is composed of narrow riband, plaited to resemble straw. *Ladies' Monthly Museum*, May 1819 ~~~ *Paille de soie* is also occasionally seen in the morning promenades; but it is more frequently worn in the evening, ... Straw hats are almost all yellow, and silk ones either white or rose-colour; but *paille de soie* are of various hues, pea-green, rose-colour, gilliflower, and the prettiest shade of lilac that I ever saw. *Repository of Arts*, July 1819

paillette – *a spangle, gold* Tardy's French Dictionary, 1799

painted – [court dress] Had on a superb dress of gold embroidery, ... the border of the festoons of satin, painted and embroidered in all the shades of the rainbow: *Lady's Magazine*, January 1797 ~~~ At Chelsea, there is established a new and beautiful manufacture of painted silk, View of the Agriculture of Middlesex, 1798 ~~~ Ridicules of painted velvet, of various constructions, and beautifully designed, are now much used by our *belles* of fashion. *La Belle Assemblée*, August 1807 ~~~ Prohibited Goods, Wares, and Merchandise. ... Dimities, painted. ... Painted silk gauze. Oriental Commerce, 1813 ~~~ Afternoon Costume. This is a very favorite style of *parure* adopted in the country, after returning from the morning walk or drive. It consists of a dress of painted Indian taffety, in white stripes on a ground of pearl-grey. Between the stripes are delicate figures in the most beautiful pencil-work, all of one color; and on the white stripes, small detached *bouquets*, remarkable for the variety and splendor of their colors. *Atheneum*, December 1, 1828 ~~~ Painted stuff is a material among our novelties for walking costume; it is pretty, but not adapted for summer wear. The painted *gros de Naples* for the public promenade, and for dinner parties, is extremely beautiful; the patterns are exquisite, and admirably painted. *La Belle Assemblée*, June 1829 ~~~ The continued warm weather has caused printed and painted muslins to be almost the only articles employed for promenade or carriage dress. The patterns introduced this season are exceedingly rich, both in design and colours. *Court Journal*, June 15, 1833 ~~~ Painted *gros de Naples* is occasionally seen both in morning and evening dress. Its costliness renders it very *recherché*. *Court Journal*, June 22, 1833 ~~~ Some new materials have appeared for evening dress. We may cite among the most beautiful those of painted pou de Soie, the tulles embroidered in application, and organdys either painted or embroidered. *New Monthly Belle Assemblée*, July 1836 ~~~ The few robes worn by women of high fashion are composed of painted Pekin. They have a white ground, flowered in running patterns of small delicate flowers, in vivid but not glaring hues. *Court Magazine*, August 1833

palmyrene – [Paris] A new material, called palmyrene, between a poplin and a *barège*, was introduced this month for dresses, and was extremely beautiful. *La Belle Assemblée*, Summary of July, 1827 ~~~ One of the prettiest materials now for dresses destined to evening parties, is a *tissue* called palmyrene. The embroidery in silk with which it is embellished, appears on it to high advantage. It is between a poplin and a *barège*, and is of a softness which causes the plaits to fall in a very graceful manner. *La Belle Assemblée*, September 1827 ~~~ [Paris evening dress] a rose-colored Palmyrene dress, with a black velvet body, has excited much admiration: *Ladies' Pocket*, January 1829 ~~~ [Paris] The rich mantles, and the warm *douillette*, have now given place to a high dress, or a spring pelisse; the first is composed of silk, or of some of the numerous light materials manufactured of silk and cotton, which have been, during some years, in favour with the Parisian belles, such as *Cotpalis, palmyriennes*, &c. *Ladies' Museum*, May 1830 ~~~ New patterns of silks, muslins, palmyriennes, and other fancy materials, are produced almost daily; and, were there as much variety in the make, as there is in the materials of dress, we should despair of being able to present even an abridgement of the fashions. ... Printed book-muslins, and palmyriennes, but particularly the latter, are also much worn in carriage dress. *La Belle Assemblée*,

July 1831 ~~~ *Palmyriennes* are more in favour than silks in dinner dress, *La Belle Assemblée*, September 1831 ~~~ Make and Materials of Half Dress. – *Chaly, palmyriennes*, and a variety of fancy silks, are in favour. *Atheneum*, November 1831 ~~~ palmoreens (a mixture of silk and cotton; there were none of these making previous to 1833 on the Jacquards) … in 1830, 1 *s*.; in 1835, 5 *d*.; <u>Reports from the Committees</u>, 1835

pamyrienne – *Pamyriennes en colonnes*, and printed gros de Naples, are much in favour in dinner dress. *Ladies' Museum*, May 1830 ~~~ *pamyriennes*, are among the new materials in half dress; they are changeable, being a mixture of silk and English wool of different colours. *Ladies' Museum*, February 1831

panache – they are adorned with a *panache*, that is to say, a plume *Repository of Arts*, May 1819

panne – *shag, plush*. <u>Dufief's French Dictionary</u>, 1810

pannuscorium – An establishment has been opened in the Strand, by Messrs. Hall and Co., for the manufacture of boots and shoes of this patent material, which they denominate *pannus corium*, or *leather cloth*; and they state that their boots and shoes will last longer than those made of curried substances, and that they are adapted to all climates, and have no tendency to crack. <u>Arcana of Science and Art</u>, 1830 ~~~ In some cases it is advisable that the shoe or boot should be made, not of ordinary leather, but of very soft and flexible buckskin, or of cloth. A material for shoes and boots is sold under the grandiloquent name of *pannuscorium*, which answers the purpose intended in these cases very well. It is really a kind of cloth, but it has the appearance of leather, and is very soft and pliable. *Boston Medical and Surgical Journal*, August 3, 1836 [see also *leather cloth*]

pano – Evening Half Dress. .. shawl of white Indian mohair or pano silk, *Jersey Magazine*, November 1810

paper – The ingenuity of manufacturers might discover many new objects, to which macerated linen might be applied. For instance, hats, and bonnets, for womens wear are formed of paper, which, for lightness, neatness, and durability, are not inferior, to those of straw, and chips. <u>Transactions of the Royal Irish Academy</u>, 1803 ~~~ *List of Patents*. George Simmonds, of —; for a method of manufacturing hats, bonnets, and other useful articles of paper. Dated May 19, 1804. <u>Repertory of Arts</u>, 1804 ~~~ [Paris] Hats made of rolled paper have lately come into vogue; the rolls are about the size of a corn stalk, and are divided at equal distances in diamonds or chequers, or in stripes only held together by a thread: these hats are mostly of a lilac or a rose colour. *La Belle Assemblée*, September 1819 ~~~ [Paris] within the last few days, some *chapeaux* have appeared made of a peculiar kind of wove paper. *Ladies' Monthly Museum*, May 1820 ~~~ [hats of] what is called rice straw, which, by the bye, is paper made to resemble straw finely plaited. *Repository of Arts*, August 1821 ~~~ Some of these large hats are now of stamped paper; the white, in imitation of chip: others are glazed, and died yellow, and have all the appearance of Leghorn. *La Belle Assemblée*, August 1828 ~~~ A certain kind of hats for ladies, called "Navarino hats," when first imported, were sold, in large quantities, at 8 or 10 dollars each; they are made of paper, and in a few weeks after their original introduction, were supplied of *American fabric* for about a dollar; and perhaps, cost not more then *fifty cents! Niles' Weekly Register*, August 30, 1828 ~~~ hats, composed of paper, which is now brought to such excellence as to offer a perfect imitation of watered silk; … paper hats are always lined with *gros de Naples*, wither blue or rose-colour; *La Belle Assemblée*, September 1831 ~~~ Every article of a lady's dress is now manufactured in paper, and many *élegantes* have a fancy for wearing aprons, *fichu*, &c. of that kind at home; these articles are a most excellent imitation of muslin, silk, &c. &c.; but, as may be supposed, they only last a few hours. However, the fair wearers cannot complain, for the price is but a few *sous. Atheneum*, September 1831

papier mache – The *papier mache* is paper reduced to the consistence of a pulp by boiling and beating, till it be of such a consistence, that, being cast in a moist state, in proper moulds, it will receive the form or impression of the figure of the mould; <u>Artist's Assistant</u>, 1801 ~~~ *To make papier mache*. This is a substance made of cuttings of white or brown paper, boiled in water, and beaten in a mortar till they are reduced to a kind of paste, and then boiled with a solution of gum arabic, or of size, to give tenacity to the paste, which is afterwards formed into different toys, &c. by pressing it into oiled moulds. When dry, it is done over with a mixture of size and lamp-black, and afterwards varnished. <u>Five Thousand Receipts</u>, 1825 ~~~ an article called by the imported "*dried pulp*," but which is known by the manufacturers of it in this country [USA], by the name of "*tip paper*," and in Europe is called "*papier mache*," being used by milliners for stiffening the tops of bonnets; by hatters for the top linings of coarse hats; *Public Documents*, January 26, 1829 ~~~ In Paris, a very economical mode of procuring the materials for *papier-maché* is now adopted – the walls being diligently stripped of the posting-bills, which thus afford both paper and paste for the moulding of snuff-boxes, &c. <u>Servant's Guide</u>, 1831

Paris cord – what we call Paris Cord, or rich Tabby, <u>Sessional Papers</u>, June 26, 1823 ~~~ an Article, called Paris Cord, which it is rather important to mention. This Work had then been recently introduced from France, and had not been before made in this Country; it is now used chiefly for Cravats; at that Time it was used for Ladies Dresses. As a new Work, Mr. Woolley considered he had a Right to pay it any Price that was satisfactory to himself and his Men, and paid accordingly a Shilling per Yard; … The Work in dispute, of which I also have a Pattern (*producing it*), is made with only Fifty-two Shutes. The Shutes in this are alternately of fine Silk and coarse Cotton, the latter making the Cord which appears on the Work. The Shutes being alternately of Cotton and of Silk, the Weaver is required to change his Shuttle every Time; <u>Sessional Papers</u>, July 2, 1823 ~~~ [ad] he has on hand a few OFFICERS REGULATION FORAGE CAPS, … BLACK ELASTIC STIFFENERS, and PARIS CORD STOCKS. *Honduras Gazette*, December 9, 1826

Paris gauze – Evening Dress. Parisian gauze dress over a white satin slip; *Repository of Fashions*, June 1829 ~~~ the coiffure is composed of the beautiful new material, called gaze de Paris; it is spotted with gold, and two birds of Paradise. *Casket*, April 1830 ~~~ For bridal dresses, the *gaze de Paris* is said to rival blonde. *Lady's Magazine*, September 1830 ~~~ full-dress … Dresses composed of *organdy* are trimmed round the bust with blond lace, or gaze de Paris, which is so good an imitation of blond lace that it can scarcely be distinguished from it. *Ladies' Museum*, October 1830 ~~~ An evening dress of light-blue *gaze de Paris*, worn over a slip of rich satin. *Royal Lady's Magazine*, March 1832

Paris net – [essay written in 1759] I could, indeed, have wished her more than an handkerchief of Paris-net to shade her beauties; <u>Miscellaneous Works of Oliver Goldsmith</u>, 1801 ~~~ A French apron of Paris net, *La Belle Assemblée*, May 1807 ~~~ Another net is known by the name of the DOUBLE PARIS NET. This net is, in every respect, both of drawing and cording, the same as the patent net, or night thought. It is wrought entirely by the first and fourth treddles, omitting the second and third. <u>Art of Weaving</u>, 1808 ~~~ In full or evening dress, Paris nets, … over satin slips, *La Belle Assemblée*, July 1810 ~~~ [court dress] A Parisian net petticoat over white satin, embroidered in wreaths of flowers; train and body green satin, worked in silver lama. *La Belle Assemblée*, May 1816 ~~~ Cap of white tulle or Paris net, *Manchester Iris*, October 4, 1823 [see *net* and *French net*]

Parisienne – a new stuff called *Parisienne*, which very much resembles *velours simulé*, *Repository of Arts*, April 1819 ~~~ A new stuff has been lately fabricated called *Parisienne*; it resembles cut velvet, but is a lighter article, and is much used for bonnets. *La Belle Assemblée*, April 1819

paroquet – Besides maraboo and ostrich feathers, we see those of the peacock, the paroquet, and the splendid plumage of the bird of paradise, all in requisition for half dress hats. *Court Magazine*, January 1836 ~~~ Other bonnets are trimmed with a *bouquet* of the feathers of parroquets and other rare foreign birds. *Ladies' Pocket*, March 1836

parrot – *aigrettes à la militaire*, formed of the green and yellow feathers of the parrot. *La Belle Assemblée*, July 1827

partridge – decorated with feathers, termed the partridge plume. *La Belle Assemblée*, October 1806 ~~~ sometimes it is a scarf, or half a garland of velvet flowers, which ornaments the crowns of these hats, or a wreath of partridge's feathers: *La Belle Assemblée*, January 1818

passementerie – The latter [private individuals] are more frequently purchasers of *passementerie*, by which is understood artificial flowers, fringes, gold and silver lace, with a variety of trifling but tasteful articles, all sufficiently adapted to a city where so much more is thought of display than of utility. <u>Encyclopædia Britannica</u>, 1824 ~~~ Though coloured muslin is much worn in *déshabille*, white dresses begin now very generally to prevail: they are embroidered, trimmed with lace, and made, every way, as expensive as possible: flounces form the chief ornament on the borders of these splendid dresses; and they are either finished at the edges with narrow lace, cotton *passementerie*, or a rich border of embroidery. *La*

Belle Assemblée, August 1827 ~~~ [Paris] Ginghams are much in favour for home costume; they are often bordered by one broad flounce, trimmed and headed by *passementerie*, (or braiding.) *Ladies' Monthly Museum*, July 1828 … *Passementerie* is now in high favour. Very few pelisses or even dresses are made without being trimmed with braiding, guimp, buttons, or frogs. *Court Journal*, September 28, 1833 ~~~ [Paris] The redingottes are trimmed down the fronts with *passementerie* (gimp) *Lady's Magazine*, October 1834 ~~~ [Paris] Many of them [robes] have a Grecian border done entirely round the dress in *passementerie*, small silk braid; and this is an improvement. *Lady's Magazine and Museum*, April 1835 [see also *gimp*]

patent lace – the Patent Lace trade, an article which was introduced at Nottingham only a few years since, but is now in considerable demand, and claims the attention of most of the manufacturers, the public encouraging it much in wide and narrow laces, in cloaks, and in vails; *Monthly Magazine*, December 1798 ~~~ *Method of washing white silk Patent Lace*. F old up the piece to the length of about a quarter of a yard, stitch it up slightly together with a needle and thread; anoint the surface of the lace with a little sweet oil upon the end of a feather, and boil it one hour in strong soap and water. When taken out it will have a snowy whiteness superior to its original colour. *Balance*, April 22, 1806 ~~~ The lace manufactory in England occupies a considerable number of persons, mostly women and girls: the principal seat of it is in Buckinghamshire. Of late years lace has been manufactured in the loom under a patent, and brought to great excellence if not perfection. The quantity worn by our ladies is very great. Patent lace is improved by a mixture of real lace, for borders, &c. Literary Panorama, 1808 ~~~ *Nottingham*. – On Sunday night last, about twelve o'clock, Mr. Orgil's patent lace manufactory, at Castle Donington, Leicestershire, was forcibly entered by a band of desperadoes, supposed ten or twelve, and the entire machinery, consisting of twelve warp lace frames, reduced to a heap of ruins, with the exception of one, which received only a partial injury. The depredators, not content with committing havoc on the machinery, cut or burnt all the valuable cotton-yarn and lace-pieces within the premises. Annual Register, 1815 ~~~ Long sleeves of fine net, entwined with quiltings round the arm, of Urling's Patent Lace, of which manufacture the net is also composed: *Kaleidoscope*, May 14, 1822 ~~~ *Nottingham* … is the centre of the silk and cotton manufactory of stockings, patent lace, and patent net: Compendium of Geography, 1822 [see *bobbin-net*, *lace*, *Nottingham* and *tulle*, also *Urling's lace*]

patent net – A train or round dress of white muslin, with a short dress of black patent net worn over it, and trimmed all round with deep lace. *Port Folio*, June 19, 1802 ~~~ The round apron of lace, or patent net, in white, or morone, with light border in silver, gold, or coloured foil, is considered as very elegant; *La Belle Assemblée*, February 1807 ~~~ *Princess Charlotte of Wales*. – A frock of pale blue patent net embroidered in silver, with a light elegant border of the same. *La Belle Assemblée*, June 1809 ~~~ in Castle Donnington and its neighbourhood, a great many of the female sex principally are employed in the manufacture of patent net lace, for lady's veils, &c. dependant I believe upon Nottingham and its neighbourhood. Agriculture of the County of Leicester, 1809 ~~~ [court dress] An elegant patent net dress, richly embroidered at the bottom in pyramids of beautiful shell work; *La Belle Assemblée*, June 1820 ~~~ this last, which is called the patent net, thought we believe without any just reason, partly because it is one of the most complicated, and also because it is the only one of real British origin, having been invented at Paisley, where it is known by the name of the *night thought*, a name probably bestowed upon it from the nocturnal meditation which it cost the inventor. Edinburgh Encyclopædia, 1830 ~~~ Patent Net, or Night Thought. This net, … consists of a gauze ground interwoven with whip. Treatise on the Art of Weaving, 1831 ~~~ one square yard of silk gauze weighs 137 grains, and one square yard of the finest patent net weighs 262 ½ grains. On the Economy of Machinery And Manufactures, 1832

patent straw – That "*patent straw*," so called, which is composed of straw and a very small quantity of silk, comes under the general classification of "all flats, braids, or plats, for the making of hats or bonnets," *Public Documents*, November 1830 [see also *satin straw*]

payne – That an article called '*Payne de L'Inde*,' composed of grass, cotton, and silk, and used in the manufacture of ladies' hats and bonnets, *Public Documents*, May 1831 ~~~ Watered silk bonnets are, upon the whole, most fashionable, but those of fine split straw, of a fancy material called *payne*, … are also worn by many elegant women. *Ladies' Museum*, September 1831 [see also *pagne*]

peacock – *The Duchess of York* – wore a suit of deep-coloured purple and silver, with the feathers of the peacock-tail on her head, which looked beautifully. *Lady's Magazine*, June 1798 ~~~ peacocks' feathers, cut short, are favourite ornaments; *La Belle Assemblée*, May 1820 ~~~ The plumage of the *wonderful Indian cock*, (Peacock,) is peculiarly beautiful; it consists of five colours, viz. black , blue, green, red, and white. The tail is composed of twelve most rich and elegant feathers. Female's Encyclopædia, 1830

pearl straw – Bonnets worn by the sea-side … a new and elegant article, called chain-pearl straw, and which is chiefly made in what is called the Anna Boleyn form, lined with fluted net or blond, and ornamented with fox-brush feathers. Bonnets of this shape are very beautiful in transparent black lace, with a full quilling or *cheveux de frise* at the edge. *Ladies' Monthly Museum*, October 1821 ~~~ [Paris] Fancy straw, Leghorn, pearl straw, chip, rose, and other coloured crapes, form the favourite materials for hats; *La Belle Assemblée*, August 1823 ~~~ Bonnet of pink *crepe lisse*; the outside fluted, and edged with three rows of pearl straw, and finished with blond lace: round crown, confined by a band of French folds, and decorated with a quadrangular trimming, edged with pearl straw and blond; *Kaleidoscope*, September 9, 1823

peas – A peignoir of organdi, embroidered in worsteds – pattern, peas, two greens, two lilacs, rose and brown, apricot and brown, or blue and brown; the peas are worked in diamonds all over the dress. You are, of course, aware that what we call "peas" are round spots, about the size of a pea. *Lady's Magazine and Museum*, July 1834

peau – *a skin, a hide*; Tardy's French Dictionary, 1799 ~~~ *Skin, hide, coat, leather, peel, pelt, husk, fell, rind.* Boniface's French Dictionary, 1828 [see **Furs**]

peau de chagrin – The first separate work of the era by which M. de Balsac wishes to be judged is *La Peau de Chagrin* [published in 1831], of which – as the groundwork is supernatural, and therefore out of our present scope – we shall say little. A young fellow – an *etudiant* we believe – having lost his last penny at play, resolves to drown himself; but failing somehow in his resolution, he postpones the catastrophe to the next night, and in the meanwhile goes into one of the curiosity shops which line the Quay Voltaire, and there *buys* – he had no money, but he pawned his soul – a magical piece *of chagrin*, or seal skin, which has the agreeable property of giving its possessor the enjoyment of all his wishes, embittered by the very disagreeable accompaniment of diminishing at every wish, and of a warning, that, when it shall be exhausted, the possessor must perish. *Quarterly Review*, April 1836 ~~~ [Paris, new materials] *La peau de chagrin.* – A silk with very narrow stripes, and satin spots at distances. *Lady's Magazine and Museum*, May 1836

peau de poule – *Peau de poule*, composed of silk and wool, is figured and quadrilled with flowers in the squares. *Court Magazine*, May 1836 [poule = hen in French; chicken skin?]

peeling satin – Exports for the Year 1770. … East India Goods exported from Leverpool to Africa. … Pelongs. History of Leverpool, 1774 ~~~ Peelings and persians are in a certain degree valuable, for the same reason [as modes]. The Irish maker has already attained such a degree of perfection in these fabrics as almost secures to him the home-market. Little or no English peelings or persians are imported. They are also a kind of goods, which, as they are used in linings, and other unimportant parts of dress, are likely to suffer few changes from the variations of fashion. Accordingly, a great number of the silk-weavers of Dublin are employed on them. Manufactures of Ireland, 1798 ~~~ [mourning dress] Petticoat of plain muslin, trimmed with a black net border; *corset* and *epaulettes* of black peeling satin; white satin sleeves covered with black net. *Lady's Magazine*, March 1797 ~~~ Evening. … Robe of red and purple peeling satin; *Lady's Magazine*, April 1797 ~~~ Some Parisian leaders of ton have lately introduced robes of very thin black crape, with a light embroidery of silver spangles. These they wear over a pale rose peeling, and the *éclat* is singularly striking. *Lady's Magazine*, November 1800 ~~~ Satinade, *silk in imitation of satin, peeling satin*. Boyer's Royal Dictionary Abridged, 1802 ~~~ Promenade Costume. … the cloak of green pelong satin, with a vandyke border, edged with white point lace; *National Register*, September 4, 1808 ~~~ Pelains, (pĕ-leīn) *m p. Chinese satins* Dufief's French Dictionary, 1810 ~~~ Cachao, the capital of Tonquin, … They manufacture many kinds of beautiful silks, pelongs, gauzes, &c., which are very cheap, Oriental Commerce, 1813 ~~~

Peeled satin, *Satinade*, <u>New Dictionary, English and French</u>, 1815 ~~~ Peeling, *s.* a kind of soft silk; Chinese, *peelam*, satin; B. *pelang*. <u>Etymons of English Words</u>, 1826 [see also *satinet*]

pegne Anglais – Riding habits … of *pegne Anglais* of light colours. *La Belle Assemblée*, August 1830

pekin – The principal silk stuffs brought from China are, plain pekins of from 11 ½ to 12 ells by 5 5/8. … Painted pekins for dresses, of from 11 ½ to 22 ells by 3/8. *New-York Magazine*, February 1795 ~~~ This is peculiarly adapted for balls. It has but one sleeve, and reaches only to the calf of the leg, close at the side, and rounded. All these latter dresses are of Florence satin, Pekin satin, muslin, plain and embroidered, painted linen, gauze, crape, &c. &c. *Port Folio*, February 6, 1802 ~~~ [Paris] Merino shawls, and even the thin Pekin wrap, spensers, and scarf shawls, made their appearance during the mild weather. *La Belle Assemblée*, April 1811 ~~~ *Tariff of the mean prices of Merchandise imported into the Ports of the Republic of Hayti.* … Pekin, black – pr ell [$] 3 00 colored … [$] 2 00 <u>Digest of the Recent Commercial Regulations</u>, 1824 ~~~ Pekin, (éstoffe de soie rayée ou brochée, qui se fabrique principalement à Lyon) *Pekin.* [cloth of silk, striped or figured, that's made mainly at Lyon] <u>Boniface's French Dictionary</u>, 1828 ~~~ the real novelty for dresses are, … the *Pékin à ramages* (the latter also worn in morning dresses), *Court Magazine*, May 1833 ~~~ [court dress] A Brussels lace dress over white satin; train of a rich green Pekin a ramages; *Court Journal*, May 11, 1833 ~~~ painted Pekin, … are fashionable materials in evening dress. … The few robes worn by women of high fashion are composed of painted Pekin. They have a white ground, flowered in running patterns of small delicate flowers, in vivid but not glaring hues. *Court Magazine*, August 1833 ~~~ The most elegant of the new materials for dinner and evening dress are the … *Pekins Chines.* These are silks of the richest kind: *Court Magazine*, May 1834 ~~~ Among the new silks that are expected to be most fashionable for robes, we may cite some *pekins* of a very soft and rich kind, *Ladies' Pocket*, April 1836 ~~~ Morning Dress Of Tissue Pekin, the cape and skirt edged with a plain fold of *gros de Naples*, *Court Magazine*, June 1836

pelian satin – the Witzchoura pelisse of black pelian satin, elegantly trimmed with that light and valuable fur, the chinchilla; *La Belle Assemblée*, March 1819 ~~~ For walking, or for the carriage, pelisses and spencers of *gros-de-Naples* or Pelian satin, are likely to be most in favour. … Another spencer of gossamer, or Pelian satin, is equally beautiful; it is of a pale primrose-colour, and is elegantly trimmed with violet-coloured satin. *La Belle Assemblée*, July 1819 [may be *pelong?* See *peeling satin*]

Pelisse Cloth – Mr. Bakewell thus describes the Saxon wool: … Will spin finer when carded, than Spanish wool, and is suited for light kerseymeres and pelisse cloths. <u>General Treatise on Cattle</u>, 1809 ~~~ Fashionable Mode of Shopping. Enter *Miss Whimsical* and her *Sister.* – Have you and pelisse cloth, Sir? Yes Miss, here is a very fine piece. What is the price of it, sir? Two dollars and a half miss; *Juvenile Port-Folio*, October 17, 1812 ~~~ [Leeds, Lancaster, &c.] So great has been the sudden revival of trade, that several merchants here find it impossible to procure pelisse cloths, shawls, and stuff goods in general, for the execution of their orders. In woollen goods, generally, a considerable rise has taken place. *Blackwood's Edinburgh Magazine*, October 1817 ~~~ [ad] The most extensive choice of Pelisse and Ladies' Habit Cloths, from 7*s.* to 20*s.* per yard. *Evangelical Magazine*, November 1821 ~~~ Large quantities of ladies' cloths, which come under the designation of pelisse-cloths, and shawls, have lately been made in this neighbourhood. [Yorkshire] <u>County of York</u>, 1822 ~~~ For the dyeing of 100 lbs. of pelisse cloth (a broad woollen cloth of thin and open texture), *Annals of Philosophy*, June 1826 ~~~ *Pelisse Cloths* – 54 inches wide, cost 2*s.* 6*d.* to 3*s.* 4 ½ *d.* – Worn by all classes. *Niles' Weekly Register*, March 8, 1828 ~~~ To the list we have just given of the various foreign cloths imported into the United States, we must add the thin fabrics, known under the name of pelisse and habit cloths – the former used almost exclusively for women's wear – the latter for women's wear and for men's summer clothing. <u>An Exposition…of the Tariff System</u>, 1832 ~~~ [ad] 2 cases pelisse cloths, and excellent article for chaise lining (very low) *New England Farmer*, September 25, 1833 ~~~ The best length of staple for the clothing or fulling species of wool is from two to three inches. But Saxony wool, though four or five inches long, admits from its tenderness of being easily broken down by carding to the proper shortness, and is preferable, on account of its variable lengths, for making kerseymeres, pelisse-cloths, shawls, and such fabrics as require fine yarn. <u>Philosophy of Manufactures</u>, 1835 [see also *ladies' cloth*] pelong – [sometimes spelled *pellong*; see *peeling satin*]

peluche – Plush, (*adj. from the* French peluche) Shag, stuff woven after the manner of velvet. Ash's English Dictionary, 1795 ~~~Pluche, *or* Peluche, *plush, shag.* Dufief's French Dictionary, 1810 ~~~ [Paris hats] a new description of *pluche* has just appeared, which promises to become very fashionable; the silk is left longer than in the other kinds of *pluche*, and has rather a curly appearance: another sort of *pluche*, which resembles granite, is also much in favour. *Repository of Arts*, November 1820 ~~~ The materials used for chapeaux, are … *pluche bouclée*; this last is a very beautiful material; it is a curled silk *pluche* which has at once a very light and rich effect. *Ladies' Monthly Museum*, January 1821 ~~~ Bonnets composed of velvet, and lined, and trimmed with *peluche*, are now more in favor than any other for walking dress. *Ladies' Pocket*, March 1830 ~~~ We see very few satin bonnets in carriage dress. *Peluche*, of a new and very beautiful kind, had been introduced in the course of the last month, but is not so much in favour as velvet; it is beginning to be employed in lining bonnets, but the greatest number are made of one material only. *La Belle Assemblée*, January 1832 ~~~ Peluche Chiné, (silk and cotton) Jones's Digest, 1835 ~~~ That light and rich material, *peluche*, will be one of the most fashionable materials for hats and bonnets. *New Monthly Belle Assemblée*, October 1836 ~~~ [Paris hats] I have already spoken to you of *Peluche*, when it is worn by unmarried ladies, it is simply trimmed with plain white satin. It is trimmed for married ladies with feathers, flowers, or *velours épinglé*. *New Monthly Belle Assemblée*, December 1836 ~~~ *Robes de chambre* appear as likely to be in high favour this winter as they were last season. A great many are composed of fine merinoes or of plain or printed Cachemérienne. They are either wadded or lined with *peluche*. Rose or cherry-coloured *peluche* is grey merinoes. If the dress is of white, blue, or light-green Cachemérienne, the lining should be *peluche* of Turkish patterns: the effect is extremely rich. *Court Magazine*, December 1836 [see also *pluche de soie* and *plush*]

pelure – Pelure (*s. from the* French) A rich kind of fur. Ash's English Dictionary, 1795 ~~~ [in dyeing] The wools of the healthy, dead, and diseased animals, … were employed separately, together, and mixed with scrapings (*pelure*,) wool of very inferior quality, and which has besides been altered by lime. Repertory of Arts and Manufactures, 1805 ~~~ Pelule, or pelure de soie, or d'ognon, (hat lining of silk) *Public Documents*, March 23, 1832 ~~~ The peel of an onion. *Peau ou pelure d'ognon*. Wilson's French Dictionary, 1833

pencilled – We may surpass the Armenian chintz-printers in the patterns, but they are fully our masters in other respects. There is a softness in the effect of their blocks, that I think more likely to be admired in competition, than the clear exact lines with which our designs are finished. … They have a method of painting muslins, by tracing them with the pencil over drawings, which produces an effect greatly superior to that of printing. It is chiefly handkerchiefs that they ornament in this way; and they render them of great value. I have seen squares of muslin not worth ten shillings, raised in value, by the labour of the painters, to upwards of a hundred. I believe we do not practise this art. Voyages and Travels, 1812 ~~~ A beautiful material for rural dress-parties, called pencilled muslin, has appeared of late; the ground is white, and figured over with the most elegantly finished pattern, of stripes, representing small flowers and foliage, clustered together. *Ladies' Monthly Museum*, October 1825 ~~~ Printed muslin dresses are still in high request *en deshabille*. The favourite ground is yellow: they are, however, no longer of that turmeric tint, which was so prevalent the last week of July; but are now of the beautiful canary yellow, and the figures are in a more delicate and pencilled style, than when in those gaudy variegated hues, which accord least of all with bright yellow. *La Belle Assemblée*, September 1827 [see *painted*; also *calico* and *chintz*]

penguin – [Paris] there appeared, on a very fashionable lady, a mantle of a light colour, trimmed with the feathers of the drake's neck called *penguin*. *La Belle Assemblée*, March 1826

pennistone – Manufactures (woollen). All ordinary Penistones, or forest whites, 12 & 13 [Yards long.] … Sorting penistones 13 & 14 [Yards long.] Whole Law Relative to the Duty and Office of a Justice of the Peace, 1794 ~~~ Annual Supplies from Great Britain and Ireland. 1st. Negro Clothing; viz. … 650 Yards of blue baize, or pennistones, for a warm frock for each negro. History … of the British Colonies in the West Indies, 1806 … Cumberland. – The manufactures of this county are … pennistons, Lex Mercatoria, 1813 ~~~ *Stores required for the use of the Belvedere estate*, 1815. Fifty-four men's Pennistone jackets ... 64 women's Pennistone wrappers ... Jamaica Trade. ... Serges. Pennistones (Indigo die) napped were at 2s. 6d. currency a yard, but are frequently sold a 3s. 4d. a yard. Review of the ... Interests and Capabilities of the Port of Plymouth, 1816 ~~~ the clothing for every man is a Pennistone jacket, an Oznabrugs shirt and trowsers, and a woollen cap or hat. The women have a full-size jacket of Pennistone, an Osnabrugs petticoat, a handkerchief and a woollen cap; on some estates they have a check chemise besides, and the children likewise an annual suit. The quantity of clothing may appear insufficient for a year, but the Negroes, or at least the industrious part of them, have ample means of procuring additional raiment, and they are always observed to be not only decently but comfortably clad. A Report of a Committee of the Council of Barbadoes, appointed to inquire into the actual condition of the slaves in this island, 1824 ~~~ Negro Men's Jackets. ... These jackets will require 2 ½ yards of 27 inch Honley or Pennystone, ... Negro Women's Bedgowns. These Gowns, we generally cut of Blue Nap, commonly called Pennystone, 27 inches wide. Sectum, 1825 ~~~ The Pennistone is the same kind of coarse flimsy woollen with the bamboo or baize. Slavery of the British West India Colonies Delineated, 1830 ~~~ There is also a very coarse Frieze, made for the foreign market, called Pennistone, from the name of a small town in Yorkshire. Analytical Dictionary, 1830 ~~~ Yearly clothes for a child: ... 1 ½ yards of Pennistones, at 2 s. 6 d. – 3 s. 9 d. Accounts and Papers, 1831 ~~~ a coarse narrow woollen cloth called Pennistones, Analysis...on the Extinction of Slavery, 1833 [see *baize*; also *forest cloth* and *frieze*]

perching – [see *flannel*]

perkale – [Paris] A Half Full Dress. ... *perkale* gloves: this half dress has been considered equally simple and elegant. *La Belle Assemblée*, March 1806 ~~~ Percale, ... cambrick muslin. Dufief's French Dictionary, 1810 ~~~ [Paris] Late as it is in the season, our promenade dresses are invariably composed of white: *perkale* is in high estimation, *Repository of Arts*, November 1816 ~~~ [Paris] Robes of *perkale*, that is to say, of cambric muslin, are most in favour; *Ladies' Monthly Museum*, October 1817 ~~~ [Paris] *Capotes* are much worn in *perkale*; the most fashionable are of unbleached *percale*, lined with rose-coloured sarsnet, and trimmed with riband to correspond. ... Dinner gowns now are mostly made of *perkale*; *Ladies' Monthly Museum*, September 1818 ~~~ At present, levantine, gros de Naples, *perkale*, and Merino cloth, are all worn indiscriminately. *Repository of Arts*, November 1820 ~~~The *perkals*, so called from a Tamul word signifying "superfine," are made in the Carnatic, of a long silky cotton, which is particularly abundant in the plain of Arcot. Universal Geography, 1825 ~~~ Cotton manufactures, viz: ... Percale; *Niles' Weekly Register*, December 2, 1820 ~~~ these percales (English manufacture of cambric muslin) Spinster's Tour in France, 1828 ~~~ A new material for half dress is called *perkale lustrée*; it resembles the printed *foulards*. These dresses have light grounds and patterns of very vivid colours. *Repository of Fashions*, September 1829 [see *cambric*]

Perline – *Satins Imperial à la Reines* and *Perline*, may be classed among the richest materials for half-dress; *New Monthly Belle Assemblée*, November 1836

persian – a kind of silk Perry's English Dictionary, 1795 ~~~ A head-dress of yellow and white persian; ... The dress yellow persian, trimmed with yellow ribands. *Ladies' Monthly Museum*, March 1802 ~~~ For full dress robes of white Persian, covered with silver nets, ... White Persian short pelices, trimmed with broad white lace, are extremely elegant; some prefer lilac or buff. *Port Folio*, August 21, 1802 ~~~ Coloured persian, two shillings and fivepence per yard. [in 1801] A Voyage Round the World, 1805 ~~~ of those [cloaks] the most elegantly attractive were of royal purple taffeta lined with Pomona green Persian, *La Belle Assemblée*, April 1806 ~~~ the latter [cottage poke bonnet] of muslin, or leno, lined with coloured Persian; *Emerald*, September 26, 1807 ~~~ [court dress] A green and silver Persian silk petticoat; drapery of beautiful Brussels lace, looped up and festooned with rich oriental amber beads; *Lady's Magazine*, June 1810 ~~~ Persian, the name of a thin, inferior kind of silken stuff, which is principally employed in the lining of garments of females. General Dictionary of Commerce, 1810 ~~~ There is the article of persian, which is the lowest article made, it is made by women and children; at times we could not get hands to make it, and then we should have been glad to pay sixpence a yard for making it; the price is now fixed at five-pence; ... is not the average retail price of Persians 2*s.* 6*d.* per yard; Minutes of Evidence... relating to Ribbon Weavers, 1818 ~~~ [ad, June

1823] pink persian, 3s. 6d. per yard, per piece; <u>British Settlements in Australasia</u>, 1824 ~~~ [ad] Extraordinary Bargains. ... Persians, 1s.; *Examiner*, April 23, 1826 ~~~ Light cloaks are often used for autumnal walking costume: when this is the case, they are composed of silk only, lined with persian, without wadding. *Lady's Magazine*, September 1830 ~~~ Persian ... is exceedingly flimsy in its texture, and has of late nearly gone out of use, its place being taken by the description next in quality, sarsnet. <u>Silk Manufacture</u>, 1832 ~~~ *robe-de-chambre* ... lined with pink, lilac, or cherry-coloured Persian, wadded and quilted. *Court Journal*, October 24, 1835... the sound made by rubbing coarse hair between the fingers, or by tearing English taffeta, or other silk, popularly called lining silk, or Persian. *London Medical and Surgical Journal*, October 8, 1836 [see also *sarsnet*]

Persian taffeta – Among the new silks that have appeared for evening and dinner dress, we may cite the Persian taffeta, one of the best imitations that has yet appeared of the silks that were fashionable between fifty and sixty years ago. The prettiest are those with a milk-white or lemon-coloured ground thickly strewed with small bouquets of roses. *Court Magazine*, January 1834

Persian yarn – Shawl Manufacture. ... Some years afterwards another step was made towards the introduction of the proper material, by preparing a weft of silk and Merino wool, which received the name of Persian yarn. This still continues partially in use. *Atheneum*, September 1826

Peruvian – Court dress ... Train of pink Peruvian net; body and sleeves of the same, *La Belle Assemblée*, June 1807... [ad] Peruvian spotted net. Very different in colour from the preceding article, yet in one respect similar, namely, that the paleness of the ground only approximates to the beauty of the blue with which it is spotted. *Repository of Arts*, July 1813 ~~~ Peruvian embossed silk and marabout gauze are favourite articles for evening dresses; ... [Paris] China silk and Peruvian gauze are much used in the fabrication of carriage hats; these gauzes are checquered with marabout down of rose colour, blue and lilac with the ground is white; jonquil on a puce coloured ground, and green on blue (a vile mixture) and blue on black, in squares ... Peruvian gauze is an article much in use for ornamenting hats; some specimens of this elegant material are sprinkled with little tufts of white down: the ribbons worn with this trimming are very broad, and are edged with small tufts of marabout feathers. *La Belle Assemblée*, April 1820 ~~~ Evening Dress. A *gaze Peruvienne* dress, a white ground figured *à calonnes*, in buds and foliage; *La Belle Assemblée*, February 1832 ~~~ [ad] Have received by the ships Hark-away and Jefferson, direct from Liverpool, ... 2 cases light stripe Peruvian jeans. *Farmer's Register*, May 1835 ~~~ Half transparent materials, of the very finest Cashmere wool, are in great request. The most fashionable are the *mousselines Peruviennes*, ... of Indian patterns, rather large, and of full colours. *Ladies' Pocket*, June 1836

petersham – What crowding and jostling to get a side-view / Of my *Petersham* breeches, and coat of *sky-blue!* <u>Pursuits of Fashion: A Satirical Poem</u>, 1810 ~~~ 1 piece Petersham coating, 47 yards – [Price $] 3.00 [Amount $] 141.00 [letter dated October 26, 1832] ... Petersham box coats – $15.00 [letter dated October 27, 1832] <u>Emigration of Indians</u>, 1835 ~~~ [ad] Petersham Surtout Coats, for £1 10s; ... at Simpson's Woollen-Drapery *Irish Monthly Magazine*, April 1833 ~~~ I wore a black hat that night, drab pantaloons, and a shaggy petersham pea jacket, of brown, with a Russia dog skin collar. <u>Trial of Ephraim K. Avery</u>, 1833 ~~~ [ad] 1 case Petershams. *New England Farmer*, December 10, 1834 ~~~ Petershams, woollen cloth, <u>Jones's Digest</u>, 1835 ~~~ [ad for men's] Great Coat, of a fine milled Petersham, for £2 2s. ... Petersham Great Coats, bound, and velvet collar. *Eminent Foreign Statesmen*, March 1836 [see *coating*; note: Petersham also is a style of coat and the name of a hat, and may be a style of breeches. Lord Petersham was synonymous with dandyism.]

Pharamond – [Paris] The evening dress silks that have appeared, are all in the superb but heavy style of Louis XIV's reign. The satins *Salomon, Esmeralda,* and *Pharamond,* are expected to be in great request; *New Monthly Belle Assemblée*, November 1836 ~~~ Evening costume is still of a light kind; several new materials have, however, appeared for it. We may cite among them the ... *Reps Corysandre* and *Pharamond*; ... These rich and beautiful materials will be in great request as soon as the winter has fairly set in. *Ladies' Pocket*, November 1836

Phillipines – Rich silks are beginning to be worn in evening-dress, particularly *Phillipines* and *gros d'Orleans*. *Maids, Wives, and Widows*, November 10, 1832 ~~~ [ad] Gros d'Orleans, Philippines, Poult de Soie, and other rich Silks, for Pelisses and Evening Dress; *Court Journal*, February 9, 1833

pic nic – [see *single press lace*]

picot – [see *purl lace*]

pignet gauze – The extreme warmth of the weather …and we consequently see crape, clear muslin, leno, pignet gauze, *La Belle Assemblée*, July 1808

pillow lace – Bone lace, flaxen lace, coarse lace <u>Perry's English Dictionary</u>, 1795 ~~~ Buckinghamshire. … The laboring inhabitants are principally employed in agricultural pursuits, or lace*-making. As the latter manufacture requires but little ingenuity, and cheap materials, there is scarcely a house or female in the town unprovided with a lace pillow, parchments, bobbins, gimps, pins, thread, and other requisites. The profits of this business to the makers, depends on their facility of execution; their daily earnings are therefore different. Some women can earn from eighteen pence to two shillings a day; others cannot get more than one shilling in the same time. Their receipts, however, have lately experienced a considerable drawback, a manufactory having been established at Nottingham, in which the lace is made with, *machinery,* and being quicker executed, is retailed at a less price; yet neither its quality nor workmanship is so good as that made by hand. * In all the accounts we have read of Buckinghamshire, it ii stated that *bone* lace is the chief manufacture; but some of the oldest makers, whom we consulted, were totally ignorant of the term. The principal sort made is fine thread-lace, black and white: the former commonly worked with a French-ground, or perfect diamond squares; the latter generally executed with a roundish hole, called the point-ground. The maker is furnished with a round pillow, on which a slip of parchment is fixed, perforated with a great number of holes, corresponding to the pattern required to be executed. These holes are filled with pins, which are placed and displaced as the bobbins are moved, or stitches finished. The thread is fixed on the top of small bobbins, or gimps; the first are used in making fine lace and ground ; and the latter for coarse lace, to work in the flowers, &c. <u>Beauties of England and Wales</u>, 1801 ~~~ In speaking of the manufactures of Bedfordshire, the authors observe, that the principal is thread-lace, "formerly know by the name of bone-lace." * … * Probably from the bones out of which the bobbins were turned. In these bobbins, the girls are very fanciful, ornamenting them at the ends with bugles, coral, and other beads, crystal buttons, rings, &c. &c. *European Magazine*, August 1808 ~~~ The poorer classes [in Finedon] have sufficient means of education, but the boys do not avail themselves of them, their parents putting them to labour in the field at an early age, and the girls are set down to the lace pillow, at five years old; … [in Stanwick] There are few of the poorer classes who cannot afford something towards the education of their children, but they put them to the lace pillow as soon as they can use their fingers; … [in Stoke] Several schools for lace making, in some of which the children are taught to read, but very imperfectly. <u>Education of the Poor</u>, 1819 ~~~ Lace, in the arts, is formed of cotton, thread, or silk, and is in the manufacture a species of weaving. … We may notice in this place, however, the manner in which it is made by hand in Bedfordshire, Buckinghamshire, &c. A pillow or cushion being furnished with a stiff piece of parchment, having a number of holes pricked in it, through these holes pins are stuck into the pillow and the threads wound upon bobbins are woven round the pins, and twisted round each other so as to form the required pattern. The process is tedious, and since the invention of the Nottingham machinery confined to a small part of the country. Still there is this difference between Nottingham and Buckinghamshire lace. In the hand-made, or pillow lace, the net or meshes may be described, by supposing a number of ropes, each formed of two or more threads twisted round each other: these are extended parallel; but, at every two or three spiral turns of these ropes, the strands or threads composing one rope are twisted around with those of its neighbour, and then return to be twisted with its own: and this reciprocally of the whole number forms a netting; the figure of the meshes depending upon the number of turns which are made, before the twist is changed from one rope to the next. To form a lace of this description, it is essential that the ends of each thread be detached, and capable of being twisted over the adjacent threads. This is easily done by the hand upon the pillow, by twisting the bobbins round each other; but has difficulties which prevent its performance by machinery. <u>London Encyclopædia</u>, 1829 ~~~ [court dress] Dress of vapeur crape, richly embroidered and trimmed with pillow blonde manufactured by her Ladyship's own tenants;

Royal Lady's Magazine, March 1831 ~~~ The manufacture of thread or pillow-lace, in the counties of Buckingham, Bedford, and Northampton, is in the same depressed and deplorable state. The miserable workers, after labouring sixteen hours a day, cannot earn more than from 1*s.* 6*d.* to 2*s.* per week! In the very best of times these poor creatures could not earn more than from 8*s.* to 10*s.* a week; but their present distressed and pauperised situation is truly piteous. *New Monthly Magazine*, October 1832 ~~~ Northampton, June 9th, 1835 ~~~ [regarding farmer George Allen] His daughter, Sarah, aged 11, could sometimes earn 1*s.* 6*d.* per week at the lace pillow, First Annual Report of the Poor Law Commissioners, 1835 ~~~ *Bone* or *pillow lace* is so called from its being made with bobbins of bone or ivory, upon a pillow, or cushion. This pillow is in shape round on one side, and straight on the other, and in substance much harder in its stuffing than the cushion of a sofa. When in use, it is supported by a kind of tripod, or three-legged stool; and the lace-maker sits before it. On the top of the cushion, in the centre, is a piece of parchment, on which the pattern of the intended lace is pricked in holes. In the back rows of these holes pins are stuck through into the cushion; and to the pins are fastened very fine threads, drawn from the bobbins on which they are wound, and which hang down in front. The bobbins, made of ivory, bone, ebony, and sometimes of boxwood, are about the length of one's finger, thin and taper at the upper end, but thick at the lower extremity for the convenience of handling, and each has some distinguishing mark. The thread is wound upon the thin end of the bobbin, and passes through a small hole at the top, to the pin upon the parchment pattern. To each pin, the threads of two bobbins are attached; and the maker, seating herself in front, divides the bobbins into two parcels, so as to have in each parcel one thread only of each pin. One of these parcels she takes between the fingers of her right hand; the other between those of her left; and then she begins throwing the bobbins from one hand to the other, so as to twist the several pairs of threads into the adjacent pairs, without allowing any one pair to be twisted together. When this operation has been performed as often as the pattern requires for the first set of pins, she takes up the bobbins of the next set, till she has completed the whole row. The back row of pins being now done with, they are taken out and placed forward in the next row of holes upon the pattern; then the bobbins are again thrown, and the threads twisted, as before, care being taken to work together, not the two bobbins which hang together from the row of pins already twisted, but one of each pair with one of the next pair. Now as the pins prevent the threads from twisting too close, the effect is, that on removing the pins, a row of small eyelet holes appear; and as the same pair do not go in the second row that went together in the first, the second row of holes is not exactly under, but between them, giving the whole the appearance of a honeycomb. Scenes of Commerce, 1836 [see also *Bedfordshire* and *Buckinghamshire*]

pilot cloth – [ad] Gentlemen's Dress. ... Also, a great variety of Pea Jackets, in Pilot Cloth, Turkey Beaver, &c. *Court Journal*, December 12, 1835 ~~~ Monthly Report of the Woollen Trade. ... The demand for double milled goods has still further been considerably affected by the substitution of pilot and mohair cloths, especially in the metropolis, where the gentlemen appear to think that bear-skins are a very appropriate accompaniment to the ladies' boas. *Farmer's Magazine*, January 1836

pine marten – The martes, or pine-martin, has the body of a dark or blackish chesnut colour, the breast and throat yellow. It inhabits the north of Europe, Asia, and America; and is more rarely found in Britain, France, Germany, and Hungary; ... The fur is far superior in fineness to that of the common kind, and is a prodigious article in commerce: Those about Mount Caucasus, with an orange throat, are more esteemed by furriers than the rest. Encyclopædia Britannica, 1797 ~~~ The term *marten*, although applied to the whole weasel tribe, is more generally used in this country to designate the pine marten ... It closely resembles the marten of Europe, by may be distinguished by its smaller size, longer legs, finer, thicker and more glossy fur, and from the throat being marked by a broad yellow spot, whilst the same part in the European marten is white. ... The fur is fine, and much used for trimmings. Upwards of 100,000 are collected annually in the fur countries. Encyclopædia Americana, 1831 ~~~ Martin, or martern, or pine martin. A fur of very general use, here for muffs and trimmings, abroad for the same purposes, and for almost all the uses to which the better kinds of furs are applied. The darkest coloured, from the rocky and woody district of the Nipigon, are the best, and go popularly by the name of sable; but the true sable is not a native of America. The wholesale price of skins of first quality is about twenty shillings a-piece. <u>Transactions of the Society</u>, 1833 [see also *marten*]

pique – Piqué, *quilted.* Coton piqué, *quilting.* <u>Dufief's French Dictionary</u>, 1810 ~~~ Bed Covers, unembroidered, of Cotton, Thread, Piqué, or wool … Cotton Goods. … With mixture of … linen yarn, wool, gold and silver, as fustian, piqué, <u>European Commerce</u>, 1818 ~~~ Cotton goods of all kinds, white, without gold and silver: (a) Cotton mitcales, and cambric muslins, printed calicoes, dimities, piquets, fustians, Manchesters, velverets, and other stuffs of this kind, plain, or with white figures woven, <u>Digest of the Commercial Regulations</u>, 1824 ~~~ One of our most stylish dandies has just been seen on horseback in the following dress: … waistcoat of *pique chamois* buttoned from the top; long small clothes, composed of *pique cotele*; [probably satire] *Casket*, January 1831 ~~~ PIQUETS. The variety of gauze generally known by the name of piquets, are simply plain gauze, omitting every third or fourth splitful of warp. They are woven in fine reeds, leaving the third, fourth, &c. interval empty; by which, two, three, or more splitfuls of warp run together in a stripe. Piquets are frequently ornamented like the gauze with spotting, spidering, lappeting, &c. Piquets, however, are at present woven on silk in the form of turkey gauze, of which an example will be given under that article. <u>Art of Weaving</u>, 1831 [see also *gauze* and *turkey gauze*]

pinking – Pink, To pierce with small holes, to work in oyletholes. [eyelet holes] <u>Ash's English Dictionary</u>, 1795 ~~~ On dresses made of sarsnet or *gros-de-Naples*, the trimming consists of strips of different kinds of stuff, placed on in festoons, and notched at the edges, like the ancient fashion of pinking. *La Belle Assemblée*, May 1819 ~~~ the silk dresses have a multitude of narrow flounces, reaching almost to the knee, except the black silks, on which the ugly fashion of shrowd-like pinking seems to prevail, and the flounces on them are in serpentine or detached wavings; *La Belle Assemblée*, January 1823 ~~~ in general a shroud, which is woven stuff of a whitish colour, is shaped to go over the body, at the edges of which are trimmings of the same stuff, pinked into ornaments, and plaited round the face, wrists, &c. <u>Scenes of British Wealth</u>, 1825 ~~~ Nearly all dresses are composed of light materials, either crape, gauze, Cachemire, or grenadine, with satin stripes, &c. As to the trimmings, they chiefly consist of flounces, bias, or *ruches*; the flounces are pinked with shell-work, and bordered with an embroidery of satin. *Ladies' Monthly Museum*, November 1826 ~~~ A favourite dress for the theatres is of taffety, of the colour of bird-of-paradise-yellow, with two broad flounces at the border, pinked in scalops; *La Belle Assemblée*, May 1827 ~~~ Carriage Dress. … The sleeves have a single large bouffant at the upper part, from thence to the wrist they are tight, with a double cuff pinked at each edge. *New Monthly Belle Assemblée*, September 1836

piping – [Paris] White satin is in very general estimation for full dress; those ladies who affect simplicity trim it only with two or three very narrow pipings of byas velvet round the bust and the bottom of the train. *Repository of Arts*, November 1816 ~~~ Walking-dress. …the bottom of the skirt ornamented with satin folds, and decorated with festoons of the same, each festoon confined with narrow bands of corded or piped satin. *Ladies' Monthly Museum*, April 1822 ~~~ Satin dresses have the lappel of velvet, and *vice versâ*; the trimming is formed of pipings of alternate velvet and satin. They are sometimes arranged in a Grecian border; and then two are of velvet, and the centre one of satin: sometimes they are put plain, one of each alternately, to the number of six or eight. *La Belle Assemblée*, February 1831 ~~~ Carriage Dress. … The [sleeve] folds are retained by a triple piping, the colour of the ground of the dress, which, we should observe, also borders the lappel. *Court Magazine*, June 1834 ~~~ [Paris] Cloak of velours d'Arménie, lined with satin and wadded. The cape … is edged with a narrow *liseré* or piping. *Lady's Magazine*, December 1834 ~~~ The pipings made of *reps* form a very pretty relief to plain silk. *Court Journal*, October 31, 1835 ~~~ Some of these *capotes* are edged with colour pipings, but then they are trimmed with *mirabouts*, *Court Magazine*, May 1836

plaid – Plaid, a checked Scotch stuff <u>Perry's English Dictionary</u>, 1795 ~~~ A striped or variegated cloth; an outer loose garment worn much by the Highlanders in Scotland. <u>Sheridan's English Dictionary</u>, 1797 ~~~ *Statistical Account of* Scotland. … A great change has taken place in dress within the last 30 years; the plaid is now almost wholly laid aside by the women, and the use of the cloak and bonnet become general. Among the men the Scotch bonnet has given place to the hat, and serving men are generally clothed with English cloth, *Gentleman's Magazine*, February 1795 ~~~ Fashions for January.

... Scotch Dress. The front and side hair dressed in small curls: *chignon* turned up plain. Bonnet of white satin and plaid silk; ... Round dress of muslin: short sleeves: the whole trimmed with plaid ribband. Scarf of plaid silk, *Lady's Magazine*, January 1797 ~~~ Plaid ribbands and scarfs have been introduced within this last fortnight; the latter is twisted round the throat, crosses the back, and falls in irregular lengths down the figure in front, the ends finished with correspondent tassels. *La Belle Assemblée*, October 1807 ~~~ The Scotch plaids, or cross-barred and party-coloured stuffs, known by that appellation, are made of silk; but more frequently of worsted. That made of silk is generally used in the formation of ladies' garments, such as pelisses, gowns, shawls, ribbons, &c. The worsted stuff is almost entirely consumed by the lower orders of people in Scotland, who make it into petticoats, cloaks, stockings, &c. Dictionary of Commerce, 1810 ~~~ One very ingenious manufacture is not included in the above enumerated articles, because it was only introduced in that year [1805], and had not then been prosecuted to any considerable extent – namely, imitations of India shawls and plaids. The materials used are silk and cotton, but more generally Merino wool, instead of cotton, as succeeding better with the public taste. These are of different sizes and different degrees of fineness. Thus, respecting size, they are 3/4 and 1/4 scarfs; 4/4 plaids and 7/4 shawls, at the following prices : – Scarfs from 10s. to 50s. / Plaids from 50s. to 180s. / Shawls from 24s. to 130s. Shire of Renfrew, 1818 ~~~ Highland clan and tartan plaids are also much worn in half dress; when worn on evenings, the sleeves are of white satin trimmed with blond; *La Belle Assemblée*, January 1820 ~~~ Since his Majesty's return from Scotland, we have noticed at most of our fashionable places of amusement, that a great number of ladies have adopted plaid sarsenets and bombazines, in honor of his Majesty's visit to that country; and we have every reason to believe that plaids of all descriptions will be generally worn on the approach of winter. *Ladies' Monthly Museum*, October 1822 ~~~ Scotch satins are used with the greatest success in grand toilet. Those which we have seen are of a brilliant and admirable reflection of light. The colours *oreille d'ours,* blue, and cherry red, predominate in the grounds, and the squares are excessively large. We must, however, except some robes of the same satin, the squares of which, crossed by narrow lines, render the stuff much more adapted to ladies of small stature. Scotch satins are also used for scarfs: they are bordered with a long fringe formed of the same stuff. [Paris] *Ladies' Monthly Museum*, February 1826 ~~~ [Paris] The reign of the Scotch plaids has not yet passed over; on the contrary, the return of spring is expected to give a fresh stimulus to the manufacturers of this favourite article. The colours acquire more brilliancy every day; the squares are enlarged, and the shades are multiplied to infinity. We see an instance of this in the *Magasin Sante Anne,* where the Scotch plaid is presented under two hundred different aspects. Nothing can equal the beauty and variety of the last assortment which M. Delisle, the proprietor of these *Magasins,* has just received. We allude, particularly, to the velvets, which are of an admirable richness and brilliancy: also the woollen stuffs for cloaks. *Ladies' Monthly Museum*, March 1826 ~~~ Lemon-colored bonnets of gros de Naples, chequered in Egyptian plaid, with yellow, pink, and purple, are much admired in carriage out-door costume: *Ladies' Pocket*, May 1829 ~~~ Plaid dresses, in sarsenet or gros de Naples, of the true tartan kind, are much worn in home costume and in half dress. *Ladies' Museum*, May 1829 ~~~ Plaid silks of dark and rich hues are worn in home costume, and in half-dress; *Lady's Magazine*, October 1829 ~~~ Evening Dress. – A gown of white and rose colored plaid gros de Naples: *Ladies' Pocket*, July 1830 ~~~ Appraisers' Office, *October* 14, 1831. Sir: The article of Scotch or tartan plaid, enclosed in a letter to the Comptroller, is composed of combed wool, with the exception of three single threads of yellow silk, running one way, and four threads of the same color, running in an opposite direction, forming a cross bar. We are of opinion that from the very trifling quantity of silk which enters into the fabric, and the material of chief value being composed of combed wool, and also from the evident use to which the article is to be applied, that it should properly be classed with worsted stuff goods paying a duty of 25 per cent. There are other reasons also which would operate on our minds to give it this direction, viz. In all the lighter fabrics of silk and worsted, such as bombasins, Norwich crapes, barege, &c. &c, paying a duty of 33 1/3 per cent it must be recollected that the entire warp is composed of silk, while in this sample of tartan plaid, the warp and filling both are entirely composed of combed wool, and that the few threads of silk which are added merely to give life and effect to the pattern, should not subject it to a higher rate of duty than Scotch or tartan plaids, or other stuff goods. *Public Documents*, October 1831 … Worsted Stuff Goods, from Manchester to New York … Plaids … actual [width] inches 18 *a* [to] 19 ~~~ Price per yard s.d. [shillings.pence] 0.7 *a* 1.0 <u>Trade between Great Britain and the United States of America</u>, 1833 ~~~ Satins and cashmeres of Scotch plaid patterns are expected to be very fashionable, both for robes and mantles. Some of the latter, intended for the promenade, are an exact imitation of the highland plaid; they have red, green, or blue grounds, with the pattern formed by black, white, or orange lines. *Court Magazine*, November 1834 [see also *tartan*]

plain velvet – There are various kinds of velvets; Plain, that is, that is uniform and smooth, without either figures or stripes. <u>General Dictionary of Commerce</u>, 1810 [see *velvet*]

plains – *British Merchandize exported, from* Jan. 5, 1792, *to* Jan. 5, 1793. … Woollen goods, … Welch plains <u>Annual Register</u>, 1799 ~~~ [in Dolgelly] a manufacture of webbing or white plains, a kind of coarse cloth undyed, chiefly for exportation. <u>Tour Through … Great Britain</u>, 1801 ~~~ *Of the Trade which Great Britain carries on with the Austrian Netherlands.* This is a very extensive and beneficial commerce, as it takes off great quantities of our products and manufactures. We supply them with a vast variety of articles, the chief of which are Yorkshire woollen cloths, particularly white plains for clothing their military; <u>Lex Mercatoria</u>, 1813 ~~~ What description of goods do you principally manufacture? – Plains, from four shillings a yard to nine or ten shillings. By plains you mean narrow cloths? – Yes, narrow cloths. <u>Reports from the Committees</u>, 1821 ~~~ The cost of keeping one negro a year on a cotton plantation: … 6 yards of plains, at 75 cents, 4.50; *Niles' Weekly Register*, December 7, 1822 ~~~ the coarse British goods called "plains," *Niles' Weekly Register*, May 10, 1823 ~~~ In the autumn of 1815, when the country had been destitute for a long time, negro cloths, (say such as Welsh plains, 7-8ths of a yard wide) averaged by the sales of that time, from 75 cents to $1, per yard. In 1816, they sold at 70 & 90 cents per yard. *Niles' Weekly Register*, November 17, 1827 ~~~ There is also a class of cloths imported, which, by this bill, falls under the 16 cents per square yard duty, called white plains, negro cloths, &c. These are from 23 to 28 inches wide, and cost in England from 12 cents to 34 cents the running yard, or from 19 to 47 cents the square yard. *Gales & Seaton's Register*, March 5, 1828 ~~~ *Plains* – width 27 inches, cost 10d. to 1s. 6d. sterling. An article of great consumption by sailors, boatmen, fishermen, and laborers. *Niles' Weekly Register*, March 8, 1828 ~~~ The chief manufactures are those of *webs,* and knit woollen stockings and socks. The former is carried on in the town of Dôlgelley, and in the surrounding country, to the distance of twelve miles, as also in the Vale of Dovey; and in these districts almost every little farmer is a manufacturer of webs, and few cottages are without a loom. These webs, called by the London drapers Welsh plains, or cottons, are a sort of thick white cloth, made in pieces of from ninety to one hundred and twenty yards long, two pieces constituting a web. The same branch of manufacture is also carried on in the western part of Montgomeryshire, and the south-eastern part of Denbighshire: but the quantity of webs produced in Dôlgelley and its neighbourhood is far greater than in either of the other districts. The Dôlgelley webs may be divided into two classes, – the coarsest, which are three-quarters of a yard wide; and the finest, seven-eighths of a yard: these, as well as those made in the district of which Machynlleth is the centre, are indiscriminately termed by the drapers *strong cloth,* to distinguish them from those of the Glyn district, near Oswestry, which are termed *small cloth,* because they are about one-eighth of a yard narrower, although of the same length. <u>Topographical Dictionary of Wales</u>, 1833 ~~~ *Tariffs* July 14, 1832 ~~~ On all milled and fulled cloth, known by the names of plains, kerseys, or kendal cottons, of which wool shall be the only material, <u>National Calendar</u>, 1834 [see also *negro cloth*]

plonkets – [see *plunkets*]

plowman net – [ad] Amidst the very extensive stock (£15,000) of elegant, fashionable, and cheap SILK MERCERY of Thomas and Co. … Gossamer and Plowman Nets, Crapes, and all other fashionable articles kept by the most respectable Silk-Mercers; *Repository of Arts*, April 1814 ~~~ [in India] we are often startled with the apparition of some obsolete manufacture, which, after having slumbered in an English warehouse during a quarter of a century, is sent out on a venture to India, under the idea that it may pass current in the upper provinces as a fashionable article. The poor deluded box-wallah [pedlar or duffer] is astonished and confounded at the contempt and horror which his Chamberry's, his Plowman's nets, and Picket muslins excite. In vain he endeavours to recommend them to notice; *Asiatic Journal*, January 1833

pluche – [see *peluche* and *plush*]

pluche de soie – The *cornette* bonnet of white satin also forms a favourite article for carriage costume; it is trimmed at the edge with the improved silk shag trimming, or *marabout plûche de soie*, … [Paris] the light swansdown … cannot yet be laid aside; and it must indeed be confessed, that it is full as light a trimming as the *plûche de soie*, which having the appearance in its improved state of a downy fur, is in high estimation as an ornament to spring pelisses, robes *à la Niobe*, and satin dresses for the Opera or evening party. *La Belle Assemblée*, April 1819 ~~~ [Paris hats] *pluche de soie*, that is to say, silk plush of different kinds, are all in favour. *Ladies' Monthly Museum*, November 1820 ~~~ The gowns are made low for dinner parties and evening dress; they are of silk of a bright summer colour, the border beautifully diversified with puckered white gauze and pink *plûche de soie*. *La Belle Assemblée*, October 1823 ~~~ trimmed at the border of the skirt with black *pluche-de-soye*, or with velvet, of a light and silky texture. *La Belle Assemblée*, September 1829 [see also *peluche* and *plush*]

pluie-d'or – Ribbons spotted with gold, called *rubans pluie-d'or*, have just been introduced for *ceintures*, scarfs, and to wear in the hair in full dress. *Repository of Arts*, April 1824

plume silk – Bonnet of either granite silk or spotted velvet, trimmed with the new plume silk trimming, with full bouquet of flowers on the left side. *La Belle Assemblée*, November 1819 ~~~ London Opera Dress. *Mantilla* of black levantine, lined throughout, and with a pelerine cape of *ponçeau* plume silk, over a dress, superbly finished, of white satin. *La Belle Assemblée*, January 1820 [see also *feathered silk*]

plume velvet – Black dresses are very prevalent this winter; a new article for matronly ladies in full dress, is much admired, called plume velvet, which is lightened by narrow saint stripes. *La Belle Assemblée*, January 1820

plunkets – Manufactures (woollen). … All *long coloured cloths*, called plunkets, azures, and blues, and long white cloths made in *Suffolk*, *Norfolk* and *Essex*, or elsewhere of like making – 29 to 32 [Yards long.] Whole Law Relative to the Duty and Office of a Justice of the Peace, 1794 ~~~ Imports into Mogodor in 1804. *Yorkshire and West County Cloths of various colours*. … 150 pieces, plunkets, about 40 yards each piece. … Imports into Mogodor in 1805. Woollen Cloths. *Yorkshire Cloths*. … Tier blue, or plunkets Account of the Empire of Marocco, 1809 ~~~ Plonkets, A kind of coarse woollen cloth. See *stat. I R* 3. c. 8. Law Dictionary, 1811

plush – *Dress of the Officers upon all Occasions*. All Officers in Quarters must wear their uniforms with lappels buttoned back, regimental small swords, with the belt under the coat, and regimental boots. Nothing is so unmilitary as seeing them walking about in plain cloaths, and it is therefore absolutely forbid by His Majesty's orders; nor must they, on any account, wear any waistcoat and breeches with their uniform, but white cloth, kerseymere, leather, or plush, with regimental buttons, and made in the regimental pattern, Rules and Regulations for the Cavalry, 1795 ~~~ A kind of villous or shaggy cloth, shag. Sheridan's English Dictionary, 1797 ~~~ Oxfordshire. Banbury. … the inhabitants are tradesmen, and manufacturers, principally, of worsted, and hair-shagg, or plush. State of the Poor, 1797 ~~~ in commerce, &c. a kind of stuff, having a sort of velvet nap or shag on one side, composed regularly of a woof of a single woollen thread and a double warp; the one wool, of two threads twisted; the other goats or camels hair; though there are some plushes entirely of worsted, and others composed wholly of hair. Encyclopædia Britannica, 1797 ~~~ [Patent granted to] Joshua Green, of Banbury, Oxfordshire, manufacturer; for a method of manufacturing corded and ribbed shags or plushes, composed of different materials, on a principle entirely new. Dated May 17. [1803] Annual Register, 1805 ~~~ Plush is manufactured, like velvet, on a loom with three treadles; … There are other kinds of plush, all of silk: some have a pretty long nap on one side, and some on the other. Some kinds of plush are likewise entirely made of worsted; these are, however, generally called shag. General Dictionary of Commerce, 1810 ~~~ [Paris] White silk beaver hats, lined with rose-colour, and ornamented with a wreath of white marabout feathers round the crown, are much in request. They resemble the silk plush, or shag silk hats, so much in vogue. *Ladies' Monthly Museum*, May 1817 ~~~ The following is a list of dresses made for her Royal Highness the Princess Elisabeth, on her nuptials with the Prince of Hesse Homberg, ... Four elegant satin and sarsnet pelisses, handsomely trimmed with satin and plush trimmings, and handsome lace ruffs. *La Belle Assemblée*, April 1818 ~~~ the most novel and striking is a carriage bonnet of that rare material the spotted moss plush; the ground is white with small spots of bright geranium. A diadem of white satin, edged with spotted moss plush, the same as the bonnet, is placed in front, *La Belle Assemblée*, November 1820 ~~~ Trimming of silk plush intermixed with velvet are very general: the trimming usually corresponds in colour with the pelisse; *Repository of Arts*, January 1823 ~~~ The newest carriage bonnet that we have seen is of fancy silk plush; the ground is in plain *gros de Naples,* and small lozenges are thrown up in plush. This material is novel and pretty. *Repository of Arts*, March 1823 ~~~ [Paris] The hats and bonnets are made of glazed plush; and this gloss has a beautiful effect, giving to the plush the same appearance as the changeable silks, now the reigning mode. *Lady's Magazine*, December 1829 ~~~ Some very fashionable hats and bonnets are made of plush; it is a heavy-looking article which we do not admire, and reminds us too much of liveries and linings of carriages to be pleased with it on a lady's head: this is one of those fashions borrowed from across the water, which, would be "more honoured in the breach than the observance." We are surprised that our countrywomen should show themselves so wanting in invention, as thus to copy every foolery because it is French! *Ladies' Museum*, January 1830 ~~~ Plush, of cotton, ... of silk and cotton, ... of wool, ... of silk, *Public Documents*, March 1832 ~~~ [court dress] An elegant embroidered aerophane dress, richly trimmed with blonde, over a petticoat of white satin; a violet satin train, trimmed with plush and blonde. *Court Journal*, March 2, 1833 [see also *pluche de soie, peluche* and *shag*]

poil – Poil, *hair.* <u>Dufief's French Dictionary</u>, 1810 ~~~ Poil, hair; beard, nap. *Etoffe à poil long*, high-napped or shagged cloth. <u>Boyer's French Dictionary</u>, 1835

poil de chevre – Goat's hair, *poil de chèvre.* <u>Dufief's French Dictionary</u>, 1810 ~~~ [men's] Some waistcoats are composed of *poil de chevre*, with patterns embroidered in silk. *Casket*, January 1831 ~~~ [Paris, new materials] *Tissue de poil de chèvre*; a material in the style of Cachemerienne, with or without figured satin stripes. *Lady's Magazine and Museum*, May 1836 ~~~ We may cite, among the most elegant evening dresses, those of a new material of the chaly kind, called *poil-de-chevre.* The pattern is ponceau, upon a fawn-coloured ground. *Ladies' Pocket,* July 1836

poil de Sanglier – Bristle, *soies,* ou *poil de sanglier* ... A wild boar, *un sanglier.* <u>Dufief's French Dictionary</u>, 1810 ~~~ [men's] During some time past the cravat of a dandy could not be brought high enough; it was supported round the throat by a stiffener in *poil de Sanglier*. This stiffener is gone out of fashion, and the cravat is now worn low and soft. [Article may be satirical] *Casket*, January 1831

point d'Angleterre – [see *English point*]

point ground – [see *pillow lace*]

point lace – in the manufactories, is a general term, used for all kinds of laces wrought with the needle; such are the point de Venice, point de France, point de Genoa, &c. which are distinguished by the particular economy and arrangement of their points. – *Point* is sometimes used for lace woven with bobbins; as English point, point de Malines, point d'Havre, &c. <u>Encyclopædia Britannica</u>, 1797 ~~~ [court dress] Double ruffles, tucker, and lappels of point lace. *Lady's Magazine*, February 1797 ~~~ [court dress] A petticoat of rich purple and grey figured silk, with a most elegant drapery of point lace; *La Belle Assemblée*, June 1807 ~~~ Lace properly so called, is essentially distinguished from *point*, (to which it bears a resemblance), by being worked upon a cushion, *with bobbins*, whereas, the *point* is invariably made with the needle, such as the French or Alençon point, the Venetian, and the Brussels point. ... some authors write, concerning Alençon *lace*, and English *point*; but, this is an error. <u>Literary Panorama</u>, 1808 ~~~ [court dress] A rich white satin petticoat, over which was worn a most beautiful point lace dress. The train was composed of rich white figured *gros de* Naples, *Ladies' Literary Cabinet,* September 22, 1821 ~~~ Point (*Com.*) or *Point-lace*, the richest and heaviest kind of lace. <u>Universal Technological Dictionary</u>, 1823 ~~~ Point lace is seldom seen now, except as a crown-piece to babies' caps. Much of it used to be done in the nunneries abroad; but we do not wish such prisons to be established again, for the sake of point lace. <u>Scenes of British Wealth</u>, 1825 ~~~ [court dress] A richly embroidered dress of black aerophane; train of watered striped satin; mantilla of point lace. *Court*

Journal, March 23, 1833 ... *Point lace* ... was formerly the chief occupation of young ladies in convents, and was very injurious to the eyes of the workers; Scenes of Commerce, 1836 [see also *Alençon*, *Brussels*, *Honiton*, *Venetian* and *lace*]

point net – [court dress] Court-train and petticoat of blush-coloured satin, the petticoat tastefully embroidered with silver, with a beautiful point net drapery embroidered with silver wreaths and sprigs; body and sleeves trimmed with rich point lace and silver belts. *Lady's Magazine*, June 1810 ~~~ Since the lace trade has failed in Nottingham, I have been under the necessity of taking a box, and going round about the country and selling lace to maintain myself and my family, so that I know pretty well the general opinion of the country people, at least Derby, Nottingham, and Lincolnshire on the subject. If I had offered them the best lace I had, what we call double press point net, or six coarse hold warp, and told them positively that those were good articles, their answer would be, they had been imposed on so often they would buy no more. People have said they would sooner give seven shillings for a yard of thread or Buckinghamshire lace, than give me sixpence for my best lace, though I considered mine nearly as good as Buckinghamshire lace. ... I will now, with the leave of the Committee, come to the point net-lace; that I think was first made about the year 1772 to 1774; it was, when first known, invented by what we now call single-press; it continued so till the year 1784, when what is called double-press was invented; ... About the year 1805, the cotton-yarn was brought to that perfection that it was fine enough to be wrought into double-press lace; upon a point net-frame it answered every purpose which the ladies required, both for beauty, elegance and durability, so much so that in 1808 there were 1,500 point net-frames; ... About this time single-press was introduced into the cotton lace, double the quantity of it could be made in the same time by the workmen who made it; this glutted the market, cast many men out of employment thereby, and it soon destroyed its own credit and the credit of that which it was an imitation of, by its own imperfections. ... the consequences which have arisen from the introduction of these two articles into point net-lace have been, that out of 1,000 Frames, which were employed in making cotton net in the year 1809, there are not more now, I suppose, than 100, I believe hardly that number. Reports from the Committees, 1812 ~~~ The Nottingham imitations of lace are of two kinds, point-net and warp-net. From the names of the machines in which they are made, they are both a species of chain-work, and the machines are varieties of the stocking frame. ... The lace in this machine is formed of one continued thread, ... These operations continued, form a net work of hexagonal meshes, which resemble lace, and when stiffened with starch, to make the meshes preserve their figure, has a very beautiful appearance. The objection to this imitation of lace is, that it becomes loose and irregular, after being washed; and if the thread breaks, the work will unravel in the same manner as stockings. Edinburgh Encyclopædia, 1830 ~~~ [court dress] White satin dress, bordered at the bottom with point net and gauze riband, *Royal Lady's Magazine*, May 1831 [see also *single press lace*]

pole cat – [see *fitch*]

poledavy – Pouldavis, (*in commerce*) A kind of course linen cloth. Ash's English Dictionary, 1795 ~~~ Poledavy, A kind of coarse cloth or canvass. Sheridan's English Dictionary, 1797 ~~~ Rates of Scavage, ... Linen, ... poldavies, per bolt . . . 1*d.* Practical Book of Customs, 1802 ~~~ canvass for wrapping wares in, sarplier, poledavy. Dictionary of the Synonymous Words, 1806 ~~~ Sort of coarse cloth; also *Poledavis* and *Pouldavis*, perhaps the name of the maker. Walker Remodeled, 1836

Polish twill – The Polish twill is also much worn for morning dresses; it is a sort of chambray, and can hardly be distinguished from sarsnet, except by the richness of texture. *Edinburgh Annual Register*, August 30, 1814

polonais – Materials .. of Demi-Toilette. ... a half-transparent woollen material, called "gaze polonais." *Casket*, September 1831 ~~~ Make and Materials of Evening Dress. – Crape, *gaze polonaise*, and *tulle*, all worn over sarsnet or *gros de Naples*, are the materials most in favor; *Atheneum*, October 1831 ~~~ Some new materials, as ... *gaze Polonais*, have recently been introduced in evening dress; the gauzes are figured, and of a very rich description; *Ladies' Museum*, November 1831 ~~~ Bonnets are, for the most part, of rich silks, as *moire*, which is most in favor, or else *gros des Indes*, or the new material, *gros Polonais*; this last is an extremely rich silk. One of the prettiest *capotes* of the month is of rose-colored *gros*

Polonais, with the material disposed in plaits upon the crown. *Atheneum*, December 1831 ~~~ Make and Materials of Evening Dress. – Among the new materials which belong to winter rather than autumn, but for which many orders have already been given, are the *satin polonais* and *à la reine*, ... The materials are of extreme richness. *Atheneum*, February 1832

pompadour – *Mousseline de laine Pompadour*, with large bunches of coloured flowers on a black ground, is also a beautiful and fashionable article for dresses. *Court Journal*, November 2, 1833 ~~~ The new materials most likely to be in favour in evening dress are, *Foulard Pompadour*, the pattern dates from Louis XV.'s time; it is rich but heavy; *Court Magazine*, April 1834 ~~~ Court Dress. .. Robe of *gros Pompadour*, vermilion ground, and rich antique pattern of gold. *Court Magazine*, June 1834 ~~~ Court costume Louis XIV., a rich white satin dress, ... train pale green Pompadour silk, lined, and trimmed with ribbon; ... [court dress] Beautiful green and white Pompadour silk, corsage and sleeves in the costume of Louis XIV., *Lady's Magazine and Museum*, May 1836 [*note*: Pompadour is also a claret color.]

Pompadour satin – the real novelty for dresses are ... Pompadour satin. *Court Magazine*, May 1833 ~~~ The newly-introduced figured Satin *à la Pompadour*, is most admired with orange or cherry-coloured designs on black grounds. *Court Journal*, November 2, 1833 ~~~ A dress of pompadour satin, richly figured in groups of natural flowers of the most brilliant hues on a black ground; *Royal Lady's Magazine*, August 1834 ~~~ The materials of evening dress continue to be of the richest description. Pompadour satins, a white ground embroidered in bouquets of different flowers in colours, are much in request. *Court Magazine*, March 1835 ~~~ [court dress] Pompadour satin dress, broché d'or a bouquets; [brocaded in gold bouquets] *Lady's Magazine and Museum*, March 1836

pompon – Pompons, (for women's head dresses, silk or wool) <u>Digest of the Recent Commercial Regulations</u>, 1824 ~~~ Some half-dress hats have the inside of the brim trimmed with a narrow wreath of ribbon disposed either in *coques*, or foliage; but *pompons*, or small knots of ribbon, are more in favour. These are not attached to the hat, but are placed in the hair under the brim; either two of different colours in the centre of the forehead, on one placed on the left side. ... [in evening dress] We also see some *coiffures* decorated with two *pompons* of blue or rose-coloured ribbons, with a diamond or pearl ornament in the centre of each. *La Belle Assemblée*, September 1831 ~~~ A trimming of blond lace, in the cap style, intermingled with *nœuds* of ribbon *en pompon*, is generally employed to decorate the inside of the brims of silk bonnets. *La Belle Assemblée*, October 1831 ~~~ [court dress] rich sky-blue satin manteau, ornee de pompons; *Lady's Magazine and Museum*, March 1836

pompose – [Paris] *Pomposes*, round bows of ribbon, made up in the style of those put into baby's caps, are very much in vogue. They are worn with two long ends, to fasten pelerines or collars at the neck; and smaller ones are worn, one at each side, beneath the fronts of the bonnets. *Lady's Magazine and Museum*, May 1836

pongee – [ad] Summer Goods, ... Pongees, ... of all colour and qualities. <u>Boston Annual Advertiser</u>, 1823 ~~~ Pongees (Canton, French or Italian silk) <u>Commercial Directory</u>, 1823 ~~~ I suspect the stuff called pongee has a mixture of this cotton in it. We use it for pillows and mattresses; but it is too elastic to be approved by the doctors for the latter. It is of a brownish color, and has more the feeling of silk than of the gossypium or common cotton. *Boston Monthly Magazine*, May 1826 ~~~ The first week in August, we put in hand, a lady's riding habit, to be made by four or five hands, of thin pongee. ... The dress made by the men was a lady's riding habit; I believe of silk and cotton Pongee. ... Width of pongee is half a yard, <u>Trial of Twenty-Four Journeymen Tailors</u>, 1827 ~~~ For the summer-uniform, each young lady must be provided with two dark slate colored pongee dresses; <u>Account of the Conflagration of the Ursuline Convent</u>, 1834 ~~~ [ad] Have received by the ships Hark-away and Jefferson, direct from Liverpool, ... 2 cases white, scarlet, crimson and fancy colored Pongee hdkfs. ... 2 cases lead, blue, black, brown and suchan pongees. *Farmer's Register*, May 1835 ~~~ The Manufacture Of Silk. – We have heretofore had occasion to speak of the success with which the power loom bad been applied by Mr. Gay to the weaving of Silk. But the only experiments which had then been made, had been made upon on old and very awkwardly constructed cotton loom. Within the last three weeks, one of the new looms, with improvements by Mr. Gay, adapted to the manufacture of silk has been put in operation upon a piece of fine white Pongee Handkerchiefs, three quarters wide.

This loom has put at rest all doubt that might before have been entertained in relation to the practicability of weaving silk in this manner. We have several times made the observation by marking the piece with a pencil, and the loom has woven an *inch and a half* of this fabric in *one minute*. Others have at different times witnessed the operation of the loom and their observation of the result has been precisely the same. The speed is regulated at one *hundred and forty* strokes of the lathe per minute, and the fabric which it turns off is in no manner inferior to the imported article. The girl who attends it is an experienced cotton weaver and one of the smartest in the country. She affirms that she can without difficulty tend four of them, and turn off *one hundred* yards of goods per day. What will Louis Phillipe say to that? *Fessenden's Silk Manual*, February 1836 ~~~ they make a species of *washing* silk, called at Canton *ponge,* which becomes more soft as it is longer used. The Chinese, 1836

popeline – Parisian Evening Dress. … A white *gaze de popeline* gown over a white satin slip; *Repository of Fashions*, February 1829 ~~~ Evening dress. A dress of *gaze popeline* over a black *gros de Naples* slip. *La Belle Assemblée*, August 1830 ~~~ *Palmyrienne, gaze popeline*, and white lace, are all fashionable in evening dress. … those of *gaze popeline* are frequently trimmed with *nœuds* of the *papillon* form, placed at some distance from each other. *La Belle Assemblée*, October 1830 ~~~ Poplin is another plain silk and worsted article, but the worsted weft is of a thicker thread than Norwich Crape. The French *papeline* has its weft of Flasksilk, *(fleuret,)* but the English imitation is with worsted. Analytical Dictionary, 1830 [see also *poplin*]

poplin – Pelisses of dove-colour poplins have a genteel appearance. *Lady's Magazine*, December 1800 ~~~ Papelin, poplin; stuff made of worsted and silk for habits, robes, &c. Dictionary … Ancient Irish, 1802 ~~~ London, Feb. 12, 1804. A most elegant article for Ladies' Gowns has made its appearance in the higher circles; it is called the Union Poplin, and combines the lustre and consistency of the Irish poplins, with the softness of the finest muslin. *Boston Weekly Magazine*, March 10, 1804 ~~~ Irish poplins have lost nothing of their attraction, but they are generally worn in light colours; bright faun, amber, drab, Clarence blue, and olive-green, are all in general request; and although various trimmings are fashionable, lace, particularly blond, is in the highest estimation; it is, however, more generally appropriated to full than to dinner dresses, except blond net, which is quilled very full on dinner dresses, the one which we are about to describe struck me as being very elegant and tasteful in no common degree. Frock of amber Irish poplin, tight to the shape, and very short in the waist, cut very low all round the bosom, and made to lace behind. *La Belle Assemblée*, November 1814 ~~~ [ad] Plain Poplins, 4s. 6d. and 5s. per yard, usually sold at 5s. 6d. and 6s. *Repository of Arts*, March 1815 ~~~ For the dress promenade, or carriage costume, velvet spencers, with tabbinet, silk, or poplin dresses, are in high estimation, *Repository of Arts*, March 1819 ~~~ Opera robe of purple poplin, trimmed with broad white blond, is much admired on our matronly ladies. *La Belle Assemblée*, May 1819 ~~~ a poplin at ten shillings per yard, which is of course of very fine quality, is superior to the best they have here [France] at eighteen or twenty francs per yard. *European Magazine*, September 1823 ~~~ Poplin dresses, both plain and figured, are much in request; the plain, being the real Irish tabinets, are reckoned the most genteel, and are worn in every style of dress: the figured, often of British manufacture, are confined to home costume. *Ladies' Pocket*, January 1829 ~~~ Poplin is another plain silk and worsted article, but the worsted weft is of a thicker thread than Norwich Crape. The French *papeline* has its weft of Flasksilk, *(fleuret,)* but the English imitation is with worsted. Analytical Dictionary, 1830 ~~~ [court dress] A white figured poplin dress, trimmed with blonde; train of blue figured silk, trimmed with tulle and satin; *Royal Lady's*, May 1831 ~~~ We understand her Excellency the Countess Mulgrave takes a lively interest in the encouragement of Irish manufactures, not only in the many orders given by her Excellency for articles justly esteemed, the manufacture of this country, as poplins, linens, damask, &c. …The first part of the order executed, we hear, is in every way a credit to our country; the ground is azure blue, with white satin stripes, which has all the effect of silver, and, contrasted on the blue, has a very chaste and elegant effect; altogether it is a credit to the manufacturers, and the taste that designed it. We must not omit noticing the brocaded poplin, quite novel in its way, designed and painted by her Excellency; the coloured flowers and sprays tastefully brocaded on the white poplin ground has a very rich and beautiful effect, and cannot fail to attract the attention of our fashionables as a splendid evening dress. We understand Irish poplins were never more sought after than at present; their richness and durability will always insure them a preference, independent of the vast good done by the employment of so many industrious artisans. ... In addition to the above, we have just heard her Royal Highness the Duchess of Kent, with that patriotic feeling which shines so conspicuous in every action, has sent a large order for poplins through her Excellency, the Countess Mulgrave, to the different manufacturers of our city. Her Royal Highness has ordered a dress of the *Mulgrave Brocaded Poplin* – the first dress was only just finished from the loom. *Court Journal*, December 26, 1835 ~~~ Poplins are likely to be very fashionable for robes of all kinds. That material offers this season great variety; it is watered and figured in all colours and in almost all patterns. Small quadrilled patterns will be much in request for undress robes. Colours for poplins are also very various: we may cite among them wood colour, grey, green, and blue. *Court Magazine*, December 1836 [see also *gaze popeline* and *tabbinet*]

porcupine – the flat and porcupine ostrich, *Lady's Magazine*, April 1800 ~~~ ornamented with porcupine feathers. *La Belle Assemblée*, April 1816 [see *feathers* and *ostrich*]

Portuguese sarsnet – The Portuguese sarsnet, an evident imitation of that beautiful article the French levantine, has lately made its appearance; but it has all the thickness of the levantine without its elegant softness, and seems best appropriated to traveling dresses. *La Belle Assemblée*, June 1812

pou – louse. *Des poux*, lice. <u>Boyer's French Dictionary</u>, 1836

pou de soie – *Paduasoy* is a similar falsification of *Podesoy*, the English offspring of the French *Poudesoie*. <u>Critical Pronouncing Dictionary</u>, 1806 ~~~ Pou-de-Soie, (grosse étoffe toute de soie [thick stuff entirely of silk) *Padesoy, a sort of farandine*. <u>Boniface's French Dictionary</u>, 1828 ~~~ Opera Dress. The robe is composed of *poux de soie, Court Magazine*, August 1833 ~~~ [ad] 1 case Pou de Soi a genteel article for ladies' summer dresses, 9d. per yd. *New England Farmer*, July 10, 1833 ~~~ Several of these umbrellas are covered with white *pou de soie. Court Journal*, July 13, 1833 ~~~ The *pou de soie dentelle* is another very pretty article, and is equally well suited to either demi-toilette or full dress. Orange, red, or green, covered with black lace patterns, has a very rich and elegant effect. *Court Journal*, December 14, 1833 ~~~ we see also several [robes] of rich plain silk, particularly *pou de soie, gros de France*, and *gros de Naples chiné*. The former of these materials is very generally employed, and is likely to continue long in favour; it drapes admirably, is rich without being heavy, and its high price will prevent it from ever becoming very common. *Court Magazine*, June 1834 ~~~ [Paris] Silks continue to be partially worn [at public breakfasts and evening *fêtes* in the open air], particularly those of watered *poi de soi* of light colours, which in many instances are trimmed with black lace. ... Silk is very little worn [for evening dress], but where it is adopted it is usually of plain triple *pou de soie. Ladies' Pocket*, July 1836 ~~~ *double pou de soie* ... begins to be employed for hats and bonnets; *Court Magazine*, May 1835 ~~~ [Paris] The newest materials for dresses are *poux de soie*, figured, striped, and cross-barred: these are frequently of two colours, or two shades of the same colour. *Lady's Magazine and Museum*, May 1836 [see also *paduasoy*]

pouldavis – [see *poledavy*]

poult de soie – [ad] Poult de Soie, and other rich Silks, for Pelisses and Evening Dress; *Court Journal*, February 9, 1833 ~~~ [court dress] White moire poult-de-soie dress; corsage and train of mauve terry, trimmed with satin; *Court Journal*, March 2, 1833 ~~~ [ad] Dry Goods at Reduced Prices. ... col'd [colored] Poult de Soie Silk, at 3s per yd, of an excellent quality, *New England Farmer*, July 1, 1835 ~~~ Some very pretty new *poults de Soie* have just appeared; they have blue *écrue*, and straw grounds, very lightly figured in black, or in darker shades than the ground. *New Monthly Belle Assemblée*, October 1836

prig – Prig, to steal cloth as a taylor <u>Perry's English Dictionary</u>, 1795

Prince of Wales plume – [Paris] Feathers are said to be placed on hats *à l'Anglaise*, when there are three in a vertical direction, in front, on account of the three feathers, called the Prince of Wales's plume. *Ladies' Museum*, October 1829

Prince's Cord – a new velvet, called Prince's Cord, are mush used in bonnets and cloaks *Lady's Magazine*, July 1800 ~~~ *The Irish Four-in-Hand Club.* ... the costume of the drivers, blue coats, buff waistcoats, and white Prince's-cord breeches; a driving coat of Yorkshire drab, *Sporting Magazine*, August 1810

prince's stuff – [at Cambridge] Bachelors of arts shall provide themselves with gowns made of prunello, or prince's stuff. *Gentleman's Magazine*, July 1750 ~~~ in the year *of Our Lord* 1789 ~~~ [goods lawfully possessed] two hundred yards of princes stuff, Complete System of Pleading, 1798 ~~~ Doctor in Divinity. ... The ordinary gown is black, either or crape, silk, or prince's stuff; Book Explaining the Ranks and Dignities of British Society, 1809 ~~~ Of some of the *ordinary* habits worn at present, a brief description may not be unacceptable. A *Master of Arts* wears a gown of Prince's stuff, and a hood of black silk, lined with crimson; the gown is remarkable for the semicircular cut at the bottom of the sleeve. *Bachelor of Arts,* Prince's stuff gown looped up at the elbow, and terminating in a point; black hood lined with fur. *Nobleman,* black silk gown with full sleeves; a tippet like that worn by the Proctors attached to the shoulders. *Gentleman Commoner,* silk gown plaited at the sleeves. *Commoner,* gown of Prince's stuff, no sleeves, a black strip appended from each shoulder reaches to the bottom of the dress, and, towards the top, is gathered into plaits. *Student of Civil Law,* plain silk gown, with lilac hood. *Scholar,* plain stuff gown with full sleeves. *Servitor,* gown like the Commoner's, but without plaits at the shoulder. Walks in Oxford, 1818 ~~~ In December 1820, ... Mr. *Bryson* possesses a Secret in the art of dying Bombazeens, Princes Stuffs, and other Goods, which is known to himself and Son-in-law, *Samuel Portlock,* only: Reports of Cases, 1824 ~~~ Stuff goods, worsted, viz.; ... princes' stuff, Trade between Great Britain and the United States of America, 1833 ~~~ [at Oxford] The Commoner's gown is made of what is called *prince's stuff;* and, together with the cap, costs about five guineas. *Tait's Edinburgh Magazine*, June 1835 ~~~ [in 1744] Weaving, ... Making goods of the same kind and equal to Lutherines, rufferines, Prince's stuffs or prunellos, by mixing a certain material with silk, instead of mohair yarn. Patents of Invention, 1857

princettas – That an article called "*princettas,*" possessing the same essential generic character with *bombasins* and *Norwich crapes,* and being composed of materials precisely similar, only combined in proportions somewhat different, *Public Documents*, January 1829 ~~~ Worsted Stuff Goods, from Manchester to New York ... Princetta do ... actual [width] inches 25 *a* [to] 26 ~~~ Price per yard s.d. [shillings.pence] 1.4 *a* 3.0 Trade between Great Britain and the United States of America, 1833 ~~~ [ad] Have received by the ships Hark-away and Jefferson, direct from Liverpool, ... 1 case fine and extra fine black and colored princettas. *Farmer's Register*, May 1835

printanière – There were also some few ladies, ... dressed in those light materials, which have been invented expressly for the summer; one of the most beautiful of these is a silk *tissu* called *printannière.* *La Belle Assemblée*, May 1830 ~~~ [Paris] The materials for bonnets, or, as they sill continue to be called, *capotes bibis,* are *moire,* satin, which this year remains a long time in favour, and a new kind of silk called *printanière*; it is printed in small squares, which present different shades of the same colour. I should observe, that it is made in all colours, but lilac, *écrue* (the colour of unbleached linen), and cherry, are most fashionable. *La Belle Assemblée*, May 1832 ~~~ Printanier, -ère, *adj.* (qui est du printemps) *Of or belonging to the spring.* Fleurs printanières, *Spring-flowers.* Boniface's French Dictionary, 1836

printed fabrics – Calico printing has been hitherto confined to linens and cottons. Of late, however, an ingenious method has been discovered, probably by the help of heat, of applying topical stains to kerseymeres for waistcoat patterns. *Monthly Review*, August 1795 ~~~ List of Patents for New Inventions. To John Nyren, of Bromley, in the county of Middlesex, muslin bleacher and tambour worker; for printing fancy patterns on silk and cotton lacenet, instead of tambouring or working them in colours. Dated September 27, 1805 *Philosophical Magazine*, October 1805 ~~~ *Selection of a Cargo suited, on a general scale, for the Spanish Settlements in America,* ... *Printed Calicoes,* 1000 *Pieces,* 28 *yards each.* 600 Pieces low priced, say, from 16d. to 22d. per yard, glaring colours and grounds, neat sprigs. More depends on the colours and shew, than on the fineness of the cloth; if they only consist of two colours, let them be gaudy and lively. 200 Pieces, from 20d. to 24d. chintz furniture patterns, sprigged, shewy, and tawdry. 200 Pieces ell wide, from 2s. to 2s. 6d. per yard, length 21 yards; all most shewy possible, to imitate the prints done by Portales in Neufchatel, Switzerland, or East India calicoes. Present State of the Spanish Colonies, 1810 ~~~ [ad] printed Cambrics and Muslins, patterns new, and singularly elegant, from 2s. to 3s. per yard, usually sold at 4s 6d; *La Belle Assemblée*, July 1807 ~~~ Parisian Walking Dress. Round dress of printed muslin, of a cerulean blue spotted with black, ... [Paris]

Printed cambric gowns are yet very fashionable; they are either striped or spotted, … muslin gowns, printed in small chequers of pink, are in high favour: *La Belle Assemblée*, August 1818 ~~~ Printed linens of all descriptions, cambrics, chintzes and muslins, are much in request; the favourite ground is bird-of-Paradise-yellow, with black figures. Hermit brown, too, is seen figured over with humming-birds. Other birds of the most resplendent and varied plumage are also seen, perched on branches of trees, which wind up the gown, in stripes. Some of these dresses have patterns remarkably small, such as the common house-flies, grains of barley, and little stars. *La Belle Assemblée*, September 1827 ~~~ Never were chintzes and printed muslins more in request than they are at present, for morning dresses: by the young they are often retained as a home attire, till the evening. Some of these are uncommonly beautiful; particularly those on a ground of canary-yellow, over which runs a pattern of miniature roses, the hues of which, together with the charmingly-shaded green foliage, are of the most delicate kind. Some of these printed materials are on white striped muslin, and the pattern consists of *bouquets,* separate from each other, of the most lively and varied colours, the flowers being correct imitations from the treasures of the garden. Though these are higher in price than the coloured chintz above mentioned, we confess that we prefer the cheaper article, from its attractive delicacy and elegance: the flowers on the striped muslin strike us as ungenteel, and are, certainly, only an old fashion revived. *La Belle Assemblée*, October 1828 ~~~ Chintzes of the most rich and beautiful patterns are much worn in home costume: their colours are so brilliant, and at the same time so soft, that many of them have the appearance of painted velvet, especially those which have a ground of bright ruby; but the most fashionable dress for home *déshabille* is of striped coloured muslin, the ground either an ethereal-blue, or the yellow of the bird-of-paradise. These are flowered over with *bouquets* of passion-flowers, auriculas, and white narcissuses; on the yellow are also seen convolvuluses; the flowers are all coloured from nature, but are smaller than in reality. A bright spring green, with sprigs of heart'-ease, is admired; and, for half dress, tartan silks are very general; the ground either buff or canary-yellow, with chequers, rather large, formed of three stripes, black, scarlet, and hare-brown. *La Belle Assemblée*, June 1829 ~~~ Nothing can be more perfect and beautiful than the designs of the printed muslins and *batistes,* which are becoming every day more in favour for morning costume whether at home or for walking. They are usually figured in columns, and being plaited full round the waist, while the width of the pattern is displayed towards the bottom of the dress, the stripes take the form of rays, and this produces an exceedingly novel effect to the eye. Patterns of this kind are not confined to muslins; printed silks are daily becoming more fashionable. It requires some taste to chuse these. There is one that seems to meet with many admirers; bird of Paradise yellow is the ground, on which is printed large red lozenges; some of our contemporaries have pronounced that it has a very piquant effect. We mention it by way of warning. It is true, it is worn: it is gaudy and unbecoming. … The new printed muslins of all sorts greatly vary in their patterns from those of last year. Arabesque designs, garlands of roses of a large size, Gothic figuring, and Etruscan vases filled with flowers, are the favourite patterns. They print many of these designs on rayed and columned muslins. The muslins *à Alhambra* are so called because they are printed with arabesques taken from that celebrated palace. *Lady's Magazine*, April 1830 ~~~ Clear muslin, printed in delicate patterns, and in colours partly full, and partly light, is fashionable for dresses, but not so much so as washing silks with white grounds, printed in very small bouquets of pink flowers. *Court Magazine*, August 1833 ~~~ *Cheapness of Female Clothing in Modern Times*. – The wife of a labouring man may buy at a retail shop a neat and good print as low as 6d. per yard, so that, allowing six yards for the dress, the whole material shall only cost three shillings. Common plain calico may be bought for 2 ½ d. per yard. Elegant cotton prints, for ladies' dresses, sell at from 10d. to 1s. 4d. per yard, and printed muslins at from 1s. to 4s., – the higher priced having beautiful patterns, in brilliant and permanent colours. Thus the humblest classes have now the means of as great neatness, and even gaiety of dress, as the middle and upper classes of the last age. *Imperial Magazine*, September 1833 [see also *calico* and *chintz*]

prunella – Prunello, a kind of stuff woven with a mixture of silk and worsted, of which clergymen's gowns are made. <u>Royal English Dictionary</u>, 1775 ~~~ Prunella, (*s. in commerce*) A kind of stuff, prunello. <u>Ash's English Dictionary</u>, 1795… Prunello, a kind of silken stuff <u>Perry's English Dictionary</u>, 1795 ~~~ [ad]

on Sale, every Article Connected with the Silk Trade, as well as Fine Prunello, Eminets, and Moreens; *Yorkshire Observer*, December 7, 1822 ~~~ Prunella, everlasting or Barbary stuff, mixed of wool and silk, of all colors and qualities and width <u>Digest of the Commercial Regulations</u>, 1824 ~~~ [ad] KEEPS constantly on hand, a general assortment of Ladies and Gentlemen's BOOTS AND SHOES, Among which, are Ladies' Prunell, Sattin, Morocco, Seal and Calf skin BOOTS, Prunell of all colours, <u>Directory for the Village of Rochester</u>, 1827 ~~~ Prunella shoes are often seen embroidered on the front with a flower in coloured silks, and sometimes with an ornamented buckle or button; *Lady's Magazine*, May 1830 ~~~ Carriage Dress. ... boots of pea-green prunella. *Royal Lady's*, January 1831 ~~~ Prunello, in pieces, worsted and silk, ... Prunello shoes *Public Documents*, March 1832 ~~~ An early morning's walk in a pair of thin prunellas will be more injurious than even the want of exercise. Unless the feet are warm and dry the body cannot be in a state of health and comfort; and the danger from wet feet is much greater where a person sits inactive, than when constantly engaged in exercise. <u>Female Student</u>, 1836 ~~~ In Europe and America, boots and shoes are commonly made of leather: in shoes for females, however, it is not unusual to use prunello, which is a kind of twilled, worsted cloth. ... The edges of fine leather shoes and boots, are trimmed with thin strips of the like material: whilst those of prunello, and other thin shoes for ladies, are bound with narrow tape. <u>Panorama of Professions and Trades</u>, 1836 ~~~ [Paris] Black silk slippers are much worn in *négligé*, and the French prunella for walking, as they are much less accessible to damp. *Blackwood's Lady's Magazine*, July 1836 [see also *lasting*]

pullicat – The Bengal ships, with two from Colombo, brought the following cargoes: ... Pullicat – 800 [pieces] *Monthly Magazine*, October 1798 ~~~ pullicats, a kind of chequered cotton handkerchiefs, *Belfast Monthly*, December 1808 ~~~ Great improvements have likewise been made in the dying of cotton, particularly by George Mackintosh, who, in 1805, having engaged M. Papillon, a dyer from Rouen, erected a large dye-house at Dalmarneck, where genuine Adrianople red is dyed; so that the Pulicat handkerchiefs made here are not inferior to those imported from the East Indies. <u>Topographical Dictionary of the United Kingdom</u>, 1808 ~~~ Glasgow. ... The manufacture of pulicats, at one time carried on by a Mr. Mackintosh, has long ceased to exist. <u>Travels through England</u>, 1820 ~~~ The article of pullicats, for which there was a great demand in India, sold, in 1814, at 9*d*. per yard; in 1817 it was reduced to 7*d*.; in 1819 to 4*d*.; in 1826 to 2 ½*d*.; and now it was only 2 ½*d*. *Fraser's Magazine*, April 1833 ~~~ Hindoos' manufactures are generally imitated in Europe, and even retain their names. Calicoes, cossacs, jaconets, boucks, chintzs, mulls, japans, ballusores, bandannas, pullcates, ginghams, &c. &c. are all Indian names, and mere imitations. <u>A Million of Facts</u>, 1835 ~~~ A kind of silk handkerchief. <u>Knowles' English Dictionary</u>, 1835 ~~~ Pullicat handkerchiefs – a style of goods first introduced at Glasgow in 1785, and manufactured exclusively there to a great extend for many years – were eventually introduced into Lancashire, but have never attained the same magnitude as in their birth-place. <u>Cotton Manufacture</u>, 1836

punjum cloth – Punjum is a kind of cloth, of a peculiar strong texture, manufactured in the Northern Circars, on the Coast of Coromandel. A punjum is the mark of quality, and consists of 120 threads, and increases by 2 punjums; the lowest is 10 in the breadth, the coarsest made, and called No. 10 Punjum, from which it increases by 2, and the finer the threads, the greater number of punjums are contained in the breadth, up to 40, the finest of this sort of cloth made. The numbers are 10, 12, 14, 16, 18, 20, and so up to 40. This kind of cloth in the lower numbers, has been lately imitated with success in the Baramhaul country; but is made up in pieces, only about half the length of the Circar cloth, and called Salempores. <u>Oriental Commerce</u>, 1813 ~~~ [ad] India Goods, viz. Nos. 14, 16, and 18, white and brown Punjams, *Colonist*, January 10, 1828 ~~~ The manufactures are wholly white cotton cloths, known here by the name of punjums, or, as we more commonly call them, calicoes, of every degree of fineness, from muslin down to sail-cloth. The quality most in demand, and of which by far the greatest quantity is made, is that which would be sold in England for a shilling a yard, but which costs nearly eighteen pence here. It is a fact established beyond all doubt, that the English manufacturers can import their cotton from India, at a great expense of time, risk, and actual cost, work it into cloths in England, return it to this country again with renewed expences of conveyance, and sell it profitably after all, at a less rate than the same kind of goods can be made for in India – where the cotton, the looms, the labourers, and the buyers, are all upon the same spot. This is owing, no doubt, to the wonderful facilities granted to manufacturers by the use of machinery. The consequences of it promise to be most important, and at Bombay and Madras, where this fact has been completely verified by importations from England, and profitable sales of such goods, among the natives themselves, I have heard several most intelligent men express their belief, that the whole of India would, bye and bye, be clothed in the manufactures of Britain. The East India Company have already lessened the amount of their supplies of these articles for the European market, since, the value which the name of *India* gave to every thing of the kind imported into England has worn off, and since the nations of the Mediterranean, who consumed so much of them, have found a substitute in the cheaper and finer manufactures of Glasgow. *Oriental Herald*, December 1829 ~~~ Madras Native Cavalry and Horse Artillery: ... 2 pair loose Punjum trousers, lined Report ... Affairs of the East-India Company, 1833 [see also *calico*]

purfle – Purfle (*v. t. from the* French, pourfiler) To embroider. Purfle (*s. from the verb*) A border, and edge of embroidery. Purfled (*p. from* purfle) Embroidered: ... Purflew (*s. from* purfle) A border, and edge of embroidery. ... Purflo (*s. from* purfle) A border, a fringe. Ash's English Dictionary, 1795

puritain – [Paris] in requisition for carriage or public promenade dress, which for us is the same thing, so will also be some new materials of Cashmere wool and silk intermingled: they are called *ècossais satins*, Waverleys, and *puritains. New Monthly Belle Assemblée*, November 1836 ~~~ [Paris] a list of new materials which have just appeared for mantles, robes, &c., ... Fancy materials, called *Waverley Puritain* and *satin Ecossiais*, will be appropriated to the promenade; *Court Magazine*, November 1836

purl – Purl, a sort of lace for borders or edging; Perry's English Dictionary, 1795 ~~~ Purl, (*s. from* purflo) A kind of puckered border. *Sidney.* ... To decorate with fringe, to embroider. Purled, (*p. from* purl) Decorated with fringe, embroidered. Ash's English Dictionary, 1795 ~~~ Picots, *purl-lace.* Dufief's French Dictionary, 1810 ~~~ The bonnet composed of alternate stripes of white ribband and straw purl, ... the mixture of ribband and straw purl is becoming general; *La Belle Assemblée*, August 1810 ~~~ Notices of New Patents. *Patent granted to* John Heathcoat, *of Tiverton, Devonshire, Lace-manufacturer, for an improved mode of producing figures or ornaments in or upon a certain description or kind of goods, manufactured from silk, cotton, flax, or other thread or yarn.* Dated February 26, 1825. The object of this patent is the use and application of purl in making figures and ornaments on lace. In the first of three methods for the above purpose, which are described in the specification, it is directed that designs of figures or ornaments, such as sprigs, bouquets, &c. be traced on the lace, previously stretched in a frame, after which the purl is to be taken, with which article it is asserted all lace-manufacturers are well acquainted, and one end of it is to be applied to one of the said figures or ornaments, and to be sewed or otherwise fastened to the lace, according to its outline and frame, and then successively to the other figures, in the same manner. In the second method the figures are to be traced on a cushion, and the purl to be then pinned on it, according to their form; after which the lace is to be laid down on the cushion, and the figures so formed with the purl to be sewed on it, and then to be detached from the cushion. In the third and last method, the figures or ornaments are to be traced upon paper, over which the purl is to be pinned, so as to represent their form, and then to be sewed to itself so as to preserve that form afterwards. The figures thus produced are then to be detached from the paper, and may be sold by themselves separately, to serve as a substitute for Brussels sprigs in ornamenting lace. We understand there is a considerable demand for Brussels sprigs. If, therefore, the article last mentioned in the specification can be made equal in beauty to the Brussels sprigs, or even sufficiently approaching to them in appearance so as to come at all in competition with them, it is evident that this circumstance will make the patent proportionally valuable. *Repertory of Patent Inventions*, November 1825 ~~~ LACE MFRS. *Marked thus * make Purl and Tatting*, ... *Carter Wm. Brown (and fast purled gimp thread edging) Rutland street. History, Gazetteer, and Directory of Nottinghamshire, 1832

Quadrilled - Quilted

quadrilled – Hat of quadrille gauze of celestial blue and black, *La Belle Assemblée*, December 1820 ~~~ [Paris] Plush silk is the favourite material for hats, both for the carriage and for the public walks; they are generally figured, and when in checquers, this article is called quadrille plush. *Ladies' Monthly Museum*, February 1821 ~~~ Among the quadrilled grenadines which are considered the prettiest, we have remarked one, in particular, of a white ground, quadrilled with red and brown; the lines imitate satin perfectly, and produce a rich and elegant effect: they form delightful dresses. *Ladies' Monthly Museum*, November 1826 ~~~ Very beautiful hats of black satin, quadrilled with large stripes of black velvet, are worn in half-toilet; but the most beautiful hat we have seen, was of a very fine satin bird of Paradise colour, embroidered with black. The ribands were half satin, of the same shade as the hat, and half black, quadrilled with yellow; *Ladies' Monthly Museum*, December 1826 ~~~ [Paris] The materials for bonnets are … satin quadrillé, cross barred in small squares. *Lady's Magazine and Museum*, December 1834 ~~~ [for hats and bonnets] It is expected that plain materials will be preferred, except for drawn bonnets, for which *gros de Naples*, quadrilled in two colours, will no doubt be very fashionable. We have already seen a good many of white and rose, white and lilac, and white and green. *Court Magazine*, May 1835 ~~~ *Peau de poule*, composed of silk and wool, is figured and quadrilled with flowers in the squares. *Court Magazine*, May 1836 ~~~ I have seen also a few quadrilled *mousselines de laine*, the ground is a dead white, the square figured in a brilliant white, is formed by a coloured stripe not thicker than a thread; the colours are different shades of blue, red, and green. *New Monthly Belle Assemblée*, October 1836 [not to be confused with the gossamer net quadrille robe of 1818, the music/dance, or the game]

queen's – Walking dress. A jaconot muslin dress; a white ground striped in green and citron. This is called the queen's pattern. *Lady's Museum*, September 1831

queen's blonde – [court dress] A handsome colonnade white satin dress, elegantly ornamented with rich gold lama, body and sleeve handsomely trimmed with Queen's blond lace; *Lady's Museum*, March 1831 ~~~ [court dress] A Queen's blonde dress à colonne, over white satin; *Court Journal*, March 23, 1833 ~~~ [court dress] An elegant dress of Queen's blonde over white satin; rich crimson velvet train, lined with white; body and sleeves handsomely trimmed with blonde; blonde sabots; *Lady's Magazine and Museum*, March 1836

queen's cloth – [exported to China] light woollens, such as queen's cloths, *Monthly Magazine*, August 1812 ~~~ Promenade or Carriage Costume. This dress, when divested of the spencer, or jacket, exhibits the Evening or Opera Costume: … consists of a round robe of morone or crimson-coloured Merino, kerseymere, or queen's cloth, *Repository of Arts*, December 1813

queen's lustre – [ad] Queen's Lustres, … for Dresses; *La Belle Assemblée*, January 1807

queen's silk – In deep mourning, this robe should be formed of black crape, and worn over black sarsnet. The ornaments and trimmings of every description must be of bugles or jet. The shoes of queen's silk. *Weekly Entertainer*, September 11, 1809 ~~~ Shoes are made in brocaded or Queen's silk. *La Belle Assemblée*, September 1810 ~~~ Brighton Walking Dress. Jaconot muslin round dress over a French grey sarsnet slip. … Over this dress is the Blandford spencer, composed of white queen's silk. *Repository of Arts*, September 1817 ~~~ The most tasteful autumnal pelisse … is one composed of queen's silk of the colour of the dead leaf; it is lined with white sarsnet, *Repository of Arts*, October 1817 ~~~ Very few dinner dresses have as yet been made in muslin, but we have seen a good many in silk, and of a texture which we consider infinitely too substantial for the season; in fact our levantines, *gros de Naples, reps*, and queen's silk, are almost as stout as the brocades, tissues, and damasks of our grandmammas. *Atheneum*, July 1820

queen's stuff – The peasant's jacket and petticoat, of fine Imperial, or Queen's stuff, occasionally blends with the white gowns for more general wear. … Know the, that after all my railing last winter against the unyielding harshness of the stuff gown, I have actually purchased one; and thus it is: – A fine scarlet bombazeen, or Queen's stuff, with five rows of white sarsnet ribbon tied round the bottom; *La Belle Assemblée*, December 1808 ~~~ A rich silk spencer … worn over a bombazeen or Queen's stuff dress, is a very fashionable and convenient carriage costume. *Jersey Magazine*, January 1810 ~~~ For

Dinner or Home Dresses, cloth, queens stuff, bombazeen, opera nets, and sarsnets are still unrivalled, *La Belle Assemblée*, October 1810

Quentin Durward – [Paris] The Quentin Durward are of a smaller pattern [than *satin Walter Scott* plaided patterns], but very rich, and in a great variety of colours. *Court Magazine*, October 1834 ~~~ Satins and cashmeres of Scotch plaid patterns are expected to be very fashionable, both for robes and mantles. … The *Quentin Durwards* are also very rich; the squares are marked by lines of very vivid colours, upon brown or marron grounds. *Court Magazine*, November 1834 ~~~ [Paris] The most fashionable materials for cloaks are – … Satins Ecossais, satins Quentin Durward, satins Marie Stuart, and plaids des Montagnards. All the above are imitations of the Scotch plaids, made in Cachemere wool and silk. *Lady's Magazine and Museum*, November 1834 [see also *plaid* and *Walter Scott*]

quilling – *Aikin's Description of the Country round Manchester*. [published 1795] … "For some time past the staple manufactory of the place and neighbourhood has been …superfine quilled everlastings, double russels, serges de Nisme and du Rome. These are all made from combing wool. *British Critic*, June 1796 ~~~ Evening Dress. … A robe of purple velvet with gold and crape ruff; white satin coat, with a double quilling of crape at the bottom. *Weekly Magazine*, March 12, 1803 ~~~ A short French apron of blond net, trimmed with a quilling of net, is considered as indispensible [sic] with this dress. *La Belle Assemblée*, December 1814 ~~~ [belonging to Princess Charlotte] Two worked dresses for the occasion; very rich scalloped borders of four rows, quilled with net at the top of each row. *Niles' Weekly Register*, June 22, 1816 ~~~ [Paris] A double quilling is a favourite trimming at the edge of hats; one is placed underneath the edge, the other over. *La Belle Assemblée*, November 1820 ~~~ Quillings, or narrow edges of lace (which was first made by the traverse-warp machine) three inches broad, were sold in 1810 for 4*s*. 6*d*. per yard, is now selling for 1½*d*. and improved in quality. History of the County of Derby, 1829 ~~~ All regular tartans are made, so that, in the folds of the kilt and plaid, which are formed in what is called quilled, or box plaiting, a particular stripe shall appear. Scottish Gaël, 1831 ~~~ BEDFORDSHIRE. *Lace-makers* … The quilling-net, which at the same time [about ten years ago] sold for two shillings and sixpence a yard, is now selling at three-halfpence! Several hundreds of thousands of pounds' worth of this article used to be exported to the continent, especially to France and to America; but the export trade is now entirely ruined – France and America not only being in the possession of English machinery, but English workmen, who are enabled not only to compete, successfully, with English-made goods, but to undersell us in foreign markets from fifteen to twenty per cent. *New Monthly Magazine*, October 1832 ~~~ Quill. *v*. To plait; to form in plaits or folds, like quills. pr. par. *quilling*; past, *quilled*. Ladies' Lexicon, 1835 ~~~ To Quill, in the language of the laundress, is to plait her frills into small tubes, which are kept from collapsing by means of the starch. This she sometimes calls Piping; Analytical Dictionary, 1835 ~~~ The narrow ribands of bobbin-net, called quilling-lace, or ruffles for cap-borders, from about the breadth of the finger to that of the hand, are worked in many breadths at a time in the same machine, … [Bobbin-net] Of late, three-fourths of our production has been exported, and chiefly in the plain state. The American trade, which has much increased, is supplied entirely in the white. Quillings are sent to the north of Europe in the white, as are also the principal part of the wide nets sent to those markets. A large quantity of wide net is sent into Belgium and into France, in the unbleached state. We have almost entirely ceased to export quillings into France, as they make an immense quantity themselves. Cotton Manufacture of Great Britain, 1836 ~~~ [Paris ball dress] white kid gloves, trimmed at the tops with a double quilling of white satin ribbon and tulle; *Lady's Magazine and Museum*, May 1836

quilted – Quiltings appear to be two distinct cloths, tied, as it were, together, by stitches which go through both cloths, and in some cases, as in bed-quilts, there is a third shuttle, which throws in a quantity of coarsely spun cotton, to serve as a kind of wadding. *Monthly Magazine*, October 1797 ~~~ [men's] The waistcoats are coloured quilting, *Union Magazine*, December 1801 ~~~ Now, Sir, the machines for which Sir Richard Arkwright obtained his patent, are only used for the spinning of [cotton] yarn of a very limited degree of fineness, such as is manufactured into quiltings, dimities, and other goods of a similar strength of fabric. *Athenæum*, July 1807 ~~~ Quilting, a method of sewing two pieces of silk, linen, or stuff, on each other, with wool or cotton between them, by working them all over in the form of chequer or diamond-work, or in flowers. The same name is also given to the stuff so worked. <u>American Edition of the British Encyclopedia</u>, 1818 ~~~ The quilting at the border of dresses is again in request, but is confined to half dress; it looks well on sarsnets, or slight satins; otherwise it ahs rather an antique appearance; or we should express ourselves better, if we called it *old-fashioned*; for many of our subscribers may recollect the quilted satin petticoats worn by their mothers or grandmothers. *La Belle Assemblée*, November 1823 ~~~ [Paris] At the ball at St. Cloud I saw a dress, the *corsage* of which was of white satin quilted and stitched like a gentleman's under-waistcoat. *La Belle Assemblée*, November 1825 ~~~ Quiltings, White and Coloured, from Manchester to New York. Nominal Width, actual, from 24 to 26 inches. Length of piece, from 15 to 30 yards. 5 Cases, containing: 150 ends, white, buff and printed quiltings, <u>Trade between Great Britain and the United States of America</u>, 1833 ~~~ in 1832, the average wages for weaving … quiltings, from 9s. to 12s., 13s., and even 15s. <u>Essay on the Rate of Wages</u>, 1835 [see also *double cloth* and *Marseilles quilting*]

Rabbit - Rustic

rabbit – Sort of Rabbits. Until of late years, the common *grey* rabbit – probably the native wild rabbit of the Island – was the only species. At present, the *silver-haired* rabbit is sought after, and has, within the few last years, been introduced into most warrens. The skin of the grey rabbit is *cut*; that is, the "wool" is pared off the pelt, as a material of *hats:* whereas that of the silver-haired rabbit is *dressed* as *fur;* which, I understand, goes principally to the East Indies. The color is a black ground, thickly interspersed with single white hairs. The skins of this variety fell for about four shillings, a dozen, more than those of the common sort; a sufficient inducement, this, for propagating it. Rural Economy of Yorkshire, 1796 ~~~ In my travels through America, I have often been surprised that no attempt has been made to introduce, for the purpose of propagation, that useful little animal, the warren rabbit, of such vast importance to the hat manufactory of England. It is chiefly owing to the fur of this animal that the English hats are so much esteemed abroad. It is a fact well known amongst the hatters, that a hat composed of one half of coney wool, one sixth old coat beaver, one sixth pelt beaver, and one sixth Vigonia wool, will wear far preferable to one made of all beaver, as it will keep its shape better, feel more firm, and wear bright and black much longer. Transactions of the Society, 1807 ~~~ *Furs used in a Hat of fine quality, according to the present improved system of making, their proportions, value, cost of manufacture, &c. &c.* FOR THE BODY. [in shillings and pence] *s. d.* ... 4 oz. of seasoned coney wool, 1*s.* 0*d.* per oz. 4 0 ... 1/2 oz. red wool - - - 2 4 [2*s.* 4*d.* per oz.] - - 1 2 ... 1/4 oz. of silk - - - 0 9 [0*s.* 9*d.* per oz.] - - 0 4 ½ FOR THE COVERING. 1 oz. of prime seasoned beaver, 8*s.* 6*d.** - - 8 6 ... * No hat can be good, or well covered, with less than one ounce of prime beaver; Lloyd's Treatise on Hats, 1819 ~~~ [ad] *Ladies' Woollen Warehouse, 28, King-street, Covent-garden.* – The utmost variety is manufactured and kept for Sale of Pelisse, Habit, Merino, Saxon, Rabbit, Seal-skin, and Vigona Cloths, in every Colour, and those of the present Fashion in particular, from 5*s.* to 25*s.* per yard, all Two yards wide. At this Warehouse nothing but Woollen Cloths are Sold, and consequently much lower than can possibly be bought at any Silk-mercer's, Linen-draper's, Haberdasher's, &c. who purchase them of the Woollen-draper to sell again. *Evangelical Magazine,* November 1821 ~~~ *The colour of the wild rabbit is dusky brown above, and paler or whitish on the under parts. In the domestic rabbit the colour is various, white, grey, black, or black and white. ...* The *fur* is a principal substance employed in the composition of hats; and such parts of it as are unfit for this purpose may advantageously be adopted for the stuffing of beds and bolsters. Rabbits' skins are also sometimes used as a cheap and warm trimming for female dress; Useful Knowledge, 1821

raccoon – Raccoon skins, undressed, the 100 skins – 13s. 9d. [import duty] Ship Owner's Manual, 1795 ~~~ Raccoon Skins are taken from an animal of the bear genus, which inhabits the northern parts of America; it is also found in some of the West-India islands. The colour of this animal is gray, the face white, and each of the eyes imbedded in a large patch of black, which forms a kind of band across the forehead, and is crossed by a dusky stripe running down the nose. The fur of the raccoon is principally used by hatters, and is considered next in merit, for their purposes, to beaver. Practice of Customs, 1812 ~~~ The fur of the racoon is much valued by hatters, being next, in fineness, to that of the beaver; it is also used as linings to dresses; gloves, and even the upper leather of shoes, are made from its skin when dressed. Anecdotes of Quadrupeds, 1831

raies – [see *mille rayes* and *rayes*]

rainbow – Rainbow. *s.* Iris. Dictionary of the Synonymous Words, 1806 ~~~ [court dress] A most beautiful rainbow green crape petticoat, with rich silver foil border; *La Belle Assemblée,* June 1807 ~~~ a scarf of the same material [net silk], diversely striped, entitled the Rainbow, or Iris scarf: it answers three purposes, being worn alternately as a turban, a sash, or a shawl. *La Belle Assemblée,* April 1816 ~~~ The skirt is trimmed with ribbon, brocaded in the colours of the rainbow; this ribbon is twisted into a rouleau, which is disposed in waves, and each wave is finished by a rosette of the ribbon: nothing can be more beautiful than the effect of this simple trimming. *Repository of Arts,* October 1817 ~~~ That useful head-dress, the Madras turban, has not yet declined in favour; but it is now no longer made of silk but of rainbow net, fabricated of raw silk. *La Belle Assemblée,* October 1819 ~~~ Straw-coloured gauze is much used in the trimming of straw hats: rainbow gauze is a favourite trimming on chip hats. *La Belle Assemblée*, June 1820 ~~~ English Carriage Dress. ... Elastic drapery scarf of rainbow *bouffont* wove silk. *La Belle Assemblée*, November 1820 ~~~ Rainbow ribbons are also much in favour for these *chapeaux*: ... close to the bow is placed a bunch of flowers, composed of the three colours of the ribbon. *Repository of Arts*, October 1821 ~~~ The materials for turbans are of the most brilliant kind, and well adapted for the mid-night glare of artificial day. ... another article for this becoming head-dress is of rainbow striped gauze, on a green ground powdered with gold; the stripes are crimson, royal blue, green, and yellow; *La Belle Assemblée*, February 1823 ~~~ [Paris ball dresses] *Crêpe lisse and gaze Iris* are also worn, but not so generally. *Repository of Arts*, March 1823 ~~~ [sea-side dress] A rainbow silk scarf, with a broad tassel fringe, to answer the colours of the shaded cross-stripes on the scarf, completes this simple, though elegant dress. *Ladies' Monthly Museum*, September 1825 ~~~ Opera Dress. ... The head-dress consists of a scarf of Iris gauze, *Ladies' Pocket*, February 1830 ~~~ [court dress] A white gauze Iris dress, lined with white satin, *Court Journal*, June 1, 1833 ~~~ [court dress] dress white gaze Iris, brode d'or, over white satin. *Lady's Magazine*, June 1836 [iris is also a blue colour, but usually written iris-blue or iris-colour]

ramaged – Ramage (*s. from the* Latin ramus *a branch*) The branches of trees. <u>Ash's English Dictionary</u>, 1795 ~~~ *Ramaged or branched velvet*, representing long stalks, branches, &c. on a satin ground, which is sometimes the of the same colour with the velvet, but more commonly of a different one. Sometimes, instead of satin, they make the ground of gold and silver. <u>General Dictionary of Commerce</u>, 1810 ~~~ Figured silks are so much worn that I cannot refrain from again mentioning it to you, although I have done so several times before. Damasks *à grands ramages* are now all the rage. We pay so high as fifty francs an ell for them, for our ancient costumes; and so much has been used that they are now very scarce at Paris. The morning dresses are not subjected to the old fashions of our fore-fathers; these fashions are confined only to ball and dinner dresses. *Court Magazine*, April 1833 ~~~ [court dress] A Brussels lace dress over white satin; train of a rich green Pekin a ramages; *Court Journal*, May 11, 1833 ~~~ The materials for morning dresses are ... plain *chalys* printed *à très grands ramages*, *Court Magazine*, May 1833

rateen – or Ratten, in commerce, a thick woollen stuff, quilled, and woven on a loom with four treddles, like serges and other stuffs that have the whale or quilling. There are some ratteens dressed and prepared like cloths; others are left simply in the hair, and others where the hair or knap is frized. Rateens are chiefly manufactured in France, Holland, and Italy, and are mostly used in linings. The frize is a sort of coarse rateen, and the drugget is a rateen half linen half woollen. <u>Encyclopædia Britannica</u>, 1797 ~~~ The clothing of the lower rank in this county is principally effected at the fairs, where they can in general supply themselves with either ratteens or frizes. The ratteens are sold at from 5*s.* to 6*s.* a yard, and are higher priced than frize, being a degree finer; they are strong, and warm wear. Frize is bought in the same fairs, at from 3*s.* 3*d.* to 4*s.* per yard, according to the quality; it takes about five yards and a half to make a coat and waistcoat. This manufacture is excellently adapted to poor people; it is strong, cheap, and warm. <u>Statistical Survey of the County Dublin</u>, 1801 ~~~ This evidence was received in the year 1803. ... 1, The finest and thinnest cloths are made for the Turkey-trade; 2, ladies' cloths are in the next degree thicker; 3, the next in thickness are made for the West India trade; 4, the next are for the Russia trade; 5, superfine cloths are thicker still; 6, the thickest of all are double milled superfine, and a species of narrow-cloths named *ratteens*. *Monthly Magazine*, March 1807 ~~~ Stradbally School. Thursday, 15th September 1808; two o'clock. ... I saw the new clothing of the children; it was of a strong thick brown stuff, called Carrick Ratteen, and was faced with bright yellow. <u>Board of Education in Ireland</u>, 1813 ~~~ Rateen (*Com.*) or *Ratten*, a thick woollen stuff, quilted and wove on a loom, with four treadles, like serges and other stuffs that have the weale or quilling. <u>Universal Technological Dictionary</u>, 1823 ~~~ That "green ratteens" or "friezes," are to be considered as coming under the general term of "baizes," within the meaning of the law, and are to pay duty accordingly. *Public Documents*, January 1829 ~~~ Drugget, Baize, Frize, and other coarse cloths are known, in commerce, by the general name of Rateens. <u>Analytical Dictionary</u>, 1835 [see also *baize* and *frieze*] ratenet – *Assistant Commissary*. – Blue coat single breasted, 8 buttons by two's, 2 rows of holes, soldiers back, lined white ratenet, scarlet cuffs, a scarlet stand-collar, Regimental Companion, 1811

rattan – Canes; viz. rattans, the thousand – 16s. 6d. [duty] Ship Owner's Manual, 1795 ~~~ Rattans, or Ratans, … are the small shoots or branches of the sugar-cane, brought to us from the East and West Indes. When polished and mounted, they are used as walking-sticks. Dictionary of Commerce, 1810 ~~~ That hats, the material of which is rattan, fairly come within the spirit and meaning of the general classification of all hats or bonnets of straw, chip, or grass, and should be charged with duty accordingly. *Public Documents*, August 15, 1826

raven duck – To those engaged in mercantile concerns, we conceive the follow price current of goods, wares, &c. as they actually were at Philadelphia in January, 1794, … Duck, Russia, per piece of 42 yards . [Dlls Cts] 14 0 — Ravens . . 11 0 View of the American United States, 1795 ~~~ On the 2d of February, [1787] a marine school was instituted and opened by the Corporation of the Trinity House, at Hull, for the reception of boys, to be bred to the sea service. The principal rules of which are as follows, viz. Boys are to be eleven years of age before they can be admitted. … They are clothed annually; have an upper and under jacket, metal buttons, bearing the house's arms, two pair of raven duck trowsers, two check shirts, two pair of shoes, two hats, and two black vellet collars. Naval Chronology, 1802 ~~~ The manufacturers of linens, sailcloth, &c. purchase the yarn of the peasants, who grow the flax, and make the yarn; it is then manufactured into ravenducks, flems, and drillings … and carries them to St. Petersburgh for sale. Voyages and Travels, 1809 ~~~ *Premium 14. – Fifteen Dollars*. For the best piece of Raven duck, in imitation of the Russian manufacture, not less than thirty yards long and twenty-eight inches wide. *Universal Magazine*, February 1809 ~~~ He went into an explanation of the difference between ravens duck and other sail duck, stating its lightness and flexibility, its use by bay and river craft, and for the lighter sails of ships, … The cotton duck was stout and heavy – ravens duck, light and flexible. *Gales & Seaton's Register*, April 15, 1828 ~~~ A statement of the work performed by the female subjects in the house of refuge from December first, 1827, to the first of December, 1828, inclusive, viz. … Ravens Duck Pantaloons, made, . . . 114 Prison Discipline Society, 1829 ~~~ Raven's Duck, *n*. (G. *ravenstuch*.) A species of sail cloth. Webster's Dictionary, 1832 ~~~ Stores for 100 Convicts [proceeding to *new South Wales* or *Van Diemen's Land* in 1832]. … Clothing for Use during the Voyage. Raven Duck Overalls. Accounts and Papers … Relating to Crime, 1834 [see also *duck*, *Ravensberg linen* and *sail cloth*]

Ravensberg linen – Ravensberg. This sort of linen was first made in the year 1800, and invented by a gentleman of the name of Ebeling, a merchant of the city of Bergholzhausen, and a considerable linen trader. It is made of the best and strongest quality of hempen tow, called Lovent linen, the quality of which is before described. A piece contains 50 Flemish ells in length. The pieces are put up single in their full width, and then committed to the press. It is of three different qualities, marked No. 1, 2, and 3; … Although it is an imitation of the Russian ravenducks, but inferior in quality, the lowest sorts of those are much finer, evener, and better than the best sort of the Ravensberg linen, because the Russians spin the yarn designed for this purpose of pure hemp, without any intermixture of tow; whilst, in the county of Ravensberg, the yarn of which the linen is made, is but partly spun of pure hemp, the weft being spun of hempen tow. However, the Ravensburg linen is very strong, and much cheaper than the Russian ravenducks. European Commerce, 1805

ravenua – A favourite article for morning dresses is the newly-invented manufacture entitled Camelias; another article styled Ravenua, is expected to be much patronized when the winter shall be more decidedly set in. *La Belle Assemblée*, November 1823

raw silk – Crape, *f*. (*crepa*, low Lat.) a light transparent manufacture resembling gauze, made of raw silk gummed and twisted in the mill, wove without crossing, and much used in mourning. Complete and Universal English Dictionary, 1799 ~~~ Silk is distinguished by different names, according to its different states, – Thus, *raw silk* is that taken from the ball, without fire, and wound without any boiling; such as is most, if not all, that is brought into England from the Levant. In the French silk-works, the greatest part of this raw silk passes for little better than a kind of fine floretta; yet, when spun, it makes a bright thread, and serves for the manufacture of stuff of moderate value and lustre.

But the raw silks of the Levant, whence most of ours come, are exceedingly fine and beautiful. This difference arises hence, that in France the best balls are spun and wound in boiling water, and only the refuse made into raw silk: whereas in the Levant, there is no such thing as spinning or winding on the fire; but the silks are all sent in bales or packs, as they are drawn from off the balls; so that they are only distinguished by their quality of fine, middling, and coarse. Guy's Pocket Cyclopædia, 1810 ~~~ DYING. *To prepare raw Silk.* Put the raw silk into a bag, that it may not entangle; and to every pound add a quarter of a pound of soap; let this boil together two hours, then take it and cleanse it well, and it is ready for all sorts of colours, being first alumed. *Another Way to prepare raw Silk.* Take it, and smear it well, putting to every pound of silk, a quarter of a pound of black or green soap; put it into a linen bag, and let it boil six or seven hours; then take it out of the bag and cool it, that you may handle it the better; after this, rinse it in a river or running water for fifteen minutes. Beat the water out very well, and then rinse it again; then dry it, and it is ready for dying. Observe, that this preparation is absolutely necessary for all raw silks before they can be died. Young Woman's Companion, 1815 ~~~ Since I closed this account I have been favoured with a sight of some very elegant articles from the magazine of Madame Leroy, amongst which I must notice some dresses made of India raw silk, not for their elegance but for their novelty. The robe is of lilac, rose-colour, or green, with a deep border of Scotch plaid, which being always of colours which look well with the ground, they are not so ridiculous as may be imagined, and they bear the stamp of high fashion. *La Belle Assemblée*, June 1816 ~~~ The Parisian ladies now wear shoes made of raw silk, half-boots and gaiters, all made of the same material. *La Belle Assemblée*, August 1820 ~~~ There are three qualities of raw silk, graduated according to their different degrees of fineness. While in that shape, and until they have undergone the operations that are to fit them for the loom, they are called first, second, and third, beginning with the finest. They assume other names as soon as they have been prepared and made fit to be used by the manufacturer. Then they have ceased to be raw silk, and they are called singles, organzine, and tram silk, according to their different degrees of fineness and the manner in which they have been passed through a certain machine called a mill. ... The next branch of the silk manufacturing business is the *organzining* or preparation of the raw silk for the weaver's loom. This is done by a number of distinct and successive operations, performed by different machines, the principal of which, the *mill,* (or *throwsting mill,* as it is called,) has never, that I have heard, been introduced into this country, and yet cannot be dispensed with. The silk, when thus prepared, is said in French to be *moulinée* or milled; in English it is called *organzined* or *thrown silk.* These operations are nice, difficult, and complicated; their methods vary according to the kind of silk that is to be produced, whether organzine or tram silk. Singles do not require to be organzined. The success of these operations depends much on the manner in which the raw silk has been prepared before it is brought to the mill. After going through these various processes, the silk is wound into short skeins, for the greater facility of the weaver; and, after being dyed, is fit to be immediately employed in the manufacture of silk stuffs. I shall not undertake hereto describe those processes, as it is entirely foreign to my object; and no descriptions that I can make could supply the place of skill, experience, and practice. *Report of the Committee on Agriculture on the Growth and Manufacture of Silk,* July 23, 1829 ~~~ [men's] Gloves of raw silk are fashionable for the morning. *Casket,* January 1831 ~~~ [Paris] Black mittens are still in request in half dress, but they are now embroidered in coloured silks, and edged with raw silk fringe. *Court Magazine,* June 1835 ~~~ From the breeder, the cocoons pass to the throwster, who casts them into a trough, filled with water as hot as the hand can well bear: this loosens the gummy matter, with which the worm had fastened the thread together; and then he whisks them about till he obtains the ends. Taking as many of these as his purpose requires, he twists them pretty firmly together into a single thread, which he thrusts through a hole in an .iron plate, fixed over the trough. On the other side of this plate is a reel, to which the thread is fastened; and by turning the reel, the whole length of the threads in the several cocoons is drawn out, adhering to each other by their own gumminess, and forming a single thread, fit for the manufacturer. At least two of the threads, as loosened from the cocoons, are required for a thread fit for the weaver: the threads of eight cocoons are necessary to make one fit for ribbons; for velvets, fourteen are requisite; and for some purposes, more than fourteen are used, up to thirty, beyond which it is difficult to make them unite. If a thread break, it is immediately joined again; or its place is supplied by another, if the cocoon from which it is drawn be expended. The length of the thread varies, some cocoons giving out as much as twelve hundred ells; but in general they yield from five to six hundred. The silk in this simple state, as wound off the cocoons, is called *raw silk*; when doubled and twisted, it has the name of *thrown silk,* or *organzine*, and forms the *warp*, or lengthwise thread of the manufactured broad silk. That which crosses it is called the *tram*, or *woof*, and is more loosely twisted. … That elegant light summer dress is of crape, an article made of raw silk, in the chain manner, and highly stiffened with wax and gum. <u>Scenes of Commerce</u>, 1836 ~~~ The two main articles sent forth from the throwing mill are "tram" and "organzine," which differ principally in the latter being more *tightly* twisted than the former. The processes are – Reeling: done by females, requires considerable skill: it is the process of winding the cocoons into a thread. Winding: from skeins to bobbins. Spinning: requires two or three successive operations: – "Singles" are formed by slightly twisting the raw silk. "Tram" is the next state, formed by twisting threads together: "tram" constitutes the *weft* for the loom. "Organzine" is the *warp*. <u>Manchester</u>, 1836 [see also *organzine, silk, singles,* and *tram*]

Ray – Raycloth, cloth never died [dyed] <u>Perry's English Dictionary</u>, 1795 ~~~ Ray, Cloth never coloured or dyed. See *stats. 17 R 2.c.3; 11 H. 4.c.6; 1 R. 3.c.8.* <u>Law Dictionary</u>, 1811

raye – Velours … rayé, *striped velvet.* <u>Dufief's French Dictionary</u>, 1810 ~~~ RAYÉ, -ÉE, … *striped, full of stripes.* … étoffe rayée, *Striped cloth, satin, stuff.* <u>Boniface's French Dictionary</u>, 1828 ~~~ Parisian Dinner Dress. Hat of apricot-coloured *gros de Naples*, with four broad striped gauze ribbons of the same colour, laid *en raye* in the inside of the front. *Lady's Magazine*, September 1830 ~~~ Morning Dress. – Dress of emerald green terry velvet *rayee satinee*, the body crossed with folds. *Casket*, February 1833 ~~~ Carriage Dress. Pelisse of green *rayé* watered silk, *Court Magazine*, April 1833

red wool – [see *vigonia*]

Redubbers – Those that buy stolen cloth, and turn it into some other colour or fashion, that it may not be known again. <u>Law Dictionary</u>, 1811

regency spots – Among the newest articles worthy the notice of the fashionable world, are the *Regency Spots*, or the beautiful Bottilla grounds, for ladies' morning dresses; these have an agreeable effect, having a pleasing fall, and giving a graceful effect to the shape. *La Belle Assemblée*, March 1811

rein-deer – The flesh of the reindeer is excellent eating; the skin, well covered with thick hair, serves the Laplander with different articles of clothing; when stripped of its hair, it becomes a supple and durable leather, of which they make gloves, waistcoats, and belts of unrivalled workmanship. *La Belle Assemblée*, January 1818 ~~~ *Amazone* or riding habit … Gloves of rein-deer skin, confined at the wrists by two buttons, similar to those on the chemisette. *Court Journal*, September 19, 1835 ~~~ *Riding Dress.* … Small manchettes and gloves of rein-deer skin. *Atkinson's Casket*, August 1836

reine – Reine, *f.* rèn. *a queen* <u>Tardy's French Dictionary</u>, 1799 ~~~ Velours … figuré, à fleurs, *or* à la reine, *figured velvet.* <u>Dufief's French Dictionary</u>, 1810 ~~~ [court dress] A rich vapeur ducape dress, … train of watered gros à la reine, embroidered with silver lama; *Royal Lady's*, June 1831 ~~~ *Chaly a la reine,* reps *Africain*, and figured *gros de Naples,* are all in equal favour for the theatres and for dinner dress. *Ladies' Museum*, December 1831 ~~~ Make and Materials of Evening Dress. – Among the new materials which belong to winter rather than autumn, but for which many orders have already been given, are the *satin polonais and a la reine,* … These material are of extreme richness. The *satin a la reine* unites the gloss of the richest satin, to the softness and graceful flow of cachemire. *Casket*, January 1832 ~~~ Another morning bonnet … is composed of a new and very rich kind of silk, called *poux de Reine. Court Magazine*, October 1833 ~~~ The materials for evening dress will be … *poux de la reine,* … [Paris] Satin *poux de la reine* and *reps*, are the materials employed both for hats and bonnets, many of the former are lined with different colours; *Court Magazine*, November 1833 ~~~ Velvet bonnets increase in favour, … *Velours epingle* and *velours de la Reine* are also very much worn; *Court Magazine*, December 1834 ~~~ [court dress] Siecle XVII., rich white velours a la Reine, with tulle and ribbons; *Lady's Magazine and Museum*, June 1836 [see also *satin à la reine*]

rep velvet – Late as it is in the season, we still see several *capotes* of rose-coloured satin; but velvet and rep velvet are materials more in favour than satin. *Court Magazine*, December 1835 ~~~ one of this prettiest of this latter kind of a hat of white rep velvet trimmed with a light blue Bird of Paradise, *Ladies' Companion*, February 1836 ~~~ *velours épinglé* (called in England rep velvet) *New Monthly Belle Assemblée*, November 1836 ~~~ Carriage-hats and bonnets are principally composed of satin and *peluche*. There are also a good many of rep velvet, and a few, but as yet very few, of velvet. *Ladies' Pocket*, December 1836 [see *velours épinglé*]

reps – [see also the word after *reps*]

reps – *Princess Charlotte's dresses.* ... A travelling dress of rich white reps silk, elegantly trimmed with flounces at the bottom, of superb Brussels point, with ruff and cuffs to correspond. *Asiatic Journal*, June 1816 ~~~ Walking Dress. Garter purple poplin pelisse, ornamented with black velvet: Mary Scot bonnet of garter purple *reps silk*, ... Next in estimation to the fine light silk velvet, are poplins and reps silk; which latter article is chiefly in requisition for half dress, *La Belle Assemblée*, October 1818 ~~~ *Gros de Naples*, levantine, *reps* silk, and plain and figured sarsnets, are all in requisition for spencers and pelisses. The exquisite beauty and richness of these silks cannot be surpassed by the productions of any foreign loom; and se see with pleasure, that our fair countrywomen no longer seek for French silks and laces, but vie with each other in encouraging our own manufactures. *Repository of Arts*, May 1819 ~~~ Shoes of painted cambric, and of reps silk, promise to be in high favour this summer. *La Belle Assemblée*, May 1820 ~~~ Very few dinner dresses have as yet been made in muslin, but we have seen a good many in silk, and of a texture which we consider infinitely too substantial for the season; in fact, our levantines, gros *de Naples, reps,* and queen's silk, are almost as stout as the brocades, tissues, and damasks of our grandmammas. *Atheneum*, July 1820 ~~~ A beautiful dinner dress has been finished by Mrs. Bell for a lady of fashion, of the beautiful article the chain *reps* silk: it is of a bright Christmas green, and is trimmed round the border with strips of satin of the same colour, set at very distinct distances from each other. *La Belle Assemblée*, December 1820 ~~~ Woollen cloths – ... Reps, Sessional Papers, 1827 ~~~ The materials used in grand costume continue to be of the richest and most varied description: nothing could be more magnificent than the dresses of the ladies who attended the drawing-room which his Majesty held to celebrate his birthday on Thursday, the 15th of June. Gold and silver tissue, coloured and white satin, both figured and plain, white and coloured *gros de Naples, reps* silk, levantine, *velours épingle*, white and coloured net, blond net, gauze, tulle, blond, and thread lace, were the materials of the dresses. *Repository of Arts*, September 1820 ~~~ [men's] Waistcoats composed of *reps de soie*, either blue or straw-color, are much in favor. *Casket*, January 1831 ~~~ [ad] Griffiths and Crick ... Silk Mercers and Irish Poplin Manufacturers to the Royal Family, respectfully acquaint the Nobility and Gentry they have now on SALE an extensive assortment of every article for WINTER COSTUME, in all the most fashionable colours. Rich flowered and plain satins, satinettes, and tissue rep d'Anglaise, adapted for Court dresses, Pelisses. &c. well worth attention. *Court Journal*, February 9, 1833 ~~~ Reps silk is likewise a fashionable article for evening dress, but the brocaded and painted satins are decidedly more elegant. *Court Journal*, February 7, 1835 ~~~ And don't you remember Miss Grover's canary-coloured reps bonnet, that looked as if it had been made in the ark. The idea of any one wearing reps! a thing that has not been seen since the flood! Only think of reps!" Laura Lovel wondered what *reps* could possibly be. Pencil Sketches, 1835 ~~~ Reps, natural silk and cotton, Jones's Digest, 1836 [see also *chain gauze, gros de Indes, Indian reps* and *royal reps*]

reps Africain – Carriage Dress. ... The mantle is composed of *reps Africain*: the ground is *terre d'Egypte* colour, printed in rosaces of bright green and rose colour; it is wadded and lined with green gros de Naples, ... The material, *reps Africain*, is of French origin, but is now made here to surpass the foreign article. ... [Paris] Mantles are in great favour, particularly those of *reps Africain*, a silk of an extremely rich kind, and of greatly varied and beautiful patterns; it has also a great advantage, that of not being spoiled by the rain. *La Belle Assemblée*, December 1831 ~~~ Morning and Carriage Dress. .. The mantle is of blue reps African, lined and trimmed with martin fur. *Day*, January 4, 1832 ~~~ Walking Dress. ... The mantle is of violet-coloured *reps Africain*, and lined with white *gros de Naples*; *Casket*, January 1832 ~~~ Make and Materials of Evening Dress. – Among the new materials which belong to winter rather than autumn, but for which many orders have already been given, are the *satin polonais* and *à la reine*, *reps Africain*, … The materials are of extreme richness. *Atheneum*, February 1832 [see also *African*]

reps Americain – [see *American silk*]

reps Atala – We have seen a very elegant pelisse composed of myrtle green *Reps Atala*, *Court Journal*, October 31, 1835

reps Corysandre – Evening costume is still of a light kind; several new materials have, however, appeared for it. We may cite among them the … *Reps Corysandre*, … These rich and beautiful materials will be in great request as soon as the winter has fairly set in. *Ladies' Pocket*, November 1836

ribaned – A number of *tulle* dresses are what is called *ribaned*, that is, large ribands fixed from the waist to the border of the dress; these ribands nearly join at the waist, and gradually widen on approaching the border of the dress, and there is a bouquet of flowers or a rosette appears to fasten each riband. *Ladies' Monthly Museum*, July 1825

riband – A fillet of silk, a narrow web of silk, which is worn for ornament. <u>Sheridan's English Dictionary</u>, 1797 ~~~ Riband, or Ribbon, a narrow sort of silk, chiefly used for head-ornaments, badges of chivalry, &c. … Ribbons of all sorts are prohibited from being imported. <u>Encyclopædia Britannica</u>, 1797 ~~~ [Paris] The ribbons in vogue are white, and shaggy, with long fringe. *Lady's Magazine*, December 1800 ~~~ Ribands used by the milliners are woven: of these there are several sorts, distinguished by different names; as the China, the sarsenet, and the satin riband. Muffs and fur tippets are sold by the milliner, but the manufacture of them from the skin is a distinct business. <u>Book of Trades</u>, 1806 ~~~ The commoner sorts of ribands are composed altogether, both warp and shoot, of Bengal silk. Those of better quality are manufactured with a mixture of Italian and Bengal silk; and the finest descriptions are made of Italian silk without any mixture. Riband is woven in pieces, each of which measures thirty-six yards. <u>Silk Manufacture</u>, 1832 ~~~ Riband, Ribband, Ribbon, s. *ruban*, m. <u>Nouveau Boyer</u>, 1834 ~~~ Ribbons, Dutch and China, Taffeta or lustring; French, satin or taffeta, plain, black, and colored, figured, dentele, gauffre, garniture, crape, gauze, or Cashmere, of silk, *Public Documents*, March 1832 ~~~ *Ribbons* are usually woven as narrow lustrings, but sometimes satin is intermingled, in stripes or flowers. These are called figured ribbons. The principal manufactory for these in England, is at Coventry and in France at Lyons. <u>Book of Commerce by Sea and Land</u>, 1834 ~~~ The bonnet, hanging upon yonder hook, is of *satin*, which has a smooth, glossy surface, produced by passing the woof over several threads of the warp at a time. Many *ribbons* are made in this manner, and have a very showy appearance; but generally they are woven as narrow lustrings; or sometimes as satin, intermingled in stripes or flowers, and then they are called *figured ribbons*. For caps, they are woven in the form of gauzes and other light fabrics. Coventry is the most celebrated town in England for the manufacture of ribbons. The machines which are in use there are capable of weaving a dozen narrow articles, such as ribbons and tapes, at one time. <u>Scenes of Commerce</u>, 1836

ribbon gauze – we must describe evening and ball dresses. A court dress of stripes of violet velvet and gold tissue possessed the most extraordinary richness of appearance. These manufactures are called ribbon gauzes, they are generally formed of rich stripes of brocade satin and alternate with a broad space of gauze. *Lady's Magazine*, March 1830 ~~~ Crape is much in favour both for married and unmarried ladies. Ribbon gauze is in great request among the former. It is so called because it is made in very broad stripes, which are alternately of gauze and satin. We have seen one dress of this description of exquisite beauty, and great price, the stripes of which were alternately of violet velvet, and of gauze that offered a perfect imitation of blond lace. *La Belle Assemblée*, April 1830

rice straw – [hats of] what is called rice straw, which, by the bye, is paper made to resemble straw finely plaited. *Repository of Arts*, August 1821 ~~~ [Paris] In the carriages … Contrary to custom, among our fair fashionables, there were but few hats of *paille de riz*, or rice-straw, but a great many of white *gros de Naples*, or white *crêpe*, *Ladies' Monthly Museum*, May 1825 ~~~ [Paris] Hats of paille de riz, trimmed with satin ribbons, are preferred; feathers are frequently to be seen in these hats. I met your friend, Madame le H –, at a soirée lately; she wore a hat of paille de riz, ornamented with black satin ribbons, *imprimés* in all the colours of the rainbow, and a splendid bouquet of – guess what, my dear – of peacock's feathers! *Lady's Magazine*, October 1834 ~~~ There is quite a rage for rice straw; we see it employed for the plain morning bonnet, … for the elegant half dress hat, … and for the evening dress *chapeau*, *Court Magazine*, June 1835 ~~~ Rice straw enjoys, if possible, a greater vogue this year for carriage-hats and bonnets than it did last season; it is equally fashionable for the small close morning bonnet, simply trimmed with white ribbon, and a white *tulle* veil, and for the half dress-hat with a wide and rather large brim; *Ladies' Pocket*, June 1836 ~~~ Rice straw hats are almost the only ones adopted in evening toilettes. *Court Magazine*, June 1836 ~~~ Hat of paille de riz, ornamented with two primrose coloured feathers, and white ribband, striped with primrose. The inside of the brim lined primrose-coloured crape, and ornamented with bows of riband and blonde. *Atkinson's Casket*, August 1836

rigotine – Rigotine, a kind of woollen cloth, Jones's Digest, 1836

riz – rice straw, *Ladies' Monthly Museum*, August 1822 [see *rice straw*]

roan – [see *morocco*]

rock silk – Among the bonnets we call on the attention of our fashionable readers to the rock bonnet, the silk texture of which is wonderful; representing the spar on rocks, when the sun shining on it gives to it a peculiar brilliancy: this bonnet is a beautiful carriage head-dress; and surmounted by a plume of white feathers, has appeared amongst the paraphernalia of a lady of high rank when on a visit to a certain amiable and highly-elevated personage. *La Belle Assemblée*, March, 1819 ~~~ Another walking bonnet is formed of the rock silk; its colour is lavender, and it is ornamented with coxcombs of red and white striped satin ribbon. *La Belle Assemblée*, June 1819

rock-work – White satin slippers, wove in a pattern of filagree, or rock-work in silver, *La Belle Assemblée*, October 1807 ~~~ materials which are called frosted, or rock-work, are much in use; the silky part of the figured velvet is most beautiful, and shines exactly like satin, while the ground resembles fine spangled velvet. It is very seldom that the same velvet or the same granite material, or rock-work, consists of two colours, though they are of every one that the rainbow can boast; but still it is rose on rose colour, and green on green, &c. *La Belle Assemblée*, November 1819 [see also *granite*]

rosadimoi – The most appropriate out-door *costume* for the first weeks of mourning, is a pelisse of black rosadimoi; a silk which is infinitely deeper than bombazin, and is worn only by widows in the very first stage of their weeds; it is also often appropriated to the fabrication of clergymen's Court robes: the material, however, of the pelisse is entirely new; and forms a truly classical and *unique costume* for the present sad occasion. The rich rosadimoi is figured; it is thereby not only rendered lighter in appearance, but also it marks a distinction between the very deep mourning for the nearest and dearest of all individual connections, and that which should be adopted for the sire of the people. *La Belle Assemblée*, February 1820

roses des Indes – [Paris] The materials for bonnets are velvet, velours épinglé, satin plain and broché, roses des Indes, *Lady's Magazine and Museum*, December 1834

rosette – *Dress of the Officers upon all Occasions.* … They must always wear a black velvet stock, without a turnover, and an-exact regimental club and rosette, tied close to the head; the rosette black and clean, like those of the men. Rules and Regulations for the Cavalry, 1795 ~~~ *Cabriolet* bonnet of light green velvet, … large rosette of pink riband in the front, and a small one behind. *Lady's Magazine*, April 1797 ~~~ Rosette, an ornamental bunch of ribands, or cut leather, which is worn both by officers and soldiers in the British service, on the upper part of their cues. New and Enlarged Military Dictionary, 1802 ~~~ A full dress laced turban, with a rosette of lace, ornamented with gold-spangled net, an *aigrette* in front, with a large row of muslin confining the whole, and a row of gold, intermixed with rosette lace, and spangled net hanging tastefully on one side of the forehead, has a rich effect. *La Belle Assemblée*, March 1806 ~~~ [full dress] Slippers of pale orange velvet, with silver rosettes, were worn with this uncommonly elegant habit – orange being the colour of which the dress was composed. *La Belle Assemblée*, December 1807 ~~~ The breast is shaded by a *fichu* of plain blond made extremely full; it comes up to the throat, and fastens behind with small lace rosettes edged with green satin; as the back is open on each side down to the bottom of the waist, these rosettes give it an uncommonly pretty finish. *Repository of Arts*, December 1816 ~~~ [Paris] A very whimsical manner prevails of ornamenting some dresses, particularly if they are white; a large rosette of ribbon is placed on each shoulder, but they are of different colours, while an end is brought to terminate in a point, each different end the same colour as one rosette, with the other different colour to the bottom of the waist in front; which is confined by a sash of two colours, the same that prevail in the rosettes. *La Belle Assemblée*, December 1823 ~~~ The Cravat which bears the name of this noble author [Byron], differs widely from most others – this difference consists in the manner in which it is first placed on the neck. It is commenced at the back of the neck – the ends are then brought in front under the chin, and fastened in a large bow, or *rosette*, at least six inches in length and four in circumference. Art of Tying the Cravat, 1829 ~~~ [court dress] A white crape dress over white satin, trimmed, en tablier, with rosettes and rouleaux of gauze riband, *Court Journal*, June 1, 1833 ~~~ [Paris] Four small rosette bows of gauze or satin ribbon give a pretty finish to the pelerine; one front and back, and one on each shoulder. *Lady's Magazine and Museum*, January 1835

Rouen linen – From France; Britannias, broad and narrow, Rouen linen, bleached, Origin of Commerce, 1801 ~~~ The articles transported by the company of merchants trading from Fas to Timbuctoo, are principally as follow: – various kinds of German linens, viz. plattilias, rouans, brettanias, *Lady's Magazine*, July 1810 ~~~ Rouens, at 40 ells, and always exceeding 36 inches in breadth. Practice of the Customs, 1812 ~~~ Rouens, real, with the crown … cotton 4-4 *a* [to] 6-4 wide, 40 *a* 50 ells … Rouens, white and dyed, real and counterfeit, of all qualities, up to one yard and a quarter wide. Digest of the Commercial Regulations, 1824 ~~~ Rouans (German, flax) *Public Documents*, March 1832 [see *linen*]

rough cloth – Rough-cloth is milled, but not dressed. Statistical Survey of the County Dublin, 1801

rouleau – [court dress] A white crape petticoat, very richly embroidered with silver; at the bottom a corkscrew trimming of white satin and silver rolio, with a flounce of silver Vandyke blond: *Lady's Magazine*, June 1807 ~~~ [Paris] Plain rouleaus of crape are also fashionable, *Repository of Arts*, December 1817 ~~~ Gowns of twilled sarsnet, trimmed round the border with *rouleaux* of the same material, set on very full, have a beautiful and novel effect; the shade formed by this manner of placing the *rouleaux* is admirable, especially when they are of satin. *Ladies' Monthly Museum*, February 1821 ~~~ [Paris] A lady of very high rank wore a dress entirely ornamented with serpents. These horrible reptiles were formed of a beautiful gauze, tiger-spotted, and were placed in *rouleaux* round the skirt. The tail, terminated by three puffs of riband, fell toward the hem, while the head ascended toward the belt, and the ruby eye was seen there to sparkle. Two serpents of the same composition, were attached to the corners of the bust, and supplied the place of drapery on the corsage, turning round the arms over the wide sleeves. A serpent surrounding the small of the waist placed its head amidst the drapery of the corsage, *à la Sevigné*, while the tail fell down at the base of the waist, like a bouquet bending downwards. *Lady's Magazine*, March 1829 ~~~ Ball Dress. … the skirt is bordered by a satin rouleau to correspond, above which is a row of lozenges formed by satin rouleaus. The tunic worn over the dress is of blond lace, embroidered in columns of flowers, and terminating with a deep double flounce arranged in waves by a satin rouleau; the point of each is adorned by a cluster of satin leaves. *Maids, Wives, and Widows*, January 5, 1833

royal reps – [Paris] Sarcenets, *gros de Naples*, and royal-reps silk, are the favourite articles for dresses in *general* request. *La Belle Assemblée*, December 1827 ~~~ *Materials and Colours.* – The different fabrics are varied much at present. Royal reps; … are the most prevailing. *Blackwood's Lady's*, December 1836 [see also *reps*]

royal tartan – The pipers wore a red tartan of very bright colours, (of the pattern known by the name of the Stewart or Royal Tartan,) so that they could be more clearly seen at a distance. Sketches of … the Highlanders of Scotland, 1822 ~~~ The mantles for walking were made of what the French call royal tartan, in very large diamond checquers. *La Belle Assemblée*, [review of the last six months] 1826 ~~~ [duchess's court dress] Train of Royal tartan velvet, trimmed with minever fur; petticoat of white satin, with trimming of minever, clasped down with diamonds; *Lady's Magazine and Museum*, April 1835

ruche – Four rows of blond, or ribband, in whole plaiting at one edge, sew together, forming a long rosette, and overcast on the other with coloured chenille, called a ruche, is a favourite addition to lace or satin caps. *Weekly Entertainer*, October 9, 1809 ~~~ it is likewise put on in three or four falls quilled together and very full, which is called a *ruche*; *Ladies' Monthly Museum*, May 1818 ~~~ [mourning for

George IV.] The trimmings most in favour, in full dress, are crape ruches, placed just above the hem; *Ladies' Museum*, August 1830 ~~~ A triple quilling, for which we have borrowed the French term *ruche*, figures under the bonnet as a small round cap, *Maids, Wives, and Widows*, February 2, 1833 [see also *quilling*]

rug – Rug (*s. from the* Swedish rugget *rough*) A course nappy kind of cloth; a coarse nappy coverlet used for mean beds; a rough woolly dog. Ash's English Dictionary, 1795 ~~~ A course nappy woollen cloth; Sheridan's English Dictionary, 1797 ~~~ RUG, a sort of carpet in which the wool is thickly worked, and the fibres are permitted to stand erect so as to form a warm foot-cloth. Rugs are generally made to fit hearth-stones, over which they are laid during the winter season. Some of these articles are beautifully executed at Kidderminster; and at the present day they are much in vogue. RUG is also a coarse nappy coverlet, generally composed of yellow and red worsted, and used as a covering for low-priced beds. Dictionary of Commerce, 1810

rugin – Rugin (*s. in* surgery) A soft kind of nappy cloth. Ash's English Dictionary, 1795

russels – *Aikin's Description of the Country round Manchester*. [published 1795] … "For some time past the staple manufactory of the place and neighbourhood has been … double russels, serges de Nisme and du Rome. These are all made from combing wool. *British Critic*, June 1796 ~~~ the following are the principal goods manufactured in and about Halifax: … plain and dyed Russels or florentines, Dictionary of Commerce, 1810 ~~~ Stuff goods, worsted, viz.; bird's eye, bombazetts, … russels, russeletts, Trade between Great Britain and the United States of America, 1833

russet – Halifax. … the principal fabrics are tammies, callimancoes, russets, broad and narrow cloths. They are generally woven by poor manufacturers, and sold in an unfinished state to the merchants, who dye and prepare them for foreign and home consumption. State of the Poor, 1797 ~~~ Perth … They likewise wash, card, spin, and weave their wool into tartan for plaids, kersies, and coarse russet cloth, for common wearing, Encyclopædia Britannica, 1797

Russia crash – [see *crash*]

Russia drab – [see *drab* and *drill*]

Russia drill – [see *drill*]

Russia duck – [see *duck*]

Russian satin – [Paris] Russian satin, resembling figured velvet, is a favorite material for hats; *Lady's Magazine*, January 1829 ~~~ [Paris] I have seen a hat of Russian satin, of forester's-green: this material appears like figured velvet: *La Belle Assemblée*, February 1829 ~~~ Bonnets of Russia satin, ornamented by a branch of lilacs, are favourite head-coverings for carriages for the Bois de Boulogne. *Ladies' Museum*, May 1829 ~~~ Some new materials, as *gaze d'Alger, satin de Russia*, … have recently been introduced in evening dress; the gauzes are figured, and of a very rich description; as is also the satin: the latter has, as yet, been very little employed, but it is expected that it will be very fashionable. *Ladies' Museum*, November 1831

rustic – [see *straw*]

Sable - Syrie

sable – The zibellina, or sable, has a great resemblance to the martin: … longer and more elegant fur. … The colour of the hair is cinereous at the bottom, and black at the tips; … The blackest are reputed the best; and sometimes sell, even in Siberia, from one to ten pounds Sterling each. Encyclopædia Britannica, 1797 ~~~ *Princess of Wales* was decorated with a very magnificent petticoat, composed of rich real silver net over white satin, ornamented with four stripes of real fable fur from the top of the right to the bottom of the left corner, with five or six real silver plumes, in imitation of ostrich feathers drooping from each stripe; *Lady's Magazine*, January 1800 ~~~ The sable is also found in North America: the fur of this kind is more glossy than the Siberian, of a bright chesnut hue, but of a courser texture. *Lady's Magazine*, October 1800 ~~~ [Paris] The new *stuff* is called *zibelline*; in effect, by the spotting, it is like the *martre-zibelline* (the martine-sable). *Lady's Magazine*, December 1807 ~~~ Zabelles, *or* zibelines, *sable skins*. Dufief's French Dictionary, 1810 ~~~ A pelisse of purple velvet to fit tight to the shape, in the wrap form, without a band, lined with royal amber, trimmed round the bottom and up the front with a border of sable five inches in width; … Half-boots of yellow Morocco, edged with sable. … Fur trimmings have taken place of gold and coloured edgings. White muffs and tippets now distinguish the woman of fashion; boots must be edged with sable. Mantles are made longer and wider, trimmed with broad sable or swansdown; *La Belle Assemblée*, January 1810 ~~~ *Zibellina,* the Sable. – This animal is very similar in its general appearance to the martin, but its fur is finer, and of a deep glossy brown; the hair being ash-coloured at the root, and black at the tips. … The skins of sables form one of the most valuable articles of the fur trade; and for these the animals are hunted with great eagerness. The hunting is usually carried on by criminals confined to the desert regions of Siberia, or by soldiers sent thither for that purpose, who generally remain there for several years. Both are obliged to furnish a certain quantity of furs. They shoot with a single ball, to injure the skin as little as possible. They frequently take them in traps, or kill them with blunt arrows. As an encouragement to the hunters, they are allowed to share among themselves whatever skins they take above the allotted number; and this, in a few years, amounts to a considerable premium. – The hunters form themselves into small troops, each of which is directed by a leader of their own choosing. The season of hunting is from November to February; for at that time the sables are in the highest perfection. Those caught at any other time of the year are full of short hairs, and are sold at inferior prices. The best skins are such as have only long hair, which is always black, and of a glossy brightness. Old furs do not retain their gloss. – Both the Russians and Chinese have a method of dyeing their furs; but the dyed sables are easily discovered, having neither the smoothness nor the brightness of the natural hair. Encyclopædia Britannica, 1810 ~~~ The fur of the sable is short, and generally of glossy and beautiful blackish brown colour: some animals, however, are of lighter colour, some have yellowish spots on the neck, and others have been found entirely white; but the skins of these are of little further value than as curiosities. There is a mode of dyeing the light-coloured furs darker, and also of dyeing other furs to imitate sables; but these are easily discovered by their having neither the smoothness nor the gloss of furs in a natural state. Useful Knowledge, 1821 ~~~ Valuable Zibeline muff, of the lightest shade of that rare and costly fur. *Lady's Magazine*, December 1825 ~~~ Sables of all countries are much worn this winter; each lady adopts them according to her means, and the *boa* seems to indicate the rank of the party. There is so great a difference of price in the qualities of this fur, that although this trimming is sought after by every one, it is sometimes of a price difficult to be attained: such is the real sable fur. *Ladies' Monthly Museum*, February 1828 ~~~ Merino pelisses of royal-blue, trimmed with light-coloured sable, are much admired for the promenade; *La Belle Assemblée*, March 1828 ~~~ Marten … *marte ou* [or] *martre*, Dictionnaire Anglais-Français, 1829 ~~~ Walking Dress. … Dress of crimson *gros de Naples*, trimmed with a deep fur of *marte Zibeline*: around the neck a *collerette of* lace. Cape, which is cut into deep points at the shoulders, boa, and muff, are of the same fur as the trimming. *Royal Lady's*, January 1831 ~~~ The Sable, *Mustela Zibellina,* is the most valuable of all the Weasel tribe. It is the size of the Martin, and inhabits the north of Asia, Siberia, and Kamtschatka. The Fur is glossy, and, usually, of a black-brown colour, except the head and throat, which are whitish. The colour of the animal, however, is various; some have been seen pure white; but the blacker the skins, the more they are esteemed: and, in all metaphorical applications, the adjective Sable is equivalent to *black*. The Russians dye the skins for the purpose of deception; but in this fraud they are far outdone by the Chinese. Sables fetch very different prices: from one to twelve pounds each. The *American* Sable, Mustela *Americana*, has a chesnut colour, but is of much less value. Analytical Dictionary, 1835 ~~~ Mantles and mantelets begin already to be trimmed with fur, and I have strong reasons to believe that when the season fairly opens, which it will in December, evening robes, particularly open ones, will be trimmed with sable or ermine. *New Monthly Belle Assemblée*, December 1836

Sacarallie – Ball Dress. A round dress, of India Sacarallie, *Ladies' Monthly Museum*, March 1818 [probably Sacharilla muslin]

sackcloth – Reading. … Sail-cloth, sacking or sack-cloth, gauze, ribbon, and pins are made here. The weavers of sacking can earn 16s. a week; State of the Poor, 1797 ~~~ Coarse stuff made of goats hair, of a dark colour, worn by soldiers and mariners; and used as a habit among the Hebrews in times of mourning. Called *sackcloth*, either because sacks were made of this sort of stuff, or because haircloaths were straight and close like a sack. New Encyclopædia, 1807

sagathee – In regard to the stuffs of wool, called … sagathis, &c. which were furnished both to France and foreigners by Darnetel, Beauvais, Amiens, Lille, Rheims, and le Mans, they must sink under the competition of the similar manufactures of England. System of Geography, 1807 ~~~ Sagathee, a slight woollen stuff, being a kind of serge, or ratteen; sometimes mixed with a little silk. It was originally manufactured at Amiens in France, but for several years past it has been wrought in England. General Dictionary of Commerce, 1810 ~~~ Sagathy, a kind of serge. Knowles' English Dictionary, 1835

sail cloth – To those engaged in mercantile concerns, we conceive the follow price current of goods, wares, &c. as they actually were at Philadelphia in January, 1794, … Sailcloth, English, No. I., per yard . . 0 40 [40 cents] — Boston, No. I., ditto [per yard] . . 0 36 [36 cents] View of the American United States, 1795 ~~~ The sail cloth is made in pieces of about forty yards each, yard-wide, and worth from fifteen to seventeen-pence *per* yard. *Universal Magazine*, November 1795 ~~~ SAIL-CLOTH, a strong texture, made of hemp, for the purpose of supplying ships with sails. –Although considerable quantities of this valuable article are annually manufactured in Britain, yet as they are not only inadequate to the demand for the navy, but, being subject to the *mildew*, are consequently less durable than the sailcloth imported from North America, we shall state the following: expedient, adopted in that country; by which the cloth may be greatly improved. It simply consists in moistening the warp, in the loom, with a decoction or gelatinous substance prepared from the refuse of neats'-feet (after the oil is expressed), which is boiled in water, till it is converted into a kind of glue. The weavers of this article, in Britain, employ a paste made of flour and water, which necessarily renders the cloth brittle; whereas, by using the *animal* preparation above mentioned, the sail-cloth will not only be rendered more durable, but the expence may be lessened, and an article, that is at present thrown away, may thus be usefully employed. Domestic Encyclopædia, 1803 ~~~ The manufacture of sail-cloth, is confined chiefly to the neighbourhood of Cork; but considerable sums are paid by the Linen Board to encourage the manufacture of sail-cloth, duck, canvas, and drilling, spun by machinery; and it is thought this part of the trade might advantageously be extended. Political State of the British Empire, 1818 ~~~ Dresses for Wildfowl Shooting. … Having put on the boots, there must be drawn over all a pair of short loose sailcloth * (or, if cold frosty weather, Flushing-coating) trowsers. … * *Sailcloth* is so strong, so durable, and such a good defence against rain, that it answers better than any thing for making game bags; Instructions to Young Sportsmen, 1825 [see also *canvas*, *duck* and *raven duck*]

Saint Vailler – Ball Dress. A dress of bright cherry-coloured *gaze de St. Valiere*, over a *gros de Naples* slip, to correspond. *La Belle Assemblée*, March 1830 ~~~ her majesty wore a dress of *gauze Saint Vallier* of salmon-colour: *La Belle Assemblée*, July 1830

salamandre – Besides those rich materials we may cite … *gaze salamandre* … for ball dresses. *Court Magazine*, November 1835

salamporis – These are silks of the richest kind: *Salamporis unis*, the which is in fact another name for a superior kind of chaly; and the *Salamporis croises*, the same description of material, but twilled. They are of different patterns. Some arabesques on a white or colour ground; others running patterns; others bouquets of flowers. *Court Magazine*, May 1834 ~~~ For in-door dress, *mousseline de laine* and *salamporis* are favourite articles. They may be trimmed with bias folds of satin or *poult de soie*. *Court Journal*, November 7, 1835

Salempores – One Year from 5th July 1809 to 5th July 1810. ... White Calicoes. Sallampores . . . Highest Price [per piece]. s. 22/6 Lowest Price s. 10/. Average Price. s. 16/10. Papers, &c. – East India Company, 1813 ~~~ For the following merchandise, delivered to Thomas Forsyth, United States' Indian agent for the Sioux, Fox, and other tribes of Indians, ... 2 pieces Salampores, 23 dollars, Letter from the Secretary of War, 1822 ~~~ "One word, however, about *clothing*. – The negroes of a Plantation in Berbice, called Profit, complained to the Fiscal, in October, 1823, of a want of fish and clothing. I will not now go into the matter of the fish, though that, too, might well illustrate the *comforts* of West India Slavery, but confine myself to the other point. The answer of the Manager, to the complaint of a want of clothing, was, that nineteen months before, each man had had a jacket, a hat, one yard of Salampore, and four yards of Osnaburg. This was deemed so adequate a supply, by the Fiscal, that two of the complainants were selected by him and flogged, for 'having failed to prove' their complaints. And yet, it would be difficult, for the most ingenious tailor in England to contrive to make even half, a suit of clothes for the merest beggar who treads our streets, out of this entire supply of a man-slave for nineteen months, and for not being content with which the said man-slave was flogged. \ "And then let us look at the value of this nineteen months' clothing of a grown man! The four yards of Osnaburg *two shillings*, the yard of Salampore *one shilling,* the hat *fifteen pence* – the jacket would be valued high at *five shillings*; in all nine *shillings and three pence*. Why, it would do no more than pay for a single pair of shoes and stockings for one of our comparatively wretched peasants. *Anti-Slavery Monthly Reporter*, September 1827 ~~~ [ad] India Goods, viz. ... white, brown, and blue Salempores, *Colonist*, January 10, 1828 ~~~ For the following goods delivered (in compliance with the provisions of the 4th article of the treaty concluded with the Pottawatamie Indians at Tippecanoe river, on the 27th October, 1832,) ... 2 pieces Salempores prints, 171 1/4 yds, at 19 cents, $32.53 3/4; 5 pieces choc. ground prints, 142 yds, at 29 cents, $41.18 Emigration of Indians, 1835 [see also *punjum cloth*]

Salisbury whites – *Salisbury*, a city of England, in the county of Wilts, ... Besides the manufactures of flannels, druggets, and the cloths called Salisbury whites, for the Turkey trade here, it is noted for the manufacture of bone lace, New Universal Gazetteer, 1798 ~~~ Salisbury was formerly celebrated for its manufactures of flannels, druggets, and the cloths called Salisbury Whites; but these branches of trade are now almost extinct, and what remains is confined to a very inconsiderable number of persons; Topographical Dictionary of England, 1831

Salomon – [Paris] The evening dress silks that have appeared, are all in the superb but heavy style of Louis XIV's reign. The satins *Salomon, Esmeralda,* and *Pharamond*, are expected to be in great request; *New Monthly Belle Assemblée*, November 1836

Samarcande – [Paris] The *tissues de Samarcande*, a slight printed silk of very pretty pattern, are expected to succeed the foulards. *New Monthly Belle Assemblée*, November 1836

Sarah – Evening costume is still of a light kind; several new materials have, however, appeared for it. We may cite among them the *satins d'Aboukir, Sarah,* and *Casanova*; ... These rich and beautiful materials will be in great request as soon as the winter has fairly set in. *Ladies' Pocket*, November 1836

sarsnet – [court dress] A white crape petticoat, ... body and train of green sarsnet trimmed with gold fringe. *Lady's Magazine*, June 1797 ~~~ Sarcenet , [pronounced:] sars-net. Fine thin woven silk. Sheridan's English Dictionary, 1797 ~~~ [Paris] In a round dress of Italian crape, of a bright lemon colour, over a white sarsnet slip. ... [London] The Woodman's hat, of figured sarsnet, in celestial blue, olive, dove-colour, or lilac, is an ornament where much taste and whim is united; *La Belle Assemblée*, April 1807 ~~~ An autumnal brown wrap-cloak, with sleeves made of rich twilled sarcenet, *Lady's Magazine*, October 1807 ~~~ Shot and figured twill sarsnets remain high in fashionable estimation. Little variety is observable in the formation of pelisses and spencers; the principal article used in their construction is twilled shot sarsnet; the favourite assortment of colours is red and green, red and brown, mazarine and red. *Weekly Entertainer*, October 9, 1809 ~~~ The Portuguese sarsnet, an evident imitation of that beautiful article the French levantine, has lately made its appearance; but it has all the thickness of levantine without its elegant softness, and seems best appropriated to travelling dresses. *Belle Assemblée*, May 1812 ~~~ [ad] Rich Figured Sarsnets, from French models, 6s. to 7s. 6d. per yard, usually sold at 7s. 6d. and 9s.; *Repository of Arts*, May 1815 ~~~ This is the most lady-like slight mourning that we have seen; we say slight, because black sarsnet can never be considered as deep mourning. *Repository of Arts*, January 1819 ~~~ For carriage airings, when the mornings are somewhat chill, a pelisse is generally worn of a pale lavender, or purple evening primrose colour: the material is of the improved twilled sarsnet, equal in richness to, thought of a still lighter appearance than the French *levantine*. *La Belle Assemblée*, August 1819 ~~~ The new materials for gowns are very beautiful, and are well adapted to the season. ... it is not unusual for a lady, when she returns from her carriage airing, to divest herself of her white dress and put on a coloured gown of slight summer sarcenet. *La Belle Assemblée*, August 1823 ~~~ [ad] they are now offering rich double Sarsnets, 2s. per yard; *Examiner*, April 23, 1826 ~~~ This, which used to form the substance of garments, is now most usually employed for lining them, giving place in its turn, as regards its former more dignified uses, to gros-de-naples. Silk Manufacture, 1832 ~~~ Sarsnets, silk . . [duty] free. — cotton, *See Cottons*, . . 25 per cent. Jones's Digest, 1836 ~~~. This pelisse is of *sarcenet*, which is a thinner, slighter kind of lustring, woven in a similar manner, and not unfrequently sold for it at a cheap rate. It is sometimes twilled. Scenes of Commerce, 1836 [see also *Florence*]

sateen – [see *satteen*]

satin – [see the word proceeding or following *satin*; example: for *satin ecossais*, see *ecossais*]

satin – Satin, a soft, close shining silk Perry's English Dictionary, 1795 ~~~ The principal silk stuffs brought from China are, ... Plain embroidered, and brocaded sattins, of from 11 ½, to 12 ells by 5/8. *New-York Magazine*, February 1795 ~~~ the dress of the Princess was changed, from a muslin gown and blue sattin petticoat, with a black beaver hat, and blue and black feathers, for a white sattin gown, and very elegant turban, cap of sattin, trimmed with crape, and ornamented with white feathers, *European Magazine*, April 1795 ~~~ *Her Majesty*. White crape petticoat, embroidered with white satin, in waves across, intersected with spotted blue shaded satin, and black velvet stars, ornamented with an elegant double border of painted satin in shaded spots, festooned and trimmed with black lace; under and upper drapery of white satin and spotted crape, trimmed with black lace, and blue shaded satin border; *Lady's Magazine*, January 1797 ~~~ His Majesty, Very richly habited in a coat of brown cloth, curiously embroidered, white satin waistcoat, and a very rich collar of the order of the Garter, sword-knot, &c. *Lady's Magazine*, May 1897 ~~~ SATIN is a kind of thick silken stuff, very smooth and shining; the warp is very fine and stands out, the woof courser and hid underneath: on which depends its gloss and beauty. Some satins are quite plain, others wrought, some flowered with gold or silk, others striped. The finest satins are those of Florence and Genoa, yet the French will not allow those of Lyons to be at all inferior. India satins or satins of China, are silken stuff, much like those manufactured in Europe. Of these some are plain, others worked, either with gold, or silk, flowered, damasked, striped, &c. They are mostly valued because of their bleaching easily, without losing any thing of their lustre. In other respects they are inferior to those of Europe. Guy's Pocket Cyclopædia, 1810 ~~~ The chief seats of this branch of manufacture, are Lyons in France, and Genoa and Florence in Italy. At these places they manufacture plain, embossed, striped, and embroidered satins, besides a great variety of other designs, whose colours and fabric have hitherto given them a decided superiority in the market. Very capital imitations of the foreign satins are made in Spitalfields, and in other parts of England; but we seldom export this article. General Dictionary of Commerce, 1810 ~~~ [ad] stout White Satins for slips, 4s. 9d. [per yard]; *Repository of Arts*, May 1815 ~~~ Two new ball dresses came under our inspection, the most beautiful we have seen for some time; one is of a figured satin of an entire new manufacture, with the figures woven among the satin in such a manner that they are transparent; *La Belle Assemblée*, January 1820 ~~~ Figured satin seems likely to be a great deal worn in full dress: it is used both for gowns and slips; it has an uncommonly beautiful effect under white lace or transparent gauze dresses. *Repository of Arts*, December 1820 ~~~ Satins of various kinds, plain, figured, striped, and watered, will, it is thought, be fashionable in dinner and evening dress. *La Belle Assemblée*, November 1831 ~~~ Satin is a twill of a peculiar description: the soft and lustrous face which it exhibits is given by keeping always a very large proportion, frequently even as much as seven out of every eight threads of the warp, visible, or as it is called, floating above the shoot. ... Satins from China are much esteemed for the quality they possess of being easily cleaned and bleached, when they resume all their original lustre; but in other respects they are found to be inferior to those manufactured in Europe. Satins of the higher qualities have long been manufactured in Spitalfields, for the supply of our eastern dependencies. Silk Manufacture, 1832 ~~~ [Paris] Rich brocaded satins of all descriptions are worn in dresses á l'antique; *Lady's Magazine*, December 1834 ~~~ The materials for evening dress rival in splendour those of several seasons past; .. satins striped, flowered and figured, some with velvet; *Court Magazine*, November 1835... Some new materials have appeared both for dinner and evening dress. ... another, composed of silk only, is a twilled and figured satin, of an excessively rich kind. *Ladies' Pocket*, January 1836

satin à la reine – a new kind of watered satin, which we have borrowed from the French, and which is styled *satin à la reine*, are all in favour for carriage hats and bonnets. *Ladies' Museum*, November 1831 ~~~ Make and Materials of Evening Dress. – Among the new materials which belong to winter rather than autumn, but for which many orders have already been given, are the *satin polonis* and *à la reine*, ... The materials are of extreme richness. The *satin à la reine* unites the gloss of the richest satin, to the softness and graceful flow of cachemire. *Atheneum*, February 1832 ~~~ Materials of Evening Dress. ... The *satin a la reine* unites the gloss of the richest satin, to the softness and graceful flow of cashmere. *Atkinson's Casket*, January 1832 ~~~ *Satins Imperial à la Reines* and *Perline*, may be classified among the richest materials for half-dress; *New Monthly Belle Assemblée*, November 1836 [see also *reine* and *watered satin*]

satin brocard – *Satin brocard*, a superb material, in which gold is interwoven with silk, is very generally employed for turbans, so also is gold gauze, *Ladies' Pocket*, January 1836

satin cachemire – [see *cashmere satin*]

satin cloth – [see *tissue satin*]

satin d'Aboukir – [see *Aboukir*]

satin d'Alger – [see *Algerian*]

satin d'Ancre – [see *Ancre*]

satin damas – [see *damask satin*]

satin de Byzance – Some new silks, of a very rich kind, will appear very shortly. They are the ... *satin de Byzance*. It is expected that, both in form and materials, the style of the seventeenth century will be revived in winter evening dress. *Court Magazine*, October 1836 ~~~ Byzantium, t. Byzance, New Pocket Dictionary, 1830 [an ancient city, now (1830) part of Constantinople]

satin de Chine – [see *Chinese satin*]

satin de Cleopatre – new materials of incomparable richness and beauty. One, called *satin de Cléopatre*, has a plain ground thickly strewed with flowers woven in the satin, but stand out like a highly raised embroidery. The ground appears as if covered with white *tulle*, but the flowers are not covered. *Court Magazine*, November 1833

satin de laine – *Troyes*, on the Seine, has a number of manufactories of woollen stuffs, such as satins, (*satins de laine*), European Commerce, 1818 ~~~ [men's] Among the new materials for pantaloons are *satin de laine*, and *estaing*, either black brown, *grenat noisette*, or *ecru*. *Casket*, January 1831 ~~~ The most fashionable materials for cloaks are – Satin de laine; a material of the texture of Cachemere, broché with satin flowers, lilac and green, orange and black, blue and black, green and black, &c.; or all one colour. *Lady's Magazine and Museum*, November 1834 ~~~ New materials already appear in crowds for the different departments of the toilette; those for morning *negligé*, travelling, &c. &c., are principally of the woollen kind, such as watered and figured *satins de laine*, *Ladies' Pocket*, November 1836 ~~~ Materials and Colours. – The different fabrics are varied much at present. ... woollen satins; *Blackwood's Lady's Magazine*, December 1836 [see also *cashmere satin*]

satin de Russia – [see *Russian satin*]

satin des Indes – [see *Indian satin*]

satin diamente – One of the prettiest novelties in head dresses is a turban of *satin diamenté*, intermixed with white crape. The satin has a black ground, flowered in the most vivid and beautiful colours; the foundation of the turban is composed of it. *Court Magazine*, January 1835

satin du Levant – [see *Levant*]

satin duchesse – Full Dress. A Round dress of white *gros des Indes*, … Over this dress is an open robe composed of satin duchesse; the color is emerald green. *La Belle Assemblée*, February, 1830

satin foulard – [see *foulard satin*]

satin Gabrielle – the most admired materials for dresses which have just appeared in Paris. … *Satin Gabrielle*: – A superb material, figured in various colours; the pattern being flowers on a rich dark ground. *Court Journal*, October 17, 1835 ~~~ [Paris] A great variety of materials have appeared for evening dress. We may cite, as likely to be fashionable, *velours Indien, satins rosiere, Montpensier, Gabrielle, Rachel*, all of which are in the rich but heavy style that we spoke of in our last number, *Court Magazine*, November 1835

satin gauze – Dinner Dress, Of thin mull muslin, … A satin gauze cap, richly trimmed with blond, *Ladies' Monthly Museum*, May 1817 ~~~ Evening Dress. A round dress, composed of satin striped gauze of a dark puce colour, *Repository of Arts*, March 1819 ~~~ a new gauze of French invention, called *gaze sattinée*, … [Paris Ball dresses] Satin-gauze, either striped or in diamonds, or rings interlaced. *Repository of Arts*, March 1823 ~~~ [ad] Quincy Tufts, … Has received … Elegant Satin Stripe Gauze Hdkfs.; *New England Farmer*, June 3, 1825 ~~~ We have seen some very pretty dancing dresses, made of striped satin gauze, and trimmed with ribands. *Ladies' Museum*, March 1830 ~~~ There are very pretty ribbons of gauze *satinée*, which produce a very pleasing effect on hats. *Royal Lady's Magazine*, January 1831 ~~~ [court dress] Dress of white satin gauze, over a white satin slip, trimmed with two flounces of queen's blonde, looped up in front with diamonds; *Royal Lady's Magazine*, April 1831 ~~~ Ribbon aprons are a new and very pretty accessory to full dress. They are composed of *gaze satinée*; *La Belle Assemblée*, May 1831 ~~~ Ball dress. A dress of *gaze satinée*, a white ground figured in a new pattern of chocolate and *vallière*. … Among the novel materials in evening dress, … *Gaze cashmere* and *gaze satinnée*, are the most in favour for young ladies. *Ladies' Museum*, January 1832 ~~~ *Gaze satin*, … are all fashionable for dancing dresses. *Court Magazine*, February 1835

satin Isabelle – [see *Isabelle*]

satin Medicis – [see *Medicis*]

satin Memphis – [see *Memphis*]

satin Montespan – [see *Montespan*]

satin moyen âge – The most novel, and in our opinion the most elegant, pelisses are those of the new rich material called *satin moyen âge*, with dark-blue grounds, and orange patterns; or else the ground black and the pattern in rose or ruby. *Court Magazine*, January 1834

satin Rachel – the most admired materials for dresses which have just appeared in Paris. … *Satin Rachele*: – A magnificent texture, falling in broad and massive folds, similar to the draperies worn by the fair daughters of Israel in the pictures of the old masters. *Court Journal*, October 17, 1835 ~~~ A great variety of materials have appeared for evening dress. We may cite, as likely to be fashionable, *velours Indien, satins rosiere, Montpensier, Gabrielle, Rachel*, all which are in the rich but heavy style that we spoke of in our last number, particularly the *satin Rachel*, which takes its name from its resemblance to the superb tissues in which the Jewish maidens of the olden time were attired in *grand parure*. *Court Magazine*, November 1835

satin royal – [Paris] Evening-Dress. A gown composed of satin royal, the color is a light shade of Chamois; *Ladies' Pocket*, March 1830 ~~~ shoes of satin royal. *Lady's Magazine and Museum*, July 1834 ~~~ but the most superb [riband] is the *satin royal* of gold tissue intermixed with colour silks. *Court Magazine*, October 1835

satin serge – For plain evening dress, a robe of *satin sergé*, the ground white, or light grey, with bunches of flowers in bring and variegated tints. *Court Journal*, October 24, 1835

satin straw – the Spanish hat, of black satin-straw, *La Belle Assemblée*, September 1807 ~~~ [Paris]

Amongst the straw hats which are at present in the highest estimation, we have particularly noticed the *Chapeau à-la-Pamela,* which is composed of satin straw, and ornamented with a large cockade of straw-coloured ribband and three feathers. *La Belle Assemblée,* July 1814 ~~~ *Satin straw,* and by some called *patent straw,* similar to that already alluded to ... but having a much greater proportion of silk in it, *Public Documents,* March 1831 ~~~ The Secretary of the Treasury has referred to me a letter addressed to him by Mr. Meigs D. Benjamin, upon the subject of the duty legally chargeable on the article called *satin straw* or *Pagne de l'Inde.* The article in question being generally (if not altogether) used in the manufacture of women's hats or bonnets, it was conceived that they were embraced in the 4th clause of the 1st section of the act of 22d May, 1824, under the general head of "all flats, braids, or plats, for making of hats or bonnets," more particularly as some of the *satin straw* is composed almost entirely of straw. *Public Documents,* December 1831 [see also *payne*]

satin Turc – [see *Turkish satin*]

satinade – [see *satinet*]

satinée – *satin-like; soft as velvet,* <u>Dufief's French Dictionary</u>, 1810 ~~~ There are very pretty ribbons of gauze *satinèe,* which produce a very pleasing effect upon hats. *Royal Lady's Magazine,* January 1831 ~~~ Morning Dress. – Dress of emerald green terry velvet *rayee satinee, Casket,* February 1833 ~~~ For evening dress, several splendid novelties have this season been introduced: among the most distinguished, are the satin satineé, *Court Journal,* January 10, 1835

satinet – a slight kind of sattin, commonly striped, and ordinarily used by the ladies for summer night-gowns. <u>Encyclopædia Britannica</u>, 1797 ~~~ The greater part of the combing wool is consumed in worsted for making what is called new drapery in the Book of Rates, viz. ... satinet, 2s. to 4s. ... per yard. <u>Origin of Commerce</u>, 1801 ~~~ Satinade, *s. f. silk in imitation of satin, peeling satin.* <u>Boyer's Royal Dictionary Abridged</u>, 1802 ~~~ *Satinet* is a kind of very light, thin satin, principally manufactured at Bruges, and usually employed in making furniture. <u>Dictionary of Commerce</u>, 1810 ~~~ Satinet or Satinade, s. (a slight thin sort of satin) <u>Chambaud's French Dictionary</u>, 1815 ~~~ The coarse cloths called satinets, ... Of the common country wool we make coarse cloths and kerscys principally for the army; we purchase some wool of Merino, of which we make satinets. ... The satinets and the negro clothing are generally about three-quarter yards wide, <u>American Tariffs</u>, 1828 ~~~ [ad] Blue Cloth and Satinet Jackets, Pants, Vests and Coatees, <u>Directory for the City of Buffalo</u>, 1832 ~~~ There is required for the supply of that manufacture, annually, 2530000 pounds of wool, 52112 pounds cotton, for warp of satinets, *Gales & Seaton's Register,* March 2, 1832 ~~~ [ad] 7 cases Satinettes, Striped, and plain of various colors *New England Farmer,* September 25, 1833 ~~~ What portion of the cost of your manufactures consists of the price of the raw material, what portion of the wages of labor, and what portion of the profits of capital? Of a yard of satinet, 50 cents for materials, 18 cents for wages, 7 cents profits and wear and tear. ... satinet from 60 cts. to 95 cts. per yard; ... Xenia Woollen Factory, in Greene county, was established in 1825; water power. About 9.000 lbs. of wool are manufactured per annum, into satinets, country cloths, &c. <u>Executive Documents,</u> 1833 ~~~ *Uniforms.* ... Of the Cadets. A coatee of grey satinet, single breasted, <u>American State Papers</u>, 1834 [see also *Bruges satin* and *peeling satin*]

satinture – [riding dress in Paris] Pantaloons, also, of cambric, trimmed at the bottom, and *bottines* of *reps* silk, or of *satinture. La Belle Assemblée,* September 1831

satteen – I have found nothing so good for a light summer jacket as what is made at Manchester, by the name of *satteen,* or *jeanett,* which is printed on each side, in imitation of cloth. This stuff far surpasses the others for lightness, comfort, durability, and every thing that can be required for warm weather; but, as there is no particular interest in making it (rather the reverse), it is not everywhere very easily procured; so that your tailor would probably be obliged to order it, in doing which he cannot choose it of too good a quality. <u>Instructions to Young Sportsmen</u>, 1816 ~~~ [ad] Pantaloons, ... Sateen, Crape, Concan, ... Summer Goods, ... Striped and Plain Satteen, ... of all colour and qualities. <u>Boston Annual Advertiser</u>, 1823 ~~~ Ladies' Corsets. ... These Corsets will take a yard of 18 inch satteen – the sizes are from 24 to 32 inches, <u>Sectum</u>, 1825 ~~~ [ad] Gentlemen's Superfine Blue, Black, Green & Brown Coats With Silk Shoulders, White Drill, Satteen & Kersemere Trowsers. *Honduras Gazette,*

July 1, 1826 ~~~ White and striped Satteen Jackets and Trowsers. *Honduras Gazette*, December 30, 1826 ~~~ [ad] To Officers, Cadets, &c. ... at Wholesale Prices, – say, White Jean and Satteen Trowsers, from 5s. to 10s.; ditto Waistcoats, 4s. to 6s.; ditto Jackets, 7s. to 11s.; *Asiatic Journal*, January 1828 ~~~ Denmark satin, or sateen, if cotton and wool is component material, 40 per cent. Denmark satin, or sateens, entirely stuff, 25 do. Tariff, 1832 ~~~ I have found nothing better for a light summer jacket than what is made at Manchester by the name of *satteen, jeanet*, or *florentine*, which is printed on each side, in imitation of cloth. This stuff far surpasses the others for lightness, comfort, durability, and every thing that can be required for warm weather; Instructions to Young Sportsmen, 1833 ~~~ Stuff goods, worsted, viz ; bird's eye, bombazetts, calimancos, camblets, Circassians, Denmark satteens, ... satteen, Trade between Great Britain and the United States of America, 1833 ~~~ [ad] Have received by the ships Hark-away and Jefferson, direct from Liverpool, ... superior satteen and jeans corsetts; *Farmer's Register*, May 1835 [see also *Denmark satin*]

satteuse – trimmings of dresses ... have mountings in bias, called *satteuses. Ladies' Monthly Museum*, July 1825

Saxon – Within the last four years cloth made from *Saxon* wool has been introduced, and it is *now* more highly esteemed than that made of Spanish wool, and bears a higher price. The emperor of Saxony raises a large quantity of wool and sends it to England. New Pocket Cyclopædia, 1813 ~~~ Of the Saxon and Prussian ordinary and middling Cloths, almost all the stocks, even those long lying in the warehouses, are already disposed of, and partly even at better prices than at the last Michaelmas fair. Even fine Saxon Cloths have been much more in demand than for a long time past. Edinburgh Annual Register, 1824 ~~~ The British manufactures which were sold at Kiachta, during last year, consisted of the following articles; viz. Woollen cloth, in imitation of Saxon cloth, 400,000 yards. Sessional Papers, 1825 ~~~ [ad] A MOST IMPORTANT FACT, connected with the following statement, should be borne in mind; viz., that the same care and expense in workmanship and trimming is bestowed on the lower as on the higher class of clothing; so that, in style and general appearance, all are alike. This, while the First Class is equal to any produced, and the Second Class but little inferior to the First, the Third Class, though not as fine, as of an excellent stout Saxon cloth, admirably adapted for Gentleman's travelling or hack wear. ... Ladies' Riding Habits, Lined with Silk, ... Saxon Wool ditto [Habit, of any colour] £5 5s.; Extra Saxon habit Cloth . £6 6s. Doudney Brothers, 1830 ~~~ [men's] A Morning Dress. This frock coat is of sky blue Saxony cloth; *Casket*, January 1831 ~~~ Philadelphia, *June 25th*, 1831. *Dear Sir*: Not many days ago I was prompted by curiosity to visit the elegant store of Mr. Van Harlingen, in Chesnut Street, where I had an opportunity of viewing his assortment of goods; but, what particularly attracted my attention, were the articles of German manufacture, consisting chiefly of beautiful damask napkins, muslins handsomely embroidered, and superfine Saxon cloths of various colors, and superbly wrought. These last are designed chiefly for table, chair, and sofa covers, and are, perhaps, unsurpassed by any goods of a similar description in the world. Letters ... in the Banner of the Constitution, 1831 ~~~ [ad] A Suit of Clothes made of the best Saxony cloth that can be produced, and of superior workmanship, for £4 5s. 3d. at four suits per year, (the old ones returned) is unique for the economy in this age of retrenchment and competition. *Athenæum*, August 11, 1832 ~~~ [ad for men's] Extra Imperial Saxony [dress coats], the best that is made . 2 £ 15s. *Eminent Foreign Statesmen*, March 1836 ~~~ Although *wool* is generally said to be the staple of England, there is very little British wool used in the English manufactories of broad cloth. All the finer sorts are brought from Saxony and other parts of Germany, and the Saxony wool is fabricated into an article which fetches a higher price than even the much-talked-of Spanish wool. It must be observed, however, that the breed of sheep from which this wool is obtained, is of Spanish origin. *Blackwood's Lady's Magazine*, August 1836 [see also *broadcloth*]

say – A kind of silk, from *soie*, Fr. A kind of woollen stuff. Royal English Dictionary, 1775 ~~~ Say, or Saye, in commerce, a kind of serge much used abroad for linings, and by the religious for shirts; with us it is employed for aprons by several sorts of artificers, being usually dyed green. Encyclopædia Britannica, 1797 ~~~ Say, or Saye, a kind of serge or woollen stuff, much used abroad for linings, and by the religious of some orders for shirts: with us it is employed as aprons, by several descriptions of artificers, being usually dyed green. Some of the manufacturers in Belgia make says of very superior quality, which are entirely formed of Segovian, or English wool. These are usually 7-8ths in breadth; but some sorts of says are only 3-4ths. The latter are made from the wools of the country itself. The denomination of say is likewise bestowed upon a remarkably stout kind of cloth, of which the Turks make short cloaks and vest for winter-wear. The only colours given to this species of stuff are bright scarlet and dark red. General Dictionary of Commerce, 1810 ~~~ The Dutch *saai*, wool, signifies also Woollencloth, and, hence, the old English Say (Scoth Sey) was the plain milled cloth of our ancestors. Analytical Dictionary, 1835

Scarron – [Paris] New Materials. – For grandes toilettes d'hirer, the newest materials are … The satin *Scarron* – a striped satin, *broché* in a large antique pattern of flowers; a perfect imitation of the satins of the time of Louis XIV. and Madame de Maintenon. *Lady's Magazine and Museum*, November 1834 ~~~ [evening dress] The *satine Scarron*, a superb material of the damask kind, intermingled with gold, are highly fashionable. Robes of these rich materials never have any trimming round the border. *Court Magazine*, March 1835

Scotch madras – [Paris] Among the generality of white dresses, two or three Scotch robes, with red and green stripes, are much distinguished. This kind of stuff is more than ever sought after by ladies of the first fashion in the choice of their apparel: thus we see daily the most elegant ladies in brilliant equipages alighting at the warehouses Sainte-Anne, for the purpose of choosing Scotch madras: so great success has determined the proprietor of these warehouses, which alone supply the material, to erect in his factory twenty new looms for this kind of stuff. We have seen some of the newest patterns and designs, which are extremely handsome. Some milliners have made robes, in the Greek style, of Scotch madras; they have a charming effect: in short, this stuff is so highly appreciated, that we have seen gentlemen of the highest rank adopting it for their cravats; and it is even said, they intend to have the same colours and design on woollen stuffs for cloaks during the ensuing winter. *Ladies' Monthly Museum*, October 1825 [see *madras*]

Scotch tartan – [see *plaid* and *tartan*]

seal skin – When the mountaineer has killed the seal, he flays him in the cavern, and takes away only the skin and fat, leaving all the rest of the animal to be devoured by the birds, or carried off by the waves. The skin being properly dressed, serves to make shoes, which are found more durable than those of neat's leather. *Weekly Magazine*, October 30, 1802 ~~~ York Mantle and Hat, seal-skin, or Gregorian cloth, edging, orange and scarlet, India-pattern. *La Belle Assemblée*, February 1806 ~~~ Walking Dress. … Regency hat of black beaver or seal-skin, ornamented with an elegant feather of the same colour, and finished by a gold button and loop on one side. – Large bear or seal skin muff; *Edinburgh Annual Register*, April 3, 1813 ~~~ The young and smaller seals yield the most oil; the largest are good for little, except the skin; indeed, our seal-catchers seldom care for killing the old ones, where they can have the others. Our tanners dress the seal's skin both for shoes and breeches, but they do not answer very well for the former, being soft and spungy; when properly managed, do well for breeches. They are likewise dressed with the hair on, for saddle-covers, and I have seen very beautiful ones made into waistcoats. *Sporting Magazine*, January 1813 ~~~ Seal skin hats and bonnets continue to be worn, but velvet or satin French hats are, beyond doubt, higher in estimation; *La Belle Assemblée*, November 1814 ~~~ For walking *costume*, a plainer dress presents itself, generally of a dark bottle-green, with a sable or seal-skin hat, *La Belle Assemblée*, February 1816 ~~~ seal skins, which have always sold for two dollars each. Reports from the Committees, 1821 ~~~ Seal *skins,* when tanned and properly dressed, are converted into a valuable leather for shoes and other uses. Useful Knowledge, 1821 ~~~ [ad] constantly on hand, a general assortment of Ladies and Gentlemen's BOOTS AND SHOES, Among which, are Ladies' Prunell, Sattin, Morocco, Seal and Calf skin BOOTS, Directory for the Village of Rochester, 1827 ~~~ On the 9th of May, 1827, I purchased a copy of this work of Jonathan Martin. He was dressed in rather an eccentric manner, having on a pair of trowsers and a waistcoat made of seals' skin, with the hair outwards; this he said was for the purpose of resisting any wet weather which he might encounter in his travels to sell his pamphlets Local Records; or Historical Register, 1833 ~~~ Seal-skin is similar, but inferior, to dog-skin; it is employed for the same purposes, but its use has much declined of late years. Transactions of the Society, 1836

seal-wool cloth – *Specification of the Patent granted to Mr., Thomas Chapman, of the Parish of Saint Mary Magdalen, Bermondsey, in the County of Surry, Skinner and Seal-wool Manufacturer; for his Method of taking or getting off the Wool or Fur from Seal and other Skins, in a more perfect State than has hitherto been done, for the Purpose of manufacturing the same into Hats, or any other Article of cloathing; whereby the Skins or Pelts are less damaged than by any other Process yet adopted, and are kept and preserved in a perfect State, for the Purpose of tanning into any Kind of Leather.* Dated June 6, 1799. ... After the above operation has been practised with effect, take the other vessel, fill it with warm water, and therein immerse the wool or fur; and thoroughly wash, cleanse, purify, and press from and out of the wool or fur, every filth or dirt that then adheres or appears to adhere thereto. After it is so cleansed, let it be dried by a slow fire-stove, or by heat of the sun, if the season will permit. After it is completely dried, pull or part it by hand, or otherwise, as it will freely part. After it is so parted, bow it with the bow-string, or other like instrument; and the wool or fur so prepared, dried, and finished, will be found to be fit for the purpose of being used in the manufacture of hats, and other articles of clothing, and to be nearly equal to every purpose for which the wool or fur called beaver is used; and is also a wool or fur of so fine a texture, and so good a staple, as to be convertible to any other article of clothing. Repertory of Arts, 1799 ~~~ Velvets, nay, even coats of kerseymere, and seal-wool cloth, are now dragged from the recesses of the wardrobe. *La Belle Assemblée*, April 1807 ~~~ When the long and coarse hair of the seal is pulled off, a fine, short, silky, and somewhat fawn-coloured down is left, which in this country is a fashionable *fur* for ornamenting ladies' dresses. This fur woven with silk, is also manufactured into shawls, which are of extremely soft and delicate texture. Useful Knowledge, 1821 ~~~ [ad] *Ladies' Woollen Warehouse, 28, King-street, Covent-garden.* – The utmost variety is manufactured and kept for Sale of Pelisse, Habit, Merino, Saxon, Rabbit, Seal-skin, and Vigona Cloths, in every Colour, and those of the present Fashion in particular, from 5*s*. to 25*s*. per yard, all Two yards wide. At this Warehouse nothing but Woollen Cloths are Sold, and consequently much lower than can possibly be bought at any Silk-mercer's, Linen-draper's, Haberdasher's, &c. who purchase them of the Woollen-draper to sell again. *Evangelical Magazine*, November 1821

sear cloth – [see *cerecloth*]

second cloth – Frome, a town of Somersetshire, ... chiefly inhabited by clothiers. The article chiefly made here is second cloths, the principal material of which is fine English wool. Universal Gazetteer, 1795 ... What sort of wool is it that you have been accustomed to, and that you have observed a. deficiency in? – The wool that makes livery cloth, and the wool that makes second cloth. Is that the long combing wool or the short? – Neither; it is a finer sort than the combing; it is wool which makes cloth from seven shillings a yard to twelve. Wool and Woollen Trade of Great Britain, 1800 ~~~ Ireland makes cloths of her own wool, as high as twelve shillings a yard. – This wool is fit to mix with the Spanish wool, in the same way as the finer and coarser English wools are mixed with it to make the second cloths. Union, Necessary to Security, 1800 ~~~ Patent Waterproof Cloth ... Though nankeens, thin casimer, and other light wearing apparel, &c. will resist a middling rain, they will not do it in the degree of a superfine broad, or second cloth, or stout beaver, such as is generally used for box and driving coats, which are thus rendered impenetrable to any rains that ever fall in any of the four quarters of the globe; Analytical Hints, 1802 ~~~ A Quaker here is easily known by his *costume*: a plain-coloured second-cloth coat, with covered buttons, long waist, and immoderately wide skirt; his breeches of the same cloth; *European Magazine*, May 1807 ~~~ The broad cloth in France, called cloth of Lovain, is as much beyond an English superfine as an English superfine is beyond a second cloth. Political Writing of Thomas Paine, 1819 ~~~ Stuff forwarded every year to make a suit of clothes for each teacher would cost but little in England, but here [Madagascar] it would cost a good deal of money. Second blue cloth for jackets, and a few yards of common scarlet cloth for collars and cuffs. *Evangelical Magazine*, March 1825 ~~~ Mr. Francis, a manufacturer of livery or second cloths, states, that in his manufactory he decreased the quantity of English wool, because, from the coarser quality of it, a less number of yards was produced; and he observes that it is growing worse for his purposes from year to year. ... The demand has gone almost from cloths made exclusively of English wool (that is, cloths called second cloths) to cloths manufactured partly, and altogether, of foreign wool. Journal of Agriculture, 1829 ~~~ An Account of the Nature and present State of the Philanthropic Society, … for the Prevention of Crimes, by the Admission of the Offspring of Convicts, and for the Reformation of Mail Children. … [in 1816] When a Boy has served Four Years of his Apprenticeship he is permitted to wear a plain Button. When he has served Five Years, provided his Industry has procured him a Balance of 5*l.* or upwards in the Book of Rewards, he is allowed a Brown Second Cloth Coat and a Toilenet Waistcoat for his Sunday Dress, otherwise this Change is deferred until his Balance amount to that Sum. When he has served Six Years, provided the Balance due to him in the Account of his Rewards shall amount to 10*l.*, he is allowed a Blue Second Cloth Coat and Toilenet Waistcoat for his Sunday Dress, and to use the Brown Coat, &c. for his working Dress, and at the Expiration of his Apprenticeship he has also a new Suit the same as the latter Sunday Dress. Reports from the Committees, 1835 [see also *livery cloth*]

seersucker – The Bengal ships, with two from Columbo, brought the following cargoes: … Seersuckers. *Monthly Magazine*, October 1798 ~~~ [describing John Quincy Adams] in warm weather wearing a striped seersucker coat, and white trowsers, and dirty waistcoat, spotted with ink, his whole dress, altogether, not worth a couple of pounds; *Atheneum*, July 15, 1824 ~~~ [ad] India Book, Mull, and Nansook Muslins, Bengals, Seersuckers, *Genius of Universal Emancipation*, February 1833 ~~~ Many substantial and beautiful fabrics are formed of a combination of silk and cotton. Varieties of vestings, varieties of heavy damask, Concan, Seersuckers, &c. &c. American Silk Grower's Guide, 1835

selvage – SELVAGE, or SELVEDGE. The edge of linen or cotton cloth. Dictionary of General Knowledge, 1833

semi-military – The semi-military plume, formed of black cock's feathers, is one of the most novel articles; it droops arch-wise over the front of the hat or bonnet, has a most peculiar lustre, and is tipped with pink, coquelicot or amber; the latter color is, however, most distinguishing of the lady of fashion. Some of these plumes are long, and droop gracefully over the left shoulder. *La Belle Assemblée*, January 1823

sephora crape – Dinner or Soiree Dress. – Dress of a new material called *séphora crape*, embroidered in coloured floss silks. *Lady's Magazine and Museum*, January 1836

Seraphine – [ad] Seraphines, Palmyrines, and many other articles for Young Ladies' wear; *Court Journal*, June 15, 1833 ~~~ Seraphine silk low dresses are now more in vogue than ever, and suit well for the display of material, both figured and coloured in the most delicate shades, and if edged with tulle or lace, is very becoming on the neck; *Blackwood's Lady's Magazine*, August 1836

serge – Serge, a kind of thin woollen cloth Perry's English Dictionary, 1795 ~~~ SERGE, a woollen quilted stuff, manufactured on a loom with four treddles, after the manner of rateens, and other stuffs that have the whale. The goodness of serges is known by the quilting, as that of cloths by the spinning. Of serges there are various kinds, denominated either from the different qualities thereof, or from the places where they are wrought. The most considerable is the London serge, now highly valued abroad, particularly in France, where a manufacture is carried on with considerable success, under the title of *serge façon de Londres*. Encyclopædia Britannica, 1797 ~~~ Fashions for Gentlemen. … The leaders of the haut-ton appear at the opera in great coats edged with Russia lamb skin, … lined throughout with silk serge. *Jersey Magazine*, February 1810 ~~~ Serge,… a woollen stuff manufactured in a loom, of which there are various kinds, denominated either from their different qualities, or from the places were they are wrought; the most considerable of which is the London serge, which is highly valued abroad. In the manufacture of London serges, the longest wool is chosen for the warp, and the shortest for the woof. General Dictionary of Commerce, 1810 ~~~ *Serges* – 27 inches wide, cost 7d to 11d. … These are used as baizes for lining jackets, great-coats, &c, and for the same purposes that coarse flannels are used. *Niles' Weekly Register*, March 8, 1828 ~~~ [ad] Serge, 3s. 6d. per yard. *Political Guardian*, April 22, 1831 ~~~ SERGE is *kersey* wove, and either white, colored, or figured. Colored serges, and figured *Duroys,* were very commonly worn by the lower orders in the west of England, some years ago; but these manufactures have been superseded by *bombazets* and printed cottons. White serge is however still in use, and is a useful and durable material, superior in strength to flannel or baize. <u>New Family Encyclopedia</u>, 1835… Serge, like Baize, is made of worsted warp and woollen weft, but it differs in being tweeled. It may be either light or milled, and is generally sold white. <u>Analytical Dictionary</u>, 1835… Serge de Rome, or drap de soie (silk) .. [duty] free. — woollen, 50 per cent. <u>Jones's Digest</u>, 1836

sewing silk – There is a great variety of what are called *imperfect cocoons,* whose threads are not susceptible of being prepared for the manufacture of silk stuffs. They are called in French by the generic name of *choquets* or *chiques.* The limits of these essays do not permit me to enumerate or describe them, nor is it necessary for the object I have in view. The material extracted from those cocoons is employed in the manufacture *of sewing silk.* This silk is of two kinds, each of which has its first and second qualities. The name of *sewing silk* is exclusively appropriated, in France, to the finest of these two species; the other is called *cordonnet* or *twist.* The sewing silk, so called, is employed in the sewing of silken stuffs; the *cordonnet* is used for working button-holes, and sewing woollen and cotton stuffs. The one is for the use of *tailors,* the other for that of *milliners* and *mantuamakers.* Tailors employ it only in their more delicate works. The raw silk for these purposes is extracted from the bad cocoons, reeled and wound into skeins, according to its different degrees of fineness, in the same manner, and by the same process .(varying only in the details) as that intended to be used for the-manufacturing of fine stuffs. It is sold in market under the name of raw silk, but does not bear so high a price as the other. To manufacture this raw silk into *cordonnet* and sewing silk, properly so called, is a nice, delicate, and very complicated work, particularly to make the finest kind, and give it the evenness of threads, the elegant twist, and the beautiful gloss, that the French sewing silks possess. Like the threads which are worked into organzine and tram silk, these are passed through the *throwsting mill.* <u>Essays on American Silk</u>, 1830

shaded – [court dress] A petticoat entirely of silver ribbon, interwoven with shaded pink stripes, with a rich drapery of Italian silver net, elegantly embroidered in silver spangles, … the train spotted silver gauze, shaded with pink and silver, as the petticoat, full sleeves of Italian silver net. *Lady's Magazine,* June 1796 ~~~ robes of superfine cloth, embroidered round the bottom, on the bosom, and sleeves, in wreaths of leaves, composed of shaded velvet. We have seem them of buff, with leaves of shaded purple velvet, each leaf veined to nature. *La Belle Assemblée,* December 1807 ~~~ In carriages, this mantle is sometimes wrought in a border of shaded chenille of well contrasted lines; *Lady's Weekly Miscellany,* December 31, 1808 ~~~ A dinner dress, composed of green sarsnet with satin stripes, the stripes shaded in three or four different shades of the same colour. *Ladies' Monthly Museum,* October 1817 ~~~ Shot colors are very fashionable. Vine-leaf green and bright crimson, orange and garter blue, and shaded colors, such as dead leaf and Etruscan brown, scarlet and *ponceau,* crimson and pink, &c. &c. *Ladies' Monthly Museum,* December 1821 ~~~ French bonnet of gros de Naples, … circular broad front, with a small rouleau of shaded terry velvet, or velours epingle, let in near the edge of the brim, *Kaleidoscope,* November 9, 1824 ~~~ Dark shaded striped silk are also much worn; the ground is of a Macassar brown; the stripes orange and scarlet, finely shaded. *Ladies' Monthly Museum,* January 1826 ~~~ For walking dresses shaded silks are becoming universal, nor will the fashion soon terminate. A rose-coloured, soft *gros de Naples,* shot with bright green, was admired the other day in the Bois de Boulogne; this was worn with a large ermine pelerine, a hat of bright green satin, lined with white plush. In the hat were two plumes, one of a bright light green, the other of a rich deep green. Those who prefer a less showy costume, wear the pelisse of green satin, trimmed with velvet or plush of a deeper shade, or a dress of green, shot with amethyst. … Plain shaded *gros de Naples* are not exclusively worn. Damasked silks, figured with flowers of various colours, on a ground shot with two colours, are great favourites. They are exceedingly rich, and if chosen tastefully, do not offend the eye by their gaudiness. *Lady's Magazine,* March 1830 ~~~ Ribbons of light green, shaded *a mille rayes,* the stripes very minute, and shot with white. *Godey's Ladies Book,* February 1830 [see also *changeable* and *shot*]

shag – *Her Majesty.* … the body and train of tea green striped shag, *Lady's Magazine,* January 1797 ~~~Oxfordshire. Banbury. … the inhabitants are tradesmen, and manufacturers, principally, of worsted, and hair-shagg, or plush. <u>State of the Poor</u>, 1797 ~~~ *Specification of the Patent granted to* Timothy Cobb, *of Banbury, in the County of Oxford, Woollen-manufacturer, for an Improvement in the Manufacture of a certain Kind of Piece Goods, called Shag or Plush.* Dated February 21, 1803. To all to whom these presents shall come, &c. Now Know Ye, that in compliance with the said proviso, I the said Timothy Cobb do hereby declare that my said invention of a certain kind of piece goods, called shag or plush, consists in the combining in the warp called the pole or pile of yarn, made from Spanish or other wool of a short staple, prepared by carding, roving, and spinning, in the common method now used in the manufacture of wool into yarn for weaving into cloth, by which the harshness, inseparable from shags made of the usual materials, is removed, the surface rendered softer, and the article of a more pliable nature. In witness whereof, &c. Observations By The Patentee. In the article described by the above specification, is combined the finest Spanish wool with cotton, so as to unite the valuable properties of each, and at the same time avoid what is objectionable in goods composed entirely of either. It is not so liable to be soiled, and discharge its colour, as goods made of cotton alone. It possesses the durability of shag without its harshness, having a soft and agreeable surface, besides the great advantage of not shrinking when wet or washed. Repertory of Arts and Manufactures, 1803 ~~~ Altringham, or Altrincham, ... The principal manufactory is worsted yarn, and worsted and hair shags; Traveller's Guide, 1805 ~~~ Walking Dress. ... French tippet of leopard silk shag. *Jersey Magazine*, November 1810 ~~~a sort of woollen stuff, smooth on one side, and velvety on the other. Shags are usually made from coarse wools, but there are some remarkably fine, with latter are used fore waistcoating of the best kind. The coarser shags are employed as different parts of wearing apparel by the lower orders of people. These articles are made in abundance in Yorkshire, General Dictionary of Commerce, 1810 ~~~ *List of Necessaries to be provided by Stoppage from the Pay of the Soldiers of Regiments of Dragoon Guards, Dragoons, and Fencible Calvary.* For one pair of leather, or two pair of shag breeches, in two years, value 1l. 6s. Regimental Companion, 1811 ~~~ Silk shag hats are quite in fashion; and all bonnets except the lining, are made of this material. *Ladies' Monthly Museum*, March 1817 ~~~Shag silk promises to be a favourite trimming this winter; it is very much improved in the manufacturing, and has now the appearance of Swansdown. *La Belle Assemblée*, October 1818 ~~~ [ad] Guthrie and Sons, Tailors, respectfully submit the following estimate of ready money prices, ... Hair Shag Breeches are charged extra [from the Drab Great Coat], 14s. each pair. *Court Journal*, February 23, 1833 [see also *plush*]

shagreen leather – The process for preparing shagreen is a very old oriental invention, not practiced in Europe, ... All kinds of horses' or asses' skin, which have been dressed in such a manner as to appear grained, are by the Tartars called *sauwer*, by the Persians *sogre*, and by the Turks *sagri*, from which the Europeans have made *shagreen* or *chagrin*. Philosophical magazine, April 1800 ~~~ Shagreen, or Chagreen, ... a kind of grained leather, prepared, as is supposed, of the skin of a species of squalus, or hound-fish, called the shagree, or shagrain, and much used in covering cases, books, &c. It is imported from Constantinople, Tunis, Tripoli, Algiers, and from some parts of Poland, where it is prepared in the following manner: the skin being stretched out is first covered over with mustard-seed, which is bruised upon it; and being thus exposed to the weather for some days, it is then tanned. The best is of a brownish colour, and the white sort is the worst. It is extremely hard; yet, when steeped in water, it becomes soft and pliable, and being fashioned into case-covers, it readily takes any colour, as red, green, yellow, black, according to the fancy of the workman. Shagreen is often counterfeited, by preparing Morocco leather in the same manner as the fish above-mentioned; such fraud may, however, be easily detected by the surface of the spurious manufacture peeling or scaling off, while that of the genuine article remains perfectly sound. It is not unusual, even in Turkey, to prepare a species of shagreen from the hides of horses, asses, and mules. Dictionary of Commerce, 1810 ~~~ A large quantity of shagreen skin is prepared here [Tabriz], an article much used in Persia for shoes. Universal Geography, 1824

shagreen silk – Chagrin, ... *shagreen; a silk stuff made rough like shagreen,* Dufief's French Dictionary, 1810 ~~~ [Paris] for half dress they [slippers] are of different colours in kid, jean, and chagrin silk. *La Belle Assemblée*, May 1812 ~~~ The twilled sarsnet gives place to the *gros de Naples*; an article adapted either to summer or winter wear, but certainly warmer than sarsnet, particularly the improved figured gros *de Naples,* called the shagreen, which is richly spotted in figures as small as the skin from whence it takes its name. *Repository of Arts*, November 1819 ~~~ For young ladies, a beautiful pink shagreen *gros-de-*

Naples, lightly ornamented with feathered silk, forms a very attractive carriage dress for morning visits of ceremony. *La Belle Assemblée*, December 1819 ~~~ Bonnet of white shagreen, dotted improved sarcenet, lined with a quilling of blond, *Kaleidoscope*, June 11, 1822 ~~~ The greatest novelty in silk dresses, is the shagreen rose-coloured silk, being a kind of rich *gros de Naples*, powdered over with extremely small spots. *Ladies' Monthly Museum*, June 1825 ~~~ [Paris, new materials] *La peau de chagrin.* – A silk with very narrow stripes, and satin spots at distances. *Lady's Magazine and Museum*, May 1836 [see also *shagreen* in **Furs**]

shalloon – A slight woollen stuff. Sheridan's English Dictionary, 1797 ~~~ *Alterations in the present uniform Clothing of the Captains and Commanders of his Majesties Fleet. … Undress.* Blue frock lappels, cuffs and collar the same, the collar to button on to the lappels, lap over behind, white shalloon lining, Naval Chronology, 1802 ~~~ Constantinople. … Shalloons have been for ages in great demand here; they are much made use of in the dress of the orientals: the consumption has, however, decreased considerably; only two hundred bales are disposed of a year. Shalloons formerly yielded a great profit, but this, like that on all other British articles, is now but small; the price is regulated according to the quality: this year it has run frum 55 to 100 piastres per piece. Travels in Turkey, 1808 ~~~ Shalloon, a slight woollen stuff, being a species of serge. It derives its appellation from the town of Chalons, in France, where the first specimens of the article were produced. At the present day, abundance of shalloons are manufactured in Northamptonshire and other parts of England, as well as at Edinburgh. The Scotch shalloons are of peculiarly excellent quality. General Dictionary of Commerce, 1810 ~~~ Shalloon (Spanish *challon,* supposed to be from Chalons, a town in France,) is also a worsted article which, like Calamanco, may be either hotpressed or unglazed; but it differs from the latter, particularly in the manner of weaving, being tweeled equally on both sides, or what is termed double-tweeled. A very fine Shalloon, always unglazed, has the Spanish name of Cubica. It is chiefly exported to Catholic countries, to be made into gowns for the Ecclesiastics, and is, therefore, dyed black, blue, Carmelite brown, &c. according to the several orders of Friars. A stouter sort of Cubicas are sometimes called Says, – but these are very different from the Say formerly mentioned. The manufacture of Shalloons, in this country, was formerly much more extensive than at present. The species called Prunella (now little known) was universally worn, as an upper dress, or gown, by the clergy; and, therefore, Mr. Pope has immortalized the term, in his famous couplet, by contrasting such robes with the leathern jerkins of the peasants. Analytical Dictionary, 1830 ~~~ *Artillery. … Cloak – blue, lined with scarlet shalloon; Army and Navy Chronicle*, December 2, 1835 [see also *prunella*]

shaly – [see *chaly*]

shamoy, shammy – [see *chamois*]

shantung silk – A particular sort of wild silk is found in the province of Shantung. It is the produce of a caterpillar which feeds indiscriminately on the mulberry and many other trees. They do not spin cocoons like the silk-worm, but they form long threads, which being driven about by the wind, are caught by the trees and bushes, whence they are carefully gathered, and spun like flax or wool. A thick sort of cloth is woven from this silk; it is very strong and durable, does not easily spoil, and is considered very valuable. *Penny Magazine*, March 26, 1836

shawl cloth – Upwards of fifteen thousand looms are constantly employed in the manufacture of linen and cotton in Perth, and as many more in the country around it. The fabrics thus manufactured consist chiefly of … cotton stuffs, such as shawl-cloths, calicoes and muslins, Journey from Edinburgh through Parts of North Britain, 1802 ~~~ The long scarf *a la Parisot*, composed of mohair, or shawl muslin in imitation, is a most distinguishing ornament. *La Belle Assemblée*, November 1806 ~~~ shawl muslins … are either of the real Indian shawl fabric, or of imitations equally rich and beautiful in effect; these [pelisses] are lined throughout with sarsnets of well contrasted colours. We have seen some of light-brown, salmon, and cream-coloured grounds, lined with pale-green, pink, and jonquille, *La Belle Assemblée*, March 1809 ~~~ what is technically termed shawl cloths, are merely calicoes of a different breadth and fineness. Edinburgh Encyclopædia, 1814 ~~~ Black satin spencers and shawl pelisses are generally worn over cambric dresses; … The pelisses which are made in imitation of Cachemire, are made in a style of uncommon simplicity: … [Paris] Muslin, so long in favour for the promenade, is now very partially worn; it has been superseded by gowns of white and coloured merino cloth and shawl dresses. *Repository of Arts*, November 1817 ~~~ one of the most curious productions ever manufactured in this country, about six yards of transparent shawl cloth, made from his Merino Teg worsted. The weight was little more than 12 ounces. *Monthly Magazine*, September 1820 ~~~ SHAWL MANUFACTURE. Accidental circumstances lately called our attention to some facts connected with the history of the shawl manufacture, a short statement of which our readers may perhaps consider not without interest – We need scarcely state, that this species of manufacture has risen almost from nothing within the last thirty years, and that little more than twenty years have passed since it was established in this city, which may now be considered as the chief seat of the finest, though not the most extensive, branch of the manufacture. Shawls were originally made in the East Indies, and they exhibit a curious example of the high perfection to which some single species of manufacture may be carried in a country where the arts in general are in a rude state. So highly are these India shawls prized in this country, that they fetch a price of 100*l.*, 200*l.*, or even 500*l.*, while the best of those of domestic manufacture can be had for 20*l.* or 30*l.* But what makes the preference shown to the foreign article the more surprising is, that no small proportion of the India shawls brought to Britain have been worn by the natives as turbans, girdles &c. before they were imported. This is no secret among dealers, for the marks of wearing are often manifest to an experienced eye, in the discoloration or roughening of the surface, the attenuation of the fabric at particular places, and now and then in actual rents and holes. Strange as it may seem, therefore, it is literally true, that our wealthy and titled dames are content to array themselves in the cast clothes of our Eastern subjects, which vestments, notwithstanding, have no small intrinsic value! There are two substances of which the body or fabric of fine shawls is made – and wool. Silk has generally been employed in Britain; but the Hindoos use an extremely fine wool, and from the use of this material the India shawls derive much of their superiority. First, it gives them an exquisite softness and warmth, to which it is impossible to approach when the fabric is chiefly of silk. Secondly, the fine wool takes a brighter colour than silk, and keeps it incomparably better. Thirdly, the woollen fabric has an advantage which is perfectly understood by the ladies; its folds dispose themselves in more graceful and flowing lines, and of course it affords a finer drapery to the figure. With regard to the patterns, it must be admitted, that till we have discovered the mode of working the figure practised by the Indians, and till our weavers can subsist on two-pence a day, and spend three or four years' labour on a single shawl, we shall scarcely be able to rival them. In the brightness of the dyes we already surpass the Hindoos, and the figures on their inferior shawls, which are sewed in or embroidered, are not nearly equal to the best of those which we execute in the loom; but in the finest of the India shawls the figures are wove in a manner which we cannot perfectly imitate, and of which our weavers only comprehend enough to perceive, that it must be extremely laborious and infinitely tedious. Indeed, it is certain, that even the smallest compartment of the figure must be worked on the principle on which we work an entire web – that the weft must be turned at each margin of the compartment, though it should be but a tenth of an inch in breadth. The best idea we can form of the process may be derived from the mode of laying in the figures of tapestry; and hence, too, the Indian mode of working enables them to sink the ground of the web more completely, and to exhibit the colours of the pattern in a more unmixed state than we possibly can. It is remarkable, too, that long practice has taught them to combine their colours with singular harmony, and to diversify their designs, without falling into extravagance or incongruity, to such a degree that the British manufacturer, with all his skill, finds it the best policy to copy their patterns, because he can seldom invent any thing better himself. In the execution of the figures, however, our manufacturers have made great progress within the last ten years; and this is not now the department in which their work has been felt to be most deficient. Latterly their leading object has been to rival the Indians in the fabric or basis of the web. Organzine silk was the material originally employed for warp, and upon this a weft of wool and silk, or of various mixtures of the two substances, was thrown in. This was succeeded, about 1804 or 1805, by spun silk, that is, the waste of Indian silk chopped into short lengths, and worked upon the same principle as wool or cotton – a process long kept secret, but now well known. It was made to resemble the Indian yarn very closely, and was deservedly considered a great improvement, though it still wanted the best properties of fine wool. Some years afterwards another step was made towards the introduction of the proper material, by preparing a weft of silk and Merino wool, which received the name of Persian yarn. This still continues partially in use. At length, about three years ago, an attempt was made to make the fabrick of wool entirely. To the substance employed, the name of Van Diemen's Land, or Indian, or Thibet wool, was given, though in reality it consisted merely of picked quantities taken from picked Saxon or English fleeces. Of this a fabric was made which surpassed those previously used, but it was still deficient in the exquisite softness and warmth which the Indian wool possesses, and what was not of less importance, no figure could be worked in upon it with accuracy and beauty. British enterprise, however, is not easily discouraged. Inquiries were set on foot in the East; and specimens of the actual material used in the fabrication of the very finest shawls were brought home. It was found to consist of the undergrowth of wool of the Thibet goat, or the down growing beneath the long rough hairs which form the exterior covering of the animal. It was found, too, that the article, though very expensive, could be procured in considerable quantities. But a new difficulty presented itself – this down was so extremely tender, that the most expert spinners in England despaired of forming it into a thread of sufficient tenacity to bear the operation of the loom. The practical skill and invention of our artisans is, however, inexhaustible; and we verily believe, that if it were required to convert spider's webs into cables, they would find means to accomplish it. An English spinner discovered a process by which he was able to form a very delicate yet firm and durable thread out of this soft material, and, according to custom, he secured his invention by a patent. Some farther difficulties remained, but not of very great magnitude. Our manufacturers had some advantages before, which the natives of the East wanted; and. having now the material in their hands which gave the others their chief superiority, they were in a condition to unite every possible excellence in their workmanship. We think we may safely say that this has been attained. We have seen shawls of the new fabric made by our townsmen, Gibb and M'Donald (who hold the first rank, we believe, in this branch of manufacture), quite admirable in point of softness, delicacy of texture, and vividness of colour, and which we have been assured by adequate judges, rival the India shawls in these, and indeed in all the leading qualities for which the latter are prized. Some superiority the Indians have still in their patterns, from the tedious process they employ; but this will be confined to shawls of the very first class. In the others we already equal or surpass them, and future improvements will probably leave us little to desire on this head. To those who know how much our manufactures contribute to our national wealth, we need scarcely say that the successful establishment of a branch of industry like this is really an object of national importance. India muslins have been already superseded by the skill of our artisans; and it is probable that India shawls are destined soon to share the same fate. Custom may keep up the old predilection for a time; but self-interest will teach people to save the two or three hundred pounds paid for an India shawl, when they can have one for ten, twenty, or thirty, so closely resembling the other in fabric and appearance, that only the practised eye of the dealer can detect the difference. Thirty years ago there was not a single shawl made in Edinburgh, and the number made in Britain was absolutely trifling. At this day, shawls are made to the value of a million sterling annually at least, and the manufacture now forms a leading branch of our national industry. *Atheneum*, September 1826 ~~~ Shawl dresses, of a fine and soft texture, with two deep flounces, each edged with a narrow brocaded riband of similar colours to the dress, but more frequently with one which, though strikingly different, is yet suitable, are the newest gowns for home costume; for which style of parure, chintzes are also much in request. *Ladies' Museum*, May 1829 ~~~ THIBET SHAWL CLOTH. A gentleman in Edinburgh has sent us two beautiful specimens of shawl cloth, manufactured at Edinburgh, of Thibet wool; one of them dyed *amber,* with an extract from the flower of the potato, and the other dyed *green*, by the application of indigo to the former colour. They are fine specimens of our manufactures, and worthy the attention of the curious. *Asiatic Journal*, January 1830 ~~~ [ad] New Merinos, Silks, Shawls, Furs, and Cloaks. … Shawl Dresses, in novel Foreign patterns; *Court Journal*, February 9, 1833 [see also *cashmere* and *Thibet wool*]

sheeting – The staple manufacture of Perth is linen; … Stout Holland sheetings of various breadths;

Statistical Account of Scotland, 1796 ~~~ blue cloth jackets and Russia sheeting trowsers, such as are worn in the West Indies, Trials of William S. Smith, and Samuel G. Ogden, 1807 ~~~ A considerable manufacture of linen has been carried on here for many ages, and is at present in a flourishing condition. ... Sheetings are also manufactured here, some of which are twenty-four yards in length, and one yard and half a quarter in breadth; others, twenty-six or twenty-eight yards in length, and one yard and quarter in breadth, all varying in price according to the comparative difference in the fineness of each. History of ... Knaresbrough, 1809 ~~~ The linen manufacture of Scotland, is, therefore, at present, nearly confined to coarse articles, such as plain sheetings, Osnaburghs, bagging, and canvas. The three first are principally exported to the West Indies and to America; General Report of the Agricultural State ... of Scotland, 1814 ~~~ Plain Sheeting is used for packing fine goods, sheets, trowsers, &c. Linen Manufacturer, 1817 ~~~ [in 1821] The common dress of the male slaves is an Osnaburgh or check frock, and a pair of Osnaburgh or sheeting trowsers, with a coarse hat. Colonial Slavery, 1824 ~~~ [ad] Russia Sheeting, 2 ½ wide, without a seam, 22d. per yard; strong servants' Sheeting, at 6½d. per yard; *Examiner*, July 16, 1826 ~~~ *Price of* 3-4 *cotton sheetings per yard from* 1812 *to* 1832. 1812, 28 cts.; 1813, 28-29 cts.;. 1814, 30-32 cts.; 1815, 28-30 cts.; 1816, 26 28 cts.; 1817, 24-27 cts.; 1818, 24 cts; 1819, 24-16 cts.; 1820, 16-14cts.; 1821, 14-12 cts.; 1822, 12-11 cts.; 1823, 11-10 cts.; 1824, 11-10 cts.; 1825, 11-10 cts.; 1826, 10 cts.; 1827, 10-9 cts.; 1828, 9 cts.; 1829, 6 1/2 cts.; 1830, 6 1/2 – 7 1/2 cts.; 1831, 8 1/2 cts.; 1832, 8 cts.; Executive Documents, 1833 ~~~ [ad] Have received by the ships Hark-away and Jefferson, direct from Liverpool, ... 3 do. [bales] 4-4 and 9-4 real Russia and brown and bleached imitation Russia sheetings. 1 case 5-4 and 6-4 Silesia and Irish sheetings. 1 case 5-4 and 6-4 Bamsley sheetings, very superior. *Farmer's Register*, May 1835 ~~~ *Uniforms*. ... Of the Cadets. ... *Pantaloons* – ... Russia sheeting or white jean for summer, without trimmings, the form the same as for winter. American State Papers, 1834 ~~~ the thousand of little articles he is obliged to purchase of the purser, to keep himself neat and comfortable, such as sheeting (duck), *Naval Magazine*, September 1836 [see also *duck, osnaburgh* and *shirting*]

shirting – *Manufactures from hemp and flax* ... white and checked shirtings, View of the United States of America, 1795 ~~~ The staple manufacture of Perth is linen; and of late, a considerable quantity of cotton-cloth. ... other coarse fabrics, manufactured in the neighbourhood; including soldiers shirtings, with a few coarse sheetings, and Osnaburgs purchased. Statistical Account of Scotland, 1796 ~~~ Cotton goods are divided into 7 different classes, each proportionally lighter the than other. The heaviest of these are, 1st. *Shirtings*, New Encyclopædia, 1807 ~~~ *Premium 10. – Twenty Dollars*. For the best piece of cotton shirting of a fine, smooth, hard texture, not apt, like muslin, to adhere to the skink by perspiration, and in all respects best calculated to supersede the use of Irish linen; to be not less than twenty-five yards long, and one yard wide. *Universal Magazine*, February 1809 ~~~ Linen is a commodity of universal use from the prince to the peasant, and a commodity that cannot be supplanted by any thing else near so commodious and agreeable for those uses to which it is applied. The use of the Indian cotton cloth his often been attempted for shirting, but to no purpose, Dictionary of Commerce, 1810 ~~~ in the state of Rhode Island, ... Cloth for Shirts and Sheeting, [sold at] 35 to 75 [cents per yd.] Sketch of the United States of North America, 1814 ~~~ *Of the making of Webs Half Linen, Half Cotton, and the Discount upon Water Twist*. In the manufacture of Linen Cloth, cheapness, beauty, and durability, ought certainly to be the principle object of the Manufacturers' study; for to attain this, different methods have been tried, ... Sheeting and Shirting ought to be made in a different way, so that it may resemble Sheeting and Shirting made wholly of Linen yarn, viz. instead of soft spun Mull yarn, the weft must be good, evenly, well twined Water Twist, and if the warp is Linen, it must be made about half a set stronger than in common cases, when both warp and weft are Linen; Sheeting and Shirting manufactured in this way, can be made considerably cheaper, having a fine appearance, and nearly equal to Linen in durability, and except by a very minute investigation, cannot be distinguished from Cloth wholly made of Linen yarn, even by the best judges, ... Shirting is distinguished into two kinds, viz. light and heavy set shirting; all the difference, if wanted light, is to put the yarn which should go into a 1300 reed into a 1200 reed; and, if wanted heavy, put the yarn which ought to go into a 1200 reed into a 1300 reed. See Irish linen, which is only a species of shirting of heavy fabric, generally made in Ireland from which it takes its name. <u>Linen Manufacturer</u>, 1817 ~~~ fine linens, what we call shirting, <u>Reports from the Committees</u>, 1820 ~~~ I have procured an account of actual sales made in this city at different periods, the qualities adjudged to he the same. In 1815 (the year of the peace) when cotton was 20 cents per pound, the sales of domestic shirtings were 25 cents per yard. The next year, 1816, cotton rose to 28 cents per lb. and shirting fell in price to 21 cents per yard. In 1818 when cotton sold at 32 cents per lb. shirting continued at 21 cents per yard. From that period till this, they have declined in price, and now when the same quality of cotton is sold at 9 1/2 cents per lb. shirtings are sold at 9 1/2 cents per yard. The present low price cannot be attributed to the fall of cotton, as one fourth of a pound of cotton will make a yard of these goods whether cotton is 9 1/2 or 20 cents per lb. it will differ less than three cents per yard. If we add 3 cents to the present price of shirtings it will make them only 12 1/2 cents per yard. *Niles' Weekly Register*, July 14, 1827 ~~~ At Blackburn, and the neighbourhood, the hand-loom weavers can weave 36 yards of shirting per diem, by working 15 hours. For this they get 1*s.* 6*d.*, subject to deduction. The Power-looms yield 1*s.* 4*d* per piece, and as a man can tend two looms of this kind at a time, they can realise twice the amount. But the hands at the Power-looms are over-stocked. <u>Lectures on the Restrictive System</u>, 1829 ~~~ [ad] Irish shirting, sheeting, and diaper, from Ralshine, 1s. to 2s. 2d. per yard. *Political Guardian*, April 22, 1831 ~~~ *The Richmond Cotton Manufactory* … The fabrics are heavy – negro shirtings, 20 inches wide, 4-4 shirtings and ¾ shirtings of No. 16 yarns, *Southern Literary Messenger*, February 1835 ~~~ Shirting, Cloth fit to be made into shirts. <u>Knowles' English Dictionary</u>, 1835 ~~~ [ad] IRISH SHIRTING CLOTH, made, without any admixture, from pure Flax. *Musical World*, September 9, 1836 [see also *British shirting*]

shoddy – Shoddy-grinders (a provincial term) are persons employed in certain districts of the West Riding of Yorkshire, as that of Batley and Dewsbury, in picking and tearing woollen rags, and afterwards manufacturing them, with the addition of new wool or worsted, into yarn. This is taken from the mill, and woven at the houses of the workmen into a coarse cloth or drugget. The only part of the manufacture which differs materially from the ordinary woollen, is the sorting and breaking up of the rags. Much dust is produced, particularly by the tearing machines, or "devils." … Mr. Brearey remarks that persons commencing or returning to the employ, are so generally attacked with head-ache, sickness, dryness of the fauces, and difficulty of breathing, that the complaint is known in the district by the name of the "shoddy fever." This disorder subsides in six or eight hours; but cough and expectoration of dirty mucus, chiefly in the morning, generally remain, and indeed are almost universal, in a greater or less degree, among those who long and steadily attend to the machines. <u>Effects of Arts, Trades, and Professions</u>, 1832 ~~~ Yet, without the loss of a day; we should like to put our fair readers upon their guard against a villanous woollen compound, made of filthy rags, and named *shoddy*, and imitating wool most abominably, with which their flannel petticoats and merino gowns are but too often adulterated, in those days of improved machinery and low prices. Dewsbury is the native place of *shoddy*; but we suspect it travels father, and is applied to more uses than are dreamed of by the purchasers of great bargains in cheap shops. … the wollen [sic] rags of which the *shoddy* or mock-wool is made. *Museum of Foreign Literature*, August 1836 ~~~ the "shoddy," as it is called, may be, as occasion requires, mixed with new wool in any proportion; so as to afford, by the help of various artists, in this free country, equal satisfaction to all parties, whether the latter be tidy or dirty by nature. … The shoddy thus prepared in the mill is afterwards subjected to the usual process of manufacture, and together with an admixture of new wool, and the help of large quantities of oil, it is passed through the discipline of the carding-machine, mules, &c, till a thread is formed, which latter is handed to the weavers. <u>Home Tour through the Manufacturing Districts of England</u>, 1836

shorling – [see *morling*]

shot silk – Were it allowable to attribute to the weavers of the middle ages the art now common amongst us, of making what are usually called *shot* silks, (or silks of two colours predominating interchangeably as in the neck of the drake or pigeon,) <u>Fabliaux or Tales</u>, 1796 ~~~ *Ceremonial of the Princess Royal.* … The Bridegroom, … in is nuptial dress, which was all alike of silk shot, with gold and silver, richly embroidered, *Lady's Magazine*, May 1797 ~~~ We have lately seen one [Hibernian vest] … of light brown [sarsnet], shot with amber, and lined with a Persian of the latter colour. *La Belle Assemblée*, March 1807 ~~~ Shot silks, except pale colours shot with white, have fallen quite into disrepute. *La Belle Assemblée*, May 1811 ~~~ Fashionable colours for the month continue the same as the last, with the exception of the pigeon's wing, a beautiful colour in shot silk; it is blue and pink, and forms one of the most striking colours we have seen. *La Belle Assemblée*, August 1814 ~~~ Shot sarsnets, particularly lilac, azure, blush-colour, and green shot with white, are in great estimation. *Repository of Arts*, September 1816 ~~~ Shot colors are very fashionable. Vine-leaf green and bright crimson, orange and garter blue, and shaded colors, such as dead leaf and Etruscan brown, scarlet and *ponçeau*, crimson and pink, &c. &c. *Ladies' Monthly Museum*, December 1821 ~~~ two elegant carriage pelisses, of *gros de Naples*, are remarkably handsome: one is of a very singular tint, being the fine grey-blue of the lavender blossom, shot with black. *Ladies' Monthly Museum*, April 1826 ~~~ Shaded and shot silks are still more universal than last month, and the skill of the manufacturer is hourly producing a new and singular union of colours, and these are employed in bonnets as well as pelisses. White *gros de Naples* shot with *mauve* (the colour of the mallow, and very fashionable for bonnets,) is richer than the whole colour called French white, and far more durable. We see Swedish blue shot with *mauve, rose-julienne* and Swedish blue, green and *feuille-mort*, and emerald green and toucan yellow. ... Dinner Dress. The hat is of shot velvet, of a rich green; *Lady's Magazine*, April 1830 ~~~ Shot *gros de Naples* is occasionally employed for hats, which are trimmed with ribbons to correspond. Pink or blue, shot with white, are very becoming to the complexion. *Court Journal*, May 18, 1833 ~~~ [court dress] velvet train of a beautiful azure blue shot with white. *Court Journal*, June 1, 1833 ~~~ [Paris] The prevailing colours are rose, blue, paille, lilac, and apple green, all shot with white; *Lady's Magazine and Museum*, July 1834 [see also *changeable*]

Siam – Cotton of Siam, [cotton thread] is a kind of silky cotton in the Antilles, so called because the grain was brought from Siam. It is of an extraordinary fineness, even surpassing silk in softness. They make hose of it there preferable to silk one for their lustre and beauty. They sell from 10 to 12 and 15 crowns a pair, but there are very few made unless for curiosity. Encyclopædia Britannica, 1797 ~~~ Evening Dress. A gown of new material; it is called Soire du Roide Siame; it is a very rich silk, the ground is a shade between lavender and grey, thickly covered with bouquets of rose-buds, in these is a mixture of gold. *Casket*, April 1830 [probably *soie du Roi de Siame*, silk of the king of Siam.] ~~~ Evening Dress. ... The robe, a little shorter than the under dress, is composed of *taffetas de Siam*, the ground in a rich shade of golden brown, with a detached pattern delicately traced in green. ... *Taffetas de Siam* ... are full dress materials of a very beautiful kind. The first is flowered, and we think the richest taffetas we have ever seen; *Court Magazine*, October 1834 ~~~ Tartan silks, tigrine, Siam taffitas, and Algiers satin, form the majority of the dresses worn at evening parties in Paris. *Court Journal*, February 7, 1835

Siberian squirrel – Foreign and Internal Trade of Russia. ... The fur of a Siberian squirrel, which in summer is red, but in winter becomes grey. The back of this animal is of a beautiful grey colour, but the belly is nearly as white as the fur of the ermine. The most beautiful and richest pelisses are composed of pieces cut from the back and the belly, joined together alternately. *Athenæum*, August 1808 ~~~ Calabar Skin, ... The Siberian Squirrel skin used in making muffs, tippets, and trimming for cloths of various colours. Dictionary of Commerce, 1810 ~~~ [ad] Russian Ermine, Chinchilla, Kolinsky, and Siberian Squirrel, at such prices as will ensure future patronage, the Stock being manufactured in the best style and newest fashion for the present season. *Court Journal*, December 26, 1835

silemia – A new woollen stuff, called *silemia*, manufactured by M. Ternaux, will also be much used this winter: it unties the double advantage of being very moderate in price, and excellent in quality. *Ladies' Monthly Museum*, November 1827

silesia – A dutchy in Germany subject to the king of Prussia. ... (*s in commerce, from the foregoing*) A kind of thin linen cloth. Ash's English Dictionary, 1795 ~~~ The printers here [Perth] have a full command of the article of Silesia linen for handkerchief printing, Statistical Account of Scotland, 1796 ~~~ *Manufacture of Linen in the Prussian States*. ... No doubt can be entertained, in point of the linen manufacture, that Silesia has gained great reputation in the world, for its durability and excellence in general. That they make of as good or better quality in Ireland, is certain; but they at one time were not equally considerate in the bleaching part. The chymical process for bleaching once introduced into that kingdom was wisely done away, otherwise it might have been detrimental; while the gentle process in Silesia has been invariably used. Their cloth is generally three and four months in bleaching, and the lyes made very mild and moderately used. … The striped and the checked sort of Silesia linen, which they call bontons, are mostly … The yarn of which the Silesia linen is made is spun by means of the spindle, which makes it almost look like cotton; and such kind of linen requires less time to bleach than any other. The Silesia linen of different manufactures is all of the same quality, and there is no other distinction in it than in its width, and in the length of the pieces. … The raw long lawns, or what are called double Silesias, are frequently sent to Harlem, in order to be bleached for the English market. The patterns of the coloured lawns are very different; sometimes they are mixed with red, sometimes with blue, and sometimes with green flowers. This coloured sort of lawn is 1 ½ Breslaw ell-wide, and from 52 to 54 ells long, the same as the white and the raw sorts. European Commerce, 1807 ~~~ Silesia is used for linings soldiers' and childrens' shirts and takes its name from a place on the Continent. Linen Manufacturer, 1817 ~~~ Kinross, [Scotland] … The principal manufacture in this county is that of coarse linens, commonly called silesias. Political State of the British Empire, 1818 ~~~ Silecia or Silezia (linen) Public Documents, March 1832 ~~~ [1783] Silesia Linens, viz : Bretagnas; Plattillas Royales; Creas a la Morlaix; Rouens Cholets; Estopilles, or Cambricks. Imitating the French Linens under the same denomination, but are one-third cheaper here [Germany]. Diplomatic Correspondence, 1833

Silesian – [Paris] The Silesian, a charming stuff, newly invented, is also worn by ladies of the first circles. Of this material are made blue and rose-coloured dresses, Ladies' Monthly Museum, October 1827 ~~~ Notwithstanding the pecuniary aid which the Minister Colbert granted to M. Cadot to establish a manufacture of broad-cloth at Sedan … but he persuaded Lewis XIV. to wear a green-striped coat of the light Pagnan fabric, and to declare in presence of his court, before setting out for the chase, that he considered that kind of dress very beautiful. Immediately the courtiers about his person, and all their dependent courtlings in the country, became so solicitous to get similar coats, that they bought up an immense quantity of cloth (which the Minister knew to be lying by in store), at such an exorbitant price, as not only to put in activity the works of Sedan, but to cause the erection of a similar manufactory at Rheims, where an analogous stuff was for a long time made, under the name of Silesian. The French are still of opinion that their broadcloth fabrics of Sedan and Louviers surpass those of all Europe in beauty and perfection. At the former place, piece-goods, especially blacks, are admirably dyed; and at the latter, the wool is dyed in a superior style, especially for blues. Philosophy of Manufactures, 1835

silk – The thread of the worm that turns afterwards to a butterfly; the stuff made of the worm's thread. Sheridan's English Dictionary, 1797 ~~~ Her Royal Highness the Duchess of York, escorted as usual – In a white silk petticoat, body and train light purple violet. Lady's Magazine, May 1797 ~~~ Silk is white, orange, yellow, and sulphur coloured. Raw Silk has only one thread; the thrown Silk is distinguished from it by having two threads, which are easily discovered by twisting them between the finger and thumb. Practice of the Customs, 1812 ~~~ Stout silk half-boots, which are made very low, and always correspond with the dress, are most in favour in the carriage costume. Repository of Arts, September 1816 ~~~ 1504, silk was manufactured in England. … Broad silk, manufactured from the raw silk, introduced into England in 1620. Literary Chronicle, September 10, 1825 ~~~ "From this period [1700s] the manufacture advanced gradually, though slowly, until about 1785 or 1790, when the general substitution of cottons for silks, in articles of dress and furniture, gave it a check, from which it did not recover for some years. So rapid was the change of fashion; that in Spitalfields only, above 4000 looms were shut up in 1793, which, when in full work, seven years before, had given employment to about 10,000 persons. "The trade began to revive in 1798 or 1800, and has made an astonishing progress within the last ten or twelve years. This has been, in no inconsiderable degree, owing to the facility with which increased supplies of raw silk are now obtained from India. American Farmer, August

24, 1827 ~~~ Silk Brocade. – Damask. ...Cafard Damask. – Persian. – Sarsnet – Gros-de-Naples. – Ducape. – Satin. – Crape. – Levantine. – Gros-des-Indes. – Watering. – Embossing. – Mixed Goods. – Bombasins. – Poplins. – Lustres. – Shawls. ... There are several descriptions of silk goods, or, to speak more correctly, several modifications of the same class, which are each known popularly by distinctive names, but which yet require no particular description. Thus the plainest mode of silk-weaving takes the name of Persian, sarsnet, gros-de-naples, ducapes, &c, varying only in the thickness of the fabric, or the quality of the material of which it is composed, and not at all differing in the arrangements of its interlacings. Silk Manufacture, 1832 ~~~ Silk is the production of a species of Moth, called the *Phalana mori* or Mulberry moth, ... Some idea may be formed of the extent to which the silk manufacture is carried on at present in England, by the fact that no less a quantity than four million, six hundred and ninety three thousand, five hundred and seventeen pounds of raw silk were imported for home consumption, in the year ending January 1831. *Saturday Magazine*, July 6, 1833 ~~~ Silk occasions a gentle stimulus, but does not sufficiently promote perspiration, though it attracts less humidity from the atmosphere than linen. Toilette of Health, Beauty, and Fashion, 1834 ~~~ Notwithstanding the extreme warmth of the weather, silk robes and pelisses are in request. *Court Magazine*, August 1834 The term *brocade* relates to any sort of silk goods richly ornamented with flowers, wove in. Anciently, these ornaments were made with gold and silver threads. Brocaded silks were much in fashion in former days; now lighter fabrics are preferred. That sort most commonly seen is called *lustring*. This is woven over and under, like a piece of calico: the warp, and the woof or tram, appearing equally on the face of it, glistening as it catches the light. It has its name from its lustre or brilliancy. It is usually the stoutest of broad silks. *Satins,* on the contrary have the woof passing over several threads of the warp at a time, presenting a very soft and glossy surface. Book of Commerce by Sea and Land, 1834 [see also *Bengal silk, raw silk, soie, shot silk,* and the various types of silk]

silk muslin – Evening Dress. A dress of rose-coloured *mousseline de soie*, over satin to correspond. *La Belle Assemblée*, March 1831 ~~~ Wedding Presents. [given to Princess Louis] ... A dress of silk muslin (one of the new French stuffs), embroidered in bunches of grapes, of which the fruit was composed of amethysts. *Schoolmaster*, October 6, 1832 ~~~ Ball dress of white mousseline de soie over satin, *Royal Lady's*, November 1832 ~~~ Silk muslin, or as it is more commonly called *mousseline de soie* a material of the half-transparent kind, which bears some resemblance to palmyrienne, is very fashionable, particularly for young ladies. *Maids, Wives, and Widows*, March 2, 1833 ~~~ [Paris] I have seen some very pretty walking dresses of silk muslin, *à desseins semés*, all of well-selected colours and patterns, and in much better taste than printed muslins, now considered exceedingly vulgar. *Court Magazine*, June 1833 ~~~ For ball dresses, light textures will be decidedly preferred this winter. *Mousseline de soie*, embroidered in silk, is very light and elegant. *Court Journal*, November 14, 1835

silk worm gut – When you fish in rivers with this bait [maggots], your line should be finer than for pool-fishing, and leaded pretty heavy: the lower link must be a single hair, or a fine silk-worm gut; Sportsman's Dictionary, 1800 ~~~ Silk-worm gut is well adapted for suture, on account of its strength, fineness, and great smoothness. *Edinburgh Medical and Surgical Journal*, November 1818 ~~~ The article of *silk worm gut* prepared by the latter, though known to the disciples of Old Isaac Walton, is a new manufacture in this country. ... Charles F. Durant, Jersey City, N. Jersey, for the first silk worm gut known to the Institute as having been manufactured in the United States. *Gold Medal. Mechanics' Magazine*, December 1836

sinchaw – [ad] Silks at Reduced Prices. ... Heavy Blk. Sinchaws from 2s. 6 to 3s. 6 [per yard] *New England Farmer*, March 25, 1835

single press lace – What is the difference of prices to the consumer between double press and single press, now? – Single press comes at about one-third lower. ... Can you describe all the kinds of single press lace? – There is single press lace made sometimes, but very rarely; ... Lace of this kind is in general made into mitts or gloves. Do you deem it a good article? – When made of three thread we deem it a good article, thought it may be made of single thread; it generally bears the name of Pic Nic. There is also another kind of single press lace which bears the name of Brussels lace, in imitation of the Brussels lace; this, when made of two or three threads we consider a good article, but not a good article when made of one; it is seldom made of one. ... Can you describe the difference between single loop and double loop, that the Committee can understand it? – I will endeavour to do it this way; double press we consider fast secure in the knotting, and single press is not so: single-press is like a false stitch in netting; double press is a double knot, and the loop keeps its width. ... It is necessary the Committee should understand that these kind of laces, both good and bad, are stiffened when got up for sale, so that the single press has not that loose appearance when in that state, it is stiffened with starch and gum; but the single press, when washed, loses this stiffening, it is then that the consumer discerns the difference between single and double press. Double press, though stiffened when offered for sale, has nearly the same appearance after it is washed as it had in the stiffened state, when it is made of double cotton; when made of single, it is a bad article; single press made of double cotton, I consider as good as double press made of single cotton. ... With regard to what has been formerly said by several of the Witnesses, with respect to single press lace, single press I believe is never made into what is termed lace, strictly speaking, it is usually made into mitts and gloves; it has a handsome appearance, there is no fraud in them, as no person can possibly be deceived by them. A mitt that is made of single press, and is intended to be made 30 inches long when sold, it runs up from the operation in making, that it is not above 6 inches long, therefore there is no fraud, every person knows what article it is; I never knew them to be stiffened with gum. Reports from the Committees, 1812

singles – Singles, called in French *le poil,* that is to say hair silk, are made of the first quality of raw silk, consequently the finest, as the name sufficiently implies. They are made of a single thread. This silk is used for the woof of the lighter stuffs, the warp of which is made of cotton thread. *Report of the Committee on Agriculture on the Growth and Manufacture of Silk,* May 24, 1830 [see also *raw silk*]

Sire – [see *Syrie*]

sleasy – Sleasy (*s. in commerce*) A thin kind of holland, a thin kind of linen imported from Silesia. Ash's English Dictionary, 1795

sleave – Sleave, silk or thread untwisted ... to untwist; reduce the thread of silk to its original fibres Perry's English Dictionary, 1795 ~~~ Sleave, *v. t.* To separate threads; or to divide a collection of threads; to sley; *a word used by weavers.* Webster's Dictionary, 1832

Sleepy – Much worn: the cloth of your coat must be extremely sleepy, for it has not had a nap this long time. Dictionary of Buckish Slang, 1811

sleeve silk – [see *filoselle* and *floss*]

Smyrne – Poil de chèvre d'Angore, de Smyrne, et d'Alep, *Persian goat's hair.* Dufief's French Dictionary, 1810 ... Parisian Dinner Dress. A gown of the new fancy material, *toile de Smyrne,* of the darkest shade of bottle green. *Repository of Fashions,* January 1829 ~~~ Dinner Party Dress. A dress of black Smyrna satin, *La Belle Assemblée,* January 1829 ~~~ Evening Dress. A gown of rose colour *gaze de Smyrne* over a slip of *gros d'été* to correspond. *Repository of Fashions,* July 1829 ~~~ [ball dress] composed of white Smyrna gauze over white satin. *Ladies' Museum,* February 1830 ~~~ Some of our fashionable west-end *magazines* have just imported from Paris an elegant assortment of cloaks, made of the new *foulard de Smyrne.* The patterns of this elegant article, which are copied from the designs of Ottoman architecture, are totally different from any of the English or French *foulards* hitherto seen. The entire width of a cloak may be formed of a single piece, without a seam, the whole edged round by a very rich border, which is continued *en colonnes* to the top of the cloak. The cape and the falling collar have the same patterns on a smaller scale. This new *foulard* may also be made into dresses, open in front in the tunic form, a fashion which is just now very prevalent. *Court Journal,* December 21, 1833 ~~~ The head-dress is a *berret* of *gaze de Smyrne,* striped in rose-colour, white, and *vapeur. La Belle Assemblée,* March 1830 ~~~ *Tissue Smyrne* of goats' hair and silk quadrilled, is a soft material, which does not crease. *Court Magazine,* May 1836

soie – *silk, bristle, hair* Tardy's French Dictionary, 1799 ~~~ Soie, *f. silk.* – crue *or* écrue, *raw silk.* – cuite, *boiled silk.* ... – organsin, *throuwn solk, organsine silk.* – trème, *frame or shot silk.* Dufief's French Dictionary, 1810

soie de Londres – [see *London silk* and *Spitalfields*]

soie en moche – *moss silk.* Dufief's French Dictionary, 1810 [see *moss silk*] soie mouchetee – [see *mouchetee*]

soire du Roide Siame – [see *Siam*]

sorshet – [court dresses] A white dress, embroidered with beetles' wings and gold; corsage and sleeves trimmed with blond sabots; train of white satin, lined with white sorshet, and finished with with and gold flowers; … train of primrose watered silk, lined with white sorshets, and finished with silver lace; *Royal Lady's Magazine*, June 1831

spangle – Spangle, (s. *from the* German spange) A small drop or boss of shining metal, any small thing that sparkles. Ash's English Dictionary, 1795 ~~~ [worn at the Prince of Wales's marriage] A crape petticoat, embroidered with silver spangles, *Gentleman's Magazine*, May 1795 ~~~ [court dress] White crape petticoat, richly embroidered with silver pearl spangles and white satin, *Lady's Magazine*, June 1798 ~~~ Spangles are small thin round leaves of metal pierced in the middle, which are sewed on as ornaments to a dress. They are made in the following manner: a wire is twisted in the form of a screw; it is then cut into single spiral rings, like those used by pin-makers; and these rings, being placed on a very smooth anvil, are flatted, and spread by a smart blow of the hammer, so that a small hole remains in the middle; and the ends of the wire, which lie over each other, are closely united. Spangles were first made in the gold and silver manufactories of France, and the method was long kept a secret: at length, however, they were successfully imitated in Germany and other parts. Book of Trades, 1806 ~~~ [court dress] A magnificent silver robe and coat, entirely covered with a shower of spangles, the draperies tied up with very large zephyr and cords, and finished with a superb silver fringe. *La Belle Assemblée*, June 1807 ~~~ [court dress] A petticoat of rich white satin, … the draperies very richly embroidered to correspond, which were peculiarly elegant and tastefully designed, festooned up, and ornamented with rich gold ropes and tassels, finishing at the bottom with double scollop flounces or net, richly spangled, intermixed with embroidered bow and gold. *La Belle Assemblée*, July 1816 ~~~ We have seen also a few blond trimmings, lightly finished at the edge with an embroidery of steel spangles in a running pattern: these trimmings had a very brilliant and beautiful effect. *Repository of Arts*, December 1821 ~~~ [court dress] The dresses were mostly of white satin, with spangled under robe, tastefully ornamented with a profusion of lama. *Ladies' Monthly Museum*, September 1822 ~~~ [court dress] Dress of white crape and spangles, body plaited, full bell sleeves, and richly trimmed with blonde; *Royal Lady's Magazine*, January 1831

spangled crape – Bride's Maids to-her Royal Highness, Dressed all alike, viz. A crape petticoat, embroidered with silver spangles, and stripes of silver foil, with fringe and tassel; white satin body and train, trimmed with silver fringe, festooned with silver cord and tassels; the cap embroidered, silver bandeau, and spangled crape, trimmed with laurel, and the Prince's plume. *Gentleman's Magazine*, May 1795 ~~~ [court dress] A white crape dress, superbly embroidered in rich stripes of spangles, … the draperies formed of spangled crape, *La Belle Assemblée*, January 1807 ~~~ The trimmings for the spangled crapes, Opera nets, and other light articles made use of for full dress at this season, are now of the slightest texture; *La Belle Assemblée*, June 1812

spangled poplin – [Paris] Rose-coloured poplins with silk spots, like those of Ireland, called there *spangled* poplins, are in high estimation, having received the peculiar patronage of the Duchesse de Berri: they are, at present, worn in full dress. *La Belle Assemblée*, January 1826

spangled straw – [Paris] Fancy straw hats are in great requisition; they are called spangled straw, and are of various shapes, patterns, and colours. Bonnets of this material are either of the poke kind for undress, or of the turban shape for carriage costume. *La Belle Assemblée*, September 1816

Spanish cloth – The so perfectly fine Spanish cloth, which has the softness of velvet and satin, and which we generally see come in presents to other countries, is not worked from the wool of Spanish sheep, but from the wool taken from the Peruvian Vigogna, Lama, or Alpaca *(camellus glama et pacos Linnæi)*, which is of the camel species, and which will scarcely (it is probable) be introduced into Europe, though it should seem that, they ought to thrive equally well on the Spanish, as on the Peruvian mountains, which are still higher, and covered with snow. Communications to the Board of Agriculture, 1797 ~~~ With respect to the woollen manufactures, there is a general mistake prevails with many even to this day, in imagining that the fine broad cloth in France is principally supported by our English run wool, seeing it is well known that the real superfine cloth everywhere must be entirely of Spanish wool, and therefor often called Spanish cloths; Annals of Commerce, 1805 ~~~ A new kind of Spanish cloth mantle, however, made its appearance, elegant in formation, and in such universal favour, many ladies resolved, at first, not to throw it off; but the elbows were cold, it looked comfortless, and the more close shielding out-door dresses resumed their station: La Belle Assemblée, April 1812 ~~~ Woollen bays ... Spanish cloth, English making, each 20 yards Digest of the Commercial Regulations, 1824 ~~~ Stuffs are coming into favour for negligé; it will, however, be only a fancy of the moment, as they are not costly enough to retain their vogue for any length of time. They are made of Spanish wool, are of an exceedingly fine kind, and generally figured. Dark hues, as brown, marron, and soot-colour are most fashionable for stuffs. Court Magazine, January 1836 [see merino and vicuna]

Spanish silk – Though the Spanish silks in general are very fine, those of Valencia are by far the best. They are all fit for any sort of manufacture; the only fault they have, is being rather too oily, which is a great detriment to the dye. History of the Settlements and Trade, 1798 ~~~ Large India shawls, or scarfs tastefully wrapt round the figure, are seen amidst the above mentioned out-door habiliments, while those of fine Spanish silk are allowed to form a most graceful appendage to the evening party. We most however here remark, that much taste is required to produce that unstudied and graceful negligence which alone can render these ornaments advantageous to their wearers. La Belle Assemblée, October 1808 ~~~ The Spanish silk is fine and strong, and nearly equal to the Italian in quality. The exportation of it in a raw state, is prohibited, in order to encourage the manufactures of the country; but as these cannot consume half of what is produced in good years, the rest is smuggled out. Statistical and Geographical Survey of Spain and Portugal, 1808 ~~~ Promenade Sea-Beach Costume. ... A marine scarf, of purple Spanish silk, with rich ends, Weekly Entertainer, September 11, 1809 ~~~ Spanish silks are all raw; and are spun, milled, &c. in England, according to the several works they are to be used in. Guy's Pocket Cyclopædia, 1810

sparterie – Nothing is now so elegant as a straw hat: ... and ornamented with an aigrette de Sparterie. Lady's Magazine, August 1800 ~~~ [Paris morning caps] The ends of the ribbons are left very long, and cut in the from of horns. The horns are particularly noticed on the Sparterie straw hats. Port Folio, January 16, 1802 ~~~ The sea shore of Spain ... the celebrated esparto grass, which, on account of its extraordinary toughness, is used for making ropes, mats, chair bottoms, and, in short, all the articles included under the French term sparterie. Modern Geography, 1806 ~~~ Hats of Sparterie are fashionable for walking when the sun is not too powerful; La Belle Assemblée, October 1823 ~~~ White Sparterie hats are trimmed with bias folds of tartan sarcenet; La Belle Assemblée, February 1826 ~~~ Spartarie, or sparterie, or willow sheets for hats. Tariff, 1832 ~~~ Sparterie, sf. mats and ropes made of Spanish broom. Cobbet's French Dictionary, 1833 ~~~ Abele Tree (Populus Alba). White Poplar, or Dutch Beech, otherwise called the Arbeel. ... By splitting the wood into thin shavings, like tape or braid, the stuff called sparterie, used for hats, is manufactured. These shavings are always made from green wood. One workman can, with the aid of a child to carry off the shavings, keep several plaiters employed. Miller's Dictionary of Gardening, October 1834

sparterie de Venise – [hats] A new material called Sparterie de Venise, which is a kind of willow, is coming into favour, but it is not yet very much worn, Court Magazine, July 1836 ~~~ Carriage Hat – Of a new fancy material, Sparterie de Venisé, the colour is a light shade of brick dust, New Monthly Belle Assemblée, July 1836

spider – fashionable for Lord Melville's trial, ... mantles, &c. &c. made of silk, with a new trimming, or silk covered with sprigged lenons, muslin, or spider-web. La Belle Assemblée, April 1806 ~~~ Dress gowns ... The long sleeve of worked muslin, or spider net, is sometimes worn in an evening, ... Caps of lace, muslin, or spider net, are much in vogue; La Belle Assemblée, August 1806 ~~~ The long sleeve, is very generally introduced in evening dress, but is ever composed of the clearest materials. Sometimes of lace, patent, or spider-net, and embroidered book muslin. La Belle Assemblée, January 1807 ~~~ [court dresses] A dress of green spider-gauze, ornamented with wreaths of oak-leaves; ...A white spider gauze dress, richly trimmed in silver, ... A superb dress of pink spider gauze, embossed with silver ... A dress of green spider-gauze, *La Belle Assemblée*, June 1807 ~~~ A net, very simple in the mounting, but which produces a very pleasing effect, is much used, and is called the SPIDER NET. This net has merely a common gauze mounting behind the reed, and the gauze is drawn through every second interval. The whip part is, usually, composed of coarser yarn than the gauze. It passes through a bead, to which two lams are attached. These lams pass through the reed, and are attached to separate shafts, so that each may be raised alternately. By these means, the whip, *or spidering*, is alternately pulled to the right and left in a zig zag direction, but the whip threads do not cross each other. On whatever side the whip is lifted, it is secured by the weft shot. Art of Weaving, 1808 ~~~ [in 1813] a species of fine gause, called by us spider's web; Journal of a Cruse, 1822 ~~~ Though of an open texture, and of silk, it is not lace: it has somewhat the appearance of a material in fashion about ten years since, named spider's net; but it is more durable, less flimsy, and more adapted to hang in elegant shawl drapery. *La Belle Assemblée*, August 1829 ~~~ Spider net, considered as cotton cloth, [may refer to a net to catch birds] Tariff, 1829 ~~~ The false spider net is thus woven in stripes of various breadths; but when it is formed into checkers or alternate squares, which seems to be the greatest extent in point of variety to which it has been carried, two sets of the through-puts are requisite, and sometimes two of the ground; ... The spider net is woven with two treadles, which produce the texture of plain gauze interwoven with the whip: Treatise on the Art of Weaving, 1831 [see also *Arachne*, *cobweb* and *gossamer net*]

spider silk – *So far as to make a suit.* I do not believe; that M. Bon carried the matter quite so far: but we are informed, in the Memoirs of the Royal Academy of Sciences, 1710, that he presented to the Academy, the year before, stockings and gloves, made of the webs of spiders. ... He found, that the webs of spiders, were by no means proper for use, because the thread of them is too delicate, requiring ninety to make a thread, equal in strength to that spun by the silk-worm, and about 18,000 of them, to compose a thread fit for sewing, as strong as the threads used for that purpose, made of silk. ... he was convinced, that spider-silk would cost infinitely more than common silk. It only remained, then, so know whether it would be more beautiful; and this, M. de Reaumur was persuaded would not be the case; on the contrary, he found that it had less lustre, and the reason he gives for this, is, that the threads which compose the silk of spiders, are more delicate, and more crisped, than those of the silk-worm. Insecto-Theology, 1799 ~~~ *Spider silk.* The secret of procuring and preparing silk of the webs of spiders, has been found. M. Bon published a dissertation on this subject. He says, the silk-spider makes a silk as beautiful, glossy, and strong as the silk-worm; it spins it out of the anus, around which are five papillæ, or small nipples, and behind these two others; all musculous, and furnished with sphincters. These nipples serve as so many wire-drawing irons, to form and mould a viscous liquor, which, when dried in the air, after being drawn through them, makes the silk. By collecting a quantity of their bags, he says, a new silk may be made, that takes all kinds of dyes, and may be made into all kinds of stuffs. M. Bon had stockings and gloves made of it, which he presented to the French Academy; and others to the Royal Society. It was, however, soon found to be impossible to rear spiders in any quantities, as they, destroyed each other whenever they had not flies to prey on. Guy's Pocket Cyclopædia, 1810

spiral wire – [see *wire*]

Spitalfields – It was ascertained, that in the neighbourhood of Spitalfields along 4,500 looms were shut up in the year 1793, which, when in full work, gave employment to 18,000 people, of whom above a half were women and children. Annals of Commerce, 1805 ... Taking the north-east part of the metropolis, we commence at those vast ranges of building, called Spitalfields, reaching from Spital Yard at Northern Fallgate, and from Artillery lane in Bishopsgate Street, with all the new streets, beginning at Hoxton and the back of Shoreditch church north, and reaching to Brick Lane, and to the end of Hare Street, on the way to Bethnal Green east; then sloping away quite to Whitechapel road south-east, containing above three hundred and twenty acres of ground, closely built, and numerously inhabited. Before this improvement, the lanes were deep, dirty, and unfrequented; that part now called Spitalfields Market was a field, with cows feeding on it, since the year 1670. London, 1805 ~~~ It having been represented to many of the nobility and gentry of this country, that the Spitalfields' weavers are not able to manufacture silk goods equal to foreigners; and in consequence of such an idea many wrought goods having been smuggled into this country, to the great injury of the silk weavers; a subscription has been opened by them, for the purpose of raising a sum of money to weave a flag, as a proof of their ability, superior to any thing ever yet executed in this or any other country. This great undertaking has been actually commenced, and is now in a state of forwardness. Its dimensions are two yards wide, the ground a rich crimson satin on both sides, and brocaded on each side alike, with appropriate colours, tastefully and elegantly shaded by the artist. Upon its surface will appear woven within an oval, a female figure, emblematic of the art of weaving, reclining with pensive aspect on a remnant of brocade, lamenting the neglected state of this manufacture. A figure of Enterprize is represented in the generous act of raising her up, and reviving her drooping spirits, by shewing her a cornucopia; pouring forth its treasure. Close to that of Enterprize, and under a representation of the all-seeing eye of Divine Providence, the figure of Genius appears erect, pointing to a flag displaying the Weaver's Arms, placed upon the temple of Fame. *Repertory of Arts*, September 1810 ~~~ *Memoir of H. R. H. the Princess Charlotte of Wales*. ... immediately after her marriage, it was intimated to her establishment that her Royal Highness expected them to wear in future none but British manufactures. At the same time she sent an order to her own dress-makers not to introduce any thing foreign into articles prepared for her, on pain of incurring her displeasure and being no longer employed. In the same spirit, when the distress among the silk manufacturers in Spitalfields was so pressing in March, 1817, her Royal Highness and her illustrious consort, in order to afford a solid relief to the poor artizans, ordered 1000*l.* to be expended in British silks, which were sent as presents to the various families of their continental connections. They also determined to furnish a suite of apartments with silk of British manufacture, and just before her last illness, the Princess had finished an apartment in yellow silk. *New Monthly Magazine*, January 1818 ~~~ Retail Spitalfields Silk Warehouse, ... He begs to say his Stock of Silks of every description for the Spring, is complete for their inspection, and full 25 per cent. lower than he could ever offer them before, as every article has been purchased for ready money; every piece of goods is selected by himself, and will be warranted to wear well. Silk Velvets, Sarsnets, Lustrings, Gros de Naples, Laventines, Gauzes, Netts, Lustres, Poplins, Bombazeens, Norwich Crapes, washing Silks, and every article connected with Mercery. *Evangelical Magazine*, April 1821 ~~~ The Starving Silk Weavers. – His Majesty has given orders that the rooms of his palace at Winsor shall be hung round with silk of the Spitalfields manufacture. It is expected that many of the nobility will testify their compassion for the unfortunate weavers in a similar manner. The distress in Spitalfields is now dreadful in the extreme; many of the wretched families are actually starving. It is said that in many parts of the kingdom the ladies have resolved to make silk and considerable portion of their dress, with the praiseworthy motive of affording relief to a class which is at this time suffering under great deprivations. *Examiner*, February 12, 1826 ~~~ English Dress. In introducing the fashions for the month, we have the satisfaction to announce that the Queen has conferred a benefit upon the trade of Spitalfields, which will be long felt and appreciated. Her Majesty has caused patterns of figured silk to be forwarded for inspection, and ordered several for ordinary purposes; and for the Royal visit to Guildhall the Queen has commanded a white silk of splendid fabric, magnificently figured with leaves and flowers; some part of the blossoms of which are to be enriched with silver woven into the silk, displaying at once what can be done by the trade of London, and originating a taste for magnificent brocade silks, which will at once become general among the higher classes, and create a new means of giving bread to thousands. We shall simply add to the following directions, that after the 9th of November, ladies will do well to adopt, in place of other material, wherever they can do so, some of the magnificent silks which will by that time become general among the higher classes. *Lady's Magazine*, October 1830 ~~~ [court dress] Superb white satin dress, skirt, and corsage, trimmed with blonde' train of beautifully figured gros de Naples of Spitalfields manufacture, trimmed with satin and blonde; *Royal Lady's Magazine*, April 1831 ~~~ in Spitalfields the wages of the silk weavers have been reduced from 16*s.* to 8*s.* since 1826 <u>Reports from the Committees</u>, 1835 ~~~ H. R. H. the Princess Victoria. Superb pink satin dress, richly brocaded in silver; body, sleeves, and front of skirt elegantly trimmed with ribbon and blonde. (Dress Spitalfields manufacture.) *Lady's Magazine and Museum*, March

1836

split straw – [patent for making Straw Plat, dated May 8, 1800 by Edward Simpson and Caleb Isbester] To make plat of split straw, presenting only the outside surface of the straw to the eye, take straw, of any size, and split and fold the same to the size wanted, ... when the outside surface of the straw only will present itself to the eye, and the same will answer every purpose of, and appear like, a curious fine straw flattened, and make the same into plat. And to make plat of split straw, laid, put, or stuck on silk, paper, or wood, take straw, and split and open the same, and lay, put, or stick the same, with paste, gum, or any other thing fit for the purpose, on silk, paper, or wood, and cut the same into any size slips, which may be wanted, and make the same into plats. Repertory of Arts, 1801 ~~~ it may be necessary to explain to some of my readers, wherein the *split straw* differs from the *Leghorn platt*. In the first, the straw is split by a machine into five or six strips, each of which is applied separately in the platting. ... In October 1802, a school was opened at Fincham, ... They are instructed twice a day in reading, and eight of them in writing. The rest of their school time, being seven hours of the day, is employed in the platting of split-straw; for which, in addition to the advantage of education, they receive pay, according to the amount of their respective earnings. ... Dr. Briggs has introduced the split-straw manufacture, as part of the girls' employment, in the Kendal schools. Several of the girls now earn 2s. and 6d. a week by it, tho they give up port of the day to needlework. Reports of the Society for Bettering the Condition and Increasing the Comforts of the Poor, 1805 ~~~ A barouche hat of diamond or split straw, trimmed with extreme broad ribband. *La Belle Assemblée*, May 1806 ~~~ Watered silk bonnets are, upon the whole, most fashionable, but those of fine split straw, ... are also worn by many elegant women. *Ladies' Museum*, September 1831

spotted – *Her Majesty*. White crape petticoat, embroidered with white satin, in waves across, intersected with spotted blue shaded satin, *Lady's Magazine*, January 1797 ~~~ Zealand robes are another article which exhibits much novel grace. These are composed of black crape, muslin, or Paris net, tamboured in large spots of *coquelicot*, crimson or orange. *La Belle Assemblée*, December 1807 ~~~ [court dress] A petticoat of rich blue spotted tissue; *La Belle Assemblée*, May 1816 ~~~ [Paris] the hats that are ornamented with a feathered edge are generally of a spotted velvet of pearl grey. Hats, also, of Mozarian red, in spotted velvet, or of spotted satin of rose-colour, are in high estimation. *La Belle Assemblée*, December 1816 ~~~ An undress *cornette* is remarkable for its novelty, elegance, and simplicity. It is composed of fine net, with embossed spots, almost rising in tufts, of lilac or light blue satin, *La Belle Assemblée*, February 1819 ~~~ Rose-colored *corsages* of spotted velvet, are much worn with white gauze dresses; *Ladies' Monthly Museum*, December 1821 ... Contrasts may be most happy, or the reverse – spots, stripes, chequers, and mixtures, have no alliance with nobility; they are trying, they are the taste and livery of the lower orders, and always seem to be contrived for economy, for a quick and ready to t the vender, to hide uncleanliness, to disguise the person for some purpose or other to the wearer. *Atheneum*, October 15, 1824 ~~~ A dress of light summer silk, of etherial[sic] blue, spotted with black, is among the novelties of the day; *La Belle Assemblée*, August 1826 ~~~ [Paris ball] A dress of rose-coloured gauze, spotted with silver; ... [court dress] A net dress, beautifully spotted with gold, *Royal Lady's*, March 1831

sprig – [in weaving] For the formation of sprigs, &c. of various colours, there are often as many shuttles as colours; or a number of little swivel-looms, such as they use for the weaving of tapes, are introduced occasionally, as many as there are sprigs in the breadth of the piece. *Monthly Magazine*, October 1797 ~~~ [tambour-work] About 50 girls are bound apprentices to a person who attends in the [work-] house, and employs them in sprigging muslin. State of the Poor, 1797 ~~~ A round dress of sprigged muslin; *Port Folio*, June 19, 1802 ~~~ saffron, or primrose sarsnet, or taffeta, covered in like manner, or tastefully worked in sprigs of tambour or embroidery, and trimmed with lace, which had an effect truly elegant. *La Belle Assemblée*, May 1806 ~~~ For dinner dresses, sprigged muslins over coloured sarsnet slips, are much worn, and have a very elegant effect. *Edinburgh Annual Register*, August 30, 1812 ~~~ Silver sprigged and spotted muslins appear in higher estimation for the approaching summer, than silks or gossamers. *Repository of Arts*, May 1814 ~~~ [court dress] Draperies of sprigged net, trimmed with blond lace, *La Belle Assemblée*, May 1816 ~~~ Morning Dress. ... Round cap of sprigged bobbinet, *Brighton Gleaner*, April 1823 ~~~ The turbans are more splendid than they have been for these two months past; they are of coloured gauze, sprigged with gold or silver, or with gold stripes interwoven among the gauze; ... [Paris] Opera Dress. A dress of Smyrna gauze of bright jonquil colour, with sprigs of red flowers, and green foliage. *Ladies' Museum*, January 1830 ~~~ [court dress] An elegant dress of white crape, sprigged with gold, body and sleeves trimmed with blonde; train of white satin, lined and trimmed with blond to correspond; *Royal Lady's Magazine*, June 1831 ~~~ Dresses of black blond, over slips of coloured satin, promise to be greatly in favour during the ensuing winter. The blond should be of a very rich sprigged pattern. *Court Journal*, October 12, 1833... Another importation of new *ancien-etoffe* has just made its appearance from Paris. It consists of taffety with embroidered flowers. Some of these silks which we have seen, of white or citron yellow, sprigged with bouquets of roses, look more like venerable relics of the last century than fashionable *novelties*. *Court Journal*, December 14, 1833

spun gold – Gold-thread, or *spun-gold*, is a flatted gold, wrapped or laid over a thread of silk, by twisting with a wheel and iron bobbins. General Dictionary of Commerce, 1810 ~~~ In ancient times, those cloths only were called brocades which were woven, both in the warp and shoot, with gold or silver threads, or with a mixture or combination of both these materials. In preparing the threads for manufacturing gold brocade, a flattened silver-gilt wire or riband was spun on silk that had been dyed, to resemble as nearly as possible the colour of the metal; and the principal excellence in the art of preparing gold threads consisted in so regulating the convolutions of the metallic covering of the silk, as that its edges should exactly touch, and form, as it were, one continued casing, without either interval or overlapping. Silk Manufacture, 1831 [see *gold thread* and *metal lace*]

spun silk – Letter XXII. *Nice, Nov.* 10, 1764. ... In about ten days aster the last moulting, the silk worm climbs upon the props of his house, and, choosing a situation among the heath, begins to spin in a most curious manner, until he is quite enclosed, and the cocon or pod of silk, about the size of a pigeon's egg, which he has produced, remains suspended by several filaments.... In preserving the cocons for breed, you must choose an equal number of males and females; and these are very easily distinguished by the shape of the cocons; that which contains the male is sharp, and the other obtuse, at the two ends. In ten or twelve days aster the cocon is finished, the worm makes its way through it, in the form of a very ugly, unwieldy, awkward butterfly, ...The silk of these cocons cannot be wound, because the animals, in piercing through them, have destroyed the continuity of the filaments. It is, therefore, first boiled, and then picked and carded like wool, and being afterwards spun, is used in the coarser stuffs of the silk manufacture. Tobias Smollett, 1800 ~~~ *Yarn and Threads.* – There are no silk throw-mills in Scotland. The yarn used for the silk trade is brought from England – also all the sewing silk. The refuse and chippings of the manufactories, after being carded, are spun on the common wheel, or hand jeanie; and the yarn being laid two or three ply, is slightly twisted. This is denominated *Spun silk*, and is used for coarse stockings, which are knitted in the usual manner. This manufacture is still carried on to a small extent in Aberdeen, &c. General Report of the Agricultural State ... of Scotland, 1814 ~~~ *Shawl Manufacture.* ... Organzine silk was the material originally employed for warp, and upon this a weft of wool and silk, or of various mixtures of the two substances, was thrown in. This was succeeded, about 1804 or 1805, by spun silk, that is, the waste of Indian silk chopped into short lengths, and worked upon the same principle as wool or cotton – a process long kept secret, but now well known. It was made to resemble the Indian yarn very closely, and was deservedly considered a great improvement, though it still wanted the best properties of fine wool. *Atheneum*, September 1826 ~~~ This waste silk, when carefully spun by a spinning wheel, is called spun silk, and the thread is not inferior to the regular silk which is wound off; indeed, the winding off the silk into a thread united by its gum, is of no advantage farther than as a preparation for spinning, from which process the thread obtains its strength. Encyclopædia Londinensis, 1828 ~~~ Do you know as a fact, that that spun silk is impregnated with cotton? – I know it as a fact: those that manufacture spun silk purchase the pieces and ends of cotton cops that cannot be wove off without waste; they card this cotton up with the waste silk, and spin it in one thread by the cotton machinery. Reports from the Committees, 1835 ~~~ Each cocoon is surrounded with a coarse kind of web, which is carefully separated from it, as being of no use to the throwster; but it is mixed with the damaged cocoons, together with the coarser parts and refuse of the good; and the whole, being carded and spun, becomes what is called *spun* or *flos silk,* which is used for many purposes, as coverings for hats, cheap stockings, and those inferior kinds of velvet, denominated *plush* and *shag.* ... Of French silks, however, it may be remarked, that though they seem stouter than the English, yet as the woof is often of spun silk, or mixed with cotton, they are less durable. Scenes of Commerce, 1836 [see also *floss*]

square net – The next article I would speak to is Square Net; this is made from the same machine as the knotted stocking is; this is a very sound and good article, but not adapted to lace: it is usually made into mitts, and such like articles; Reports from the Committees, 1812 ~~~ The first machine for making lace from a stocking frame was constructed in 1777, ... Various kinds of network were made from the stocking frame prior to the time you name, none of which, however, much resembled lace-net until the invention of a fabric called square net, for which Mr. Robert Frost had a patent. This was superseded by the invention of point-net, the most perfect description of net-work ever produced from the stocking frame. Cotton Manufacture, 1836

squirrel – There are five sorts of squirrels in North America; the red, the grey, the black, the variegated, and the flying. The two former are exactly the same as those of Europe; the black are somewhat larger; and as to the rest, differ from them only in colour. The variegated also resemble them in shape and figure, and are very beautiful; being finely striped with white or grey, and sometimes with red or black. The American flying Squirrel, is much less than the European, being not above five inches long, and of a russet, grey, or ash colour on the back, and white on the under parts. Dictionary of Merchandise, 1805 ~~~ Walking Dress. A Polish Robe of purple velvet, ... the whole trimmed entirely round with the red fox, mole, leopard spot, or grey squirrel. *La Belle Assemblée,* February 1807 ~~~ Pelerines of fur are only partially worn; and those *élégantes* who do adopt them, have them very large. Swansdown, sable, and squirrel's skin, are the favourite furs. *Ladies' Monthly Museum,* March 1818 ~~~ The winter pelisses are chiefly of cachemire, of a light colour, lined with bright pink satin, and trimmed with a broad border of grey squirrel-skin; this elegant pelisse, generally of a cream-colour, is fastened down the front with pink bows, and has a high French collar. Another winter pelisse is of *gros de Naples,* and of a dark, changeable colour, approaching to the plum, but rather lighter; this is lined with white, with a broad fur at the border of the black squirrel, and is fastened with bows down the front, of a colour to suit the pelisse. *Ladies' Monthly Museum,* February 1821 ~~~ when that [the pelisse] is without trimming, they are of the grey squirrel of America, ermine, or the black Muscovy fox: all are equally fashionable. *Ladies' Museum,* February 1829 ~~~ Among the new fancy articles of the season, we must not omit to mention the *sac manchons.* The lower part of these bags is of fur, either sable, squirrel, lynx, or any other kind, so that they may, if required, match the boa or pelerine with which they are to be worn. *Court Journal,* December 21, 1833 [see also *American squirrel, chinchilla, flying squirrel, grey squirrel* and *Siberian squirrel*]

St. Maur – [1789] His things had previously been packed up in a bundle, and were taken down to put in the trunk. The effects were as follow: ... An old waistcoat of Rag de St. Maur. *Tomahawk,* January 23, 1796 ~~~ [Paris] Undress and half-dress gowns are made of a fine thin black cloth, which is called *drap de St. Maur.* this cloth is considered by the Parisians as the deepest mourning. *Repository of Arts,* December 1817 ~~~ [Paris court mourning] *Drap de St. Maur,* which we are obliged to substitute for bombazine, is worn in undress, very full trimmed with black crape. *Repository of Arts,* January 1819

stamine – Stamen, Stamin (s. *obsolete*) Hemp; coarse cloth made of hemp. ... Stamine (s. *in commerce*) A kind of French stuff. Ash's English Dictionary, 1795 ~~~ *Tariff of Duties.* ... Dyed cloths, stamines, kerseys, duftles, serges, frizes, kerseymeres, flag cloth, (1806 and 1807) *Tradesman,* March 1814 ~~~ Woollen cloths – ... Stamines, Sessional Papers, 1827 ~~~ Taminy, *s.* (*estamine,* Fr., whence our old word *stamin,* which see.) A kind of woollen stuff: called also *tammie* and *tammy.* Encyclopædia Londinensis, 1828

stamped – in Cumberland: ... Women's dress generally consists of ... a linen bed-gown, (stamped with blue) mostly of the home manufacture; this usually costs in the shops about 5s. 6d.: *Monthly Review,* July 1797 ~~~ Lace and satin caps, with stamped satin flowers, of correspondent colours with the dress, are the usual coverings for the head; but it should be observed, that they are better adapted to the gay parade, or the retirement of parks and pleasure-grounds, than to the less consecrated promenade. *La Belle Assemblée*, June 1810 ~~~ A mantle of French grey satin, with collar fastened on the right shoulder with black broach, and trimmed entirely round with a rich stamped velvet, lined with the same colour. A bonnet to correspond, with stamped velvet flower in front. *La Belle Assemblée*, December 1810 ~~~ but black satin stamped with a rich black velvet, upon a new principle, lined with rose-colour sarsnet, has just been introduced by Mrs. Bell, and made for a lady of the first rank and fashion. This pelisse is certainly a novelty, and the most elegant pelisse made this season. *La Belle Assemblée*, November 1814 ~~~ Morning Walking Dress. Black velvet slip, finished at the bottom with a double row of perfectly novel trimming. ... The trimming, which is at once superb and tasteful, is composed of stamped velvet; it is infinitely superior to embroidery, for which it is intended as a substitute. If we may venture to judge of the estimation in which it is held, by the demand there is for it, we may safely pronounce it likely to rival all other trimmings for pelisses. Its novelty must render it desirable to ladies of taste in dress; who, if they consult the annals of fashion, will find that nothing similar has ever been introduced before, and its effect is at once rich, striking, and tasteful; but in fact, we cannot do it justice in description, and this we are sure will be acknowledged by every lady who has seen the original pelisse. *La Belle Assemblée*, December 1814 ~~~ there is, at this moment, being manufactured at Lyons, stamped velvet, with broad stripes, of different colours, in order to form a material for winter hats. *Ladies' Monthly Museum*, November 1825 ~~~ Dinner Dress. ... White kid gloves, stamped and tied at the wrist; *Atheneum*, April 15, 1829 ~~~ Walking Dress. – Cloak of blue merino cloth, stamped with a black figure; *Godey's Ladies Book*, January 1831 ~~~ [court dress] A white watered silk dress, stamped in gold stripes, body with mantilla of blonde; train of ruby-coloured velvet, lined with white, and trimmed with velvet and satin; *Royal Lady's Magazine*, June 1831 ~~~ Neglige for the Theatre. – A black satin, *en redingote*, stamped with crimson and blue flowers. *Casket*, March 1835 [see also *calico*, *chintz*, and *printed*]

stifling cloth – If a woollen cloth were constantly kept in nurseries and sitting rooms, especially when there are fires, laid loose upon the table or other piece of furniture, this being always at hand, might be easily resorted to in case of accident, and being wrapped tight round the flames, or strongly pressed against them, would, by excluding the air, no doubt, in many instances, soon extinguish the fire. A green baize cloth, being very pliable, and likewise a neat cover to furniture, is recommended for this purpose; and if such were known in the family by the name of the Stifling Cloth, it probably would as readily be used when there was occasion for it, as fire-engines or buckets now are. Care must be taken to procure baize of a close texture. *Gentleman's Magazine*, March 1803

stocking net – 1589, the year after the defeat of the *Spanish* armada, the stocking frame, which has brought such wealth to the inhabitants of this place, was invented. ... The Nottingham branch, which is in general the finest, and consequently of the most valuable goods, has rapidly increased of late years. An enterprizing spirit pervades every branch of the stocking manufactory, and industry is a marking feature in the place. In 1641, Deering informs us that there were only two framework-knitters in this place; in his time fifty; now fifty times fifty may be computed, there and in its neighbourhood. History of Nottinghamshire, 1797 ~~~ *Sutton*, in its neighbourhood, has also a thriving manufactory of the same kind [stocking manufacture], which extends to a greater variety of articles than any other in the kingdom; such as milled woollen caps, for the Canadian and other markets, and pieces for waistcoats, &c. of fancy patterns, woven in the stocking frame, which are exported to France, Germany, and other parts of Europe. England Delineated, 1800 ~~~ Stockings are manufactured of silk, cotton, thread, or worsted; being either knit with needles, or woven on a loom; but the most proper material is *wool*, which is doubtless warmer, and more natural clothing for the human body, particularly during the winter, than that of any other texture. ... But silk stockings ought, on no account, to be worn *next the skin*; because they not only expose the person wearing them to frequent colds and catarrhs, but are also in other respects very unfavourable to health, especially in scorbutic habits. In July, 1799, a patent was granted to Mr. John Eaton, for his invention of a piece of machinery to be added to a stocking-frame, for manufacturing *hose-pieces*, *gloves*, &c. in a more neat, simple, and expeditious manner, than can be effected by the common method. <u>Domestic Encyclopædia</u>, 1802 ~~~ Nottingham, … Lace is made here on the stocking frame; and it would be a laudable object of the encouragement of those ladies, whose rank in life enables them to lead the fashion, in order to banish the other kind of lace, which ruins the eyes of the women who make it, especially if women would take up the business of making the frame-work lace. <u>Annals of Commerce</u>, 1805 ~~~ [men's] For Morning Wear. … From the extreme heat of the weather, few have been seen in riding breeches and boots, but we have observed many in stocking pantaloons, made of the finest stocking web, which from their flexibility and lightness are certainly well adapted for summer wear. *National Register*, July 31, 1808 ~~~ 31st May, 1810. … He had worn, in the morning, a dark-coloured coat and pantaloons; he changed them for an old blue coat, and an old light-coloured pair of stocking web pantaloons, which he had thrown aside for nearly a year before. It was in this last dress he made his murderous attack on the Duke, and, with whose blood, it was covered in numerous large spots. <u>A Minute Detail of the Attempt to Assassinate His Royal Highness the Duke of Cumberland</u>, 1810 ~~~ Worsted webbing or stockinet, for pantaloons, is to be regarded in the light of *woollen manufactures*, <u>National Calendar</u>, 1820 ~~~ Barragon, for flowered woollen stuffs, to one yard and one third wide – watered or plain, to one yard – stockinet, plain or ribbed, of all colors, to two-thirds of a yard wide <u>Digest of the Commercial Regulations</u>, 1824 ~~~ The stays which I recommend for young ladies (children require none), consist of the fine white woollen stocking web, such as is used for gentlemen's pantaloons. The web, doubled, is cut and formed into stays, in the same manner as any other material; and instead of bones or steel being added to them, there are strips of jean stitched closely down on both sides, in the places where these injurious bars are generally put. The strips of jean, stitched in the manner described, give sufficient firmness to the stays, while the elastic web between them admits of the free motion of the body in all directions. <u>Pathological Observations on the Rotated or Contorted Spine</u>, 1824 ~~~ Each Gentleman Cadet, at his admission, must be provided, at his own expense, with … Four pairs of Stocking-web Drawers. <u>Dictionary of the Military Science</u>, 1830 ~~~ [Patent January 17, 1833] The first of these improvements I effect by preparing knitting frames, or other similar machines, in the usual way for the production of the knitted materials called stocking fabric; <u>Journal of the Franklin Institute</u>, 1834 ~~~ Bandage … Of late years, ribbons of stocking-net, commonly called elastic web bandages, have been much used, and they appear peculiarly adapted for the purpose, as their elasticity prevents injurious consequences on any sudden increase of the size of the part to which they are applied. <u>Penny Cyclopædia</u>, 1835 [see also *webbing*]

stormant – *Stormont-field Bleach-field*. … There is here bleached, in a very satisfactory manner, a great quantity of britannias, diapers, and every other sort of cotton and linen cloth. <u>Statistical Account of Scotland</u>, 1796 ~~~ [October 1832] *for the use of the Pottawatamie nation of Indians, bought of A. Drouillard* … 1 piece twilled stormet 23 ¾ yards – 35 [cents/yard, totaling] $8 40 <u>Emigration of Indians</u>, 1835 ~~~ [story] I am now an old woman, [but when she was twelve,] My aunt brought with her a maid-servant, … I thought I could not enough admire a yellow stormant gown with green trimmings and flounces, that she wore, which, it afterward appeared, had descended to her from her lady, <u>Works of Mrs. Sherwood</u> 1834 ~~~ [ad] Have received by the ships Hark-away and Jefferson, direct from Liverpool, … 2 cases heavy dark striped and random Hamilton stormants. *Farmer's Register*, May 1835 ~~~ Stormont rugs are also formed with tufts put in as they are in Axminster carpets; … In all these carpets the warp and weft, or, as they are called, chain and shoot, which are both of linen, are altogether concealed from the upper surface, the tufts of worsted or woollen being the only part that is visible. <u>Penny Cyclopædia</u>, 1836

straights – Straights (*in commerce*) A kind of narrow kersey cloth. <u>Ash's English Dictionary</u>, 1795 ~~~ [during the reign of Elizabeth] Concerning making of woollen cloths in the counties of Devon and Cornwall, called plain white straights, and pinned white straights. <u>Parliamentary History of England</u>, 1806

straw – Straw'hat (*s. from* straw, *and* hat) A woman's hat made of straw. <u>Ash's English Dictionary</u>, 1795 ~~~ Parisian Fashions. Nothing is now so fashionable as the straw-hat. *Lady's Magazine*, June 1800… A new invented plain straw bonnet, much finer than the finest Leghorn; the form a poke, and peculiar for its lightness, not weighing more than an ounce; is likely to be very generally worn. *Lady's Magazine*, November 1800 ~~~ About Stevenage, spinning has given place to plaiting straw, by which they earn three or four times as much. The same is to be found at Hatfield; but Redburn is the place where the manufacture is most prevalent; where women will earn 1l. 1s. a week, and where a pound of prepared straw is sold as high as 6d. After six weeks learning, a girl has earned 8s. a week; and some clever little girls even 15s.* The farmers complain of it, as doing mischief, for it makes the poor saucy, and no servants can be procured, or any field-work done, where this manufacture establishes itself. There may be some inconvenience of this sort, but good earnings are a most happy circumstance, which I wish to see universal. At St. Albans I saw much plaiting: here are women that will earn 5s. a day. Little or none is found at Watford; much at Berkhamsted; the beginning of this spring (1801), a good hand could earn from 14s. to 18s. a week, which was the price of thirty yards of twist; but now it sells only at 4s. per score. Mrs. Muns, at Market-Street, is a great purchaser: she buys the twist of the poor, and makes it up into various fabricks, chiefly bonnets. Luton, in Bedfordshire, is also a considerable mart for it. Black lace making has been carried on at Berkhamsted time immemorial; these fabricks, especially the straw, render the women averse to husbandry work, and are said to make them bad servants, from their ignorance of every thing else. It is, however, highly beneficial to the poor: a child can begin at four or five years old. Some men employ themselves in getting straw for their wives. Some women have earned 2l. 2s. a week but that lasted only a short time. ... * This appears to be very high indeed. General View ... of Hertfordshire, 1804 ~~~ There are few manufactures in the kingdom in which so little capital is wanted, or the knowledge of the art so soon acquired, as in that of *Straw-platting*. One guinea is quite sufficient for the purchase of the machines and materials, for employing 100 persons for several months. Two machines cost 4*s*.; a few dozen pounds of brimstone, and the remaining sum in straw, is all that is required; the expense of a teacher excepted, will be from 7*s*. to 10*s*. a week, with board and travelling charges. One of the young women of Avebury went to Devizes and taught a school of about 30 persons for six weeks, for which she received two guineas; ... In selecting the straw, which is of wheat, the best platters are very choice and particular. The straws should be as free from blight and spots as possible, and small, short, soft straws, are reckoned best. The straw is cut or broken at the joints, and the outer covering being removed, is sorted of equal sizes, and formed in short bundles of eight or ten inches in length, and a foot in circumference. It is dipped once or twice in water and shaken a little, so as not to retain too much moisture; and the bundles are placed on their edges, in a box, which is sufficiently close to prevent the evaporation of smoke. In the middle of the box an earthen dish is placed, containing a pound of brimstone, broken in pieces: this is set on fire, and the box covered over. It should remain eight or ten hours, and this process should never be suffered to be done within doors. Two days after, or as soon as the straw is moderately dry, it is fit to be used. It will then be necessary to re-examine the bundles, and to select those straws which are best blanched, free from spots, and are of the same degree of softness. A tough straw and a pliant one will not work up well together. Reports of the Society for Bettering the Condition and Increasing the Comforts of the Poor, 1805 ~~~ The simple and elegant material of straw still maintains its ground — and turbans, hats, and bonnets of that fabric, with artificial roses, or sprigs of other flowers, seemed to be the prevailing favourites. *La Belle Assemblée*, April 1806 ~~~ Never were straw hats so much in vogue as at this moment, it would be impossible to describe their various forms; every *élégante* wishes to have a straw hat according to her own *gout*; the mob straw hat, tied under the chin, and ornamented with a lace trimming, is a very novel straw hat, and appears to be confined to the higher classes of *élégantes*. ... [Paris] Straw hats are in the highest degree of favour; they wear yellow straw hats without any ornaments whatever, but a bunch of lilac or a ribbon of pink or white, which flows loosely. *La Belle Assemblée*, May 1806 ~~~ There is nothing in which the French ladies more display their versatility of taste than in their hats. One of fancy straw, of a very whimsical kind, has lately made its appearance: it is wrought in diamonds, formed with chenille, and bound with straw-coloured ribband striped with green, or with ribband in large plaits. A few cane hats have also appeared worked in diamonds. Some ladies, who affect simplicity, wear straw hats without either lining or ribband, others have a double row of plaiting at the edges, and the crown is formed of a colour in sarsnet to answer the ribband, and finished by a wreath of flowers which are in season of various sorts. *La Belle Assemblée*, July 1816 ~~~ Straw bonnets, as they are made in New England, are a most beautiful and valuable article of dress. ... Formerly, the straw was split, flattened by a hot iron, and pasted upon cloth or paper. The plate, this formed, was cut into patterns, and made up and trimmed with ribbons. This was not a very durable fabric, and was therefore little esteemed. The ladies are indebted to the acute observation of a young gentleman of this town, who is now no more, for their knowledge of the elegant and durable manner in which the bonnets are now made. Some twenty years ago, this young gentleman was in one of the Southern States, whither commercial enterprise had called him, and lodged in a boarding house where were tow English females who made and sold bonnets of the celebrated Dunstable braid. [Which he learned to make by observation.] ... A farmer who has a crop of rye which is large, and bright, and fit for bonnets, can get twice as much for the straw in the milk, as for the ripened grain. *New England Farmer*, May 4, 1827 ~~~ Hats and bonnets are now worn placed very far back on the head. Some are of fancy straw; they are composed of very fine split straw, mixed with an open work formed of narrow tresses of Leghorn straw. *La Belle Assemblée*, June 1832 ~~~ BEDFORDSHIRE. *Lace-makers and Straw-plat Workers.* – The poor straw-plat workers in Dunstable, and the surrounding villages, are in the most dreadful state of misery, destitution, and want. The very same straw-plat for which they were paid, a few years since, half-a-crown a score, they can now only get sevenpence halfpenny a score for – barely sufficient to keep the poor creatures from actual starvation; and those who get this remuneration for their labour, are what are called "tip-top workers." Inferior workers can, with difficulty, get three halfpence the score. Straw bonnets, which some time ago would have fetched from 10*s.* to 12*s.*, may now be procured for 3*s. New Monthly Magazine*, October 1832 ~~~ The first attempts to divide the straw, were by means of knives; but this was a work that occupied much time. About thirty years ago, a mode was invented of dividing the entire straw into equal parts, by means of little instruments called "MACHINES," and then platting the divided parts. The ingenuity of the inventor (a great benefactor to his country,) was rewarded by realising a fortune of 30,000*l.*; and from that time may be dated the use of the plat made from divided straws. The Straw-platting *Districts* include Bedfordshire, Buckinghamshire, Hertfordshire, and Essex. In many other counties the platting is partially followed, and it may be well adopted in other districts for the supply of the neighbourhood. The *material* generally used is ripe wheat-straw; but rye and other straws have been used, and within the last ten years large quantities of Italian straw, said to be both of corn and grass, have been imported, and worked up into what are called Tuscan plat. ... Of the different *plats,* which are numerous, the principal are the following. First: the Dunstable, or whole straw; a considerable improvement has taken place in the imitation; as 2nd. the *Rustic,* of four coarse straw : this is a large plat, and used in making very common bonnets and hats; 3rd. *the Pearl,* of four small straw , not much used, being very expensive; 4th. *the Devonshire* of seven straws; 5th. the *fine-seven;* 6th. the *Backbone,* also worked in seven; 7th. the *Double-seven:* the straws are in the doubles wetted and laid together, and worked double; 8th. the *Eleven Straw;* 9th. the *Double Eleven;* 10th. the *Lustre, or* shining, of seventeen straws; 11th. the *Wave,* of twenty-two straws, the straws appear as if worked one way; 12th. the *Diamond,* of twenty-three straws. *Saturday Magazine*, January 26, 1833 ~~~ Straw Plat For Hats And Bonnets. – The cause of the decline in our own manufacture of hats and bonnets is said to be the importation from Italy. The straw hats and bonnets of Italy are said to be greatly superior in durability and beauty to those made m England. The plat made in England is splits, and the main circumstance is, that it is made of the straw of *ripened grass*; while the Italian plat is made of the straw of grain, or grass, *cut green.* Now the straw of ripened grain or grass is brittle, or, rather, rotten. It dies while standing; and, in point of toughness, the difference between it and straw from plats cut green is much about the same as the difference between a stick that has died and one that has been *cut from the tree.* But, besides the difference in point of toughness, strength, and durability, there is the difference in beauty. The colour of the Italian plat is better, and brighter; and the Italian straws are *small whole* straws, instead of small straws made by the *splitting* of *large ones*; there is a roundness in them, that gives *light* and *shade* to the plat, which cannot be given by our *flat bits* of straw. The grass must generally used is the smooth-stalked meadow grass. *Lady's Magazine and Museum*, July 1834 ~~~ [Paris] Hats And

Capottes. – The most fashionable, as well as the most elegant, hats, are those of paille de riz; the crowns are not worn very high, but the fronts are very large, and as long as possible at the sides. These hats are ornamented with flowers, and trimmed with Foulard or crystal ribbons, pink, light green, paille, or lilac. Paille d'Italie or Leghorn hats are much worn, especially by young ladies; they are lined and trimmed with either straw colour or white, enfin, as plain as possible. *Lady's Magazine and Museum*, June 1835 ~~~ [Paris] We have little to say of hats and bonnets; those of rice straw have at length become second rate, for though still highly fashionable, and indeed adopted by a majority of *élégantes*, they yet yield the *pas* to those of *paille d'Italie* – we mean, of course, those of high price – for no others are fashionable. *Ladies' Pocket*, September 1836 [see also *cottage straw, Dunstable, imitation Leghorn, Italian straw, Leghorn, rice straw, split straw, Tuscan straw*, also see *chip, pagne, patent straw, satin straw, sparterie*, and *willow*]

straw gauze – A carriage bonnet of straw gauze is justly admired; the material is entirely new; *La Belle Assemblée*, June 1820 ~~~ [Paris] A tissue of straw and silk is in much requisition for bonnets; and those formed of this material are lined with lilac or with rose colour. *La Belle Assemblée*, August 1820 ~~~ Hats of tissue straw, and silk, are not numerous, but they are always seen on the heads of very elegant females. *La Belle Assemblée*, September 1820 ~~~ Leghorn bonnets, though very fashionably, are not so generally worn in promenade dress, as straw, and a new kind of straw tissue; this last has a very light appearance: the trimming of bonnets composed of it is always a mixture of the same material with the ribbons. *Ladies' Pocket*, June 1830 ~~~ [mourning hat] *Tissue-de-paille*, gauze figured with black straw, *Lady's Magazine*, June 1830 ~~~ a new material, which, though it has but just appeared in Paris, is to be had at most of our stylish milliners' – we mean *tissu de paille*: it is composed of silk and soft straw, and is really very beautiful. *La Belle Assemblée*, July 1830 ~~~ [Paris promenade bonnets] There are also several made of straw tissue, and even of straw gauze, … straw gauze, a material composed of a mixture of silk and straw, figured in leaves or rings. A bonnet of this last material, which has been very much admired, has the brim disposed in large deep plaits, and bordered with a plait of straw; *Ladies' Museum*, June 1831 ~~~ Straw Ornaments, viz. – Straw Bands and Flowers, and Straw Gauze, (fit for ornaments only and not for making Hats or Bonnets.) to be entered as manufactured goods not otherwise enumerated. Ship-Master's Assistant, 1832

striped – *The Queen*. … the train of purple and black striped velvet, *Lady's Magazine*, January 1796 ~~~ Equal striped cambric muslins are coming into fashion for morning dresses, *La Belle Assemblée*, May 1806 ~~~ Coloured striped muslins may probably be considered to homely a style of dress for notice, they are likely, however, to become very general at our most fashionable watering-places. *La Belle Assemblée*, August 1810… Stripes are formed upon cloth, either by the warp or by the woof. When the former of these ways is practised, the variation of the process is chiefly the business of the warper: in the latter case it is that of the weaver. By unravelling any shred of striped cloth, it may easily be discovered, whether the stripes have been produced by the operations of the warper or those of the weaver. Circle of the Mechanical Arts, 1813 ~~~ [court dress] White satin petticoat, decorated with rich white and gold stripes; purple satin train. *La Belle Assemblée*, May 1816 ~~~ [Paris] A new and fashionable muslin, with large stripes, two inches broad; the one white, the other rose, blue, or lilac, which are placed aslant, or ray-like. The dress-makers who make use of this muslin, cut the front and the back, the points and the sleeves, in such a manner, that the rays appear to form an entire diagonal, that is to say a single sloping ray embraces the whole circumference. The *corsage* is formed of two points or rays which unite in the middle of the back, and in the front. *Ladies' Monthly Museum*, July 1822 ~~~ Plain colors in silks are now preferred to stripes; but the latter look well with bias folds, and neither that way of trimming nor the stripes are yet entirely laid aside. *Lady's Magazine*, September 1825 ~~~ [Paris] At the benefit performed for the sufferers by the fire at the Bazaar Boufflers, Her Royal Highness, Madame, wore a striped dress of gros des Indes; the stripes very broad, cherry-colour, white, and Saxon green: these stripes against the white had the appearance of velvet, while on the white were lightly painted flowers mingled with gold. *Ladies' Museum*, May 1829 ~~~ Striped muslins are in high favour, either white or coloured; those which are coloured have the stripes of the same shade as the muslin; but they are often figured over in patterns of separate bouquets, both between and on the stripes, which are of various colours; *Ladies' Museum*, June 1829 ~~~ Another new material is striped Cachemire: although but just introduced, it is already in great request. *La Belle Assemblée*, July 1830 ~~~ [Paris] White organdi, or India muslin, either plain or embroidered, or striped in thick or thin stripes, is extremely fashionable. *Court Magazine*, August 1833 ~~~ We have seen too some [robes] in marbled stripes; these last are exceedingly pretty. *Court Magazine*, November 1833 ~~~ The dress of the convicts is a striped roundabout coat, vest and trousers, made of cotton warp and woollen filling, with the stripes running round the body and limbs, a cap of the same cloth, ... their shirts are cotton, striped with blue. <u>Documents of the Senate of the State of New York</u>, 1834 ~~~ Morning Dress. *Gros de Naples* robe, a white ground striped obliquely in wreaths of green foliage; *Court Magazine*, April 1835 ~~~ The prison dress or uniform in winter is made of cotton and wool, with alternate stripes of black and white about an inch wide. In summer the dress is of cotton only. <u>Reports and Papers of the House of Commons</u>, 1836 ~~~ Carriage-dress offers great variety, ... silks, and those even of dark colours, striped in two different shades of the same hue, are in request; *New Monthly Belle Assemblée*, July 1836

stuff – cloth or texture of any kind; textures of wool thinner and slighter than cloth; <u>Sheridan's English Dictionary</u>, 1797 ~~~ in commerce, a general name for all kinds of fabrics of gold, silver, silk, wool, hair, cotton, or thread, manufactured on the loom; of which number are velvets, brocades, mohairs, satins, taffetas, cloths, serges, &c. <u>Encyclopædia Britannica</u>, 1797 ~~~ Parisian Fashions. Silk stuffs are adopted for full dress for the winter, and muslins for undress. *Port Folio*, January 30, 1802 ~~~ Dinner dresses are mostly made of cloth or stuff, high in the neck, with a falling collar of fine embroidered muslin or frill of lace; *La Belle Assemblée*, January 1810 ~~~ In deshabille, stuff dresses, of a very fine texture, are much worn, some of them are painted to imitate Indian chintz, and they are named *woollen chintz. Ladies' Museum*, February 1829 ~~~ Dresses for dishabille are made of a mixture of silk and stuff; *Ladies' Pocket*, November 1829 ~~~ A few hints, delivered in a kind, and not peremptory manner, might suggest to a female servant that the following materials of dress are the most suitable to her situation, and only can be permitted. Muslin, not lace-caps; cotton and stuff gowns, and petticoats of the same texture; <u>Domestic Duties</u>, 1829 ~~~ STUFF. Any sort of thin cloth made of wool or other matter. <u>Dictionary of General Knowledge</u>, 1833 ~~~ Stuff goods, worsted, viz.; bird's eye, bombazetts, calimancos, camblets, Circassians, Denmark satteens, durants, lastings, lustres, moreens, princes' stuff, rattinetts, russels, russeletts, satteen, Scotch plaids, shalloons, tamboreens, tartans, wildbore, &c. <u>Trade between Great Britain and the United States of America</u>, 1833 [see also *wool* and *worsted*]

Suede – That excellent Swedish leather, so superior to all other, of which not only boots are made, but also breeches, and great coats capable of resisting the most violent rains, is prepared in Jæmtland with hot water. <u>Repertory of Arts</u>, 1794 ~~~ Suède, s. f. Sweden. <u>Boyer's French Dictionary</u>, 1827 ~~~ Morning Dresses. ... gloves, *peau de Suède*; *Royal Lady's*, January 1831

Sumatra – *Sumatra Tissue.* – A supple brilliant material, which never rumples. ... *Out-Door Costume, New Materials for Mantle Dresses.* ... Among the new materials for dresses we cite the *tissue of Sumatra;* it is extremely soft and brilliant, and has the advantage of never creasing. *Maids, Wives, and Widows*, November 10, 1832

summer cloth – Drap, *cloth, sheet*. ... Eté, *summer*. Un jour d'été, *a summer day*. <u>Tardy's French Dictionary</u>, 1799 ~~~ Châlons [France] ... manufactures summer cloths, serges, stuffs, <u>Itinerary of France and Belgium</u>, 1816 ~~~ *List of French Patents.* [in 1823] ... for a stuff which they call *drap d'été* (summer-cloth). *Repertory of Arts*, November 1824 ~~~ [ad] Ladies' Riding Habits, Lined with Silk, and finished by first-rate workmen. Summer Cloth Habits . . £2 18s. ... [men's] Chesterfields, of light Summer Cloth, or stout Camblet . . 18s. <u>Doudney Brothers</u>, 1830 ~~~ An extra premium is due to Joseph Ripka, of Philadelphia, for his green summer cloth, (No. 141,) cotton and worsted; the only imitation of the English, of this description, which has come under our notice. *Journal of the Franklin Institute*, November 1831 ~~~ Information having been received from sources entitled to entire confidence, that impositions have been practised, and will continue to be practised, on the revenue, by invoicing and entering the articles known by the names of "*Summer Cloth*," and "*Brochellas*," under the name of "*Worsted stuff good*" when, according to the materials of which they are both composed, (say worsted or *combed wool* and *cotton*) they are not entitled to that classification, but are liable to the *Woollens duty*, it becomes necessary that measures be adopted at the customhouses, in the examination and inspection of such goods, to detect and prevent impositions of the kind in future. *American Railroad Journal*, March 23, 1833 ~~~ *The United States bought of Jordan Virgus*: ... 1 piece of Saxony summer cloth, 33 yds - $2.50 [per yard] Emigration of Indians, 1835

summer satin – Ball dresses, for the private ball-room, have experienced but little change since last month; the bodices worn with them consist of white or coloured summer satins, according to the fancy of the wearer. *La Belle Assemblée*, August 1820 ~~~ Silk dresses now are either of levantine or gros-de-Naples; and gossamer summer satin is much in favour for the evening dress of married ladies and matrons: *Ladies' Monthly Museum*, September 1828 ~~~ For evening and dinner-party dresses, those of slight Summer satins and of gros de Naples are preferred; *Ladies' Pocket*, June 1829 ~~~ White lace dresses over white satin are much in favour for young people, at evening visits of ceremony; and summer satins, or gros-de-Naples, of light colours, with broad flounces of white blond, are frequently seen on married ladies. *Ladies' Museum*, July 1829 [see also *ete*]

superfine – [usually refers to wool, but can mean any product] ... Superfine. (*from the adj.*) The best kind of woollen cloth, a piece of the finest cloth. Ash's English Dictionary, 1795 ~~~ Superfine, in the manufactories, a term used to express the superlative fineness of a stuff: thus a cloth, a camblet, &c. are said to be superfine when made of the finest wool, &c. or when they are the finest that can be made. Encyclopædia Britannica, 1797... [letter dated: Jan. 18th, 1794] upon the whole, it may, I think, be ranked with the best superfine cloth manufactured in England; if I except a few pieces made at a very high price, and merely out of curiosity. I find it stouter than our superfine cloth in general, and am of opinion that such cloth is well worth nineteen shillings a yard, or more. View of the Agriculture of Middlesex, 1798 ~~~ This evidence was received in the year 1803. ... 1, The finest and thinnest cloths are made for the Turkey-trade; 2, ladies' cloths are in the next degree thicker; 3, the next in thickness are made for the West India trade; 4, the next are for the Russia trade; 5, superfine cloths are thicker still; 6, the thickest of all are double milled superfine, and a species of narrow-cloths named *ratteens*. *Monthly Magazine*, March 1807 ~~~ In the style of dress gowns, we have a crowd of information; at the head of which may be properly placed robes of superfine cloth, embroidered round the bottom, on the bosom, and sleeves, in wreaths of leaves, composed of shaded velvet. *La Belle Assemblée*, December 1807 ~~~ There is no branch of our intercourse with England, in which we have fallen into so servile a dependence upon her, as that of superfine cloths; especially in cities, where a fastidious refinement in dress is indulged. The cloths of England are annually used to a very great value in the United States; and, notwithstanding the embargo, it is said, vast quantities have this year been smuggled through our Canadian frontier. The cloths of France, though so much preferable on every account, are seldom to be met with. French cloths now cost more than English. Whether they did or not, before the annihilation of their exports, I am not able to say. But they are finer, softer, stronger, and handsomer than the English, and more than reimburse their greater price, in their greater durability. There is probably more good wool in them than in the English. View of the Rights and Wrongs, Power and Policy, of the United States of America, 1808 ~~~ It had been, as I understand, a point long settled with the manufacturers, that superfine broad cloth could only be made of Spanish wool, and that any admixture of British wool degraded the quality of the cloth, and disgraced the Manufacturer. *Agricultural Museum*, December 7, 1810 ~~~ THE ENGLISH WITZCHOURA. Is the greatest novelty and most useful appendage to dress for the present season that can be conceived: it protects the wearer from the inclemency of the weather, preserves the dress worn under from being rumpled, and forms a most elegant exterior covering, either for riding, walking, or evening parties. ... It is composed of a superfine lilac and white mixture cloth, lined with silk. *Ladies' Monthly Museum*, January 1817 ~~~ Clothing is dear. A superfine cloth coat will cost from 30 to 35 dollars, or from 6*l*. 15*s* to 7*l*. 17*s*. 6*d*.; ... A superfine blue coat will cost from twelve to fifteen dollars per yard; An Account of the United States of America, 1823 ~~~ [men's evening dress] The pantaloons are of a dark fawn superfine cloth, made full projecting well over the boot, and are fastened underneath by a strap. *Casket*, April 1830 ~~~ [ad] 1 case of superfine London Broadcloths, consisting of the following shades of color, viz. – drakeneck, adelaide, invisible green, olive, olive-brown, russet brown, blue, black, &c. *New England Farmer*, December 10, 1834 ~~~ By this rolling and beating, the cloth shrinks in its superficies and thickens in solidity, on the principle of Felting. A web of the best sort, which is termed Superfine Cloth, is thus milled until it be reduced to less than one half of its original surface, and it might be raised to a much more solid consistence, if required. Analytical Dictionary, 1835 ~~~ For the last 20 years, therefore, superfine cloth has been made of wool imported from Hamburgh and Bremen, called *Saxony wool*. A Million of Facts, 1835 ~~~ The fabrics formed of wool are very various: *superfine broad cloths* stand at the head of the list. These are chiefly worn at home, where the prevailing colours are blue and black. Scenes of Commerce, 1836 [see also *broadcloth, merino* and *Saxon*]

swan feathers / fur – Swan skins, undressed, the piece – 11d. [import duty] Ship Owner's Manual, 1795 ~~~ Morning Dresses. ... White satin cloak, trimmed with swan-down. ... Afternoon Dresses. ... Swan-down muffs. *Lady's Magazine*, January 1797 ~~~ Evening or opera dress; made of white sattin and trimmed with swansdown fur. A mantle of the same, trimmed also with swansdown. *Port Folio*, April 10, 1802 ~~~ Edgings of swan-down still the most fashionable. *Gentleman's Monthly*, March 1, 1803 ~~~ *Swan's Down or Feathers*. Among the wild swans there are some whose plumage is entirely white like that of the domestic swans; others, and these are the most numerous, are more grey than white, and this grey when darker appears almost brown upon the head and back. The domestic swans are plucked, like the geese, twice a year; they afford a down which is esteemed for its softness, and used for filling cushions and beds. It is known that the same substance, which is extremely fine and softer than silk, forms also powder-puffs: likewise beautiful muffs and fur linings, equally elegant and warm, are made of it. The feathers of the wings are preferable to those of the goose, for writing and forming the tubes of pencils. *Repertory of Arts*, February 1805 ~~~ Parisian Opera Dress. An evening or dinner robe, of white muslin; ... A loose robe pelisse, of celestial blue satin or velvet, trimmed down each side and round the neck with a full swansdown fur, and negligently confined in the center of the bosom. *Repository of Arts*, November 1812 ~~~ In the carriage costume sarsnet pelisses are still much worn; ... they are trimmed, in general, with swansdown, and worn either with a swansdown tippet, or a small India or silk scarf tied round the throat. We saw one the other day composed of pale lavender levantine, lined with white sarsnet, and trimmed with swansdown. *Repository of Arts*, November 1816 ~~~ [Paris] the light swansdown, though we are on the verge of the generally warm and delightful month of May, cannot yet be laid aside; and it must indeed be confessed, that it is full as light a trimming is the *pluche de soie,* which having the appearance in its improved state of a downy fur, is in high estimation as an ornament to spring pelisses, robes *à la-Niobe,* and satin dresses for the Opera or evening party. *La Belle Assemblée*, April 1819 ~~~ Muffs have already made their appearance: they are, at present, of swansdown; they, therefore, do not affright us by their wintry appearance. The grey squirrel, the sable, and the ounce, as the cold sets in, will, no doubt, succeed to the delicate cygnet. *Repository of Arts*, November 1819 ~~~ a pelisse of sky-blue levantine, lined throughout with swansdown; *La Belle Assemblée*, December 1820 ~~~ There are some feathers of the swan, and of the white turkey, which cost, at first, about ten *centimes,* or less, but which sell for twenty *francs* each, on account of the miniatures of birds and butterflies, &c., which are placed on them, in the most beautiful colours. *La Belle Assemblée*, August 1828 ~~~ Many curative virtues were attributed by the ancients to the swan's skin, but modern practice only sanctions its use as a defence against rheumatic affections; in fact, the only worth of the very few wild swans which reach a market, consists in their skins. Poultry, Cows, Swine, and Other Domestic Animals, 1832 ~~~ [court dress] A rich aerophane dress, embroidered in gold, over white satin; train of Irish tabinet, trimmed with swansdown, and lined with white satin. *Court Journal*, March 2, 1833 ~~~ [Paris] *Cygnet* swan's-down is coming into favour with our belles. *Lady's Magazine and Museum*, December 1834 ~~~ It is to the Trumpeter that the bulk of the Swan-skins imported by the Hudson's Bay Company belong. Manual of the Ornithology, 1834 ~~~ Some pelisses ... are trimmed with swan's down. This delicate fur will, we have reason to believe, continue in favour during the month. *Court Magazine*, April 1836

swansdown, swanskin – Swanskin. A kind of soft flannel. Ash's English Dictionary, 1795 ~~~ Haggerty's dress was a velveteen jacket, swansdown waistcoat, and velveteen breeches. [Haggerty was executed

Feb. 23, 1807] <u>Murder of Mr. Steele</u>, 1807 ~~~ White stoved swanskins for vests, untwilled or plain, raised, about 7-8 of a yard wide, at 2 shillings per yard, *Weekly Register*, September 21, 1811 ~~~ [written in 1793] "There is a manufactory in the neighbourhood of Shaftesbury of a kind of flannel called swanskin, which is a coarse white woollen cloth, used for soldiers' cloathing, and made from 18*d.* to 2*s.* a yard; but this is of little consequence to Shaftesbury, the chief trade in this article being carried on at Sturminster Newton, where about 1200 people are employed in it, and where between 4000 and 5000 pieces, containing 35 yards in length, in a piece, yard wide, are annually made." – *Claridge*. <u>Agriculture of the County of Dorset</u>, 1812 ~~~ Swansdown, a fine soft woollen cloth Swanskin, a fine soft kind of flannel <u>Webster's Dictionary</u>, 1817 ~~~ A kind of coarse white woollen cloth or flannel, called swanskin or swansdown, is made at Starminster-Newton; <u>Edinburgh Gazetteer</u>, 1822 ~~~ Dresses for Wildfowl Shooting. ... Under the waistcoat, should be worn a Flushing frock, and over it, a short jacket, of either drab cloth, or swanskin. ... *swanskin*, should be previously wetted and dried, to prevent shrinking), <u>Instructions to Young Sportsmen</u>, 1825 ~~~ [ad] a great variety of toilonet and swansdown waistcoating; *Colonial Times*, January 13, 1826 ~~~ friezes (Swanskins) <u>Sessional Papers</u>, 1827 ~~~ *Swansdown* – 27 niches wide, cost 8d. to 3s. ... It is not manufactured in the United Stales. Used by the farming, mechanic, and laboring interests. The quality principally consumed costs about 1s. 2d. sterling, *Niles' Weekly Register*, March 8, 1828 ~~~ That "*Swansdown vestings*," composed of *wool* and *cotton*, and some of *wool*, *silk* and *cotton*, *Public Documents*, January 1829 ~~~ Swansdown, (an English woollen cloth) ... Swanskin, (a thick stout woollen) *Public Documents*, March 1832 ~~~ Swansdown. A fine, soft, thick linen cloth. Swanskin. A soft kind of flannel. <u>Knowles' English Dictionary</u>, 1835 ~~~1 do [piece] crimson spotted swanskin, 44 yards – [Price $] 1.00 [Amount $] 44.00 <u>Emigration of Indians</u>, 1835 ~~~ The fabrics formed of wool ... we have *swansdown*, a loose and woolly but warm fabric, for waistcoats; <u>Scenes of Commerce</u>, 1836

Swedish leather – [see *suede*]

Swiss chintz – *A Treatise on Callicoe Printing*. ... Something here too might reasonably have been said on the very evident superiority of the reds and chocolates in the swiss chintzes. *Analytical Review*, July 1794 ~~~ *Birmingham Institution*. ... it is said that our cotton printers borrow some of their most approved designs from the chintz patterns of the Swiss, *Edinburgh Magazine*, March 1821 ~~~ Families Furnishing will experience a great saving in them, and likewise in rich Merino Damasks, Tabarets, Moreens, &c. but more especially in the profusion of tasteful designs (for 1833) in Indian and Swiss Chintz furnitures. Last years patterns they are disposing of at irresistibly low prices. *Court Journal*, February 16, 1833

Swiss muslin – The muslin manufactories, established some years since in Ireland and Scotland, cause considerable uneasiness to the Swiss; as the machines used in those countries for spinning cotton considerably lessen the expence, and consequently enable the Scotch and Irish to under-sell the Swiss. The latter already draw a great deal of cotton yarn from Scotland and Ireland; and the author thinks it not improbable that, whenever a general peace shall have given full scope to industry and trade, the Swiss muslin manufactories, being then no longer able to cope with those of Scotland and Ireland, will entirely be superseded by them. *Monthly Review*, Appendix, 1798 ~~~ *Morning Promenade Dress* – Dove-colored or lilac silk spencer, over a dress of plain Swiss muslin, flounced with rows of same material; ... Dress of figured green Gros de Naples, open in front, rich figured Swiss muslin under dress; *Ladies' Museum*, August 13, 1825 ~~~ [ad] Have received by the ships Hark-away and Jefferson, direct from Liverpool, ...1 case 9-8 and 6-4 plain Swiss muslins and bishop lawns. 1 case rich figured Swiss muslins, dotted and large patterns. 1 cartoon rich worked cambric and Swiss muslin edgings and insertings. *Farmer's Register*, May 1835 ~~~ Walking Dress. Pelisse of Swiss muslin, lined with primrose silk, *Court Magazine*, August 1835

sylphide – the ballet was [Taglioni's] La Sylphide, *United Service Journal*, May 1832 ~~~ Head-dresses in Dinner Dress. – Turbans of crapes, *gaze sylphide*, and trimmed with a single feather, or two *esprits*, are in favour; *Day*, February 6, 1832 ~~~ Ball Dress. The material is white Mousseline Sylphide: *Ladies' Museum*, May 1832 ~~~ Materials of Evening Dresses. ... *Mousseline Sylphidi*, with *moire* patterns, is a light and very elegant material which promises to become very fashionable. *Day*, May 5, 1832 ~~~

Sylphide Satin is a pretty material, as supple as cashmere, and as brilliant as *Donna Maria* gauze, and is employed for millinery and dress robes. Some are with stripes of *ribbon designs*; others are embroidered with small detached *bouquets*. ... *Make and Materials of Evening Dress*. ... the prettiest of the new materials is the *Satin Sylphide*; it is exceedingly soft and brilliant; those of ribbon patterns will be most in favour. ... *Make and Materials of Evening Dress*. – Some rich gauzes and figured *gros de Naples* have already appeared; but the prettiest of the new materials is the *Satin Sylphide*; it is exceedingly soft and brilliant; those of ribbon patterns will be most in favour. *Maids, Wives, and Widows*, November 10, 1832 ~~~ [Paris] Something quite new and very pretty for walking bonnets, is the *tissu Sylphide*. It is made of different colours, and all look well. *Court Magazine*, June 1833 ~~~ Scarf of *gaze sylphide*, embroidered round the border in a very light pattern. *Court Magazine*, November 1833 ~~~ Evening Dresses. ... The robe is composed of pale blue *gaze sylphide* over *pou de soie* to correspond. *Court Magazine*, May 1835 ~~~ [court dress] dress of sylphide gauze, over a rich poult de soie slip; *Lady's Magazine and Museum*, April 1836 ~~~ Turbans are expected to continue in favour in evening dress: two new materials, *tul-Sylphide*, and *tul-Danae* have just appeared for them. *Court Magazine*, May 1836 ~~~ [court dress] mantilla, lappets, and sabots of rich French Sylphide blonde. *Lady's Magazine and Museum*, June 1836 ~~~ [Paris] Scarfs of this latter material [pou de soie] are also in request, and so likewise are those of tulle Sylphide and tulle Arachne, both in white and colours, but those of black lace are more decidedly in favour. *Ladies' Pocket*, July 1836

sylvestrine – An entirely new material for bonnets has been introduced, called *Sylvestrine*. It is a stuff resembling silk, made in every fashionable colour, but in reality formed of wood. This new tissue is said to be very durable, and has already superseded those embossed in straw, which were so much worn last season. *Godey's Ladies Book*, June 1831 ~~~ Public Promenade Dress. ... Hat of the new material *sylvestrine*, trimmed with blond gauze ribbons, and *aigrettes*. *Atheneum*, August 1831

sypers – Silk wrought, viz. ... Sypers, of Silk, broad, the dozen yards, ... narrow, each 24 yards <u>Ship-Master's Assistant</u>, 1795 ~~~ *Sypers* – i.e. *Cyprus*; thin stuff of which women's veils were made. <u>Ancient British Drama</u>, 1810 [see *cyprus*]

Syrie – Syria (region), *la Syrie*. <u>Nugent's French Dictionary</u>, 1827 ~~~ Opera Dress. A dress of emerald-green *gaze de Sire*, over satin of the same shade; *Royal Lady's Magazine*, April 1831 ~~~ Evening Dress. ... The head-dress is a toque of white spotted *gaze de Syrie*, a low foundation, and front arranged in high and full folds, the ends of the gauze trimmed with gold fringe droop at the sides. *New Monthly Belle Assemblée*, December 1836 ~~~ Half transparent materials, of the very finest Cashmere wool, are in great request. The most fashionable are ... *tissue de Syrie*. ... of delicate colours, and flowered patterns. *Ladies' Pocket*, June 1836

Tabanet - Tyrolienne

tabanet – [see *tabbinet*]

tabaret – [see *taboret*]

tabbinet – The other exports from Ireland are, … fine tabbinets and poplins (which last exceed those of any other country), <u>Elements of Geography</u>, 1797 ~~~ In tabinets and poplins, particularly, Ireland has long been superior to her competitors; but as of these a large part of the material, viz. the warp, is silk, they may seem not properly to rank under the head of woollen manufacture. <u>Manufactures of Ireland</u>, 1798 ~~~ It may not be improper to observe in this place, that when a parcel is not fit for broad cloth it is applied to the manufacture of worsteds, the finest part to hose and to worsteds for mixing with silk: viz. poplins and tabinets from 1s. 3d. to 6s. 6d. per yard; crapes from 1s. 2d. to 4s. per yard. … In many of these branches Ireland excels: her poplins and tabinets are universally known and admired, particularly with respect to their colours. <u>Origin of Commerce</u>, 1801 ~~~ Her Grace the Duchess of Richmond wore a white tabinet dress, richly ornamented with silver, *Scots Magazine*, February 1810 ~~~ The silk manufactures of Ireland have been carried to a degree of high perfection in their handkerchiefs; and in articles mixed with wool, such as tabbinets, they even excel those of Spitalfields, Paisley, or Norwich. <u>System of Modern Geography</u>, 1811 ~~~ [ad] Figured Tabbinets of matchless brilliancy, 5s. and 6s. per yard, usually sold at 7s. and 8s. *Repository of Arts*, March 1815 ~~~ At present, the beautiful tabinet triumphs, and as an article of dress for the social party, is likely to be long unrivalled. *Repository of Arts*, November 1819 ~~~ Morning Dress. A mulberry-coloured tabbinet round gown, made half high; … Cambric-muslin is still worn in morning dress; but plain poplins, lustres, and tabbinets, are much more in request. *Ladies' Monthly Museum*, December 1819 ~~~ [ad] The real Irish Tabbinets – from 4*s*. 6*d*. to 5*s*. *Evangelical Magazine*, April 1822 ~~~ The real Irish tabinet will never be common, as it is rather an expensive material, for what it is only calculated for, half-dress: it is worn only by a certain set for that sort of costume, who admire its beauty, and are by their independent station in life entitled to wear what they please. The wretchedly-wearing imitations of this beautiful produce of the Irish looms are fast going out of date; and the real tabinet is not likely, at present, to be very general. *La Belle Assemblée*, October 1826 ~~~ [mourning for the Duke of York] One evening dress we much admired; it was a beautiful black tabinet; which is quite deep enough for mourning, and is far preferable to bombazin, both from its jet-like colour, and the glossy richness of its texture. *La Belle Assemblée*, February 1827 ~~~ [court dress] A rich white and gold Irish tabinet, trimmed with beautiful point lace, *Royal Lady's*, March 1831 ~~~ Ireland has been celebrated for a manufacture of mixed silk and worsted, known in the country by the name of tabbinet, and in Great Britain by that of Irish poplin. For a long period this fabric was much sought after both at home and in the foreign market; but the fluctuation of female fashion has latterly considerably diminished the demand for it. <u>Universal Geography</u>, 1833 ~~~ [ad] a variety of GOLD and SILVER TABINET, for Court Dresses and Gentlemen's Waistcoats, and at prices considerably lower than before. *Court Journal*, March 2, 1833 ~~~ We feel much gratification in stating that the Royal Family and principal nobility in England have shewn a decided disposition to encourage and patronize Irish manufacture. Tabinet is becoming so much in fashion in the highest circles, that it is expected to be the prevailing court and evening dress during the ensuing season. Notwithstanding the extreme elegance of this beautiful fabric, the country is much indebted to the persevering exertions of Miss Elliott, *Court Journal*, December 28, 1833 ~~~ TABINET, (Compare Tabby.) A kind of silk gauze. <u>Walker Remodelled</u>, 1836 ~~~ [court dress] Superb dress of French blonde, over rich white satin petticoat; cerulean blue tabinet, manteau a la Reine, *Lady's Magazine and Museum*, May 1836 [see also *poplin*]

tabboreen – Tabboreens, a stuff. <u>Commercial Directory</u>, 1823 ~~~ *Taboret* or *taborine*. … Also spelt *taffeta*. <u>Manual of Orthoepy</u>, 1832 ~~~ Tabboreens (a worsted stuff) *Public Documents*, March 1832 [see also *taboret*]

tabby – Tabby, in commerce, is a rich silk which has undergone the operation of tabbying… passing the silk or stuff under a calendar, the rolls of which are made of iron or copper variously engraven, which bearing unequally on the stuff renders the surface thereof unequal, so as to reflect the rays of light differently, making the representation of waves thereon. Encyclopædia Britannica, 1797 ~~~ The tabby is a species of undulated silk. The more bright a tabby is, in the greater request it is. It must be well grained in the weaving, because the finer the grain is, the more glossy it becomes under the calender. View of the Commerce of Greece, 1800 ~~~ [court mourning for Prince Henry of Prussia] The Ladies to wear … [for] Undress – White or grey lutestrings, tabbies or damasks. *Corbett's Weekly*, September 4, 1802 ~~~ TABBY; in commerce, a kind of coarse taffety, watered. It is manufactured like the common taffety, excepting, that it is stronger and thicker both in the woof and warp. The watering is given it by means of a calender; the rollers are of iron, or copper variously engraven, which bearing unequally on the stuff, render the surface thereof unequal, so as to reflect the rays of light differently. It is usual to tabby mohairs, ribbands, &c. Tabbying is performed without the addition of any water, or dye, and furnishes the modern philosophers with a strong proof that colours are only appearances. Guy's Pocket Cyclopædia, 1810 ~~~ [court mourning for the Duchess of York] For head-dress, black or grey unwatered tabbies. *Repository of Arts*, September 1820 ~~~ [court dress] train of white watered tabby trimmed with gold and blonde; *Royal Lady's*, June 1831 [see also *watered*]

taboret – Tabboretts, - 25 per cent. [duty] Tariff, 1824 ~~~ *Taboret* or *taborine*. … Also spelt *taffeta*. Manual of Orthoepy, 1832 ~~~ [court dresses] Tulle dresses over white satin, trimmed with blonde; trains, white figured tabaret, lined with white satin; *Court Journal*, June 1, 1833 ~~~ Tabboretts, (a worsted stuff) Jones's Digest, 1836 [see also *tabboreen*]

taffeta – A thin silk. Sheridan's English Dictionary, 1797 ~~~ Taffety or Taffeta, in commerce, a fine smooth silken stuff, remarkably glossy. There are taffeties of all colours, some plain, and others striped with gold, silver, &c. others chequered, others flowered, &c. according to the fancy of the workmen. Encyclopædia Britannica, 1797 ~~~ Evening dress of peach-coloured taffety; *Boston Weekly*, May 21, 1803 ~~~ [court dress] A gold and white taffety petticoat and train, with crape draperies, *La Belle Assemblée*, June 1807 ~~~ taffetas d'armoisin, *Persian*. … taffetas lustré, *lustring, lutestring*. Dufief's French Dictionary, 1810 ~~~ TAFFETY, or TAFFETA, …a fine smooth silken stuff, remarkable for its gloss or lustre. The *taffetas noir lustre,* or black and glossed taffety, is what the English call alamode or mode: and the *non lustre* or *unglossed* of the former *lustring*. India furnishes very excellent taffetas, but they are by no means comparable to those of France or Italy, in point of durability and the excellence of the workmanship. Taffetas are of different qualities, according to the different places in which they are manufactured, and from which places they obtain the various appellations of Lyonese, English, Italian, and Florentine taffetas, &c. In the manufacture of taffety the best kind of Italian silk is usually employed, and it is said, that the peculiar quality of the water used, has considerable influence upon the fabric; thus the admirably beautiful gloss of the Lyonese taffety, is generally attributed to a property resident in the water of the Sane, which the manufacturers of Lyons invariably employ. Dictionary of Commerce, 1810 ~~~ TAFFETY; a kind of fine, smooth silken stuff, having usually a remarkable gloss. There are tafteties of all colours, some plain, others striped with gold, silver, silk, &c. others chequered or flowered. There are three things that contribute to the perfection of taffeties, the silk, the water, and the fire. The silk is not only to be of the finest kind, but it mast be worked, a long time and very much before it be used. The watering, seems only intended to give it that fine lustre, by a peculiar property not found in all waters, and lastly, the perfection of the stuff, greatly depends on the particular application of the fire. Guy's Pocket Cyclopædia, 1810 ~~~ Taffeta, *s*. (a thin silk) … Striped taffeta, *Taffetas rayé*. Taffeta of raw silk, *Taffetas de gaze*. Three quarter taffety, *Taffetas laize*. Ondulated taffety, *Taffetas flambé*. Taffety of two colours, *Taffetas de doubleté*. English taffety five eighths wide, *Taffetas d'Angleterre*. Chambaud's French Dictionary, 1815 ~~~ [court mourning] Wrapping dresses for home dishabille, of black taffety, are even at present more prevalent than the warm crape or bombazin, *Ladies' Monthly Museum*, September 1821 ~~~ The new materials for gowns are very beautiful, and are well adapted to the season. … taffeties of the most delicate colours, particularly of a light silver grey, have been seen on some very distinguished females. *La Belle Assemblée*, August 1823 ~~~ *Evening Dresses*. – Silk begins to appear slowly; some plaided taffetas, in large squares, and tranquiller colours; … are both now highly fashionable: *Blackwood's Lady's*, October 1836

Talma ribbon – [Paris] We often now see black and pink ribbons mingled together in the trimmings of some hats, which seem to warn us of the approach of winter, when these two colours blended are generally in requisition. *La Belle Assemblée*, November 1826 ~~~ Hats of plush silk, the colour of the bird-of-paradise, were worn in morning walks. They were trimmed with Talma ribbons. [November] *La Belle Assemblée*, Review, 1826 ~~~ [Paris] and fastened down the front of the skirt with rosettes of tartan ribbon; the colours black and rose colour: these ribbons formed fancy mourning for Talma. ... The most tasteful and becoming bonnet I have yet seen, is of white satin, lined with rose-colour, with Talma-ribbons, as they are still called, of rose-colour and black. *La Belle Assemblée*, February 1827

tamboreen – Stuff goods, worsted, viz ; bird's eye, bombazetts, ... tamboreens, Trade between Great Britain and the United States of America, 1833 [see also *tabboreen*]

tambour – Two tambour factories were lately erected here. The one employs 36 girls, who are bound for three years, and have 1s. 6d. a-week the first year, 2s. the second, and 2s. 6d. the third. At the other, 50 are engaged for the same time, who receive each 2d. more a-week. Statistical Account of Scotland, 1795 ~~~ the principal novelties of dress which attracted observation were mantles of the Egyptian stile, of various colours and materials; some of purple sarsnet or taffeta, covered by a transparent veil of white lace, or thin tamboured muslin, and trimmed with broad rich lace; others of saffron, or primrose sarsnet, or taffeta, covered in like manner, or tastefully worked in sprigs of tambour or embroidery, and trimmed with lace, which had an effect truly elegant. *La Belle Assemblée*, May 1806 ~~~ During a time of good trade, a superior tradesman can earn three guineas per week, and some of the tambouring girls fifteen shillings in the same period. *Scots Magazine*, August 1806 ~~~ The coloured tambour, or shawl bordering, is making rapid advances in the sphere of fashion; when attached to a printed dress, the latter ornament must ever be considered as a redundant and vulgar addition, but a border of tambour or embroidery in well-chosen and well-arranged colours, on cambric muslin, or even a delicate printed border on plain jaconet, or mull muslin, has an animated and pleasing effect. *La Belle Assemblée*, August 1806 ~~~ Tambour, a species of embroidery. The tambour frame is an instrument of a spherical form, upon which is stretched, by a string and a buckle, or other appropriate appendage, a piece of silk, muslin, linen, &c. which is wrought with a needle of a particular form, and by means of silken or gold and silver threads, into leaves, flowers, or other figures. Dictionary of Commerce, 1810 ~~~ About twelve years ago, a successful attempt was made at Glasgow to tambour muslin by machinery, for which the inventor obtained a patent. A manufactory wad then established; and, at present, there are sixteen frames in full employment. Twelve of them having each 54 needles, one inch asunder, tambour 6-4ths muslins; the other four, with 100 needles each, 3-4ths of an inch asunder, are intended for either 8-4ths muslins, or two webs of 4-4ths each. The whole are wrought by power from a steam engine; and a female attends each, who performs as much work as eighteen girls could accomplish by hand-sewing. *Scots Magazine*, December 1814 ~~~ The principal materials on which Tambour-work is employed, are muslin and net, and the Embroidery is generally done in coloured crewels, white twisted cotton, or gold thread. Young Lady's Book, 1829 ~~~ *Tambouring Muslin*. After some delay, on account of the numerous interruptions from visitors, we were admitted to see the celebrated tambouring machine for working sprigs and flowers upon muslins. A row of needles, with threads attached to them, are made to perforate the muslin, stretched upon a small frame; and after making a sort of stitch, they are again withdrawn, to repeat the operation in another spot. Each movement is so regulated as to bring the points of the row of needles against the proper place upon the muslin, where the sprig is to be wrought. In consequence of the superiority of the work executed by hand, we were informed that this branch of business is not carried on to the extent it once was. State of the Useful Arts, 1833

tammy – Tammy. (*s. in commerce*) A kind of thin woollen stuff. Ash's English Dictionary, 1795 ~~~ Taminy (*s. in commerce, but not a common spelling*). Tammy, a kind of woollen stuff. Ash's English Dictionary, 1795 ~~~ Halifax. ... the principal fabrics are ... tammies, ... They are generally woven by poor manufacturers, and sold in an unfinished state to the merchants, who dye and prepare them for foreign and home consumption. ... there was formerly a tammy manufacture [in Kibworth-beauchamp], which is now nearly laid aside; State of the Poor, 1797 ~~~ TAMMY, a species of woollen stuff, which is manufactured in the best possible manner in England. The wool of our own country is employed in this manufacture, in which the warp and woof are nearly equal. The material of the warp for 46 yards of this stuff ought to weigh from 10 lbs. to 10 ½ lbs. Exeter and Norwich are the chief seats of the manufacture of tammies, which, in time of peace, we export to almost every part of the world with which we trade. Dictionary of Commerce, 1810 ~~~ though bombazin is not equally unknown as tammy and camblet, still mentioned in the court circulars, it is equally unwearable at Midsummer. *Lady's Magazine*, July 1830 ~~~ Tamy, Taminy, or Tamine, is a light thin plain stuff, dyed green, blue, or other colours, and sold for window-curtains, screens, &c. or exported to the West Indies for Negro clothing. – The French *estame* signifies worsted, but *ettamine*, from which Tamine is derived, is not only a thin worsted fabric, for wear, but such a tissue as is used for separating flour from its bran, or as a search for purifying liquors, whether that cloth be made of worsted, linenyarn, hair, or any other substance. ... Buntin, or Bunting, which is used for ships' colours, is also a stout sort of Tamy. Analytical Dictionary, 1830

tape – Tape, (*s. from the* Sax. tappan) A kind of fine inkle, a narrow fillet. Ash's English Dictionary, 1795 ~~~ Of late, Sir John has added a piece of stay-tape to his wig, which attaches on the other side, passing under his chin; from this circumstance, some persons might infer that he is rather chop-fallen; an inference by no means fair, if we still consider the gay complexion of his advertisements and addresses to the ladies. Kirby's Wonderful and Scientific Museum, 1803 ~~~ A sort of ribbon or narrow band, made either from flaxen or cotton thread. Tape is woven upon a small loom in the manner of linen, &c. and the only difference between it and linen or calico is, that its warp is narrower. General Dictionary of Commerce, 1810 ~~~ The Roman mantle, in orange, scarlet, or blue Georgian cloth, edged with a narrow gold tape, is a very graceful and convenient defence against the night air. *Port Folio*, march 1810 ~~~ [ad] reel cotton, black and coloured sewing silk, stay tape, silk and cotton ferret; *Colonial Times*, September 8, 1826 ~~~ HINTS respecting the various departments and branches of neckcloth tying. ... After the knot is made, take a piece of white tape and tie one end of it tight to one end of your neckcloth; then carry the tape under your arm, behind your back, under the other arm, and fasten it tightly to the other end of the neckcloth. The tape must *not* be visible. This way prevents the knot from flying up, which would thereby shorten the length of the cloth, and, in short, greatly injure its appearance. On putting on the neckcloth, take that part which is immediately under the ears with your thumb and finger, and pull it up till it reaches the ear, and contrive to make it maintain permanently that position. Nothing displays more *mauvais gout* than seeing a cloth forming a *straight* line from the chin to the ear. Whole Art of Dress, 1830 ~~~ The edges of fine leather shoes and boots, are trimmed with thin strips of the like material: whilst those of prunello, and other thin shoes for ladies, are bound with narrow tape. The binding is applied by females with thread, by means of a common needle. Panorama of Professions and Trades, 1836

tape-lace – [probably obsolete] ... Tape-lace, *dentelle faite avec tissu*, [lace made with fabric] Boyer's Royal Dictionary, 1802 ~~~ Dentelle de lin [linen lace], *tape-lace*. Dufief's French Dictionary, 1810 ~~~ Tape-lace, *Dentelle dont le fond est un ruban de fil.* [Lace where the background is a thread (linen?) ribbon] Chambaud's French Dictionary, 1815 ~~~ Twist, tape-lace, and twine of all kinds, of cotton, silk, and any other materials – prohib'd [for import] Digest of the Commercial Regulations, 1824 ~~~ "Thursday, December 9, 1703. – Near Dundee, at Dudhope, there is to be taught, by a gentlewoman from London, the following works, *viz.* ... True point or tape lace. Traditions of Edinburgh, 1825

tapestry – Cloth woven in regular figures. Sheridan's English Dictionary, 1797 ~~~ At present any stuff of silk, satin or even simple tapestry, when wrought and enriched with flowers, &c. obtains the appellation of brocade. Guy's Pocket Cyclopædia, 1810 ~~~ TAPESTRY is a curious kind of manufacture, formerly used to adorn a chamber or other apartment, by hanging or lining the walls. The term is appropriated to a kind of woven hangings of wool and silk, frequently raised and enriched with gold and silver, representing figures of men, animals, landscapes, &c. Two methods are adopted in weaving tapestry: in the *high warp* the cloth is woven *perpendicularly*, in the low warp *horizontally*. The low warps in Flanders have been said to exceed those of France. New Family Encyclopedia, 1831

tarpaulin – [1792] We know that the cook was lying asleep in a tarpauling great coat, stretched along the rough-tree, just before the accident happened; African Memoranda, 1805 ~~~ Tarpaulings, are made of strong canvas, thoroughly tarred, and cut into different size, according to their several uses in the field; New and Enlarged Military Dictionary, 1810 ~~~ Tarpawlin. A coarse cloth tarred over: also, figuratively, a sailor. Dictionary of Buckish Slang, 1811 ~~~ A sailor's summer uniform is a white hat, duck frock with blue-striped and starred bosoms and collars, duck trowsers and blue-striped belt. His winter uniform is a black tarpaulin hat, blue cloth jacket and trowsers, with the same frock and belt as in summer. He is always obliged to appear at muster, dressed in uniform. Two Years and a Half in the American Navy, 1833 ~~~ Few, indeed, now of those who assume the jacket, trousers, and tarpaulin hat, are seamen; and the public ought to be upon their guard accordingly. *Chambers's Edinburgh Journal*, August 29, 1835

tartan – Tartan, a kind of woollen stuff Perry's English Dictionary, 1795 ~~~ *Tartan*, cross striped stuff of various colours, checkered. The Highland plaid. [from the Glossary of the play *The Gentle Shepherd*] Bell's British Theatre, 1796 ~~~ Letter *from an* Antiquary *to the* Colonel *of a* Highland Regiment, *on the* Highland Dress. In compliance with your desire, I have now the honour to send you a few remarks on the Highland dress. When I first saw in the papers, that you had appeared at court in a new highland dress, substituting trowsers or pantaloons for the philibeg, I was highly pleased with the improvement. The highland dress is, in fact, quite modern, and any improvement may be made without violating antiquity. ... Nothing can reconcile the tasteless regularity, and vulgar glare, of tartan to the eye of fashion, and every attempt to introduce it has failed. But in your uniform, by using only two tints of a colour proverbially mild, and without glare, all such objections are avoided, and the general effect rendered very pleasing. *Monthly Magazine*, June 1798 ~~~ The tartan plaid is just introduced, and it is thought will remain a favourite during the winter. *La Belle Assemblée*, October 1807 ~~~ Tartan, or Tartan cloth, a kind of cloth, made generally of woollen, sometimes of linen, and often of silk, of various colour; at blue, red, green, white, black, and yellow, &c. running in parallel lines, and crossing each other; and this forming various coloured squares, parallelograms and parallelopipeds. Encyclopædia Perthensis, 1816 ~~~ It is well known how difficult it is to make a Tartan dress, because every stripe and colour (of which there are many) must fit each other with mathematical exactness: hence it is that very few tailors, who enjoy their sight, are capable of executing this task. *Manchester Iris*, December 21, 1822 ~~~ Tartan silk dresses, in great variety, are much worn in half dress; their lively colours produce a good effect by candle-light; for which reason they are very prevalent at the theatres. *Ladies' Monthly Museum*, March 1827 ~~~ the new tartan silks were often on a black ground. The innovation of these patterns is curious: nothing can bear a more decided and classical feature then *Scotch* tartan – woe to the clan that would change it! The French often boast of their classical knowledge in costume; we wish they would study this: a lively tartan pattern on a *black* ground, would excite not only laughter, but anger in a true-born Scot, to see his favourite fabric so profaned. *La Belle Assemblée*, [review of the first six months] 1827 ~~~ Worsted Stuff Goods, from Manchester to New York ... Tartans ... actual [width] inches 24 *a* 25 ~~~ Price per yard s.d. [shillings.pence] 1.4 *a* [to] 1.8 Trade between Great Britain and the United States of America, 1833 ~~~ The Tartan of the Scotch Highlanders is strong worsted stuff, tweeled in the manner of Shalloon, but never glazed. The name is from the Erse *tarsin*, across; because it is made of yarn of different colours, both in the warp and weft, which are arranged so as to produce a chequered cloth, now varying in its appearance as directed by the fancy of the wearer, but, in former times, specifically fixed according to the clan to which each chequer peculiarly belonged. The finer Tartans are woven with double-twisted yarn, both warp and weft, and some are made wholly of silk. There are also cotton imitations. Analytical Dictionary, 1835 ~~~ tartans are no longer adopted by élégantes of distinguished taste. *Court Magazine*, January 1835 [see also *plaid*]

tartanelle – *Materials and Colours.* – The different fabrics are varied much at present. ... tartanelles; *Blackwood's Lady's Magazine*, December 1836 [possibly a combination of tiretaine and brocatelle, which each can mean linsey-woolsey]

tassel – [court dress] White crape petticoat, with gold fringe, and drapery embroidered with gold, and tied with gold cord and tassels. *Lady's Magazine*, June 1796 ~~~ An ornamental bunch of silk, or glittering substances. Sheridan's English Dictionary, 1797 ~~~ [court dress] A dress of white crape, magnificently embroidered with silver roses; at the bottom of the petticoat a very rich Vandyke embroidered border, and at the bottom of each Vandyke was a silver tassel; *La Belle Assemblée*, June 1807 ~~~ The mantle of scarlet kerseymere, reaching to the feet, with a high standing collar, confined round the throat with a rich cord and tassels, which reach to the bottom of the waist. ... [Paris evening dress] A fine silver filagree net was extended over the bust in front, somewhat like, the bibs worn by the antients; and it was terminated at the bottom of the waist with an elastic band, and large acorn tassels of silver. *La Belle Assemblée*, October 1807 ~~~ [court dress] A dress of pale pink twilled sarsnet, ... ornamented with superb bunches of fringed tassels. *Lady's Miscellany*, August 22, 1812 ~~~ Evening Dress. White British net dress over a soft white satin slip. The body is composed of white satin, disposed in folds, and rich letting-in lace. The sleeve, which is very short and full, is composed of the same materials: the lace is brought very full in front of the arm, and divided by tucks into full compartments, which are finished by small pearl tassels. *Repository of Arts*, October 1817 ~~~ Tassel is also the name of a bunch of silk or gold fringe, and is an addition to the strings of mantles, and robes of state. Universal Technological Dictionary, 1823 ~~~ [court dress] White crape dress, ... body and train of white and silver brocades, ornamented with tassels of pearls and blonde. *Court Journal*, April 20, 1833

tassel fringe – *Princess Sophia.* ... with gold and silver tasseled fringe; *Lady's Magazine*, January 1797 ~~~ *The Princess of Wales* – Wore as superb a dress as we have ever seen. The petticoat was of azure blue sarsnet, elegantly embroidered with polished steel and silver, which formed large bunches and wreaths of flowers; the bottom was trimmed round with an entire new rich silver tassel fringe; the train very magnificently embroidered to correspond, *Scots Magazine*, June 1804 ~~~ the points of the cymar trimmed with tassel fringe or beads. *La Belle Assemblée*, March 1812 ~~~ [Paris] worn on coming out of the theatres, or from other evening amusements; and from dress-parties, or public concerts, mantles of white *gros de Naples,* with round collars, and trimmed with tassel fringe, are considered extremely elegant, as envelopes against the night-air. *La Belle Assemblée*, November 1825

tatting – each flounce is edged with a very narrow silk gimp of the same colour: it is pointed, and resembles exactly what you call in England *tatting*. *Repository of Arts*, August 1819 ~~~ her mother who was quietly settled in a corner of the sofa nodding over her tatting – the lady-like employment which of all others comes nearest to doing nothing – Our Village, 1832 ~~~ Stapleford is a large village, ... Here are upwards of 100 machines employed in making *tatting and warp lace*. History, Gazetteer, and Directory of Nottinghamshire, 1832 ~~~ Mrs. Danby stayed in the tent with Lady Portbury, where she made several yards of tatting; [novel] Aims and Ends, 1833

taw – to dress leather white, commonly called *alum* leather, in contradistinction from *tan* leather, which is dressed with bark. Perry's English Dictionary, 1805

tease – Tease, *v a.* to comb wool; vex, torment. Teasel, *s.* a plant with which cloth is dressed. Teaseing, *s.* the act of raising the nap on woollen cloth. Perry's English Dictionary, 1795 ~~~ Tease, to scratch cloth to level the nap; Complete and Universal English Dictionary, 1799 ~~~ The teasel, a species of thistle, *(disacus carduus fullonum)* is propagated by sowing the seeds in March, upon a well prepared soil. About one peck of seed is sufficient for an acre, as the plants must have room to grow, otherwise the heads will not be large enough, nor in great quantity. ... The teasel is of singular use in raising the nap upon woollen cloth. For this purpose the heads are fixed round a large broad wheel, which is made to revolve, two men holding the teasel frame, as it is called, and work the cloth as it hangs up in a vertical position, drawing it down in portions as they proceed. The whole forms an instrument resembling a currycomb, and which is used in a similar manner to draw out all loose ends of the fibres of the wool. *Journal of the Franklin Institute*, March 1833

Tecklenburg linen – The importation also of dowlas, osnabrucks, ticklenburgs, and other german linens, and of Haerlem stripes, and tapes, from Bremen, Hamburgh, and Amsterdam, with the manufactory of every ton of hemp, and almost every ton of flax, which we raise or import, together with some cotton, has very much affected the british and irish linen trade*. ... * The use of cotton shirts is extending in America, being thought very favourable to health. A. D. 1793. View of the United States of America, 1795 ~~~ Tecklenburg. This is a very strong and lasting sort of hempen linen, manufactured in the county of Tecklenburg, the materials of which are the same as those of the Lovent linen, and made in the very same manner; yet it looks not so fine, on account of its not being calandered, after it has been measured at the staple office. The length of the pieces are very unequal, and contain from 70 to 100 double ells a piece, and sometimes more than that. Its width is the same as that of the Lovent linen. European Commerce, 1805 ~~~ German Linen … Ticklenburgs are known by that word being stamped on the Cloth. The length of the pieces generally *exceeds* the English ell, Practice of the Customs, 1812 ~~~ The denominations of Osnaburghs and Tecklenburghs being frequently misapplied, it is to be observed, that the former are made of flaxen, and the latter of hempen yarn, and of course much stouter. European Commerce, 1818 ~~~ Oznaburgs and Ticklenburgs are essential to the summer clothing of the slaves and laborers, and for bags for the cotton. Message from the President of the United States, 1826 ~~~ [ad] Have received by the ships Hark-away and Jefferson, direct from Liverpool, … 2 do. 3-4 German ticklenburgs. 3 do bleached Scotch ticklenburgs. *Farmer's Register*, May 1835

tenter – a machine used in the cloth manufactory, to stretch out the pieces of cloth, stuff, &c. or only to make them even and set them square. Encyclopædia Britannica, 1797 ~~~ Tenter; a railing used in the cloth manufacture, to stretch out the pieces of cloth, stuff, &c., or only to make them even, and set them square. It is usually about four feet and a half high, and in length exceeds the longest piece of cloth. It consists of several long pieces of wood, placed so that the lower cross piece may be raised or lowered, as is found requisite, to be fixed at any height by means of pins. Along the cross pieces, both the upper and under one, are hooked nails, called *tenter-hooks,* from space to space. In England, it is made felony, without benefit of clergy, to steal cloth on the tenters in the night time, by 22 Car. II, c. 5; and having in possession any cloth stolen from the tenters, and not giving a good account of the manner of becoming possessed, is subjected to transportation by 15 Geo. II, c. 27. Encyclopædia Americana, 1832

terre velure – [men's] The waistcoat is of *terre velure*, with broad satin and velvet stripes; *Casket*, January 1831 ~~~ [court dress] Rich dress of white crape, trimmed with gold lama, worn over a white satin slip; train of white terre velvet, trimmed with gold lama. *Ladies' Museum*, March 1831 [probably *terry velvet*]

terry velvet – Spencers of Terry velvet over muslin and cambric dresses, are reckoned most elegant for the promenade. … and the Terry velvet bonnet, superbly ornamented with a towering plume of white feathers, is esteemed the most appropriate carriage head-dress for the morning ride, *La Belle Assemblée*, February 1819 ~~~ Promenade Dress. Pelisse of levantine silk, or Terry velvet, … The velvet (*velours épinglé*), which promises to be very fashionable this winter, has not been worn for many years: it looks like very narrow cords, and forms elegant trimmings for silk pelisses: … Terry velvet boots, the colour of the pelisse. *Repository of Arts*, January 1824 ~~~ [court dress] A superb blonde dress, … a train of pink terry velvet, lined with white satin, trimmed with silver; *Royal Lady's*, May 1831 ~~~ Hats and bonnets in carriage dress are compose of velvet, of stain lined, and partly trimmed with velvet – terry velvet, called by the French *velours épinglé*, *Maids, Wives, and Widows*, December 1, 1832 ~~~ [ad] Terry Velvets, and coloured Silk Velvets, for Bonnets. *Court Journal*, February 9, 1833 ~~~ [court dress] White moire poult-de-soie dress; corsage and train of mauve terry, trimmed with satin; *Court Journal*, March 2, 1833 ~~~ [court dress] Train superb terry lilac velvet, richly trimmed with ribbon; body and sleeves to correspond, *Lady's Magazine and Museum*, May 1836 [see also *velours epingle*]

Thessalienne – Make and Materials of Out-Door Costume. … Dresses are composed of a variety of new spring silks, as *Gros de Naples, Bayadères, Thessaliennes Chines Perses*, and *Foulard du Bengale*, a mixture of silk and thread, and a perfect imitation of Indian materials. *Atheneum*, July 15, 1831

Thibet – Even the thinnest of the woollen fabrics possess a considerable degree of warmth, as appears in those very delicate cloths called shawls. The real shawls are made of the sine wool of Tibet, in the eastern part of Asia, and are sold at higher prices than almost any other wearing manufacture. They have, however, been well imitated by the product of some of our English looms. Arts of Life, 1802 ~~~ [Paris] the magnificent shawls manufactured by Messrs. Ternaux with Thibet wool, and which rival, if not in fineness, as least in beauty, the Cachemires of India. *London Literary Gazette*, September

13, 1823 ~~~ Morning Dress. – Dress of fawn-coloured Thibet cloth, or English twilled cachemire; a warm and beautiful article for winter wear, falling into graceful folds, and unaffectedly displaying the elegance of form; *Kaleidoscope*, November 9, 1824 ~~~ At length, about three years ago, an attempt was made to make the fabrick [shawl cloth] of wool entirely. To the substance employed, the name of Van Diemen's Land, or Indian, or Thibet wool, was given, though in reality it consisted merely of picked quantities taken from picked Saxon or English fleeces. Of this a fabric was made which surpassed those previously used, but it was still deficient in the exquisite softness and warmth which the Indian wool possesses, and what was not of less importance, no figure could be worked in upon it with accuracy and beauty. British enterprise, however, is not easily discouraged. Inquiries were set on foot in the East; and specimens of the actual material used in the fabrication of the very finest shawls were brought home. It was found to consist of the undergrowth of wool of the Thibet goat, or the down growing beneath the long rough hairs which form the exterior covering of the animal. It was found, too, that the article, though very expensive, could be procured in considerable quantities. But a new difficulty presented itself – this down was so extremely tender, that the most expert spinners in England despaired of forming it into a thread of sufficient tenacity to bear the operation of the loom. The practical skill and invention of our artisans is, however, inexhaustible; and we verily believe, that if it were required to convert spider's webs into cables, they would find means to accomplish it. An English spinner discovered a process by which he was able to form a very delicate yet firm and durable thread out of this soft material, and, according to custom, he secured his invention by a patent. *Atheneum*, September 1826 ~~~ Cloaks are very universal in out-door costume; many ladies, therefore, we believe, think them too common; for a wonderful predilection among our great ones is shown to the large Cachemire shawl, especially when really of oriental manufacture, and we have seen some of these which are rarely superb; this has increased the price of our own beautiful Thibets, which are a charming imitation. *Ladies' Pocket*, December 1829 ~~~ Some [shawls], of Thibet wool, have just been introduced, which have a very undress look, but are extremely light, soft, and warm; they will, probably, come into favour as the weather grows colder. *Ladies' Museum*, December 1831 ~~~ [men's] There are also imitations of the Thibet shawl, for waistcoats, with is in the mixing of cotton and silk as a substitute for the fine hair of the Cashmere goat. A judge of these things easily detects the cheat by the feel. *Day*, February 10, 1832 ~~~ A Thibet gauze dress, plain ground, with arabesque designs. … *Thibet Cashmere* – Has the fineness of the richest cashmere. This material can be employed for *negligé* or evening dresses, according to the ground shades. It is of great solidity, and will, it is expected, meet with great success. *Maids, Wives, and Widows*, November 10, 1832 ~~~ Among ladies of the highest fashion in Paris, the *peignoirs* now supersede every other kind of morning dress. Those most generally worn are of white cashmere or thibet, lined with coloured silk. *Court Journal*, April 11, 1835 ~~~ [in 1834] three-fourths wide thibets, No. 6, 32*s*.; six-fourths wide, 60*s*. Practical Mercantile Correspondence, 1836 [see also *cashmere* and *shawl cloth*]

Thibitian – *Merinos* promise this winter to be very much in favour, but under many new names. We have Thibetians, Indostan, and Ganges dresses, all of which are *merinos* of different patterns, either printed or figured. *La Belle Assemblée*, December 1831 ~~~ High Dresses composed of Cashmere wool, under the names of *Indonstans* and *Thibitians*, begin to be worn in the promenades. They are painted and figured in various patterns; *Casket*, January 1832

Thickset – Thicksets, corduroys, velveteens, &c. are cut upon long tables, with a knife, of a construction somewhat like the sting of a wasp, terminating in a very sharp point defended on each side by a sort of sheath. This point is introduced under the upper course of threads, which are intended to be cut, and with great ease carried forward the whole length of the table. *Monthly Magazine*, October 1797 ~~~ In the higher price thicksets, or velveteens, we cannot stand a competition either in quality or price with Manchester. Manufactures of Ireland, 1798 ~~~ Some of the young people wear chorded thicksets, and Manchester waistcoats, Statistical Survey of the County of Donegal, 1802 ~~~ At present, the fact is, that vast quantities, of cotton warp, and weft must, of necessity, be imported into this country, to answer the demand of the looms that are employed, in all the various kinds of cotton fabricks, from muslins and callicoes, down to thicksets. Transactions of the Royal Irish Academy, 1803 ~~~

Statement Of British Cotton Manufactures Suitable For Sicily. ... Thicksets. – The consumption very considerable. Best time for sale, September and October. Those invoiced at *2s.* are in greatest request. Blues, blacks, and bottle-greens, are the colours which suit. Genoa thicksets stand too high to answer well: the twilled ones are quite unsaleable at any price. Voyages and Travels, 1812 ~~~ Breeches worn by elderly people are commonly of frize, the same as the coat and waistcoat; but the young men are ambitious of getting thicksets or cords of different fading colours; the beaux are fond of black or pearl colour, made so very tight about the knees that they get very little wear from them: you will frequently see one at the top of the fashion with his stockings gartered below the knee, and the knees of his black breeches open, and a profusion of long black tape strings hanging loose about his legs. It seems to be a universal practice with most country tailors to make every article of dress too light; probably it may be by the directions of the rustic dandies. Statistical ... Survey of the County of Galway, 1824

thread – *Thread Manufacture*. – In the article of thread, particularly white and coloured pound threads, the Scotch stand unrivalled, and they must maintain their superiority by local advantages, which no other country at present can possess, and the manufacture is carried on to an extent equal to any demand. Aberdeen exceeds in quantity that of any other town in Scotland; and none have surpassed, if they have yet come up to, their fabric in quality. All the threads made here are sent to the English market, and for the greatest part direct to London, and from thence to many different places abroad. Besides pound thread there is made here a considerable quantity of the finer threads, called *ounce* or *nun's* thread, from their having been made by nuns in France and Flanders before the manufacture was introduced into this country. The principal thread manufacturers in Aberdeen are, Milne, Cruden and Company, for stitching and ounce threads; Leys, Masson and Company, for stitching and coloured threads; and Young and Walker, for coloured threads only. Statistical Account of Scotland, 1797 ~~~ a very great variety of fancy-work, in silk, worsted, cotton, and thread is made, Origin of Commerce, 1801 [Unless specified, *thread* usually means flax or linen thread. See also *sewing silk*.]

thread lace – Thread'lace, (*s. from* thread, *and* lace) Lace made of thread. Ash's English Dictionary, 1795 ~~~ Thread Lace is of various kinds, denominated either from the place where it is manufactured, or from the particular method of working, such as Point, Brussels, or Flanders Lace, manufactured in the Netherlands. Practice of the Customs, 1812 ~~~ Nottingham lace, or machine lace, has always a cut selvage at the sides; the bobbin or thread lace has a pearl edge. Reports from the Committees, 1812 ~~~ Caps of thread lace for home costume are more in favour, at present, than those of blond. *La Belle Assemblée*, October 1829 ~~~ Several elegant women have lately adopted a *fichu canezou* of white lace in dinner dress; ... If worn over a muslin dress the lace is thread, but if the dress is silk it is blond; these *canezous* look particularly well on slight figures, and as they partially shade the neck and bosom, they are at once delicate and graceful. *Ladies' Museum*, June 1830 ~~~ Brussels lace (thread lace) ... Valenciennes (thread lace) ... Thread, mecklin (thread laces, narrow, or in pieces quite whole for gowns, caps, &c. *Public Documents*, March 23, 1832 ~~~ [Paris] The pelerines, of coloured muslin to match the dresses, are trimmed round with a narrow Valenciennes, Mechlin, or any fine thread lace, such as is put in pocket handkerchiefs. *Lady's Magazine and Museum*, July 1834 ~~~ Thread lace is of various kinds, denominated either from the place where it is manufactured, or from the particular method of working. That which is woven with bobbins, made of bone or ivory, is called bone-lace. Book of Commerce by Sea and Land, 1834 [see *bone lace* and *pillow lace*; also *Bedfordshire* or *Buckinghamshire*]

thread net – The breakfast *cornette*, of fine thread net and Brussels lace, simply finished by rouleaux of lilac satin, is a very becoming deshabille to every face: *La Belle Assemblée*, August 1818 ~~~ *tulle*, thread net, *Linguist*, July 30, 1825 ~~~ Every kind friend, therefore, will have an opportunity of shewing her approbation of this cause, without taking a mite from other good objects. To those who may not have much money to offer, I would suggest, that any kind of work upon thread-net, such as collars, cuffs, frills, children's caps, frock-bodies, sleeves, &c. would find here an immediate sale, greatly to the advantage of our resources. *Missionary Register*, July 1825 ~~~ [Paris] The Tuileries now form the favorite evening promenade; and then the most fashionable out-door covering is a canezou spencer of thread tulle over a dress of printed muslin; *Lady's Magazine*, July 1825 ~~~ The marriage vail is always white, its material is thread net embroidered round with flowers and different patterns of needle or woven work, and is sufficiently large to extend nearly to the knees. *Whitby Panorama*, August 1827 ~~~ [Paris] Ball Dress. Dress of white Grecian thread-net, ... over a white satin slip; *Lady's Magazine*, August 1830 ~~~ [Paris] The bride wore a robe of *tulle-de-fil*, extremely fine, *Court Journal*, September 5, 1835 ~~~ [Paris] At the Opera, ... robes are in application of Brussels or fine thread net, *Court Magazine*, October 1836 [see also *net* and *tulle*]

threepile – Threepile (*s. in commerce*) A kind of stout velvet. Ash's English Dictionary, 1795 ~~~ Threepile, an old name for good velvet. Critical Pronouncing Dictionary, 1807

thule – [see *tulle*]

Tibet wool – [see *Thibet wool*]

ticking – Ticken, Ticking, *s.* (*in commerce*) tick, a sort of strong linen for beds. Perry's English Dictionary, 1795 ~~~ The prices of checks run from 6d. to 1s. 6d. per yard; of ticks, from 7d. to 2s. 6d. Statistical Account of Scotland, 1796 ~~~ Tickens, cheap corduroys, &c. are commonly worn for waistcoat and breeches. Statistical Survey of the County of Tyrone, 1802 ~~~ Tick, or Ticking, ... a sort of texture used for covering bedding. Ticking is made either from hemp or flax, being woven in the loom in the same manner as linen, from which, however, it differs both in quality and appearance, being coarse and stiff, though close, and presenting a surface marked with narrow blue and white stripes alternately. General Dictionary of Commerce, 1810 ~~~ I saw the new clothing for the year, ... it consisted of ... ticken trowsers 2 pair for each boy, Board of Education in Ireland, 1813 ~~~ in the state of Rhode Island, ... Bed Ticking, sold at 55 to 90 cents per yd. Sketch of the United States of North America, 1814 ~~~ *Directions to Travellers on Foot, Botanists, Mineralogists, &c.* In order to travel comfortably on foot, you must wear no knee-buckles, neither must, you garter tight. Be provided with a jacket of some light but strong stuff, such as ticking, and a pair of pantaloons. These latter should come sloping gradually below the knee, so as to fit tight round the leg and foot; a pair of tight half-gaiters, made of either cloth, ticking, or leather, and which may be worn either over or under the pantaloons, and reach the calf of the leg. These articles are indispensably necessary to prevent the stones getting into the traveller's shoes, an inconvenience to which he would continually be exposed on descending from the mountains. Traveller's Guide through Switzerland, 1820 ~~~ Tickings, plain, striped and clouded colors, including those known as Cholets and Arabias, of all qualities, up to one yard wide. Digest of the Commercial Regulations, 1823 ~~~ Bed Ticking, Flax ... Bed Ticking, Cotton Tariff, 1824 ~~~ Gaiters are very fashionable, either in cloth or ticking; many ladies dance in them; *La Belle Assemblée*, August 1826

ticklematch or ticklemoth grass – [see *imitation Leghorn*]

Ticklenburg – [see *Tecklenburg linen*]

tiffany – Tiffany, a very thin kind of silk Perry's English Dictionary, 1795 ~~~ Gold and silver spotted tiffanies are much used in turbans. *Lady's Magazine*, April 1800 ~~~ Coloured borders to represent natural flowers, on white crape, tiffany, muslin or velvet, are amidst the most elegant embellishments for full dress. *La Belle Assemblée*, November 1806 ~~~ [ad] Ribbons and Broad Silks, such as Sarcenets, Satins, Persians, Tiffanies, Crapes, &c.; *La Belle Assemblée*, January 1807 ~~~ The newest articles that have issued from the manufactory are the striped sarsnets and imperial bombazeens; gossamer gauzes, Italian tiffanies, spotted cambrics, and fine tamboured muslins, are still much worn in full dress. ... The simple pelerine, in white tiffany, lined with satin and trimmed with swan's-down, is truly elegant. *Weekly Entertainer*, October 9, 1809 ~~~ a sort of transparent gauze, stiffened with gum and pressed. It is much employed in the making of artificial flowers, &c. The best tiffany is made in this country; which is so excellent, that even the French eagerly purchase it, though its importation is prohibited in France. General Dictionary of Commerce, 1810 ~~~ *Tiffany* is a very thin silk, having some stiffness given it. It was formerly used for trimmings, but it is now out of fashion. Book of Commerce by Sea and Land, 1834

tigrine – Pelisse robe of pale blue *tigrine*; ... Another half dress material, called *tigrine,* is a mixture of silk and cashmere; it has something of the appearance of twilled satin, and is remarkably soft and supple. The grounds are thickly covered, and the patterns are an intermixture of two colours, as orange and black, green and brown, &c. &c. *Court Magazine*, November 1834 ~~~ TIGRINE, ti-grĭ n, a. Resembling a tiger. <u>Knowles' English Dictionary</u>, 1835 ~~~ Among the new materials likely to become fashionable, we may cite *tigrine*; it is a levantine of the very richest kind, spotted like a tiger's skin. ... for evening dress. *Court Magazine*, January 1835 ~~~ Tartan silks, tigrine, Siam taffitas, and Algiers satin, form the majority of the dresses worn at evening parties in Paris. *Court Journal*, February 7, 1835

Tillicoultry Serge – Tillicoultry has been long famous for weaving a course woolen cloth, called *Tillicoultry Serge*. It is a species of shaloon, having *worsted* warp and *yarn* [linen] waft, and is reported to have been wrought here, as early as the reign of Mary Queen of Scots. The average price is 1s. Sterling per yard. Though the manufacture has now, in a great measure, left us, and gone to Alva, (*like the arts and sciences, from East to West,*) yet all the cloth of this kind is sold in the markets, under the name of *Tillicoutry Serge*. It is much to be regretted, that more attention is not paid to this manufacture in the place where is was invented, or at least brought to the greatest perfection. <u>Statistical Account of Scotland</u>, 1795 ~~~ Tillicoultry *Serge* has been manufactured here since the days of Queen Mary; it commonly sells at 1s. per yard. <u>Traveller's Guide</u>, 1798

tinsel – Tinsel, lace resembling gold <u>Perry's English Dictionary</u>, 1795 ~~~ A kind of shining cloth; any thing shining with false lustre, any thing showy and of little value. <u>Sheridan's English Dictionary</u>, 1797 ~~~ Copper, and lace inferior to *silver*, is to be spun upon thread, yarn or incle, and not on silk; but this does not extend to *Tinsel* apparel, used in theatre. <u>Law-Dictionary</u>, 1797 ~~~ [from a 1788 lawsuit] 7th Count, selling another quantity less than one ounce of copper (being a material inferior to silver) gilt and *flatted* into plat, and made into a certain material called *tinsel* (the same tinsel being a material then and there used in the making of buttons in the gold and silver lace manufactory) <u>Complete System of Pleading</u>, 1798 ~~~ Parisian Fashions. ... The robes are all in the Turkish style, trimmed in satin *applique*, or tinsel. *Lady's Magazine*, July 1800

tip paper – [see *papier mache*]

tissu – Tissu, *m. tissue, any thing interwoven*; ... Gauze, *gaze* (*tissu trés-clair*) [very light fabric] <u>Dufief's French Dictionary</u>, 1810

tissu Cachemire – [see *cashmere gauze*]

tissu Cachemire – [see *cashmere gauze*]

tissu Chantilly – Two new materials have just been introduced for the evening *negligé*, the one called *tissu Chantilly*, is exceedingly pretty; it has a *gros de Naples* ground, generally of a light colour, as emerald-green, pale rose, *oiseau*, or azure blue; it is strewed with small bouquets woven in black net work, which has very much the appearance of blond lace; *La Belle Assemblée*, June 1832

tissu de coton – [Paris] Bonnets of *tissu de coton* are made with gauze trimmings of the poppy color, *Ladies' Monthly Museum*, July 1822 ~~~ [Paris] At the last sitting of the *Institut*, the hats were chiefly white: they were of rice straw, cotton *tissu*, and silk, *gauffrée*; *La Belle Assemblée*, August 1823 ~~~ White hats of *paille de riz* and *tissu de coton*, are very much worn. *Ladies' Monthly Museum*, August 1823 ~~~ *tissus de coton*, ... *Cotton manufactured* goods, <u>British and Foreign State Papers</u>, 1828 [see also *cotton straw*]

tissu de paille – [see *straw gauze*]

tissue – Tissue (*s. from the French*) Cloth interwoven with gold or silver. ... To interweave, to variegate. <u>Ash's English Dictionary</u>, 1795 ~~~ *The Princess Royal.* – A crape petticoat superbly embroidered with old foil, the train a most beautiful gold brocaded tissue. We cannot help remarking the extreme richness and brilliancy of the various tints displayed in the superb dress, which, we understand, is of Persian manufacture, being part of the presents from the Ottoman ambassador. *Lady's Magazine*, January 1796 ~~~ Princess Elizabeth. – A superb dress of apricot and silver tissue. *La Belle Assemblée*, June 1807 ~~~ Tissue-cloth, *Brocard*, <u>Dictionnaire Français-Anglais</u>, 1816 ~~~ [Paris] *Tulle* is still very fashionable for full dress, but white silk tissue is more so. *Ladies' Monthly Museum*, August 1818 ~~~ Very few dinner dresses have as yet been made in muslin, but we have seen a good many in silk, and of a texture which we consider infinitely too substantial for the season; in fact our levantines, *gros de Naples, reps*, and queen's silk, are almost as stout as the brocades, tissues, and damasks of our grandmammas. *Atheneum*, July 1820 ~~~ Tissue (*Com.*) stuff made of silk and silver. <u>Universal</u>

<u>Technological Dictionary</u>, 1823 ~~~ some woollen tissue of a very fine texture, such as Lyonese crape, or double Merino: *Atheneum*, February 15, 1830 ~~~ [court dress] A silver tissue dress, trimmed with silver palms, fastened with silver wheat ears; *Royal Lady's*, May 1831 ~~~ [ad for men's] DRESS WAISTCOATS. Vary in Prices from the rich Silk at 14s. to the most superb Embroidered Satins, Velvets, and Tissues, at Two and Three Guineas each. *Eminent Foreign Statesmen*, March 1836 ~~~ We may cite among the new silks for evening dress those with a dead ground and satin stripes, and also quadrilled changeable silks, but those most likely to be highly fashionable, are the rich tissues imitating the old fashioned brocades. *Ladies' Pocket*, December 1836

tissue gauze – Her Majesty. – A petticoat of rich white and silver tissue gauze, with silver wreath ornaments and tassels, diamond bows and tassels. *Edinburgh Magazine*, June 1802 ~~~ for evening dress velvets, French silks, particularly the rich levantine, are most in requisition for the matron ladies, while the younger sport the Cosmo gauze, or the lately imported new article of beautiful texture, the tissue gauze, the most favoured of which has amber flowers on a white ground; this material is peculiarly calculated for ball dresses: it as a lustre in the flowers little inferior to gold, and dazzles without being glaring. *La Belle Assemblée*, November 1816 ~~~ [Paris] Silver tissue gauze, of a very light and elegant description, is a favourite material for these head-dresses, [toques] *Repository of Arts*, July 1817 ~~~ We are happy, however, to see that most becoming of all head-dresses for matronly ladies, and even those who are elderly who go much in company, the turban, now so much in request; these distinguished head-dresses are of richly striped and beautifully figured gauze of various and brilliant colours; they are worn at all times of the day; and for the evening dress party are of velvet, or gold and silk tissue-gauze, with plumage of the aigrette kind. *Ladies' Museum*, December 1829

tissue Memphis – [see *Memphis*]

tissue Pekin – [see *pekin*]

tissue satin – Her Majesty – Wore a scarlet velvet petticoat, ornamented with black lace, thrown over in tasteful draperies tied up with diamond rows; ... superb gold and white leopard tissue satin train and petticoat, richly embroidered, ... the drapery and pocket-holes of royal purple and gold tissue satin, with a most superb border all round to correspond with the petticoat and train; the body and sleeves of gold tissue satin, embroidered and inlaid with rich colored stones to correspond with the train and petticoat: *Lady's Magazine*, January 1809 ~~~ For dinner dresses velvets are considered as the most elegant; next to this in estimation is satin cloth; but sarsnets, both plain and twilled, satins (white particularly,) Merino cloth, and rich worked muslins, are likewise worn. *Edinburgh Annual Register*, December 31, 1812 ~~~ For dinner dresses, ... tissue satin cloth, are worn. This last article is exceedingly elegant, and perfectly novel; it has all the richness of those silks which were worn in old times, without their heaviness; it is indeed particularly appropriate for the time of the year, and we have no doubt it will become very general. *Edinburgh Annual Register*, February 1, 1813 ~~~ For dinner-dress, black and coloured velvets, satins, and French double-sided silks, are, we think, highest in request; but Irish poplins, sarsnets, and satin cloths are also much worn. *La Belle Assemblée*, December 1814

tissue straw – [see *straw gauze*]

tissue Syrie – [see *Syrie*]

tobine – There are likewise lutestring tobines, which commonly are striped with flowers in the warp, and sometimes between the tobine stripes, with brocaded sprigs. Some have likewise a running trail with the colour of the ground, as other lutestrings. <u>Laboratory</u>, 1799 ~~~ English Winter Carriage Costume. ... Pelisse of rich Tobine silk striped, of Christmas holly-berry colour and bright grass green, trimmed round the collar, cuffs, and down the front with very broad swansdown. ... For the carriage rich Tobine silks, and those generally striped of different colours, are reckoned most fashionable; *La Belle Assemblée*, February 1818 ~~~ the more matronly adopt the rich Tobine sarsnet, either striped or plain, *La Belle Assemblée*, January 1819 ~~~ [ad] Gros de Naples and Tobines, 2s. 4d. to 2s. 9d.; rich ditto, 3s. 4d.; the richest make, 4s. 6d.; *Examiner*, June 18, 1826 ~~~ figured silks, such as Florets, Tobines, Tissues, and Damasks; *New England Farmer*, July 1, 1835

toile – *cloth, linen cloth*. ...— ouvrée, *huckaback*. — à voile, *sail-cloth*. ... — d'or *or* d'argent, *gold or silver tissue*.

... — de coton (toile Indienne), *calico*. — de soie, *silk cloth*. <u>Dufief's French Dictionary</u>, 1810... Parisian Dinner Dress. A gown of the new fancy material, *toile de Smyrne*, of the darkest shade of bottle green. *Repository of Fashions*, January 1829 ~~~ Toile, *sf.* cloth, linen-cloth, linen. *Toile peinte*, printed calico. *Toile cirée*, oil-cloth. *Toile de Hollande*, Holland cloth. *Toile d'araignée*, cobweb. *Marchand de toile*, a linen-draper. *La toile est levée*, the curtain is drawn up. ... Toilé, *sm.* the ground of lace. <u>Cobbett's French Dictionary</u>, 1833 ~~~ The most fashionable *toilette de matin* worn at Paris, consists of a *negligé* of *foulard*, *toile de laine*, *white jaconnot*, or *batiste*. *Court Journal*, June 29, 1833 ~~~ [Paris] Walking Dress. ... The hat is of *toile de soie*; *Lady's Magazine and Museum*, May 1835

toile de Smyrne – [see *Smyrne*]

toilenet – [in Leeds] more recently very large quantities of fancy articles have been made, such as swan-downs, toilonets, and kerseymeres; <u>Pocket Gazetteer of England and Wales</u>, 1807 ~~~ [men's] *For Morning Dress* ... plain buff kerseymere or stripe toilinet waistcoats still take the lead in preference to scarlet; *National Register*, February 28, 1808 ~~~. Silk and cotton toilinette, appropriate for evening or full dress, and worn with a bodice of pink, or white satin, or velvet, has a rich and elegant appearance. *Repository of Arts*, January 1815 ~~~ Valentias and toilenettes, composed of wool and cotton and sometimes contain silk, liable to an ad valorem duty of 25 per cent. <u>National Calendar</u>, 1820 ~~~ What is the particular line you are in? – I am working toilinettes at present. What do you earn at present? – I can make about 12*s.* independently of bobbin and winding. In how many hours? – I generally work fourteen or fifteen hours a day. <u>Report from the Committee</u>, 1825 ~~~ [ad] KEEPS constantly on hand, an elegant assortment of Shepherd's best Black, Blue, Mixed and Olive Broadcloths, Kerseymeres, Cut Velvets, Toilinet, Valencia and Silk Vestings, &c. <u>Directory for the Village of Rochester</u>, 1827 ~~~ *Toilinets* – 27 inches wide, cost 8d to 5s. ... This article is consumed by all classes. *Niles' Weekly Register*, March 8, 1828 ~~~ Previous to the tariff of 1828 there was a considerable importation of various fancy stuffs used for vest-coats, known by the name of valencias, toilenets, &c, the component materials of which are wool and silk, or worsted and silk. <u>Exposition of the ... Tariff System</u>, 1832

topaz gauze – [see *metallic gauze*]

toucan – trimming consists of a mixture of Astracan fur and the small feathers of the toukan, orange-colour and red. *Ladies' Monthly Museum*, April 1828 ~~~ Robe of white satin, bordered above the hem with a trimming of *toucan* feathers. These feathers bear a close resemblance to fur, from their extreme shortness. They are red and yellow. *Royal Lady's Magazine*, January 1831

tow – Tow, flax or hemp beaten and combed into a filamentous substance. <u>Sheridan's English Dictionary</u>, 1797

tow cloth – *Manufactures from hemp and flax* ... tow cloth, <u>View of the United States of America</u>, 1795 ~~~ CORONER'S REPORTS. Yesterday morning a colored man (apparently about 40 years old) was taken with fits and died instantly, near the corner of Broadway and Warren street. He had on a homespun drab cloth jacket, dark colored under vest, tow cloth shirt, blue pantaloons, and shoetees laced in front: supposed to belong on Long-Island. *Lady's Miscellany*, November 17, 1810 ~~~ From the earliest ages of the West Indies slaves have been improperly clothed, with flax and tow cloths of British, or German imported manufactory; for the selfish restrictions, of the mother country have kept them in the sad alternative, to accept these or nakedness. Nor has their qualities evidenced the integrity of the tradesmen, for they have sunk as their prices have risen, and become a nominal raiment. *Tradesman*, February 1, 1811 ~~~ *Tow Cloth.* – There is no article of domestic manufacture so much wanted as stout Tow Cloth. The filling and the warp should be of equal firmness and size, and full forty inches wide, as this article is principally wanted for bailing up Domestic Cotton Goods. It need not be very fine, but it should be very stout and firm. Our New Hampshire friends are particularly requested to attend to these remarks, as the Tow Cloth which comes from that State is so thin and *sleazy* that no manufacturer of Cotton Goods will buy it. *New England Farmer*, August 9, 1823 ~~~ John Gilbert, a native of Wales. Had on when drowned tow cloth pantaloons, red flannel shirt, striped vest; *New-York Mirror*, August 30, 1823 ~~~ *List of prices paid for Indian goods in England,* ... Tow cloth – pr. yard 6s. ½d. *Public Documents*, March 5, 1832

Trafalgar – Trafalgar Dress, white satin, trimmed with gold, or silver lace. *La Belle Assemblée*, February 1806 ~~~ the plain kerseymere coat, trimmed down the front, round the bottom, collar, and cuffs, with Trafalgar trimming of the same colour; *La Belle Assemblée*, December 1806 ~~~ [court dress] A white crape petticoat, with rich silver foil border, the drapery richly embroidered with Trafalgar net border; *La Belle Assemblée*, June 1807 ~~~ [court dress] A white crape petticoat, ... the left drapery is beautifully embroidered with silver roses, with the same border, and edged with Trafalgar fringe; *Lady's Magazine*, June 1807 ~~~ the silk cords, or Trafalgar trimmings, are a bright relief, and have a more light effect [than trimming with skin (fur)]. ... The waist and sleeve of this dress are usually worn plain, and over a satin under-waist. No trimming but Trafalgar, or a border of netting of floss silk. ... [Paris] The pelisse is composed of superfine mazarine cloth, ... The whole trimmed with rich silk Trafalgar of the same colour. *La Belle Assemblée*, December 1807 ~~~ White Embroidery comprises the art of working flowers, and other ornamental designs, on muslin, for dresses, or their trimmings; capes, collars, handkerchiefs, &c. There are two sorts of cotton proper for this work; that which is most generally used, because it washes the best, is the dull cotton; sometimes called Trafalgar, or Indian. The other sort is the glazed, or English cotton, and is only proper to be used on thin muslin; although it looks infinitely the more beautiful of the two, previously to its being washed, yet that operation destroys its beauty, and removes all its gloss; nor is it so smooth and pleasant to use as the other. Young Lady's Book, 1829 ~~~ the biassed or diagonal patterns formed by four sets have obtained the name of tweeled gauze. There are patterns woven likewise in the diamond draught, forming bird-eye figures, with a barley-corn spot in the centre of each diamond, which have been named Trafalgars, in compliment to that great victory: and these appear to be the chief varieties which have been woven on this principle. ... TRAFALGARS. It was formerly observed, that the patterns which have assumed this name, were merely the tweeled gauze turned into a bird-eye or lozenge figure, with a small barleycorn spot in the centre. Treatise on the Art of Weaving, 1831

tram – The silks of Naples, Sicily, and Reggio, whether in organzin or in tram, are all ordinary silks; but they are useful, and even necessary for brocades, for embroidery, and for all works that require strong silk. History of the Settlements and Trade of the Europeans in the East and West Indies, 1798 ~~~ Tram Silk is considered in London as *thrown* Silk, but *not* as *organzine thrown Silk*. This article is prohibited. Practice of the Customs, 1812 ~~~ *Tram silk,* called in French *la trame,* or *soie de trame,* which means *woof silk,* is the thickest of the three, and is the thread of which is made the woof of silk stuffs. It seems that the English have preferred retaining the French name to translating it. *Report of the Committee on Agriculture on the Growth and Manufacture of Silk,* May 24, 1830 ~~~ Tram is formed by twisting together, but not very closely, two or more threads of raw silk, and usually constitutes the weft or shoot of manufactured goods. Treatise on ... Silk Manufacture, 1832 [see also *raw silk*]

transparent dress – Both travellers and the French Journalists agree in depicting the city of Paris profligate and dissipated in the extreme. The Ladies have revived the transparent, Lacedemonian dress, because, in their expressive phrase, "it *marks* and identifies the shape." Madame Tallien lately appeared at a concert in the dress of a Roman lady; but not, the Journalist remarks, like one of those matrons, whose principal attire was their native modesty. At balls the ladies wear silk pantaloons to which the antient sock is appended with diamonds glittering on the toes. In dancing they must have realized the description of the poet, and "Glance their many twinkling feet." Spirit of the Farmers' Museum, 1801 ~~~ on the fashionable promenades in Hyde Park and Kensington Gardens for the last few Sundays, ... The under dresses were generally of white or coloured muslins, with trains extremely long, and not a few beautiful and elegant figures were attired in dresses of cloud coloured crape or transparent muslin, whose filmy texture changing in tint and shade from the ever-varying folds of this gossamer drapery, seemed to wrap the elegant wearers in robes of light impalpable *ether,* and impress the gazing throng rather with the idea of *celestial* than of *earthly* beings. *La Belle Assemblée*, June 1806 ~~~ Princess Charlotte of Wales' Wedding Dress ... The wedding dress is a slip of white and silver atlas, worn under a dress of transparent silk net elegantly embroidered is silver lama, *Niles' Weekly Register*, June 22, 1816 ~~~ Transparent dresses are much in vogue, and are of bright colours over white: those of amber and bright jonquil are most in favour. *La Belle Assemblée*, October 1826 ~~~ We may now consider the texture of dress. Fineness and thinness are of course generally preferable to their reverse. Their roughness or smoothness admits of some observation. In general, fine surfaces which are somewhat rough, form a good contrast with the smoothness of the skin, as in velvet, crape, lace, &c. The opacity or transparency of materials also deserves consideration. With regard to the figure in general, an opaque dress is better suited to an *en-bon-point* figure; and a transparent dress to a thin one. With regard to the face in particular, transparency of the dress which comes in contact with it, is in general preferable. Rough and transparent crape has a better effect upon it than smooth and opaque cambric. *Ladies' Museum*, February 1829 ~~~ For dinner parties or *petites soirées* nothing is more elegant than a robe of *mousseline de soie*, cashmere muslin, or any other transparent material, *Court Journal*, May 11, 1833 ~~~ [court dress] A transparent dress over white satin; blue satin train, trimmed with tulle. *Court Journal*, June 22, 1833 ~~~ The most approved ball dresses are robes of *tulle*, trimmed with flowers and ribbons; or of *crape blonde*, worked like *tulle*. All these transparent dresses should be worn over slips of the richest white satin. *Court Journal*, January 17, 1835 ~~~ The excessive heat of the weather renders dresses of light and transparent texture universal. For morning, white and printed muslins are much worn. White open robes of book or mull muslin are made with broad hems at the bottom and up the fronts. *Court Journal*, August 22, 1835

transparent – I have seen two or three hats ornamented with what our *plumassiers* call transparent feathers; I think them frightful; they remind me of an ostrich moulting; very large leaves where the fibres are all discovered, can alone give you an idea of these feathers. ... Dress hats of rose-coloured crape are much in favour at dinner parties, ornamented with transparent feathers if worn at a dinner of ceremony. *La Belle Assemblée*, January 1820

transparent hat – [in hats, "transparent" often means "unlined" thin fabric] ... [walking dress] The Spanish scarf, and Chili girdle, together with simple scarfs of coloured Italian crape, twisted fancifully round the figure, and worn with small transparent bonnets of the same, are all articles which rank high amidst a fashionable selection. *La Belle Assemblée*, August 1807 ~~~ The most fashionable for the carriage, or dress promenade, are either wholly or partly transparent; the first are composed of either net or gauze; the shape is formed by satin welts; the others have a satin or *gros de Naples* crown, with a transparent brim; they are finished at the edge by blond, and always adorned with flowers. *Ladies' Monthly Museum*, July 1819 ~~~ The few hats that are made in crape or gauze are in general transparent: sometimes, however, these materials are laid over silk; *Repository of Arts*, August 1820 ~~~ Small dress caps of blond, with various flowers, are much worn by married ladies at the theatres; and these often wear transparent dress hats of white crape or stiffened net. *Lady's Magazine*, October 1825 ~~~ We may now make a few remarks on some of the particular forms of female attire, beginning with that of the head. The veil must be noticed first. It is the most elegant of all. Its loose and easy folds are at once beautiful in themselves, and form a fine contrast with the contour of the countenance. Its shade, moreover, at once heightens the beholder's interest, and, by concealing all the asperities of the face, gives it that smoothness and polish which are essential to a high degree of beauty. To this the transparent bonnets which have prevailed so much of late, more or less approach. ... We now arrive at an important point in female costume – the lining of bonnets which reflect their colour on the face, or transparent bonnets which transmit that colour, and equally tinge it. In both these cases, the colour should no longer be that which is placed around the face, and acts on it by contrast, but the opposite. As green around the face would heighten a faint red in the cheeks by contrast, so the pink lining of the bonnet would aid it by reflection. *Ladies' Museum*, February 1829

transparent satin – An exquisite material, called transparent satin, has been lately invented at Paris, which must be much worn when known. *Lady's Magazine*, October 1830 ~~~ Some of the most elegant of the latter [turbans] are of transparent satin, *Casket*, July 1832 ~~~ The new ribands for bonnets and evening dress hats are of transparent satin, or else of foulard, *Court Magazine*, December 1834

trellis – trellis, *buckram* [in: A Mercantile Vocabulary of the French] Commercial Letters, 1794 ~~~ Terliz, *m. ticken for beds*; *trellis*. First Dictionary of Two Languages, 1811 ~~~ Buckram, a kind of cloth stiffened with gum; but formerly called *trellis* from its lattice-like texture; Etymons of English Words, 1826 ~~~ Flax and hemp ... trellis, ... Ticking and Trellis. See Flax Manufacture. Ship-Master's

Assistant, 1826

trianon – Several new materials for robes have already appeared, one of the most elegant for the promenade, and even for *demi toilette* is *satin trianon*. The patterns are something like those of the Indian foulards, but it is more brilliant, and will fall much more gracefully in drapery. *Court Magazine*, October 1833 ~~~ the most admired materials for dresses which have just appeared in Paris. *Reps Trianon*: – A beautiful article adapted to full dress. It consists of white satin foliage on a ground of dark reps. *Court Journal*, October 17, 1835

tricot – Tricoter, *v.a. to knit; weave (lace)* Boyer's Royal Dictionary, 1802 ~~~ [France] In the middling class of woollens, which compromises the tricots and small stuffs, we have a marked inferiority [to England]. The wools of which these are made are with us less fine, less brilliant, and higher priced. But this evil is not without a remedy. System of Geography, 1807 ~~~ [Patent] To Messrs. Pouillot, Fayolle, and Hullin, of Paris, for five years, for a machine for making the lace, called *tricot de Berlin, toile d'araignée, oeil de perdrix. Monthly Magazine*, November 1809 ~~~ Tricot, a small town in the north of France, department of the Oise, with 1200 inhabitants. Here are manufactures of woollen stuffs, and various knitted articles, in very general use in France, and called from this place Tricots. Edinburgh Gazetteer, 1822 ~~~ Fancy Silk Net or Tricot, Public General Acts, 1823 ~~~ Wool, viz. … cassimeres, rateen, worsted-tricot, and half-cloth, Ship-Master's Assistant, 1826 ~~~ At the ball at the *Hotel de Ville* … Several ladies appeared in long gloves of open *tricot de soie*, either white or black. *Court Journal*, August 31, 1833 [see also *arachne* and *net*]

triple satin – London Evening Dress. – The robe is a pale straw-coloured satin, of that rich kind called triple satin. *Ladies' Pocket*, January 1836 ~~~ [mantles] We have seen some lined and bordered with sable; others, and the latter are more numerous, of black velvet, or that very rich material *triple satin*, lined with rose, emerald green, or Swedish blue gros de Naples, *Court Magazine*, February 1836

tropic bird – Walking dress. … Mary Scot bonnet of garter purple *reps* silk, ornamented at the edge with a cordon of purple and black flowers, and surmounted by a full plume of tropic birds' feathers, variegated in black and purple. … a dress hat … of white satin, ornamented with the feathers of the tropic bird, a new and *unique* article of taste and value. *La Belle Assemblée*, October 1818

tuffelus – [Paris] Silks are the only materials for promenade robes and *redingotes*; … Furry tuffelus, striped, plaided, and plain, figured, quadrilled, *gros de Naples*, and *pou de soie* of different kinds, seem all equal in favour. *Court Magazine*, May 1835

tuft – A number of threads or ribbands, flowery leaves, or any small bodies joined together; a cluster, a clump. Sheridan's English Dictionary, 1797 ~~~ 'the Pomeranian mantle,' was formed of pea green gauze, cut in irregular pointed drapery, and trimmed with a silver tufted fringe; it was worn over a Gossamer satin under dress, *La Belle Assemblée*, July 1807 ~~~ Tuft, … *Velouté, peluché*, Chambaud's French Dictionary, 1815 ~~~ [Paris] yesterday she appeared in a *chapeau* of tufted gauze over white satin; *Repository of Arts*, August 1821 ~~~ Close morning bonnets of dark-coloured satin, surrounded by a *fichu* of blonde quilling or tufted silk, are often seen in walking costume. *Lady's Magazine*, December 31, 1830

tul Danae – [see *Danae*]

tull sylphide – [see *sylphide*]

tulle – Parisian Fashions. … A *tulle* is still employed in ornamenting robes and hats. *Monthly Mirror*, August 1802 ~~~ A Morning high Dress of Cambric Muslin. Train moderately long; robe flowing from the shoulder, lace collar, trimmed with *tulle*, … A Morning cap of white lace trimmed with *tulle*, *La Belle Assemblée*, April 1806 ~~~ The French have lately manufactured a trimming which they call *tulle*, and we believe it is the same which we call patent lace, but of a much finer and more valuable texture. This *tulle* is not made on a cushion, according to the tedious process of lace-making; but on a machine, in the same manner as our British lace; and we rather imagine that our idea of making patent lace was taken from it; for the Sieur Genton produced the first specimens of this invention thirty years ago. In 1791, a brevet of invention (similar to our patents), was given to Monsieurs Jolivet and Cochet, of Lyons, for the fabrication of *tulle. La Belle Assemblée*, March 1811 ~~~ a plaiting of *tulle*, (letting-in lace,) *La Belle Assemblée*, July 1814 ~~~ Full Dress. A celestial blue crape frock, over a white satin slip, ornamented round the bottom with a deep border of tull or net lace, *Repository of Arts*, January 1815 ~~~ The attention of the wealthy *elegante* will be well repaid when given to the dress she has just completed, named the Saxe-Cobourg robe; ... a tucker is worn with this dress, the most *unique* and elegant; it is formed of *tulle,* or Parisian patent net, partially exposing the bust in front, from each side of which depend two points finished by tassels of gold. *La Belle Assemblée*, February 1816 ~~~ Thule, see Tulle. ... Tulle de Berline, Tulle de Flandre, (Thread Lace Gowns) ... Tulle, or Tull Lace, narrow, or even if in pieces quite wide (French) Black, White, Plain, Worked, Embroidered or Stamped. Commercial Directory, 1823 ~~~ Tulle, or any other article fairly coming under the denomination of *lace,* whether wove on the loom, or manufactured by the hand, and whether made of *silk, cotton or thread,* or a mixture of these different materials, is considered as coming under the general classification of "*all other laces,*" and entitled to an entry at 12 ½ per cent,, but when made up into gowns or dresses, then they are to pay an ad valorem duty of 30 per cent. *Public Documents*, December 1824 ~~~ *Tulle* and different kinds of silk are worn in full dress. *Tulle* dresses are always worn over silk slips to correspond, and are frequently embroidered; but the embroidery is either in different colors, or if it is in one color only, it contrasts very strongly with that of the dress. The most novel, as well as the most elegant, gowns of this description, are of white *tulle* embroidered in feather-stitch, either in wreaths or bouquets of roses, auriculas, camelias, or fruit blossoms. We have seen also some dresses embroidered in bouquets of lilac, at regular distances, and drooping a little to one side; this last style of trimming is remarkably elegant. *Ladies' Pocket*, July 1830 ~~~ [court dress] A handsome white tulle dress, ornamented with silver tissue, over white satin; *Royal Lady's*, April 1831 ~~~ The French tulle is made in the exact manner termed by the workman single press point net, against which the Luddites, from 1812 to 1816, directed so much of their vengeance, when made of cotton, as being a fraudulent article. History, Gazetteer, and Directory of Nottinghamshire, 1832 ~~~ Plain Silk Lace or Net, called Tulle. ... Note. There are a considerable number of articles which are made in France, but which we should nevertheless prefer getting from England if it were not for the prohibitions and excessive duties. Irish linens are in this latter situation; and as to English tulle, called bobbinet, and cotton twist, we join all those who have any knowledge of the transactions which take place in these articles in deploring bitterly, that in consequence of a system which we will not denominate, these prohibited articles have been for many years clandestinely introduced in immense quantities, instead of having contributed by a duty, established on justice and reason, to the revenue of the Treasury. We are, convinced that this state of things is on the eve of a close, but it is 15 years too late! ... Since 1825-6, the export of tulle (silk net) from France has diminished two-thirds. ... In 1826, 7, 8, and 9, England was by far the largest purchaser of this article, having regularly imported one-third to one-fourth of the whole export. Commercial Relations, 1834 ~~~ The most approved ball dresses are robes of *tulle,* trimmed with flowers and ribbons; or of *crape blonde,* worked like *tulle.* All these transparent dresses should be worn over slips of the richest white satin. *Court Journal,* January 17, 1835 [see also *bobbin-net, single press lace* and *thread net*]

tulle arachne – [see *arachne*]

tulle blond – [see *blond net*]

tulle de Cambray – [see *Cambray* and *chambray gauze*]

tulle de fil – [see thread net]

tulle filet de Vulcain – [see *filet de Vulcain*]

tulle grec, grecque – [see *Grecian net*]

tulle illusion – [see *illusion*]

tulle Lara – [see *Lara*]

Turin – Different kinds of gauze are worn in evening dress, particularly gaze de Chine, and gaze de Turin; the first is of uncommon richness; the other of a lighter description, and much in favour for ball dresses. Both kinds of gauze are striped, spotted, and figured in a great variety of patterns. *Ladies' Museum*, December 1830 ~~~ Ball Dress. A rose-coloured *gaze de Turin* dress, over white *gros de Naples*; ... Some of the newest ball dresses are of *gaze de Turin*, a material which is likely to be much in favour. It is embroidered in a light style: one to the prettiest that we have seen was embroidered in citron and brown, in a small, light pattern; *La Belle Assemblée*, April 1832 … Ball Dress. *Gauze de Turin* is the only novel material, it is worn plain and embroidered; *The Day*, April 5, 1832

turkey feathers – There are some feathers of the swan, and of the white turkey, which cost, at first, about ten *centimes*, or less, but which sell for twenty *francs* each, on account of the miniatures of birds and butterflies, &c., which are placed on them, in the most beautiful colours. *La Belle Assemblée*, August 1828

Turkey gauze – [13 *Geo.* 3. c. 68] Aldermen of the said city of London, … declare the price of work of journeymen weavers working within their said jurisdiction in the said manufacture for making and manufacturing of Turkey Gauze, of the width of 36 inches or under, with one thread in the reed, made with the warp double silk raw, and containing 3000 counts or under, with 96 shoots or less to an inch, at the sum of 9*d.* by the yard; Law and Practice of Summary Convictions, 1814 ~~~ TURKEY GAUZE. This variety of fancy gauze is woven on the same principle, nearly, as crape. In the Turkey gauze, however, there are sometimes three, four, five, and even six threads in one interval of the reed, which are all twisted together in the gauze parts; but when they are spread out in the plain parts, they form a more solid and substantial fabric than can be produced on crape. Turkey gauze has a very beautiful appearance when woven on silk: for the natural elasticity of this substance allows it to expand, and fill the interstices of the plain parts, while it is easily compressed into a fine transparent fabric by the gauze twist. Cotton yarn, however, does not possess this property in such a high degree as silk; and therefore, the attempts which have been made to introduce it into the cotton manufacture, has not been attended with that success which was to be desired. Art of Weaving, 1831 ~~~ [1756-1760] what they call Turkey gauze, that looks like sarcenet: Life of Robert Lord Clive, 1836

turkey red – [a color and a dye, and occassionally the fabric so dyed] … Cotton-yarn bleached by your process takes, very advantageously, the red dye called the Turkey red; Repertory of Patent Inventions, 1795 ~~~ *Turkey-red*, &c. – The beautiful and permanent colour termed Turkey, or Adrianople red, is the most expensive and difficult to be given of all the cotton dyes. General Report of the Agricultural State … of Scotland, 1814 ~~~ The Turkey or Adrianople red has been long admired on account of its brightness, beauty, and durability; but it is communicated by a tedious and complicated process. This colour, the beauty of which is ascribed to the superior quality of the madder produced in a more genial climate, is so permanent that it resists the action of aquafortis for nearly an hour without any perceptible change. Elements of Chemistry, 1820 ~~~ Turkey red chintz *Asiatic Journal*, February 1832 ~~~. 4 pieces Turkey red, 135 yards – 50 [cents, total $] 67.50 [letter dated October 27, 1832] Emigration of Indians, 1835

Turkish brocade – [court dress] A Turkish gold brocade dress, embroidered in columns and ornamented with blonde; corsage of gold, with blonde mantilla, and sabots to correspond. *Royal Lady's*, June 1831 ~~~ [court dress] White and gold Turkish brocade dress; rich green velvet, trimmed with blonde and filets en or; *Lady's Magazine and Museum*, June 1836

Turkish satin – Rate of Scavage. … Turkey Satin, the doz. yards 1d. Ship-Master's Assistant, 1795 ~~~ Roubaix, a considerable town in the north-east of France, … has considerable manufactures of woollens, Turkish satins, camelots, Edinburgh Gazetteer, 1822 ~~~ [ad] A. S. And Co. are likewise selling the remainder of their stupendous and splendid collection of Winter Articles, at such reduced prices as never before were submitted to purchasers. … the most elegant Ducape and Satin Turc ditto [cloaks], 70s. and 80s.; *Examiner*, February 5, 1826 ~~~ [ad] A. Shears & Co. beg to apprize the Nobility, Gentry and the Public … the much admired Gros des Indes and Satin Turc, so justly celebrated for their warmth, are greatly in demand for Winter Pelisses; *Examiner*, November 19, 1826 ~~~ Evening Dress. Dress of white *crepe lisse*, over a lavender-colour Turkish satin-slip; *Ariel*, May 5, 1827 ~~~ A second novelty is a mantle intended for the Opera, or dress parties. It is composed of *satin turc*; the colour *bleu Adelaide,* a rich silk ground with broad satin stripes, on which are figured very light wreaths of foliage in white. *La Belle Assemblée*, April 1831 ~~~ [ad] Turc Satins, *New England Farmer*, April 27, 1831 ~~~ [court dress] A dress of pink satin Turc à l'Espagnolle: train of black satin; black lace Spanish mantilla. *Court Journal*, June 1, 1833 ~~~ [ad] Heavy Blk Turk Satins (4-4 in width) 6s. 5 [per yard] *New England Farmer*, March 25, 1835

Turkish satin leather – Half-boots are now again very general for the promenade; they are dark blue, dark screen, jean color, or black; they are of a fine new kind of morrocco leather, called Turkish satin. *La Belle Assemblée*, May 1823 ~~~ In out-door costume … The half-boots are of turkish satin. *Ladies' Monthly Museum*, June 1828 [see also *morocco*]

Turkish silk – The Queen. As usual on her own Birth-day, was not so splendidly dresses as on that of his Majesty. Her dress was composed of British point, interspersed with gold Turkish tissue. *National Register*, January 24, 1808 ~~~ Princess Augusta. – Petticoat of amber-color tissue, … a mantle of Turkish silk, a late present from the Ottoman court to his majesty. This dress was peculiarly beautiful. *Lady's Magazine*, June 1809 ~~~ [court dress] train of Turkish material, tissued in gold and green silk; *Royal Lady's*, May 1831

Turkish velvet – Dresses of Turkish velvet are now in high repute for evening parties: they are made without plaits round the shape, the thickness of the stuff not admitting them. *Ladies' Monthly Museum*, February 1828 ~~~ *Satins Imperial à la Reines* and *Perline*, may be classed among the richest materials for half-dress; for which also I may cite some new kinds of rich silks under the names of *Velours turc*, *Huguenots* and Indostan. *New Monthly Belle Assemblée*, November 1836

turquoises – *Manufactures of Picardy*. … Serges, minorques, turquoises, &. Voyages and Travels, 1809 ~~~ The greater part of these cloths bear the names of the various places in which they are fabricated; but these distinctions in regard to names operate in a very small degree with respect to the qualities of the articles. In the second class are comprised camlets of different descriptions, bolting-cloths, baizes, kerseys, serges of Aumale, Blicomt, &c. callimancoes, turquoises, knaps, silesias, malboroughs, &c. Dictionary of Commerce, 1819 ~~~ we shall make three classes: first, fine cloths, second, light fine cloths; third, coarse stuffs. … The second will contain the cassimeres, the royal cloths, silesias, fine ratteens, camlets, striped flannels, serges, (*les *prunelles* and *turquoises),* wollens in imitation of crape, &c. &c.. … * Some of the technical words, names of manufactured cloths, cannot be translated by the help of Boyer's Dictionary. *Tr.* [translator] *Analectic Magazine*, May 1820

Tuscan – Our attention has lately been attracted by the novelty of a bonnet, manufactured in this country, from grass imported from Italy, which, combining durability with much elegance, is likely to become a favourite in the fashionable world. In addition to its beautiful appearance, the Tuscan grass bonnet has also a powerful claim to the patronage of the ladies, from the circumstance of its giving employment to many thousands of British manufacturers who are principally females. *La Belle Assemblée*, May 1827 ~~~ The new Tuscan grass bonnets, and the coarse straw and Dunstable, so much the present rage, all yield to the superiority of those of gros-de-Naples; *Ladies' Monthly Museum*, July 1828 ~~~Tuscan bonnets – why they are so called we know not, since they are made of English straw – are partially worn as morning bonnets. *La Belle Assemblée*, May 1831 ~~~ within the last ten years large quantities of Italian straw, said to be both of corn and grass, have been imported, and worked up into what are called Tuscan plat. *Saturday Magazine*, January 26, 1833 ~~~ A straw factory near Boston yet employs between 150 and 200 persons, chiefly females in weaving straw, by hand looms, &c. after the manner of what is called the *Tuscany*, as imported from the Mediterranean. We hope that a knowledge of the fact that the chief part of the *Tuscany bonnets* used in the United States are made in New England, will not render them less fashionable than they have been; but the much *reduced price* has already caused this beautiful manufacture to be rejected by some, who will not wear any thing that is common. *Niles' Weekly Register*, May 17, 1834 ~~~ TUSCAN HATS. The beauty, durability, and above all, the fashion of ladies' Tuscan hats, have introduced them into this country, and, it is probable, they will continue to be an important and profitable branch of the silk manufacture. These hats are made of a fabric the warp of which is silk, and the woof Tuscan straw. This straw is the product of a variety of beardless wheat, bleached by the sterility of the soil on which it grows, it is cultivated on the unmanured calcareous soil in Tuscany, sowed thick, and harvested before it is quite ripe. … At the silk factory in Hartford, Connecticut, this article is manufactured in large quantities. About one hundred young ladies are constantly engaged upon it, occupying as many looms. It requires some little time for a young lady to acquire the art of weaving skilfully and dexterously, but when acquired she will weave twenty yards a day, for which she is paid from three to seven cents a yard, and receiving for her week's work, from $3 to $5. The young ladies in the factory are in fine health, and manifestly enjoying a buoyance and elasticity of spirits to which less industrious females are strangers. The factory turns out weekly about 6,000 yards of this article, which is sold as fast as manufactured, at an average price of 20 cents a yard. *Niles' Weekly Register*, December 5, 1835 [see also *Leghorn* and *Italian straw*]

Tussah – coarse silks, spun by the wild tussah <u>Transactions of the Society</u>, 1805 ~~~ The Tusseh silk, which is coarse and very durable, is produced by a phalæna call paphia by Linnæus. It is a native of Bengal, Bahar, Assam, &c. and feeds on the leaves of rhamnus jujuba *Monthly Magazine*, July 1805 ~~~ There are two other kinds of worms which produce silk in Bengal, *viz.* the Tusseh and Arrindy worms: the former are found in such abundance over many parts of Bengal, and the adjoining provinces, as to have afforded to the natives, from time immemorial, a considerable supply of a most durable, coarse, dark-coloured silk, commonly called Tusseh silk, which is woven into a kind of cloth called Tusseh dooties, much worn by Bramins, and other sects of Hindoos. This substance would, no doubt, be highly useful to the inhabitants of many parts of America, and the south of Europe, where a cheap, light, cool, durable dress, such as this silk makes, is much wanted. This species cannot be domesticated. <u>Oriental Commerce</u>, 1813 ~~~ A coarse kind of silk, known by the name of *tussar*, is produced there [Currucdea, India] in large quantities. <u>Sketches of Indian Field Sports</u>, 1827

tweed – [ad for men's] Tweed Travelling Trousers . . 16s. *Alexander's East India and Colonial Magazine*, December 1835 ~~~ [ad] Cloth and Tweed Fishing or Travelling Trousers, 13s. 6d. per pair. *Musical World*, September 2, 1836

tweel – [see *twill*]

twill – *The clothing given yearly to the children* [in the charity school] *is as follows*: … Girls. A grey linen shift, with white linen sleeves, a linsey-woolsey petticoat, an olive coloured twilled cotton gown, a check apron. <u>Reports … for Promoting the Comforts of the Poor</u>, 1800 ~~~Tweeling is, in many instances, applied to the weaving of cloths which require a great portion of strength, thickness, and durability. For instance, in the linen manufacture, every description of bed and table linen, is generally tweeled; sometimes with ornaments, and sometimes without them. In the silk, tweeling is very common. Sometimes it is employed for the sake of strength, but, more frequently, for the display of colour. In the woollen, strength is the general object; and in the cotton, it is most commonly the same. It may be necessary in this place, to inquire shortly into the causes which render tweeled cloths stronger than plain, and to ascertain the difference. In so far as the strength of tweeled cloths depends solely on the mode of weaving, that strength will be rather diminished than increased, when compared with plain cloth, containing an equal quantity of similar materials. For, in the texture of plain cloth, every thread is constantly interwoven; whilst in that of tweels, they are only interwoven at intervals. Now, in the latter case, the threads can derive no mutual support from each other, except at the intervals where they are interwoven; and that part of them which is flushed, must depend entirely on the strength of the individual threads; those of the warp being flushed upon one side, and those of the weft upon the other. <u>Art of Weaving</u>, 1807 ~~~ In the morning costume … Shot and figured twill sarsnets remain high in fashionable estimation. *Weekly Entertainer*, October 9, 1809 ~~~ Twilled silks are no longer even candidates for approbation, it is so generally allowed that they cast a shade over the complexion which make them extremely unbecoming. *La Belle Assemblée*, April 1811 ~~~ *Pullicates, Ginghams, and Tweels* are very dull, and the number of hands employed in their manufacture are reducing daily. *Weavers' Magazine*, April 1819 ~~~ There is another mode of throwing the woof, not over every thread of the warp, but suffering two, three, or many more threads of the warp to lie on the face of the fabric, and shooting the woof under them, except every second, third, &c. which comes over, to bind it down. Cloth thus woven are said to be tweeled or twilled. <u>Scenes of British Wealth</u>, 1825 ~~~ Merino dresses for home costume are very much in favor; though the fine double merino is certainly expensive, yet we would advise the purchasing of this beautiful article, which appears like a very fine and light cloth, not discovering the twill, which, in the other merinos, always imparts the idea of a stuff gown; *Ladies' Pocket*, December 1829 ~~~ Next to plain texture, tweeling is the most extensive in its application to every branch of the cloth manufacture: it not only serves as a ground on which other decorations are woven, but it forms, purely on its own principles, some of the most beautiful patterns which can be produced in the art of weaving. The number of tweels, which may be woven by varying the succession of the draught, plan of cording, or order of treading, is very extensive; but they may, for the sake of distinction, be treated of under the following heads, namely, biassed or regular tweels, broken or satin tweels, and fancy tweels. ... Damask, like the diaper, is merely a branch of fancy tweeling; or rather, it is the principle of diaper weaving conducted on a more extensive scale by means of the draw loom. Damask patterns, therefore, are formed on the cloth merely by reversing the tweel, Treatise on the Art of Weaving, 1831 ~~~ Twilled fabrics are thicker than plain ones when of the same fineness, and more flexable when of the same thickness. They are also more susceptible of ornamental variations. Jeans, dimoties, serges, &c., are specimens of this kind of texture. Encyclopædia Americana, 1833 ~~~ Morning Dress. Pelisse robe of green twilled satin. *Court Magazine*, December 1834 ~~~ In weaving *tweeled*, or *twilled, fabrics,* the woof, instead of passing over every second thread of the warp, is shot over two, three, or more threads at a time, so as to leave a kind of figured surface on the cloth. Scenes of Commerce, 1836

twin ribbons – Broad ribbons of two colours, sewn together, continue to be worn: they are called twin ribbons; *La Belle Assemblée,* June 1827

twine cloth – *Specification of the Patent granted to* John Millard, *of Cheapside, in the City of London, Linen Draper; for a Method of manufacturing Cotton-Wool free from Mixture into Cloth, for the Purpose of regulating Perspiration.* Dated July 14, 1813. To all to whom these presents shall come, &c. Now know ye, that in compliance with the said proviso, I the said John Millard do hereby declare that the manner or method of manufacturing my cotton twine cloth, for regulating the perspiration and prevention of taking cold, is as follows: That the purest and choicest cotton wool, of East India or Brazil growth, be selected, prepared, and spun, *Repertory of Arts,* March 1814 ~~~ No. 2 is a specimen of the new patent twine cloth, for sheeting, yard and half wide; possessing those rarely united qualities of great delicacy, economy, and conduciveness to health. It is equal in appearance to the fine Holland, yet without the chilly properties of the latter, whilst it is obtained at one half the expense. The mathematical principle on which it is manufactured, renders it at once durable and delicate. *Repository of Arts,* November 1813 ~~~ [ad] The new PATENT TWINE CLOTH, brought out by the House of Millard last year, for the purpose of Sheeting, and for Shirting, obtains universal notice; several Families of distinction having *experienced their benefit* as well as economy, have given it their unqualified approbation; there being not a doubt but they are a great promoter of health, not only to the most delicate constitution, but also to that of the robust. *Repository of Arts,* February 1814 ~~~ [ad] MILLARD'S Imperial Patent Twine CLOTH for SHIRTING. Patronized by both the late and present Governors-General of India, and which is found to be not only the cheapest, but most conducive to health to wear in the West and East Indies, as well as in this and the colder Climates.--- J. Millard very respectfully informs Merchants and Families, the sale of the above Cloth is removed from Cheapside to his East India and French Establishment, in the Quadrant, No. 99, where alone it can be obtained genuine, stamped with his name, number of the Warehouse, &c. by the Piece of 26 to 32 Yards each, in the various numbers, commencing at 18*d.* per yard. Edinburgh Review, 1827

twist – Dress cloaks are generally made of white satin, with the hood embellished by semi-circular folds, relieved by a splendid intermixture of gold twist. *Lady's Magazine,* December 1800 ~~~ The staple trade of the town [of Macclesfield] is that of wrought buttons in silk, mohair, and twist. The use of them may be traced nearly two hundred years backwards: they were once curiously wrought with the needle, and used in the decoration of full trimmed suits. Macclesfield was always considered as the center of this trade; and mills were erected long ago, both here and at Stockport, for winding silk, and making twist, and trimming, suitable to the buttons. Beauties of England and Wales, 1801 ~~~ [court dresses] A puce velvet petticoat, embroidered round the bottom with twist and spangles, ... Petticoat of fawn-coloured satin, covered by a crape one of the same colour, ... train of fawn-coloured twist, with a rich border, the same as the petticoat. *La Belle Assemblée,* January 1807 ~~~ [1807 clothing for the troops] The twist, cord, lace, arid trimmings, with every other mark, distinguishing the different ranks on the musters, to be carefully observed by the contractor; and the clothing to be prepared, in every respect, equal in size, and the materials to be equal in quality to the musters. Asiatic Annual

Register, 1809 ~~~ [Pairs spencers] the front adorned with numerous rows of buttons intermixed with silk twist. *Ladies' Monthly Museum*, November 1817 ~~~ [Paris] Silk *pluche* hats are ornamented sometimes with ostrich, sometimes with down, feathers; they are lined in general with satin, and finished round the edge of the brim with the same material twisted: the short down feather edging, which formerly used to trim the brims of bonnets, is sometimes mingled with this twist; it has a bad effect; you see the little bits of feathers peeping out here and there in an irregular manner, which gives the hat the appearance of not being properly trimmed. *Repository of Arts*, January 1819 ~~~ Silk twist is spun in the same manner [as sewing silk], except that it is always of three cords. Growth and Manufacture of Silk, 1828 ~~~ [Parisian ball dress] *Cordeliére* of silver twist *a gros grains. Repository of Fashions*, April 1829 ~~~ The name of *sewing silk* is exclusively appropriated, in France, to the finest of these two species; the other is called *cordonnet* or *twist*. The sewing silk, so called, is employed in the sewing of silken stuffs; the *cordonnet* is used for working button-holes, and sewing woollen and cotton stuffs. The one is for the use of *tailors,* the other for that of *milliners* and *mantuamakers*. Tailors employ it only in their more delicate works. Essays on American Silk, 1830 ~~~ [Paris walking dress] The top of the redingote is trimmed with twist, *Casket*, January 1831 ~~~ *Uniforms ... of the General Staff. The coat* – Single breasted, with ten buttons, and button holes worked with blue twist in front, five inches long at the top and three at the bottom, American State Papers, 1834 [see also *gimp* and *sewing silk*; for straw-related twist, see *straw*]

twist lace – [May 20, 1812] The particular points I wish now to state, are the nature of the Twist Lace, which is new invented, made by a machine, and Fleecy Hosiery. With respect to twist lace, it has been the unwearied application of a number of the most ingenious mechanics in Nottinghamshire to make this twist lace, and hitherto it is thought to be almost an impossibility. All the sorts of lace made by a machine are looped, this is twisted, but still this lace, though equal in every respect to that made by hand, is liable to be mistaken for two-course hole warp or single press; the reason is, because all lace made with a machine, when sold in breadths, is cut, therefore all cut lace is supposed by the consumers to be bad, as they cannot distinguish the twist lace from two-course hole or single press, all being cut alike. Reports from the Committees, 1812 ~~~ [in a lawsuit over the 1811 patent for] the manufacture of bobbin lace, or twist-net, (which is another phrase by which the commodity is described), similar to, and resembling the Buckinghamshire lace-net, and French lace-net, as made by the hand with pillows. In Buckinghamshire the women make this species of lace called bobbin lace, or twisted net, by the hand, upon the pillows; and the object of this machine is to make that through the medium of machinery which by them is made by the hand: the benefit derived from it is expedition; it also makes it much more perfect and better; but whether it makes it better than that made by hand would be no question in this cause, because the patent is for a machine, of the particular description specified, to produce the commodity which formerly was produced by hand. A Collection of the Most Important Cases Respecting Patents of Invention, 1816 [see *bobbin-net, French net* and *Nottingham*]

twisted fringe – *Dresses of the French Constituted Authorities. ...* Staff of the Army. 1. General and Commander in Chief. Blue coat, ... a scarf, by was of a girdle, across the middle, of white and red, ending in a fringe of twisted gold. *Monthly Magazine*, June 1797 ~~~ Epaulets, fine gold, with twisted fringe, [$]4 00 per pair. – false gold, 1 00. – plain, 1 60... fine silver, with twisted fringe, 2 40 Commercial Regulations, 1819 ~~~ Twisted fringe is a favourite trimming on dresses of *gros de Naples*: it is simple, and well adapted to half dress. *La Belle Assemblée*, February 1829 ~~~ pelisses of this kind [gros de Chine] are trimmed with twisted fringe, shaded in various colors, to correspond with the Cachemire patterns, with which the ground of the dress is figured. *Ladies' Pocket*, November 1829 ~~~ Sword knots, gold, and with twisted fringe, $1 00 each. American State Papers, 1834

Tyrolienne – Boas begin to give place to scarfs, they are of China crapes with *tissu de Cachemire*, and *tissu Tyrolienne*; these last resemble grenadine gauze in richness, softness, and brilliancy, but they are thicker. ... A new fancy silk called *Tyrolienne*, is coming much into request for hats and bonnets; *La Belle Assemblée*, May 1832 ~~~ Light materials, as *gaze Tyrolienne* and clear muslin, are adopted in evening dress; the first is a half transparent material of silk and wool printed in *chaly* patterns, *Atheneum*, December 1832

Umbrella cloth - Urling's lace

umbrella cloth – Umbrella cloth is dyed green, blue, &c. prepared with wax, and made into umbrellas, window blinds, hat covers, &c. but is now much disused, on account of cotton and silk being used for that purpose. Linen Manufacturer, 1817 ~~~ Edinburgh, ... *Umbrella Cloth*, a considerable quantity of which is manufactured here, has been reduced one shilling the piece in the weaving price. *Weavers' Magazine*, March 1819 ~~~ *Umbrella Cloth* has again been reduced in the weaving price, *Weavers' Magazine*, April 1819 ~~~ Perth, June 30th, 1819. Trade is in a miserable situation here. ... Cosaes, Cambrics and Umbrella Cloth have been reduced in a most unprecedented manner. The most of the Weavers are as yet employed, but our prospects are getting daily worse. *Weavers' Magazine*, June 1819 ~~~ The extensive County of Perth, ... where Silk is also converted into Umbrella Cloth, and more expensive Fabricks; Enumeration Abstract, 1833 ~~~ [August 7, 1833] What did the weavers get eight or nine years ago at Perth? – They were not much better eight or nine years ago than they are just now. I have wrought at umbrella cloth at different periods; in 1806 I wrought a piece per week, which came to 25*s.* 4*d.* ... Could a man make one piece in a week? – Yes; one piece was just my work in a week. ... What length was the piece? – Twenty-four yards and a quarter. About the end of the year 1811 it fell to 17*s.*; in 1817 I wrought the same work at 12*s.*; in 1828 it was 8*s.* 6*d.*; and there was another kind that was 7*s.* 11*d.* Now I have just wrought two harness webs since I left umbrella work, and they are of the same price now that they were in 1828, that is 8*s.* 6*d.* Reports and Papers of the House of Commons, 1836

Union drill – [see *drill*]

urban fleuri – Ceinture with long ends fastened in front of urban fleuri, a rich flowered ribbon. *Lady's Magazine and Museum*, August 1834

Urling's lace – From its intrinsic merits, it met with the most distinguished personal encouragement from her late Majesty, who, on the 23d July, 1817, affixed her royal signature to a special warrant, entering us as Lace-Manufacturers to her Majesty upon the list of the household: ... we presume now to inclose you specimens of our PATENT THREAD, of which our Lace is fabricated, for comparison with the rough and fibrous Cotton Thread used in manufacturing every other description of British Lace; and to state, that we have OPENED the House as below for the RETAIL Disposal of our Manufacture, of which we have a most elegant and extensive Assortment, comprising *Figured and Plain Nets, Quillings, Dresses, Scarfs, Veil, Handkerchiefs, Laces, Honiton Flowers, Brussels Sprigs*, and every other description of Lace whatsoever. ... its exquisite clearness and transparency, its beautiful color and durability (all of which it retains after repeated washing), *Repository of Arts*, November 1819 ~~~ Urling's patent lace, which for it lightness, durability, and elegance forms a valuable article of fashion: a specimen of this lace, with its thread, was given in our last Number. *La Belle Assemblée*, January 1820 ~~~ Evening Dress. A low dress, composed of Urlings' lace, figured in a leaf pattern: it is worn over a white satin slip; *Atheneum*, July 1820 ~~~ [ad] one Urling lace veil, 15*s.*; *Colonial Times*, March 3, 1826 ~~~ Among the English Laces, Urling's Lace-Net has, latterly, obtained the greatest celebrity, for the beauty of its patterns, and its cheapness. It is made by means of machinery, and the Net is cleared from all its loose fibrous parts by being passed over the flame of gas. It is applied to all the purposes of other Laces, as well as to veils and dresses. All the plain Net which is now to be had, for embroidering and other ornamental purposes, is of this kind. Young Lady's Book, 1829... [court dress] A rich Urling's lace dress, with a handsome flounce, headed by a silver fringe, *Royal Lady's*, May 1831 ~~~ [December 8, 1830] Have you any employment in your parish for the women and children? We had, very recently, lace-making for the children, to a great extent. Does that continue? It is very nearly stopped; it must stop. Urling's lace takes away all the profit. Poor Laws, 1831

Valencia - Vulture

valencia – Both, valentias and toilenettes, are composed of wool and cotton, and in some there is a small mixture of silk, *Niles' Weekly Register*, May 15, 1819 ~~~ [ad] MARSEILLES AND VALENCIA VESTINGS. 2 cases of the latest London fashions, comprising a beautiful assortment of entire new figures, superior to any hitherto imported both in point of fabric, and richness and brilliancy of colours – plain white and buff do. – rich striped do. &c. … Vests. Rich Figured Valencia, Do. [ditto rich] Plaid do. [ditto Valencia] Do. Striped do. Do. Super. White, Buff and Black. Boston Annual Advertiser, 1823 ~~~ [men's] For morning waistcoats the casinette and the figured Valentia in a variety of patterns are the most prevailing materials. *Casket*, January 1831 ~~~ [Huddersfield, York] The silk valentias, now so commonly exposed in the shops of the drapers throughout the kingdom, are the produce of this neighbourhood, and, for beauty of design and texture, possess superior merit. An immense quantity of these articles is exported to the continent, and their manufacture affords employment to several thousand individuals. Topographical Dictionary of England, 1831 ~~~ Previous to the tariff of 1828 there was a considerable importation of various fancy stuffs used for vest-coats, known by the name of valencias, toilenets, &c, the component materials of which are wool and silk, or worsted and silk. Exposition of the … Tariff System, 1832 ~~~ Valencias, from Manchester to New York. Nominal Width, ¾ yard, octual do. ordinary quality, 24 to 25 inches, fine do. 26 to 27 inches. Length of the piece, 20 to 30 yards. 2 cases Valencia vestings, worsted, or worsted and silk, containing 70 ends, measuring 2100 yds. @ 3s. 3d. § yard. Trade between Great Britain and the United States of America, 1833 ~~~ [ad for men's] Silk Valencia Dress Waistcoats . 10s. *Eminent Foreign Statesmen*, March 1836

Valenciennes lace – Riding-dress of blue cloth. Double plaiting of Valenciennes lace round the neck. *Lady's Magazine*, May 1797 ~~~ The Valenciennes laces are made with bobbins. They are less rich and shewy but more solid than the Mechlin laces, and this advantage alone renders them dearer than the latter. Their extreme fineness, joined to that equality of texture which distinguishes them, forms an appropriate species of beauty; to which we may add their whiteness, in which they excel all others. … An ordinary workwoman usually takes *ten months* to make a pair of real Valenciennes ruffles; the prices for these ruffles are, generally, from £5. to £14. sterling, per pair, Literary Panorama, 1808 ~~~ Her Majesty. – A green and silver tissue, with lace draperies, richly ornamented with diamonds, festoons of Valenciennes lace, and beautiful diamond tassels; *Edinburgh Annual Register*, June 4, 1809 ~~~ Those ladies who chuse to display their throats wear this dress with a small white lace handkerchief put on inside the dress: those who do not, wear a lace shirt, but either way it is extremely tasteful, novel, and becoming. When made in washing silks it is similar, but if in muslin it is indeed a most expensive dishabille, as few ladies content themselves with a letting-in of muslin, and where it is of lace, as is generally the case, the breadth of it, the quantity that is used, and the fine Valenciennes edging which is put on at each side, renders it amazingly expensive; it certainly looks very elegant and striking in muslin when trimmed in this expensive way, but it is not by any means so appropriate to the season as in silk or chintz. *La Belle Assemblée*, October 1814 ~~~ Full Dress. A pink figured satin slip, terminated at the bottom by a full rouleau of *gros de Naples* to correspond, over which is a white lace dress of Urling's manufacture, finished at the bottom by a very full fall of imitation Valenciennes lace, headed by a narrow rouleau of pink figured satin; *Repository of Arts*, December 1820 ~~~ Morning caps are trimmed with a profusion of Valenciennes lace; with this *I* find fault; for though valuable, that lace has a thickness which renders it requisite to be used sparingly near the face; and it is heavy, and unfit for the *trimming* of caps; it should, certainly, be confined to the borders of dresses, *bonets-de-Nuits*, and other night-clothes. *La Belle Assemblée*, November 1826 ~~~ Valenciennes Lace is noted for its strength and durability. Its ornamental sprigs and flowers are woven like those before described; but they have not, usually, any outline of thicker thread. Young Lady's Book, 1829 ~~~ The lace made at Valenciennes is very highly esteemed, but is not manufactured in England. All the six sides of the hexagon are plaited; but two of the sides of each mesh are so small, that they appear like lozenges. Edinburgh Encyclopædia, 1830 ~~~ Valenciennes is at present the lace *comme il faut*. It is employed for trimming pocket-handkerchiefs, whether embroidered or simply hemmed. It is also used for trimming pelerines of Scotch cambric and undress caps; in short, for everything which may be denominated *lingerie*. *Court Journal*, June 8, 1833

valentia – [see *valencia*]

valentine – Habit de Reception. – A *redingote* of lilac valentine, *Casket*, January 1834 ~~~ Rhode Island Silk. A few months since, we gave some account of the operations of the Valentine Silk Company, in this city. They were at that time just getting their plantation of Mulberry trees under way, and had commenced operating some machinery by way of experiment. Since that time, they have manufactured a considerable quantity of rich and beautiful goods, and have been so fully satisfied with the result of their experiment, that they have fitted up, in the vicinity of the Steam Cotton Factory, in this city, a building, thirty feet by ninety, three stories high, with a basement, to be devoted hereafter to the manufacture of Silk. An engine of six horse power, is already up, and the machinery will be in operation, in the course of a week. Thus as Rhode Island led the way in the manufacture of Cotton, so does she lead in the manufacture of Silk – and we do not doubt that the latter enterprize will prove to be even more beneficial to New England, than the former has ever been. *Silk Manual*, June 1835

Valliere – One of the most elegant dresses we ever saw was of *gauze de Valliere*, embroidered at the knees in silver *adiante*, (the grass called maiden-hair). *Lady's Magazine*, March 1830 ~~~ [Paris] mantles, which are composed of a great variety of materials, both silk and woollen. The latter are all imitations of cashmere, but of different patterns. Some are of an onyx ground, with a zigzag in relief, of claret-colour; others have a *Valliere* ground, thickly strewed with bouquets of fancy flowers of very vivid colours, and of a *bizarre*, we had almost said a grotesque, appearance: these last are very fashionable. *Ladies' Museum*, February 1832 [*Valliere* is also a color]

Van Diemen's Land – [see *thibet wool*]

vandyke – [court dress] A white satin petticoat trimmed with a drapery of rich embroidered crape in stars, bordered with a rich vandyke, and edged with a beautiful sable, *Lady's Magazine*, January 1796 ~~~ Petticoat of light blue satin, in deep Vandyke scallops. *Lady's Magazine*, January 1797 ~~~ Dresses and robes are often seen in plain coloured muslins, ornamented with Vandyke lace; … [court dresses] A white crape petticoat, with a rich Vandyke silver foil border, …An elegant dress … a very rich embroidered border, with Vandyke silver fringe; *La Belle Assemblée*, June 1807 ~~~ The British zigzag, or the modern Vandyke pattern, *Monthly Magazine*, December 1812 ~~~ *Spring Promenade Costume*. – A round dress of fine cambric or India muslin, trimmed round the border with three Vandyke flounces, set or [on?] plain, of muslin richly embroidered, and each point edged with narrow lace of Urling's manufacture. *European Magazine*, April 1823 ~~~ The open net-like Vandyke lace is still much in favour for home cornettes; it has lasted longer than we expected; it is, however, very becoming, and that is the most important consideration. *Lady's Magazine*, August 1825 ~~~ Morning Dress. – Cape of Brussels lace, ornamented with pink gauze ribbon, cut in vandykes. … Carriage Dress. – The hat, which is ornamented with two white esprit plumes, is of buff watered silk, nearly lined with Vandyke blonde, and is trimmed with striped gauze ribands of the same colour. *Godey's Ladies Book*, May 1831 ~~~ Pelerines of worked muslin or net are now lined with silk of any light tint, such as pink, blue, straw-colour, &c. If they are vandyked at the edge, the lining must be cut out and fitted to the points, which is very troublesome, whenever they require washing. For this reason a trimming of lace is frequently preferred. *Court Journal*, June 22, 1833

veletine – A beautiful blue veletine, adapted principally for the pelisse and spencer, when the ball fringe, or gymp, or fancy trimming, to correspond, is both a requisite and tasteful addition. Its superior texture and excessive neatness render it the most elegant article we have ever seen. Its beautiful simplicity cannot fail to attract great notice amongst the fair sex. *Repository of Arts*, August 1812

vellum gauze – Shot and figured sarsnets, Spanish gause, imperial and vellum net, … each of various shades and colours, are offered for dress gowns; and are worn over white gossamer satin, sarsnet, or glazed cambric. *La Belle Assemblée*, April 1809 ~~~ Evening, or Full Dress. … A Gallician Robe, with demi-train of pale-blue or pea-green crape, vellum gause or leno; the edged finished with broad double foldings and cord. *La Belle Assemblée*, May 1809 ~~~ a robe of green vellum gauze, Mirror of the Graces, 1811 vellum lace – GOLD and SILVER LACE and Thread, Persons that sell orrice lace, mixed with other metals or materials than *gold, silver,* silk and vellum, shall forfeit 2*s.* 6*d.* for every ounce: Law-Dictionary, 1797 ~~~ Guipure, … *gimp, vellum lace,* Tardy's French Dictionary, 1799 ~~~ At a Court of Assistants of the Honourable Artillery Company, held at the Armoury-house, on Monday, the 20th of June 1803, … The following Orders for the uniform-dress, arms, and accoutrements of the battalion, were unanimously agreed to, viz. UNIFORM-JACKET. *Jacket* of superfine scarlet, … and stand-up collar, edged with white kerseymere and laced with broad vellum-lace; History of the Honourable Artillery Company of the City of London, 1804 ~~~ Vellum-lace, *Guipure, ouvrage guipé,* sorte de dentelle de soie. [a kind of silk lace] Chambaud's French Dictionary, 1815 ~~~ instituted Sept. 22, 1812 ~~~ The uniform of the Company shall be as follows; – a dark blue coat, … the skirts of the coat to reach the middle of the thigh, and to be cut away narrow, and a vellum lace diamond on the extremities; a standing collar to hook in front, and to be edged all round with gold vellum lace; wings of blue cloth stuffed and edged with vellum lace and buttoning to the collar on the shoulders. Constitution of the New England Guards, 1824 [see *gimp*]

vellum net – [see *vellum gauze*]

Velo di Festa – For opera and evening dresses, a new, light, and transparent article, called *Velo de Festa,* of the softest and most brilliant colours, is now introducing by Maynard and Pyne, of Ludgate-street. We have just seen a dress of this beautiful material, which is extremely well adapted for evening parties and visits. – The ground is of bright jonquil, figured with blossoms of coloured heath, of striking colours, delicately grouped together, form a pattern resembling those sprigs that are on the cachemire shawls. *Ladies' Monthly Museum,* May 1825

velonti – [Paris] *Velonti Carlina* and *Velonti de la Mosquée* are new and very beautiful silks for evening dress. *Ladies' Pocket,* November 1836 [see *veloute*]

velorine – Walking Dress, … A bonnet composed of *black Velorine,* lined with black *gros de Naples, Ladies' Monthly Museum,* December 1822

velours – Velours, *s. m.* velvet. Boyer's Royal Dictionary, 1802 ~~~ [court dress] White satin dress, with a flounce of blonde; manteau and boddice of pink velours, trimmed with blonde and gauze riband. *Court Journal,* May 11, 1833 [see *velvet*]

velours a mille raies – [see *mille rayes*]

velours cachemire – [Paris, grande dress] Another dress is of *velours cachemire*; it is striped in very broad stripes of emerald green and white: on the first is a gothic pattern in black; the other has a large cachemire pattern woven in the stuff. *Repository of Fashions,* September 1829

velours Chinois – [see *Chinese velvet*]

velours d'Afrique – [see *African*]

velours d'Armenie – [see *Armenian*]

velours d'Ispahan – [see *Ispahan velvet*]

velours de coton – [see *cotton velvet, Manchester, velveteen,* and *velveret*]

velours de la reine – [see *reine*]

velours de Liban – Paris Evening Dress. – Robe of a new and very rich material, *Velours de Liban,* a pink ground strewed with roses; *Ladies' Pocket,* January 1836

velours des Indes – [see *Indian velvet*]

velours epingle – [court dress] A petticoat of white satin, … train of a rich geranium velvet *épingle,* elegantly trimmed with silver and blond. *La Belle Assemblée,* April 1818 ~~~ Bonnets at present are composed chiefly of *gros de Naples*; we have, however, seen a few made of those rich silks which have stripes or spots thrown up in imitation of velvet, and which the French call *velours épingle, velours natté,* &c.: *Repository of Arts,* November 1820 ~~~ The pelisse is composed of the French material called *Velours epingle,* or, rather we should say, of our imitation of it, which is now perfectly equal to the foreign article; it is a silk of the richest description, with spots thrown up in imitation of fancy velvet; *Ladies' Monthly Museum,* January 1821 ~~~ *Velours épingle,* a new kind of spotted silk of the Lyons manufacture, … are the silks at present most in favour. *Repository of Arts,* June 1823 ~~~ The velvet (*velours épingle*), which promises to be very fashionable this winter, has not been worn for many years: it looks like very narrow cords, and forms elegant trimmings for silk pelisses: *Repository of Arts*, January 1824 ~~~ [Paris] A species of cut velvet, *velours épinglé*, is recherché, and, in dark colours, looks very well for hats. *Royal Lady's*, February 1831 ~~~ [court dress] A dress of figured vapeur China crape, elegantly trimmed with blonde; train of cerise velours epingle, lined and trimmed to correspond; *Royal Lady's*, May 1831 ~~~ *Velours épinglé* and *Velours des Indes* are two of the most elegant and fashionable materials for dresses. In pale colours they produce brilliant effects of light and shade. In pink and light blue they make beautiful evening dresses, without any other ornament than blonde *sabots* to the short sleeves, and a few bows of gauze riband on the pointed corsage. *Court Journal*, March 9, 1833 ~~~ [court dress] Pink velours train epingle, richly trimmed with blonde, satin, and flowers; *Lady's Magazine and Museum*, June 1836 ~~~ *velours épinglé* (called in England rep velvet) *New Monthly Belle Assemblée*, November 1836 ~~~ [Paris] *Velours épinglé* less rich, but also not so heavy as velvet, will be in great request. *New Monthly Belle Assemblée*, December 1836 [see also *rep velvet*]

velours Grec – [see Greek velvet]

velours Indien – [see *Indian velvet*]

velours Medicis – [see *Medicis*]

velours mousseline – [Paris] She wore a dress of *velours mousseline*, *dalia* colour; *Casket*, February 1833 ~~~ Another novelty is *velours mousseline*, one of the richest half transparent materials that has yet appears; both are for evening dress. *Court Magazine*, January 1835

velours nalta – *Velours simulé*, *velours nalta*, and chenille stuff, are the materials most used for bonnets; the two first are silks, made in imitation of fancy velvet; *Ladies' Monthly Museum*, February 1820 [probably *velours natté*]

velours natte – [for winter chapeaux] new and very beautiful stuffs. One is called *velours natté*; it is figured, and has all the softness of satin, with the richness of velvet. *Repository of Arts*, December 1819 ~~~ There are so many materials used for *chapeaux*, that it is rather difficult to say which is most fashionable. *Gros de Naples* and other kinds of silk, to which the French give the name of *velours simulé*, *velours natte*, and *velours epingle*, ... are all in favour. Velvet is not yet considered decidedly fashionable, but it begins to be worn. *Ladies' Monthly Museum*, November 1820 ~~~ we have, however, seen a few made of those rich silks which have stripes or spots thrown up in imitation of velvet, and which the French call *velours épingle*, *velours natté*, &c.: these bonnets have in general a mixture of satin. *Repository of Arts*, November 1820 ~~~ Natte, ... *a mat; a twist*. <u>Dufief's French Dictionary</u>, 1810 [see also *velours épingle*]

velours simule – [Paris] The favourite materials for *chapeaux* are, *pluche*, velvet, satin, down, and the stuff called *velours simulé*. *Repository of Arts*, March 1819 ~~~ *Velours simulé*, ... are the materials most used for bonnets; the two first are silks, made in imitation of fancy velvet; *Ladies' Monthly Museum*, February 1820 ~~~ The material which the French call *velours simulé*: has recently been very much used both for pelisses and dresses: there is a new kind, which has lately been much worn: it is a singularly durable and beautiful stuff; it has the appearance of rich silk, but in reality is composed of one half cotton, and the other silk: it is, however, so very well made, that the materials can only be known by the touch. There is much variety in this sort of stuff: it is figured, corded, and spotted. There is also another description of *velours simulé*, which, though, has been for some time in fashion, is still in very great estimation: we mean that very rich silk, the ground of which is thrown up so as to resemble velvet: this is also of various patterns. *Repository of Arts*, December 1820 ~~~ Velvet pelisses are fashionable in carriage costume; but they are not so much worn as pelisses made of that rich silk called *velours simulé*, of which there are a great many different kinds. ... We have noticed among these pelisses, one made in black *velours simulé*: the trimming was a cording of scarlet satin, which went all round; *Repository of Arts*, January 1823 ~~~ Simule, ée, ... *Fictitous*. ... Dévotion simulée, *Pretended devotion*. Simuler, ... *To feign, pretend*. <u>Boniface's French Dictionary</u>, 1828

velours veloutie – [see *veloute*]

veloute – Ruban velouté, *m. velvet riband*. Velouté, *m. velvet lace*. <u>Dufief's French Dictionary</u>, 1810 ~~~ Dinner Dress. ... A *ceinture* of *velours veloutie*, rose colour lined with blue. *Casket*, February 1831 *La Belle Assemblée*, January 1831 ~~~ Velouté, *adj* velvet, velveted, tufty, ... *sm* velvet-lace. <u>Cobbett's French</u>

Dictionary, 1833 ~~~ We see among the evening dress materials, a peculiarly rich kind of silk, to which the name of *velouté* is given; as *velouté Arnanda, de la Juive, guirlandes et bouquets*, and *clochette*, this last is figured. *Court Magazine*, May 1836 [see also *Carlina*]

veloutine – The dress-makers have lately introduced a material for gowns, called *veloutine*: generally, the article is checquered of two colours, that is to say, the ground is of one tint, the squares of another. *La Belle Assemblée*, May 1827

velure – Vellure. See Fustians. Ship-Master's Assistant, 1795 ~~~ Velure, ... Velvet. An old word. Sheridan's English Dictionary, 1797 ~~~ [men's] The waistcoat is of *terre velure*, with broad satin and velvet stripes; ... For dress waistcoats the silk *velure*, or velvet of Genoa, in stripes or running sprigs. *Casket*, January 1831

veluteen – [ad] rich French Veluteens for Pelisses and Spencers. *Repository of Arts*, May 1815 [see also *veletine*]

velveret – [1789] His things had previously been packed up in a bundle, and were taken down to put in the trunk. The effects were as follow: ... A second-hand dyed black velveret coat. *Tomahawk*, January 23, 1796 ~~~ [patent granted] *for a new Manufacture of mixed and coloured Cotton Velvets, Velveteens, Velverets, Thicksets, Cords, and other Cotton Pile Goods, commonly called Fustians*. Dated April 5, 1803 *Repertory of Arts*, March 1804 ~~~ Velveret, (Ger. *Manchester*, ... a species of cotton velvet, chiefly manufactured at Manchester, and in its neighbourhood. General Dictionary of Commerce, 1810 ~~~ raised *velverets*, which were made as a middle species between velvets and thicksets, to a rivalship with the former, *Tradesman*, September 1810 ~~~ *Selection of a Cargo suited, on a general scale, for the Spanish Settlements in America*, ... *Velverets. All Half Ell wide, none Half Yards*, 100 *Pieces*. 2 Black. 4 Blue. 1 Yellow. 1 Purple. 1 Rose. 1 Sky blue. – 10 Pieces in each trunk, from 2s. 3d. to 3s. 6d. per yard. Present State of the Spanish Colonies, 1810 ~~~ [exported in 1819] Manchester velveteens, 120,000 yards. Manchester velverets, 40,000 yards. *Asiatic Journal*, June 1822 ~~~ Thickset, velveret, and velveteen, are varieties of it [corduroy]; London Encyclopædia, 1829 [see also *cotton velvet, fustian, Manchester*, and *velveteen*]

velvet – Silk with a short fur or pile upon it. Sheridan's English Dictionary, 1797 ~~~ [court dress] body and train purple velvet, richly trimmed with bronze. ... Morning Dresses. ... *cabriolet* bonnet covered with white, black, and blue striped velvet; *Lady's Magazine*, January 1797 ~~~ *Flowered velvets*, except those designed for furniture, are commonly but small designs; the uncut bordering the cut velvet, the ground is but little seen, which is satin, and is chiefly designed to part the flowers and leaves from each other. The patterns fro velvets are drawn much in the same manner for gentlemen's wear; but when for a lady's winter dress, they are done with an open ground, and larger flowers. From what has been advanced it will appear that ornaments, stalks, flowers, and leaves, are the principal objects in designing of weaving patterns; they seem the most becoming for embellishing a lady's dress; and notwithstanding that for many years past, the manufacturers have puzzled both their own, and tortured the pattern-drawer's brains to contrive new fashions and uncommon devices, ... Whims have been carried to an extravagant rate, and no jack-pudding on a mountebank's stage ever had more ridiculous trumperies on his jacket, than have been imitated on silk. Pitchforks, and hangers, ropes and ladders, sea-shells upon trees, have been, by some weavers, thought proper devices for a lady's dress. Laboratory, 1799 ~~~ Black velvet slippers, covered with a net-work of silver, are likewise worn by those with whom *Fashion* is on the best *footing*. *Lady's Magazine*, November 1800 ~~~ ... [men's] pantaloon's [are of] striped velvet. *Union Magazine*, December 1801 ~~~ The *Bronti* hat, made of silver grey embossed velvet, with a small band of the same, ... is esteemed elegant. *La Belle Assemblée*, March 1806 ~~~ The velvets are woven, at first without any of that downy coating, which makes them so pleasant to the touch. The threads which are to form this shag, are, in the first instance, inserted at both ends in the very texture of the cloth, so as to produce a vast number of small loops, running in rows, from one end of the piece to the other. These loops are cut by hand. The cloth is extended horizontally on a machine, and the artist inserts among the loops a long slender knife, much resembling a very delicate sword; this, guided by one hand only, he pushes along so dexterously, as to cut the whole series of loops for several yards, at one thrust, without piercing the cloth, unless a knot or other obstacle turns his instrument aside. This operation being repeated along every thread in the whole breadth of the piece, a shag is at length raised over the whole surface. But it would be very rough and inelegant if left in this state. To remove its roughnesses, the whole piece is made to pass rather slowly over a red hot iron cylinder, and in absolute contact with it; and during the whole operation, the iron is maintained at a red heat, by the aid of a furnace. I would not assert a thing seemingly so incredible, had I not witnessed the process; Journal of Travels, 1806 ~~~ There are various kinds of velvets; *Plain*, that is uniform and smooth, without either figures or stripes. *Figured velvet*, that is, adorned and worked with divers figures, though the ground is the same with the figures, that is the whole surface velveted. *Ramaged or branched velvet*, representing long stalks, branches, &c. on a satin ground, which is sometimes the of the same colour with the velvet, but more commonly of a different one. Sometimes, instead of satin, they make the ground of gold and silver. *Shorn velvet*, is that wherein the threads that make the velveting, have been ranged in the channelled ruler, but not cut there. Striped velvet is that wherein there are stripes of different colours running along the warp, whether these stripes are partly velvet or all velveted. *Cut velvet*, is that whereon the ground is a kind of taffety, or *gros de tours*, and the figures velvet. General Dictionary of Commerce, 1810 ~~~ The principal and best manufactories of velvet or in England and France; there are others in Italy, as at Venice, Milan, Florence, Genoa, and Lucca, and in Holland, at Haerlem, those in China are the worst of all. Guy's Pocket Cyclopædia, 1810 ~~~ [ad] a most extensive assortment of Silk Velvets, of the richest hues, from 10s. to 16s. per yard, is now on sale at Sutton's, *Repository of Arts*, March 1815 ~~~ [Paris] Spotted velvet, velvet striped in shades, and a beautiful new kind of gauze with velvet spots, are now the materials considered most tonish for head-dresses. *Repository of Arts*, November 1817 ~~~ [Paris] A new material for dresses in *grande parure* is of velvet, on which are imprinted palm leaves in gold. … Although velvet does not confer any advantage on the feet, making them always appear larger than they really are, yet the Parisian ladies of fashion wear velvet shoes this winter, in preference to any other, particularly in carriage morning airings. *Ladies' Museum*, January 1829 ~~~ Rich figured velvets of crimson, and black stripes and cloudings, promise to be general; but the heaviness attached to this material will confine it to matronly females, without it is lined and relieved by white, or light and delicate colours. *Lady's Magazine*, October 1830 ~~~ The use of the trevat in cutting the pile calls for a certain amount of skilfulness or sleight of hand, only to be fully acquired through care and after long practice, while the minutest deviation from the proper line in performing this part of the process would infallibly injure, if even it did not destroy, the goods; and the movements to be made throughout the entire operation are, as has been shown, so numerous, and require such constant changing of the hand from one action to another, that the weaver is greatly and unavoidably retarded in his progress. It is considered to amount to a very good day's work, when as much as one yard of plain velvet has been woven. For this the workman is usually paid five times the price charged for weaving gros-de-naples. … Velvet is sometimes woven with stripes which run in the direction of the shoot, and which are produced, at regular intervals, by leaving uncut such a number of loops of the pile as are sufficient to make up the breadth of the intended stripe. The wire employed for forming these uncut loops is unlike that described, being of a simple cylindrical form: the appearance of velvet thus woven is rich and pleasing. Silk Manufacture, 1832 ~~~ That rich crimson pelisse, so comfortable for cold weather, is of *velvet*, a silken fabric, in weaving which the warp is brought over a thin wire, so as to form a line of fine loops; before the wire is withdrawn, the loops are cut open, which gives the fabric a rich shaggy texture, very deep in its colour, and affording an appearance suited to occasions of ceremony, and fit for persons of the highest rank. Genoa, Venice, Milan, Florence, and Lucca, were once celebrated for their velvets; French velvet, however, now excels them in beauty, but this is rivalled by our own manufacturers of Spitalfields. Some of the velvets, especially English, are made of silk and cotton; others of cotton only; but these do not keep their colour equally well with the silk velvets. Scenes of Commerce, 1836 [see also *Chinese velvet*, *Indian velvet*, *velveret*, and *velveteen*]

velvet gauze – [Paris] A charming velvet gauze, in large checquers, is much used for ball dresses; *La Belle Assemblée*, November 1819 ~~~ Velvet gauze in checquer work is a very fashionable material for hats; the checquers are richly embossed; *La Belle Assemblée*, July 1820

velvet netting – Crape or velvet netting, plain, spangled, beaded, and bugled, are much introduced into caps and bonnets, with flowers to match. For the use of milliners, the netting may be had separate, in small squares. *Lady's Magazine*, April 1800

velveteen – The fustian trade has also been improved, by the addition of velveteens fifteen years since, approaching nearer to real velvets than velverets; *British Critic*, May 1796 ~~~ M. De la Haye fabricates both velvets and velveteens, which are frequently sold as velvets, though essentially different; … The shag of the velvet is cut in the loom cross-ways; whereas the velveteens come out close shorn. … It is easy to distinguish the velveteens from velvets. The ground of the parts, that are not cut in shag, and the selvages, resemble satin; whereas in the velvets the texture of the selvages is plain, like those of the cloth. On opening the pieces that are cut shag-fashion, and on folding the stuff, it is perceived, that in velvets the nap divides itself breadth-ways, whereas in velveteens it separated lengthways. *Monthly Magazine*, April 1804 ~~~ Haggerty's dress was a velveteen jacket, swansdown waistcoat, and velveteen breeches. [Haggerty was executed Feb. 23, 1807 for murder] Murder of Mr. Steele, 1807 ~~~ We all know, that a jean, nankeen, or any kind of thin jacket, is the pleasantest wear for September, one of fustian for October, and one of velveteen for the winter; Instructions to Young Sportsmen, 1816 ~~~ Velveteen, cloth of cotton and linen Webster's Dictionary, 1817 ~~~ I should take a piece of velveteen, which is the heaviest goods which I am aware of made in this country: I got a piece, which was stated to be the average quality which is usually sold for exportation to the continent, weighed since I came to London; the length of the piece was twenty-eight yards, the price it was selling at was 2*s.* a yard, the weight of the piece when finished was eight pounds eight ounces, Reports from the Committees, 1818 ~~~ The miners, or, as they call themselves, the colliers, … Their holiday clothes are generally of cotton velvet, or velveteen as I believe the drapers call it, decorated with a prolusion of shining metal buttons; *Manchester Iris*, October 11, 1823 ~~~ [1820] Speirs had a dark jacket, either velveteen or corduroy – I think it was velveteen; that is different from fustian – the fustian is lighter. Trials for High Treason, in Scotland, 1825 ~~~ [fashionable men's] Shooting Dress. This coat is of light green mohair or velveteen. *Casket*, January 1831 ~~~ [ad] Very Best Liveries. A Footman's Suit complete, with Sleeves to Waistcoat and Velveteen Breeches £4 5s. *Alexander's East India and Colonial Magazine*, December 1835… Velveteens 27 inches wide. As they leave the loom, with a downy surface on the one side and tweeled on the other. … Dyed and finished as black velveteens; a beautiful fabric. Price from 1*s.* 4*d.* to 2*s.* 9*d.* per yard. Cotton Manufacture of Great Britain, 1836 [see also *cotton velvet* and *fustian*]

velveteen satin – The turbans worn at evening-parties are magnificent, and in the true Eastern style: they are formed of folds of colored velveteen satin, and gold or silver gauze; *Lady's Magazine*, May 1829

Venetian gauze – Dresses of Venetian gauze, a peculiarly elegant article, over white satin are most in favour for evening parties, *La Belle Assemblée*, June 1816 ~~~ Summer Recess Ball Dress. Frock of white crape, Venetian gauze, or fine net, *La Belle Assemblée*, July 1818 ~~~ Two evening dresses for the present mournful occasion are peculiarly elegant; the one is a frock of beautiful black Venetian gauze, with a profusion of narrow flounces at the border, toughing each other. … Slight silks will be much in favour for the autumnal season; and the ball dresses will chiefly consist of fine net or Venetian gauze, *La Belle Assemblée*, August 1820 ~~~ Evening Dress. A Venetian gauze frock over a white satin slip: *Ladies' Monthly Museum*, December 1820

Venetian net – [the Prince of Wales's marriage] The Princess, In her nuptial habit; namely, A royal robe; silver tissue petticoat, covered with silver and Venetian net and silver tassels, *Gentleman's Magazine*, May 1795 ~~~ I have ordered for the ensuing hall at Brighton, a drapery of venetian net, which is most gracefully disposed over a round under dress of pale crimson satin. The sleeve short, is formed in oblique stripes of the same satin, blended with the venetian net, and trimmed with point lace in antique scollop; which also forms the tucker to which is attached an imperial ruff. *La Belle Assemblée*, October 1808 ~~~ [Dress gowns] These robes were round, with demi-train, and formed of white Venetian net, worn over white sarsnet; *La Belle Assemblée*, May 1809

Venetian velvet – Evening Dress. … A robe of black Venetian velvet with short Circassian sleeve, *Lady's Miscellany*, March 16, 1811

Venus – A new material, and one likely to become very fashionable, has lately appeared for full dress gowns: it is called *Gaze de Venus*; and is worn in cherry-red, pale rose-color, and lilac: *Ladies' Monthly Museum*, October 1823 ~~~ Evening Dress. – Round dress of rose-coloured *gaze de Venus*, trimmed with white tulle disposed in three rows of three deep folds called *wolves' teeth*, *New-York Mirror*, October 4, 1823 ~~~ A beautiful silvery kind of gauze has been lately fabricated for ball-dresses: it is called *La Voile de Venus;* it is soft, and hangs like the finest India muslin. *Lady's Magazine*, May 1825

vestings – The cotton cloths made [in America] are bed-ticking, stripes and checks, ginghams, cloth for shirts and sheeting, counterpanes, webbing and coach-laces, diapers, jeans, vesting, cotton kerseymeres, fustians, cords, and velvets. <u>American Universal Geography</u>, 1812 ~~~ [ad] MARSEILLES AND VALENCIA VESTINGS. 2 cases of the latest London fashions, comprising a beautiful assortment of entire new figures, superior to any hitherto imported both in point of fabric, and richness and brilliancy of colours – plain white and buff do. – rich striped do. &c. CASSIMERE VESTINGS, super white, black, buff, &c. <u>Boston Annual Advertiser</u>, 1823 ~~~ Vesting, n. Cloth for vests; vest patterns. *U. States.* <u>Webster's Dictionary</u>, 1830 ~~~ The *filoselle,* or floss silk, which will issue from the filatures, and needs not be thrown, but only carded and spun in the usual way, will be immediately employed by our industrious workmen in making stockings, caps, vestings, and other kinds of hosiery. <u>Essays on American Silk</u>, 1830 ~~~ Printed cotton vestings, from the Hamilton Manufacturing Company, is a fair low priced article, for the increased manufacture of which there is great room, as the demand is very extensive. An improvement in this article is deemed desirable. <u>Journal of the Franklin Institute</u>, 1834 ~~~ At the establishment of the Harmony Society, at Economy, in Pennsylvania, on the Ohio River, silk is cultivated, and some figured silk vestings have been produced which may vie with the most beautiful fabrics of Europe. ... At Providence the Valentine Company have just commenced with new and elegant machinery which is moved chiefly by the steam-engine; ... I was here shewn beautiful patterns of vestings which had been wove by the power loom, some were composed wholly of silk, and some of silk for the warp, and cotton for the woof, with the appearance of entire silk. <u>American Silk Grower's Guide</u>, 1835 ~~~ [October 1832] *for the use of the Pottawatamie nation of Indians, bought of Samuel Lewis.* ...1 piece silk vesting 36 yards - $2 50 [per yard, totaling] $81 00 <u>Emigration of Indians</u>, 1835 [see also *Marseilles, swansdown* and *Valencia*]

Victoria silk – [court dress] A magnificent white satin dress, splendidly trimmed with blonde; a train of blue Victoria, handsomely trimmed; *Royal Lady's Magazine*, April 1831 ~~~ [court dress] A white aerophane crape dress, ornamented with wreaths of riband and flowers; train of beautiful rose-coloured Victoria silk. ... [court dress] A white Victoria silk dress, *Royal Lady's*, June 1831 ~~~ [court dress] Manteau of silver-grey Victoria satin, lined with white silk, *Lady's Magazine and Museum*, June 1835

victory – Fancy Gauze. ... The patterns which are to be treated of under this head are formed by combining either plain texture, or flushing, with gauze, as a ground. By the former of these methods, are woven those varieties which are known by the several names of purles, victories, crapes, and Turkey gauze; by the latter, chambries, gauze tweels, and Trafalgars. ... VICTORIES. By thus combining gauze and plain cloth, in different ways, arise that species of fancy gauze, called victories, which were manufactured some time ago in great quantities and variety. Their most predominant appearance is a number of small gauze spaces, interspersed with plains; sometimes checked by the weft, at others, thrown into small alternate checkers, though not always square. Some of these patterns were woven by one set of gauze mounting and a plain stripe, the gauze parts resembling lino; others, by two sets of gauze mounting, making these small gauze spaces alternate, the plains consisting of three or five shots, succeeded by the key shot, or by a few shots of gauze. These spaces or stripes of gauze were sometimes separated by a cord of coarse yarn, or more frequently by two splitfills of warp drawn into two adjacent intervals of the reed, while the other intervals were alternately full and empty. These varieties were frequently increased by the addition of another gauze mounting for veining; whence these patterns were called veined victories. <u>Art of Weaving</u>, 1831

vicuna – [see *vigonia*]

vigonia – Vigogna or Vicugna cloths, however, are said to be frequently adulterated by a mixture of sheep's wool, or beaver. <u>Communications to the Board of Agriculture</u>, 1797 ~~~ The northern part of Peru produces wine in great plenty. Wool is another article of its produce, and is no less remarkable for its fineness than for the animals on which it grows; these they call Lamas and Vicunnas. ... The Vicunna is smaller and swifter than the Lama, and produces wool still finer in quality. In the Vicunna too is found the Bezoar stones, regarded as a specific against poisons. New Geographical, Historical, and Commercial Grammar, 1801 ~~~ Pelisses and mantles of fine Vigonia cloth (an elegant and entirely novel manufacture of Spanish wool,) kerseymere, and double twilled sarsnet, are now introduced as appropriate and seasonable articles; ... Vigonia cloth, which latter article will most probably become a reigning favourite during the winter; in softness and warmth is resembles the texture of the Indian shawl; and its graceful pliability, as it waves round the figure, must render it a most becoming and acceptable article for train robes, *La Belle Assemblée*, October 1808 ~~~ The fine wool, called Vigonia wool, that sells so high, and of which the Vigonia cassimere is made, is the produce of animals of the above species. *Athenæum*, December 1808 ~~~ Guadalaxara is the only place in Spain where the famous Vigonia cloth is manufactured; it is made from a precious wool imported from the colonies of Buenos Ayres and Peru, which is no where else to be found. An attempt has been made to weave this wool in France, and those who have compared our Vigonia cloth with that made at Guadalaxara, agree that ours is more agreeable to the eye, but that made in Spain possesses more durability, either because the Spanish weavers are better acquainted with the management of it, or because they keep the finest Vigonia wool to themselves. These cloths are not yet in general use among the Spaniards, and cannot consequently be procured, unless ordered several months before they are really wanted. Some of these Vigonias are manufactured at the ex pence of the King, who sends them as presents to foreign courts. In the year 1782 Charles the third sent twenty pieces to the Grand Signior, on the conclusion of a treaty with the Porte. *Modern State of Spain*, 1808 ~~~ The Vicuna is most similar to the above description of the Lama: two of them are at present in London; one, a female, at Brooke's, in Piccadilly, and the other, a male, at another place of exhibition (No 207) in the same street. The fine wool, called Vigonia wool, that sells so high, and of which the Vigonia cassimere is made, is the produce of animals of the above species. Mr. Bakewell, in his interesting tract on wool, strongly advises the introduction of these animals; he mentions that some of them are nearly white, and that he has little doubt "that with proper attention they would grow a fleece free from the long coarse hair with which the downy coat is frequently intermixed. The wool, when clear from these hairs, would be worth 30s. a pound; and the flesh, if we may judge from the appearance of the animal, would be equal to venison" *Atheneum*, December 1808 ~~~ Vigogne, *vigon, vicugna wool*. Dufief's French Dictionary, 1810 ~~~ Vicunna wool is only occasionally brought to England; Dictionary of Commerce, 1810 ~~~ "Deep Vigonia, or red wool, is from its fineness, and soft silky nature, the most valuable fleece produced from any animal in the world. Those of Caramania were generally considered in the first light, and they were for that reason, reserved for the uses of the priests; but the Vicuna wool was in like manner, monopolized by the Incas. This species confessedly exceeds the preceding, surpasses that of Cachemire, or the Lamb wool of Bucharia; and is better suited to the manufacture of fine shawls, than any of the wools of Persia. A quantity of what is denominated Camelia wool, was imported into England by the East India company, seven years ago, but it only sold for 3s. 6d. per lb. and from having both scurf and hair in it, was not suited for the manufacture of hats. It was perhaps shorn at an unseasonable moment, for had it been divested of these two objections, it would have been worth 10s. to the hat trade, or of an equal value with Vigonia. "The only objection that can be brought against the Vigonia, or red wool, is its colour, which prevents it from being introduced into light coloured, and fancy cloths, shawls, or ladies' habit cloths, for which it is admirably well suited. The dyers of this country, have not however yet found out the secret of giving it colour, for besides black, we have seen both the Vigonia and Alpaca wools of a brilliant scarlet hue, and of the latter we are even possessed of samples. We presume nevertheless that both were from white wools; but the Peruvians even give that which is red, a black colour; as is in a most conspicuous manner evinced in their hats, which could not be surpassed in Europe, and of which we can produce a specimen. *Agricultural Magazine*, October 1811 ~~~ *The Thanks of the Society were this Session given to Mr. W. Pritchard, of Castle Street, in the Borough, for the introduction of a* New Material For Hats, *instead of Vigonia*

Wool. The felt of the finer kinds of hats is made of rabbits' hair; but as hair alone will not undergo the process of felting, it is necessary for this purpose to mix with the rabbits' hair, a certain, but small proportion of the finer kinds of wool. That which has upon the whole been in most esteem for this purpose, is the wool of the Vicuña, a species of camel indigenous in Peru and Chili; which is known in commerce by the name of Vigonia wool, or red wool (from the peach-blossom tinge which it naturally possesses). This substance however, is brought here by a long navigation, and is often, from various circumstances, at an extravagant price. In consequence of this, the finer sorts of Merino wool, especially the Saxon, have been employed as a substitute with tolerable success. Transactions of the Society, 1821 ~~~ This wool [cashmere], which is more beautiful than that of Vigonia, Edinburgh Encyclopædia, 1832 [see also *lama*, *paco* and *Spanish cloth*]

vigontine – [Paris] cloaks of *Vigontine* (a sort of superfine Castorine) and those of cloth of the first quality, are adopted by ladies of high fashion. *Ladies' Monthly Museum*, December 1825 ~~~ Wool … vigontines, Philosophy of Manufactures, 1835

Virginia cloth – The exile mantle is now much in esteem. It is composed of fine Virginia cloth, of a very dark green, lined throughout with rose-coloured, or amber sarsanet. *Edinburgh Annual Register*, February 1, 1809 ~~~ The Domestic Warehouse and other stores in Baltimore, have now for sale the following wearing articles of home manufacture, drawn from various parts of the Union; viz. … Virginia cloth; *Agricultural Museum*, August 15, 1810 ~~~ *Petersburg, July* 9, 1789. Virginia cloth – of excellent quality, and very cheap – may be purchased almost every day, of the country people who come to town, for the purpose of making sale of it. It is infinitely superior to any thing of the kind imported, and wears remarkably well. The cloth is made of cotton, woven with great taste, and, by the ingenuity of our fair, has been brought to such perfection as to be preferred by many to the European manufactures. Several gentlemen have furnished themselves with full suits of this cloth; and as many others are anxious to obtain it, we hope that every one, who professes himself to be a Virginian, will be distinguished by his cloth, as it will be promoting the manufactures of our own country, and giving that encouragement to industry which it ought ever to meet with. *Niles' Weekly Register*, September 1, 1832 ~~~ Petersburg is also much indebted for her prosperity to her *cotton factories*; … some part of it [cotton yarn] is woven at the factory into a heavy cotton cloth called "oznaburgs," and is stamped "*Virginia cloth*" in consequence of the likeness between this and the cotton cloth formerly so well known in this state by that name. Gazetteer of the State of Virginia, 1835

voile de Venus – [see *Venus*]

volans – Walking Dress. A Pelisse of *grot de Naples* of a pomegranate-red. A full wadded *rouleau* finishes the skirt next the feet; over this *rouleau*, at a suitable distance, and down each side of the front, is a trimming, *en volan*, pinked at the edge, and set on in a serpentine wave; the trimming headed by a narrow *rouleau*. *La Belle Assemblée*, November 1826 ~~~ Ball Dress. … Two *volans* (narrow flounces) of blond gauze at the knees. *Lady's Magazine*, September 1830 ~~~ The skirts of dresses are much ornamented with volans, more particularly the lighter sorts, as lace, muslin, tulle, &c. *Blackwood's Lady's Magazine*, August 1836

vulture – When plumage is adopted on carriage bonnets, the feathers are very short, closely grouped together over the front, and are of the vulture or marabout kind. *La Belle Assemblée*, July 1823

Wadded - Worsted

wadded – Wadding, A kind of soft stuff loosely woven, with which the skirts of coats were formerly stuffed out; Sheridan's English Dictionary, 1797 ~~~ Short wadded coats, of coloured sarsnet, trimmed all round with fur or broad lace, are worn by the highest *belles* of fashion. *Lady's Magazine*, February 1800 ~~~ *Belles Douillettes à Russienne*. These cloaks are of three cuts, and three different sorts of wadding, according as the wearer is more or less delicate, from rude health, to an invalid state. ... Spencers of double Florence, wadded, are also in repute. *Port Folio*, January 30, 1802 ~~~ This mantle will be found particularly desirable for delicate women in the present severe weather, from its being wadded round the shoulders and bosom, a circumstance, however, which by no means prevents its displaying the shape to the utmost advantage in that respect; indeed it claims a decided preference, since nothing can be more elegantly becoming. *La Belle Assemblée*, December 1814 ~~~ We have to remark, among our Parisian belles this month a ball dress, of a glossy rose-colored crape, with a rouleau of rose satin wadded with cotton; *Ladies' Monthly Museum*, April 1822 ~~~ *Evening Dress*. – Dress of plain net over a gold-coloured satin slip, lined throughout; the hem and two tucks wadded. *Manchester Iris*, December 7, 1822 ~~~ [Paris] Pelisses, composed of Levantine, are very much worn: they have not a wintry appearance, but being wadded, are rendered very comfortable. *Ladies' Monthly Museum*, December 1822 ~~~ Wadded shoes are worn in home dress; the most elegant are of cachemere, lined with white satin; they lace up the instep, and have there a bow of satin riband. *Ladies' Museum*, January 1829 ~~~ [men's] Morning Dress. ... the sleeve has wadding in the top, which carries the cape well off, and gives the shoulders a square appearance. *Casket*, April 1830 ~~~ At a recent Parisian ball a lady of distinguished elegance appeared in the following dress: – A slip of rich white *gros-de-Naples*, with a deep wadded hem. *Court Journal*, October 3, 1835 ~~~ Mantles, both of velvet and satin, wadded and lined with satin, and the lining quilted either in small quadrilled pattern, or what is still prettier, in sprigs of foliage, and other fancy patterns, begin to come into favour, and will be more so in the course of the month; they are worn both in carriage-dress and for the Opera: I shall cite two that I think extremely elegant; the one is crimson satin, lined with white satin, and bordered with swansdown; the other, garter blue satin, lined with pale pink satin, and trimmed with light sable. ... High dresses and *douillettes*, as our wadded pelisses are called, are also in favour for home *negligé*. *New Monthly Belle Assemblée*, December 1836

wale – A rising part in cloth. Sheridan's English Dictionary, 1797

Walter Scott – The most remarkable of the new autumnal materials are the *satins Walter Scott*, they are of plaided patterns, but vary exceedingly both in size and colours. Some are of very small squares traced in black or blue, or violet and green. Others, called Marie Stuart patterns, are of an excessive size and damasked. The Quentin Durward are of a smaller pattern, but very rich, and in a great variety of colours. *Court Magazine*, October 1834

warp – The thread thus spun, is reeled, and made into skeins. That designed for the woof is wound on little tubes, pieces of paper, or rustles, so disposed as that they may be easily put in the eye of the shuttle. That for the warp is wound on a kind of large wooden bobbins, to dispose it for warping. When warped, it is stiffened with size; the best of which is that made of shreds of parchment; and when dry, is given to the weavers, who mount it on the loom. The warp thus mounted, the weavers, who are two to each loom, one on each side, tread alternately on the treddle, first on the right step, and then on the left, which raises and lowers the threads of the warp equally; between which they throw transversely the shuttle from the one to the other: and every time that the shuttle is thus thrown, and a thread of the woof inserted within the warp, they strike it conjunctly with the same frame, wherein is fastened the comb or reed, between whose teeth the threads of the warp are passed, repeating the stroke as often as is necessary. Encyclopædia Britannica 1797 ~~~ Warp, in the manufactures, the threads whether of silk, wool, linen, hemp, &c. that are extended lengthwise on the weaver's loom; and across which the workman, by his shuttle, passes the threads of the woof, to form a cloth, ribband, fustian, or the like. New Encyclopædia, 1807 [see also *weft*]

warp lace – I will next advert to Warp Lace. There is a great variety of different kinds of warp lace made, some having four times the labour in it as others; these are ten-course hole made, and two-course hole made; what I mean by so many course holes is, the number of loopings the workmen have to complete a hole; the more pressings there is to a hole in warp lace, the firmer the article is, and the least liable to lose its form in washing. Warp lace, from the nature of the principle upon which it is worked, can make a harder twisted material than what the point frame can; warp lace has not been long invented, I think it was invented in the year 1804. At that time the lace was principally made of silk, which was extremely fine; afterwards it was made of cotton; it was made much finer than the point will make it. This was generally made with six courses to the hole, though a considerable quantity was made with eight courses to the hole. Warp lace made with six or eight courses to the hole, if made of two-thread cotton material, is a good article; they then gradually go down to four courses to the hole, and lastly they degenerated to two courses to the hole. This two-course hole is made by lapping four times and pressing twice to the hole; this when stretched out in what is termed the getting-up frame, has the handsomest appearance of any kind of machine lace made, though when washed it runs up, and frequently appears like cloth. The warp lace frame is calculated to carry improvements in lace to a very great extent, joined to which, it can be made very cheap. Upon the best principle, the very best lace can be made forty-four inches wide, and a yard long material, and all for about 28s. that is the very best article that can be made, and it is very little inferior to foreign lace; the only difference is, foreign lace is made of thread, and this is made of cotton: the workmen are positive they could work thread if their masters would give them thread to make in that branch of business. Reports from the Committees, 1812 ~~~Warp lace was invented in 1804; and, in the year 1805, cotton-yarn (for this lace is made of cotton) was wrought fine enough to be made into double press lace, … The Nottingham imitations of lace are of two kinds, point-net and warp-net. From the names of the machines in which they are made, they are both a species of chain-work, and the machines are varieties of the stocking frame. The warp frame makes a very close imitation of the Brussels lace, but has very little durability. … In the warp-frame, the piece of lace is not formed of one continued thread, as in the point-net frame; but there are as many different threads are there are needles in the frame. These threads are warped, or wound upon a roller or beam, the same as a loom; and it is from this circumstance that the machine is called warp-frame. Edinburgh Encyclopædia, 1830 [see also *Nottingham* and *single press lace*]

washers – Manufactures (woollen). … All kerseys called washers or wash whites, made in the counties of *York*, *Lancaster*, or elsewhere, of like making, being half thickened – 17 & 18 [Yards long.] And being quarter thickened – 18 & 19 [Yards long.] Whole Law Relative to the Duty and Office of a Justice of the Peace, 1794

washing materials – The dress of the white inhabitants of Jamaica is so similar to that which is worn in Britain, that it would be difficult to induce any young man to prefer another. But new settlers ought, as much as possible, to wear kerseymeres, and other light washing materials, such as dimity. They should, on all occasions, prefer the use of cotton, to that of linen, for shirts; [from An History of Jamaica, 1807] *British Critic*, March 1807 ~~~ The dresses form a most pleasing variety. Washing materials of every kind, from the slight sarcenet, of fast-standing colours, to the lively chintz, both of Indian and home manufacture. *La Belle Assemblée*, August 1828

washing leather – The Officers … must on all occasions wear proper wash-leather gloves with their uniforms, which must be clean. Rules and Regulations for the Cavalry, 1795 ~~~ [ad] Ladies' Wash Leather Drawers for riding. *Repository of Arts*, June 1814 ~~~ *Shammoyed Leather*, is generally sheep or doeskin, prepared in the way mentioned for alum and tawed leather, and dyed if necessary, and then finished in oil. This forms the common wash leather, breeches leather, &c. and is the only kind which, when dyed, will bear washing without the colour being materially injured. Pantologia, 1818 ~~~ Parisian Walking Dress. Slippers of blue kid, and washing leather gloves. *La Belle Assemblée*, August 1818 ~~~ The continued severity of the weather induces the writer to reiterate his recommendation of wash-leather waistcoats. It is only they who have tried the expedient that can conceive the comfort of it. The Reporter would almost as soon part with his own skin as the additional one he has adopted. Till he wore the material in question, he scarcely knew the feeling of warmth during the winter season; he now, with less exterior clothing than before, finds himself comparatively indifferent to the temperature of the air. "God's blessing (says Sancho Panza,) be upon that man who first invented sleep; *it covers one all over like a garment*." So does wash leather, says the writer of these Reports; and so will every one say who shall make an essay of its virtue. *Atheneum*, April 15, 1823 ~~~ wash leather (chamois skin) London Journal of Arts and Sciences, 1825 ~~~ [6th April, 1830] The cheaper kinds of wash-leather, for breeches gloves under-waistcoats and other articles of dress, are of sheep-skin; Transactions of the Society, 1836 [see also *chamois*]

washing net – We see with pleasure that British washing net, of extreme fineness and clearness, begins to be used by very genteel women for morning caps. *Maids, Wives, and Widows*, April 13, 1833

washing silk – London Evening and Full Dress. ... the newly-invented washing silk; *Lady's Magazine*, March 1809 ~~~ Kensington Garden Dress. ... Robe dress, walking length, of white washing sarsnet, with an embroidered border. *La Belle Assemblée*, June 1809 ~~~ on a few mild days we have remarked upon some light pelisses made of washing silks, of a shawl pattern. *La Belle Assemblée*, March 1812 ~~~ high dresses of French washing silk, ... are all worn in the walking costume. ... French washing silks, as they are called, though of their possessing the economical quality we must be permitted to doubt, *La Belle Assemblée*, July 1814... [ad] Patent Washing Ditto, [satin for slips, per yard] 4s. 6d.; ... An extensive stock of Washing Silks, with the unrivalled Vive le Roi Dresses, at 30s. to 48s. each. *Repository of Arts*, May 1815 ~~~ At the change of mourning, black spencers of satin, or *gros de Naples*, are expected to be very prevalent over white dresses; and plaid washing silks of black and grey, with black and white chintzes, elegantly ornamented with black fringe, are already in preparation. *Ladies' Monthly Museum*, September 1821 ~~~ An article has been introduced, in almost endless variety, for walking and dinner-dresses. It is a rich washing silk, with printed, chintz, and other patterns; it was partially tried last season with great success, by Thresher, the King's hosier and silk manufacturer; and he has this season produced still more elegant patterns and fabrics, the entire work of British hands. *Lady's Magazine*, February 1830... Nothing can exceed the beauty of some of the newly imported French *foulards* or washing silks. The richness of their designs, and the freshness of their colours, render them suitable even for full dress. For morning and out-door costume, those with small patterns, and one or two colours only, are generally adopted. *Court Journal*, July 6, 1833 ~~~ Clear muslin, printed in delicate patterns, and in colours partly full, and partly light, is fashionable for dresses, but not so much so as washing silks with white grounds, printed in very small bouquets of pink flowers. *Court Magazine*, August, 1833

watered – Water, the gloss, ray or waves on died silk ... Watering, ... act of glossing silk Perry's English Dictionary, 1795 ~~~ [Paris] It is reported that our *élégantes* have resolved to explode white – an event very probable, as a vast number of commissions have been received for watered stuffs, of a new kind. *Lady's Magazine*, April 1800 ~~~ [Paris] The materials for hats and bonnets ... have given place to silk *pluche*, which is of a new description: it is striped and watered, and is really uncommonly pretty: it is in general mixed with satin. *Repository of Arts*, November 1817 ~~~ Watered *gros-de-Naples* is a favourite material for hats; hats made of this material are generally white, *La Belle Assemblée*, September 1820 ~~~ Parisian Ball Dress. One of the most elegant ball dresses we have lately seen consists of a rose-colored watered silk; *Atheneum*, June 15, 1830 ~~~ [court dresses] train of white watered tabby trimmed with gold and blonde; ... A ducape watered dress, ... train of watered shot silk; ... a pomona green watered gros de Naples train, ... train of rich white pau de soi, lined with sarcenet watered in colonnades, *Royal Lady's*, June 1831 ~~~ The process which is called watering silk, and which gives to its surface a peculiar and unequal wavy appearance, is effected by placing together, lengthwise, one on the other, two pieces of silk, and passing them, thus circumstanced, between two cylindrical metal rollers, one of which is made hollow for the purpose of containing a heated iron in its cavity. Smooth and even as the surface and texture of the woven fabric appear to our imperfect vision, it has in reality many thicknesses and as many inequalities as there are crossings of the warp and shoot. These inequalities are not brought to coincide in the two pieces of silk when they are placed together, so that such portion of the face of each as is thereby subjected to severer pressure will receive a greater gloss or polish than other portions, and the wavy appearance results entirely from this unequal degree of pressure. The appearance here described is sometimes produced when it is not wished to do so, and is the result of an unequal pressure used in winding the woven silk upon the breast roll of the loom. The only means of preventing this accident is by using a proper degree of carefulness in rolling the silk. Silk Manufacture, 1832 ~~~ [court dress] A dress of watered silk, richly trimmed with blonde; watered lilac silk train, trimmed with blonde. *Court Journal*, March 2, 1833 ~~~ watering – by which the surface assumes a variety of shades, as if the cloth were covered with a multitude of waving and intersecting lines. This effect is thus produced: The piece, or web, of cloth is folded, from one end to the other, in triangular folds, without attending to regularity, and being thus reduced to a comparatively small length, it is put upon a roller and rolled under a calender of very great weight. When taken out, the strong threads of the weft are found to have impressed lines upon both surfaces, which are variously waved in consequence of the foldings above described. As it is only intended to have one side waved, the web is made up, for the press, with pasteboards between each second fold, so as to allow one side of the web to be wholly without the pasteboards. The web is then hotpressed and that side, which was covered with pasteboard, comes out glazed, while the other remains Watered. When it is wanted to be creased, it is folded, in the first instance, selvage to selvage. Another operation is, to pass the cloth over a hot brass, cylinder, on which are engraved various flowers, or other fancy figures. While passing over this cylinder, the cloth is pressed by two wooden rollers, and thus its surface is indented with those figures. This sort is called Embossed Moreen. From the preceding account, it is plain that the phrase, "To Water Stuffs," has no connection with "to Water," in the sense of to Wash. The term is a Gallicism, having been translated from the old French *onder,* which (from *onde,* a wave of the sea, &c.) was metaphorically applied, like the English *wave,* to denote any undulating line. The French speak of *la moire ondée,* which our manufacturers have chosen to call Watered Moreen. Tabby (French *tabis, – tafetas onde,*) is a silk stuff, waved in a similar manner. To Tabby is another expression for "to Water;" and the adjective Tabby, usually referring to a brindled cat, signifies streaked with waving lines. Analytical Dictionary, 1835 [see also *moire, moreen* and *tabby*]

watered gauze – The new gauze, called water gauze, first made its appearance; [in May 1822] Museum of Foreign Literature, 1823 ~~~ [Paris] A dress hat was also seen of gold-colored, watered gauze; *La Belle Assemblée*, April 1823 ~~~ [Paris] On crape or poux de soie hats, the ribbons are watered gauze ribbons; *Lady's Magazine and Museum,* July 1834

watered satin – a new material, called watered satin, the figures on which are different from those on watered silks, for on the satin they are regular, and consist of the patterns of those creeping plants that are entwined round lattice work: others are covered with the branches bearing blossoms and small fruits: the hats that are made of this satin are trimmed with plush silk, *La Belle Assemblée*, November 1820 ~~~ We have seen some new full dresses made in watered satin, *Repository of Arts*, February 1823 ~~~ a new kind of watered satin, which we have borrowed from the French, and which is styled *satin à la reine,* are all in favour for carriage hats and bonnets. *Ladies' Museum,* November 1831 ~~~ [court dress] A dress of figured blonde gauze over black satin, trimmed with blonde; train of rich watered black satin. *Court Journal*, March 23, 1833

waterproof – WATER-PROOF, a term applied to those stuffs, which have undergone certain chemical or mechanical processes, and thus become impermeable to moisture. ... In July, 1797, a patent was granted to Mr. Henry Johnson, for his invention of a vegetable liquid, the design of which is to bleach and cleanse woollen, or other stuffs; to prepare them for the reception of a certain compound, calculated to render them not only water-proof, but also more durable and elastic, when manufactured into articles of dress, which he terms *Hydrolaines.* – In order to obtain first the vegetable liquid the patentee directs horse-chesnuts, or the rinds and kernels of oranges, that are usually thrown away, or the offals and gall of fish, to be boiled for four or five hours; after which they are suffered to cool and settle, for a few days: ... In 1801, another patent was granted to Messrs. Ackermann, Suardy, and Co. for their invention of a process, by which every species of cloth may be rendered *water-proof.* – As the patentees have not thought proper to publish the particulars of their process (though such concealment is contrary to the nature of *Letters Patent),* we shall briefly remark from our own observation, that their method appears to be a simple impregnation of cloth with wax previously dissolved; and incorporated with water, by the addition of pure vegetable alkali, or pot-ash. This being the cheapest and most expeditious mode of reducing wax to a fluid state, we are farther inclined to believe that our conjecture is well founded; because all the woollen cloth prepared in the manufactory of Messrs. Ackermann; Suardy, and Co. *feels* somewhat harder than such as has not been *waxed*: for the same reason, it will stand a shower of rain only so long as it has not been subject to friction; and we understand from those who have worn *patent waterproof coats,* that in the sleeves particularly, they are very apt to admit moisture through the different folds. Nevertheless, their process is entitled to attention; and it deserves to be adopted principally in those cases, where the manufacture is not liable to be impaired by friction; such as coverings for tents; for horses exposed to the rain when at rest; and especially for paper in which gunpowder, or steel and other goods, are to be packed. Domestic Encyclopædia, 1802 ~~~ Many people foolishly recommend strong fustian or waterproof cloth jackets for shooting; but this is a most useless and unnecessary encumbrance. *Emerald*, August 2, 1806 ~~~ Silks and muslin have almost entirely disappeared, the most fashionable article for ladies' dresses is *waterproof* cloth. An elegant *full* dress, made of this material, may be seen in Ackermann's Repository. It is very becoming, that is, very *decorous*; and will probably secure the wearers from many injurious *aspersions*. Although some malicious persons, no doubt with a view to injure the manufacturers of this article, assert, that it proves of no service against the effects of *eau de vie. Literary Chronicle*, August 30, 1823 ~~~ [ad] *Waterproof Leather Dresses* – It has long been a great desideratum to render cloth, leather, &c., completely waterproof, and we have made some experiments with several specimens, none of which we found completely to resist a long exposure to water. Some of the waterproof stuff is rendered so stiff by the process as to crack at the folds, or to prevent the wearer from working or moving so freely as is desirable. Ramsay's Leather Waterproof Dresses, advertised in another part of this day's *Kaleidoscope*, are entirely free from all these objections; as, independently of their being completely impervious to water, they are as pliant as a glove, and therefore keep the wearer warm as well as dry, by wrapping closely round his body. To seamen, coachmen, waggoners, watchmen, and all persons much exposed to the weather, these dresses are invaluable. They may be had at our office, as it will be seen, by the advertisement, that we have been appointed agents; and we have only to add, that, previously to accepting the agency, we experimentally satisfied ourselves of the excellence of the invention. Attached to the advertisement will be found a strong certificate in their favour, by the crew of one of the Carron Company's vessels, after having had eighteen months' experience of their efficacy. *Kaleidoscope*, February 17, 1829 ~~~ [ad] New Fashions for Autumn – A new material has been introduced by BROWN and CO. Silk Mercers, 234 Regent street, called CACHMERE. DE COUVENT. It is light and durable for Dresses, is also made waterproof for Cloaks, and moderate in price. *Court Journal*, October 19, 1833 [see also *Indian rubber* and *leather cloth*]

wave silk – another carriage hat is of wave silk of the June rose-colour, *La Belle Assemblée*, July 1819 [last month this was *Circassian wave silk*]

Waverley – [Paris] new materials which have just appeared for mantles, ... Some new patterns of quadrilled and figured Cashmere have appeared for *negligé* or travelling. Fancy materials, called *Waverley Puritain* and *satin Ecossais*, will be appropriated to the promenade; *Court Magazine*, November 1836 ~~~ [Paris] in requisition for carriage or public promenade dress, which for us is the same thing, so will also be some new materials of wool and silk intermingled: they are called *ècossais satins*, Waverleys, and *puritains. New Monthly Belle Assemblée*, November 1836 [see also *plaid*, *Quentin Durward* and *Walter Scott*]

weasel – [see *fitch* and *marten*]

web – A Full Dress. A splendid web Fourreau, Grecian front, sleeves and train bound with embossed ribband, and trimmed with *tulle*; a white satin slip is worn underneath. *La Belle Assemblée*, April 1806 ~~~ Web, a tissue, or texture, formed of threads interwoven with each other; some whereof are extended in length, and called the warp; and others drawn across, and called the woof. ... [in Dolgelly, Wales, they make] fabric of coarse, undyed woollens, called webbing, or white plains; Dictionary of Commerce, 1810 ~~~ [Trial for murder in Ireland] the pantaloons, which were stocking-web, were remarkable from a hole in the knee having been mended with black thread. *AntiJacobin Review*, May 1817 ~~~ Worsted webbing or stockinet, for pantaloons, is to be regarded in the light of *woollen manufacture*, or of which wool is the material of chief value, and chargeable with duty accordingly.

National Calendar, 1820 ~~~ [military general orders in Calcutta, officer's dress] Loose trowsers or
overalls, with ancle boots, have been permitted as an undress, but on all occasions of dress and
ceremony, tight pantaloons (of white kerseymere, web, or cotton, according to the season), and half-
boots are to be worn. *Asiatic Journal*, December 1822 [see also *plains, stocking net* and *worsted*]

weed crape – The plain Cypress robe, elegantly trimmed with weed crape, forms the chief dress; *La Belle
Assemblée*, October 1816 [weed might mean black]

weeds – The progress of *widowed grief*, in dress, and person, is exactly this; the dress changes from weeds to
black, from black to grey, and from grey to white and the countenance from dismal to sorrowful, from
sorrowful to sad, and from sad to serious and then comes a *second husband. Sporting Magazine*, May 1795
~~~ Weeds formerly meant any kind of dress; but is now confined to the morning dresses of widows,
which are called their *weeds*. Poetry Explained for the Use of Young People, 1802

weepers – Weeper, a mourner, a white border of linen Perry's English Dictionary, 1795 ~~~ Gentlemen
not in uniform, wear what are called weepers in deep mourning, which are merely cambric cuffs, with
broad hems turned back on the sleeves. Book Explaining the Ranks and Dignities of British Society,
1809 ~~~ [court mourning] We observe that weepers, composed either of clear muslin or long lawn,
are very general in undress. *Repository of Arts*, December 1817 ~~~ At present, the *allée des Veuves* is
deserted; the Parisian widows support their bereavement with greater cheerfulness; and it is far from
uncommon to see the crape and weepers of dowagers associated, at the Opera, with plumes and
diamonds. History of Paris, 1825 ~~~ WEEPERS. Pieces of white cambric, crape, or muslin, sewed
upon the sleeves in deep mourning. Dictionary of General Knowledge, 1833

weft – Woof (s. *from* wove) The set of threads which cross the warp, the weft; texture, cloth. Ash's English
Dictionary, 1795 ~~~ On inspecting a piece of plain cloth, it is found to consist of two distinct sets of
threads running perpendicularly to each other. Of these, the longitudinal threads constitute the warp,
while the transverse threads are called the *woof, weft*, or *filling*, and consist of a single thread passing
backwards and forwards. Encyclopædia Americana, 1833 ~~~ Weaving is the art of making cloth by
the rectangular decussation of flexible fibres, of which the longitudinal are called the warp or chain,
and the transverse the woof or weft. The former extends through the whole length of the web, the
latter only over its breadth. The outside thread on each side of the warp, round which the woof-thread
returns in the act of decussation, is called the selvage or list. Cotton Manufacture of Great Britain,
1836 [see also *warp*]

Welsh plains – [see *plains*]

whalebone – Baleine, *ou* côte de baleine, *a whale bone.* Boyer's Royal Dictionary, 1794 ~~~ What is called
Whalebone, adheres to the upper jaw of the whale, and is formed of thin parallel laminæ, some of the
longest four yards in length. Of these there are commonly three hundred and fifty on each side, but in
very old fish more; about five hundred of them are of a length fit for use, the others being too short.
Dictionary of Merchandise, 1805 ~~~ [Patent] Dated October 30, 1807. To all to whom these
presents shall come, &c. Now know ye, that in compliance with the said proviso, I the said Robert
Bowman do hereby declare, that my said invention is described as follows; that is to say: the process of
making hats, caps, and bonnets of whalebone, for men and women, consists of making the whalebone
soft and flexible, by means of heat, which may be produced either by steam, furnace, immersion in
boiling water, or in any way the workman may find most convenient. And whilst the whalebone is in
that state it is to be cut into such breadths as may be necessary and proper for the purposes for which
it is to be used. For example; in making hats for military men, or other persons, the breadth of the
whalebone should be such, that one breadth may answer for the sides, one for the crown, and one or
more pieces for the brim. These, after being rasped, filed and scraped, are brought into the form,
required, while the whalebone is in a soft and flexible state, by working them on a block of the exact
shape or form wanted; and observe, either the block or the whalebone must be warm before it be
attempted to put the hat or other thing into the form wanted. When the whalebone becomes cold it
will retain the shape it received from the block; which last may either consist of wood, metal, or any
other proper material. The joinings of the pieces of whalebone are to be fastened either by sewing, or
by applying an adhesive gum or cement, or by soldering with parts of itself, as is done in

manufacturing articles of tortoiseshell. … Hats for military men, or other persons, manufactured as above, will prove to be very light and durable, and, besides, will be found to be incapable of being penetrated by the cut of a sword, or other weapon. They will also be impervious to water, be thereby comfortable to the soldier, and will free him from much labour and attention he was formerly obliged to bestow. The hats may be made of such a quality as to suit persons in the highest rank of life. The process of manufacturing hats, caps, and bonnets, similar to those made of straw and of chip, commonly called Leghorn hats, &c. consists in separating the whalebone, while in its soft and flexible state, produced by heat as before described, into such breadths as may be wished to have the plaiting in fineness. The splits are varied accordingly, as may be judged necessary to suit a fine or coarse plaiting or webbing; previous to which the splits are to be reduced to a certain thinness and breadth, either by means of a knife by the hand, or by the aid of machinery, as may be deemed most prudent and convenient. They are then to be plaited into a plaiting or webbing (as straw or chip are plaited or woven while either in a cold or hot state), which plaiting or webbing is to be stitched or sewed up into the form of hats, caps or bonnets for men or women; to accomplish which, the same process is to be pursued as is usual in the manufacturing straw, chip or Leghorn hats, caps, bonnets, &c. by sewing, or otherwise forming it; after which they may be dyed, stained, or varnished, so as to make them water-proof. They also may be lined with silk, leather, or other material, as fancy may direct. *Repertory of Arts*, November 1807 ~~~ A new kind of hat has just appeared, made in white whalebone, which, to all the delicacy of the chip, from its transparent quality, has the appearance of being lighter; *La Belle Assemblée*, August 1810 ~~~ Hats made of fine Whalebone are now become extremely fashionable, the most elegant and becoming shape is the Cobourg Hat, formed of transparent white whalebone. There is a delicacy in the material, and novelty in the shape, superior to any that we have seen this season. We understand that this invention is patronized by Her Royal Highness. *Ladies' Monthly Museum*, April 1816 ~~~ *Whalebone.* – This singular substance, when softened in hot water, or simply by heating it before a fire, has the property of retaining any shape which may then be given to it, provided it be secured in the required form until it becomes cold. This property, together with its great elasticity and flexibility, renders it capable of being applied to many useful purposes. The first way in which it seems to have been employed was in the stays of ladies. Its application to this purpose, was, at one period, when the quantity imported was small, so general that it attained, in the wholesale way, the price of 700 *l. per* ton. Subsequently, however, it has become less valuable, and of late it has fallen somewhat into disrepute, some ladies having superseded it use in stays, by supporting themselves with plates of steel. There has, for many years, been an extensive consumption of this article in the manufacture of umbrellas and parasols. The white enamel (found in some specimens of whalebone) has recently been fabricated into ladies hats, and into a variety of ornamental forms, as head-dresses; <u>Account of the Arctic Regions</u>, 1820 ~~~ [Paris, in May] first made its appearance; and the *osier baleine*, for summer hats. <u>Museum of Foreign Literature</u>, 1823 ~~~ With regard to any little defects in my dress, all my friends tell me, that to wear no whalebone in my stays is the greatest; and which, I am informed, makes me look like a sack of flour with a string tied round the middle; yet to this I have submitted to please some whimsical notions which Hezekiah entertains about the order of nature, and the symmetry of the human figure. But, as soon as this letter appears in print, I will resume my whalebone, though at the expense of this supposed symmetry. *Manchester Iris*, February 1, 1823 ~~~ ON Mr. GIBSON'S PATENT ELASTIC HATS. It is always with pleasure that we turn to inventions which receive their birth in our own city. The invention of Mr. Gibson consists of a flexible and elastic fabric, applicable to a variety of purposes, but chiefly as a material in the manufacture of hats. This fabric is made in the following method: Whalebone is split down into long pieces, commonly about the thickness of a hay-straw. This operation is performed by those persons whose business it is to break whalebone down into fibres, like hairs, to be used in the manufacture of brushes. Those long pieces of whalebone are then woven into a very open gauze-like fabric; which, from the nature of its materials, is exceedingly flexible and elastic. This is Mr. Gibson's new patent fabric. *Glasgow Mechanics' Magazine*, July 1824 ~~~ [ad] a large assortment whalebone and rattan, for bonnets, constantly on hand, by the gross or dozen; – whalebone for stays constantly on hand, and cut to any pattern, – at the lowest cash prices. *New*

England Farmer, May 27, 1825 ~~~ [Paris] A very brilliant assembly was lately collected together at the salon of the Société des Bonnes-Lettres; several ladies wore dresses, of which the corsages were *à la Sevigné;* quite tight to the shape, and laced behind. On each side, and in front, this tightness was preserved by pieces of whalebone. *Ladies' Monthly Museum,* July 1828 ~~~ [Paris ball dresses] The breadth of the cuffs at the waists of long sleeves is so immense, that the dressmakers are obliged to keep them in shape with whalebone placed between the lining and the outside. A dress of gros-de-Naples appeared lately where the cuff was laced exactly like a little corset. *Ladies' Monthly Museum,* September 1828 ~~~ A material of a still more singular kind has just been introduced for *chapeaux;* it is a light transparent stuff called *gaze de baleine,* because it is manufactured from whalebone; it is made in a variety of colours. We have seen these hats variously ornamented, but now trimming suits them so well as gauze ribands, because they accord best with the gloss and lightness of the *chapeau. Repository of Fashions,* September 1829 ~~~ Opera Dress. A dress of olive green satin. The *corsage* is of velvet, and shaped *en corset.* This body is of an entirely new description, and has only been executed by the first dressmakers in Paris. A particular degree of skill is necessary in the disposition of the whalebones, so as to give it a graceful shape and style of fit. *Royal Lady's,* April 1832 ~~~ [Paris] I must here mention a revival of the ancient modes, and which with the *Polonaise* ensures our comfort sertant du bal – that is, the *calash,* made of silk and whalebone, and exactly such as our grandmothers wore, it does not in the least derange the hair, nor any coiffure, however high – enfin il n'y a rien de plus *comfortable. Lady's Magazine and Museum,* March 1835 ~~~ [ad] Have received by the ships Hark-away and Jefferson, direct from Liverpool, ... 3 cases black, brown, green and blue whalebone, and best finished cotton umbrellas. *Farmer's Register,* May 1835

Whip net – When the principle of gauze weaving is thoroughly understood, its application to the weaving of fancy nets, may be easily acquired. Many varieties of net work are used; but a few, which form the ground work upon which the rest are formed, will be sufficient to elucidate the general principle, and the limits, to which it is necessary to restrict this work, will not admit of more particular details. The most simple of these is known by the name of the WHIP NET. The term *whip* is used by weavers, to denote a species of warp rolled upon a separate beam, and slackened, as may be required, to form fanciful patterns. In this net, the whole warp is of this description, and, therefore, only one beam, or roll, is required. The mounting of the whip net is, in every respect, the same as common gauze, and the connections are formed exactly in the same way. Art of Weaving, 1808 ~~~ the most simple kind of ornamental net-work produced in the loom. It is called a whip-net by weavers, who use the term *whip* for any substance interwoven in cloth for ornamental purposes, when it is distinct from the ground of the fabric. Edinburgh Encyclopædia, 1832 [see also *gauze* and *net*]

white chintz – This is a most useful and economical article, of a delicate texture, termed white chintz, which we have been favoured with by the house of Millard, in the city, where only it is to be obtained, and by whom it is manufactured. It contains three dresses in each piece, and is sold, we learn, at two guineas the piece, reducing the price of the dresses to fourteen shillings each. It is admirably adapted for the different articles of morning costume and of children's wear. We understand this article is unrivalled for durability, and for retaining a beautiful snowy white it equals the hummum and chorea, and surpasses the percoula and izzaree, of Oriental produce, possessing a more elegant fall. *Repository of Arts,* August 1812 ~~~ [Paris] The prettiest dishabille I have seen is composed of white chintz, and worn with a petticoat of the same material; *Repository of Arts,* February 1819 [see *chintz*]

white plains – [see *plains*]

whited-brown –*All unbleached, or brown, is called Bridges Thread; and half bleached Thread, whited brown,* New Merchant's Guide, 1798 ~~~ [British tariff] whited-brown thread, the dozen lbs. 0 18 0 [18*s.*] *Niles' Weekly Register,* October 29, 1825 ~~~ You may actually get there thread made of flax, from the gouty, uneven, clumsy, shiny fabric yclept [called] whited-brown, Our Village, 1828

whittle – [see *kerseymere*]

wildbore – The introduction of stuff-making, as tammies, wildbores, and camblets, with the improvement of the woollen branch, has amazingly increased the population of the town and neighbourhood. [of Wakefield] Tour through the Whole Island of Great Britain, 1801 ~~~ *Wool Trade. Leeds, April 20.* ...

Mr. Jeremiah Naylor said he had made a calculation of the comparative profit to this country of exporting ten packs of wool in the raw and the manufactured state; in the raw state, including the expences of shipping, it would fetch about 232*l.*; if manufactured into a species of stuff called wildbores, it would sell for about 631*l.*; which, allowing 30*l.* for the materials used, would leave an increase of upwards of 400*l.* for the labour bestowed upon it; and which, if the wool had been exported in the raw state, would have been lost to the country. *Literary Panorama*, May 1816 ~~~ Worsted and stuff goods, such as ... wildboars, ... &c. which are composed entirely of wool are subject to an ad valorem duty of 15 per cent. National Calendar, 1820

willow – Osier, a tree of the willow kind, growing by the water. Sheridan's English Dictionary, 1797 ~~~ Advert – 'It may be requisite to explain to those, who are not acquainted with the produce of *Cambridgeshire,* and the manners of the people, that rearing osiers, for making baskets, hats, &c. is a profitable branch of trade, and peeling them for use, a favourite employment of the young women at a certain time of the year. When they have completed their work, they go in procession, dressed in their holy-day clothes, decorated with the strips peeled from the rods; they collect contributions, and with them make a feast and. a dance. 'The delicate willow hats, of late so fashionable, are made of Cambridgeshire osiers.' [ad for *Mary, the Osier-Peeler, a simple but true Story: a Poem,* published in 1798] *Analytical Review,* December 1798 ~~~ Round hat of striped willow. *Boston Magazine,* September 24, 1803 ~~~ *Patent-method of making Hats water proof, by Mr. William Hance, of Tooley-street.* In the usual mode of making Hats, they are stiffened with glue, which, when they are exposed to rain, fastens down the nap, and causes them to look old and greasy. Mr. Hance's hats are free from this defect, as no glue or stiffening of any sort is used in finishing their external parts. The felted part of these hats is made so thin, that it could not support itself without the internal part, which is formed of willow, or some other matter of sufficient stiffness. *Athenæum,* June 1807 ~~~ A Morning, or Walking Dress. ... A Helmet hat of basket willow, ornamented with amber-coloured ribband, *La Belle Assemblée,* October 1807 ~~~ Walking bonnets of willow shavings are very general, and extremely neat. *Edinburgh Annual Register,* July 1, 1813 ~~~ The most fashionable bonnets at present are composed of French willow, and made in the French form, *Ladies' Monthly Museum,* October 1817 ~~~ Round hats are made of willow, in imitation of straw plait; small pieces of whalebone being used to give them support. These are called *osier valiene.* [probably *baleine*] *Ladies' Monthly Museum,* May 1822 ~~~ *SALIX, Ozier, Sallow or Withy, and Willow,* ... *Salix Amygdalina,* Almon, or Peach-leaved, is the most common, and generally known by the appellation of Huntingdonshire Willow; for which there has been a great demand for making Willow Hats, for Gentlemen's summer wear, split and worked the same as Straw for Bonnets. Forest Trees, 1827 [see also *chip*]

willow feather – When feathers are worn in silk bonnets – and they begin to prevail – they droop, in the weeping-willow-style, over the back of the crown; *La Belle Assemblée,* November 1825

wincie – the mixing of Cotton with Linen has been tried with success, sometimes the warp made of Linen and sometimes the weft, but if the weft is made Linen and the warp Cotton, the Weaver must have his shuttle made so that it draw the weft shot well in at the selvedges, as they are particularly difficult to make neat, and if proper care is not taken, they will resemble the teeth of a saw, but when the weft is Cotton this is not the case; the principle fabrics with which Cotton is mixed are Damasks Diaper, Sheeting, Shirting, and Wincie. In Damasks, Diaper, and Wincie, the Cotton used must be soft or Mull spun yarn, and of a size so as to make the figures of just and proportionable dimensions, for if the weft was too small, the figures would be too short, and if the weft be too heavy, the figure will be too long, therefore care must be taken that the size of the weft for every set be proportioned, to make the figures uniform and just in all their parts; Wincie needs only weft to make a stout Cloth, and cover the warp, ... Wincie is used for gowns, petticoats, &c. and has a much better appearance, if the warp is slightly dyed. Linen Manufacturer, 1817

wire – the little elastic brass cylinder, which is used in making suspenders, and was formerly worn by sailors as a hat-band. Journal of travels in England, Holland and Scotland, 1810 ~~~ The only novelty in head-dresses is the gipsey cap, the form of which is that of a small gipsey hat, but it is composed entirely of lace; round the edge it is wired to keep it in shape, and trimmed so as to conceal the wire with a plaiting of net; *Edinburgh Annual Register*, October 29, 1812 ~~~ the spiral wire of the suspenders which form at this time an article of every gentleman's dress <u>Elements of Surgery</u>, 1813 ~~~ transparent bonnets of crape, or *tulle,* are frequently seen in carriages, and are much worn in half dress at the theatres: these transparent bonnets are generally ornamented with rose-coloured ribbands, which are placed in twists or flutings over the wires that quarter the brims. *La Belle Assemblée,* November 1816 ~~~ English Carriage Dress. ... with Etruscan facings ... The Etruscan points of the facings are edged with wire chain fringe of a pink colour, and each point terminated by a tassel. *Kaleidoscope,* March 6, 1821 ~~~ Cornettes, well wired, and extending wide from the temples, over which is placed, on one side, a small full blown rose, on the other a bunch of auriculas, are much in favour for receiving friendly dinner parties at home: they are made of beautiful blond lace, and the caul is of pink satin, *Ladies' Monthly Museum,* November 1824 ~~~ Among the recent inventions at Paris – an elastic stiffening of a vegetable substance has been invented, instead of that spiral brass wire now used for shoulder-straps, glove-tops, corsets, &c.: it is valuable, because it neither cuts the cloth that covers it, nor corrodes with verdigris: it is said to be made of Indian rubber, *Lady's Magazine,* September 1830

wired riband – *Regulation of Silk Manufacturers' Wages.* ... WIRE RIBBON. This is work with wires in the body, show with silk or cotton. Under and up to ¼ of an inch, not exceeding 18 leishes with two wires 0*s.* 7*d.* From ¼ to ½ an inch, not exceeding 34 leiches with three wires 0*s.* 10*d.* From ½ up to ¾ of an inch, not exceeding 50 leishes with four wires 1*s.* 1*d. Tradesman,* August 1810 ~~~ These flounces are disposed in waves; they are put on at some distance from each other; the edge of every flounce is finished with a piping of satin to correspond in colour with the dress; a wire riband is passed through this piping to make each flounce stand a little out from the other. *Ladies' Monthly Museum,* February 1819 ~~~ The cornettes for home *déshabille* still continue to be set out wide from the temples, by means of wired ribbon; they are composed chiefly of fine net and blond, *La Belle Assemblée,* September 1823 ~~~ Very broad ribands are now used in the trimming of blond caps; they are so broad that they take three rows of wired riband, to keep the puffs or bows in shape; flowers in wreaths conceal this stiffening. *Lady's Magazine,* September 1829

wolf fur – while the account of ornamental articles which our country does not produce, and we cannot wish it to produce, continues, upon the whole, to rise, in spite of all the caprices of fancy and fashion. Of this kind are the different furs* used for muffs, trimmings, and linings, which, as the chief of the kind, I shall particularize. ... * Furs. ... The skins here selected from the Custom-House Accounts are, *Black Bear, Ordinary Fox, Marten, Mink, Musquash, Otter, Raccoon,* and *Wolf.* <u>Third Letter to a Member of the Present Parliament</u>, 1797 ~~~ By some information of due authority which has been recently made public, we learn, that the *fur-trade* of the British Canadian Provinces, is now in a flourishing state. Its produce in the year 1798, consisted of ... 3800 wolf skins, *Monthly Magazine,* January 1802... [Paris] The fashionable furs are the fox, the white wolf of Siberia, and chinchilla: the fur tippets have very long ends. *La Belle Assemblée,* January 1823 ~~~ Muffs of the skin of the grey wolf are much in favour. *La Belle Assemblée,* January 1826

wolves teeth – [Paris] Puckers made to resemble wolves teeth are fancifully dispersed at the bottom of most fashionable gowns. *La Belle Assemblée,* June 1806 ... [Paris] Gauze and crape hats are trimmed round the edge of the brim with a piece of the same material cut byas, and disposed plaits of a peculiar shape, which the Parisians call *wolves' mouths. Ladies' Monthly Museum,* September 1818 ~~~ [Paris] The brims of *chapeaux* are variously ornamented: some have a trimming of gauze in wolves' mouths, a style of trimming which has for some time been exploded, but is now again become fashionable; *Repository of Arts,* August 1819 ~~~ Velvet bonnet to correspond: the front at the edges is trimmed, within and without, with fluted velvet, and interspersed with wolves' teeth, or velvet points, edged with two rows of *gros de Naples* cord: *Manchester Iris,* December 7, 1822 ~~~ [Paris] The brims of *chapeaux* are variously ornamented: some have a trimming of gauze in *wolves' mouths,* a style of trimming which has for some time been exploded, but is now again becoming fashionable; *Repository of Arts,* August 1819 ~~~ They are trimmed round *en dents de loups* (wolves'-teeth), *Ladies' Monthly Museum,* February 1824 ~~~ [Paris] Dresses of plain tulle are trimmed with two or three flounces, figured with *dents de loup;*

these *dents* are very large, and bordered with a large stripe, marked in the tulle, by six or seven large flat welts, placed at a short distance from each other. These welts are arranged in zig-zags, above the trimming on the petticoat. This kind of embroidery is much used in tulle this year: it has the advantage of being executed quickly, and producing a pretty effect. *Ladies' Monthly Museum*, June 1827 ~~~ [Paris] The trimming mostly adopted for the skirts of promenade dresses, is a deep flounce with a broad heading; the latter is either arranged in festoons, or disposed in those large round plaits, called *dents de loup*. *Ladies' Pocket*, March 1830 ~~~ We see also many blond lace caps, or rather head-dresses, composed of blond lace: they are arranged on wire ribands in the large deep plaits called *dents de loup*; *Ladies' Museum*, March 1831

Woodstock – [see *doe skin*]

woof – [see *weft*]

wool – Great-Britain sends [to Brazil] woollen manufactures, such as fine broad medley cloths, fine Spanish cloths, scarlet and black cloths, serges, duroys, druggets, sagathies, shalloons, camblets, and Norwich stuffs, black Colchester bays, says, and perpetuanas, called long ells, hats, stockings and gloves. Historical, Geographical, Commercial, and Philosophical View of the United States of America, 1795 ~~~ The stable jackets are to be of white woollen, with white-raised metal buttons, double-breasted, high fall-down collar, two buttons at the sleeve, and edged with the colour of the facing of the Regiment, with pockets. Rules and Regulations for the Cavalry, 1795 ~~~ The wool of the above sheep [Leonese] was of the sort, which the English call *clothing wool,* which is very soft, greasy, curly or rather wavy, thick matted together at the top, and is preferred by the clothiers, because it *felts* better, and makes a finer cloth, than the sort which is dry, hairy, pointed at the extremities, bushy, and commonly longer and thinner. The wool of the less fortunate cargoes of Spanish sheep, resembled more the last described, or Andalusian species, though considerably finer than the Barbary, Roman, or English sorts of wool, which are called *combing wools*. Communications to the Board of Agriculture, 1797 ~~~ [Paris] The most elegant [shawls] are of wool or cotton, on a white ground, with a slight embroidery along the edge, and a bunch of flowers on each corner. *Lady's Magazine*, December 1800 ~~~ Wool, in the fleece, is classed under two heads or denominations, the one combing, or long stapled; the other clothing, or short stapled wool; each fleece, when sub-divided, produces different degrees of fineness, in both classes. And some fleeces produce wool, which maybe used in either (but unprofitably); hence proceed all the different qualities of manufacture, which we fee made of wool, and after these forts are separated by the wool stapler.* The manufactures of the combing, and of the clothing wool, are a distinct business, as those of silk and wool. Of combing wool is made *worsted*, and of it serges, poplins, stuffs, calamancoes, stockings, &c. And of clothing wool is made yarn, and of it broad cloth, frize, blankets, &c. And of yarn and worsted, when manufactured together in the same web, are made cassimeres, drugget, carpets, &c. † * The wool-stapler is the person, who separates the fleece into its different degrees of fineness. † Let this idea strike you, and you'll better understand those distinctions, when you conceive that in goods, made of worsted, the excellence consists in having as *few as possible* of the ends of the wool lying out of the stuff. And in goods, made of yarn, the excellence lies in the *greatest quantity* of the ends of the wool being brought out on the surface, having regard to the texture. From which it is to be concluded, that the finer and shorter the wool is, that is used in cloth, the greater number of ends of wool may be brought to the surface, without robbing the thread of sufficient substance, and which gives a rich downy feel and appearance to cloth: besides, the greater number of small parts a thread is composed of, the greater strength and permanency it will have. Statistical Survey of the County Dublin, 1801 ~~~ Spanish and British wools are continually worked up together in the manufacture of fine cloths. It is a common question in the cloth-halls of Yorkshire, in England, to ask, – How much Spanish wool is there in this piece? – and the answer generally is, – half and half; – that is, half Spanish and half English wool. Neither is it true, as Mr. Livingston also roundly asserts, that the British native wool is only capable of being made into coarse cloths. Fine broad cloth, up to the price of fifteen or sixteen shillings a yard, is, every day, made entirely of English wool; – cloth, from fifteen to twenty shillings a yard, is made of Spanish and English wool mixed; and superfine cloth, from twenty to thirty shillings a yard and upwards, is made altogether of Spanish wool.

These prices relate to cloth in its *undressed* state; when it comes to the hand of the consumer, of course, the cost is considerably enhanced. Hints on the National Bankruptcy of Britain, 1809 ~~~ *English Wool.* – The wools of England have always been in the highest repute; and that more abroad than at home. Some we have, which manufactured by our own clothiers, both for softness and fineness vies with the choicest silks. *Spanish wools,* indeed, bear a great price; but it is certain that much the greater part of that, which, when manufactured, our clothiers, &c. call *Spanish cloth,* grows in England. – It is allowed the goodness of the Spanish wools is owing to a few English sheep sent over, into Spain, as a present, by Henry II. of England; or, as others will have it, though we think erroneously, by Edward IV. in 1465. The fineness and plenty of our wools is owing, in some measure, to the sweet, short grass in many of our pastures and downs; though the advantage of our sheep feeding on this grass all the year, without being obliged to be shut up in the folds during the winter, or to secure them from wolves at other times, contributes not a little to its excellence. Of late, the English fleece has been greatly improved by crossing the breed with Spanish merino and English fine-woolled sheep; the offspring of this mixed breed yielding wool in some respects superior to the best in Spain. The English sheep are of two kinds; one which yields fine short clothing, the other which produces coarse long combing, wool. The South Down, Hereford, and Norfolk breeds, belong to the former class: the Lincoln and Leicestershire to the latter. English wool has also been improved by greasing the skins of sheep, and cutting them during winter. Guy's Pocket Cyclopædia, 1810 ~~~ but does it not shew that, beyond the powers of increasing the human species, the other sex are intended merely for the comfort of the labouring sex; with full liberty, that unbounded duty being performed, to attend to the trifling business of buying or selling blond, gauze, caps, &c.; from which, however, all other human beings, not wearing petticoats, should be excluded. Notwithstanding ladies wear pelisses and riding-habits, made of cloth, never does a female make her appearance behind the counters of the respectable woollen-drapers, for the very reason that the tailors are left to procure the patterns. *La Belle Assemblée,* April 1818 ~~~ We know not how to approach a delicate female in woollen, the very idea of the touch of wool is unfeminine – masculine. Even the riding habit is scarcely justified by its apparent necessity (for it is not necessary); *Atheneum,* October 1825 ~~~ The fabrics formed of wool are very various. The *superfine broad cloth,* of which our coats are made, stands at the head of the list; then come *narrow cloths,* which are of a coarser texture. Flannels, blankets &c. are also made of wool; indeed so many are its uses, that it would be tedious to enumerate them. Many elegant fabrics are formed by a small mixture of wool with other articles. Poplins and lustres have some silk in them; and some flannels have a little cotton mingled. Book of Commerce by Sea and Land, 1834 ~~~ *Animal Wool.* Articles of dress composed of this substance produce moderate warmth, owing to the stimulus and gentle friction it occasions on the skin. By its use, animal electricity is elicited, perspiration promoted, the perspired humors are absorbed, and again easily evaporated, on account of its porous properties. Toilette of Health, Beauty, and Fashion, 1834 ~~~ Woollen cloths vary in price, not only in regard to fineness but to colors, from 13*s.* to 30*s.* for blacks and blues; from 2*l.* 2*s.* to 3*l.* 3*s.* for scarlets; from 2*l.* 10*s.* to 4*l.* 4*s.* for orange; and from 1*l.* 4*s.* to 2*l.* 5*s.* for crimson and French grey. One yard of superfine woollen cloth weighs 1lb. 2oz.; and 1 yard kerseymere 11 ½ oz. A Million of Facts, 1835 ~~~ The fabrics formed of wool are very various: *superfine broad cloths* stand at the head of the list. These are chiefly worn at home, where the prevailing colours are blue and black. *Narrow cloths,* which are half the breadth of the broad, are generally of stronger fabric, and not so fine. Of these a great exportation takes place. *Kerseymeres,* which are generally narrow, are twilled, and of various thicknesses. *Kerseys* are nearly of the same fabric with the last mentioned, but much thicker and stouter. *Coatings,* which are of a coarse open texture, are used for great coats and other inferior purposes. Besides these, we have *swansdown,* a loose and woolly but warm fabric, for waistcoats; *flannels* and *fleecy hosiery,* for invalids; *stockings,* upper and under; *calimancoes,* for women's shoes; and *stuffs,* of various degrees of fineness, for gowns. The latter used to be worn mostly by servants and poor people, who now prefer cotton; and the genteeler part of society have taken to them, under the names of *merinos,* &c. "In addition to the fabrics already noticed, our attention should be drawn towards two inferior articles, which, though far from splendid, give employment to a great number of hands, at Sudbury, in Suffolk; these are *buntine* for flags, and *shrouds* for the dead. "*Buntine* is a thin open sort of woollen stuff, very pliable, though strong; it is woven in stripes, blue, white, red, &c. which stripes are afterwards sewed strongly together, in the form required for any particular flag; their different shapes and the arrangement of the colours having specific meanings. "To encourage the growth of wool, a law was made, in an early period of our history, enjoining all bodies to be buried in wool, under a heavy penalty. To meet this law, the manufacture of shrouds took place, consisting of a very thin stuff, of a whitish colour, of which a dress for the dead is made up. But since cotton has become of equal importance with wool, in a commercial point of view, this law has been abrogated by act of parliament. Yet though people may now bury their dead in what habiliments they please, the manufacture of shrouds is still considerable. Scenes of Commerce, 1836 … Over this dress is thrown a loose robe, *à l'orientale*, composed of a tissue of light wool, striped and figured with silk; the lining is of blue taffeta. *Royal Lady's*, May 1832 [see also *cashmere*, *lamb's wool*, *merino*, *Saxon*, and *thibet*]

wool gauze – Evening Dress. … Head-dress, a coronation hat, composed of *gaze de laine*. *Repository of Arts*, August 1821 ~~~ [Paris] Bonnets … are generally ornamented with white down feathers; the lappets are of white *crêpe lisse* or white *gauze de laine*. *Ladies' Monthly Museum*, March 1825 ~~~ [Paris] Young ladies wear white dresses of woollen gauze. This very clear gauze is a medium between organdy and crape, and is of a delightful freshness; it corresponds admirably with the lightness required by the *ruches* placed at the bottom of the dresses, in four or five rows, *Ladies' Monthly Museum*, August 1826 ~~~ Evening Dress. A gown of rose-coloured gaze de laine, over a satin slip of a corresponding shade. *Casket*, April 1830 ~~~ Where the cap is composed of blond net, or of *gaze de laine* (a kind of woollen gauze, extremely light and fine), the trimming is a double quilling of plain blond net *Maids, Wives, and Widows*, February 9, 1833 [see also *foulard de laine* and *mousseline de laine*]

woolenet – [ad for men's clothing] Summer Goods, … Woolenetts, … of all colour and qualities. … Vestings, … Woolinets Boston Annual Advertiser, 1823 ~~~ Woollenets, Tariff, 1829

woolfel – a sheep's skin not stripped of the wool. Perry's English Dictionary, 1805

woollen – Made of wool not finely dressed, and thence used likewise for any thing coarse; it is likewise used in general for *made of wool*, as distinct from *linen*. Encyclopædia Perthensis, 1816 [see *wool*]

woollen chintz – In deshabille, stuff dresses, of a very fine texture, are much worn, some of them are painted to imitate Indian chintz, and they are named *woollen chintz*. *Ladies' Museum*, February 1829

woollen muslin – [see *mousseline de laine*]

woollen satin – [see *satin de laine*]

woolsey – [awarded in 1795] Third Rate Premium [loosely: third place prize] … Gown and woolsey petticoat. … That two surveyors be from time to time appointed by the committee out of their own body, who are … to buy wool for woolsey, State of the Poor, 1797 ~~~ A parish-officer, who was mindful of this, would never purchase a cotton or linen gown for the poor instead of a woolsey one, which is much stronger, cheaper, and more comfortable; History of the Poor, 1797 [see also *linsey-woolsey*]

worsted – Worsted, yarn spun from combed wool. Perry's English Dictionary, 1795 ~~~ It has often been observed, that when we wear worsted under-stockings, and silk over them, if we chance to draw off the silk stocking in the dark, the bright electric fluid is seen flashing from every part of the worsted under-stocking. Philosophy of Medicine, 1799 ~~~ The spinner forms the wool into threads, which are more or less twisted, according to the manufacture for which they are designed. The more twisted is called *worsted*; the looser, *yarn*. Arts of Life, 1802 ~~~ [1794] Mr. *Joseph Jennings* being examined, said, He is a Worsted Manufacturer, and lives in the City of *London*; he knows the different Sorts of Wool used in this Country, and that there is a Sort of Wool called Long Wool, that is selected from the Short for the sole Purpose of being combed. … And being asked, What Sort of Articles in the Woollen Manufactory must necessarily be made of the Combing Wool? he said, Sagathies, Duroy plain, Duroy figured, Draughts, Estamanes, Shalloons, Serge plain, Tamies, Poplins, Lastings, Bombazines, Bombazette, Callimanco, Harratines, Stuff Damask, Barragon, Camblets, Sattinette, Crapes, *English* Shawls, Moncriefs, Russells, Buntings, Grograms, Carpeting, Worsted Plush, Worsted Hose, Worsted Fringe, Lace and Bindings, Worsted Crewels, Drugetts, Rackers, Long Ells, *German* Serge, Sanfords,

Frays, Coarse Ells, and Baize. Journals of the House of Commons, 1803 ~~~ *It resembled a soldier's hat to me, it was bound round with worsted binding, and the worsted binding was ragged.* Murder of Mr. Steele, 1807 ~~~ he said, that was the hat left by one of his companions; it had the appearance of an old soldier's hat, with worsted binding, and that binding was ragged; Murder of Mr. Steele, 1807 ~~~ *Army Estimates.* ... Laughable as this seemed, it was the fact; the heavy dragoon was to have white worsted web pantaloons, and on home service, blue worsted web pantaloons! This might do very well for Bond-street, but certainly it was very unfit for foreign service. Now, the reason for making these alterations was, that the colonel of a regiment, on the new articles, made a profit of about 700*l.* per annum, *Parliamentary Debates*, March 8, 1813 ~~~ The little village of Worsted is remarkable for giving a name to a kind of cloths made of wool, differently dressed from those denominated woollens; the yarn of the former being spun from combed, and of the latter from carded wool. New British Traveller, 1819 ~~~ [Paris] Shawls of Cachemire, and those of fine worsted, in imitation of the Oriental ones, are favorite out-door envelopes. *Lady's Magazine*, April 1829 ~~~ Worsted bindings, gloves, mits, hose, stockings, socks or half stockings, ...Worsted drawers, Tariff, 1829 ~~~ Cloths, that are woven of worstedyarn, have the general name of Worsted-Stuffs, or simply Stuffs, and are specifically denominated according to the manner in which they are severally manufactured. Most of these articles have been made in imitation of the fabrics of France and Spain, and, in consequence, their names are, for the greater part, imported from those countries. The following are the principal denominations: [bunting, bombazet, calamanco, durant, lasting, shalloon, taminy, tartan] Analytical Dictionary, 1830 ~~~ There is also a *worsted lace,* of a similar texture [stout and close], commonly wrought with various patterns in colors. This was formerly much used on liveries, and may still be seen occasionally on the lining of carriages. New Family Encyclopedia, 1831 ~~~ *Worsted*, a thread spun of wool that has been combed, and which, in the spinning, is twisted harder than ordinarily. New Universal Gazetteer, 1832 ~~~ [Paris] For evening dress black or white mittens or gloves, à jours. Pocket handkerchiefs embroidered in English coloured worsted, a Persian, Cashmere, or Greek pattern, are much worn. *Lady's Magazine and Museum*, July 1834 ~~~ This was a suit to recover $30,100 paid at different periods by plaintiff as duties on merchandise which he imported, and which duties he contended were illegal. The articles in question were worsted shawls with cotton borders sewed on, and worsted suspenders, with cotton straps. ... it was admitted that wool when combed loses its appellation of wool, and is called worsted; that that woollen and worsted goods are distinctly understood by merchants and traders to be two different articles. *Niles' Weekly Register*, November 22, 1834 ~~~ Long Wool is straightened and the hairs separated, lengthwise, with a steel comb, by the Woolcomber. This combed Wool is divided into small parcels, or Slavers, which are drawn out into smaller stripes, called Plucks, and then spun, always preserving the fibres in their longitudinal direction. This yarn is Worsted, so termed, as it is said, from a town of that name, in the county of Norfolk. Worstedyarn is manufactured into calamancoes, shalloons, bombazets and other light stuffs, of which the threads are visible, not being covered with a pile. The Worsted Stockings of the Hosier are wrought with this material. Analytical Dictionary, 1835 ~~~ The manufacture of *wool* is divided into two distinct classes, – long wool, or worsted-spinning, and short wool, or woollen-yarn-spinning. ... In spinning *worsted* by hand, the portion of wool plucked from the sliver was placed across the fingers of the left hand, and from the thick part of it the fibres were drawn and twisted as the hand was withdrawn from the end of the spindle, to which it had been previously attached. The revolution of the wheel, effected by the right hand, conveyed by a band to the wheel, or pulley on the spindle, produced the requisite to give firmness to the thread; and by a very gentle motion of the same wheel, the thread being brought nearly perpendicular to the spindle, it was wound upon the spindle to form the cop. From this it was transferred to the reel, and became a hank, of a definite length, but varying in weight with the thickness of the thread. In this state it was transferred to the manufacturer, to be converted into shalloons, bombazin, or whatever other fabric *worsted* is applicable to. ... In spinning worsted by machinery, a sliver of wool is laid upon the drawing-frame, from whence it is conducted through several pairs of rollers, of which the operation of the first and last are the essential ones, the intermediate rollers moving with equal velocities, and serving merely to conduct the skin, which is received into a cylindrical can; three such skins being passed through another drawing-frame, and stretched in their progress, become fitted for roving, – the last step in the preparatory process. The spinning, which is the concluding process, is effected by means of two pair of rollers moving with equal velocities, and intermediate auxiliaries. <u>Engineer's and Mechanic's Encyclopædia</u>, 1836

Xuassed - Xuassed

Xuassed – The materials for *Chapeaux* are various, and some new ones have been introduced, but we cannot yet say how far they will become fashionable; … a third is called *Xuassed*, it is split straw manufactured in a new manner. *Ladies' Monthly Museum*, May 1819

York beaver - York tan

York beaver – A warm cloak of "York beaver," a new and handsome manufacture of woollen cloth. <u>Register of Arts</u>, 1828 [see also *beaver cloth*]

York tan – Riding-dress … York tan gloves. *Lady's Magazine*, May 1797 ~~~ the apples are sliced thin and dried in the sun, till they take the consistence and appearance of slips of leather, of that kind and colour usually called the York tan. <u>Account of Travels into the Interior of Southern Africa</u>, 1801 ~~~ Morning Dresses. … York tanned gloves; and a bear-skin muff. *Ladies' Monthly Museum*, January 1802 ~~~ White kid gloves form an indispensable part of full dress; York tan, or Limerick, is most esteemed on other occasions; *La Belle Assemblée*, March 1807 ~~~ Except in full dress, gloves are left entirely to individual choice; but pale colours in French kind, we think, have lately succeeded to the York tan, and Limerick of universal adoption. *Lady's Weekly Miscellany*, December 31, 1808 ~~~ Promenade Walking Dress. … with York tanned gloves; *Jersey Magazine*, August 1810 ~~~ Sketches of English Manners. The Female Charioteer. … Driving one day in the Circular Road, near Dublin, her horses pulled very hard, and would have blistered common fingers, but, protected by the stiff York tan, and hardened by the management of the whip, she stood up and punished them, crying, "I'll take the *shine* out of you before I have done with you!" *Robinson's Magazine*, December 18, 1818 ~~~ Gentlemen's gloves are of that yellow, known by the name of *York tan,* or they are of various shades of olive green or drab. <u>Scenes of Commerce</u>, 1836

Zalia - Zig-zag

zalia – [ad] Dresses of various designs for Morning, Dinner, Evening, and Ball Costume, in China Silk, ... Velvet, Zalia, *Declaration of the Catholic Bishops*, September 1826 [see also *zelia*]

zebra – *Zebra Dresses* are much in request, and a number of weavers have been engaged for them. Price of weaving paid by the Plaid regulation. The warps are spun silk. *Weavers' Magazine*, December 1818 ~~~ *Zebra Dresses and Shawls* are very flat, and the manufacturers are discharging their weavers. *Weavers' Magazine*, April 1819 ~~~ Zebra gauze is also much used in the fabrication of hats; the stripes are of lilac, rose-colour, and green. *La Belle Assemblée*, September 1819 ~~~ and jaconot zebra muslin is a favourite article for blouses [blouse dresses] with flounces of embroidered muslin. *La Belle Assemblée*, September 1823 ~~~Cross Zebras are also a kind of double damask, which have their patterns running in stripes across the cloth. The spotting is sometimes flushed between the figures, and sometimes incorporated with the warp. Art of Weaving, 1831 ~~~ Zebra weaving – harness-loom. Draw boy, aged about nine. Works fourteen hours a day. Stands barefooted on earthen damp-floor constantly. Never can sit except whilst the weaver is dressing his web, for about a quarter of an hour four times a day. Cannot read. Is paid 2*s.* 1*d.* per week; the penny for himself, by way of encouragement. Appears dull; but says he is in health. Reports from Commissioners, 1833 ~~~ The fashionable colors for gentlemen's dresses at Paris are blue and bottle green, the latter with ornamental buttons; shawl waistcoats; yellow gloves; kerseymere pants, striped *à la zebra*. *Bookseller's Advertiser*, December 1834 ~~~ The ribands of French manufacture which have this year been imported, are among the most splendid articles of winter fashion. They are in Arabesque, Mosaic, and Zebra patterns, and the colours are the most brilliant imaginable. These ribands have a superb effect when employed for trimming dresses, a use to which they are now very generally assigned. *Court Journal*, October 31, 1835 ~~~ In Glasgow, connected with the cotton trade, there are, according to the Directory, 1835: ... Zebra Dress Makers ... 5 General Statistics of the British Empire, 1836

zebra feather – surmounted by a plume of Zebra feathers, of peach colour and black. *La Belle Assemblée*, August 1816

zelia – Walking-Dress. ... A bonnet of French white *gros de Naples*, lined with gauze *lissé*, tastefully trimmed with Zelia gauze, and an elegant Marabout feather placed across the crown. *Ladies' Monthly Museum*, May 1823 ~~~ [ad] Quincy Tufts, ... Has received ... Elegant Satin Stripe Gauze Hdkfs.; Zelas do. [ditto, handkerchiefs]; *New England Farmer*, June 3, 1825 ~~~Zelias, (silk) *Public Documents*, March 1832

zephercene – [see *zephyrine*]

zephyr – [court dress] A magnificent dress of apple-green crape, richly embroidered in silver, ... and trimmed with large silver zephyr and Vandyke fringe, *La Belle Assemblée*, June 1807 ~~~ The most favourite hat for walking is ... finished at the edge with a novel trimming of the zephyr kind, made of the satin and gossamer straw, which form a beautiful contrast. ... [Paris] Dress hats are ... ornamented with full blown roses, or a plume of the zephyr or down feathers. *La Belle Assemblée*, July 1816 ~~~ cloaks of a fine woollen cloth, called *zephyr*, are very much in request; *Ladies' Pocket*, February 1830 ~~~ Zephyrs (light silk shawls) Commercial Directory, 1823 ~~~ Some wear little square shawls of soft crape, called zephyrs, these are of the most lively colours; *Lady's Magazine*, May 31, 1830 ~~~ Ball Dress. – Gauzes seem most in favour this month, particularly *gaze zephyr*. ... We may cite as one of the most elegant, a dress of rose-coloured *gaze zephyr* embroidered about the hem in a wreath of vine leaves in green silk; *Day*, February 6, 1832 ~~~ [Paris] One of the most elegant half dresses that I have remarked, is of blue *moire*, ... the sleeves were *en gigot* of white gauze zephyr. *La Belle Assemblée*, April 1832 ~~~ [Paris dinner party] Her scarf was of tulle *zephyr blanc*. *Court Magazine*, January 1833 ~~~ [court dress] A black zephyr gauze petticoat over black satin, trimmed with bugles; a black train of moire silk, lined with black satin, and embroidered in bugles. *Court Journal*, June 22, 1833 ~~~ [ad] To Ladies. – A. Gotto having this day received from her agents in Berlin, a large assortment of patterns, and Zephyr Lambswool, of the most splendid tints, etc., and replenished her Stock of French Decker, Floss, Netting, and other Silks, in every variety of shade. *Court Journal*, July 4, 1835 ~~~ Zephyrs, silk Jones's Digest, 1836 ~~~ Evening Dress. ... Zephyr scarf richly embroidered. *Court Magazine*,

October 1836

zephyr feather – a new kind of feather, called the zephyr plume, *La Belle Assemblée*, April 1819

zephyrine – The pelisse worn with this dress is composed of the beautiful new silk called *zephyreene*; *Atheneum*, July 1, 1818 ~~~ Court Dress. … The robe is blue *zephyrine*; … The new silk called *zephyrine* is also a good deal used in trimmings; its light and soft texture renders it very well adapted for that purpose. *Repository of Arts*, July 1820 ~~~ Some additions have been made to our stock of silks: one of these is the material called zephyreene, *Atheneum*, July 1820 ~~~ Walking dress. … the spencer worn with this dress is composed of lavender coloured *zephercene*. The body is tight to the shape; the waist is the usual length. A large collar, lined with pink *zephercene* falls very low in the neck. *Ladies' Monthly Museum*, August 1820 ~~~ Evening Dress. A round dress composed of pale pink *soi de Londres*, trimmed with pink zephyreen fluted in a scroll pattern. *Kaleidoscope*, March 6, 1821 ~~~ [court dress] A white satin dress, covered with a white zephyrine dress, embroidered with violet and gold; *Court Journal*, March 2, 1833

zibelline – [see *sable*]

zig-zag – *Princess of* Wales. – White crape petticoat, richly embroidered with silver in stripes, with silver spangles between, ornamented with a rich border of silver embroidered scarlet satin in zig-zag, and silver lace: *Lady's Magazine*, January 1797 ~~~ Zigzag, Having many short turns, turning this way and that. They are words of ludicrous formation, but frequently used by the best authors. Sheridan's English Dictionary, 1797 ~~~ [Paris] Dark blue muslins, and white muslins, embroidered in zig-zags, are worn. *Lady's Magazine*, December 1800 ~~~ richly decorated with lace, put on in a novel and rather whimsical manner in four zig-zag rows, laid one above another, *Repository of Arts*, June 1818 ~~~ Materials for dresses are white muslin and printed muslins, mostly large stripes or rays on a white ground. A new pattern was much noticed of large zigzags in columns, with wreaths of flowers between these marks. *Lady's Magazine*, May 31, 1830

Bibliography

Books

A Calvary Officer. The Whole Art of Dress: or, The Road to Elegance and Fashion. London: Effingham Wilson, 1830

A Gentleman of the Inner Temple. The Ship-Master's Assistant and Owner's Manual. London: David Steel, 1795

A Lady of Distinction. The Mirror of the Graces; or, the English Lady's Costume. London: 1811

A Lady of Distinction. The Mirror of the Graces; or, the English Lady's Costume. New York: I. Riley, 1813

A Lady of Distinction. The Mirror of the Graces; or, the English Lady's Costume. Edinburgh: 1830

Adjutant General's Office. Rules and Regulations for the Cavalry. London: J. Walter, 1795

Aiken, J. The Arts of Life. London: J. Johnson, 1802

Anderson, Adam. An Historical and Chronological Deduction of the Origin of Commerce, from the Earliest Accounts. London: J. Write, 1801 [referred to as Origin of Commerce, 1801]

Ash, John. The New and Complete Dictionary of the English Language. London: Vernor and Hood, 1795 [referred to as Ash's English Dictionary, 1795]

Babbage, Charles. On the Economy of Machinery And Manufactures. London: Charles Knight, 1832

Baines, Edward. History of the Cotton Manufacture of Great Britain. London: H. Fisher, R. Fisher, and P. Jackson, 1836

Barclay, James. A Complete and Universal English Dictionary. London: G. G. and J. Robinson et al, 1799 [referred to as Barclay's English Dictionary, 1799]

Beawes, Wyndham and Joseph Chitty. Lex Mercatoria: or, a Complete Code of Commercial Law. London: P. C. and J. Rivington et al, 1813

Bee, Jon. Slang. A Dictionary of the Turf, the Ring, the Chase, the Pit, of Bon-Ton, and the Varieties of Life. London: T. Hughes, 1823

Bearcroft, William . Practical Orthography, or the Art of Teaching Spelling by Writing. New York: Mahlon Day, 1828

Bell, James. A New and Comprehensive Gazetteer of England and Wales. Glasgow: A. Fullarton & Co., 1836

Brewster, David. Edinburgh Encyclopædia. Edinburgh: William Blackwood, 1830

Boniface, Antoine Alexander. Dictionnaire Français-Anglais et Anglais-Français. Paris: De Belin Mandar et Devaux, 1828 [referred to as Boniface's French Dictionary, 1828]

Booth, David. An Analytical Dictionary of the English Language. London: James Cochrane and Co., 1835

Brayley, Edward Wedlake and John Britton. The Beauties of England and Wales, or, Original Delineations, Topographical, Historical, and Descriptive, of Each County. London: Vernor, Hood & Sharpe, 1801

Britton, John. The Beauties of England and Wales, or, Original Delineations, Topographical, Historical, and Descriptive, of Each County. London: Vernor, Hood & Sharpe, 1807

Brookes, R. and John Marshall. A New Universal Gazetteer, or Geographical Dictionary. New York: W. W. Reed & Co., 1832

Brown, Thomas. Union Gazetteer for Great Britain and Ireland. London: Vernor, Hood, and Sharpe, 1807

Burke, Edmund. A Third Letter to a Member of the Present Parliament, on the Proposals for Peace with the Regicide Directory of France. London: F. and C. Rivington, 1797

Butler, William. Arithmetical Questions, on a New Plan. London: William Butler, 1795

Byfield, Robert. Sectum: Being the Universal Directory in the Art of Cutting. London: H. S. Mason, 1825

Campbell, Alexander. Journey from Edinburgh through Parts of North Britain. London: T. N. Longman and O. Rees, 1802

Campbell, James. Tariff, or Rates of Duties, payable after the 30th of June, 1828, on all Goods, Wares, and Merchandise, imported into the United States of America in American Vessels. New York: Edward B. Gould, 1828

Campbell, James. Tariff, or Rates of Duties, payable on Goods, Wares, and Merchandise, imported into the United States of America. New York: Mahlon Day, 1832

Chambaud, Lewis, and J. Th. H. Des Carrieres. New Dictionary, English and French and French and English. London: Cadell and Davies, et al, 1815 [referred to as Chambaud's French Dictionary, 1815]

Cobbett, William. A New French and English Dictionary. London: Mills, Jowett, and Mills, 1833 [referred to as Cobbett's French Dictionary, 1833]

Crabb, George. <u>A Dictionary of General Knowledge, or an Explanation of Words and Things Connected with All the Arts and Sciences</u>. London: T. T. and J. Tegg, 1833

Crabb, George. <u>Universal Technological Dictionary, or Familiar Explanation of the Terms Used in All Arts and Sciences</u>. London: Baldwin, Cradock, and Joy, 1823

Curtis, Thomas. <u>London Encyclopædia: or, Universal Dictionary Of Science, Art, Literature, and Practical Mechanics</u>. London: Thomas Tegg, 1829

Dufief, N. G. <u>A New Universal and Pronouncing Dictionary of the French and English Languages</u>. Philadelphia: T. & G. Palmer, 1810 [referred to as <u>Dufief's French Dictionary</u>]

Duncan, John. <u>Practical and Descriptive Essays on the Art of Weaving</u>. Glasgow: James and Andrew Duncan, 1808

Eden, Frederic Morton. <u>The State of the Poor: or, An History of the Labouring Classes in England</u>. London: B. & J. White et al, 1797

Fenning, Daniel. <u>Royal English Dictionary</u>, 1775

Fenwick de Porquet, Louis. <u>A Dictionary of the English & French and French & English Languages</u>. London: Fenwick de Porquet and Cooper, 1832 [referred to as <u>Fenwick de Porquet's French Dictionary</u>, 1832]

Force, Peter. <u>A National Calendar for 1820</u>. Washington: Davis and Force, 1820

Gaul, John. <u>Voyages and Travels in the Years 1809, 1810, and 1811</u>. London: T. Cadell and W. Davies, 1812

Goodrich, Charles A. <u>A New Family Encyclopedia; or Compendium of Universal Knowledge</u>. Connecticut: T. Belknap, 1835

Grimshaw, William. <u>The Ladies' Lexicon and Parlour Companion</u>. Philadelphia: John Grigg, 1835

Guthrie, William. <u>A New Geographical, Historical, and Commercial Grammar; and Present State of the Several Kingdoms of the World</u>. London: Vernor & Hood, et al, 1801

Guy, Joseph. <u>Guy's Pocket Cyclopædia, or Miscellany of Useful Knowledge</u>. London: C. Cradock and W. Joy, 1810

Hawker, P. <u>Instructions to Young Sportsmen in all that Relates to Guns and Shooting</u>. London: Longman et al, 1825 and 1833

Herbert, L. <u>The Register of Arts, and Journal of Patent Inventions</u>. London: B. Steill, 1828

House of Commons. <u>American Tariffs: Papers Relative to Tariffs Published in the United States</u>, 1828

House of Commons. <u>Reports from the Committees</u>. 1812, 1816, 1818, 1820, 1821, 1824, 1835

House of Commons. <u>Reports from the Commissioners of the Board of Education in Ireland</u>. 1813

House of Lords. <u>Sessional Papers</u>. 1822 – 1825

Jackson, Robert. <u>A Systematic View of the Formation, Discipline, and Economy of Armies</u>. London: John Stockdale, 1804

Jacob, Giles and T. E. Tomlins. <u>The Law-Dictionary: Explaining the Rise, Progress, and Present State, of the English Law</u>. New York: I Riley, 1811

Johnson, Samuel. <u>A Dictionary of the English Language</u>. London: A. Wilson, 1812 [referred to as <u>Johnson's English Dictionary</u>, 1812]

John C. Kayser & Co. <u>Commercial Directory</u>. Philadelphia: J. C. Kayser Co., 1823

Kenrick, William. <u>American Silk Grower's Guide, or, the Art of Raising the Mulberry and Silk</u>. Boston: George C. Barrett, 1835

Knowles, James. <u>A Pronouncing and Explanatory Dictionary of the English Language</u>. London: F. de Porquet and Cooper, 1835 [referred to as <u>Knowles' English Dictionary</u>, 1835]

Lardner, Dionysius. <u>A Treatise on the Origin, Progressive Improvement, and Present State of the Silk Manufacture</u>. Philadelphia: Carey & Lea, 1832 [referred to as <u>Silk Manufacture</u>, 1832]

Leslie, James. <u>Dictionary of the Synonymous Words and Technical Terms in the English Language</u>. Edinburgh: James Leslie, 1806

Lieber, Francis. <u>Encyclopædia Americana, a Popular Dictionary</u>. Philadelphia: Carey and Lea, 1831

Lewis, Samuel. <u>A Topographical Dictionary of England</u>. London: S. Lewis & Co., 1811

Lowrie, Walter and Walter S. Franklin. <u>American State Papers. Documents, Legislative and Executive, of the Congress of the United States</u>. Washington: Gales and Seaton, 1834

Macpherson, David. <u>Annals of Commerce, Manufactures, Fisheries, and Navigation</u>. London: Nichols and Son, et al, 1805

Middleton, John. <u>View of the Agriculture of Middlesex</u>. London: G. Nicol, 1798

Milburn, William. <u>Oriental Commerce</u>. London: Black, Parry, & Co., 1813

Millard, John. <u>The New Pocket Cyclopædia: or, Elements or Useful Knowledge, Methodically Arranged</u>. London: Sherwood, Neely, and Jones, 1813

Morse, Jedidiah and Richard C. Morse. <u>A New Universal Gazetteer, or Geographical Dictionary</u>. New Haven: S. Converse, 1823

Mortimer, Thomas. A General Dictionary of Commerce, Trade, and Manufactures. London: Richard Phillips, 1810 [referred to as Dictionary of Commerce, 1810]

Murphy, John. A Treatise on the Art of Weaving. Glasgow: Blackie & Son, and A. Fullarton & Co., 1831

Nicholson, William. The British Encyclopedia: or, Dictionary of Arts and Sciences. London: Longman, Hurst, Rees, and Orme, 1809

Oddy, J. Jepson. European Commerce. London: J. and J. Richardson, 1805

Onesimus. The Footman's Directory, And Butler's Remembrancer; or, the Advice of Onesimus to his Young Friends. London: Printed for the Author, 1823

Partington, Charles. British Cyclopædia of the Arts and Sciences. London: Orr & Smith, 1835

Peddie, Alexander. Linen Manufacturer, Weaver, and Warper's Assistant. Glasgow: W. Sommerville, A. Fullarton, J. Blackie & Co., 1817

Perry, William. The Synonymous, Etymological, and Pronouncing English Dictionary. London: John Walker et all, 1805 [referred to as Perry's English Dictionary, 1805]

Perry, William. A General Dictionary of the English Language. London: John Stockdale, 1795 [referred to as Perry's English Dictionary, 1795]

Pinkerton, John. A General Collection of the Best and Most Interesting Voyages and Travels in all Parts of the World. London: Longman, Hurst, Rees, and Orme, 1809 [referred to as Voyages and Travels, 1809]

Prieur, J. C. Boyer's Royal Dictionary: French and English. London: 1794

Raymond, Par F. Des Termes Appropriés Aux Arts et Aux Sciences. Paris: Masson et Fils, 1824

Religious Tract Society. Introduction to the Study of Birds; or, the Elements of Ornithology on Scientific Principles, with a Particular Notice of the Birds Mentioned in Scripture. London: Religious Tract Society, 1835

Rordansz, C. W.. European Commerce, or Complete Mercantile Guide to the Continent of Europe. London: Baldwin, Cradock, and Joy, 1818

Reuss, W. F. Calculations and Statements Relative to the Trade between Great Britain and the United States of America. London: Effingham Wilson, 1833

Salmon, N. Boyer's Royal Dictionary Abridged. London: Johnson et all, 1802

Salmon, N. Dictionnaire Français-Anglais et Anglais-Français, Abrégé. Paris: Lefevre, 1816

Sampson, Ezra. The Youth's Companion, or an Historical Dictionary. Albany: Websters and Skinners, 1813

Sears, W. J. The Female's Encyclopædia of Useful and Entertaining Knowledge: Comprising Every Branch of Domestic Economy. London: W. J. Sears, 1830

Sheridan, Thomas. A Complete Dictionary of the English Language, Both with regard to Sound and Meaning. London: Printed for Charles Dilly, 1797 [referred to as Sheridan's English Dictionary, 1797]

Silliman, Benjamin. Journal of Travels in England, Holland, and Scotland, and of two Passages over the Atlantic, in the years 1805 and 1806. Boston: Howe and Deforest, 1820

Sinclair, John. The General Report of the Agricultural State, and Political Circumstances, of Scotland. Edinburgh: David Willison, 1814

Sinclair, John. Statistical Account of Scotland. Edinburgh: William Creech, 1795 – 1799

Smith, G. The Laboratory; or, School of Arts. London: H. D. Symons et al, 1799

Smyth, James. The Practice of the Customs in the Entry, Examination, and Delivery of Goods and Merchandize, Usually Imported from Foreign Parts. London: John Richardson, 1812

Society for bettering the Condition of the Poor. Reports of the Society in Dublin for Promoting the Comforts of the Poor. London: Society for bettering the Condition of the Poor, 1800

Society Instituted at London for the Encouragement of Arts, Manufactures, and Commerce. Transactions of the Society Instituted at London for the Encouragement of Arts, Manufactures, and Commerce. London: The Society, 1795, 1805, 1821, 1829, 1833, and 1836

Stewarton, Lewis Goldsmith. The Female Revolutionary Plutarch. London: J. Murray, 1808

Tardy, L'Abby. An Explanatory Pronouncing Dictionary of the French Language. 1799 [referred to as Tardy's French Dictionary, 1799]

Taylor, C. The Literary Panorama. London: C. Taylor, 1807

Taylor, I. Scenes of British Wealth, in Produce, Manufactures, and Commerce. London: J. Harris, 1825

Taylor, Isaac. Scenes of Commerce, by Land and Sea; or, "Where Does It Com From?". London: John Harris, 1836

Taylor, Isaac. Scenes of Wealth, or, Views and Illustrations Of Trades – Manufactures – Produce and Commerce. London: Harris and Son, 1826

Thomson, John. Etymons of English Words. Edinburgh: Oliver & Boyd, 1826

Timbs, John. Knowledge for the People: or, the Plain Why and Because. Boston: Lilly & Wait, and Carter & Hender, 1832

United States House of Representatives. The Digest of the Recent Commercial Regulations of the Different Foreign Nations. Washington: House of Representatives, 1824

United States House of Representatives. Growth and Manufacture of Silk. Washington: House of Representatives, 1828 and 1830

United States House of Representatives. Reports of the Committee. Washington: House of Representatives, 1831

Ure, Andrew. The Cotton Manufacture of Great Britain, London: Charles Knight, 1836

Vernon, William H. A Methodical Treatise on the Cultivation of the Mulberry Tree, on the Raising of Silk Worms, and on Winding the Silk from the Cocoons. Boston: Hilliard, Gray, & Co., 1828

Villiers, George and John Bowring. First Report on the Commercial Relations between France and Great Britain. London: William Clowes, 1834 [referred to as Commercial Relations, 1834]

Walker, John. Critical Pronouncing Dictionary and Expositor of the English Language. London.: J. Johnson, 1806

Walker, John. Critical Pronouncing Dictionary and Expositor of the English Language. Hartford, Con.: Andrus, Judd, & Franklin, 1837

Walker, John. Elements of Geography, and of Natural and Civil History. Dublin: Thomas Morton Bates, 1797

Walker, John. The Universal Gazetteer. London: Darton and Harvey, 1795

Wallace, Thomas. An Essay on the Manufactures of Ireland. Dublin: Campbell and Abes, 1798

Walsh, Robert Jr. The Museum of Foreign Literature and Science. Philadelphia: E. Littell, 1823

Walton, William. Present State of the Spanish Colonies. London: Longman, Hurst, Rees, Orme, and Brown, 1810

Webster, Noah. A Dictionary of the English Language; compiled for the Use of Common Schools in the United States. Hartford: George Goodwin & Sons, 1817 [referred to as Webster's Dictionary, 1817]

Wentworth, John. A Complete System of Pleading. London: G. G. and J. Robinson, 1798

White, George S. Memoir of Samuel Slater, the Father of American Manufacture, connected with a History of the Rise and Progress of the Cotton Manufacture in England and America. Philadelphia, 1836

White, William. History, Gazetteer, and Directory of Nottinghamshire. Sheffield: William White, 1832

Willich, A. F. M. Domestic Encyclopædia; or, a Dictionary of Facts, and Useful Knowledge. Philadelphia: William Young Birch and Abraham Small, 1803

Wilson, Joseph. A French and English Dictionary. London: Joseph Ogle Robinson, 1833 [referred to as Wilson's French Dictionary, 1833]

United States Senate. Correspondence on the Subject of the Emigration of Indians. Washington: Duff Green, 1835

Unknown editor. The Annual Register, or a View of the History, Politics, and Literature for the Year 1794. London: W. Otridge and Son, et al, 1799

Unknown editor. The Annual Register, or a View of the History, Politics, and Literature for the Year 1767. London: W. Otridge and Son, et al, 1800

Unknown editor. The Annual Register, or a View of the History, Politics, and Literature for the Year 1769. London: W. Otridge and Son, et al, 1800

Unknown editor. The Annual Register, or a View of the History, Politics, and Literature for the Year 1803. London: W. Otridge and Son, et al, 1805

Unknown editor. The Annual Register, or a View of the History, Politics, and Literature for the Year 1817. London: Baldwin, Cradock, and Joy, 1818

Unknown editor. The Annual Register, or a View of the History, Politics, and Literature for the Year 1819. London: Baldwin, Cradock, and Joy, 1820

Unknown editor. A Book Explaining the Ranks and Dignities of British Society, London: Tabart and Co., 1809 [referred to as British Society]

Unknown editor. The Book of Commerce by Sea and Land. Boston: Allen and Ticknor, 1834

Unknown editor. The Book of English Trades, and Library of the Useful Arts. London: Richard Phillips, 1818

Unknown editor. The Book of Trades, or Library of the Useful Arts. London: Tabart and Co., 1806

Unknown editor. Boston Annual Advertiser annexed to the Boston Directory. Boston: C. Stimpson, Jr. and J. H. A Frost, 1823

Unknown editor. Boyer's French Dictionary. Boston: Hilliard, Gray and Co., 1835

Unknown editor. Bulletins of State Intelligence, &c. Westminster: 1834

Unknown editor. The Cabinet; or, a Natural History of Quadrupeds, Birds, Fishes and Insects. Edinburgh: W. J. & J. Richardson, 1801

Unknown editor. Dictionary of Merchandise, and Nomenclature in All Languages. Philadelphia: James Humphreys, 1805

Unknown editor. Doudney Brothers. 1830

Unknown editor. Edinburgh Gazetteer, or Geographical Dictionary. Edinburgh: Archibald Constable and Co., 1822

Unknown editor. <u>Encyclopædia Britannica, or Dictionary of Arts, Sciences, and Miscellaneous Literature</u>. Edinburgh: A Bell and C. MacFarqunar, 1797

Unknown editor. <u>Encyclopædia Perthensis; or Universal Dictionary of the Arts, Sciences, Literature, &c. Intended to Supersede the Use of Other Books of Reference</u>. Edinburgh: Printed by John Brown, 1816

Unknown editor. <u>Fourth Book of Lessons, for the use of the Irish National Schools</u>. Dublin: Philip Dixon Hardy, 1835

Unknown editor. <u>The Literary Panorama</u>. London: C. Taylor, 1808

Unknown editor. <u>The New Encyclopædia; or, Universal Dictionary of Arts and Sciences</u>. London: Vernor, Hood, and Sharpe, 1807

Unknown editor. <u>Repertory of Arts and Manufactures: consisting of Original Communications, Specifications of Patent Inventions, and Selections of Useful Practical Papers from the Transactions of the Philosophical Societies of All Nations</u>. London: Proprietors, 1801

Unknown editor. <u>Repertory of Arts and Manufactures. Consisting of Original Communications, Specifications of Patent Inventions, Practical and Interesting Papers, from the Transactions of the Philosophical Societies of All Nations</u>. London: J. Wyatt, 1802, 1804 – 1806

Unknown editor. <u>Spirit of the Public Journals for 1798</u>. Volume 2. London: James Ridgeway, 1799

Unknown editor. <u>The Ship Owner's Manual, or, Sea-Faring Man's Assistant</u>. Newcastle-Upon-Tyne: D. Akenhead and Sons, 1795

Unknown editor. <u>Spirit of the Public Journals, or, Beauties of the American Newspapers, for 1805</u>, Balitimore: Geo. Dobbin & Murphy, 1806

Unknown editor. <u>Spirit of the Public Journals for 1807</u>. Volume XI. London: James Ridgeway, 1808

Unknown editor. <u>The Toilette of Health, Beauty, and Fashion</u>. Boston: Allen and Ticknor, 1834

Unknown editor. <u>The Young Lady's Book: a Manual of Elegant Recreations, Exercises, and Pursuits</u>. London: Vizetelly, Branston, and Co., 1829

Periodicals, Magazines and Journals

Agricultural Magazine, or Farmer's Monthly Journal of Husbandry and Rural Affairs, 1811
Agricultural Museum: Designed to be a Repository of Valuable Information to the Farmer and Manufacturer, 1810, 1811
American Farmer; Rural Economy, Internal Improvements, Price Current, 1821, 1825, 1827, 1828
American Mechanics' Magazine, 1825
Analytical Review, or History of Literature, Domestic and Foreign, 1794, 1797, 1798
Army and Navy Chronicle, 1835, 1836
Asiatic Journal and Monthly Register for British India and its Dependencies, 1816, 1821, 1822, 1828, 1830, 1832, 1833, 1836
Athenæum, a Magazine of Literary and Miscellaneous Information, 1807, 1808
Atheneum, or Spirit of the English Magazines, 1818 – 1820, 1827 – 1831
Atheneum, Journal of English Literature and the Fine Arts, 1832
Atkinson's Casket, 1832 – 1836
La Belle Assemblée, 1806 – 1812, 1814, 1816, 1818 – 1820, 1823, 1825 – 1832
Blackwood's Lady's Magazine, 1836
Boston Weekly Magazine, 1803, 1805
Brighton Gleaner; or, General Repository, 1823
British Critic, A New Review, 1796, 1807
Casket, 1829 – 1831, 1833, 1834
Colonial Times, and Tasmanian Advertiser, 1826
Court Journal, 1833, 1835
Court Magazine, 1833 – 1836
Critical Review, or Annals of Literature, 1812
Day, a Morning Journal of Literature, Fine Arts, Fashion, &c., 1832
Edinburgh Annual Register, 1809 – 1814
Edinburgh Magazine, or Literary Miscellany, 1802
Emerald, or Miscellany of Literature, 1806, 1807
Eminent Foreign Statesmen, 1836
European Magazine, and London Review, 1795, 1808, 1823
Evangelical Magazine, 1821 – 1823, 1825
Examiner, a Sunday Paper, 1826

Examiner, and Journal of Political Economy, 1835

Farmer's Magazine: a Periodical Work, exclusively devoted to Agriculture and Rural Affairs, 1807

Farmer's Magazine, 1835, 1836

Farmer's Register, 1835

Figaro in London, 1836

Freemason's Magazine, 1795

Gales & Seaton's Register, 1827, 1828

Gazette of Fashion, and Magazine of the Fine Arts and Belle Lettres, 1822

Gentleman's Magazine: and Historical Chronicle, 1795, 1796, 1798, 1799, 1801, 1803, 1804

Gentleman's Monthly Miscellany, 1803

Guardian, 1797

Jersey Magazine, or Monthly Recorder, 1810

Kaleidoscope, 1820 – 1825

Ladies' Companion, 1836

Ladies' Monthly Museum; or, Polite Repository of Amusement and Instruction, 1802, 1816 – 1828

Ladies' Museum, 1829 – 1832

Ladies' Pocket Magazine, 1829, 1830, 1836

Lady's Book, 1831 – 1833, 1836 [referred to as *Godey's Ladies Book*]

Lady's Magazine: or, Entertaining Companion for the Fair Sex, 1794, 1796 – 1798, 1800, 1807, 1809, 1810, 1829

Lady's Magazine, or Mirror of the Belles Lettres, Music, Fine Arts, Drama, Fashions, &c.. 1825, 1829, 1830

Lady's Magazine and Museum of the Belles Lettres, Music, Fine Arts, Drama, Fashions, &c., 1834 – 1836

Lady's Miscellany, or the Weekly Visitor, 1810 – 1812

Lady's Weekly Miscellany, 1808, 1809

London Literary Gazette, and Journal of Belles Lettres, Arts, Politics, etc., 1818, 1831

Maids, Wives, and Widows Penny Magazine, 1832, 1833

Manchester Iris, 1822, 1823

Mirror of Literature, Amusement, and Instruction, 1829

Monthly Epitome, 1797, 1798

Monthly Magazine, or British Register, 1797 – 1799, 1803 – 1805, 1808, 1818

Monthly Mirror, 1802, 1804

Museum of Foreign Literature, Science and Art, 1836

National Register, 1808

New Annual Register, or General Repository of History, Politics, and Literature, 1811

New England Farmer, 1822 – 1824, 1831, 1833 – 1835

New Monthly Belle Assemblée, 1836

New Monthly Magazine, and Literary Journal, 1822, 1826, 1832

New Monthly Magazine, and Universal Register, 1817, 1818

New-York City-Hall Recorder, 1816

New-York Magazine, 1795

New-York Mirror, and Ladies' Literary Gazette, 1823, 1827

Niles' Weekly Register, 1815, 1816, 1820, 1826, 1828, 1829, 1831, 1833 – 1835

Penny Magazine, 1836

Port Folio, 1802, 1809, 1810

Public Documents Printed by the Order of the Senate of the United States, 1827 – 1835

Repertory of Arts, Manufactures, and Agriculture, 1804, 1805, 1810, 1811, 1818

Repertory of Patent Inventions, 1795, 1825, 1833, 1835

Repository of Arts, Literature, Commerce, Manufactures, Fashions, and Politics., 1812 – 1815

Repository of Arts, Literature, Fashions, &c., 1816 – 1821, 1823 – 1824

Repository of Fashions, 1829

Philosophical Magazine, 1805, 1808

Royal Lady's Magazine, 1831 – 1833

Saturday Magazine, 1833, 1835, 1836

The Schoolmaster, and Edinburgh Weekly Magazine, 1833

Scots Magazine; or, General Repository of Literature, History, and Politics, 1795, 1797, 1801

Scots Magazine; and Edinburg Literary Miscellany, 1804, 1806, 1810, 1814

Spirit of the Times, 1825

Sporting Magazine, 1794, 1795, 1798 – 1801, 1810, 1813, 1830, 1831
Tait's Edinburgh Magazine, 1835
Tomahawk, or, Censor General, 1796
Tradesman, 1810, 1811, 1814
Union Magazine and Imperial Register, 1801
Universal Magazine, 1809 – 1811
Weekly Entertainer, 1809
Weekly Magazine, 1798, 1802, 1803
Weekly Register, 1811, 1813
Yorkshire Observer, 1822

About the Editor

I'm the owner of the Mantua-Maker Historical Sewing Patterns, established in 1994. My costuming career began early – making dresses for my sister's dolls. I discovered costuming at the BayCon masquerade, a science fiction convention held in ~~1885~~ 1985, and soon thereafter fell in love with historical costuming. After many years of collecting historical clothing terms, I decided to assemble and share them with other costume historians.

Five Rivers Publishing, based in Canada, published my first nonfiction work,
Elephant's Breath & London Smoke: Historic Colour Names, Definitions & Uses in 2009.

Through CreateSpace, SmashWords, and my website you can find my next work:
Victorian Bathing and Bathing Suits:
The Culture of the Two-Piece Bathing Dress from 1837 – 1901

Although I grew up in Northern California, I've lived in England and Colorado, and currently reside in sunny Central Texas. I've been a receptionist, a waitress, a computer programmer, a warranty clerk, a real estate assistant, an inept archer, a costume maker and a dressmaker.

www.ingramcontent.com/pod-product-compliance
Lightning Source LLC
Chambersburg PA
CBHW081058290526
45795CB00006B/1899